Family Maps
of
Crenshaw County, Alabama
Deluxe Edition

With Homesteads, Roads, Waterways, Towns, Cemeteries, Railroads, and More

by Gregory A. Boyd, J.D.

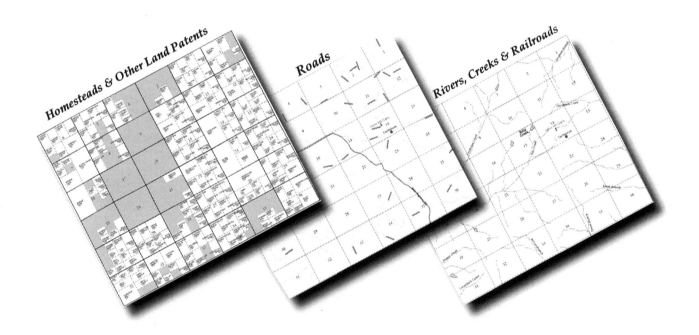

Featuring 3 *Maps Per Township...*

Arphax Publishing Co.
www.arphax.com

Family Maps of Crenshaw County, Alabama, Deluxe Edition: With Homesteads, Roads, Waterways, Towns, Cemeteries, Railroads, and More.
by Gregory A. Boyd, J.D.

ISBN 1-4203-1315-0

Published by Arphax Publishing Co., 2210 Research Park Blvd., Norman, Oklahoma, USA 73069
www.arphax.com

First Edition

ATTENTION HISTORICAL & GENEALOGICAL SOCIETIES, UNIVERSITIES, COLLEGES, CORPORATIONS, FAMILY REUNION COORDINATORS, AND PROFESSIONAL ORGANIZATIONS: Quantity discounts are available on bulk purchases of this book. For information, please contact Arphax Publishing Co., at the address listed above, or at (405) 366-6181, or visit our web-site at www.arphax.com and contact us through the "Bulk Sales" link.

—LEGAL—

The contents of this book rely on data published by the United States Government and its various agencies and departments, including but not limited to the General Land Office–Bureau of Land Management, the Department of the Interior, and the U.S. Census Bureau. The author has relied on said government agencies or re-sellers of its data, but makes no guarantee of the data's accuracy or of its representation herein, neither in its text nor maps. Said maps have been proportioned and scaled in a manner reflecting the author's primary goal—to make patentee names readable. This book will assist in the discovery of possible relationships between people, places, locales, rivers, streams, cemeteries, etc., but "proving" those relationships or exact geographic locations of any of the elements contained in the maps will require the use of other source material, which could include, but not be limited to: land patents, surveys, the patentees' applications, professionally drawn road-maps, etc.

Neither the author nor publisher makes any claim that the contents herein represent a complete or accurate record of the data it presents and disclaims any liability for reader's use of the book's contents. Many circumstances exist where human, computer, or data delivery errors could cause records to have been missed or to be inaccurately represented herein. Neither the author nor publisher shall assume any liability whatsoever for errors, inaccuracies, omissions or other inconsistencies herein.

This book is dedicated to my wonderful family:

Vicki, Jordan, & Amy Boyd

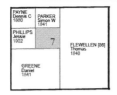

Contents

- Part I -

The Big Picture

- Part II -

Township Map Groups

(each Map Group contains a Patent Index, Patent Map, Road Map, & Historical Map)

Appendices

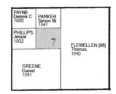

Preface

The quest for the discovery of my ancestors' origins, migrations, beliefs, and life-ways has brought me rewards that I could never have imagined. The *Family Maps* series of books is my first effort to share with historical and genealogical researchers, some of the tools that I have developed to achieve my research goals. I firmly believe that this effort will allow many people to reap the same sorts of treasures that I have.

Our Federal government's General Land Office of the Bureau of Land Management (the "GLO") has given genealogists and historians an incredible gift by virtue of its enormous database housed on its web-site at glorecords.blm.gov. Here, you can search for and find millions of parcels of land purchased by our ancestors in about thirty states.

This GLO web-site is one of the best FREE on-line tools available to family researchers. But, it is not for the faint of heart, nor is it for those unwilling or unable to to sift through and analyze the thousands of records that exist for most counties.

My immediate goal with this series is to spare you the hundreds of hours of work that it would take you to map the Land Patents for this county. Every Crenshaw County homestead or land patent that I have gleaned from public GLO databases is mapped here. Consequently, I can usually show you in an instant, where your ancestor's land is located, as well as the names of nearby land-owners.

Originally, that was my primary goal. But after speaking to other genealogists, it became clear that there was much more that they wanted. Taking their advice set me back almost a full year, but I think you will agree it was worth the wait. Because now, you can learn so much more.

Now, this book answers these sorts of questions:

- Are there any variant spellings for surnames that I have missed in searching GLO records?
- Where is my family's traditional home-place?
- What cemeteries are near Grandma's house?
- My Granddad used to swim in such-and-such-Creek—where is that?
- How close is this little community to that one?
- Are there any other people with the same surname who bought land in the county?
- How about cousins and in-laws—did they buy land in the area?

And these are just for starters!

The rules for using the *Family Maps* books are simple, but the strategies for success are many. Some techniques are apparent on first use, but many are gained with time and experience. Please take the time to notice the roads, cemeteries, creek-names, family names, and unique first-names throughout the whole county. You cannot imagine what YOU might be the first to discover.

I hope to learn that many of you have answered age-old research questions within these pages or that you have discovered relationships previously not even considered. When these sorts of things happen to you, will you please let me hear about it? I would like nothing better. My contact information can always be found at www.arphax.com.

One more thing: please read the "How To Use This Book" chapter; it starts on the next page. This will give you the very best chance to find the treasures that lie within these pages.

My family and I wish you the very best of luck, both in life, and in your research.   Greg Boyd

How to Use This Book - A Graphical Summary

Part I
"The Big Picture"

Map A ▸ Counties in the State

Map B ▸ Surrounding Counties

Map C ▸ Congressional Townships (Map Groups) in the County

Map D ▸ Cities & Towns in the County

Map E ▸ Cemeteries in the County

Surnames in the County ▸ Number of Land-Parcels for Each Surname

Surname/Township Index ▸ Directs you to Township Map Groups in Part II

The *Surname/Township Index* can direct you to any number of **Township Map Groups**

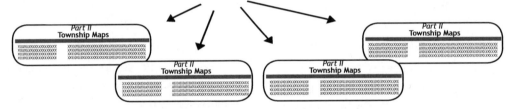

Part II
Township Map Groups
(1 for each Township in the County)

Each Township Map Group contains all four of of the following tools . . .

Land Patent Index ▸ Every-name Index of Patents Mapped in this Township

Land Patent Map ▸ Map of Patents as listed in above Index

Road Map ▸ Map of Roads, City-centers, and Cemeteries in the Township

Historical Map ▸ Map of Railroads, Lakes, Rivers, Creeks, City-Centers, and Cemeteries

---

Appendices

Appendix A ▸ Congressional Authority enabling Patents within our Maps

Appendix B ▸ Section-Parts / Aliquot Parts (a comprehensive list)

Appendix C ▸ Multi-patentee Groups (Individuals within Buying Groups)

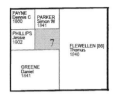

How to Use This Book

The two "Parts" of this *Family Maps* volume seek to answer two different types of questions. Part I deals with broad questions like: what counties surround Crenshaw County, are there any ASHCRAFTs in Crenshaw County, and if so, in which Townships or Maps can I find them? Ultimately, though, Part I should point you to a particular Township Map Group in Part II.

Part II concerns itself with details like: where exactly is this family's land, who else bought land in the area, and what roads and streams run through the land, or are located nearby. The Chart on the opposite page, and the remainder of this chapter attempt to convey to you the particulars of these two "parts", as well as how best to use them to achieve your research goals.

Part I
"The Big Picture"

Within Part I, you will find five "Big Picture" maps and two county-wide surname tools.

These include:

• Map A - Where Crenshaw County lies
     within the state
• Map B - Counties that surround Crenshaw
     County
• Map C - Congressional Townships of
     Crenshaw County (+ Map Group
     Numbers)
• Map D - Cities & Towns of Crenshaw
     County (with Index)
• Map E - Cemeteries of Crenshaw County
     (with Index)
• Surnames in Crenshaw County Patents
     (with Parcel-counts for each surname)
• Surname/Township Index (with Parcel-
     counts for each surname by Township)

The five "Big-Picture" Maps are fairly self-explanatory, yet should not be overlooked. This is particularly true of Maps "C", "D", and "E", all of which show Crenshaw County and its Congressional Townships (and their assigned Map Group Numbers).

Let me briefly explain this concept of Map Group Numbers. These are a device completely of our own invention. They were created to help you quickly locate maps without having to remember the full legal name of the various Congressional Townships. It is simply easier to remember "Map Group 1" than a legal name like: "Township 9-North Range 6-West, 5th Principal Meridian." But the fact is that the TRUE legal name for these Townships IS terribly important. These are the designations that others will be familiar with and you will need to accurately record them in your notes. This is why both Map Group numbers AND legal descriptions of Townships are almost always displayed together.

Map "C" will be your first intoduction to "Map Group Numbers", and that is all it contains: legal Township descriptions and their assigned Map Group Numbers. Once you get further into your research, and more immersed in the details, you will likely want to refer back to Map "C" from time to time, in order to regain your bearings on just where in the county you are researching.

Remember, township boundaries are a completely artificial device, created to standardize land descriptions. But do not let them become a boundary in your mind when choosing which townships to research. Your relative's in-laws, children, cousins, siblings, and mamas and papas, might just as easily have lived in the township next to the one your grandfather lived in—rather than in the one where he actually lived. So Map "C" can be your guide to which other Townships/Map Groups you likewise ought to analyze.

Of course, the same holds true for County lines; this is the purpose behind Map "B". It shows you surrounding counties that you may want to consider for further reserarch.

Map "D", the Cities and Towns map, is the first map with an index. Map "E" is the second (Cemeteries). Both, Maps "D" and "E" give you broad views of City (or Cemetery) locations in the County. But they go much further by pointing you toward pertinent Township Map Groups so you can locate the patents, roads, and waterways located near a particular city or cemetery.

Once you are familiar with these *Family Maps* volumes and the county you are researching, the "Surnames In Crenshaw County" chapter (or its sister chapter in other volumes) is where you'll likely start your future research sessions. Here, you can quickly scan its few pages and see if anyone in the county possesses the surnames you are researching. The "Surnames in Crenshaw County" list shows only two things: surnames and the number of parcels of land we have located for that surname in Crenshaw County. But whether or not you immediately locate the surnames you are researching, please do not go any further without taking a few moments to scan ALL the surnames in these very few pages.

You cannot imagine how many lost ancestors are waiting to be found by someone willing to take just a little longer to scan the "Surnames In Crenshaw County" list. Misspellings and typographical errors abound in most any index of this sort. Don't miss out on finding your Kinard that was written Rynard or Cox that was written Lox. If it looks funny or wrong, it very often is. And one of those little errors may well be your relative.

Now, armed with a surname and the knowledge that it has one or more entries in this book, you are ready for the "Surname/Township Index." Unlike the "Surnames In Crenshaw County", which has only one line per Surname, the "Surname/Township Index" contains one line-item for each Township Map Group in which each surname is found. In other words, each line represents a different Township Map Group that you will need to review.

Specifically, each line of the Surname/Township

Index contains the following four columns of information:

1. Surname
2. Township Map Group Number (these Map Groups are found in Part II)
3. Parcels of Land (number of them with the given Surname within the Township)
4. Meridian/Township/Range (the legal description for this Township Map Group)

The key column here is that of the Township Map Group Number. While you should definitely record the Meridian, Township, and Range, you can do that later. Right now, you need to dig a little deeper. That Map Group Number tells you where in Part II that you need to start digging.

But before you leave the "Surname/Township Index", do the same thing that you did with the "Surnames in Crenshaw County" list: take a moment to scan the pages of the Index and see if there are similarly spelled or misspelled surnames that deserve your attention. Here again, is an easy opportunity to discover grossly misspelled family names with very little effort. Now you are ready to turn to . . .

Part II
"Township Map Groups"

You will normally arrive here in Part II after being directed to do so by one or more "Map Group Numbers" in the Surname/Township Index of Part I.

Each Map Group represents a set of four tools dedicated to a single Congressional Township that is either wholly or partially within the county. If you are trying to learn all that you can about a particular family or their land, then these tools should usually be viewed in the order they are presented.

These four tools include:

1. a Land Patent Index
2. a Land Patent Map
3. a Road Map, and
4. an Historical Map

As I mentioned earlier, each grouping of this sort is assigned a Map Group Number. So, let's now move on to a discussion of the four tools that make up one of these Township Map Groups.

Land Patent Index

Each Township Map Group's Index begins with a title, something along these lines:

MAP GROUP 1: Index to Land Patents
Township 16-North Range 5-West (2nd PM)

The Index contains seven (7) columns. They are:

1. ID (a unique ID number for this Individual and a corresponding Parcel of land in this Township)
2. Individual in Patent (name)
3. Sec. (Section), and
4. Sec. Part (Section Part, or Aliquot Part)
5. Date Issued (Patent)
6. Other Counties (often means multiple counties were mentioned in GLO records, or the section lies within multiple counties).
7. For More Info . . . (points to other places within this index or elsewhere in the book where you can find more information)

While most of the seven columns are self-explanatory, I will take a few moments to explain the "Sec. Part." and "For More Info" columns.

The "Sec. Part" column refers to what surveryors and other land professionals refer to as an Aliquot Part. The origins and use of such a term mean little to a non-surveyor, and I have chosen to simply call these sub-sections of land what they are: a "Section Part". No matter what we call them, what we are referring to are things like a quarter-section or half-section or quarter-quarter-section. See Appendix "B" for most of the "Section Parts" you will come across (and many you will not) and what size land-parcel they represent.

The "For More Info" column of the Index may seem like a small appendage to each line, but please

recognize quickly that this is not so. And to understand the various items you might find here, you need to become familiar with the Legend that appears at the top of each Land Patent Index.

Here is a sample of the Legend . . .

LEGEND

"For More Info . . . " column

A = Authority (Legislative Act, See Appendix "A")

B = Block or Lot (location in Section unknown)

C = Cancelled Patent

F = Fractional Section

G = Group (Multi-Patentee Patent, see Appendix "C")

V = Overlaps another Parcel

R = Re-Issued (Parcel patented more than once)

Most parcels of land will have only one or two of these items in their "For More Info" columns, but when that is not the case, there is often some valuable information to be gained from further investigation. Below, I will explain what each of these items means to you you as a researcher.

A = Authority
(Legislative Act, See Appendix "A")

All Federal Land Patents were issued because some branch of our government (usually the U.S. Congress) passed a law making such a transfer of title possible. And therefore every patent within these pages will have an "A" item next to it in the index. The number after the "A" indicates which item in Appendix "A" holds the citation to the particular law which authorized the transfer of land to the public. As it stands, most of the Public Land data compiled and released by our government, and which serves as the basis for the patents mapped here, concerns itself with "Cash Sale" homesteads. So in some Counties, the law which authorized cash sales will be the primary, if not the only, entry in the Appendix.

B = Block or Lot (location in Section unknown)
A "B" designation in the Index is a tip-off that the EXACT location of the patent within the map is not apparent from the legal description. This Patent will nonetheless be noted within the proper

Section along with any other Lots purchased in the Section. Given the scope of this project (many states and many Counties are being mapped), trying to locate all relevant plats for Lots (if they even exist) and accurately mapping them would have taken one person several lifetimes. But since our primary goal from the onset has been to establish relationships between neighbors and families, very little is lost to this goal since we can still observe who all lived in which Section.

C = Cancelled Patent

A Cancelled Patent is just that: cancelled. Whether the original Patentee forfeited his or her patent due to fraud, a technicality, non-payment, or whatever, the fact remains that it is significant to know who received patents for what parcels and when. A cancellation may be evidence that the Patentee never physically re-located to the land, but does not in itself prove that point. Further evidence would be required to prove that. *See also*, Re-issued Patents, *below*.

F = Fractional Section

A Fractional Section is one that contains less than 640 acres, almost always because of a body of water. The exact size and shape of land-parcels contained in such sections may not be ascertainable, but we map them nonetheless. Just keep in mind that we are not mapping an actual parcel to scale in such instances. Another point to consider is that we have located some fractional sections that are not so designated by the Bureau of Land Management in their data. This means that not all fractional sections have been so identified in our indexes.

G = Group
(Multi-Patentee Patent, see Appendix "C")

A "G" designation means that the Patent was issued to a GROUP of people (Multi-patentees). The "G" will always be followed by a number. Some such groups were quite large and it was impractical if not impossible to display each individual in our maps without unduly affecting readability. EACH person in the group is named in the Index, but they won't all be found on the Map. You will find the name of the first person in such a Group

on the map with the Group number next to it, enclosed in [square brackets].

To find all the members of the Group you can either scan the Index for all people with the same Group Number or you can simply refer to Appendix "C" where all members of the Group are listed next to their number.

O = Overlaps another Parcel

An Overlap is one where PART of a parcel of land gets issued on more than one patent. For genealogical purposes, both transfers of title are important and both Patentees are mapped. If the ENTIRE parcel of land is re-issued, that is what we call it, a Re-Issued Patent (*see below*). The number after the "O" indicates the ID for the overlapping Patent(s) contained within the same Index. Like Re-Issued and Cancelled Patents, Overlaps may cause a map-reader to be confused at first, but for genealogical purposes, all of these parties' relationships to the underlying land is important, and therefore, we map them.

R = Re-Issued (Parcel patented more than once)

The label, "Re-issued Patent" describes Patents which were issued more than once for land with the EXACT SAME LEGAL DESCRIPTION. Whether the original patent was cancelled or not, there were a good many parcels which were patented more than once. The number after the "R" indicates the ID for the other Patent contained within the same Index that was for the same land. A quick glance at the map itself within the relevant Section will be the quickest way to find the other Patentee to whom the Parcel was transferred. They should both be mapped in the same general area.

I have gone to some length describing all sorts of anomalies either in the underlying data or in their representation on the maps and indexes in this book. Most of this will bore the most ardent reseracher, but I do this with all due respect to those researchers who will inevitably (and rightfully) ask: *"Why isn't so-and-so's name on the exact spot that the index says it should be?"*

In most cases it will be due to the existence of a Multi-Patentee Patent, a Re-issued Patent, a Cancelled Patent, or Overlapping Parcels named in separate Patents. I don't pretend that this discussion will answer every question along these lines, but I hope it will at least convince you of the complexity of the subject.

Not to despair, this book's companion web-site will offer a way to further explain "odd-ball" or errant data. Each book (County) will have its own web-page or pages to discuss such situations. You can go to www.arphax.com to find the relevant web-page for Crenshaw County.

Land Patent Map

On the first two-page spread following each Township's Index to Land Patents, you'll find the corresponding Land Patent Map. And here lies the real heart of our work. For the first time anywhere, researchers will be able to observe and analyze, on a grand scale, most of the original land-owners for an area AND see them mapped in proximity to each one another.

We encourage you to make vigorous use of the accompanying Index described above, but then later, to abandon it, and just stare at these maps for a while. This is a great way to catch misspellings or to find collateral kin you'd not known were in the area.

Each Land Patent Map represents one Congressional Township containing approximately 36-square miles. Each of these square miles is labeled by an accompanying Section Number (1 through 36, in most cases). Keep in mind, that this book concerns itself solely with Crenshaw County's patents. Townships which creep into one or more other counties will not be shown in their entirety in any one book. You will need to consult other books, as they become available, in order to view other countys' patents, cities, cemeteries, etc.

But getting back to Crenshaw County: each Land Patent Map contains a Statistical Chart that looks like the following:

Township Statistics

Parcels Mapped	:	173
Number of Patents	:	163
Number of Individuals	:	152
Patentees Identified	:	151
Number of Surnames	:	137
Multi-Patentee Parcels	:	4
Oldest Patent Date	:	11/27/1820
Most Recent Patent	:	9/28/1917
Block/Lot Parcels	:	0
Parcels Re-Issued	:	3
Parcels that Overlap	:	8
Cities and Towns	:	6
Cemeteries	:	6

This information may be of more use to a social statistician or historian than a genealogist, but I think all three will find it interesting.

Most of the statistics are self-explanatory, and what is not, was described in the above discussion of the Index's Legend, but I do want to mention a few of them that may affect your understanding of the Land Patent Maps.

First of all, Patents often contain more than one Parcel of land, so it is common for there to be more Parcels than Patents. Also, the Number of Individuals will more often than not, not match the number of Patentees. A Patentee is literally the person or PERSONS named in a patent. So, a Patent may have a multi-person Patentee or a single-person patentee. Nonetheless, we account for all these individuals in our indexes.

On the lower-righthand side of the Patent Map is a Legend which describes various features in the map, including Section Boundaries, Patent (land) Boundaries, Lots (numbered), and Multi-Patentee Group Numbers. You'll also find a "Helpful Hints" Box that will assist you.

One important note: though the vast majority of Patents mapped in this series will prove to be reasonably accurate representations of their actual locations, we cannot claim this for patents lying along state and county lines, or waterways, or that have been platted (lots).

Shifting boundaries and sparse legal descriptions in the GLO data make this a reality that we have nonetheless tried to overcome by estimating these patents' locations the best that we can.

Road Map

On the two-page spread following each Patent Map you will find a Road Map covering the exact same area (the same Congressional Township).

For me, fully exploring the past means that every once in a while I must leave the library and travel to the actual locations where my ancestors once walked and worked the land. Our Township Road Maps are a great place to begin such a quest.

Keep in mind that the scaling and proportion of these maps was chosen in order to squeeze hundreds of people-names, road-names, and place-names into tinier spaces than you would traditionally see. These are not professional road-maps, and like any secondary genealogical source, should be looked upon as an entry-way to original sources—in this case, original patents and applications, professionally produced maps and surveys, etc.

Both our Road Maps and Historical Maps contain cemeteries and city-centers, along with a listing of these on the left-hand side of the map. I should note that I am showing you city center-points, rather than city-limit boundaries, because in many instances, this will represent a place where settlement began. This may be a good time to mention that many cemeteries are located on private property, Always check with a local historical or genealogical society to see if a particular cemetery is publicly accessible (if it is not obviously so). As a final point, look for your surnames among the road-names. You will often be surprised by what you find.

Historical Map

The third and final map in each Map Group is our attempt to display what each Township might have looked like before the advent of modern roads. In frontier times, people were usually more determined to settle near rivers and creeks than they were near roads, which were often few and far between. As was the case with the Road Map, we've included the same cemeteries and city-centers. We've also included railroads, many of which came along before most roads.

While some may claim "Historical Map" to be a bit of a misnomer for this tool, we settled for this label simply because it was almost as accurate as saying "Railroads, Lakes, Rivers, Cities, and Cemeteries," and it is much easier to remember.

In Closing . . .

By way of example, here is *A Really Good Way to Use a Township Map Group*. First, find the person you are researching in the Township's Index to Land Patents, which will direct you to the proper Section and parcel on the Patent Map. But before leaving the Index, scan all the patents within it, looking for other names of interest. Now, turn to the Patent Map and locate your parcels of land. Pay special attention to the names of patent-holders who own land surrounding your person of interest. Next, turn the page and look at the same Section(s) on the Road Map. Note which roads are closest to your parcels and also the names of nearby towns and cemeteries. Using other resources, you may be able to learn of kin who have been buried here, plus, you may choose to visit these cemeteries the next time you are in the area.

Finally, turn to the Historical Map. Look once more at the same Sections where you found your research subject's land. Note the nearby streams, creeks, and other geographical features. You may be surprised to find family names were used to name them, or you may see a name you haven't heard mentioned in years and years—and a new research possibility is born.

Many more techniques for using these *Family Maps* volumes will no doubt be discovered. If from time to time, you will navigate to Crenshaw County's web-page at www.arphax.com (use the "Research" link), you can learn new tricks as they become known (or you can share ones you have employed). But for now, you are ready to get started. So, go, and good luck.

– Part I –

The Big Picture

Map A - Where Crenshaw County, Alabama Lies Within the State

——— Legend ———

State Boundary

County Boundaries

Crenshaw County, Alabama

——— Helpful Hints ———

1 We start with Map "A" which simply shows us where within the State this county lies.

2 Map "B" zooms in further to help us more easily identify surrounding Counties.

3 Map "C" zooms in even further to reveal the Congressional Townships that either lie within or intersect Crenshaw County.

Map B - Crenshaw County, Alabama and Surrounding Counties

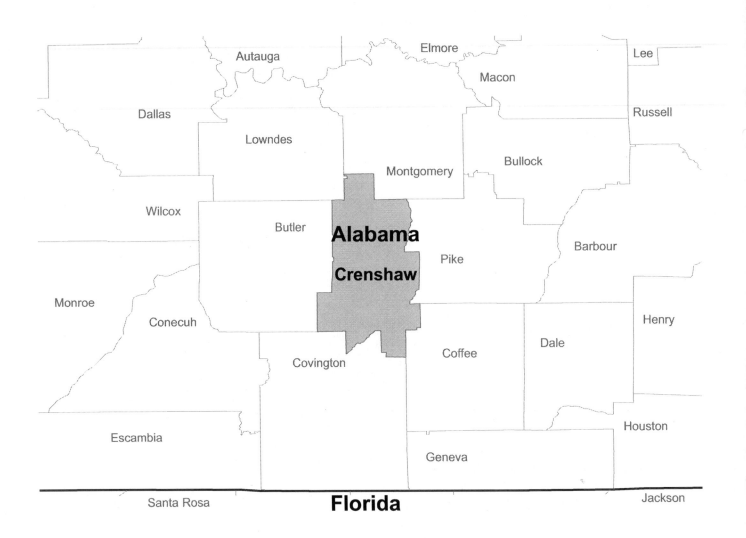

——— Legend ———

——— State Boundaries (when applicable)

——— County Boundary

——— Helpful Hints ———

1 Many Patent-holders and their families settled across county lines. It is always a good idea to check nearby counties for your families.

2 Refer to Map "A" to see a broader view of where this County lies within the State, and Map "C" to see which Congressional Townships lie within Crenshaw County.

Map C - Congressional Townships of Crenshaw County, Alabama

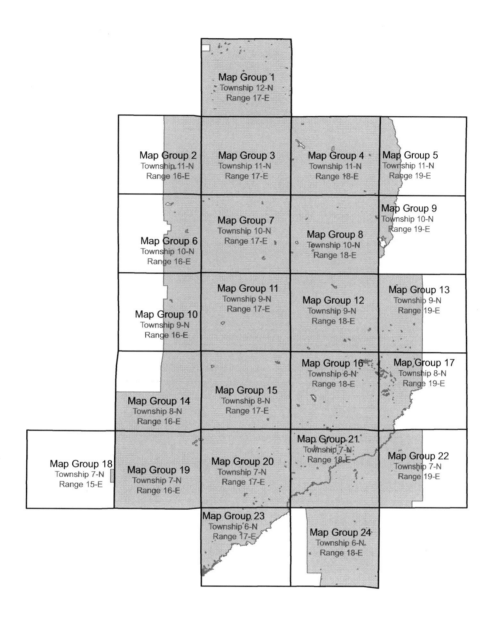

Map Group	Township	Range
Map Group 1	Township 12-N	Range 17-E
Map Group 2	Township 11-N	Range 16-E
Map Group 3	Township 11-N	Range 17-E
Map Group 4	Township 11-N	Range 18-E
Map Group 5	Township 11-N	Range 19-E
Map Group 6	Township 10-N	Range 16-E
Map Group 7	Township 10-N	Range 17-E
Map Group 8	Township 10-N	Range 18-E
Map Group 9	Township 10-N	Range 19-E
Map Group 10	Township 9-N	Range 16-E
Map Group 11	Township 9-N	Range 17-E
Map Group 12	Township 9-N	Range 18-E
Map Group 13	Township 9-N	Range 19-E
Map Group 14	Township 8-N	Range 16-E
Map Group 15	Township 8-N	Range 17-E
Map Group 16	Township 8-N	Range 18-E
Map Group 17	Township 8-N	Range 19-E
Map Group 18	Township 7-N	Range 15-E
Map Group 19	Township 7-N	Range 16-E
Map Group 20	Township 7-N	Range 17-E
Map Group 21	Township 7-N	Range 18-E
Map Group 22	Township 7-N	Range 19-E
Map Group 23	Township 6-N	Range 17-E
Map Group 24	Township 6-N	Range 18-E

──── Legend ────

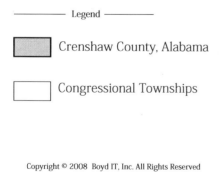

Crenshaw County, Alabama

Congressional Townships

Helpful Hints

1 Many Patent-holders and their families settled across county lines. It is always a good idea to check nearby counties for your families (See Map "B").

2 Refer to Map "A" to see a broader view of where this county lies within the State, and Map "B" for a view of the counties surrounding Crenshaw County.

Map D Index: Cities & Towns of Crenshaw County, Alabama

The following represents the Cities and Towns of Crenshaw County, along with the corresponding Map Group in which each is found. Cities and Towns are displayed in both the Road and Historical maps in the Group.

City/Town	Map Group No.
Bradleyton	4
Brantley	21
Bullock	22
Carmen	17
Centenary	11
Center Ridge	6
Cherokee Village	11
Clearview	1
Danielsville	2
Dozier	23
Fullers Crossroads	7
Garnersville	8
Glenwood	17
Helicon	4
Highland Home	3
Honoraville	6
Ivy Creek	11
Joquin	13
Leon	20
Live Oak	8
Luverne	12
Magnolia Shores	4
Merrill Mill	19
Moodys Crossroads	11
Mulberry	19
New Hope	20
Panola	1
Patsburg	12
Peacock (historical)	21
Petrey	8
Robinson Crossroads	11
Rutledge	11
Sardis	3
Saville	3
Searight	23
Shirleys Crossroads	13
Social Town	13
Theba	20
Vernledge	12
Vidette	13
Weed Crossroad	24

Map D - Cities & Towns of Crenshaw County, Alabama

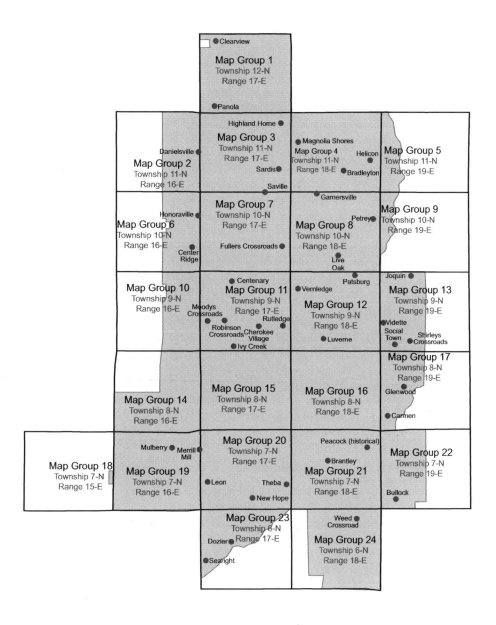

——— Legend ———

Crenshaw County, Alabama

Congressional Townships

——— Helpful Hints ———

1 Cities and towns are marked only at their center-points as published by the USGS and/or NationalAtlas.gov. This often enables us to more closely approximate where these might have existed when first settled.

2 To see more specifically where these Cities & Towns are located within the county, refer to both the Road and Historical maps in the Map-Group referred to above. See also, the Map "D" Index on the opposite page.

Map E Index: Cemeteries of Crenshaw County, Alabama

The following represents many of the Cemeteries of Crenshaw County, along with the corresponding Township Map Group in which each is found. Cemeteries are displayed in both the Road and Historical maps in the Map Groups referred to below.

Cemetery	Map Group No.
Armstrong Cem.	1
Bethel Cem.	16
Black Rock Cem.	10
Cauthens Cem.	3
Clark Cem.	23
Clarke Cem.	15
Davis Cem.	21
Dozier Cem.	23
Dry Cem.	3
Emmaus Cem.	12
Friendship Cem.	19
Green Cem.	12
Hopewell Cem.	2
Hudson Cem.	4
Leon Cem.	20
Lightfoot Cem.	11
Magnolia Cem.	1
Mitchell Cem.	7
Mitchell Cem.	24
Mount Pleasant Cem.	7
Oak Grove Cem.	6
Oak Grove Cem.	21
Panola Cem.	3
Petrey Cem.	8
Providence Cem.	17
Rocky Mount Cem.	1
Rutledge Cem.	12
Saint Lukes Cem.	19
Sardis Cem.	3
Siloam Cem.	11
Thompson Cem.	8
Vernledge Cem.	12

Map E - Cemeteries of Crenshaw County, Alabama

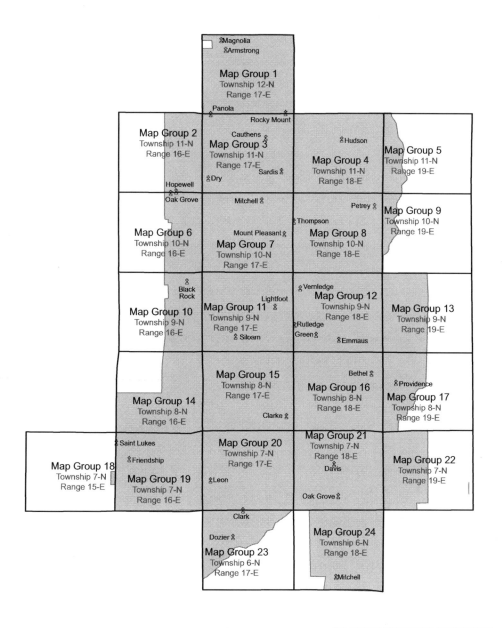

Legend

Crenshaw County, Alabama

Congressional Townships

Copyright © 2007 Boyd IT, Inc. All Rights Reserved

Helpful Hints

1 Cemeteries are marked at locations as published by the USGS and/or NationalAtlas.gov.

2 To see more specifically where these Cemeteries are located, refer to the Road & Historical maps in the Map-Group referred to above. See also, the Map "E" Index on the opposite page to make sure you don't miss any of the Cemeteries located within this Congressional township.

Surnames in Crenshaw County, Alabama Patents

The following list represents the surnames that we have located in Crenshaw County, Alabama Patents and the number of parcels that we have mapped for each one. Here is a quick way to determine the existence (or not) of Patents to be found in the subsequent indexes and maps of this volume.

Surname	# of Land Parcels	Surname	# of Land Parcels	Surname	# of Land Parcels	Surname	# of Land Parcels
ACREE	6	BOAN	15	CALLENS	1	COTHRAN	1
ADAMS	17	BODIE	2	CAMERON	1	COTTINGHAM	1
ADDISON	2	BODIFORD	18	CAMPBELL	10	COTTLE	1
ADKISON	2	BOGGS	2	CANDLE	1	COURTNEY	4
ALBRITTON	3	BOLAN	4	CANNON	12	COWART	6
ALFORD	4	BOLLING	1	CAPPS	31	COWLES	8
ALLEN	5	BOND	9	CARLILE	3	COX	4
ALSABROOKS	1	BONHAM	5	CARNES	1	CRAWFORD	2
AMASON	9	BONNER	2	CARPENTER	8	CRITINTUN	1
ANDERSON	10	BOON	6	CARR	6	CROXTON	17
ANDRESS	5	BOONE	3	CARTER	15	CULPEPPER	1
ANTHONY	4	BOOTH	3	CARTLIDGE	4	CUMBIE	1
ARCHER	6	BOOTHE	6	CASSITY	1	CURETON	5
ARMSTRONG	21	BORDEAUX	1	CASTELLAW	2	CURTIS	11
ARNOLD	3	BOSWELL	2	CASTILLAW	2	DANIEL	102
ARRINGTON	2	BOYD	1	CATHCART	1	DANNELLEY	2
ASKEW	1	BOYETER	1	CATLIN	8	DANNELLY	1
ATHEY	5	BOYETT	26	CAULEY	2	DAUPHIN	5
ATKINSON	6	BOYKIN	1	CAUTHAN	1	DAVIDSON	1
ATKISON	5	BOYT	2	CAUTHEN	7	DAVIS	108
AXSON	1	BOYTER	3	CAUTHRAN	2	DAVISON	4
BAILEY	5	BOZEMAN	13	CAUTHRON	3	DE BREE	15
BAILY	1	BRADLEY	24	CAWTHEN	1	DEAN	5
BAIN	3	BRADY	1	CHAMPION	36	DEASON	1
BAKER	3	BRANAN	1	CHANDLER	5	DEAY	1
BALDWIN	3	BRANDON	5	CHAPMAN	6	DEES	2
BALL	5	BRANEN	2	CHASSER	1	DEESON	1
BANKS	2	BRANNAN	2	CHESHIRE	6	DELOACH	3
BARKLEY	11	BRANTLEY	1	CHESSER	17	DEMING	2
BARNES	5	BRAWDAWAY	3	CHESTER	3	DENDY	22
BARRETT	4	BRAZIL	1	CHILDERS	3	DEPRIEST	4
BARROW	1	BREAKER	2	CHILDRE	5	DEVLIN	1
BARTERFORD	1	BREWER	2	CHILDRES	3	DEWITT	1
BARTON	7	BRIDGES	5	CHISSER	2	DICKERSON	1
BASS	2	BRIGGS	11	CHURCHWELL	13	DILLARD	5
BATTLE	2	BRIGHT	5	CLAGHORN	1	DOCKINS	4
BAYGENTS	2	BRISTOW	3	CLANCY	24	DORMAN	12
BEASLEY	1	BROOKS	6	CLARK	14	DOUGLASS	3
BEAVERS	4	BROWDER	8	CLARKE	3	DOWNING	2
BEAZELY	1	BROWN	12	CLAYTON	1	DOZIER	17
BECK	3	BROWNING	6	CLEGHORN	3	DRISKELL	2
BEDGOOD	5	BRUNDIGE	1	CLEMENTS	5	DRISKILL	1
BEDSOLE	12	BRUNSON	35	CODY	10	DRIVER	2
BELL	14	BRYAN	12	COFFIELD	1	DRY	4
BENBOW	9	BRYANT	4	COKER	6	DUKE	19
BENNETT	6	BUCK	4	COLEMAN	11	DUKES	1
BENSON	8	BUCKELEW	12	COLLINS	3	DUNCAN	4
BENTLEY	7	BULLARD	3	COLQUITT	2	DUNKIN	1
BERDEAUX	2	BURGESS	12	COLVIN	6	DYER	7
BERRY	6	BURGIN	3	COMPTON	19	DYKES	2
BEST	9	BURK	9	CONE	1	EDDINS	8
BIDSOLE	1	BURKE	4	CONNOR	1	EDWARDS	2
BIRD	33	BURKS	1	COOK	16	EILAND	20
BISHOP	9	BURNETT	1	COON	2	ELISOR	1
BLACK	8	BURNETTE	1	COOPER	8	ELLINGTON	15
BLACKBURN	1	BURNS	11	CORDRAY	4	ELLIS	8
BLACKMAN	3	BURT	2	CORLEY	2	ELLISON	4
BLACKMON	3	BUSH	8	CORNET	3	ENGRAM	1
BLACKSHEAR	1	BUTLER	7	CORNETT	1	ETHERIDGE	2
BLAIR	2	BYRD	2	COSBY	1	EUBANKES	2
BLAKENEY	1	CALDWELL	5	COSTON	2	EUBANKS	5
BLOCKER	1	CALLAWAY	1	COTHEN	1	EVANS	3

Surname	# of Land Parcels	Surname	# of Land Parcels	Surname	# of Land Parcels	Surname	# of Land Parcels
EVERAGE	1	GREGG	3	HOPPER	3	LAYTON	2
EVERIDGE	5	GREGORY	2	HORN	13	LEAIRD	8
EVRIDGE	3	GRIFFIN	3	HOUGH	1	LEAK	4
EYLAND	1	GRIGG	1	HOWARD	3	LEAKE	1
FAGIN	1	GUY	4	HUDSON	4	LEE	5
FAIL	14	HALE	1	HUETT	1	LEFLORE	1
FAIRCLOTH	1	HALL	26	HUGHES	14	LEGG	1
FAISON	1	HALLFORD	5	HUNT	1	LEGGETT	2
FANNIN	6	HAMBRICK	6	HURLEY	4	LEVERETT	2
FAULK	2	HAMIL	2	HURT	6	LEWIS	23
FEAGIN	13	HAMILTON	8	HURTT	4	LIGHTFOOT	1
FENDLEY	1	HAMMONDS	2	HUTCHISON	3	LILES	3
FICKLIN	7	HAMMONS	2	HUTTO	2	LINDSEY	1
FICKLING	5	HAMRICK	6	HYNES	1	LINTON	5
FIELDER	1	HANCHEY	3	INGRAM	4	LITTLE	4
FINKLEA	1	HANCOCK	3	ISHAM	1	LLOYD	2
FINLAY	11	HANDLEY	13	ISOM	8	LOCK	1
FINLEY	1	HANSHAW	1	JACKSON	25	LOCKHART	11
FLEMING	3	HARBIN	3	JAMES	12	LOFTIN	5
FLOWERS	8	HARDCASTLE	3	JAY	2	LOLLIS	3
FLOYD	6	HARDIN	3	JAYROE	2	LONG	27
FOLMAR	8	HARRELL	10	JEFCOAT	40	LONGFELLOW	1
FORREST	1	HARRELSON	1	JEFFCOATE	1	LOUNSBURY	1
FOSKETT	8	HARRIS	17	JEFFERS	3	LOWE	2
FOSTER	1	HARRISON	10	JETER	2	LOWREY	16
FOWLE	1	HARRISS	1	JOHNS	1	LOWRIE	1
FOWLER	7	HART	3	JOHNSON	52	LOWRY	3
FRANKLIN	33	HARTEN	1	JOHNSTON	1	LUKER	1
FRAZER	7	HARTIN	4	JONES	75	LUMPKIN	1
FRAZIER	5	HARWELL	1	JONSON	1	MACK	2
FROST	9	HASTING	1	JORDAN	47	MACKEY	3
FULLER	15	HATHEWAY	1	JOSEY	3	MADDOX	4
FUNK	2	HATHHORN	2	JOURDAN	1	MAHONE	27
FURR	4	HATHORN	5	JUNE	8	MAINOR	1
FURRH	3	HATTAWAY	1	KEENER	6	MAJOR	2
FUTRILL	1	HAWKINS	2	KELLEY	15	MALLOY	7
GABLE	5	HAWTHORNE	1	KELLY	7	MALONE	2
GAINER	13	HAYGOOD	1	KELY	1	MALOY	7
GAINES	7	HAYNES	5	KENNEDY	8	MANNING	2
GAINEY	3	HEAD	1	KENNINGTON	2	MANSELL	2
GALLOPS	9	HEARTSILL	4	KENNON	1	MANSILL	1
GALLUPS	4	HELMS	2	KENT	29	MAPES	3
GAMBLE	3	HELTON	4	KERBY	2	MARCHANT	6
GANEY	6	HELTOR	1	KERSEY	4	MARLOW	2
GARDNER	8	HEMPHILL	2	KETCHAND	2	MARSH	1
GARRETT	1	HENDERSON	4	KETTLER	2	MARSHALL	26
GATLIN	4	HENLEY	1	KIDD	2	MARTIN	28
GHOLSON	2	HENLY	1	KILCREASE	14	MASH	2
GIBBS	2	HERNDON	1	KIMBRO	3	MASTIN	8
GIBSON	12	HESTER	1	KING	24	MATHEWS	1
GILCHRIST	9	HICKMAN	2	KIRKLAND	5	MATTHEWS	1
GILCREASE	4	HICKS	3	KIRKPATRICK	1	MAY	10
GILL	1	HIGHNATE	1	KIRVEN	1	MAYHAR	3
GILLIS	2	HIGHSMITH	6	KIRVIN	1	MAYNARD	1
GILMER	1	HIGHTOWER	3	KITES	2	MCADAMS	11
GIPSON	7	HILBUN	2	KNIGHT	8	MCALPIN	3
GLASS	3	HILL	23	KNOTTS	3	MCCARTER	1
GODIN	1	HILLIARD	2	KNOWLEN	1	MCCARTY	10
GODWIN	7	HINDES	1	KNOWLING	3	MCCORMACK	9
GOGGANS	1	HOLDER	3	KNOWLS	4	MCCURLEY	1
GOLDEN	2	HOLLADAY	2	KOLB	2	MCCURRY	1
GOLDTHWAITE	5	HOLLAND	25	LANDERS	1	MCDANIEL	6
GOODSON	9	HOLLEY	10	LANE	4	MCDONALD	8
GOODWIN	4	HOLLINGSHEAD	1	LANGLEY	1	MCDUGALD	14
GORE	5	HOLLIS	4	LANIER	1	MCGEHEE	5
GOULD	1	HOLLY	3	LANSDON	12	MCGINNEY	2
GRAHAM	9	HOLMES	4	LARANCE	2	MCGOUGH	8
GRANT	4	HOLMS	1	LASSITER	2	MCHENRY	2
GRAVES	1	HOOD	3	LAWRENCE	13	MCILWAIN	5
GREEN	7	HOOKS	3	LAWSON	1	MCKEE	2

Surname	# of Land Parcels	Surname	# of Land Parcels	Surname	# of Land Parcels	Surname	# of Land Parcels
MCKETHAN	1	NICHOLS	21	RAINER	4	SHOWES	1
MCKEY	2	NICKOLS	1	RAMBO	1	SHOWS	13
MCKINZIE	2	NIX	4	RAMICK	1	SIKES	3
MCLEAN	1	NOBLES	4	RAY	2	SILER	10
MCLEOD	7	NORMAN	2	REAVES	16	SIMMONS	13
MCMICHEL	2	NORSWORTHY	3	REDMON	1	SIMPSON	2
MCMILLAN	2	NORTON	1	REDMOND	2	SIMS	15
MCMULLAN	1	ODEAY	2	REED	1	SKAIN	5
MCMULLEN	1	ODUM	1	REESE	12	SKAINS	26
MCNEAL	16	ODWYER	2	REEVES	18	SKINNER	1
MCNEIL	1	OGDEN	2	REID	3	SKIPPER	17
MCNEILL	1	OGLESBE	1	REIVES	1	SLOANE	2
MCQUEEN	6	OGLESBY	2	REYNOLDS	2	SMILIE	4
MCQWEEN	1	OLIVE	4	RHOADES	3	SMITH	62
MCREE	1	OLIVER	3	RHODES	40	SMYTH	11
MCTYEIRE	1	ONEILL	6	RIALS	1	SOLOMAN	1
MCWILLIAMS	1	OROXTON	1	RICHARDSON	10	SOLOMON	8
MEASLES	1	OWEN	22	RICHBOURG	1	SORRELL	2
MEDLEY	1	OWENS	11	RICHBURG	4	SORRELLS	3
MELTON	1	PARDUE	2	RIDGEWAY	2	SOWELL	7
MENEES	3	PARHAM	1	RIDGWAY	8	SPEAR	1
MERCHANT	1	PARKER	6	RIEVES	4	SPEIR	5
MERREES	1	PARMER	12	RILEY	1	SPENCER	4
MERRELL	1	PARRISH	1	RIVES	1	SPIVEY	4
MERRILL	35	PATE	4	ROACH	15	SPORT	3
MERRITT	4	PATENT	1	ROAN	1	SPRADLEY	4
MIDDLEBROOKS	1	PATTERSON	3	ROBBINS	8	SPRAGGINS	8
MILES	5	PAUL	1	ROBERTS	1	SPRAGINS	6
MILIGAN	1	PAYNE	8	ROBINS	2	SPURLIN	2
MILLER	8	PEACOCK	4	ROBINSON	5	SPURLOCK	2
MILLIGAN	5	PEAVY	4	RODGERS	26	STAGGERS	17
MILLS	10	PEEK	1	ROGERS	54	STALLINGS	12
MILTON	1	PELHAM	2	ROIAL	2	STANALAND	5
MIMS	1	PENDREY	10	ROPER	9	STANDLEY	1
MINARD	1	PENTON	5	ROSS	4	STANLEY	15
MINYARD	3	PERDUE	10	ROSTICK	1	STARK	1
MITCHEL	2	PERKINS	6	ROUSE	4	STARLING	1
MITCHELL	43	PERRITT	6	ROWELL	1	STARR	6
MONK	1	PERRY	7	ROYAL	4	STEPHENS	2
MONTGOMERY	13	PERRYMAN	1	ROYALS	1	STEPHENSON	5
MOODY	15	PETERSON	2	ROZEAR	2	STEVENS	1
MOON	2	PETRY	5	RUSSELL	1	STEVENSON	2
MOORE	29	PETTY	9	RUTLEDGE	3	STEWART	24
MORELAND	1	PHARAOH	8	RYALS	5	STINSON	17
MORGAN	23	PHAROAH	3	RYLANDER	1	STOCKARD	3
MORRIS	3	PHAROH	4	SALTER	5	STOKES	3
MORRISON	2	PHILLIPS	3	SANDERS	6	STONE	1
MORROW	2	PICKETT	10	SANKEY	2	STOUGH	11
MOSELEY	8	PINTON	2	SARLES	1	STRAUGHN	1
MOSELY	2	PITMAN	1	SARTON	1	STREET	2
MOTES	1	PLATT	4	SARTOR	6	STRICKLAN	1
MOTHERSHEAD	16	POLK	7	SASSEN	1	STRICKLIN	6
MOTHERSHED	3	POLLARD	19	SASSER	31	STRINGER	12
MOUNT	3	PONDER	7	SAUNDERS	6	STRIPLING	2
MOYE	2	POPE	6	SCARBOROUGH	1	STURGIS	7
MULLINS	2	PORTER	3	SCHOFIELD	4	STYRON	1
MURPHEY	1	POTTER	6	SCIPPER	6	SUMMERLIN	15
MURPHY	3	POUNCEY	8	SCOFIELD	1	SUMMERLINE	1
MURRAY	1	POUNCY	3	SCOTT	2	SURLES	3
MYEARS	1	POWELL	13	SEALS	1	SWANER	1
NANSWORTHY	1	PRESCOAT	1	SEARCY	1	SWANNER	22
NEEL	1	PRESCOTT	2	SELLERS	1	TALLEY	1
NEESE	2	PRICE	5	SEWELL	1	TARVER	3
NEIL	2	PRIER	4	SEXTON	7	TATE	2
NEILL	1	PRIESTER	2	SHANKS	3	TAUNTON	7
NELSON	5	PRUITT	1	SHAW	9	TAYLOR	70
NEVES	4	PYNES	1	SHEHEAN	1	TERRELL	1
NEWMAN	3	QUARLES	1	SHELL	6	TETER	1
NEWSOM	3	RABB	3	SHEPHERD	1	THAGARD	29
NICHOLLS	1	RABURN	3	SHINE	9	THAGGARD	1

Surname	# of Land Parcels	Surname	# of Land Parcels
THAWER	1	WHIDON	1
THOMAS	7	WHITE	2
THOMASSON	6	WHITTINGTON	1
THOMPKINS	2	WICKER	2
THOMPSON	8	WILKERSON	2
THORNTON	1	WILKINSON	1
THROWER	10	WILLETT	2
THURMAN	1	WILLHELM	3
THURSTON	1	WILLIAMS	53
TIDWELL	1	WILLIAMSON	65
TILLERY	3	WILLS	1
TILLIS	1	WILSON	3
TIMS	2	WINDHAM	1
TIPPET	2	WINGARD	26
TIPPETT	1	WIROSDICK	1
TISDALE	35	WISE	9
TISON	2	WOOD	7
TODD	9	WOODS	2
TOMLINSON	11	WORTHINGTON	1
TRANUM	1	WREN	3
TRUM	1	WRIGHT	21
TUCKER	39	WYATT	4
TULLIS	1	WYCHE	11
TUNNELL	2	WYROSDICK	19
TURBEVILLE	1	YARBROUGH	3
TURMAN	7	YOUNG	2
TURMON	3		
TURNER	8		
TUTRILL	1		
TYPETT	1		
TYSON	4		
UNDERWOOD	18		
UPSHAW	2		
UPTING	1		
VAN PELT	5		
VANN	3		
VEAZEY	6		
VENDERVEER	2		
VICKERY	11		
VINCENT	2		
VINES	4		
VINSON	9		
WADDILL	1		
WADE	8		
WAGERS	2		
WALKER	8		
WALL	11		
WALLACE	2		
WALLER	1		
WALLIS	9		
WARD	3		
WARREN	9		
WARRICK	4		
WASDIN	4		
WATKINS	1		
WATSON	3		
WAYNE	4		
WEATHERFORD	5		
WEBB	7		
WEED	2		
WEIL	4		
WELCH	20		
WELLBORN	1		
WELLS	9		
WEST	5		
WESTER	1		
WETHERFORD	1		
WHALEY	1		
WHEELER	2		
WHIDDON	1		

Surname/Township Index

This Index allows you to determine which *Township Map Group(s)* contain individuals with the following surnames. Each *Map Group* has a corresponding full-name index of all individuals who obtained patents for land within its Congressional township's borders. After each index you will find the Patent Map to which it refers, and just thereafter, you can view the township's Road Map and Historical Map, with the latter map displaying streams, railroads, and more.

So, once you find your Surname here, proceed to the Index at the beginning of the **Map Group** indicated below.

Surname	Map Group	Parcels of Land	Meridian/Township/Range
ACREE	**1**	4	St Stephens 12-N 17-E
" "	**6**	2	St Stephens 10-N 16-E
ADAMS	**22**	8	St Stephens 7-N 19-E
" "	**19**	5	St Stephens 7-N 16-E
" "	**3**	3	St Stephens 11-N 17-E
" "	**1**	1	St Stephens 12-N 17-E
ADDISON	**3**	2	St Stephens 11-N 17-E
ADKISON	**19**	2	St Stephens 7-N 16-E
ALBRITTON	**16**	2	St Stephens 8-N 18-E
" "	**20**	1	St Stephens 7-N 17-E
ALFORD	**15**	4	St Stephens 8-N 17-E
ALLEN	**6**	4	St Stephens 10-N 16-E
" "	**3**	1	St Stephens 11-N 17-E
ALSABROOKS	**21**	1	St Stephens 7-N 18-E
AMASON	**15**	8	St Stephens 8-N 17-E
" "	**13**	1	St Stephens 9-N 19-E
ANDERSON	**21**	4	St Stephens 7-N 18-E
" "	**20**	3	St Stephens 7-N 17-E
" "	**7**	1	St Stephens 10-N 17-E
" "	**16**	1	St Stephens 8-N 18-E
" "	**13**	1	St Stephens 9-N 19-E
ANDRESS	**2**	4	St Stephens 11-N 16-E
" "	**1**	1	St Stephens 12-N 17-E
ANTHONY	**6**	4	St Stephens 10-N 16-E
ARCHER	**1**	6	St Stephens 12-N 17-E
ARMSTRONG	**1**	11	St Stephens 12-N 17-E
" "	**19**	4	St Stephens 7-N 16-E
" "	**14**	3	St Stephens 8-N 16-E
" "	**15**	2	St Stephens 8-N 17-E
" "	**3**	1	St Stephens 11-N 17-E
ARNOLD	**11**	2	St Stephens 9-N 17-E
" "	**14**	1	St Stephens 8-N 16-E
ARRINGTON	**2**	2	St Stephens 11-N 16-E
ASKEW	**22**	1	St Stephens 7-N 19-E
ATHEY	**15**	5	St Stephens 8-N 17-E
ATKINSON	**4**	4	St Stephens 11-N 18-E
" "	**8**	1	St Stephens 10-N 18-E
" "	**9**	1	St Stephens 10-N 19-E
ATKISON	**8**	5	St Stephens 10-N 18-E
AXSON	**12**	1	St Stephens 9-N 18-E
BAILEY	**24**	5	St Stephens 6-N 18-E
BAILY	**24**	1	St Stephens 6-N 18-E
BAIN	**24**	3	St Stephens 6-N 18-E
BAKER	**16**	3	St Stephens 8-N 18-E

Surname	Map Group	Parcels of Land	Meridian/Township/Range		
BALDWIN	**4**	2	St Stephens	11-N	18-E
" "	**3**	1	St Stephens	11-N	17-E
BALL	**7**	5	St Stephens	10-N	17-E
BANKS	**15**	2	St Stephens	8-N	17-E
BARKLEY	**3**	8	St Stephens	11-N	17-E
" "	**1**	3	St Stephens	12-N	17-E
BARNES	**1**	3	St Stephens	12-N	17-E
" "	**8**	2	St Stephens	10-N	18-E
BARRETT	**14**	3	St Stephens	8-N	16-E
" "	**2**	1	St Stephens	11-N	16-E
BARROW	**15**	1	St Stephens	8-N	17-E
BARTERFORD	**3**	1	St Stephens	11-N	17-E
BARTON	**13**	7	St Stephens	9-N	19-E
BASS	**14**	2	St Stephens	8-N	16-E
BATTLE	**16**	2	St Stephens	8-N	18-E
BAYGENTS	**20**	1	St Stephens	7-N	17-E
" "	**15**	1	St Stephens	8-N	17-E
BEASLEY	**10**	1	St Stephens	9-N	16-E
BEAVERS	**1**	4	St Stephens	12-N	17-E
BEAZELY	**3**	1	St Stephens	11-N	17-E
BECK	**17**	3	St Stephens	8-N	19-E
BEDGOOD	**10**	4	St Stephens	9-N	16-E
" "	**19**	1	St Stephens	7-N	16-E
BEDSOLE	**1**	12	St Stephens	12-N	17-E
BELL	**6**	9	St Stephens	10-N	16-E
" "	**20**	3	St Stephens	7-N	17-E
" "	**23**	2	St Stephens	6-N	17-E
BENBOW	**16**	6	St Stephens	8-N	18-E
" "	**21**	3	St Stephens	7-N	18-E
BENNETT	**14**	2	St Stephens	8-N	16-E
" "	**11**	2	St Stephens	9-N	17-E
" "	**1**	1	St Stephens	12-N	17-E
" "	**16**	1	St Stephens	8-N	18-E
BENSON	**14**	8	St Stephens	8-N	16-E
BENTLEY	**11**	7	St Stephens	9-N	17-E
BERDEAUX	**1**	2	St Stephens	12-N	17-E
BERRY	**16**	3	St Stephens	8-N	18-E
" "	**1**	2	St Stephens	12-N	17-E
" "	**9**	1	St Stephens	10-N	19-E
BEST	**3**	6	St Stephens	11-N	17-E
" "	**4**	3	St Stephens	11-N	18-E
BIDSOLE	**1**	1	St Stephens	12-N	17-E
BIRD	**1**	26	St Stephens	12-N	17-E
" "	**8**	4	St Stephens	10-N	18-E
" "	**3**	1	St Stephens	11-N	17-E
" "	**4**	1	St Stephens	11-N	18-E
" "	**17**	1	St Stephens	8-N	19-E
BISHOP	**22**	4	St Stephens	7-N	19-E
" "	**16**	3	St Stephens	8-N	18-E
" "	**7**	1	St Stephens	10-N	17-E
" "	**19**	1	St Stephens	7-N	16-E
BLACK	**10**	8	St Stephens	9-N	16-E
BLACKBURN	**4**	1	St Stephens	11-N	18-E
BLACKMAN	**3**	2	St Stephens	11-N	17-E
" "	**1**	1	St Stephens	12-N	17-E
BLACKMON	**11**	2	St Stephens	9-N	17-E
" "	**4**	1	St Stephens	11-N	18-E
BLACKSHEAR	**3**	1	St Stephens	11-N	17-E
BLAIR	**22**	2	St Stephens	7-N	19-E
BLAKENEY	**19**	1	St Stephens	7-N	16-E

Surname	Map Group	Parcels of Land	Meridian/Township/Range		
BLOCKER	**24**	1	St Stephens	6-N	18-E
BOAN	**10**	12	St Stephens	9-N	16-E
" "	**11**	2	St Stephens	9-N	17-E
" "	**13**	1	St Stephens	9-N	19-E
BODIE	**5**	2	St Stephens	11-N	19-E
BODIFORD	**3**	12	St Stephens	11-N	17-E
" "	**16**	3	St Stephens	8-N	18-E
" "	**4**	2	St Stephens	11-N	18-E
" "	**7**	1	St Stephens	10-N	17-E
BOGGS	**15**	1	St Stephens	8-N	17-E
" "	**12**	1	St Stephens	9-N	18-E
BOLAN	**7**	3	St Stephens	10-N	17-E
" "	**11**	1	St Stephens	9-N	17-E
BOLLING	**8**	1	St Stephens	10-N	18-E
BOND	**9**	9	St Stephens	10-N	19-E
BONHAM	**12**	5	St Stephens	9-N	18-E
BONNER	**8**	2	St Stephens	10-N	18-E
BOON	**7**	5	St Stephens	10-N	17-E
" "	**4**	1	St Stephens	11-N	18-E
BOONE	**4**	3	St Stephens	11-N	18-E
BOOTH	**21**	2	St Stephens	7-N	18-E
" "	**24**	1	St Stephens	6-N	18-E
BOOTHE	**21**	3	St Stephens	7-N	18-E
" "	**22**	2	St Stephens	7-N	19-E
" "	**8**	1	St Stephens	10-N	18-E
BORDEAUX	**1**	1	St Stephens	12-N	17-E
BOSWELL	**21**	1	St Stephens	7-N	18-E
" "	**15**	1	St Stephens	8-N	17-E
BOYD	**15**	1	St Stephens	8-N	17-E
BOYETER	**11**	1	St Stephens	9-N	17-E
BOYETT	**10**	9	St Stephens	9-N	16-E
" "	**3**	6	St Stephens	11-N	17-E
" "	**21**	6	St Stephens	7-N	18-E
" "	**24**	3	St Stephens	6-N	18-E
" "	**4**	2	St Stephens	11-N	18-E
BOYKIN	**23**	1	St Stephens	6-N	17-E
BOYT	**3**	2	St Stephens	11-N	17-E
BOYTER	**11**	3	St Stephens	9-N	17-E
BOZEMAN	**1**	7	St Stephens	12-N	17-E
" "	**2**	2	St Stephens	11-N	16-E
" "	**3**	2	St Stephens	11-N	17-E
" "	**13**	2	St Stephens	9-N	19-E
BRADLEY	**4**	14	St Stephens	11-N	18-E
" "	**20**	6	St Stephens	7-N	17-E
" "	**13**	2	St Stephens	9-N	19-E
" "	**15**	1	St Stephens	8-N	17-E
" "	**12**	1	St Stephens	9-N	18-E
BRADY	**1**	1	St Stephens	12-N	17-E
BRANAN	**22**	1	St Stephens	7-N	19-E
BRANDON	**21**	5	St Stephens	7-N	18-E
BRANEN	**23**	2	St Stephens	6-N	17-E
BRANNAN	**20**	2	St Stephens	7-N	17-E
BRANTLEY	**22**	1	St Stephens	7-N	19-E
BRAWDAWAY	**3**	3	St Stephens	11-N	17-E
BRAZIL	**1**	1	St Stephens	12-N	17-E
BREAKER	**16**	2	St Stephens	8-N	18-E
BREWER	**15**	2	St Stephens	8-N	17-E
BRIDGES	**22**	4	St Stephens	7-N	19-E
" "	**7**	1	St Stephens	10-N	17-E
BRIGGS	**11**	9	St Stephens	9-N	17-E

Surname	Map Group	Parcels of Land	Meridian/Township/Range
BRIGGS (Cont'd)	**15**	2	St Stephens 8-N 17-E
BRIGHT	**19**	5	St Stephens 7-N 16-E
BRISTOW	**13**	3	St Stephens 9-N 19-E
BROOKS	**1**	3	St Stephens 12-N 17-E
" "	**15**	2	St Stephens 8-N 17-E
" "	**20**	1	St Stephens 7-N 17-E
BROWDER	**11**	8	St Stephens 9-N 17-E
BROWN	**14**	3	St Stephens 8-N 16-E
" "	**11**	3	St Stephens 9-N 17-E
" "	**12**	3	St Stephens 9-N 18-E
" "	**3**	2	St Stephens 11-N 17-E
" "	**15**	1	St Stephens 8-N 17-E
BROWNING	**20**	3	St Stephens 7-N 17-E
" "	**15**	2	St Stephens 8-N 17-E
" "	**16**	1	St Stephens 8-N 18-E
BRUNDIGE	**19**	1	St Stephens 7-N 16-E
BRUNSON	**16**	15	St Stephens 8-N 18-E
" "	**15**	10	St Stephens 8-N 17-E
" "	**20**	8	St Stephens 7-N 17-E
" "	**21**	2	St Stephens 7-N 18-E
BRYAN	**7**	4	St Stephens 10-N 17-E
" "	**11**	3	St Stephens 9-N 17-E
" "	**20**	2	St Stephens 7-N 17-E
" "	**2**	1	St Stephens 11-N 16-E
" "	**23**	1	St Stephens 6-N 17-E
" "	**22**	1	St Stephens 7-N 19-E
BRYANT	**21**	3	St Stephens 7-N 18-E
" "	**2**	1	St Stephens 11-N 16-E
BUCK	**3**	4	St Stephens 11-N 17-E
BUCKELEW	**22**	5	St Stephens 7-N 19-E
" "	**16**	4	St Stephens 8-N 18-E
" "	**8**	3	St Stephens 10-N 18-E
BULLARD	**1**	3	St Stephens 12-N 17-E
BURGESS	**5**	12	St Stephens 11-N 19-E
BURGIN	**14**	2	St Stephens 8-N 16-E
" "	**24**	1	St Stephens 6-N 18-E
BURK	**11**	7	St Stephens 9-N 17-E
" "	**16**	2	St Stephens 8-N 18-E
BURKE	**15**	3	St Stephens 8-N 17-E
" "	**11**	1	St Stephens 9-N 17-E
BURKS	**8**	1	St Stephens 10-N 18-E
BURNETT	**19**	1	St Stephens 7-N 16-E
BURNETTE	**20**	1	St Stephens 7-N 17-E
BURNS	**4**	7	St Stephens 11-N 18-E
" "	**10**	4	St Stephens 9-N 16-E
BURT	**1**	1	St Stephens 12-N 17-E
" "	**22**	1	St Stephens 7-N 19-E
BUSH	**11**	5	St Stephens 9-N 17-E
" "	**14**	2	St Stephens 8-N 16-E
" "	**20**	1	St Stephens 7-N 17-E
BUTLER	**24**	5	St Stephens 6-N 18-E
" "	**10**	2	St Stephens 9-N 16-E
BYRD	**13**	2	St Stephens 9-N 19-E
CALDWELL	**10**	5	St Stephens 9-N 16-E
CALLAWAY	**14**	1	St Stephens 8-N 16-E
CALLENS	**6**	1	St Stephens 10-N 16-E
CAMERON	**20**	1	St Stephens 7-N 17-E
CAMPBELL	**8**	4	St Stephens 10-N 18-E
" "	**1**	4	St Stephens 12-N 17-E
" "	**21**	1	St Stephens 7-N 18-E

Surname	Map Group	Parcels of Land	Meridian/Township/Range		
CAMPBELL (Cont'd)	14	1	St Stephens	8-N	16-E
CANDLE	7	1	St Stephens	10-N	17-E
CANNON	5	6	St Stephens	11-N	19-E
" "	8	3	St Stephens	10-N	18-E
" "	4	1	St Stephens	11-N	18-E
" "	20	1	St Stephens	7-N	17-E
" "	12	1	St Stephens	9-N	18-E
CAPPS	15	21	St Stephens	8-N	17-E
" "	16	4	St Stephens	8-N	18-E
" "	17	4	St Stephens	8-N	19-E
" "	21	1	St Stephens	7-N	18-E
" "	12	1	St Stephens	9-N	18-E
CARLILE	21	2	St Stephens	7-N	18-E
" "	22	1	St Stephens	7-N	19-E
CARNES	15	1	St Stephens	8-N	17-E
CARPENTER	22	4	St Stephens	7-N	19-E
" "	23	2	St Stephens	6-N	17-E
" "	21	2	St Stephens	7-N	18-E
CARR	14	6	St Stephens	8-N	16-E
CARTER	23	8	St Stephens	6-N	17-E
" "	20	2	St Stephens	7-N	17-E
" "	21	2	St Stephens	7-N	18-E
" "	22	1	St Stephens	7-N	19-E
" "	15	1	St Stephens	8-N	17-E
" "	13	1	St Stephens	9-N	19-E
CARTLIDGE	15	4	St Stephens	8-N	17-E
CASSITY	4	1	St Stephens	11-N	18-E
CASTELLAW	4	2	St Stephens	11-N	18-E
CASTILLAW	4	2	St Stephens	11-N	18-E
CATHCART	11	1	St Stephens	9-N	17-E
CATLIN	19	8	St Stephens	7-N	16-E
CAULEY	1	1	St Stephens	12-N	17-E
" "	21	1	St Stephens	7-N	18-E
CAUTHAN	4	1	St Stephens	11-N	18-E
CAUTHEN	4	3	St Stephens	11-N	18-E
" "	1	3	St Stephens	12-N	17-E
" "	3	1	St Stephens	11-N	17-E
CAUTHRAN	4	2	St Stephens	11-N	18-E
CAUTHRON	4	3	St Stephens	11-N	18-E
CAWTHEN	1	1	St Stephens	12-N	17-E
CHAMPION	3	15	St Stephens	11-N	17-E
" "	1	13	St Stephens	12-N	17-E
" "	4	7	St Stephens	11-N	18-E
" "	7	1	St Stephens	10-N	17-E
CHANDLER	24	5	St Stephens	6-N	18-E
CHAPMAN	20	4	St Stephens	7-N	17-E
" "	21	2	St Stephens	7-N	18-E
CHASSER	4	1	St Stephens	11-N	18-E
CHESHIRE	7	3	St Stephens	10-N	17-E
" "	1	2	St Stephens	12-N	17-E
" "	4	1	St Stephens	11-N	18-E
CHESSER	4	10	St Stephens	11-N	18-E
" "	5	6	St Stephens	11-N	19-E
" "	8	1	St Stephens	10-N	18-E
CHESTER	15	3	St Stephens	8-N	17-E
CHILDERS	11	3	St Stephens	9-N	17-E
CHILDRE	23	5	St Stephens	6-N	17-E
CHILDRES	10	3	St Stephens	9-N	16-E
CHISSER	17	2	St Stephens	8-N	19-E
CHURCHWELL	8	8	St Stephens	10-N	18-E

Surname	Map Group	Parcels of Land	Meridian/Township/Range		
CHURCHWELL (Cont'd)	**3**	5	St Stephens	11-N	17-E
CLAGHORN	**14**	1	St Stephens	8-N	16-E
CLANCY	**11**	11	St Stephens	9-N	17-E
" "	**15**	10	St Stephens	8-N	17-E
" "	**8**	3	St Stephens	10-N	18-E
CLARK	**8**	7	St Stephens	10-N	18-E
" "	**23**	5	St Stephens	6-N	17-E
" "	**19**	2	St Stephens	7-N	16-E
CLARKE	**23**	3	St Stephens	6-N	17-E
CLAYTON	**8**	1	St Stephens	10-N	18-E
CLEGHORN	**14**	3	St Stephens	8-N	16-E
CLEMENTS	**12**	3	St Stephens	9-N	18-E
" "	**13**	2	St Stephens	9-N	19-E
CODY	**12**	8	St Stephens	9-N	18-E
" "	**22**	2	St Stephens	7-N	19-E
COFFIELD	**1**	1	St Stephens	12-N	17-E
COKER	**3**	5	St Stephens	11-N	17-E
" "	**17**	1	St Stephens	8-N	19-E
COLEMAN	**1**	9	St Stephens	12-N	17-E
" "	**16**	2	St Stephens	8-N	18-E
COLLINS	**3**	2	St Stephens	11-N	17-E
" "	**2**	1	St Stephens	11-N	16-E
COLQUITT	**24**	2	St Stephens	6-N	18-E
COLVIN	**1**	6	St Stephens	12-N	17-E
COMPTON	**15**	7	St Stephens	8-N	17-E
" "	**16**	5	St Stephens	8-N	18-E
" "	**21**	3	St Stephens	7-N	18-E
" "	**13**	2	St Stephens	9-N	19-E
" "	**20**	1	St Stephens	7-N	17-E
" "	**17**	1	St Stephens	8-N	19-E
CONE	**12**	1	St Stephens	9-N	18-E
CONNOR	**19**	1	St Stephens	7-N	16-E
COOK	**14**	4	St Stephens	8-N	16-E
" "	**10**	4	St Stephens	9-N	16-E
" "	**21**	2	St Stephens	7-N	18-E
" "	**3**	1	St Stephens	11-N	17-E
" "	**4**	1	St Stephens	11-N	18-E
" "	**1**	1	St Stephens	12-N	17-E
" "	**22**	1	St Stephens	7-N	19-E
" "	**15**	1	St Stephens	8-N	17-E
" "	**13**	1	St Stephens	9-N	19-E
COON	**24**	2	St Stephens	6-N	18-E
COOPER	**17**	3	St Stephens	8-N	19-E
" "	**8**	2	St Stephens	10-N	18-E
" "	**14**	2	St Stephens	8-N	16-E
" "	**13**	1	St Stephens	9-N	19-E
CORDRAY	**15**	4	St Stephens	8-N	17-E
CORLEY	**3**	2	St Stephens	11-N	17-E
CORNET	**12**	3	St Stephens	9-N	18-E
CORNETT	**13**	1	St Stephens	9-N	19-E
COSBY	**22**	1	St Stephens	7-N	19-E
COSTON	**24**	2	St Stephens	6-N	18-E
COTHEN	**4**	1	St Stephens	11-N	18-E
COTHRAN	**3**	1	St Stephens	11-N	17-E
COTTINGHAM	**1**	1	St Stephens	12-N	17-E
COTTLE	**24**	1	St Stephens	6-N	18-E
COURTNEY	**12**	2	St Stephens	9-N	18-E
" "	**4**	1	St Stephens	11-N	18-E
" "	**15**	1	St Stephens	8-N	17-E
COWART	**14**	3	St Stephens	8-N	16-E

Surname	Map Group	Parcels of Land	Meridian/Township/Range		
COWART (Cont'd)	**10**	3	St Stephens	9-N	16-E
COWLES	**1**	8	St Stephens	12-N	17-E
COX	**22**	2	St Stephens	7-N	19-E
" "	**4**	1	St Stephens	11-N	18-E
" "	**16**	1	St Stephens	8-N	18-E
CRAWFORD	**17**	2	St Stephens	8-N	19-E
CRITINTUN	**4**	1	St Stephens	11-N	18-E
CROXTON	**1**	12	St Stephens	12-N	17-E
" "	**3**	5	St Stephens	11-N	17-E
CULPEPPER	**24**	1	St Stephens	6-N	18-E
CUMBIE	**20**	1	St Stephens	7-N	17-E
CURETON	**23**	5	St Stephens	6-N	17-E
CURTIS	**16**	8	St Stephens	8-N	18-E
" "	**17**	2	St Stephens	8-N	19-E
" "	**3**	1	St Stephens	11-N	17-E
DANIEL	**7**	50	St Stephens	10-N	17-E
" "	**3**	20	St Stephens	11-N	17-E
" "	**2**	11	St Stephens	11-N	16-E
" "	**1**	8	St Stephens	12-N	17-E
" "	**6**	5	St Stephens	10-N	16-E
" "	**20**	4	St Stephens	7-N	17-E
" "	**8**	1	St Stephens	10-N	18-E
" "	**4**	1	St Stephens	11-N	18-E
" "	**23**	1	St Stephens	6-N	17-E
" "	**15**	1	St Stephens	8-N	17-E
DANNELLEY	**24**	2	St Stephens	6-N	18-E
DANNELLY	**23**	1	St Stephens	6-N	17-E
DAUPHIN	**23**	5	St Stephens	6-N	17-E
DAVIDSON	**20**	1	St Stephens	7-N	17-E
DAVIS	**15**	25	St Stephens	8-N	17-E
" "	**1**	20	St Stephens	12-N	17-E
" "	**11**	13	St Stephens	9-N	17-E
" "	**13**	9	St Stephens	9-N	19-E
" "	**3**	7	St Stephens	11-N	17-E
" "	**6**	5	St Stephens	10-N	16-E
" "	**7**	5	St Stephens	10-N	17-E
" "	**21**	5	St Stephens	7-N	18-E
" "	**8**	4	St Stephens	10-N	18-E
" "	**10**	4	St Stephens	9-N	16-E
" "	**24**	3	St Stephens	6-N	18-E
" "	**17**	3	St Stephens	8-N	19-E
" "	**14**	2	St Stephens	8-N	16-E
" "	**9**	1	St Stephens	10-N	19-E
" "	**2**	1	St Stephens	11-N	16-E
" "	**12**	1	St Stephens	9-N	18-E
DAVISON	**6**	3	St Stephens	10-N	16-E
" "	**10**	1	St Stephens	9-N	16-E
DE BREE	**19**	11	St Stephens	7-N	16-E
" "	**12**	4	St Stephens	9-N	18-E
DEAN	**1**	2	St Stephens	12-N	17-E
" "	**6**	1	St Stephens	10-N	16-E
" "	**3**	1	St Stephens	11-N	17-E
" "	**5**	1	St Stephens	11-N	19-E
DEASON	**13**	1	St Stephens	9-N	19-E
DEAY	**17**	1	St Stephens	8-N	19-E
DEES	**19**	2	St Stephens	7-N	16-E
DEESON	**2**	1	St Stephens	11-N	16-E
DELOACH	**21**	3	St Stephens	7-N	18-E
DEMING	**16**	2	St Stephens	8-N	18-E
DENDY	**19**	8	St Stephens	7-N	16-E

Surname	Map Group	Parcels of Land	Meridian/Township/Range
DENDY (Cont'd)	**14**	8	St Stephens 8-N 16-E
" "	**7**	3	St Stephens 10-N 17-E
" "	**3**	2	St Stephens 11-N 17-E
" "	**10**	1	St Stephens 9-N 16-E
DEPRIEST	**7**	4	St Stephens 10-N 17-E
DEVLIN	**16**	1	St Stephens 8-N 18-E
DEWITT	**12**	1	St Stephens 9-N 18-E
DICKERSON	**13**	1	St Stephens 9-N 19-E
DILLARD	**4**	4	St Stephens 11-N 18-E
" "	**7**	1	St Stephens 10-N 17-E
DOCKINS	**7**	4	St Stephens 10-N 17-E
DORMAN	**3**	4	St Stephens 11-N 17-E
" "	**2**	3	St Stephens 11-N 16-E
" "	**17**	2	St Stephens 8-N 19-E
" "	**12**	2	St Stephens 9-N 18-E
" "	**13**	1	St Stephens 9-N 19-E
DOUGLASS	**3**	3	St Stephens 11-N 17-E
DOWNING	**16**	2	St Stephens 8-N 18-E
DOZIER	**23**	14	St Stephens 6-N 17-E
" "	**20**	3	St Stephens 7-N 17-E
DRISKELL	**22**	2	St Stephens 7-N 19-E
DRISKILL	**22**	1	St Stephens 7-N 19-E
DRIVER	**16**	2	St Stephens 8-N 18-E
DRY	**2**	2	St Stephens 11-N 16-E
" "	**3**	2	St Stephens 11-N 17-E
DUKE	**4**	11	St Stephens 11-N 18-E
" "	**15**	4	St Stephens 8-N 17-E
" "	**5**	2	St Stephens 11-N 19-E
" "	**12**	2	St Stephens 9-N 18-E
DUKES	**4**	1	St Stephens 11-N 18-E
DUNCAN	**4**	2	St Stephens 11-N 18-E
" "	**1**	1	St Stephens 12-N 17-E
" "	**24**	1	St Stephens 6-N 18-E
DUNKIN	**4**	1	St Stephens 11-N 18-E
DYER	**9**	4	St Stephens 10-N 19-E
" "	**17**	3	St Stephens 8-N 19-E
DYKES	**11**	2	St Stephens 9-N 17-E
EDDINS	**13**	8	St Stephens 9-N 19-E
EDWARDS	**6**	1	St Stephens 10-N 16-E
" "	**15**	1	St Stephens 8-N 17-E
EILAND	**22**	14	St Stephens 7-N 19-E
" "	**24**	3	St Stephens 6-N 18-E
" "	**17**	2	St Stephens 8-N 19-E
" "	**21**	1	St Stephens 7-N 18-E
ELISOR	**1**	1	St Stephens 12-N 17-E
ELLINGTON	**7**	12	St Stephens 10-N 17-E
" "	**15**	3	St Stephens 8-N 17-E
ELLIS	**21**	7	St Stephens 7-N 18-E
" "	**22**	1	St Stephens 7-N 19-E
ELLISON	**1**	4	St Stephens 12-N 17-E
ENGRAM	**20**	1	St Stephens 7-N 17-E
ETHERIDGE	**23**	1	St Stephens 6-N 17-E
" "	**21**	1	St Stephens 7-N 18-E
EUBANKES	**21**	2	St Stephens 7-N 18-E
EUBANKS	**17**	3	St Stephens 8-N 19-E
" "	**22**	2	St Stephens 7-N 19-E
EVANS	**4**	3	St Stephens 11-N 18-E
EVERAGE	**21**	1	St Stephens 7-N 18-E
EVERIDGE	**21**	3	St Stephens 7-N 18-E
" "	**2**	2	St Stephens 11-N 16-E

Surname	Map Group	Parcels of Land	Meridian/Township/Range		
EVRIDGE	21	3	St Stephens	7-N	18-E
EYLAND	22	1	St Stephens	7-N	19-E
FAGIN	21	1	St Stephens	7-N	18-E
FAIL	6	11	St Stephens	10-N	16-E
" "	24	2	St Stephens	6-N	18-E
" "	23	1	St Stephens	6-N	17-E
FAIRCLOTH	5	1	St Stephens	11-N	19-E
FAISON	20	1	St Stephens	7-N	17-E
FANNIN	20	6	St Stephens	7-N	17-E
FAULK	3	2	St Stephens	11-N	17-E
FEAGIN	23	10	St Stephens	6-N	17-E
" "	19	2	St Stephens	7-N	16-E
" "	20	1	St Stephens	7-N	17-E
FENDLEY	1	1	St Stephens	12-N	17-E
FICKLIN	7	4	St Stephens	10-N	17-E
" "	3	3	St Stephens	11-N	17-E
FICKLING	7	4	St Stephens	10-N	17-E
" "	6	1	St Stephens	10-N	16-E
FIELDER	16	1	St Stephens	8-N	18-E
FINKLEA	19	1	St Stephens	7-N	16-E
FINLAY	17	7	St Stephens	8-N	19-E
" "	16	3	St Stephens	8-N	18-E
" "	13	1	St Stephens	9-N	19-E
FINLEY	17	1	St Stephens	8-N	19-E
FLEMING	3	3	St Stephens	11-N	17-E
FLOWERS	7	7	St Stephens	10-N	17-E
" "	8	1	St Stephens	10-N	18-E
FLOYD	21	6	St Stephens	7-N	18-E
FOLMAR	13	8	St Stephens	9-N	19-E
FORREST	4	1	St Stephens	11-N	18-E
FOSKETT	22	4	St Stephens	7-N	19-E
" "	16	3	St Stephens	8-N	18-E
" "	19	1	St Stephens	7-N	16-E
FOSTER	15	1	St Stephens	8-N	17-E
FOWLE	11	1	St Stephens	9-N	17-E
FOWLER	8	4	St Stephens	10-N	18-E
" "	19	2	St Stephens	7-N	16-E
" "	3	1	St Stephens	11-N	17-E
FRANKLIN	16	11	St Stephens	8-N	18-E
" "	15	10	St Stephens	8-N	17-E
" "	14	5	St Stephens	8-N	16-E
" "	19	2	St Stephens	7-N	16-E
" "	21	2	St Stephens	7-N	18-E
" "	12	2	St Stephens	9-N	18-E
" "	17	1	St Stephens	8-N	19-E
FRAZER	3	3	St Stephens	11-N	17-E
" "	2	2	St Stephens	11-N	16-E
" "	4	2	St Stephens	11-N	18-E
FRAZIER	2	4	St Stephens	11-N	16-E
" "	3	1	St Stephens	11-N	17-E
FROST	23	6	St Stephens	6-N	17-E
" "	20	2	St Stephens	7-N	17-E
" "	10	1	St Stephens	9-N	16-E
FULLER	7	8	St Stephens	10-N	17-E
" "	8	7	St Stephens	10-N	18-E
FUNK	3	2	St Stephens	11-N	17-E
FURR	3	4	St Stephens	11-N	17-E
FURRH	3	3	St Stephens	11-N	17-E
FUTRILL	17	1	St Stephens	8-N	19-E
GABLE	11	5	St Stephens	9-N	17-E

Surname	Map Group	Parcels of Land	Meridian/Township/Range		
GAINER	**21**	10	St Stephens	7-N	18-E
" "	**22**	3	St Stephens	7-N	19-E
GAINES	**21**	7	St Stephens	7-N	18-E
GAINEY	**15**	3	St Stephens	8-N	17-E
GALLOPS	**20**	5	St Stephens	7-N	17-E
" "	**16**	4	St Stephens	8-N	18-E
GALLUPS	**20**	4	St Stephens	7-N	17-E
GAMBLE	**5**	2	St Stephens	11-N	19-E
" "	**4**	1	St Stephens	11-N	18-E
GANEY	**23**	5	St Stephens	6-N	17-E
" "	**15**	1	St Stephens	8-N	17-E
GARDNER	**13**	4	St Stephens	9-N	19-E
" "	**8**	3	St Stephens	10-N	18-E
" "	**23**	1	St Stephens	6-N	17-E
GARRETT	**15**	1	St Stephens	8-N	17-E
GATLIN	**6**	2	St Stephens	10-N	16-E
" "	**4**	2	St Stephens	11-N	18-E
GHOLSON	**6**	1	St Stephens	10-N	16-E
" "	**2**	1	St Stephens	11-N	16-E
GIBBS	**8**	1	St Stephens	10-N	18-E
" "	**24**	1	St Stephens	6-N	18-E
GIBSON	**15**	9	St Stephens	8-N	17-E
" "	**17**	2	St Stephens	8-N	19-E
" "	**21**	1	St Stephens	7-N	18-E
GILCHRIST	**22**	8	St Stephens	7-N	19-E
" "	**21**	1	St Stephens	7-N	18-E
GILCREASE	**15**	4	St Stephens	8-N	17-E
GILL	**3**	1	St Stephens	11-N	17-E
GILLIS	**10**	2	St Stephens	9-N	16-E
GILMER	**13**	1	St Stephens	9-N	19-E
GIPSON	**11**	7	St Stephens	9-N	17-E
GLASS	**3**	2	St Stephens	11-N	17-E
" "	**6**	1	St Stephens	10-N	16-E
GODIN	**17**	1	St Stephens	8-N	19-E
GODWIN	**19**	5	St Stephens	7-N	16-E
" "	**17**	1	St Stephens	8-N	19-E
" "	**13**	1	St Stephens	9-N	19-E
GOGGANS	**4**	1	St Stephens	11-N	18-E
GOLDEN	**17**	1	St Stephens	8-N	19-E
" "	**13**	1	St Stephens	9-N	19-E
GOLDTHWAITE	**5**	5	St Stephens	11-N	19-E
GOODSON	**14**	4	St Stephens	8-N	16-E
" "	**4**	2	St Stephens	11-N	18-E
" "	**15**	2	St Stephens	8-N	17-E
" "	**5**	1	St Stephens	11-N	19-E
GOODWIN	**17**	2	St Stephens	8-N	19-E
" "	**13**	2	St Stephens	9-N	19-E
GORE	**8**	4	St Stephens	10-N	18-E
" "	**4**	1	St Stephens	11-N	18-E
GOULD	**11**	1	St Stephens	9-N	17-E
GRAHAM	**1**	3	St Stephens	12-N	17-E
" "	**3**	2	St Stephens	11-N	17-E
" "	**10**	2	St Stephens	9-N	16-E
" "	**5**	1	St Stephens	11-N	19-E
" "	**24**	1	St Stephens	6-N	18-E
GRANT	**17**	4	St Stephens	8-N	19-E
GRAVES	**1**	1	St Stephens	12-N	17-E
GREEN	**22**	3	St Stephens	7-N	19-E
" "	**7**	1	St Stephens	10-N	17-E
" "	**8**	1	St Stephens	10-N	18-E

Surname	Map Group	Parcels of Land	Meridian/Township/Range		
GREEN (Cont'd)	11	1	St Stephens	9-N	17-E
" "	13	1	St Stephens	9-N	19-E
GREGG	6	2	St Stephens	10-N	16-E
" "	2	1	St Stephens	11-N	16-E
GREGORY	19	2	St Stephens	7-N	16-E
GRIFFIN	6	3	St Stephens	10-N	16-E
GRIGG	2	1	St Stephens	11-N	16-E
GUY	8	4	St Stephens	10-N	18-E
HALE	11	1	St Stephens	9-N	17-E
HALL	1	10	St Stephens	12-N	17-E
" "	4	3	St Stephens	11-N	18-E
" "	5	3	St Stephens	11-N	19-E
" "	21	2	St Stephens	7-N	18-E
" "	15	2	St Stephens	8-N	17-E
" "	16	2	St Stephens	8-N	18-E
" "	12	2	St Stephens	9-N	18-E
" "	7	1	St Stephens	10-N	17-E
" "	19	1	St Stephens	7-N	16-E
HALLFORD	20	5	St Stephens	7-N	17-E
HAMBRICK	2	5	St Stephens	11-N	16-E
" "	1	1	St Stephens	12-N	17-E
HAMIL	19	2	St Stephens	7-N	16-E
HAMILTON	21	7	St Stephens	7-N	18-E
" "	22	1	St Stephens	7-N	19-E
HAMMONDS	10	2	St Stephens	9-N	16-E
HAMMONS	16	2	St Stephens	8-N	18-E
HAMRICK	8	6	St Stephens	10-N	18-E
HANCHEY	12	3	St Stephens	9-N	18-E
HANCOCK	15	2	St Stephens	8-N	17-E
" "	16	1	St Stephens	8-N	18-E
HANDLEY	23	12	St Stephens	6-N	17-E
" "	20	1	St Stephens	7-N	17-E
HANSHAW	7	1	St Stephens	10-N	17-E
HARBIN	3	3	St Stephens	11-N	17-E
HARDCASTLE	12	3	St Stephens	9-N	18-E
HARDIN	15	3	St Stephens	8-N	17-E
HARRELL	12	8	St Stephens	9-N	18-E
" "	16	1	St Stephens	8-N	18-E
" "	11	1	St Stephens	9-N	17-E
HARRELSON	19	1	St Stephens	7-N	16-E
HARRIS	3	9	St Stephens	11-N	17-E
" "	12	4	St Stephens	9-N	18-E
" "	1	2	St Stephens	12-N	17-E
" "	22	1	St Stephens	7-N	19-E
" "	11	1	St Stephens	9-N	17-E
HARRISON	7	6	St Stephens	10-N	17-E
" "	20	4	St Stephens	7-N	17-E
HARRISS	1	1	St Stephens	12-N	17-E
HART	19	3	St Stephens	7-N	16-E
HARTEN	7	1	St Stephens	10-N	17-E
HARTIN	7	2	St Stephens	10-N	17-E
" "	2	2	St Stephens	11-N	16-E
HARWELL	8	1	St Stephens	10-N	18-E
HASTING	10	1	St Stephens	9-N	16-E
HATHEWAY	20	1	St Stephens	7-N	17-E
HATHHORN	7	1	St Stephens	10-N	17-E
" "	12	1	St Stephens	9-N	18-E
HATHORN	7	3	St Stephens	10-N	17-E
" "	21	2	St Stephens	7-N	18-E
HATTAWAY	24	1	St Stephens	6-N	18-E

Surname	Map Group	Parcels of Land	Meridian/Township/Range
HAWKINS	**12**	2	St Stephens 9-N 18-E
HAWTHORNE	**12**	1	St Stephens 9-N 18-E
HAYGOOD	**20**	1	St Stephens 7-N 17-E
HAYNES	**8**	5	St Stephens 10-N 18-E
HEAD	**8**	1	St Stephens 10-N 18-E
HEARTSILL	**2**	4	St Stephens 11-N 16-E
HELMS	**2**	2	St Stephens 11-N 16-E
HELTON	**20**	3	St Stephens 7-N 17-E
" "	**3**	1	St Stephens 11-N 17-E
HELTOR	**19**	1	St Stephens 7-N 16-E
HEMPHILL	**22**	2	St Stephens 7-N 19-E
HENDERSON	**20**	2	St Stephens 7-N 17-E
" "	**5**	1	St Stephens 11-N 19-E
" "	**22**	1	St Stephens 7-N 19-E
HENLEY	**23**	1	St Stephens 6-N 17-E
HENLY	**24**	1	St Stephens 6-N 18-E
HERNDON	**11**	1	St Stephens 9-N 17-E
HESTER	**10**	1	St Stephens 9-N 16-E
HICKMAN	**1**	2	St Stephens 12-N 17-E
HICKS	**20**	3	St Stephens 7-N 17-E
HIGHNATE	**12**	1	St Stephens 9-N 18-E
HIGHSMITH	**19**	3	St Stephens 7-N 16-E
" "	**21**	2	St Stephens 7-N 18-E
" "	**20**	1	St Stephens 7-N 17-E
HIGHTOWER	**7**	2	St Stephens 10-N 17-E
" "	**13**	1	St Stephens 9-N 19-E
HILBUN	**2**	2	St Stephens 11-N 16-E
HILL	**12**	12	St Stephens 9-N 18-E
" "	**15**	7	St Stephens 8-N 17-E
" "	**3**	1	St Stephens 11-N 17-E
" "	**4**	1	St Stephens 11-N 18-E
" "	**1**	1	St Stephens 12-N 17-E
" "	**23**	1	St Stephens 6-N 17-E
HILLIARD	**1**	2	St Stephens 12-N 17-E
HINDES	**1**	1	St Stephens 12-N 17-E
HOLDER	**24**	3	St Stephens 6-N 18-E
HOLLADAY	**16**	2	St Stephens 8-N 18-E
HOLLAND	**20**	12	St Stephens 7-N 17-E
" "	**15**	8	St Stephens 8-N 17-E
" "	**19**	2	St Stephens 7-N 16-E
" "	**16**	2	St Stephens 8-N 18-E
" "	**7**	1	St Stephens 10-N 17-E
HOLLEY	**23**	5	St Stephens 6-N 17-E
" "	**4**	2	St Stephens 11-N 18-E
" "	**21**	2	St Stephens 7-N 18-E
" "	**20**	1	St Stephens 7-N 17-E
HOLLINGSHEAD	**3**	1	St Stephens 11-N 17-E
HOLLIS	**20**	4	St Stephens 7-N 17-E
HOLLY	**23**	2	St Stephens 6-N 17-E
" "	**19**	1	St Stephens 7-N 16-E
HOLMES	**16**	2	St Stephens 8-N 18-E
" "	**17**	2	St Stephens 8-N 19-E
HOLMS	**17**	1	St Stephens 8-N 19-E
HOOD	**4**	3	St Stephens 11-N 18-E
HOOKS	**13**	2	St Stephens 9-N 19-E
" "	**16**	1	St Stephens 8-N 18-E
HOPPER	**16**	2	St Stephens 8-N 18-E
" "	**15**	1	St Stephens 8-N 17-E
HORN	**16**	9	St Stephens 8-N 18-E
" "	**17**	4	St Stephens 8-N 19-E

Surname	Map Group	Parcels of Land	Meridian/Township/Range
HOUGH	**16**	1	St Stephens 8-N 18-E
HOWARD	**8**	3	St Stephens 10-N 18-E
HUDSON	**24**	2	St Stephens 6-N 18-E
" "	**3**	1	St Stephens 11-N 17-E
" "	**15**	1	St Stephens 8-N 17-E
HUETT	**22**	1	St Stephens 7-N 19-E
HUGHES	**4**	6	St Stephens 11-N 18-E
" "	**20**	3	St Stephens 7-N 17-E
" "	**16**	2	St Stephens 8-N 18-E
" "	**8**	1	St Stephens 10-N 18-E
" "	**9**	1	St Stephens 10-N 19-E
" "	**18**	1	St Stephens 7-N 15-E
HUNT	**9**	1	St Stephens 10-N 19-E
HURLEY	**21**	2	St Stephens 7-N 18-E
" "	**22**	2	St Stephens 7-N 19-E
HURT	**23**	4	St Stephens 6-N 17-E
" "	**15**	2	St Stephens 8-N 17-E
HURTT	**5**	4	St Stephens 11-N 19-E
HUTCHISON	**17**	3	St Stephens 8-N 19-E
HUTTO	**8**	2	St Stephens 10-N 18-E
HYNES	**9**	1	St Stephens 10-N 19-E
INGRAM	**15**	2	St Stephens 8-N 17-E
" "	**1**	1	St Stephens 12-N 17-E
" "	**11**	1	St Stephens 9-N 17-E
ISHAM	**3**	1	St Stephens 11-N 17-E
ISOM	**3**	7	St Stephens 11-N 17-E
" "	**4**	1	St Stephens 11-N 18-E
JACKSON	**11**	9	St Stephens 9-N 17-E
" "	**19**	4	St Stephens 7-N 16-E
" "	**8**	3	St Stephens 10-N 18-E
" "	**23**	2	St Stephens 6-N 17-E
" "	**14**	2	St Stephens 8-N 16-E
" "	**13**	2	St Stephens 9-N 19-E
" "	**5**	1	St Stephens 11-N 19-E
" "	**21**	1	St Stephens 7-N 18-E
" "	**22**	1	St Stephens 7-N 19-E
JAMES	**15**	4	St Stephens 8-N 17-E
" "	**10**	4	St Stephens 9-N 16-E
" "	**9**	3	St Stephens 10-N 19-E
" "	**11**	1	St Stephens 9-N 17-E
JAY	**21**	2	St Stephens 7-N 18-E
JAYROE	**21**	2	St Stephens 7-N 18-E
JEFCOAT	**9**	12	St Stephens 10-N 19-E
" "	**12**	11	St Stephens 9-N 18-E
" "	**13**	11	St Stephens 9-N 19-E
" "	**8**	5	St Stephens 10-N 18-E
" "	**5**	1	St Stephens 11-N 19-E
JEFFCOATE	**9**	1	St Stephens 10-N 19-E
JEFFERS	**23**	3	St Stephens 6-N 17-E
JETER	**7**	1	St Stephens 10-N 17-E
" "	**4**	1	St Stephens 11-N 18-E
JOHNS	**19**	1	St Stephens 7-N 16-E
JOHNSON	**3**	17	St Stephens 11-N 17-E
" "	**21**	12	St Stephens 7-N 18-E
" "	**16**	10	St Stephens 8-N 18-E
" "	**20**	4	St Stephens 7-N 17-E
" "	**7**	3	St Stephens 10-N 17-E
" "	**15**	2	St Stephens 8-N 17-E
" "	**13**	2	St Stephens 9-N 19-E
" "	**8**	1	St Stephens 10-N 18-E

Surname	Map Group	Parcels of Land	Meridian/Township/Range
JOHNSON (Cont'd)	**14**	1	St Stephens 8-N 16-E
JOHNSTON	**4**	1	St Stephens 11-N 18-E
JONES	**21**	21	St Stephens 7-N 18-E
" "	**12**	11	St Stephens 9-N 18-E
" "	**8**	9	St Stephens 10-N 18-E
" "	**1**	7	St Stephens 12-N 17-E
" "	**20**	5	St Stephens 7-N 17-E
" "	**2**	4	St Stephens 11-N 16-E
" "	**7**	3	St Stephens 10-N 17-E
" "	**3**	3	St Stephens 11-N 17-E
" "	**24**	3	St Stephens 6-N 18-E
" "	**11**	3	St Stephens 9-N 17-E
" "	**17**	2	St Stephens 8-N 19-E
" "	**5**	1	St Stephens 11-N 19-E
" "	**23**	1	St Stephens 6-N 17-E
" "	**22**	1	St Stephens 7-N 19-E
" "	**13**	1	St Stephens 9-N 19-E
JONSON	**15**	1	St Stephens 8-N 17-E
JORDAN	**4**	20	St Stephens 11-N 18-E
" "	**8**	10	St Stephens 10-N 18-E
" "	**19**	7	St Stephens 7-N 16-E
" "	**7**	3	St Stephens 10-N 17-E
" "	**2**	3	St Stephens 11-N 16-E
" "	**11**	2	St Stephens 9-N 17-E
" "	**5**	1	St Stephens 11-N 19-E
" "	**13**	1	St Stephens 9-N 19-E
JOSEY	**21**	3	St Stephens 7-N 18-E
JOURDAN	**15**	1	St Stephens 8-N 17-E
JUNE	**17**	7	St Stephens 8-N 19-E
" "	**16**	1	St Stephens 8-N 18-E
KEENER	**1**	5	St Stephens 12-N 17-E
" "	**4**	1	St Stephens 11-N 18-E
KELLEY	**3**	8	St Stephens 11-N 17-E
" "	**2**	3	St Stephens 11-N 16-E
" "	**11**	2	St Stephens 9-N 17-E
" "	**4**	1	St Stephens 11-N 18-E
" "	**10**	1	St Stephens 9-N 16-E
KELLY	**3**	5	St Stephens 11-N 17-E
" "	**4**	1	St Stephens 11-N 18-E
" "	**11**	1	St Stephens 9-N 17-E
KELY	**3**	1	St Stephens 11-N 17-E
KENNEDY	**15**	6	St Stephens 8-N 17-E
" "	**21**	2	St Stephens 7-N 18-E
KENNINGTON	**10**	2	St Stephens 9-N 16-E
KENNON	**2**	1	St Stephens 11-N 16-E
KENT	**11**	12	St Stephens 9-N 17-E
" "	**8**	8	St Stephens 10-N 18-E
" "	**12**	5	St Stephens 9-N 18-E
" "	**7**	2	St Stephens 10-N 17-E
" "	**22**	1	St Stephens 7-N 19-E
" "	**16**	1	St Stephens 8-N 18-E
KERBY	**24**	2	St Stephens 6-N 18-E
KERSEY	**12**	2	St Stephens 9-N 18-E
" "	**16**	1	St Stephens 8-N 18-E
" "	**13**	1	St Stephens 9-N 19-E
KETCHAND	**22**	2	St Stephens 7-N 19-E
KETTLER	**10**	2	St Stephens 9-N 16-E
KIDD	**24**	2	St Stephens 6-N 18-E
KILCREASE	**24**	7	St Stephens 6-N 18-E
" "	**14**	6	St Stephens 8-N 16-E

Surname	Map Group	Parcels of Land	Meridian/Township/Range		
KILCREASE (Cont'd)	21	1	St Stephens	7-N	18-E
KIMBRO	20	3	St Stephens	7-N	17-E
KING	12	8	St Stephens	9-N	18-E
" "	22	3	St Stephens	7-N	19-E
" "	13	3	St Stephens	9-N	19-E
" "	3	2	St Stephens	11-N	17-E
" "	16	2	St Stephens	8-N	18-E
" "	17	2	St Stephens	8-N	19-E
" "	8	1	St Stephens	10-N	18-E
" "	2	1	St Stephens	11-N	16-E
" "	4	1	St Stephens	11-N	18-E
" "	1	1	St Stephens	12-N	17-E
KIRKLAND	20	5	St Stephens	7-N	17-E
KIRKPATRICK	6	1	St Stephens	10-N	16-E
KIRVEN	1	1	St Stephens	12-N	17-E
KIRVIN	3	1	St Stephens	11-N	17-E
KITES	16	2	St Stephens	8-N	18-E
KNIGHT	4	6	St Stephens	11-N	18-E
" "	11	2	St Stephens	9-N	17-E
KNOTTS	8	3	St Stephens	10-N	18-E
KNOWLEN	24	1	St Stephens	6-N	18-E
KNOWLING	24	3	St Stephens	6-N	18-E
KNOWLS	2	4	St Stephens	11-N	16-E
KOLB	22	2	St Stephens	7-N	19-E
LANDERS	5	1	St Stephens	11-N	19-E
LANE	19	2	St Stephens	7-N	16-E
" "	15	2	St Stephens	8-N	17-E
LANGLEY	22	1	St Stephens	7-N	19-E
LANIER	21	1	St Stephens	7-N	18-E
LANSDON	4	7	St Stephens	11-N	18-E
" "	8	4	St Stephens	10-N	18-E
" "	5	1	St Stephens	11-N	19-E
LARANCE	12	2	St Stephens	9-N	18-E
LASSITER	24	2	St Stephens	6-N	18-E
LAWRENCE	4	6	St Stephens	11-N	18-E
" "	2	4	St Stephens	11-N	16-E
" "	1	2	St Stephens	12-N	17-E
" "	12	1	St Stephens	9-N	18-E
LAWSON	21	1	St Stephens	7-N	18-E
LAYTON	21	2	St Stephens	7-N	18-E
LEAIRD	8	4	St Stephens	10-N	18-E
" "	11	3	St Stephens	9-N	17-E
" "	12	1	St Stephens	9-N	18-E
LEAK	9	2	St Stephens	10-N	19-E
" "	5	2	St Stephens	11-N	19-E
LEAKE	4	1	St Stephens	11-N	18-E
LEE	17	2	St Stephens	8-N	19-E
" "	11	2	St Stephens	9-N	17-E
" "	20	1	St Stephens	7-N	17-E
LEFLORE	4	1	St Stephens	11-N	18-E
LEGG	2	1	St Stephens	11-N	16-E
LEGGETT	22	2	St Stephens	7-N	19-E
LEVERETT	8	1	St Stephens	10-N	18-E
" "	12	1	St Stephens	9-N	18-E
LEWIS	8	13	St Stephens	10-N	18-E
" "	3	3	St Stephens	11-N	17-E
" "	4	3	St Stephens	11-N	18-E
" "	5	2	St Stephens	11-N	19-E
" "	12	2	St Stephens	9-N	18-E
LIGHTFOOT	22	1	St Stephens	7-N	19-E

Surname	Map Group	Parcels of Land	Meridian/Township/Range		
LILES	**7**	3	St Stephens	10-N	17-E
LINDSEY	**3**	1	St Stephens	11-N	17-E
LINTON	**17**	3	St Stephens	8-N	19-E
" "	**11**	2	St Stephens	9-N	17-E
LITTLE	**15**	4	St Stephens	8-N	17-E
LLOYD	**19**	2	St Stephens	7-N	16-E
LOCK	**15**	1	St Stephens	8-N	17-E
LOCKHART	**21**	5	St Stephens	7-N	18-E
" "	**24**	3	St Stephens	6-N	18-E
" "	**16**	2	St Stephens	8-N	18-E
" "	**17**	1	St Stephens	8-N	19-E
LOFTIN	**7**	5	St Stephens	10-N	17-E
LOLLIS	**21**	2	St Stephens	7-N	18-E
" "	**22**	1	St Stephens	7-N	19-E
LONG	**11**	12	St Stephens	9-N	17-E
" "	**19**	11	St Stephens	7-N	16-E
" "	**10**	3	St Stephens	9-N	16-E
" "	**13**	1	St Stephens	9-N	19-E
LONGFELLOW	**11**	1	St Stephens	9-N	17-E
LOUNSBURY	**24**	1	St Stephens	6-N	18-E
LOWE	**2**	2	St Stephens	11-N	16-E
LOWREY	**7**	15	St Stephens	10-N	17-E
" "	**16**	1	St Stephens	8-N	18-E
LOWRIE	**17**	1	St Stephens	8-N	19-E
LOWRY	**16**	2	St Stephens	8-N	18-E
" "	**7**	1	St Stephens	10-N	17-E
LUKER	**1**	1	St Stephens	12-N	17-E
LUMPKIN	**1**	1	St Stephens	12-N	17-E
MACK	**22**	2	St Stephens	7-N	19-E
MACKEY	**1**	3	St Stephens	12-N	17-E
MADDOX	**24**	4	St Stephens	6-N	18-E
MAHONE	**12**	11	St Stephens	9-N	18-E
" "	**11**	9	St Stephens	9-N	17-E
" "	**16**	6	St Stephens	8-N	18-E
" "	**15**	1	St Stephens	8-N	17-E
MAINOR	**15**	1	St Stephens	8-N	17-E
MAJOR	**19**	2	St Stephens	7-N	16-E
MALLOY	**21**	4	St Stephens	7-N	18-E
" "	**24**	3	St Stephens	6-N	18-E
MALONE	**24**	2	St Stephens	6-N	18-E
MALOY	**24**	4	St Stephens	6-N	18-E
" "	**21**	3	St Stephens	7-N	18-E
MANNING	**15**	2	St Stephens	8-N	17-E
MANSELL	**19**	2	St Stephens	7-N	16-E
MANSILL	**23**	1	St Stephens	6-N	17-E
MAPES	**7**	2	St Stephens	10-N	17-E
" "	**12**	1	St Stephens	9-N	18-E
MARCHANT	**3**	4	St Stephens	11-N	17-E
" "	**4**	1	St Stephens	11-N	18-E
" "	**1**	1	St Stephens	12-N	17-E
MARLOW	**10**	2	St Stephens	9-N	16-E
MARSH	**4**	1	St Stephens	11-N	18-E
MARSHALL	**15**	13	St Stephens	8-N	17-E
" "	**11**	13	St Stephens	9-N	17-E
MARTIN	**12**	11	St Stephens	9-N	18-E
" "	**4**	9	St Stephens	11-N	18-E
" "	**8**	3	St Stephens	10-N	18-E
" "	**21**	3	St Stephens	7-N	18-E
" "	**5**	1	St Stephens	11-N	19-E
" "	**23**	1	St Stephens	6-N	17-E

Surname	Map Group	Parcels of Land	Meridian/Township/Range
MASH	**11**	2	St Stephens 9-N 17-E
MASTIN	**2**	6	St Stephens 11-N 16-E
" "	**3**	1	St Stephens 11-N 17-E
" "	**1**	1	St Stephens 12-N 17-E
MATHEWS	**1**	1	St Stephens 12-N 17-E
MATTHEWS	**21**	1	St Stephens 7-N 18-E
MAY	**5**	6	St Stephens 11-N 19-E
" "	**4**	4	St Stephens 11-N 18-E
MAYHAR	**21**	3	St Stephens 7-N 18-E
MAYNARD	**3**	1	St Stephens 11-N 17-E
MCADAMS	**12**	7	St Stephens 9-N 18-E
" "	**13**	4	St Stephens 9-N 19-E
MCALPIN	**22**	3	St Stephens 7-N 19-E
MCCARTER	**6**	1	St Stephens 10-N 16-E
MCCARTY	**7**	4	St Stephens 10-N 17-E
" "	**1**	4	St Stephens 12-N 17-E
" "	**3**	1	St Stephens 11-N 17-E
" "	**11**	1	St Stephens 9-N 17-E
MCCORMACK	**6**	7	St Stephens 10-N 16-E
" "	**3**	2	St Stephens 11-N 17-E
MCCURLEY	**24**	1	St Stephens 6-N 18-E
MCCURRY	**5**	1	St Stephens 11-N 19-E
MCDANIEL	**1**	2	St Stephens 12-N 17-E
" "	**17**	2	St Stephens 8-N 19-E
" "	**4**	1	St Stephens 11-N 18-E
" "	**24**	1	St Stephens 6-N 18-E
MCDONALD	**4**	4	St Stephens 11-N 18-E
" "	**20**	2	St Stephens 7-N 17-E
" "	**3**	1	St Stephens 11-N 17-E
" "	**12**	1	St Stephens 9-N 18-E
MCDUGALD	**16**	8	St Stephens 8-N 18-E
" "	**21**	3	St Stephens 7-N 18-E
" "	**17**	3	St Stephens 8-N 19-E
MCGEHEE	**11**	5	St Stephens 9-N 17-E
MCGINNEY	**6**	1	St Stephens 10-N 16-E
" "	**12**	1	St Stephens 9-N 18-E
MCGOUGH	**3**	8	St Stephens 11-N 17-E
MCHENRY	**17**	2	St Stephens 8-N 19-E
MCILWAIN	**3**	2	St Stephens 11-N 17-E
" "	**4**	2	St Stephens 11-N 18-E
" "	**1**	1	St Stephens 12-N 17-E
MCKEE	**16**	2	St Stephens 8-N 18-E
MCKETHAN	**1**	1	St Stephens 12-N 17-E
MCKEY	**1**	2	St Stephens 12-N 17-E
MCKINZIE	**9**	2	St Stephens 10-N 19-E
MCLEAN	**14**	1	St Stephens 8-N 16-E
MCLEOD	**13**	7	St Stephens 9-N 19-E
MCMICHEL	**20**	2	St Stephens 7-N 17-E
MCMILLAN	**24**	2	St Stephens 6-N 18-E
MCMULLAN	**6**	1	St Stephens 10-N 16-E
MCMULLEN	**7**	1	St Stephens 10-N 17-E
MCNEAL	**8**	8	St Stephens 10-N 18-E
" "	**9**	7	St Stephens 10-N 19-E
" "	**14**	1	St Stephens 8-N 16-E
MCNEIL	**8**	1	St Stephens 10-N 18-E
MCNEILL	**8**	1	St Stephens 10-N 18-E
MCQUEEN	**3**	6	St Stephens 11-N 17-E
MCQWEEN	**3**	1	St Stephens 11-N 17-E
MCREE	**1**	1	St Stephens 12-N 17-E
MCTYEIRE	**19**	1	St Stephens 7-N 16-E

Surname	Map Group	Parcels of Land	Meridian/Township/Range
MCWILLIAMS	**2**	1	St Stephens 11-N 16-E
MEASLES	**9**	1	St Stephens 10-N 19-E
MEDLEY	**3**	1	St Stephens 11-N 17-E
MELTON	**4**	1	St Stephens 11-N 18-E
MENEES	**8**	2	St Stephens 10-N 18-E
" "	**7**	1	St Stephens 10-N 17-E
MERCHANT	**2**	1	St Stephens 11-N 16-E
MERREES	**7**	1	St Stephens 10-N 17-E
MERRELL	**19**	1	St Stephens 7-N 16-E
MERRILL	**19**	21	St Stephens 7-N 16-E
" "	**20**	13	St Stephens 7-N 17-E
" "	**23**	1	St Stephens 6-N 17-E
MERRITT	**21**	4	St Stephens 7-N 18-E
MIDDLEBROOKS	**8**	1	St Stephens 10-N 18-E
MILES	**23**	3	St Stephens 6-N 17-E
" "	**11**	2	St Stephens 9-N 17-E
MILIGAN	**7**	1	St Stephens 10-N 17-E
MILLER	**7**	5	St Stephens 10-N 17-E
" "	**22**	1	St Stephens 7-N 19-E
" "	**14**	1	St Stephens 8-N 16-E
" "	**11**	1	St Stephens 9-N 17-E
MILLIGAN	**3**	5	St Stephens 11-N 17-E
MILLS	**20**	3	St Stephens 7-N 17-E
" "	**15**	3	St Stephens 8-N 17-E
" "	**8**	2	St Stephens 10-N 18-E
" "	**11**	1	St Stephens 9-N 17-E
" "	**13**	1	St Stephens 9-N 19-E
MILTON	**23**	1	St Stephens 6-N 17-E
MIMS	**8**	1	St Stephens 10-N 18-E
MINARD	**3**	1	St Stephens 11-N 17-E
MINYARD	**3**	2	St Stephens 11-N 17-E
" "	**7**	1	St Stephens 10-N 17-E
MITCHEL	**7**	1	St Stephens 10-N 17-E
" "	**2**	1	St Stephens 11-N 16-E
MITCHELL	**1**	9	St Stephens 12-N 17-E
" "	**24**	7	St Stephens 6-N 18-E
" "	**7**	6	St Stephens 10-N 17-E
" "	**5**	6	St Stephens 11-N 19-E
" "	**4**	4	St Stephens 11-N 18-E
" "	**14**	4	St Stephens 8-N 16-E
" "	**9**	3	St Stephens 10-N 19-E
" "	**13**	2	St Stephens 9-N 19-E
" "	**8**	1	St Stephens 10-N 18-E
" "	**21**	1	St Stephens 7-N 18-E
MONK	**1**	1	St Stephens 12-N 17-E
MONTGOMERY	**21**	7	St Stephens 7-N 18-E
" "	**1**	3	St Stephens 12-N 17-E
" "	**20**	2	St Stephens 7-N 17-E
" "	**3**	1	St Stephens 11-N 17-E
MOODY	**16**	6	St Stephens 8-N 18-E
" "	**24**	4	St Stephens 6-N 18-E
" "	**12**	4	St Stephens 9-N 18-E
" "	**8**	1	St Stephens 10-N 18-E
MOON	**20**	2	St Stephens 7-N 17-E
MOORE	**17**	9	St Stephens 8-N 19-E
" "	**8**	4	St Stephens 10-N 18-E
" "	**16**	4	St Stephens 8-N 18-E
" "	**19**	3	St Stephens 7-N 16-E
" "	**9**	2	St Stephens 10-N 19-E
" "	**4**	2	St Stephens 11-N 18-E

Surname	Map Group	Parcels of Land	Meridian/Township/Range		
MOORE (Cont'd)	1	2	St Stephens	12-N	17-E
" "	24	1	St Stephens	6-N	18-E
" "	10	1	St Stephens	9-N	16-E
" "	11	1	St Stephens	9-N	17-E
MORELAND	12	1	St Stephens	9-N	18-E
MORGAN	24	8	St Stephens	6-N	18-E
" "	6	7	St Stephens	10-N	16-E
" "	19	3	St Stephens	7-N	16-E
" "	10	3	St Stephens	9-N	16-E
" "	2	1	St Stephens	11-N	16-E
" "	1	1	St Stephens	12-N	17-E
MORRIS	19	2	St Stephens	7-N	16-E
" "	24	1	St Stephens	6-N	18-E
MORRISON	12	2	St Stephens	9-N	18-E
MORROW	24	2	St Stephens	6-N	18-E
MOSELEY	2	4	St Stephens	11-N	16-E
" "	8	3	St Stephens	10-N	18-E
" "	4	1	St Stephens	11-N	18-E
MOSELY	8	1	St Stephens	10-N	18-E
" "	4	1	St Stephens	11-N	18-E
MOTES	4	1	St Stephens	11-N	18-E
MOTHERSHEAD	3	8	St Stephens	11-N	17-E
" "	1	8	St Stephens	12-N	17-E
MOTHERSHED	1	2	St Stephens	12-N	17-E
" "	3	1	St Stephens	11-N	17-E
MOUNT	16	2	St Stephens	8-N	18-E
" "	21	1	St Stephens	7-N	18-E
MOYE	11	2	St Stephens	9-N	17-E
MULLINS	22	2	St Stephens	7-N	19-E
MURPHEY	23	1	St Stephens	6-N	17-E
MURPHY	23	3	St Stephens	6-N	17-E
MURRAY	2	1	St Stephens	11-N	16-E
MYEARS	1	1	St Stephens	12-N	17-E
NANSWORTHY	2	1	St Stephens	11-N	16-E
NEEL	1	1	St Stephens	12-N	17-E
NEESE	20	2	St Stephens	7-N	17-E
NEIL	24	1	St Stephens	6-N	18-E
" "	13	1	St Stephens	9-N	19-E
NEILL	1	1	St Stephens	12-N	17-E
NELSON	24	4	St Stephens	6-N	18-E
" "	16	1	St Stephens	8-N	18-E
NEVES	4	4	St Stephens	11-N	18-E
NEWMAN	8	2	St Stephens	10-N	18-E
" "	7	1	St Stephens	10-N	17-E
NEWSOM	23	2	St Stephens	6-N	17-E
" "	20	1	St Stephens	7-N	17-E
NICHOLLS	7	1	St Stephens	10-N	17-E
NICHOLS	15	7	St Stephens	8-N	17-E
" "	7	4	St Stephens	10-N	17-E
" "	3	3	St Stephens	11-N	17-E
" "	21	3	St Stephens	7-N	18-E
" "	1	2	St Stephens	12-N	17-E
" "	13	2	St Stephens	9-N	19-E
NICKOLS	20	1	St Stephens	7-N	17-E
NIX	10	4	St Stephens	9-N	16-E
NOBLES	23	3	St Stephens	6-N	17-E
" "	5	1	St Stephens	11-N	19-E
NORMAN	2	2	St Stephens	11-N	16-E
NORSWORTHY	2	3	St Stephens	11-N	16-E
NORTON	23	1	St Stephens	6-N	17-E

Surname	Map Group	Parcels of Land	Meridian/Township/Range
ODEAY	**17**	2	St Stephens 8-N 19-E
ODUM	**1**	1	St Stephens 12-N 17-E
ODWYER	**11**	2	St Stephens 9-N 17-E
OGDEN	**20**	2	St Stephens 7-N 17-E
OGLESBE	**9**	1	St Stephens 10-N 19-E
OGLESBY	**24**	1	St Stephens 6-N 18-E
" "	**21**	1	St Stephens 7-N 18-E
OLIVE	**16**	4	St Stephens 8-N 18-E
OLIVER	**9**	3	St Stephens 10-N 19-E
ONEILL	**1**	4	St Stephens 12-N 17-E
" "	**3**	2	St Stephens 11-N 17-E
OROXTON	**1**	1	St Stephens 12-N 17-E
OWEN	**5**	7	St Stephens 11-N 19-E
" "	**4**	6	St Stephens 11-N 18-E
" "	**8**	2	St Stephens 10-N 18-E
" "	**23**	2	St Stephens 6-N 17-E
" "	**19**	2	St Stephens 7-N 16-E
" "	**12**	2	St Stephens 9-N 18-E
" "	**1**	1	St Stephens 12-N 17-E
OWENS	**19**	7	St Stephens 7-N 16-E
" "	**7**	2	St Stephens 10-N 17-E
" "	**2**	1	St Stephens 11-N 16-E
" "	**24**	1	St Stephens 6-N 18-E
PARDUE	**15**	2	St Stephens 8-N 17-E
PARHAM	**4**	1	St Stephens 11-N 18-E
PARKER	**20**	4	St Stephens 7-N 17-E
" "	**6**	1	St Stephens 10-N 16-E
" "	**23**	1	St Stephens 6-N 17-E
PARMER	**15**	7	St Stephens 8-N 17-E
" "	**8**	2	St Stephens 10-N 18-E
" "	**3**	2	St Stephens 11-N 17-E
" "	**14**	1	St Stephens 8-N 16-E
PARRISH	**23**	1	St Stephens 6-N 17-E
PATE	**12**	4	St Stephens 9-N 18-E
PATENT	**8**	1	St Stephens 10-N 18-E
PATTERSON	**7**	1	St Stephens 10-N 17-E
" "	**15**	1	St Stephens 8-N 17-E
" "	**12**	1	St Stephens 9-N 18-E
PAUL	**15**	1	St Stephens 8-N 17-E
PAYNE	**4**	3	St Stephens 11-N 18-E
" "	**24**	2	St Stephens 6-N 18-E
" "	**21**	2	St Stephens 7-N 18-E
" "	**8**	1	St Stephens 10-N 18-E
PEACOCK	**21**	3	St Stephens 7-N 18-E
" "	**24**	1	St Stephens 6-N 18-E
PEAVY	**21**	4	St Stephens 7-N 18-E
PEEK	**20**	1	St Stephens 7-N 17-E
PELHAM	**13**	2	St Stephens 9-N 19-E
PENDREY	**23**	4	St Stephens 6-N 17-E
" "	**16**	4	St Stephens 8-N 18-E
" "	**15**	2	St Stephens 8-N 17-E
PENTON	**4**	3	St Stephens 11-N 18-E
" "	**1**	2	St Stephens 12-N 17-E
PERDUE	**15**	7	St Stephens 8-N 17-E
" "	**6**	1	St Stephens 10-N 16-E
" "	**2**	1	St Stephens 11-N 16-E
" "	**11**	1	St Stephens 9-N 17-E
PERKINS	**16**	3	St Stephens 8-N 18-E
" "	**11**	2	St Stephens 9-N 17-E
" "	**21**	1	St Stephens 7-N 18-E

Surname	Map Group	Parcels of Land	Meridian/Township/Range
PERRITT	11	4	St Stephens 9-N 17-E
" "	8	2	St Stephens 10-N 18-E
PERRY	20	3	St Stephens 7-N 17-E
" "	2	2	St Stephens 11-N 16-E
" "	15	2	St Stephens 8-N 17-E
PERRYMAN	3	1	St Stephens 11-N 17-E
PETERSON	21	2	St Stephens 7-N 18-E
PETRY	4	4	St Stephens 11-N 18-E
" "	8	1	St Stephens 10-N 18-E
PETTY	7	7	St Stephens 10-N 17-E
" "	2	1	St Stephens 11-N 16-E
" "	11	1	St Stephens 9-N 17-E
PHARAOH	7	8	St Stephens 10-N 17-E
PHAROAH	7	3	St Stephens 10-N 17-E
PHAROH	7	4	St Stephens 10-N 17-E
PHILLIPS	20	1	St Stephens 7-N 17-E
" "	21	1	St Stephens 7-N 18-E
" "	15	1	St Stephens 8-N 17-E
PICKETT	14	5	St Stephens 8-N 16-E
" "	10	4	St Stephens 9-N 16-E
" "	11	1	St Stephens 9-N 17-E
PINTON	4	2	St Stephens 11-N 18-E
PITMAN	11	1	St Stephens 9-N 17-E
PLATT	16	3	St Stephens 8-N 18-E
" "	15	1	St Stephens 8-N 17-E
POLK	1	3	St Stephens 12-N 17-E
" "	2	2	St Stephens 11-N 16-E
" "	3	2	St Stephens 11-N 17-E
POLLARD	7	18	St Stephens 10-N 17-E
" "	3	1	St Stephens 11-N 17-E
PONDER	16	5	St Stephens 8-N 18-E
" "	12	2	St Stephens 9-N 18-E
POPE	24	3	St Stephens 6-N 18-E
" "	15	2	St Stephens 8-N 17-E
" "	1	1	St Stephens 12-N 17-E
PORTER	21	3	St Stephens 7-N 18-E
POTTER	19	2	St Stephens 7-N 16-E
" "	12	2	St Stephens 9-N 18-E
" "	21	1	St Stephens 7-N 18-E
" "	14	1	St Stephens 8-N 16-E
POUNCEY	3	4	St Stephens 11-N 17-E
" "	1	2	St Stephens 12-N 17-E
" "	7	1	St Stephens 10-N 17-E
" "	2	1	St Stephens 11-N 16-E
POUNCY	14	3	St Stephens 8-N 16 E
POWELL	1	6	St Stephens 12-N 17-E
" "	4	3	St Stephens 11-N 18-E
" "	10	3	St Stephens 9-N 16-E
" "	5	1	St Stephens 11-N 19-E
PRESCOAT	12	1	St Stephens 9-N 18-E
PRESCOTT	24	2	St Stephens 6-N 18-E
PRICE	20	5	St Stephens 7-N 17-E
PRIER	14	4	St Stephens 8-N 16-E
PRIESTER	21	2	St Stephens 7-N 18-E
PRUITT	5	1	St Stephens 11-N 19-E
PYNES	12	1	St Stephens 9-N 18-E
QUARLES	10	1	St Stephens 9-N 16-E
RABB	12	3	St Stephens 9-N 18-E
RABURN	24	3	St Stephens 6-N 18-E
RAINER	11	4	St Stephens 9-N 17-E

Surname	Map Group	Parcels of Land	Meridian/Township/Range
RAMBO	**11**	1	St Stephens 9-N 17-E
RAMICK	**24**	1	St Stephens 6-N 18-E
RAY	**1**	2	St Stephens 12-N 17-E
REAVES	**7**	5	St Stephens 10-N 17-E
" "	**14**	5	St Stephens 8-N 16-E
" "	**6**	2	St Stephens 10-N 16-E
" "	**11**	2	St Stephens 9-N 17-E
" "	**17**	1	St Stephens 8-N 19-E
" "	**10**	1	St Stephens 9-N 16-E
REDMON	**12**	1	St Stephens 9-N 18-E
REDMOND	**12**	2	St Stephens 9-N 18-E
REED	**12**	1	St Stephens 9-N 18-E
REESE	**12**	8	St Stephens 9-N 18-E
" "	**7**	2	St Stephens 10-N 17-E
" "	**15**	1	St Stephens 8-N 17-E
" "	**10**	1	St Stephens 9-N 16-E
REEVES	**6**	9	St Stephens 10-N 16-E
" "	**10**	6	St Stephens 9-N 16-E
" "	**3**	1	St Stephens 11-N 17-E
" "	**17**	1	St Stephens 8-N 19-E
" "	**11**	1	St Stephens 9-N 17-E
REID	**18**	3	St Stephens 7-N 15-E
REIVES	**17**	1	St Stephens 8-N 19-E
REYNOLDS	**8**	1	St Stephens 10-N 18-E
" "	**4**	1	St Stephens 11-N 18-E
RHOADES	**19**	2	St Stephens 7-N 16-E
" "	**7**	1	St Stephens 10-N 17-E
RHODES	**8**	12	St Stephens 10-N 18-E
" "	**15**	7	St Stephens 8-N 17-E
" "	**20**	5	St Stephens 7-N 17-E
" "	**12**	5	St Stephens 9-N 18-E
" "	**7**	4	St Stephens 10-N 17-E
" "	**13**	3	St Stephens 9-N 19-E
" "	**14**	2	St Stephens 8-N 16-E
" "	**10**	2	St Stephens 9-N 16-E
RIALS	**7**	1	St Stephens 10-N 17-E
RICHARDSON	**16**	6	St Stephens 8-N 18-E
" "	**8**	1	St Stephens 10-N 18-E
" "	**1**	1	St Stephens 12-N 17-E
" "	**14**	1	St Stephens 8-N 16-E
" "	**12**	1	St Stephens 9-N 18-E
RICHBOURG	**17**	1	St Stephens 8-N 19-E
RICHBURG	**20**	3	St Stephens 7-N 17-E
" "	**12**	1	St Stephens 9-N 18-E
RIDGEWAY	**19**	2	St Stephens 7-N 16-E
RIDGWAY	**11**	8	St Stephens 9-N 17-E
RIEVES	**13**	4	St Stephens 9-N 19-E
RILEY	**21**	1	St Stephens 7-N 18-E
RIVES	**6**	1	St Stephens 10-N 16-E
ROACH	**15**	8	St Stephens 8-N 17-E
" "	**20**	4	St Stephens 7-N 17-E
" "	**23**	3	St Stephens 6-N 17-E
ROAN	**10**	1	St Stephens 9-N 16-E
ROBBINS	**23**	5	St Stephens 6-N 17-E
" "	**24**	1	St Stephens 6-N 18-E
" "	**20**	1	St Stephens 7-N 17-E
" "	**11**	1	St Stephens 9-N 17-E
ROBERTS	**1**	1	St Stephens 12-N 17-E
ROBINS	**24**	2	St Stephens 6-N 18-E
ROBINSON	**5**	3	St Stephens 11-N 19-E

Surname	Map Group	Parcels of Land	Meridian/Township/Range		
ROBINSON (Cont'd)	**24**	1	St Stephens	6-N	18-E
" "	**11**	1	St Stephens	9-N	17-E
RODGERS	**11**	13	St Stephens	9-N	17-E
" "	**7**	7	St Stephens	10-N	17-E
" "	**23**	3	St Stephens	6-N	17-E
" "	**20**	2	St Stephens	7-N	17-E
" "	**19**	1	St Stephens	7-N	16-E
ROGERS	**7**	10	St Stephens	10-N	17-E
" "	**23**	9	St Stephens	6-N	17-E
" "	**4**	8	St Stephens	11-N	18-E
" "	**11**	7	St Stephens	9-N	17-E
" "	**21**	4	St Stephens	7-N	18-E
" "	**24**	3	St Stephens	6-N	18-E
" "	**18**	3	St Stephens	7-N	15-E
" "	**19**	3	St Stephens	7-N	16-E
" "	**14**	3	St Stephens	8-N	16-E
" "	**20**	2	St Stephens	7-N	17-E
" "	**3**	1	St Stephens	11-N	17-E
" "	**16**	1	St Stephens	8-N	18-E
ROIAL	**1**	2	St Stephens	12-N	17-E
ROPER	**6**	4	St Stephens	10-N	16-E
" "	**2**	3	St Stephens	11-N	16-E
" "	**3**	1	St Stephens	11-N	17-E
" "	**1**	1	St Stephens	12-N	17-E
ROSS	**1**	4	St Stephens	12-N	17-E
ROSTICK	**12**	1	St Stephens	9-N	18-E
ROUSE	**13**	4	St Stephens	9-N	19-E
ROWELL	**23**	1	St Stephens	6-N	17-E
ROYAL	**20**	3	St Stephens	7-N	17-E
" "	**1**	1	St Stephens	12-N	17-E
ROYALS	**1**	1	St Stephens	12-N	17-E
ROZEAR	**17**	2	St Stephens	8-N	19-E
RUSSELL	**7**	1	St Stephens	10-N	17-E
RUTLEDGE	**8**	2	St Stephens	10-N	18-E
" "	**12**	1	St Stephens	9-N	18-E
RYALS	**1**	3	St Stephens	12-N	17-E
" "	**2**	2	St Stephens	11-N	16-E
RYLANDER	**4**	1	St Stephens	11-N	18-E
SALTER	**3**	4	St Stephens	11-N	17-E
" "	**12**	1	St Stephens	9-N	18-E
SANDERS	**20**	3	St Stephens	7-N	17-E
" "	**15**	2	St Stephens	8-N	17-E
" "	**5**	1	St Stephens	11-N	19-E
SANKEY	**4**	2	St Stephens	11-N	18-E
SARLES	**1**	1	St Stephens	12-N	17-E
SARTON	**16**	1	St Stephens	8-N	18-E
SARTOR	**16**	6	St Stephens	8-N	18-E
SASSEN	**20**	1	St Stephens	7-N	17-E
SASSER	**24**	12	St Stephens	6-N	18-E
" "	**20**	12	St Stephens	7-N	17-E
" "	**21**	7	St Stephens	7-N	18-E
SAUNDERS	**20**	6	St Stephens	7-N	17-E
SCARBOROUGH	**20**	1	St Stephens	7-N	17-E
SCHOFIELD	**3**	4	St Stephens	11-N	17-E
SCIPPER	**11**	3	St Stephens	9-N	17-E
" "	**7**	2	St Stephens	10-N	17-E
" "	**19**	1	St Stephens	7-N	16-E
SCOFIELD	**9**	1	St Stephens	10-N	19-E
SCOTT	**2**	1	St Stephens	11-N	16-E
" "	**21**	1	St Stephens	7-N	18-E

Surname	Map Group	Parcels of Land	Meridian/Township/Range		
SEALS	**13**	1	St Stephens	9-N	19-E
SEARCY	**6**	1	St Stephens	10-N	16-E
SELLERS	**8**	1	St Stephens	10-N	18-E
SEWELL	**7**	1	St Stephens	10-N	17-E
SEXTON	**2**	4	St Stephens	11-N	16-E
" "	**7**	3	St Stephens	10-N	17-E
SHANKS	**21**	3	St Stephens	7-N	18-E
SHAW	**17**	6	St Stephens	8-N	19-E
" "	**1**	1	St Stephens	12-N	17-E
" "	**21**	1	St Stephens	7-N	18-E
" "	**22**	1	St Stephens	7-N	19-E
SHEHEAN	**19**	1	St Stephens	7-N	16-E
SHELL	**7**	6	St Stephens	10-N	17-E
SHEPHERD	**10**	1	St Stephens	9-N	16-E
SHINE	**19**	7	St Stephens	7-N	16-E
" "	**18**	2	St Stephens	7-N	15-E
SHOWES	**7**	1	St Stephens	10-N	17-E
SHOWS	**7**	8	St Stephens	10-N	17-E
" "	**8**	2	St Stephens	10-N	18-E
" "	**14**	2	St Stephens	8-N	16-E
" "	**4**	1	St Stephens	11-N	18-E
SIKES	**8**	2	St Stephens	10-N	18-E
" "	**7**	1	St Stephens	10-N	17-E
SILER	**16**	8	St Stephens	8-N	18-E
" "	**12**	2	St Stephens	9-N	18-E
SIMMONS	**1**	11	St Stephens	12-N	17-E
" "	**24**	2	St Stephens	6-N	18-E
SIMPSON	**3**	2	St Stephens	11-N	17-E
SIMS	**2**	9	St Stephens	11-N	16-E
" "	**7**	3	St Stephens	10-N	17-E
" "	**9**	1	St Stephens	10-N	19-E
" "	**23**	1	St Stephens	6-N	17-E
" "	**12**	1	St Stephens	9-N	18-E
SKAIN	**15**	5	St Stephens	8-N	17-E
SKAINS	**15**	22	St Stephens	8-N	17-E
" "	**16**	3	St Stephens	8-N	18-E
" "	**11**	1	St Stephens	9-N	17-E
SKINNER	**4**	1	St Stephens	11-N	18-E
SKIPPER	**6**	7	St Stephens	10-N	16-E
" "	**7**	3	St Stephens	10-N	17-E
" "	**19**	3	St Stephens	7-N	16-E
" "	**11**	2	St Stephens	9-N	17-E
" "	**8**	1	St Stephens	10-N	18-E
" "	**10**	1	St Stephens	9-N	16-E
SLOANE	**1**	2	St Stephens	12-N	17-E
SMILIE	**4**	2	St Stephens	11-N	18-E
" "	**5**	1	St Stephens	11-N	19-E
" "	**13**	1	St Stephens	9-N	19-E
SMITH	**24**	20	St Stephens	6-N	18-E
" "	**21**	10	St Stephens	7-N	18-E
" "	**12**	8	St Stephens	9-N	18-E
" "	**19**	6	St Stephens	7-N	16-E
" "	**10**	6	St Stephens	9-N	16-E
" "	**14**	3	St Stephens	8-N	16-E
" "	**20**	2	St Stephens	7-N	17-E
" "	**15**	2	St Stephens	8-N	17-E
" "	**2**	1	St Stephens	11-N	16-E
" "	**1**	1	St Stephens	12-N	17-E
" "	**22**	1	St Stephens	7-N	19-E
" "	**16**	1	St Stephens	8-N	18-E

Surname	Map Group	Parcels of Land	Meridian/Township/Range		
SMITH (Cont'd)	11	1	St Stephens	9-N	17-E
SMYTH	10	4	St Stephens	9-N	16-E
" "	11	3	St Stephens	9-N	17-E
" "	19	2	St Stephens	7-N	16-E
" "	14	2	St Stephens	8-N	16-E
SOLOMAN	8	1	St Stephens	10-N	18-E
SOLOMON	8	4	St Stephens	10-N	18-E
" "	19	2	St Stephens	7-N	16-E
" "	11	1	St Stephens	9-N	17-E
" "	12	1	St Stephens	9-N	18-E
SORRELL	20	2	St Stephens	7-N	17-E
SORRELLS	21	2	St Stephens	7-N	18-E
" "	11	1	St Stephens	9-N	17-E
SOWELL	11	6	St Stephens	9-N	17-E
" "	2	1	St Stephens	11-N	16-E
SPEAR	17	1	St Stephens	8-N	19-E
SPEIR	17	5	St Stephens	8-N	19-E
SPENCER	20	3	St Stephens	7-N	17-E
" "	16	1	St Stephens	8-N	18-E
SPIVEY	22	3	St Stephens	7-N	19-E
" "	11	1	St Stephens	9-N	17-E
SPORT	23	3	St Stephens	6-N	17-E
SPRADLEY	6	1	St Stephens	10-N	16-E
" "	7	1	St Stephens	10-N	17-E
" "	8	1	St Stephens	10-N	18-E
" "	4	1	St Stephens	11-N	18-E
SPRAGGINS	14	4	St Stephens	8-N	16-E
" "	3	3	St Stephens	11-N	17-E
" "	1	1	St Stephens	12-N	17-E
SPRAGINS	1	4	St Stephens	12-N	17-E
" "	3	2	St Stephens	11-N	17-E
SPURLIN	20	1	St Stephens	7-N	17-E
" "	15	1	St Stephens	8-N	17-E
SPURLOCK	8	2	St Stephens	10-N	18-E
STAGGERS	11	6	St Stephens	9-N	17-E
" "	12	5	St Stephens	9-N	18-E
" "	15	2	St Stephens	8-N	17-E
" "	10	2	St Stephens	9-N	16-E
" "	3	1	St Stephens	11-N	17-E
" "	4	1	St Stephens	11-N	18-E
STALLINGS	19	10	St Stephens	7-N	16-E
" "	18	2	St Stephens	7-N	15-E
STANALAND	21	5	St Stephens	7-N	18-E
STANDLEY	22	1	St Stephens	7-N	19-E
STANLEY	20	9	St Stephens	7-N	17-E
" "	19	3	St Stephens	7-N	16-E
" "	22	2	St Stephens	7-N	19-E
" "	5	1	St Stephens	11-N	19-E
STARK	4	1	St Stephens	11-N	18-E
STARLING	11	1	St Stephens	9-N	17-E
STARR	11	4	St Stephens	9-N	17-E
" "	15	2	St Stephens	8-N	17-E
STEPHENS	12	1	St Stephens	9-N	18-E
" "	13	1	St Stephens	9-N	19-E
STEPHENSON	12	3	St Stephens	9-N	18-E
" "	8	2	St Stephens	10-N	18-E
STEVENS	13	1	St Stephens	9-N	19-E
STEVENSON	8	2	St Stephens	10-N	18-E
STEWART	23	8	St Stephens	6-N	17-E
" "	12	7	St Stephens	9-N	18-E

Surname	Map Group	Parcels of Land	Meridian/Township/Range
STEWART (Cont'd)	**13**	7	St Stephens 9-N 19-E
" "	**9**	1	St Stephens 10-N 19-E
" "	**24**	1	St Stephens 6-N 18-E
STINSON	**17**	11	St Stephens 8-N 19-E
" "	**16**	3	St Stephens 8-N 18-E
" "	**3**	2	St Stephens 11-N 17-E
" "	**4**	1	St Stephens 11-N 18-E
STOCKARD	**12**	3	St Stephens 9-N 18-E
STOKES	**15**	2	St Stephens 8-N 17-E
" "	**20**	1	St Stephens 7-N 17-E
STONE	**1**	1	St Stephens 12-N 17-E
STOUGH	**3**	5	St Stephens 11-N 17-E
" "	**8**	4	St Stephens 10-N 18-E
" "	**4**	2	St Stephens 11-N 18-E
STRAUGHN	**23**	1	St Stephens 6-N 17-E
STREET	**12**	2	St Stephens 9-N 18-E
STRICKLAN	**12**	1	St Stephens 9-N 18-E
STRICKLIN	**21**	5	St Stephens 7-N 18-E
" "	**23**	1	St Stephens 6-N 17-E
STRINGER	**2**	8	St Stephens 11-N 16-E
" "	**22**	3	St Stephens 7-N 19-E
" "	**7**	1	St Stephens 10-N 17-E
STRIPLING	**20**	2	St Stephens 7-N 17-E
STURGIS	**8**	7	St Stephens 10-N 18-E
STYRON	**15**	1	St Stephens 8-N 17-E
SUMMERLIN	**8**	11	St Stephens 10-N 18-E
" "	**4**	4	St Stephens 11-N 18-E
SUMMERLINE	**8**	1	St Stephens 10-N 18-E
SURLES	**1**	3	St Stephens 12-N 17-E
SWANER	**16**	1	St Stephens 8-N 18-E
SWANNER	**15**	15	St Stephens 8-N 17-E
" "	**17**	5	St Stephens 8-N 19-E
" "	**16**	1	St Stephens 8-N 18-E
" "	**12**	1	St Stephens 9-N 18-E
TALLEY	**8**	1	St Stephens 10-N 18-E
TARVER	**9**	2	St Stephens 10-N 19-E
" "	**8**	1	St Stephens 10-N 18-E
TATE	**15**	2	St Stephens 8-N 17-E
TAUNTON	**20**	7	St Stephens 7-N 17-E
TAYLOR	**23**	18	St Stephens 6-N 17-E
" "	**20**	17	St Stephens 7-N 17-E
" "	**4**	11	St Stephens 11-N 18-E
" "	**21**	11	St Stephens 7-N 18-E
" "	**2**	5	St Stephens 11-N 16-E
" "	**8**	3	St Stephens 10-N 18-E
" "	**9**	2	St Stephens 10-N 19-E
" "	**19**	1	St Stephens 7-N 16-E
" "	**15**	1	St Stephens 8-N 17-E
" "	**13**	1	St Stephens 9-N 19-E
TERRELL	**1**	1	St Stephens 12-N 17-E
TETER	**4**	1	St Stephens 11-N 18-E
THAGARD	**7**	12	St Stephens 10-N 17-E
" "	**11**	12	St Stephens 9-N 17-E
" "	**12**	4	St Stephens 9-N 18-E
" "	**15**	1	St Stephens 8-N 17-E
THAGGARD	**11**	1	St Stephens 9-N 17-E
THAWER	**4**	1	St Stephens 11-N 18-E
THOMAS	**10**	4	St Stephens 9-N 16-E
" "	**16**	2	St Stephens 8-N 18-E
" "	**3**	1	St Stephens 11-N 17-E

Surname	Map Group	Parcels of Land	Meridian/Township/Range		
THOMASSON	**24**	5	St Stephens	6-N	18-E
" "	**15**	1	St Stephens	8-N	17-E
THOMPKINS	**21**	2	St Stephens	7-N	18-E
THOMPSON	**13**	4	St Stephens	9-N	19-E
" "	**1**	2	St Stephens	12-N	17-E
" "	**8**	1	St Stephens	10-N	18-E
" "	**16**	1	St Stephens	8-N	18-E
THORNTON	**2**	1	St Stephens	11-N	16-E
THROWER	**4**	10	St Stephens	11-N	18-E
THURMAN	**22**	1	St Stephens	7-N	19-E
THURSTON	**20**	1	St Stephens	7-N	17-E
TIDWELL	**24**	1	St Stephens	6-N	18-E
TILLERY	**21**	3	St Stephens	7-N	18-E
TILLIS	**24**	1	St Stephens	6-N	18-E
TIMS	**7**	2	St Stephens	10-N	17-E
TIPPET	**12**	2	St Stephens	9-N	18-E
TIPPETT	**12**	1	St Stephens	9-N	18-E
TISDALE	**21**	18	St Stephens	7-N	18-E
" "	**16**	13	St Stephens	8-N	18-E
" "	**12**	2	St Stephens	9-N	18-E
" "	**13**	2	St Stephens	9-N	19-E
TISON	**20**	2	St Stephens	7-N	17-E
TODD	**2**	7	St Stephens	11-N	16-E
" "	**3**	1	St Stephens	11-N	17-E
" "	**1**	1	St Stephens	12-N	17-E
TOMLINSON	**2**	5	St Stephens	11-N	16-E
" "	**3**	5	St Stephens	11-N	17-E
" "	**15**	1	St Stephens	8-N	17-E
TRANUM	**7**	1	St Stephens	10-N	17-E
TRUM	**22**	1	St Stephens	7-N	19-E
TUCKER	**5**	18	St Stephens	11-N	19-E
" "	**4**	15	St Stephens	11-N	18-E
" "	**12**	6	St Stephens	9-N	18-E
TULLIS	**24**	1	St Stephens	6-N	18-E
TUNNELL	**9**	2	St Stephens	10-N	19-E
TURBEVILLE	**23**	1	St Stephens	6-N	17-E
TURMAN	**22**	7	St Stephens	7-N	19-E
TURMON	**22**	3	St Stephens	7-N	19-E
TURNER	**21**	3	St Stephens	7-N	18-E
" "	**2**	2	St Stephens	11-N	16-E
" "	**20**	2	St Stephens	7-N	17-E
" "	**15**	1	St Stephens	8-N	17-E
TUTRILL	**17**	1	St Stephens	8-N	19-E
TYPETT	**12**	1	St Stephens	9-N	18-E
TYSON	**20**	4	St Stephens	7-N	17-E
UNDERWOOD	**12**	8	St Stephens	9-N	18-E
" "	**19**	2	St Stephens	7-N	16-E
" "	**16**	2	St Stephens	8-N	18-E
" "	**13**	2	St Stephens	9-N	19-E
" "	**20**	1	St Stephens	7-N	17-E
" "	**21**	1	St Stephens	7-N	18-E
" "	**15**	1	St Stephens	8-N	17-E
" "	**17**	1	St Stephens	8-N	19-E
UPSHAW	**15**	2	St Stephens	8-N	17-E
UPTING	**15**	1	St Stephens	8-N	17-E
VAN PELT	**19**	5	St Stephens	7-N	16-E
VANN	**10**	3	St Stephens	9-N	16-E
VEAZEY	**6**	6	St Stephens	10-N	16-E
VENDERVEER	**4**	2	St Stephens	11-N	18-E
VICKERY	**1**	6	St Stephens	12-N	17-E

Surname	Map Group	Parcels of Land	Meridian/Township/Range		
VICKERY (Cont'd)	**3**	5	St Stephens	11-N	17-E
VINCENT	**2**	1	St Stephens	11-N	16-E
" "	**1**	1	St Stephens	12-N	17-E
VINES	**21**	4	St Stephens	7-N	18-E
VINSON	**1**	6	St Stephens	12-N	17-E
" "	**7**	2	St Stephens	10-N	17-E
" "	**3**	1	St Stephens	11-N	17-E
WADDILL	**20**	1	St Stephens	7-N	17-E
WADE	**21**	8	St Stephens	7-N	18-E
WAGERS	**24**	2	St Stephens	6-N	18-E
WALKER	**1**	4	St Stephens	12-N	17-E
" "	**16**	3	St Stephens	8-N	18-E
" "	**3**	1	St Stephens	11-N	17-E
WALL	**19**	11	St Stephens	7-N	16-E
WALLACE	**20**	2	St Stephens	7-N	17-E
WALLER	**4**	1	St Stephens	11-N	18-E
WALLIS	**20**	9	St Stephens	7-N	17-E
WARD	**4**	3	St Stephens	11-N	18-E
WARREN	**22**	6	St Stephens	7-N	19-E
" "	**17**	3	St Stephens	8-N	19-E
WARRICK	**24**	2	St Stephens	6-N	18-E
" "	**20**	2	St Stephens	7-N	17-E
WASDIN	**22**	4	St Stephens	7-N	19-E
WATKINS	**4**	1	St Stephens	11-N	18-E
WATSON	**11**	2	St Stephens	9-N	17-E
" "	**4**	1	St Stephens	11-N	18-E
WAYNE	**15**	2	St Stephens	8-N	17-E
" "	**16**	2	St Stephens	8-N	18-E
WEATHERFORD	**23**	5	St Stephens	6-N	17-E
WEBB	**15**	3	St Stephens	8-N	17-E
" "	**16**	3	St Stephens	8-N	18-E
" "	**2**	1	St Stephens	11-N	16-E
WEED	**24**	2	St Stephens	6-N	18-E
WEIL	**12**	4	St Stephens	9-N	18-E
WELCH	**12**	9	St Stephens	9-N	18-E
" "	**7**	5	St Stephens	10-N	17-E
" "	**8**	5	St Stephens	10-N	18-E
" "	**15**	1	St Stephens	8-N	17-E
WELLBORN	**22**	1	St Stephens	7-N	19-E
WELLS	**23**	9	St Stephens	6-N	17-E
WEST	**16**	4	St Stephens	8-N	18-E
" "	**17**	1	St Stephens	8-N	19-E
WESTER	**7**	1	St Stephens	10-N	17-E
WETHERFORD	**4**	1	St Stephens	11-N	18-E
WHALEY	**22**	1	St Stephens	7-N	19-E
WHEELER	**2**	2	St Stephens	11-N	16-E
WHIDDON	**6**	1	St Stephens	10-N	16-E
WHIDON	**6**	1	St Stephens	10-N	16-E
WHITE	**16**	2	St Stephens	8-N	18-E
WHITTINGTON	**10**	1	St Stephens	9-N	16-E
WICKER	**22**	2	St Stephens	7-N	19-E
WILKERSON	**21**	2	St Stephens	7-N	18-E
WILKINSON	**21**	1	St Stephens	7-N	18-E
WILLETT	**1**	2	St Stephens	12-N	17-E
WILLHELM	**4**	3	St Stephens	11-N	18-E
WILLIAMS	**21**	25	St Stephens	7-N	18-E
" "	**23**	8	St Stephens	6-N	17-E
" "	**19**	8	St Stephens	7-N	16-E
" "	**16**	3	St Stephens	8-N	18-E
" "	**3**	2	St Stephens	11-N	17-E

Surname	Map Group	Parcels of Land	Meridian/Township/Range		
WILLIAMS (Cont'd)	**15**	2	St Stephens	8-N	17-E
" "	**10**	2	St Stephens	9-N	16-E
" "	**20**	1	St Stephens	7-N	17-E
" "	**12**	1	St Stephens	9-N	18-E
" "	**13**	1	St Stephens	9-N	19-E
WILLIAMSON	**17**	16	St Stephens	8-N	19-E
" "	**8**	13	St Stephens	10-N	18-E
" "	**12**	12	St Stephens	9-N	18-E
" "	**16**	8	St Stephens	8-N	18-E
" "	**4**	5	St Stephens	11-N	18-E
" "	**20**	4	St Stephens	7-N	17-E
" "	**11**	4	St Stephens	9-N	17-E
" "	**21**	3	St Stephens	7-N	18-E
WILLS	**19**	1	St Stephens	7-N	16-E
WILSON	**20**	2	St Stephens	7-N	17-E
" "	**13**	1	St Stephens	9-N	19-E
WINDHAM	**8**	1	St Stephens	10-N	18-E
WINGARD	**9**	16	St Stephens	10-N	19-E
" "	**5**	10	St Stephens	11-N	19-E
WIROSDICK	**12**	1	St Stephens	9-N	18-E
WISE	**16**	7	St Stephens	8-N	18-E
" "	**21**	2	St Stephens	7-N	18-E
WOOD	**16**	2	St Stephens	8-N	18-E
" "	**13**	2	St Stephens	9-N	19-E
" "	**5**	1	St Stephens	11-N	19-E
" "	**14**	1	St Stephens	8-N	16-E
" "	**15**	1	St Stephens	8-N	17-E
WOODS	**1**	1	St Stephens	12-N	17-E
" "	**13**	1	St Stephens	9-N	19-E
WORTHINGTON	**13**	1	St Stephens	9-N	19-E
WREN	**15**	3	St Stephens	8-N	17-E
WRIGHT	**11**	7	St Stephens	9-N	17-E
" "	**12**	5	St Stephens	9-N	18-E
" "	**8**	4	St Stephens	10-N	18-E
" "	**19**	2	St Stephens	7-N	16-E
" "	**7**	1	St Stephens	10-N	17-E
" "	**1**	1	St Stephens	12-N	17-E
" "	**21**	1	St Stephens	7-N	18-E
WYATT	**8**	2	St Stephens	10-N	18-E
" "	**9**	1	St Stephens	10-N	19-E
" "	**23**	1	St Stephens	6-N	17-E
WYCHE	**7**	5	St Stephens	10-N	17-E
" "	**6**	4	St Stephens	10-N	16-E
" "	**11**	2	St Stephens	9-N	17-E
WYROSDICK	**8**	15	St Stephens	10-N	18-E
" "	**12**	4	St Stephens	9-N	10 E
YARBROUGH	**3**	3	St Stephens	11-N	17-E
YOUNG	**16**	2	St Stephens	8-N	18-E

– Part II –

Township Map Groups

Map Group 1: Index to Land Patents

Township 12-North Range 17-East (St Stephens)

After you locate an individual in this Index, take note of the Section and Section Part then proceed to the Land Patent map on the pages immediately following. You should have no difficulty locating the corresponding parcel of land.

The "For More Info" Column will lead you to more information about the underlying Patents. See the *Legend* at right, and the "How to Use this Book" chapter, for more information.

```
                    LEGEND
            "For More Info . . . " column
A = Authority (Legislative Act, See Appendix "A")
B = Block or Lot (location in Section unknown)
C = Cancelled Patent
F = Fractional Section
G = Group  (Multi-Patentee Patent, see Appendix "C")
V = Overlaps another Parcel
R = Re-Issued (Parcel patented more than once)

(A & G items require you to look in the Appendixes referred
to above. All other Letter-designations followed by a number
require you to locate line-items in this index that possess
the ID number found after the letter).
```

ID	Individual in Patent	Sec.	Sec. Part	Date Issued	Other Counties	For More Info . . .
235	ACREE, Nathaniel	5	W½SW	1837-08-10		A1
237	" "	7	E½SW	1837-08-10		A1
238	" "	7	W½SE	1837-08-10		A1
236	" "	6	SW	1838-07-28	Lowndes	A1
6	ADAMS, Abram	13	E½NW	1831-11-30		A1
343	ANDRESS, William J	28	E½NE	1860-09-01		A1
57	ARCHER, David	29	NWSW	1837-08-09		A1
150	ARCHER, James H	17	SWNE	1834-10-21		A1
151	" "	29	NESW	1834-10-21		A1
197	ARCHER, John M	17	W½SW	1831-11-30		A1
196	" "	17	SESW	1834-09-04		A1
308	ARCHER, William	20	NWNW	1834-09-04		A1
76	ARMSTRONG, Franklin	7	E½NE	1833-06-04		A1
73	" "	19	NWNE	1835-04-02		A1
78	" "	8	E½NW	1837-05-20		A1
75	" "	6	E½SE	1837-08-02	Lowndes	A1
77	" "	7	W½NE	1837-08-02		A1
74	" "	5	E½NW	1837-08-08		A1
152	ARMSTRONG, James M	4	E½SW	1852-12-01		A1
304	ARMSTRONG, William A	6	NW	1837-05-20	Lowndes	A1 V306, 303
306	" "	6	W½NW	1837-05-20	Lowndes	A1 V304
305	" "	6	NWSE	1837-08-02	Lowndes	A1
303	" "	6	E½NW	1837-08-10	Lowndes	A1 V304
113	BARKLEY, Hugh	30	SW	1837-08-10		A1
114	" "	31	E½NE	1837-08-10		A1
115	" "	32	E½SE	1838-07-28		A1 V254
64	BARNES, Ebenezer	12	SESW	1838-07-28		A1
65	" "	3	SWSE	1838-07-28		A1
272	BARNES, Stephen	10	NWNE	1837-08-10		A1
92	BEAVERS, Henry	24	NWNW	1835-04-02		A1
89	" "	13	SESW	1837-05-15		A1
91	" "	23	E½NE	1837-08-10		A1
90	" "	13	SWSW	1838-07-28		A1
100	BEDSOLE, Henry	2	W½SE	1833-09-16		A1
99	" "	2	SESW	1834-08-05		A1
94	" "	11	SENW	1837-04-15		A1
96	" "	11	W½NE	1837-04-15		A1
103	" "	3	SESE	1837-04-15		A1
93	" "	11	SENE	1837-05-15		A1
95	" "	11	SWNW	1837-08-12		A1
98	" "	14	SESE	1837-08-12		A1
97	" "	11	W½SE	1838-07-28		A1
101	" "	3	NENE	1852-02-02		A1
102	" "	3	SENE	1852-02-02		A1
277	BEDSOLE, Thomas	14	NESE	1834-08-05		A1
62	BENNETT, Duke	35	SENE	1835-04-15		A1

ID	Individual in Patent	Sec.	Sec. Part	Date Issued	Other Counties	For More Info . . .
345	BERDEAUX, William J	10	SENE	1850-04-01		A1
344	" "	10	NWSE	1852-12-01		A1
230	BERRY, Mastin E	28	SWNW	1858-11-01		A1
231	" "	29	NESE	1858-11-01		A1
104	BIDSOLE, Henry	11	NENW	1834-08-20		A1
58	BIRD, David	21	NWNE	1834-08-20		A1
105	BIRD, Henry G	25	NE	1831-12-01		A1
106	" "	25	NENW	1834-09-04		A1
107	" "	25	SWSE	1837-05-20		A1
118	BIRD, Hugh	24	E½SW	1833-06-04		A1
120	" "	26	E½SE	1833-06-04		A1
125	" "	36	N½NE	1834-08-20		A1
116	" "	23	E½SW	1834-09-04		A1
123	" "	26	W½SE	1837-04-10		A1
124	" "	35	NENE	1837-04-10		A1
126	" "	36	NW	1837-05-20		A1
117	" "	23	NWSE	1837-08-14		A1
121	" "	26	SWNE	1837-08-14		A1
122	" "	26	W½NW	1837-08-14		A1
119	" "	25	NWSW	1852-12-01		A1
139	BIRD, James	25	SWSW	1837-04-10		A1
138	" "	23	SWSE	1837-08-01		A1
177	BIRD, John	26	NWNE	1837-05-20		A1
174	" "	24	SWSW	1849-09-01		A1
173	" "	23	SESE	1852-12-01		A1
175	" "	25	SESW	1852-12-01		A1
176	" "	26	NENE	1854-10-02		A1
239	BIRD, Neri P	24	E½NW	1833-06-04		A1
241	" "	24	SWNW	1835-10-16		A1
240	" "	24	NWSW	1837-08-01		A1
346	BIRD, William J	23	SWSW	1854-10-02		A1
328	BLACKMAN, William D	36	NESE	1837-08-01		A1
347	BORDEAUX, William J	10	NESE	1852-02-02		A1
46	BOZEMAN, Daniel C	9	SESE	1852-02-02		A1
70	BOZEMAN, Etheldred	18	SWSE	1835-04-15		A1
69	" "	18	SESW	1837-05-15		A1
214	BOZEMAN, Joseph D	18	NESW	1850-08-10		A1
218	BOZEMAN, Josiah	9	W½SE	1834-01-21		A1
217	" "	4	W½SE	1835-10-08		A1
216	" "	4	E½SE	1837-08-02		A1
140	BRADY, James	4	SWNE	1852-12-01		A1
220	BRAZIL, Kindred	30	NWNW	1837-08-01		A1
1	BROOKS, Aaron	8	E½SW	1831-11-30		A1
2	" "	8	W½SE	1834-01-21		A1
3	" "	9	W½NE	1837-08-02		A1
23	BULLARD, Andrew J	14	NWNE	1852-02-02		A1
275	BULLARD, Stephen W	22	NESE	1854-10-02		A1
278	BULLARD, Thomas	13	NWNW	1852-02-02		A1
141	BURT, James C	13	NENE	1837-08-12		A1
179	CAMPBELL, John C	7	NWNW	1835-10-08		A1
178	" "	7	NENW	1835-10-16		A1
180	" "	7	SWNW	1837-05-20		A1
181	" "	7	W½SW	1837-05-20		A1
47	CAULEY, Daniel	29	W½SE	1837-08-18		A1
15	CAUTHEN, Alexander	27	NWSW	1858-11-01		A1
112	CAUTHEN, Hiram	33	S½NW	1837-05-15		A1
111	" "	21	W½SE	1837-08-08		A1
16	CAWTHEN, Alexander	28	SESE	1860-10-01		A1
43	CHAMPION, Claiborn	18	W½SW	1835-10-14		A1
44	" "	19	NW	1835-10-14		A1
134	CHAMPION, Jacob	27	E½SE	1833-08-02		A1
135	" "	27	S½NE	1835-10-14		A1
133	" "	26	W½SW	1837-05-15		A1
136	" "	27	W½SE	1837-08-08		A1
258	CHAMPION, Robert	34	E½NW	1837-08-18		A1
259	" "	34	SENE	1838-07-28		A1
260	" "	34	W½NE	1838-07-28		A1
261	" "	34	W½NW	1838-07-28		A1
279	CHAMPION, Thomas C	24	SENE	1835-10-15		A1
312	CHAMPION, William	35	NENW	1838-07-28		A1
313	" "	35	SWNE	1843-02-01		A1
144	CHESHIRE, James	13	NESW	1848-04-01		A1
145	" "	23	SWNE	1850-04-01		A1

ID	Individual in Patent	Sec.	Sec. Part	Date Issued	Other Counties	For More Info . . .
27	COFFIELD, Bembrey	22	NWNE	1848-04-01		A1
320	COLEMAN, William	6	SWSE	1835-10-08	Lowndes	A1
321	" "	8	W½NW	1835-10-08		A1
317	" "	17	W½SE	1837-05-20		A1
318	" "	18	E½NE	1837-05-20		A1
319	" "	18	NESE	1837-05-20		A1
314	" "	10	W½SW	1837-08-09		A1
315	" "	15	NW	1837-08-09		A1
316	" "	15	W½NE	1837-08-09		A1
322	" "	9	E½NW	1837-08-09		A1
146	COLVIN, James	15	E½NE	1840-10-10		A1
147	" "	15	SWSW	1840-10-10		A1
297	COLVIN, Timothy S	17	N½NE	1837-08-09		A1
298	" "	18	NWNE	1837-08-09		A1
299	" "	8	SENE	1837-08-09		A1
300	" "	9	SWNW	1837-08-09		A1
296	COOK, Thomas W	23	NENW	1852-02-02		A1
167	COTTINGHAM, James W	4	NWNE	1852-02-02		A1
8	COWLES, Alexander A	21	NESW	1834-08-20		A1
10	" "	22	NESW	1845-07-01		A1
14	" "	27	NWNE	1850-08-10		A1
13	" "	27	N½NW	1852-02-02		A1
9	" "	21	SESW	1854-07-15		A1
12	" "	22	SWSE	1854-07-15		A1
7	" "	21	NESE	1860-04-02		A1
11	" "	22	NWSW	1860-04-02		A1
28	CROXTON, Benjamin	17	SESE	1834-10-21		A1
29	" "	20	NENE	1835-10-16		A1 R323
42	CROXTON, Calvestus	34	NESW	1851-04-10		A1
66	CROXTON, Elijah M	34	SESE	1837-05-20		A1
67	" "	35	SWSW	1837-05-20		A1
226	CROXTON, Lewis A	21	SESE	1858-11-01		A1
227	" "	22	SWSW	1858-11-01		A1
324	CROXTON, William	21	NWSW	1834-08-12		A1
323	" "	20	NENE	1834-10-21		A1 R29
325	" "	21	SWSW	1835-10-16		A1
326	" "	22	E½NE	1837-05-20		A1
327	" "	23	SWNW	1837-05-20		A1
348	CROXTON, William J	33	SWSE	1858-11-01		A1
148	DANIEL, James	19	E½SW	1837-08-01		A1
149	" "	19	NWSW	1837-08-01		A1
329	DANIEL, William	19	NESE	1834-08-12		A1
330	" "	19	NWSE	1835-10-14		A1
332	" "	19	SWSE	1837-05-20		A1
331	" "	19	SESE	1837-08-01		A1
333	" "	20	SWSW	1837-08-01		A1
334	" "	31	W½NW	1838-07-28		A1
17	DAVIS, Alexander	10	SWSE	1852-02-02		A1
71	DAVIS, Everet	10	SESE	1854-07-15		A1
72	DAVIS, Evert	14	E½NE	1848-04-01		A1
109	DAVIS, Henry I	11	SESE	1838-07-28		A1
110	" "	12	SWSW	1838-07-28		A1
127	DAVIS, Isaac	11	NWNW	1834-08-12		A1
130	" "	2	SWSW	1834-08-12		A1
129	" "	14	W½SE	1837-05-20		A1
128	" "	14	SWSW	1837-08-12		A1
168	DAVIS, Jesse	4	SENE	1837-08-12		A1
183	DAVIS, John	3	SESW	1838-07-28		A1
182	" "	27	SENW	1858-11-01		A1
229	DAVIS, Marmaduke	15	SESW	1853-08-01		A1
233	DAVIS, Micajah	11	NESE	1837-04-10		A1
265	DAVIS, Sampson	14	S½NW	1837-05-20		A1
266	" "	14	SWNE	1838-07-28		A1
264	" "	14	NENW	1850-08-10		A1
335	DAVIS, William	2	NENW	1835-04-08		A1
336	" "	2	SWNE	1835-04-08		A1
337	" "	2	SWNW	1837-05-15		A1
153	DEAN, James M	18	SESE	1837-05-15		A1
154	" "	18	SWNE	1837-05-15		A1
19	DUNCAN, Anderson	18	NWSE	1834-09-04		A1
18	ELISOR, Alexander	28	SWSE	1854-07-15		A1
185	ELLISON, John	20	E½SW	1833-06-04		A1
186	" "	20	NWSW	1835-09-12		A1

ID	Individual in Patent	Sec.	Sec. Part	Date Issued	Other Counties	For More Info . . .
184	ELLISON, John (Cont'd)	19	SWNE	1835-09-19		A1
187	" "	29	SENW	1837-08-12		A1
253	FENDLEY, Randolph	3	N½SW	1852-12-01		A1
190	GRAHAM, John	28	SESE	1858-11-01		A1
188	" "	28	NESW	1860-10-01		A1
189	" "	28	SENW	1860-10-01		A1
108	GRAVES, Henry	36	SENE	1852-02-02		A1
4	HALL, Aaron	10	SWNW	1835-10-08		A1
5	" "	9	SENE	1837-05-15		A1
219	HALL, Kenan	12	NWSW	1837-08-01		A1 F
249	HALL, Raford	3	SWSW	1850-08-10		A1
250	" "	9	NESE	1852-02-02		A1
251	HALL, Raiford	10	E½NW	1837-08-02		A1
252	" "	10	NWNW	1837-08-02		A1
341	HALL, William	11	NENE	1835-04-08		A1
342	" "	2	E½NE	1835-04-08		A1
369	HALL, Wilson	5	NWNE	1837-08-08		A1
228	HAMBRICK, Louisa	20	SENE	1838-07-28		A1
80	HARRIS, George T	36	SWSW	1858-11-01		A1
338	HARRIS, William H	20	SWNE	1835-09-12		A1
339	HARRISS, William H	30	SWNW	1834-08-20		A1
170	HICKMAN, Jesse	8	E½SE	1833-11-14		A1
169	" "	17	NESW	1835-04-02		A1
81	HILL, George W	10	SESW	1852-12-01		A1
25	HILLIARD, Bartlett	13	NESE	1835-10-16		A1
26	" "	13	SENE	1835-10-16		A1
234	HINDES, Moses	2	NWNW	1852-12-01		A1
33	INGRAM, Benjamin R	29	SWSW	1858-09-01		A1
48	JONES, Daniel	1	SW	1837-08-09		A1
49	" "	1	SWSE	1837-08-09		A1
50	" "	2	E½SE	1837-08-09		A1
193	JONES, John	14	NWSW	1837-04-10		A1
192	" "	14	NWNW	1837-04-15		A1
191	" "	14	E½SW	1837-08-02		A1
340	JONES, William H	3	W½NW	1837-08-12		A1
221	KEENER, Lawson J	21	NWNW	1837-08-08		A1
222	" "	27	E½SW	1837-08-08		A1
223	" "	33	NESW	1837-08-08		A1
224	" "	33	NWNW	1837-08-08		A1
225	" "	33	W½SW	1837-08-08		A1
282	KING, Thomas	2	NESW	1835-10-15		A1
283	KIRVEN, Thomas	31	SWSE	1837-08-12		A1
273	LAWRENCE, Stephen	24	E½SE	1833-06-04		A1 V248
274	" "	24	W½SE	1833-06-04		A1
171	LUKER, Jesse	30	SENW	1835-04-02		A1
284	LUMPKIN, Thomas	1	NE	1837-05-20		A1
199	MACKEY, John	34	NENE	1837-05-15		A1
201	" "	35	SENW	1837-05-15		A1
200	" "	34	NESE	1838-07-28		A1
232	MARCHANT, Mercer	33	SESW	1835-10-01		A1
351	MASTIN, William	31	NWSW	1852-02-02		A1
202	MATHEWS, John	18	N½NW	1837-08-10		A1
254	MCCARTY, Rhody	32	SESE	1858-11-01		A1 V115
255	" "	33	NWSE	1858-11-01		A1
256	" "	33	SESE	1858-11-01		A1
257	" "	34	W½SW	1858-11-01		A1
52	MCDANIEL, Daniel	2	SENW	1834-10-21		A1
51	" "	2	NWNE	1835-11-20		A1
285	MCILWAIN, Thomas	1	NESE	1835-10-14		A1
45	MCKETHAN, Cyrus	23	NWSW	1852-02-02		A1
281	MCKEY, Thomas J	36	SWNE	1858-11-01		A1
280	" "	28	NWSE	1860-12-01		A1
41	MCREE, Caleb P	5	E½SE	1849-09-01		A1
30	MITCHELL, Benjamin	12	E½SE	1833-09-16		A1
31	" "	12	SWSE	1834-08-05		A1
32	" "	13	SESE	1834-08-05		A1
55	MITCHELL, Daniel	12	W½NE	1834-05-12		A1
53	" "	1	SESE	1835-10-08		A1
56	" "	24	W½NE	1837-05-20		A1
54	" "	12	E½NE	1837-08-12		A1
59	MITCHELL, David	23	NWNE	1837-05-20		A1
248	MITCHELL, Peter	24	NESE	1837-08-12		A1 V273
368	MONK, Willis	18	S½NW	1837-08-07		A1

ID	Individual in Patent	Sec.	Sec. Part	Date Issued	Other Counties	For More Info . . .
309	MONTGOMERY, William C	21	SWNW	1835-10-16		A1
310	" "	33	NENW	1837-05-20		A1
311	" "	33	W½NE	1837-05-20		A1
137	MOORE, Jacob	21	SENE	1840-10-10		A1
205	MOORE, John S	3	NWNE	1837-05-20		A1
352	MORGAN, William	31	NESE	1837-08-10		A1
155	MOTHERSHEAD, James	21	E½NW	1835-10-16		A1
156	" "	21	SWNE	1837-04-10		A1
271	MOTHERSHEAD, Simeon	35	NWSW	1837-04-10		A1
287	MOTHERSHEAD, Thomas	35	E½SW	1833-06-04		A1
286	" "	26	SESW	1837-04-10		A1
288	" "	35	NWNE	1837-04-10		A1
289	" "	35	W½NW	1837-04-10		A1
290	" "	35	W½SE	1837-05-20		A1
291	MOTHERSHED, Thomas	26	E½NW	1837-05-20		A1
292	" "	26	NESW	1837-05-20		A1
85	MYEARS, Green B	25	SWNW	1858-11-01		A1
22	NEEL, Andrew H	4	NENE	1837-05-20		A1
158	NEILL, James O	36	SWSE	1835-04-15		A1
157	NICHOLS, James	34	SESW	1838-07-28		A1
142	NICHOLS, James C	29	W½NW	1845-07-01		A1
203	ODUM, John	30	NESE	1845-07-01		A1
162	ONEILL, James	36	SESW	1834-08-05		A1
159	" "	35	E½SE	1837-04-10		A1
160	" "	36	NESW	1837-08-09		A1
161	" "	36	NWSE	1837-08-09		A1
68	OROXTON, Elijah M	34	W½SE	1837-08-15		A1
263	OWEN, Robert F	36	SESE	1835-04-02		A1
353	PENTON, William	20	SESE	1834-08-20		A1
354	" "	21	NENE	1834-08-20		A1
164	POLK, James	33	NENE	1852-12-01		A1
165	" "	33	SENE	1858-11-01		A1
163	" "	28	NESE	1860-12-01		A1
293	POPE, Thomas	4	W½NW	1837-08-02		A1
349	POUNCEY, William J	3	E½NW	1834-10-21		A1
350	" "	3	SWNE	1834-10-21		A1
172	POWELL, Jesse T	9	SESE	1835-10-08		A1
370	POWELL, Zacheus	17	E½NW	1833-06-04		A1
371	" "	17	W½NW	1833-06-04		A1
373	" "	8	W½SW	1833-06-04		A1
374	" "	9	W½SW	1833-06-04		A1
372	" "	7	E½SE	1833-11-14		A1
194	RAY, John L	22	NWNW	1840-10-10		A1
195	" "	22	SWNW	1841-05-20		A1
307	RICHARDSON, William A	23	NESE	1848-04-01		A1
204	ROBERTS, John	7	SENW	1834-09-04		A1
86	ROIAL, Hardy	1	E½NW	1831-12-01		A1
87	" "	1	NWSE	1835-10-15		A1
215	ROPER, Joseph F	25	NESE	1852-02-02		A1
358	ROSS, William T	20	W½SE	1833-06-04		A1
355	" "	20	E½NW	1833-11-14		A1
356	" "	20	NWNE	1834-09-04		A1
357	" "	20	SWNW	1835-09-19		A1
88	ROYAL, Hardy	1	W½NW	1833-06-04		A1
270	ROYALS, Samuel S	31	SESE	1858-09-01		A1
267	RYALS, Samuel	31	E½NW	1852-02-02		A1
268	" "	31	E½SW	1852-02-02		A1
269	" "	31	SWNE	1852-02-02		A1
38	SARLES, Bright	9	NESW	1837-08-12		A1
24	SHAW, Archibald	19	E½NE	1833-06-04		A1
79	SIMMONS, Gellis W	11	NWSW	1852-02-02		A1
82	SIMMONS, Gillis	15	NWSW	1837-05-15		A1
83	SIMMONS, Gillis W	12	NWSE	1848-04-01		A1
84	" "	15	SWSE	1854-07-15		A1
206	SIMMONS, John	2	NWSW	1834-10-21		A1
207	" "	3	NESE	1835-04-08		A1
244	SIMMONS, Paul	12	E½NW	1834-08-05		A1
246	" "	12	NWNW	1837-05-15		A1 R247
247	" "	12	NWNW	1837-08-09		A1 R246
245	" "	12	NESW	1837-08-12		A1
242	SIMMONS, Paul C	11	SESW	1852-02-02		A1
243	" "	11	SWSW	1852-12-01		A1
39	SLOANE, Bryan W	8	NWNE	1845-07-01		A1

ID	Individual in Patent	Sec.	Sec. Part	Date Issued	Other Counties	For More Info . . .
40	SLOANE, Bryan W (Cont'd)	8	SWNE	1845-07-01		A1
208	SMITH, John	17	SENE	1837-05-20		A1
301	SPRAGGINS, Whitfield	29	NWNE	1837-08-09		A1
143	SPRAGINS, James C	30	SWNE	1837-08-18		A1
294	SPRAGINS, Thomas	28	NWSW	1837-05-15		A1
295	" "	29	NENW	1837-05-15		A1
302	SPRAGINS, Whitfield	29	SENE	1837-08-18		A1
276	STONE, Thomas B	30	NENE	1835-10-01		A1
60	SURLES, Dorsey	22	NWSE	1850-08-10		A1
61	" "	22	SWNE	1852-02-01		A1
262	SURLES, Robert D	22	E½NW	1858-11-01		A1
166	TERRELL, James	27	SWSW	1837-08-18		A1
359	THOMPSON, William	28	NENW	1858-11-01		A1
360	" "	28	W½NE	1858-11-01		A1
361	TODD, William	31	NWSE	1848-04-01		A1
209	VICKERY, John	32	NWNE	1837-08-18		A1
198	VICKERY, John M	33	NESE	1858-11-01		A1
210	VICKERY, Jonathan	29	SESE	1837-08-08		A1
213	" "	32	NENE	1837-08-08		A1
212	" "	29	SWNE	1837-08-12		A1
211	" "	29	SESW	1837-08-18		A1
20	VINCENT, Anderson P	32	SENE	1852-02-02		A1
21	VINSON, Anderson P	32	SWNE	1858-09-01		A1
362	VINSON, William	22	SESW	1837-08-09		A1
363	" "	31	NWNE	1851-04-10		A1
366	" "	32	W½NW	1854-07-15		A1
365	" "	32	SENW	1858-09-01		A1
364	" "	32	NENW	1858-11-01		A1
34	WALKER, Beverley A	30	NWSE	1845-07-01		A1
35	" "	30	SENE	1845-07-01		A1
37	WALKER, Beverly A	30	SWSE	1849-09-01		A1
36	" "	30	SESE	1850-08-10		A1
131	WILLETT, Isaac	10	NENE	1835-10-16		A1
132	" "	10	SWNE	1835-10-16		A1
63	WOODS, Dulana M	26	SENE	1848-05-03		A1
367	WRIGHT, William	17	NESE	1837-05-20		A1

Patent Map

T12-N R17-E
St Stephens Meridian

Map Group 1

Township Statistics

Parcels Mapped	:	374
Number of Patents	:	353
Number of Individuals	:	186
Patentees Identified	:	186
Number of Surnames	:	118
Multi-Patentee Parcels	:	0
Oldest Patent Date	:	11/30/1831
Most Recent Patent	:	12/1/1860
Block/Lot Parcels	:	0
Parcels Re - Issued	:	2
Parcels that Overlap	:	7
Cities and Towns	:	2
Cemeteries	:	3

Lowndes

Crenshaw

Section 6
ARMSTRONG William A 1837
ARMSTRONG William A 1837
ARMSTRONG William A 1837
ARMSTRONG William A 1837
ACREE Nathaniel 1838
COLEMAN William 1835

Section 5
HALL Wilson 1837
ARMSTRONG Franklin 1837
ACREE Nathaniel 1837
MCREE Caleb P 1849

Section 4
POPE Thomas 1837
COTTINGHAM James W 1852
NEEL Andrew H 1837
BRADY James 1852
DAVIS Jesse 1837
ARMSTRONG James M 1852
BOZEMAN Josiah 1835
BOZEMAN Josiah 1837

Section 7
CAMPBELL John C 1835
CAMPBELL John C 1835
CAMPBELL John C 1837
ROBERTS John 1834
ARMSTRONG Franklin 1837
CAMPBELL John C 1837
ACREE Nathaniel 1837
ACREE Nathaniel 1837
POWELL Zacheus 1833

Section 8
COLEMAN William 1835
ARMSTRONG Franklin 1833
ARMSTRONG Franklin 1837
SLOANE Bryan W 1845
SLOANE Bryan W 1845
COLVIN Timothy S 1837
POWELL Zacheus 1833
BROOKS Aaron 1831
BROOKS Aaron 1834
HICKMAN Jesse 1833

Section 9
COLVIN Timothy S 1837
COLEMAN William 1837
BROOKS Aaron 1837
HALL Aaron 1837
SARLES Bright 1837
HALL Raford 1852
POWELL Zacheus 1833
POWELL Jesse T 1835
BOZEMAN Josiah 1834
BOZEMAN Daniel C 1852

Section 18
MATHEWS John 1837
COLVIN Timothy S 1837
COLEMAN William 1837
MONK Willis 1837
DEAN James M 1837
CHAMPION Claiborn 1835
BOZEMAN Joseph D 1850
DUNCAN Anderson 1834
COLEMAN William 1837
BOZEMAN Etheldred 1837
BOZEMAN Etheldred 1835
DEAN James M 1837

Section 17
POWELL Zacheus 1833
POWELL Zacheus 1833
COLVIN Timothy S 1837
ARCHER James H 1834
SMITH John 1837
HICKMAN Jesse 1835
WRIGHT William 1837
ARCHER John M 1831
ARCHER John M 1834
COLEMAN William 1837
CROXTON Benjamin 1834

Section 16

Section 19
CHAMPION Claiborn 1835
ARMSTRONG Franklin 1835
SHAW Archibald 1833
ELLISON John 1835
DANIEL James 1837
DANIEL James 1837
DANIEL William 1835
DANIEL William 1837
DANIEL William 1834
DANIEL William 1837

Section 20
ARCHER William 1834
ROSS William T 1835
ROSS William T 1833
ELLISON John 1835
ELLISON John 1833
DANIEL William 1837
HARRIS William H 1835
ROSS William T 1833
PENTON William 1834

Section 21
ROSS William T 1834
CROXTON William 1834
CROXTON Benjamin 1835
KEENER Lawson J 1837
MOTHERSHEAD James 1835
BIRD David 1834
PENTON William 1834
HAMBRICK Louisa 1838
MONTGOMERY William C 1835
MOTHERSHEAD James 1837
MOORE Jacob 1840
CROXTON William 1834
COWLES Alexander A 1834
CROXTON William 1835
COWLES Alexander A 1854
COWLES Alexander A 1860
CAUTHEN Hiram 1837
CROXTON Lewis A 1858

Section 30
BRAZIL Kindred 1837
STONE Thomas B 1835
HARRISS William H 1834
LUKER Jesse 1835
SPRAGINS James C 1837
WALKER Beverley A 1845
BARKLEY Hugh 1837
WALKER Beverley A 1845
ODUM John 1845
WALKER Beverly A 1849
WALKER Beverly A 1850

Section 29
SPRAGINS Thomas 1837
SPRAGGINS Whitfield 1837
NICHOLS James C 1845
ELLISON John 1837
VICKERY Jonathan 1837
SPRAGINS Whitfield 1837
ARCHER David 1837
ARCHER James H 1834
CAULEY Daniel 1837
BERRY Mastin E 1858
VICKERY Jonathan 1837
INGRAM Benjamin R 1858
VICKERY Jonathan 1837

Section 28
THOMPSON William 1858
BERRY Mastin E 1858
GRAHAM John 1860
THOMPSON William 1858
ANDRESS William J 1860
SPRAGINS Thomas 1837
GRAHAM John 1860
MCKEY Thomas J 1860
POLK James 1860
GRAHAM John 1858
ELISOR Alexander 1854
CAWTHEN Alexander 1860

Section 31
DANIEL William 1838
RYALS Samuel 1852
VINSON William 1851
BARKLEY Hugh 1837
RYALS Samuel 1852
MASTIN William 1852
TODD William 1848
MORGAN William 1837
RYALS Samuel 1852
KIRVEN Thomas 1837
ROYALS Samuel S 1858

Section 32
VINSON William 1854
VINSON William 1858

Section 33
VINSON William 1858
VICKERY John 1837
VICKERY Jonathan 1837
KEENER Lawson J 1837
MONTGOMERY William C 1837
POLK James 1852
VINSON Anderson P 1858
VINCENT Anderson P 1852
CAUTHEN Hiram 1837
POLK James 1858
BARKLEY Hugh 1838
KEENER Lawson J 1837
KEENER Lawson J 1837
MCCARTY Rhody 1858
VICKERY John M 1858
MCCARTY Rhody 1858
MARCHANT Mercer 1835
CROXTON William J 1858
MCCARTY Rhody 1858

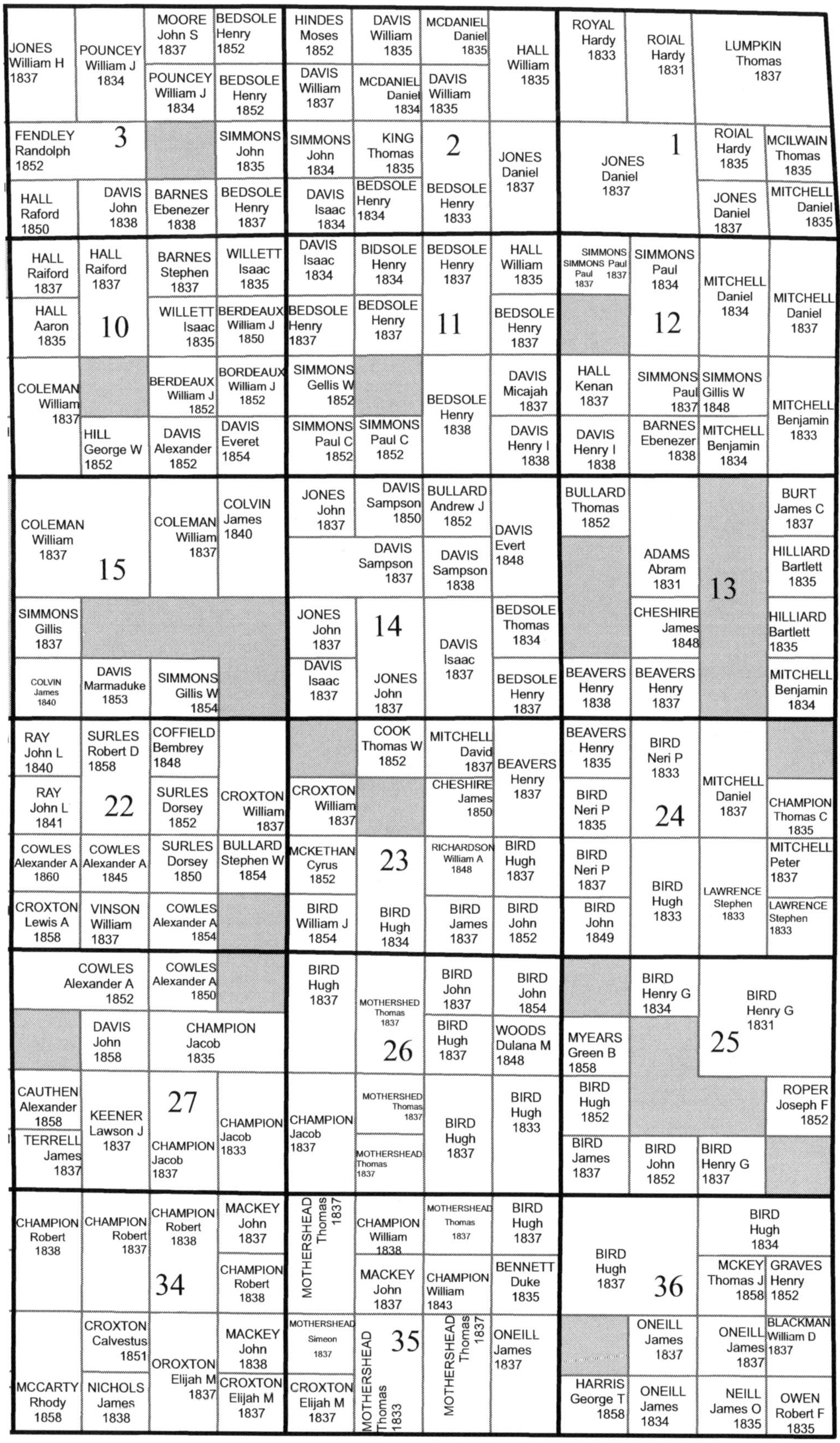
JONES William H 1837
POUNCEY William J 1834
MOORE John S 1837
BEDSOLE Henry 1852
POUNCEY William J 1834
BEDSOLE Henry 1852
HINDES Moses 1852
DAVIS William 1835
MCDANIEL Daniel 1835
DAVIS William 1837
MCDANIEL Daniel 1834
DAVIS William 1835
HALL William 1835
ROYAL Hardy 1833
ROIAL Hardy 1831
LUMPKIN Thomas 1837
FENDLEY Randolph 1852
3
SIMMONS John 1835
SIMMONS John 1834
KING Thomas 1835
2
JONES Daniel 1837
JONES Daniel 1837
1
ROIAL Hardy 1835
MCILWAIN Thomas 1835
HALL Raford 1850
DAVIS John 1838
BARNES Ebenezer 1838
BEDSOLE Henry 1837
DAVIS Isaac 1834
BEDSOLE Henry 1834
BEDSOLE Henry 1833
JONES Daniel 1837
MITCHELL Daniel 1835
HALL Raiford 1837
HALL Raiford 1837
BARNES Stephen 1837
WILLETT Isaac 1835
DAVIS Isaac 1834
BIDSOLE Henry 1834
BEDSOLE Henry 1837
HALL William 1835
SIMMONS Paul 1837
SIMMONS Paul 1837
SIMMONS Paul 1834
MITCHELL Daniel 1834
MITCHELL Daniel 1837
HALL Aaron 1835
10
WILLETT Isaac 1835
BERDEAUX William J 1850
BEDSOLE Henry 1837
BEDSOLE Henry 1837
11
BEDSOLE Henry 1837
12
COLEMAN William 1837
BERDEAUX William J 1852
BORDEAUX William J 1852
SIMMONS Gellis W 1852
BEDSOLE Henry 1838
DAVIS Micajah 1837
HALL Kenan 1837
SIMMONS Paul 1837
SIMMONS Gillis W 1848
MITCHELL Benjamin 1833
HILL George W 1852
DAVIS Alexander 1852
DAVIS Everet 1854
SIMMONS Paul C 1852
SIMMONS Paul C 1852
DAVIS Henry I 1838
DAVIS Henry I 1838
BARNES Ebenezer 1838
MITCHELL Benjamin 1834
COLEMAN William 1837
15
COLEMAN William 1837
COLVIN James 1840
JONES John 1837
DAVIS Sampson 1850
BULLARD Andrew J 1852
DAVIS Evert 1848
BULLARD Thomas 1852
ADAMS Abram 1831
13
BURT James C 1837
DAVIS Sampson 1837
DAVIS Sampson 1838
HILLIARD Bartlett 1835
SIMMONS Gillis 1837
JONES John 1837
14
DAVIS Isaac 1837
BEDSOLE Thomas 1834
CHESHIRE James 1848
HILLIARD Bartlett 1835
COLVIN James 1840
DAVIS Marmaduke 1853
SIMMONS Gillis W 1854
DAVIS Isaac 1837
JONES John 1837
BEDSOLE Henry 1837
BEAVERS Henry 1838
BEAVERS Henry 1837
MITCHELL Benjamin 1834
RAY John L 1840
SURLES Robert D 1858
COFFIELD Bembrey 1848
COOK Thomas W 1852
MITCHELL David 1837
BEAVERS Henry 1837
BEAVERS Henry 1835
BIRD Neri P 1833
MITCHELL Daniel 1837
RAY John L 1841
22
SURLES Dorsey 1852
CROXTON William 1837
CROXTON William 1837
CHESHIRE James 1850
BIRD Neri P 1835
24
CHAMPION Thomas C 1835
COWLES Alexander A 1860
COWLES Alexander A 1845
SURLES Dorsey 1850
BULLARD Stephen W 1854
MCKETHAN Cyrus 1852
23
RICHARDSON William A 1848
BIRD Hugh 1837
BIRD Neri P 1837
BIRD Hugh 1833
LAWRENCE Stephen 1833
MITCHELL Peter 1837
CROXTON Lewis A 1858
VINSON William 1837
COWLES Alexander A 1854
BIRD William J 1854
BIRD Hugh 1834
BIRD James 1837
BIRD John 1852
BIRD John 1849
LAWRENCE Stephen 1833
COWLES Alexander A 1852
COWLES Alexander A 1850
BIRD Hugh 1837
MOTHERSHED Thomas 1837
BIRD John 1837
BIRD John 1854
BIRD Henry G 1834
BIRD Henry G 1831
DAVIS John 1858
CHAMPION Jacob 1835
26
BIRD Hugh 1837
WOODS Dulana M 1848
MYEARS Green B 1858
25
CAUTHEN Alexander 1858
KEENER Lawson J 1837
27
CHAMPION Jacob 1833
CHAMPION Jacob 1837
MOTHERSHED Thomas 1837
BIRD Hugh 1837
BIRD Hugh 1833
BIRD Hugh 1852
ROPER Joseph F 1852
TERRELL James 1837
CHAMPION Jacob 1837
MOTHERSHEAD Thomas 1837
BIRD James 1837
BIRD John 1852
BIRD Henry G 1837
CHAMPION Robert 1838
CHAMPION Robert 1837
CHAMPION Robert 1838
MACKEY John 1837
MOTHERSHEAD Thomas 1837
CHAMPION William 1838
MOTHERSHEAD Thomas 1837
BIRD Hugh 1837
BIRD Hugh 1837
BIRD Hugh 1834
34
CHAMPION Robert 1838
MACKEY John 1837
CHAMPION William 1843
BENNETT Duke 1835
36
MCKEY Thomas J 1858
GRAVES Henry 1852
CROXTON Calvestus 1851
MACKEY John 1838
MOTHERSHEAD Simeon 1837
35
MOTHERSHEAD Thomas 1837
ONEILL James 1837
ONEILL James 1837
ONEILL James 1837
BLACKMAN William D 1837
OROXTON Elijah M 1837
CROXTON Elijah M 1837
CROXTON Elijah M 1837
MOTHERSHEAD Thomas 1833
MOTHERSHEAD Thomas 1837
MCCARTY Rhody 1858
NICHOLS James 1838
HARRIS George T 1858
ONEILL James 1834
NEILL James O 1835
OWEN Robert F 1835

Helpful Hints

1. This Map's INDEX can be found on the preceding pages.
2. Refer to Map "C" to see where this Township lies within Crenshaw County, Alabama.
3. Numbers within square brackets [ ] denote a multi-patentee land parcel (multi-owner). Refer to Appendix "C" for a full list of members in this group.
4. Areas that look to be crowded with Patentees usually indicate multiple sales of the same parcel (Re-issues) or Overlapping parcels. See this Township's Index for an explanation of these and other circumstances that might explain "odd" groupings of Patentees on this map.

Legend

Patent Boundary

Section Boundary

No Patents Found (or Outside County)

1., 2., 3., ... Lot Numbers (when beside a name)

[ ] Group Number (see Appendix "C")

Scale: Section = 1 mile X 1 mile (generally, with some exceptions)

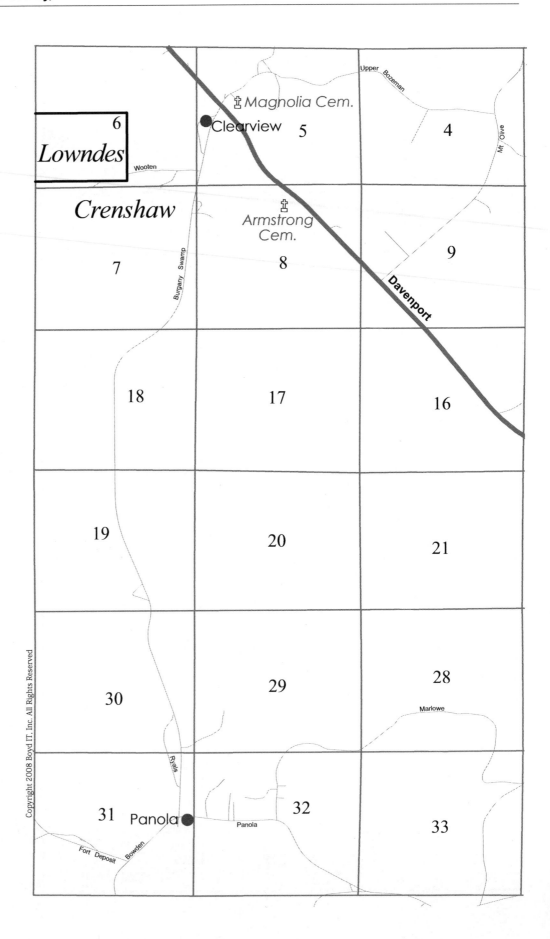

Road Map

T12-N R17-E
St Stephens Meridian

Map Group 1

Cities & Towns
Clearview
Panola

Cemeteries
Armstrong Cemetery
Magnolia Cemetery
Rocky Mount Cemetery

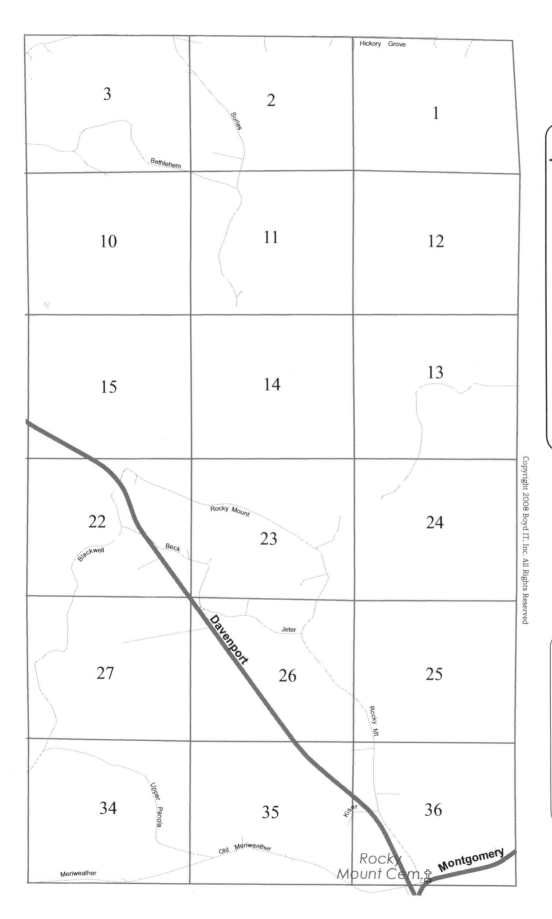

3

2

Hickory Grove

1

Surles

Bethlehem

10

11

12

15

14

13

22

Rocky Mount

23

Beck

Blackwell

24

Davenport

Jeter

27

26

25

Rocky Mt.

34

Upper Panola

35

Kiser

36

Old Meriweather

Meriweather

Rocky Mount Cem. ✝

Montgomery

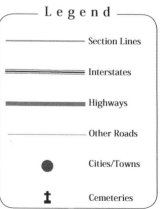

Helpful Hints

1. This road map has a number of uses, but primarily it is to help you: a) find the present location of land owned by your ancestors (at least the general area), b) find cemeteries and city-centers, and c) estimate the route/roads used by Census-takers & tax-assessors.

2. If you plan to travel to Crenshaw County to locate cemeteries or land parcels, please pick up a modern travel map for the area before you do. Mapping old land parcels on modern maps is not as exact a science as you might think. Just the slightest variations in public land survey coordinates, estimates of parcel boundaries, or road-map deviations can greatly alter a map's representation of how a road either does or doesn't cross a particular parcel of land.

L e g e n d

——————— Section Lines

══════════ Interstates

▓▓▓▓▓▓▓▓ Highways

——————— Other Roads

● Cities/Towns

✝ Cemeteries

Scale: Section = 1 mile X 1 mile
(generally, with some exceptions)

Historical Map

T12-N R17-E
St Stephens Meridian

Map Group 1

Cities & Towns
Clearview
Panola

Cemeteries
Armstrong Cemetery
Magnolia Cemetery
Rocky Mount Cemetery

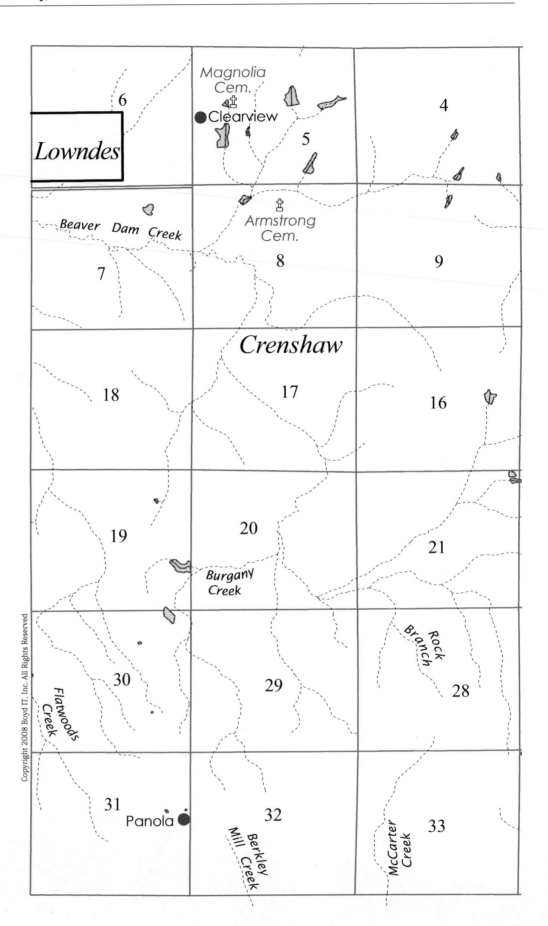

Magnolia Cem.

6

Lowndes

●Clearview

5

4

Beaver Dam Creek

Armstrong Cem.

7

8

9

Crenshaw

18

17

16

19

20

21

Burgany Creek

Rock Branch

Flatwoods Creek

30

29

28

31

Panola ●

32

33

Berkley Mill Creek

McCarter Creek

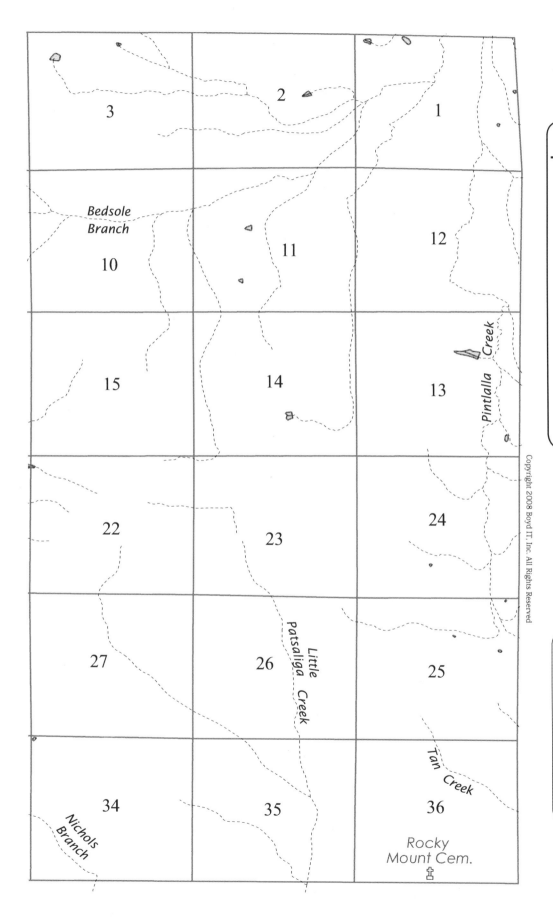

3

2

1

Helpful Hints

1. This Map takes a different look at
the same Congressional Township
displayed in the preceding two
maps. It presents features that
can help you better envision the
historical development of the area:
a) Water-bodies (lakes & ponds),
b) Water-courses (rivers, streams,
etc.), c) Railroads, d) City/town
center-points (where they were
oftentimes located when first
settled), and e) Cemeteries.

2. Using this "Historical" map in
tandem with this Township's
Patent Map and Road Map, may
lead you to some interesting
discoveries. You will often find
roads, towns, cemeteries, and
waterways are named after nearby
landowners: sometimes those
names will be the ones you are
researching. See how many of
these research gems you can find
here in Crenshaw County.

Bedsole
Branch

10

11

12

15

14

13

Pintlalla Creek

22

23

24

27

26

Little
Patsaliga Creek

25

34

35

Nichols
Branch

36

Tan Creek

Rocky
Mount Cem.

Legend

———— Section Lines

+++++++ Railroads

▨ Large Rivers &
Bodies of Water

-------- Streams/Creeks
& Small Rivers

● Cities/Towns

✝ Cemeteries

Scale: Section = 1 mile X 1 mile
(there are some exceptions)

Map Group 2: Index to Land Patents

Township 11-North Range 16-East (St Stephens)

After you locate an individual in this Index, take note of the Section and Section Part then proceed to the Land Patent map on the pages immediately following. You should have no difficulty locating the corresponding parcel of land.

The "For More Info" Column will lead you to more information about the underlying Patents. See the *Legend* at right, and the "How to Use this Book" chapter, for more information.

ID	Individual in Patent	Sec.	Sec. Part	Date Issued	Other Counties	For More Info . . .
435	ANDRESS, Jeremiah	27	NENE	1854-07-15		A1
433	" "	23	SWSW	1858-11-01		A1
434	" "	26	NWNW	1858-11-01		A1
436	" "	27	NENW	1858-11-01		A1
465	ARRINGTON, Mary	10	NESE	1860-10-01		A1
466	" "	10	SENE	1860-10-01		A1
381	BARRETT, Andrew J	36	N½NW	1849-09-01		A1
460	BOZEMAN, Joseph D	14	SWSW	1858-11-01		A1
461	" "	23	W½NW	1858-11-01		A1
494	BRYAN, Waid	3	E½NW	1837-08-02		A1
495	BRYANT, Waid	3	W½NE	1837-08-08		A1
414	COLLINS, Isaac	15	E½SE	1837-08-02		A1
399	DANIEL, Elias	1	E½NW	1843-02-01		A1
400	" "	1	NE	1843-02-01		A1
401	" "	2	SENE	1843-02-01		A1
506	DANIEL, William	14	SESE	1850-08-10		A1
505	" "	14	NESE	1852-02-02		A1
503	" "	13	S½NW	1858-11-01		A1
504	" "	13	SW	1858-11-01		A1
507	" "	23	SESE	1858-11-01		A1
508	" "	24	N½NE	1858-11-01		A1
509	" "	24	N½NW	1858-11-01		A1
511	DANIEL, William I	36	SE	1858-11-01		A1
484	DAVIS, Rowland	3	E½NE	1838-07-28		A1
377	DEESON, Abraham	10	SWNW	1835-09-12		A1
429	DORMAN, James T	35	SESE	1858-11-01		A1
430	" "	36	S½NW	1875-04-20		A1
431	" "	36	SW	1875-04-20		A1
468	DRY, Mathias	25	S½SE	1858-11-01		A1
469	" "	36	N½NE	1858-11-01		A1
440	EVERIDGE, John	27	NWSW	1837-08-18		A1
441	" "	27	SWNW	1837-08-18		A1
382	FRAZER, Annie	1	E½SE	1858-11-01		A1 V415
383	" "	1	NWSE	1858-11-01		A1 V415
384	FRAZIER, Anny	12	N½SE	1860-10-01		A1
385	" "	12	NE	1860-10-01		A1
386	" "	12	NESW	1860-10-01		A1
387	" "	12	SENW	1860-10-01		A1
523	GHOLSON, William S	34	SWSW	1852-12-01		A1
392	GREGG, Daniel	10	SWSE	1852-02-02		A1
393	GRIGG, Daniel	10	NENE	1850-08-10		A1
407	HAMBRICK, Franklin A	11	NWNW	1852-02-02		A1
472	HAMBRICK, Meshach	2	W½SW	1837-08-02		A1
473	" "	3	SESE	1837-08-02		A1
470	" "	2	E½SW	1837-08-08		A1
471	" "	2	NW	1837-08-08		A1

ID	Individual in Patent	Sec.	Sec. Part	Date Issued	Other Counties	For More Info . . .
416	HARTIN, James C	14	NWSE	1861-05-01		A1
417	" "	14	SWNE	1861-05-01		A1
375	HEARTSILL, Abner T	22	N½NE	1880-02-20		A2
376	" "	22	N½NW	1880-02-20		A2
474	HEARTSILL, Nathan H	14	SESW	1880-02-20		A2
475	" "	14	SWSE	1880-02-20		A2
379	HELMS, Andrew	26	NENW	1861-05-01		A1
380	" "	26	NWNE	1861-05-01		A1
408	HILBUN, Frederick	10	E½NW	1837-05-15		A1
409	" "	10	NWNW	1837-05-15		A1
487	JONES, Seaborn	26	NESW	1858-11-01		A1
488	" "	26	NWSE	1858-11-01		A1
489	" "	26	S½NW	1858-11-01		A1
490	" "	27	SENE	1858-11-01		A1
410	JORDAN, Hardy	22	SENE	1895-10-22		A2
476	JORDAN, Nathan	1	E½SW	1852-12-01		A1
477	" "	1	SWSE	1852-12-01		A1 F
405	KELLEY, Elisha	36	S½NE	1860-12-01		A1
412	KELLEY, Hosea	10	NWNE	1852-02-02		A1
413	" "	3	SWSE	1852-02-02		A1
510	KENNON, William H	15	NWNW	1849-09-01		A1
391	KING, Benjamin	26	SWNE	1852-02-02		A1
479	KNOWLS, Robert	35	NESW	1852-02-02		A1
480	" "	35	SENW	1858-11-01		A1
481	" "	35	SESW	1858-11-01		A1
482	" "	35	SWSE	1858-11-01		A1
419	LAWRENCE, James M	23	E½SW	1858-11-01		A1
420	" "	23	NWSE	1858-11-01		A1
421	" "	23	NWSW	1858-11-01		A1
422	" "	23	SWNE	1858-11-01		A1
378	LEGG, Albert	34	NWNW	1837-08-18		A1
411	LOWE, Henry W	14	E½NE	1880-02-20		A2
464	LOWE, Lucy	14	N½NW	1880-02-20		A2
512	MASTIN, William	13	E½SE	1837-05-20		A1
515	" "	23	N½NE	1837-08-09		A1
513	" "	13	W½SE	1838-07-28		A1
516	" "	27	E½SE	1838-07-28		A1
517	" "	27	NWNE	1838-07-28		A1
514	" "	23	E½NW	1848-04-01		A1
423	MCWILLIAMS, James	10	S½SW	1861-05-01		A1
395	MERCHANT, Drayton	1	W½SW	1852-02-02		A1
447	MITCHEL, John M	12	N½NW	1858-11-01		A1
439	MORGAN, John D	3	N½SE	1837-08-02		A1
453	MOSELEY, John	26	SWSW	1852-02-02		A1
454	" "	27	NWSE	1852-02-02		A1
451	" "	26	NWSW	1858-11-01		A1
452	" "	26	SESW	1858-11-01		A1
390	MURRAY, Barnes	35	NESE	1852-12-01		A1
424	NANSWORTHY, James	15	NENE	1858-11-01		A1
394	NORMAN, David R	24	S½	1860-12-01		A1
425	NORMAN, James	27	SENW	1849-09-01		A1
437	NORSWORTHY, John A	2	NESE	1852-12-01		A1
478	NORSWORTHY, Presley	1	W½NW	1853-08-01		A1
518	NORSWORTHY, William	2	SWNE	1852-02-02		A1
415	OWENS, Jacob	1	N½SE	1902-02-03		A2 V382, 383
493	PERDUE, Sovereign T	10	NWSW	1852-02-02		A1
491	PERRY, Simeon G	22	S½SE	1858-11-01		A1
492	" "	22	S½SW	1858-11-01		A1
418	PETTY, James F	10	SESE	1902-02-03		A2
396	POLK, Eldridge S	12	NWSW	1880-02-20		A2
397	" "	12	SWNW	1880-02-20		A2
455	POUNCEY, John	27	SWNE	1834-08-20		A1
449	ROPER, John M	3	SW	1837-08-01		A1
450	" "	3	SWNW	1837-08-01		A1
448	" "	3	NWNW	1837-08-08		A1
485	RYALS, Samuel	14	NWSW	1852-02-02		A1
486	RYALS, Samuel S	14	NESW	1858-11-01		A1
524	SCOTT, William	14	NWNE	1861-05-01		A1
402	SEXTON, Elias	25	NWSE	1850-04-01		A1
403	" "	25	S½NE	1858-11-01		A1
404	" "	25	S½NW	1858-11-01		A1
483	SEXTON, Robert M	10	NWSE	1885-03-30		A2
526	SIMS, William	34	E½NW	1837-08-18		A1

ID	Individual in Patent	Sec.	Sec. Part	Date Issued	Other Counties	For More Info . . .
527	SIMS, William (Cont'd)	34	E½SW	1837-08-18		A1
530	" "	34	SWNW	1837-08-18		A1
532	" "	34	W½NE	1837-08-18		A1
529	" "	34	NWSW	1838-07-28		A1
525	" "	27	SWSE	1852-02-02		A1
528	" "	34	NENE	1852-02-02		A1
531	" "	34	SWSE	1858-11-01		A1
533	" "	35	W½NW	1858-11-01		A1
467	SMITH, Mary	14	SWNW	1875-04-20		A1
426	SOWELL, James R	14	SENW	1860-04-02		A1
458	STRINGER, John	15	W½SW	1837-08-09		A1
456	" "	15	NWSE	1837-08-12		A1
457	" "	15	SWNE	1837-08-12		A1
438	STRINGER, John A	27	NWNW	1858-11-01		A1
519	STRINGER, William R	22	N½SE	1858-09-01		A1
520	" "	22	N½SW	1858-09-01		A1
521	" "	22	S½NW	1858-09-01		A1
522	" "	22	SWNE	1858-09-01		A1
432	TAYLOR, James	26	SWSE	1858-11-01		A1
427	TAYLOR, James R	35	NWSE	1858-11-01		A1
428	" "	35	S½NE	1858-11-01		A1
459	TAYLOR, John	34	NWSE	1838-07-28		A1
462	TAYLOR, Joseph	26	E½SE	1858-11-01		A1
398	THORNTON, Eli	27	NESW	1849-09-01		A1
496	TODD, William D	13	SWNE	1853-08-01		A1
497	" "	23	NESE	1858-11-01		A1
498	" "	23	SENE	1858-11-01		A1
500	" "	24	S½NE	1858-11-01		A1
501	" "	24	S½NW	1858-11-01		A1
499	" "	23	SWSE	1860-04-02		A1
502	" "	26	NENE	1860-04-02		A1
444	TOMLINSON, John L	13	E½NE	1837-08-10		A1
442	" "	12	S½SE	1858-11-01		A1
443	" "	12	S½SW	1858-11-01		A1
445	" "	13	N½NW	1858-11-01		A1
446	" "	13	NWNE	1858-11-01		A1
388	TURNER, Argalous	11	NENE	1854-07-15		A1
389	" "	2	SWSE	1858-11-01		A1
463	VINCENT, Joseph	11	NENW	1837-08-12		A1
406	WEBB, Foster C	11	SWSW	1852-12-01		A1
535	WHEELER, William	2	NWNE	1852-02-02		A1
534	" "	2	NENE	1854-10-02		A1

Map — Township 11-N Range 16-E

Section 3
ROPER John M 1837
ROPER John M 1837
BRYAN Waid 1837
BRYANT Waid 1837
DAVIS Rowland 1838
ROPER John M 1837
MORGAN John D 1837
KELLEY Hosea 1852
HAMBRICK Meshach 1837

Section 2
HAMBRICK Meshach 1837
HAMBRICK Meshach 1837
HAMBRICK Meshach 1837
TURNER Argalous 1858

Section 1
HAMBRICK Meshach 1837
WHEELER William 1852
WHEELER William 1854
NORSWORTHY Presley 1853
DANIEL Elias 1843
NORSWORTHY William 1852
DANIEL Elias 1843
NORSWORTHY John A 1852
DANIEL Elias 1843
MERCHANT Drayton 1852
JORDAN Nathan 1852
JORDAN Nathan 1858
FRAZIER Annie 1858
OWENS Jacob 1902
FRAZIER Annie 1858

Section 10
HILBUN Frederick 1837
DEESON Abraham 1835
HILBUN Frederick 1837
PERDUE Sovereign T 1852
KELLEY Hosea 1852
GRIGG Daniel 1850
ARRINGTON Mary 1860
SEXTON Robert M 1885
ARRINGTON Mary 1860
MCWILLIAMS James 1861
GREGG Daniel 1852
PETTY James F 1902

Section 11
HAMBRICK Franklin A 1852
VINCENT Joseph 1837
WEBB Foster C 1852

Section 12
TURNER Argalous 1854
MITCHEL John M 1858
FRAZIER Anny 1860
POLK Eldridge S 1880
FRAZIER Anny 1860
POLK Eldridge S 1880
FRAZIER Anny 1860
FRAZIER Anny 1860
TOMLINSON John L 1858
TOMLINSON John L 1858

Section 15
KENNON William H 1849
STRINGER John 1837
NANSWORTHY James 1858
STRINGER John 1837
STRINGER John 1837
COLLINS Isaac 1837

Section 14
LOWE Lucy 1880
SMITH Mary 1875
SOWELL James R 1860
SCOTT William 1861
HARTIN James C 1861
LOWE Henry W 1880
RYALS Samuel 1852
RYALS Samuel S 1858
HARTIN James C 1861
BOZEMAN Joseph D 1858
HEARTSILL Nathan H 1880
HEARTSILL Nathan H 1880
DANIEL William 1850

Section 13
TOMLINSON John L 1858
TOMLINSON John L 1858
TOMLINSON John L 1858
DANIEL William 1858
TODD William D 1858
TOMLINSON John L 1837
MASTIN William 1838
MASTIN William 1837
DANIEL William 1852
DANIEL William 1858
DANIEL William 1858

Section 22
HEARTSILL Abner T 1880
STRINGER William R 1858
HEARTSILL Abner T 1880
STRINGER William R 1858
JORDAN Hardy 1895
STRINGER William R 1858
STRINGER William R 1858
PERRY Simeon G 1858
PERRY Simeon G 1858

Section 23
BOZEMAN Joseph D 1858
MASTIN William 1848
MASTIN William 1837
LAWRENCE James M 1858
TODD William D 1858
LAWRENCE James M 1858
LAWRENCE James M 1858
TODD William D 1858
ANDRESS Jeremiah 1858

Section 24
DANIEL William 1858
DANIEL William 1858
TODD William D 1858
TODD William D 1858
TODD William D 1860
DANIEL William 1858
NORMAN David R 1860

Section 27
STRINGER John A 1858
ANDRESS Jeremiah 1858
MASTIN William 1838
ANDRESS Jeremiah 1854
EVERIDGE John 1837
NORMAN James 1849
POUNCEY John 1834
JONES Seaborn 1858
EVERIDGE John 1837
THORNTON Eli 1849
MOSELEY John 1852
SIMS William 1852
MASTIN William 1838

Section 26
ANDRESS Jeremiah 1858
HELMS Andrew 1861
HELMS Andrew 1861
TODD William D 1860
JONES Seaborn 1858
KING Benjamin 1852
MOSELEY John 1858
JONES Seaborn 1858
JONES Seaborn 1858
MOSELEY John 1852
MOSELEY John 1858
TAYLOR James 1858
TAYLOR Joseph 1858

Section 25
SEXTON Elias 1858
SEXTON Elias 1858
SEXTON Elias 1850
DRY Mathias 1858

Section 34
LEGG Albert 1837
SIMS William 1837
SIMS William 1837
SIMS William 1852
SIMS William 1837
TAYLOR John 1838
SIMS William 1837
SIMS William 1838
SIMS William 1837
GHOLSON William S 1852
SIMS William 1858

Section 35
SIMS William 1858
KNOWLS Robert 1858
KNOWLS Robert 1852
KNOWLS Robert 1858
TAYLOR James R 1858
TAYLOR James R 1858
KNOWLS Robert 1858
TAYLOR James R 1852
MURRAY Barnes 1852
KNOWLS Robert 1858
DORMAN James T 1858

Section 36
BARRETT Andrew J 1849
DRY Mathias 1858
DORMAN James T 1875
KELLEY Elisha 1860
DORMAN James T 1875
DANIEL William I 1858

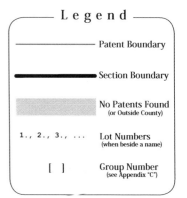

Patent Map
T11-N R16-E
St Stephens Meridian

Map Group 2

Township Statistics

Parcels Mapped	:	161
Number of Patents	:	114
Number of Individuals	:	81
Patentees Identified	:	81
Number of Surnames	:	64
Multi-Patentee Parcels	:	0
Oldest Patent Date	:	8/20/1834
Most Recent Patent	:	2/3/1902
Block/Lot Parcels	:	0
Parcels Re - Issued	:	0
Parcels that Overlap	:	3
Cities and Towns	:	1
Cemeteries	:	1

Note: the area contained in this map amounts to far less than a full Township. Therefore, its contents are completely on this single page (instead of a "normal" 2-page spread).

Legend

─── Patent Boundary

━━━ Section Boundary

▒▒▒ No Patents Found (or Outside County)

1., 2., 3., ... Lot Numbers (when beside a name)

[ ] Group Number (see Appendix "C")

Scale: Section = 1 mile X 1 mile (generally, with some exceptions)

Road Map

T11-N R16-E
St Stephens Meridian

Map Group 2

Note: the area contained in this map amounts to far less than a full Township. Therefore, its contents are completely on this single page (instead of a "normal" 2-page spread).

Cities & Towns
Danielsville

Cemeteries
Hopewell Cemetery

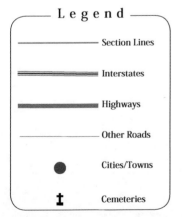

Legend

_____ Section Lines

▬▬▬▬▬ Interstates

▬▬▬▬▬ Highways

_____ Other Roads

● Cities/Towns

✝ Cemeteries

Scale: Section = 1 mile X 1 mile
(generally, with some exceptions)

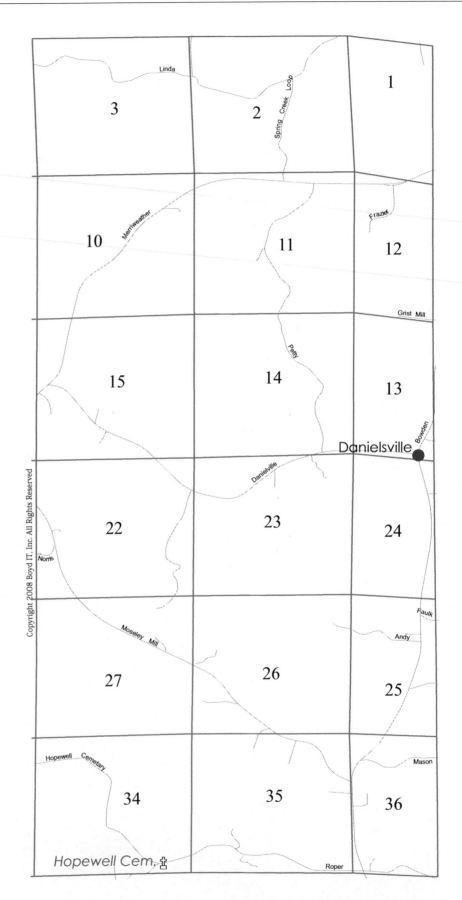

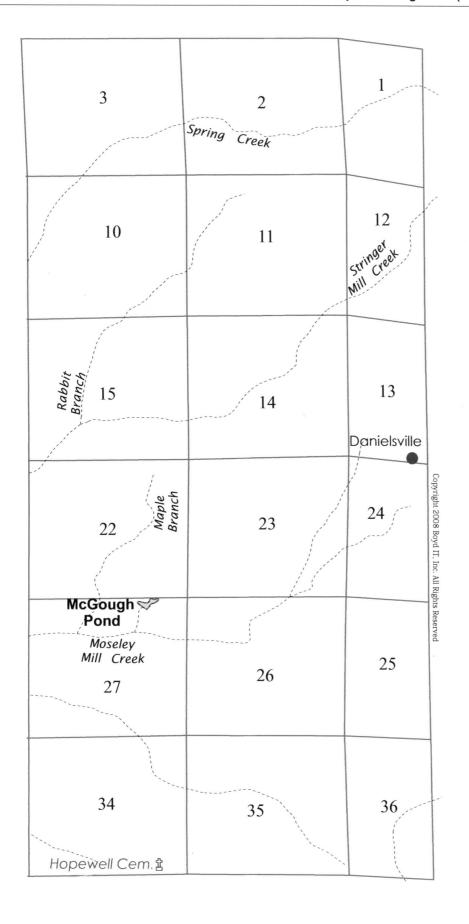

Historical Map

T11-N R16-E
St Stephens Meridian

Map Group 2

Note: the area contained in this map amounts to far less than a full Township. Therefore, its contents are completely on this single page (instead of a "normal" 2-page spread).

Cities & Towns
Danielsville

Cemeteries
Hopewell Cemetery

L e g e n d

——————— Section Lines

+ + + + + + + + Railroads

Large Rivers & Bodies of Water

- - - - - - - - Streams/Creeks & Small Rivers

● Cities/Towns

✝ Cemeteries

Scale: Section = 1 mile X 1 mile
(there are some exceptions)

Map Group 3: Index to Land Patents

Township 11-North Range 17-East (St Stephens)

After you locate an individual in this Index, take note of the Section and Section Part then proceed to the Land Patent map on the pages immediately following. You should have no difficulty locating the corresponding parcel of land.

The "For More Info" Column will lead you to more information about the underlying Patents. See the *Legend* at right, and the "How to Use this Book" chapter, for more information.

```
                    LEGEND
           "For More Info . . . " column
A = Authority (Legislative Act, See Appendix "A")
B = Block or Lot (location in Section unknown)
C = Cancelled Patent
F = Fractional Section
G = Group  (Multi-Patentee Patent, see Appendix "C")
V = Overlaps another Parcel
R = Re-Issued (Parcel patented more than once)

(A & G items require you to look in the Appendixes referred
to above. All other Letter-designations followed by a number
require you to locate line-items in this index that possess
the ID number found after the letter).
```

ID	Individual in Patent	Sec.	Sec. Part	Date Issued	Other Counties	For More Info . . .
541	ADAMS, Abraham	13	SENW	1834-10-21		A1
542	" "	13	W½NW	1835-10-08		A1
784	ADAMS, Samuel M	20	SENE	1838-07-28		A1
539	ADDISON, Abijah	4	E½SE	1861-05-01		A1
540	" "	4	NWSE	1861-05-01		A1
642	ALLEN, James G	6	NWSE	1838-07-28		A1
599	ARMSTRONG, Franklin	32	SENE	1854-10-02		A1
617	BALDWIN, Henry	1	W½SE	1852-02-02		A1
623	BARKLEY, Hugh	5	NESW	1835-10-14		A1
624	" "	5	SENW	1835-10-14		A1
627	" "	5	W½SE	1835-10-14		A1
626	" "	5	W½NW	1837-05-20		A1
621	" "	5	NE	1837-08-08		A1
622	" "	5	NENW	1837-08-08		A1
625	" "	5	SESW	1837-08-08		A1
800	BARKLEY, Thomas	5	E½SE	1837-05-20		A1
536	BARTERFORD, Aaron	25	NESE	1852-02-02		A1
543	BEAZELY, Alexander	33	SENW	1858-11-01		A1
611	BEST, George M	20	NWNE	1860-10-01		A1
610	" "	20	N½NW	1861-05-01		A1
612	" "	20	SWNW	1861-05-01		A1
628	BEST, Humphrey	2	NWSE	1837-05-15		A1
629	" "	26	NENW	1852-02-02		A1
630	" "	26	SENW	1852-02-02		A1
585	BIRD, David	3	SE	1831-12-01		A1
825	BLACKMAN, William D	28	NENW	1837-08-07		A1
826	" "	28	W½NE	1837-08-07		A1 G3
824	BLACKSHEAR, William	1	SESW	1841-05-20		A1
537	BODIFORD, Aaron	36	SWNW	1854-07-15		A1
547	BODIFORD, Alexander	25	W½NW	1837-08-12		A1
549	" "	25	W½SW	1837-08-12		A1
550	" "	26	SENE	1837-08-12		A1
544	" "	24	SW	1838-07-28		A1
545	" "	25	E½NW	1838-07-28		A1
546	" "	25	E½SW	1838-07-28		A1
548	" "	25	W½SE	1838-07-28		A1
551	" "	26	W½NE	1838-07-28		A1
554	BODIFORD, Aley	11	NWSE	1858-11-01		A1
555	" "	11	S½SE	1858-11-01		A1
556	" "	12	SWSW	1858-11-01		A1
635	BOYETT, James	22	NWSE	1852-02-02		A1
636	" "	22	SESW	1852-02-02		A1
634	" "	22	NESE	1854-07-15		A1
637	" "	26	NWNW	1854-07-15		A1
638	" "	27	NWNE	1854-07-15		A1
801	BOYETT, Thomas	23	NWSW	1858-11-01		A1

ID	Individual in Patent	Sec.	Sec. Part	Date Issued	Other Counties	For More Info . . .
639	BOYT, James	23	E½SW	1852-02-02		A1
640	" "	23	W½SE	1852-02-02		A1
641	BOZEMAN, James C	34	SESE	1858-11-01		A1
817	BOZEMAN, Travis H	35	NWSW	1862-04-10		A1
806	BRAWDAWAY, Thomas J	11	E½NW	1858-11-01		A1
807	" "	11	E½SW	1858-11-01		A1
808	" "	14	NENW	1858-11-01		A1
618	BROWN, Henry	4	S½SW	1861-05-01		A1
725	BROWN, Martha	34	SWNW	1858-11-01		A1
564	BUCK, Augustus	36	NWSE	1852-12-01		A1
695	BUCK, John	36	SENE	1850-04-01		A1
696	" "	36	SESE	1852-02-02		A1
694	" "	36	NESE	1858-11-01		A1
781	CAUTHEN, Samuel	10	NWSE	1852-12-01		A1
761	CHAMPION, Robert	2	W½SW	1833-08-02		A1 V615
762	" "	3	E½SW	1837-04-10		A1
764	" "	3	SWNE	1837-08-18		A1
758	" "	10	NENE	1843-02-01		A1
763	" "	3	NENE	1849-09-01		A1
759	" "	11	NESE	1858-11-01		A1
760	" "	12	NWSW	1858-11-01		A1
766	CHAMPION, Robert G	35	E½NE	1852-02-02		A1
767	" "	35	NWSE	1852-02-02		A1
768	" "	35	SWSW	1852-02-02		A1
765	" "	12	SWNW	1852-12-01		A1
833	CHAMPION, William J	1	SESE	1854-07-15		A1
834	" "	12	NENE	1854-07-15		A1
836	" "	12	W½NE	1854-07-15		A1
835	" "	12	SENE	1858-11-01		A1
684	CHURCHWELL, Jesse	33	NESE	1848-05-03		A1
683	" "	28	SESE	1852-02-02		A1
685	" "	34	NWNW	1852-02-02		A1
686	" "	34	SESW	1852-02-02		A1
682	" "	28	NESE	1858-11-01		A1
561	COKER, Allis	32	NWNE	1838-07-28		A1
632	COKER, Jackson	18	W½NE	1861-05-01		A1
698	COKER, John	29	NWNW	1849-09-01		A1
693	COKER, John B	29	SENE	1837-08-09		A1
692	" "	29	NESE	1838-07-28		A1
690	COLLINS, John A	20	S½SE	1858-11-01		A1
691	" "	20	SESW	1858-11-01		A1
782	COOK, Samuel	11	NE	1858-11-01		A1
688	CORLEY, Joab	10	SENE	1837-08-18		A1
689	" "	11	NWNW	1837-08-18		A1
783	COTHRAN, Samuel	10	NWNW	1852-02-02		A1
559	CROXTON, Allen	2	SENW	1834-08-20		A1
560	" "	2	W½NW	1837-04-10		A1
558	" "	2	NESW	1837-05-20		A1
557	" "	2	NENW	1837-08-01		A1 F
565	CROXTON, Benjamin	2	SWSE	1838-07-28		A1
572	CURTIS, Churchwell	1	SENW	1841-05-20		A1
538	DANIEL, Abel	34	W½SW	1837-08-08		A1
602	DANIEL, Gazaway T	18	NESW	1904-07-02		A2
827	DANIEL, William	18	SESW	1858-11-01		A1
828	" "	19	N½NW	1858-11-01		A1
845	DANIEL, William J	32	NESW	1840-10-10		A1
849	" "	32	SENW	1840-10-10		A1
840	" "	31	NESE	1850-08-10		A1
851	" "	32	SWNW	1850-08-10		A1
841	" "	31	SENE	1852-02-02		A1
852	" "	32	SWSW	1852-02-02		A1
838	" "	30	W½SE	1854-07-15		A1
842	" "	31	SESE	1854-07-15		A1
846	" "	32	NWNW	1854-07-15		A1
848	" "	32	NWSW	1854-07-15		A1
837	" "	30	E½SE	1858-11-01		A1
839	" "	31	NENE	1858-11-01		A1
843	" "	31	SW	1858-11-01		A1
844	" "	31	W½SE	1858-11-01		A1
847	" "	32	NWSE	1858-11-01		A1
850	" "	32	SWNE	1858-11-01		A1
586	DAVIS, David	21	NWNW	1858-11-01		A1
740	DAVIS, Ransom L	17	E½NW	1858-11-01		A1

ID	Individual in Patent	Sec.	Sec. Part	Date Issued	Other Counties	For More Info . . .
741	DAVIS, Ransom L (Cont'd)	17	NENE	1858-11-01		A1
742	" "	17	NWNW	1858-11-01		A1
743	DAVIS, Reuben G	27	SESE	1875-04-20		A1
744	" "	34	NENE	1875-04-20		A1
745	" "	35	N½NW	1875-04-20		A1
799	DEAN, Sumter	35	NWNE	1858-11-01		A1
566	DENDY, Buford W	34	NWSE	1860-09-01		A1
567	" "	34	SWNE	1860-09-01		A1
596	DORMAN, Ephraim D	26	NESE	1884-12-05		A2
674	DORMAN, James P	34	NESE	1852-02-02		A1
675	" "	34	SENE	1852-02-02		A1
681	DORMAN, James T	35	SWNW	1852-02-02		A1
649	DOUGLASS, James M	17	NESW	1858-11-01		A1
650	" "	17	SWNE	1858-11-01		A1
651	" "	17	W½SE	1858-11-01		A1
727	DRY, Mathias	30	NESW	1858-11-01		A1
728	" "	30	W½SW	1858-11-01		A1
735	FAULK, Nancy	35	SWSE	1843-02-01		A1
831	FAULK, William F	30	W½NW	1861-05-01		A1
803	FICKLIN, Thomas	33	SENE	1852-02-02		A1
804	" "	33	SWNE	1852-02-02		A1
802	" "	33	E½SW	1858-11-01		A1
720	FLEMING, Leonard	36	NWSW	1852-02-02		A1
719	" "	36	NENE	1858-11-01		A1
721	" "	36	SESW	1858-11-01		A1
805	FOWLER, Thomas	34	NESW	1854-10-02		A1
562	FRAZER, Annie	6	NWSW	1858-11-01		A1
563	" "	7	NWNW	1858-11-01		A1
633	FRAZER, Jacob	6	SWSW	1854-07-15		A1
792	FRAZIER, Silas	6	NESW	1858-11-01		A1
605	FUNK, George	8	E½SE	1834-10-21		A1
606	" "	8	S½NE	1834-10-21		A1
607	FURR, George	8	NESW	1837-08-08		A1
609	" "	8	W½SE	1837-08-08		A1
608	" "	8	S½SW	1858-11-01		A1
700	FURR, John	5	W½SW	1852-12-01		A1
588	FURRH, David	8	N½NE	1835-10-08		A1
587	" "	8	E½NW	1837-08-08		A1
589	" "	8	W½NW	1838-07-28		A1
577	GILL, Claibourn	24	SENW	1858-11-01		A1
643	GLASS, James	33	N½NE	1858-11-01		A1
644	" "	33	NWSE	1858-11-01		A1
590	GRAHAM, David	10	SWNW	1837-08-09		A1
704	GRAHAM, John	10	NENW	1837-05-20		A1
591	HARBIN, Dominic S	1	SWSW	1858-11-01		A1
592	" "	12	NWNW	1858-11-01		A1
593	" "	2	SESE	1858-11-01		A1
574	HARRIS, Claiborn	27	SESW	1852-02-02		A1
576	HARRIS, Claiborne	27	NESE	1852-02-02		A1
575	" "	22	NWNW	1860-10-01		A1
597	HARRIS, Ezekiel	27	SENE	1852-02-02		A1
598	" "	35	SWNE	1852-02-02		A1
619	HARRIS, Henry C	20	NESW	1890-07-03		A2
697	HARRIS, John C	15	W½SW	1858-11-01		A1
753	HARRIS, Richard	10	SENW	1838-07-28		A1
754	" "	15	NWNW	1838-07-28		A1
832	HELTON, William	36	SWSW	1838-07-28		A1
631	HILL, Isaac	25	NENE	1852-02-02		A1
705	HOLLINGSHEAD, John	30	E½NE	1860-04-02		A1
646	HUDSON, James J	21	NWSE	1858-11-01		A1
746	ISHAM, Reuben	17	E½SE	1837-04-10		A1
699	ISOM, John D	21	SENW	1852-02-02		A1
747	ISOM, Reuben	17	SENE	1837-08-08		A1
748	" "	9	E½SW	1837-08-08		A1
750	" "	9	W½SE	1837-08-08		A1
751	" "	9	W½SW	1837-08-18		A1 R776
749	" "	9	SWNE	1849-09-01		A1
755	ISOM, Richard	6	E½NE	1858-11-01		A1
580	JOHNSON, Cullen D	10	E½SW	1861-05-01		A1
581	" "	10	NESE	1861-05-01		A1
582	" "	10	SESE	1861-05-01		A1
583	" "	10	SWSE	1861-05-01		A1
778	JOHNSON, Rufus G	14	SENW	1860-10-01		A1

ID	Individual in Patent	Sec.	Sec. Part	Date Issued	Other Counties	For More Info . . .
780	JOHNSON, Rufus G (Cont'd)	14	W½NW	1860-10-01		A1
777	" "	14	NENE	1860-12-01		A1
779	" "	14	W½NE	1860-12-01		A1
859	JOHNSON, William	23	SENW	1837-05-15		A1
861	" "	23	W½NE	1837-05-15		A1 G25
855	" "	14	SWSE	1849-09-01		A1
858	" "	23	NENW	1849-09-01		A1
860	" "	23	SWSW	1854-07-15		A1
853	" "	14	N½SE	1858-11-01		A1
854	" "	14	SW	1858-11-01		A1
856	" "	15	NESE	1858-11-01		A1
857	" "	23	NENE	1858-11-01		A1
706	JONES, John	32	SESW	1858-11-01		A1
707	" "	33	SWNW	1858-11-01		A1
708	" "	33	SWSW	1858-11-01		A1
600	KELLEY, Gallant	22	SWSE	1837-05-20		A1
601	" "	27	NENE	1837-08-12		A1
648	KELLEY, James	22	NWNE	1858-11-01		A1
647	" "	22	NENW	1875-04-20		A1
788	KELLEY, Seaborn	27	NESW	1852-02-02		A1
818	KELLEY, Tyre	22	NENE	1834-10-21		A1 G28
863	KELLEY, William	22	SWNE	1837-08-12		A1
862	" "	22	SENE	1838-07-28		A1
573	KELLY, Cinthea	22	SWNW	1858-11-01		A1
789	KELLY, Seaborn	34	E½NW	1852-02-02		A1
790	" "	34	NWNE	1852-02-02		A1
820	KELLY, Tyre	28	SESW	1834-08-05		A1
819	" "	15	SESE	1837-04-10		A1
791	KELY, Seaborn	27	W½SW	1858-11-01		A1
614	KING, Hardy H	10	NWSW	1849-09-01		A1
615	" "	2	SWSW	1852-02-02		A1 V761
809	KIRVIN, Thomas	6	NWNE	1837-08-02		A1
795	LEWIS, Stephen	25	SWNE	1850-08-10		A1
793	" "	25	NWNE	1852-02-02		A1
794	" "	25	SENE	1852-02-02		A1
864	LINDSEY, William	35	E½SW	1837-08-18		A1
594	MARCHANT, Draton	4	NWNE	1837-08-09		A1
729	MARCHANT, Mercer	4	NENW	1835-10-01		A1
757	MARCHANT, Richard	1	NESE	1837-05-20		A1 F
756	" "	1	E½NE	1837-08-02		A1
865	MASTIN, William	18	W½SW	1837-05-20		A1
653	MAYNARD, James	28	SENW	1858-11-01		A1
752	MCCARTY, Rhody	3	NWNW	1858-11-01		A1
578	MCCORMACK, Crawford	12	SESW	1896-10-28		A1
579	" "	12	SWSE	1896-10-28		A1
552	MCDONALD, Alexander	12	NESE	1837-08-01		A1
654	MCGOUGH, James	20	NENE	1852-02-02		A1
655	" "	20	NESE	1852-02-02		A1
656	" "	20	SWNE	1852-02-02		A1
660	" "	29	SWNE	1852-02-02		A1
657	" "	29	N½NE	1858-11-01		A1
658	" "	29	NWSE	1858-11-01		A1
659	" "	29	SENW	1858-11-01		A1
661	" "	29	SWNW	1858-11-01		A1
811	MCILWAIN, Thomas	25	SESE	1838-07-28		A1
810	MCILWAIN, Thomas L	18	E½NW	1861-05-01		A1
553	MCQUEEN, Alexander	13	SESW	1837-05-20		A1
716	MCQUEEN, Joseph A	13	NESW	1837-08-14		A1
717	" "	13	SWSE	1837-08-14		A1
723	MCQUEEN, Margaret M	13	NWSE	1858-11-01		A1
724	" "	13	NWSW	1858-11-01		A1
829	MCQUEEN, William E	14	SESE	1849-09-01		A1
830	MCQWEEN, William E	24	NWNW	1854-07-15		A1
687	MEDLEY, Jesse H	26	SWNW	1897-01-29		A1
701	MILLIGAN, John G	24	NESE	1850-08-10		A1
702	" "	24	SESE	1850-08-10		A1
703	" "	24	SWSE	1850-08-10		A1
861	MILLIGAN, Martha	23	W½NE	1837-05-15		A1 G25
726	" "	23	SENE	1837-05-20		A1
662	MINARD, James	21	SESW	1850-08-10		A1
812	MINYARD, Thomas	32	E½SE	1837-08-10		A1
813	" "	32	SWSE	1837-08-18		A1
722	MONTGOMERY, Marcus	4	E½NE	1860-10-01		A1

ID	Individual in Patent	Sec.	Sec. Part	Date Issued	Other Counties	For More Info . . .
569	MOTHERSHEAD, Christopher C	28	NESW	1858-11-01		A1
570	" "	28	W½SW	1858-11-01		A1
666	MOTHERSHEAD, James	27	SWNE	1850-08-10		A1
665	" "	27	S½NW	1852-02-02		A1
663	" "	22	W½SW	1858-11-01		A1
664	" "	27	N½NW	1858-11-01		A1
667	" "	28	NENE	1858-11-01		A1
668	" "	28	SENE	1858-11-01		A1
571	MOTHERSHED, Christopher C	33	NWNW	1854-07-15		A1
669	NICHOLS, James	10	W½NE	1837-08-01		A1
670	" "	3	E½NW	1837-08-08		A1
671	" "	3	SWNW	1838-07-28		A1
672	ONEILL, James	1	W½NW	1837-08-09		A1
673	" "	2	E½NE	1837-08-15		A1
739	PARMER, Pickens B	24	NWSE	1858-11-01		A1
866	PARMER, William	13	NENW	1858-09-01		A1
821	PERRYMAN, Walter D	28	W½NW	1861-05-01		A1
769	POLK, Robert	4	NWSW	1837-08-08		A1
770	" "	4	SWSE	1838-07-28		A1
595	POLLARD, Elizabeth	33	S½SE	1858-11-01		A1
568	POUNCEY, Calvin B	18	W½SE	1860-10-01		A1
603	POUNCEY, George B	30	E½NW	1860-10-01		A1
604	" "	30	W½NE	1860-10-01		A1
714	POUNCEY, John	34	SWSE	1837-08-12		A1
787	REEVES, Sarah J	18	E½NE	1885-06-30		A2
620	ROGERS, Henry	7	E½NE	1858-11-01		A1
718	ROPER, Joseph F	1	NENW	1852-02-02		A1
676	SALTER, James	30	SESW	1837-08-10		A1
677	" "	31	E½NW	1837-08-10		A1
678	" "	31	NWNW	1837-08-10		A1
679	" "	31	W½NE	1837-08-10		A1
680	SCHOFIELD, James	11	SWNW	1858-11-01		A1
771	SCHOFIELD, Robert	4	NESW	1858-11-01		A1
772	" "	4	SENW	1858-11-01		A1
773	" "	4	SWNE	1858-11-01		A1
736	SIMPSON, Peter	29	S½SE	1858-11-01		A1
737	" "	32	NENE	1858-11-01		A1
814	SPRAGGINS, Thomas	29	W½SW	1858-11-01		A1
822	SPRAGGINS, Whitfield	20	NWSW	1852-02-02		A1
823	" "	20	SENW	1852-02-02		A1
816	SPRAGINS, Thomas	32	NENW	1850-08-10		A1
815	" "	29	NESW	1854-07-15		A1
652	STAGGERS, James M	2	W½NE	1843-02-01		A1
826	STINSON, Micajah	28	W½NE	1837-08-07		A1 G3
730	" "	1	W½NE	1837-08-18		A1
584	STOUGH, Daniel	13	SESE	1858-11-01		A1
731	STOUGH, Michael M	12	NESW	1861-05-01		A1
732	" "	12	NWSE	1861-05-01		A1
733	" "	12	SESE	1861-05-01		A1
734	" "	13	N½NE	1861-05-01		A1
774	THOMAS, Robert	6	SESW	1850-08-10		A1
616	TODD, Hayward C	26	NWSE	1858-11-01		A1
710	TOMLINSON, John L	18	SWNW	1837-05-20		A1
711	" "	7	NWSW	1837-05-20		A1
709	" "	18	NWNW	1858-11-01		A1
712	" "	7	SWNW	1858-11-01		A1
715	TOMLINSON, John S	7	SWSW	1835-04-02		A1
613	VICKERY, George	9	E½SE	1837-08-01		A1
818	VICKERY, James H	22	NENE	1834-10-21		A1 G28
645	" "	9	SENE	1837-08-18		A1
776	VICKERY, Robert	9	W½SW	1835-04-02		A1 R751
775	" "	9	SENW	1837-08-08		A1
738	VINSON, Peter	4	W½NW	1837-08-08		A1
713	WALKER, John N	35	SENW	1858-11-01		A1
785	WILLIAMS, Samuel	21	N½SW	1858-11-01		A1
786	" "	21	SWNW	1858-11-01		A1
796	YARBROUGH, Stokes A	15	E½SW	1858-11-01		A1
797	" "	15	SWSE	1858-11-01		A1
798	" "	22	NESW	1858-11-01		A1

Patent Map

T11-N R17-E
St Stephens Meridian

Map Group 3

Township Statistics

Parcels Mapped	:	331
Number of Patents	:	267
Number of Individuals	:	166
Patentees Identified	:	168
Number of Surnames	:	108
Multi-Patentee Parcels	:	3
Oldest Patent Date	:	12/1/1831
Most Recent Patent	:	7/2/1904
Block/Lot Parcels	:	0
Parcels Re - Issued	:	1
Parcels that Overlap	:	2
Cities and Towns	:	3
Cemeteries	:	4

Section 6
- KIRVIN Thomas 1837
- ISOM Richard 1858
- FRAZER Annie 1858
- FRAZIER Silas 1858
- ALLEN James G 1838
- FRAZER Jacob 1854
- THOMAS Robert 1850

Section 5
- BARKLEY Hugh 1837
- BARKLEY Hugh 1837
- BARKLEY Hugh 1835
- BARKLEY Hugh 1837
- FURR John 1852
- BARKLEY Hugh 1835
- BARKLEY Hugh 1835
- BARKLEY Hugh 1837
- BARKLEY Thomas 1837

Section 4
- VINSON Peter 1837
- MARCHANT Mercer 1835
- MARCHANT Draton 1837
- MONTGOMERY Marcus 1860
- SCHOFIELD Robert 1858
- SCHOFIELD Robert 1858
- POLK Robert 1837
- SCHOFIELD Robert 1858
- ADDISON Abijah 1861
- ADDISON Abijah 1861
- BROWN Henry 1861
- POLK Robert 1838

Section 7
- FRAZER Annie 1858
- TOMLINSON John L 1858
- TOMLINSON John L 1837
- TOMLINSON John S 1835
- ROGERS Henry 1858

Section 8
- FURRH David 1838
- FURRH David 1837
- FURRH David 1835
- FUNK George 1834
- FURR George 1837
- FURR George 1837
- FUNK George 1834
- FURR George 1858

Section 9
- VICKERY Robert 1837
- ISOM Reuben 1849
- VICKERY James H 1837
- VICKERY Robert 1835
- ISOM Reuben 1837
- ISOM Reuben 1837
- ISOM Reuben 1837
- VICKERY George 1837

Section 18
- TOMLINSON John L 1858
- TOMLINSON John L 1837
- MCILWAIN Thomas L 1861
- COKER Jackson 1861
- REEVES Sarah J 1885
- MASTIN William 1837
- DANIEL Gazaway T 1904
- DANIEL William 1858
- POUNCEY Calvin B 1860

Section 17
- DAVIS Ransom L 1858
- DAVIS Ransom L 1858
- DAVIS Ransom L 1858
- DOUGLASS James M 1858
- ISOM Reuben 1837
- DOUGLASS James M 1858
- DOUGLASS James M 1858
- ISHAM Reuben 1837

Section 16

Section 19
- DANIEL William 1858

Section 20
- BEST George M 1861
- BEST George M 1860
- MCGOUGH James 1852
- DAVIS David 1858
- BEST George M 1861
- SPRAGGINS Whitfield 1852
- MCGOUGH James 1852
- ADAMS Samuel M 1838
- WILLIAMS Samuel 1858
- ISOM John D 1852
- SPRAGGINS Whitfield 1852
- HARRIS Henry C 1890
- MCGOUGH James 1852
- WILLIAMS Samuel 1858
- HUDSON James J 1858
- COLLINS John A 1858
- COLLINS John A 1858
- MINARD James 1850

Section 21

Section 30
- FAULK William F 1861
- POUNCEY George B 1860
- POUNCEY George B 1860
- HOLLINGSHEAD John 1860
- DRY Mathias 1858
- DANIEL William J 1854
- DRY Mathias 1858
- SALTER James 1837
- DANIEL William J 1858

Section 29
- COKER John 1849
- MCGOUGH James 1858
- MCGOUGH James 1858
- MCGOUGH James 1852
- COKER John B 1837
- MCGOUGH James 1858
- SPRAGINS Thomas 1854
- MCGOUGH James 1858
- COKER John B 1838
- SPRAGGINS Thomas 1858
- SIMPSON Peter 1858

Section 28
- PERRYMAN Walter D 1861
- BLACKMAN William D 1837
- MOTHERSHEAD James 1858
- MOTHERSHEAD James 1858
- MAYNARD James 1858
- BLACKMAN [3] William D 1837
- MOTHERSHEAD Christopher C 1858
- MOTHERSHEAD Christopher C 1858
- CHURCHWELL Jesse 1858
- KELLY Tyre 1834
- CHURCHWELL Jesse 1852

Section 31
- SALTER James 1837
- SALTER James 1837
- SALTER James 1837
- DANIEL William J 1858
- DANIEL William J 1858
- DANIEL William J 1858

Section 32
- DANIEL William J 1854
- SPRAGINS Thomas 1850
- COKER Allis 1838
- SIMPSON Peter 1858
- DANIEL William J 1852
- DANIEL William J 1850
- DANIEL William J 1840
- DANIEL William J 1858
- ARMSTRONG Franklin 1854
- DANIEL William J 1850
- DANIEL William J 1854
- DANIEL William J 1840
- DANIEL William J 1858
- MINYARD Thomas 1837
- DANIEL William J 1852
- JONES John 1858
- MINYARD Thomas 1837

Section 33
- JONES John 1858
- BEAZELY Alexander 1858
- FICKLIN Thomas 1858
- FICKLIN Thomas 1852
- GLASS James 1858
- GLASS James 1858
- CHURCHWELL Jesse 1848
- JONES John 1858
- FICKLIN Thomas 1858
- POLLARD Elizabeth 1858

MCCARTY Rhody 1858	NICHOLS James 1837	CHAMPION Robert 1849	CROXTON Allen 1837	CROXTON Allen 1837	STAGGERS James M 1843	ONEILL James 1837	ONEILL James 1837	ROPER Joseph F 1852	STINSON Micajah 1837 / MARCHANT Richard 1837

Section 3 (top-left area)

- MCCARTY Rhody 1858
- NICHOLS James 1837
- NICHOLS James 1838
- CHAMPION Robert 1849
- CHAMPION Robert 1837
- CHAMPION Robert 1837
- **3**
- BIRD David 1831

Section 2
- CROXTON Allen 1837
- CROXTON Allen 1837
- CROXTON Allen 1834
- STAGGERS James M 1843
- ONEILL James 1837
- **2**
- CHAMPION Robert 1833
- CROXTON Allen 1837
- BEST Humphrey 1837
- KING Hardy H 1852
- CROXTON Benjamin 1838
- HARBIN Dominic S 1858

Section 1
- ONEILL James 1837
- ROPER Joseph F 1852
- CURTIS Churchwell 1841
- STINSON Micajah 1837
- MARCHANT Richard 1837
- **1**
- MARCHANT Richard 1837
- BALDWIN Henry 1852
- CHAMPION William J 1854
- HARBIN Dominic S 1858
- HARBIN Dominic S 1858
- BLACKSHEAR William 1841

Section 10
- COTHRAN Samuel 1852
- GRAHAM John 1837
- NICHOLS James 1837
- CHAMPION Robert 1843
- GRAHAM David 1837
- HARRIS Richard 1838
- **10**
- CORLEY Joab 1837
- KING Hardy H 1849
- JOHNSON Cullen D 1861
- CAUTHEN Samuel 1852
- JOHNSON Cullen D 1861
- JOHNSON Cullen D 1861
- JOHNSON Cullen D 1861

Section 11
- CORLEY Joab 1837
- BRAWDAWAY Thomas J 1858
- COOK Samuel 1858
- SCHOFIELD James 1858
- CORLEY Joab 1837
- **11**
- BRAWDAWAY Thomas J 1858
- BODIFORD Aley 1858
- CHAMPION Robert 1858
- BODIFORD Aley 1858

Section 12
- HARBIN Dominic S 1858
- CHAMPION William J 1854
- CHAMPION William J 1854
- CHAMPION Robert G 1852
- CHAMPION William J 1858
- CHAMPION Robert 1858
- STOUGH Michael M 1861
- STOUGH Michael M 1861
- MCDONALD Alexander 1837
- **12**
- BODIFORD Aley 1858
- MCCORMACK Crawford 1896
- MCCORMACK Crawford 1896
- STOUGH Michael M 1861

Section 15
- HARRIS Richard 1838
- **15**
- HARRIS John C 1858
- YARBROUGH Stokes A 1858
- JOHNSON William 1858
- YARBROUGH Stokes A 1858
- KELLY Tyre 1837

Section 14
- BRAWDAWAY Thomas J 1858
- JOHNSON Rufus G 1860
- JOHNSON Rufus G 1860
- JOHNSON Rufus G 1860
- JOHNSON Rufus G 1860
- **14**
- JOHNSON William 1858
- JOHNSON William 1849

Section 13
- PARMER William 1858
- STOUGH Michael M 1861
- ADAMS Abraham 1835
- ADAMS Abraham 1834
- **13**
- MCQUEEN Margaret M 1858
- MCQUEEN Joseph A 1837
- MCQUEEN Margaret M 1858
- MCQUEEN Alexander 1837
- MCQUEEN Joseph A 1837
- STOUGH Daniel 1858

Section 22
- HARRIS Claiborne 1860
- KELLEY James 1875
- KELLEY James 1858
- KELLEY [28] Tyre 1834
- KELLY Cinthea 1858
- **22**
- KELLEY William 1837
- KELLEY William 1838
- MOTHERSHEAD James 1858
- YARBROUGH Stokes A 1858
- BOYETT James 1852
- BOYETT James 1854
- BOYETT James 1852
- KELLEY Gallant 1837

Section 23
- JOHNSON William 1849
- JOHNSON William 1837
- JOHNSON [25] William 1837
- BOYETT Thomas 1858
- **23**
- JOHNSON William 1854
- BOYT James 1852

Section 24
- JOHNSON William 1858
- MILLIGAN Martha 1837
- MCQWEEN William E 1854
- GILL Claibourn 1858
- **24**
- BOYT James 1852
- BODIFORD Alexander 1838
- PARMER Pickens B 1858
- MILLIGAN John G 1850
- MILLIGAN John G 1850
- MILLIGAN John G 1850

Section 27
- MOTHERSHEAD James 1858
- BOYETT James 1854
- KELLEY Gallant 1837
- MOTHERSHEAD James 1852
- MOTHERSHEAD James 1850
- HARRIS Ezekiel 1852
- KELLEY Seaborn 1852
- **27**
- HARRIS Claiborne 1852
- KELY Seaborn 1858
- HARRIS Claiborn 1852
- DAVIS Reuben G 1875

Section 26
- BOYETT James 1854
- BEST Humphrey 1852
- BODIFORD Alexander 1838
- MEDLEY Jesse H 1897
- BEST Humphrey 1852
- BODIFORD Alexander 1837
- **26**
- TODD Hayward C 1858
- DORMAN Ephraim D 1884

Section 25
- BODIFORD Alexander 1837
- BODIFORD Alexander 1838
- LEWIS Stephen 1852
- HILL Isaac 1852
- LEWIS Stephen 1850
- LEWIS Stephen 1852
- **25**
- BODIFORD Alexander 1838
- BARTERFORD Aaron 1852
- BODIFORD Alexander 1837
- BODIFORD Alexander 1838
- MCILWAIN Thomas 1838

Section 34
- CHURCHWELL Jesse 1852
- KELLY Seaborn 1852
- KELLY Seaborn 1852
- DAVIS Reuben G 1875
- BROWN Martha 1858
- **34**
- DENDY Buford W 1860
- DORMAN James P 1852
- DANIEL Abel 1837
- FOWLER Thomas 1854
- DENDY Buford W 1860
- DORMAN James P 1852
- CHURCHWELL Jesse 1852
- POUNCEY John 1837
- BOZEMAN James C 1858

Section 35
- DAVIS Reuben G 1875
- DEAN Sumter 1858
- CHAMPION Robert G 1852
- DORMAN James T 1852
- WALKER John N 1858
- HARRIS Ezekiel 1852
- BOZEMAN Travis H 1862
- **35**
- CHAMPION Robert G 1852
- CHAMPION Robert G 1852
- LINDSEY William 1837
- FAULK Nancy 1843

Section 36
- BODIFORD Aaron 1854
- FLEMING Leonard 1858
- FLEMING Leonard 1852
- HELTON William 1838
- BUCK Augustus 1852
- **36**
- FLEMING Leonard 1858
- FLEMING Leonard 1858
- BUCK John 1850
- BUCK John 1858
- BUCK John 1852

Helpful Hints

1. This Map's INDEX can be found on the preceding pages.

2. Refer to Map "C" to see where this Township lies within Crenshaw County, Alabama.

3. Numbers within square brackets [ ] denote a multi-patentee land parcel (multi-owner). Refer to Appendix "C" for a full list of members in this group.

4. Areas that look to be crowded with Patentees usually indicate multiple sales of the same parcel (Re-issues) or Overlapping parcels. See this Township's Index for an explanation of these and other circumstances that might explain "odd" groupings of Patentees on this map.

Legend

——————— Patent Boundary

━━━━━━━ Section Boundary

▓▓▓▓▓▓▓ No Patents Found (or Outside County)

1., 2., 3., ... Lot Numbers (when beside a name)

[ ] Group Number (see Appendix "C")

Scale: Section = 1 mile X 1 mile (generally, with some exceptions)

Road Map

T11-N R17-E
St Stephens Meridian

Map Group 3

Cities & Towns
Highland Home
Sardis
Saville

Cemeteries
Cauthens Cemetery
Dry Cemetery
Panola Cemetery
Sardis Cemetery

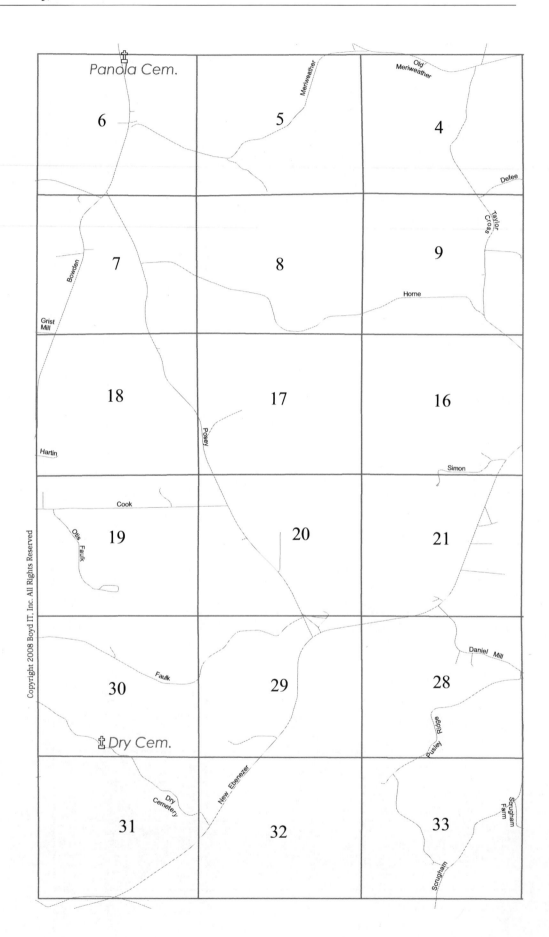

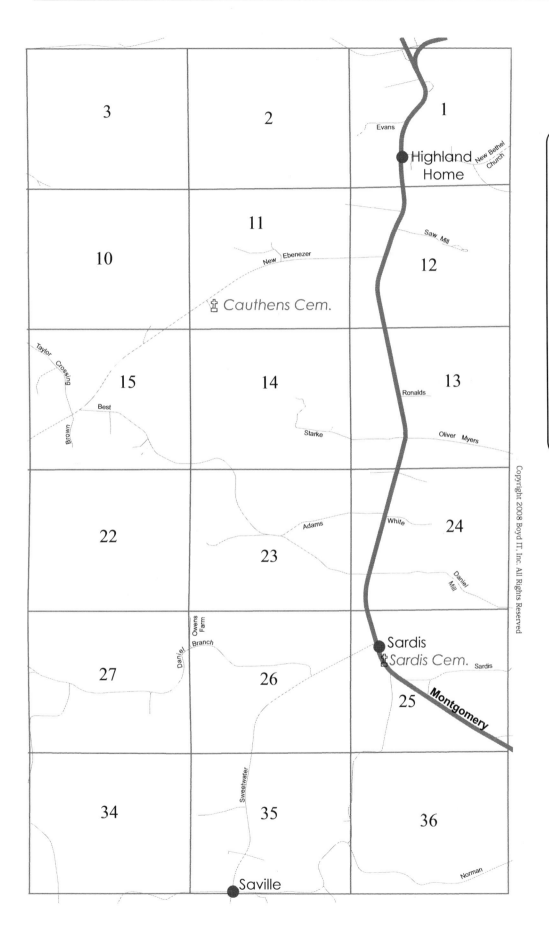

3

2

1

Evans

Highland Home

New Bethel Church

11

10

New Ebenezer

Saw Mill

12

✝ *Cauthens Cem.*

Taylor Crossing

15

14

Ronalds

13

Best

Brown

Starke

Oliver Myers

22

Adams

White

24

23

Daniel Mill

Owens Farm

Daniel

Branch

Sardis

✝ *Sardis Cem.*

Sardis

27

26

25

Montgomery

Sweetwater

34

35

36

Norman

Saville

Copyright 2008 Boyd IT, Inc. All Rights Reserved

Helpful Hints

1. This road map has a number of uses, but primarily it is to help you: a) find the present location of land owned by your ancestors (at least the general area), b) find cemeteries and city-centers, and c) estimate the route/roads used by Census-takers & tax-assessors.

2. If you plan to travel to Crenshaw County to locate cemeteries or land parcels, please pick up a modern travel map for the area before you do. Mapping old land parcels on modern maps is not as exact a science as you might think. Just the slightest variations in public land survey coordinates, estimates of parcel boundaries, or road-map deviations can greatly alter a map's representation of how a road either does or doesn't cross a particular parcel of land.

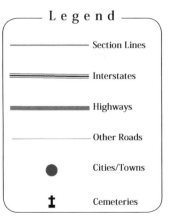

L e g e n d

———————— Section Lines

═══════════ Interstates

▬▬▬▬▬▬ Highways

———————— Other Roads

● Cities/Towns

✝ Cemeteries

Scale: Section = 1 mile X 1 mile
(generally, with some exceptions)

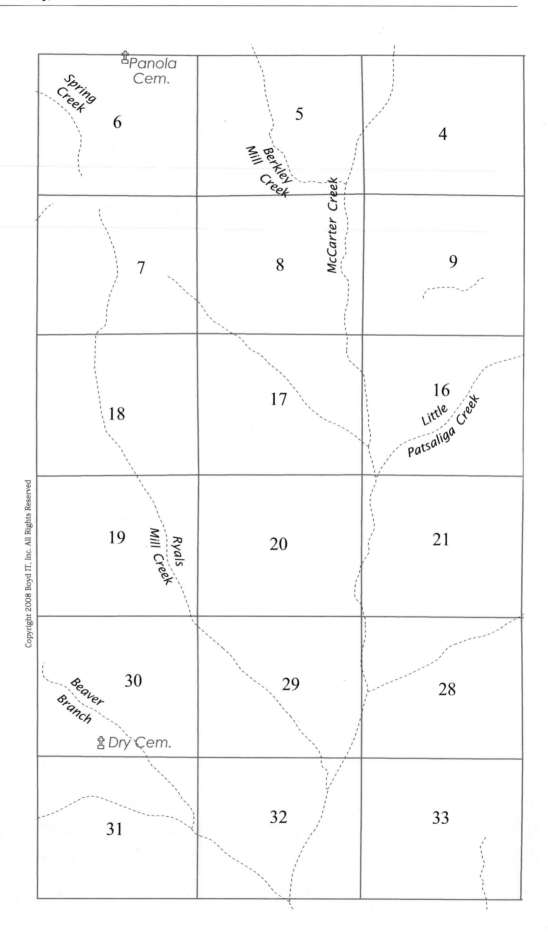

Historical Map

T11-N R17-E
St Stephens Meridian

Map Group 3

Cities & Towns
Highland Home
Sardis
Saville

Cemeteries
Cauthens Cemetery
Dry Cemetery
Panola Cemetery
Sardis Cemetery

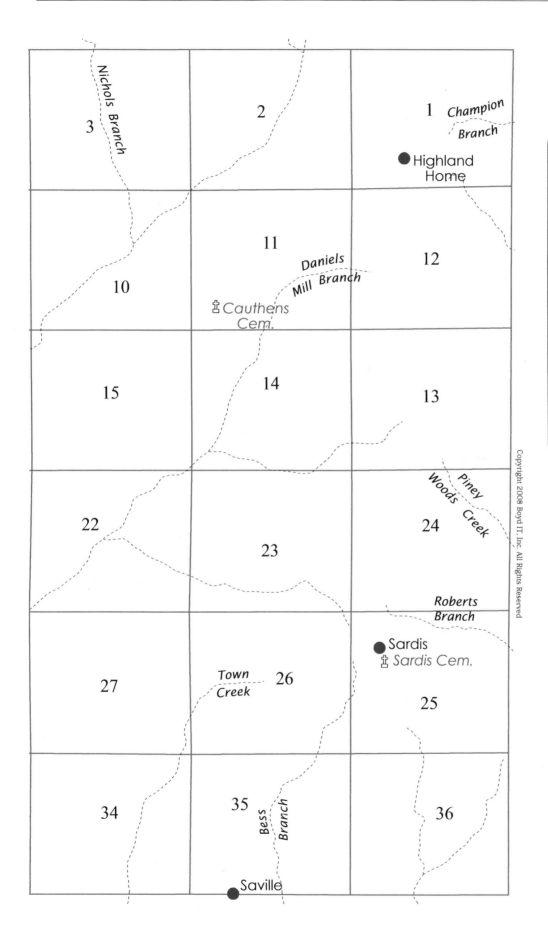

3

2

Nichols Branch

1 Champion Branch

● Highland Home

11

Daniels Mill Branch

12

10

☩ Cauthens Cem.

15

14

13

22

Piney Woods Creek

24

23

Roberts Branch

● Sardis
☩ Sardis Cem.

27

Town Creek

26

25

34

35

Bess Branch

36

● Saville

Copyright 2008 Boyd IT, Inc. All Rights Reserved

Helpful Hints

1. This Map takes a different look at the same Congressional Township displayed in the preceding two maps. It presents features that can help you better envision the historical development of the area: a) Water-bodies (lakes & ponds), b) Water-courses (rivers, streams, etc.), c) Railroads, d) City/town center-points (where they were oftentimes located when first settled), and e) Cemeteries.

2. Using this "Historical" map in tandem with this Township's Patent Map and Road Map, may lead you to some interesting discoveries. You will often find roads, towns, cemeteries, and waterways are named after nearby landowners: sometimes those names will be the ones you are researching. See how many of these research gems you can find here in Crenshaw County.

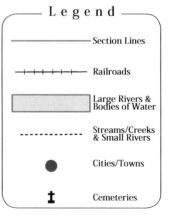

L e g e n d

———— Section Lines

+++++ Railroads

Large Rivers & Bodies of Water

- - - - - Streams/Creeks & Small Rivers

● Cities/Towns

☩ Cemeteries

Scale: Section = 1 mile X 1 mile
(there are some exceptions)

Map Group 4: Index to Land Patents

Township 11-North Range 18-East (St Stephens)

After you locate an individual in this Index, take note of the Section and Section Part then proceed to the Land Patent map on the pages immediately following. You should have no difficulty locating the corresponding parcel of land.

The "For More Info" Column will lead you to more information about the underlying Patents. See the *Legend* at right, and the "How to Use this Book" chapter, for more information.

```
┌─────────────────────────────────────────────────────────┐
│                        LEGEND                           │
│             "For More Info . . . " column               │
│  ─────────────────────────────────────────────────────  │
│  A = Authority (Legislative Act, See Appendix "A")      │
│  B = Block or Lot (location in Section unknown)         │
│  C = Cancelled Patent                                   │
│  F = Fractional Section                                 │
│  G = Group  (Multi-Patentee Patent, see Appendix "C")   │
│  V = Overlaps another Parcel                            │
│  R = Re-Issued (Parcel patented more than once)         │
│                                                         │
│  (A & G items require you to look in the Appendixes referred │
│  to above. All other Letter-designations followed by a number │
│  require you to locate line-items in this index that possess │
│  the ID number found after the letter).                 │
└─────────────────────────────────────────────────────────┘
```

ID	Individual in Patent	Sec.	Sec. Part	Date Issued	Other Counties	For More Info . . .
873	ATKINSON, Alexander	8	E½NE	1834-08-12		A1
875	" "	9	W½NW	1834-08-12		A1
874	" "	9	NENW	1837-05-15		A1
968	ATKINSON, Howell	5	S½NE	1837-08-09		A1
1039	BALDWIN, Joseph A	13	NESW	1858-11-01		A1
1040	" "	13	NWSE	1858-11-01		A1
891	BEST, Benedict	6	SWSE	1835-10-16		A1
890	" "	6	NWSW	1837-05-15		A1
969	BEST, Humphrey	6	SESE	1835-10-16		A1
945	BIRD, George L	33	E½SE	1854-10-02		A1
1123	BLACKBURN, Thomas	26	SWNE	1852-12-01		A1
1112	BLACKMON, Solomon	2	N½NW	1837-05-20		A1
1177	BODIFORD, Wright	30	NENW	1891-05-29		A2
1178	" "	30	NWNE	1891-05-29		A2
1050	BOON, Mathew	22	SWNE	1854-07-15		A1
1051	BOONE, Mathew	23	SWNE	1852-12-01		A1
1096	BOONE, Samuel	22	NENW	1837-08-18		A1
1097	" "	22	SENW	1845-07-01		A1
912	BOYETT, David	10	W½SE	1837-04-10		A1
911	" "	10	SESW	1837-05-20		A1
914	BRADLEY, David	4	E½SW	1837-05-20		A1 G6
913	" "	4	W½SW	1837-08-02		A1
1004	BRADLEY, John	22	SWSW	1837-04-10		A1
1001	" "	11	W½SW	1837-05-20		A1
1003	" "	22	N½SW	1837-08-07		A1
1000	" "	10	W½NE	1845-06-01		A1
1002	" "	2	SWNW	1852-02-02		A1
1005	" "	3	SENE	1852-02-02		A1 R1124
1049	BRADLEY, Mary C	12	SENE	1852-12-01		A1
1075	BRADLEY, Robert	11	SESW	1837-05-20		A1
1077	" "	14	NENW	1837-08-01		A1 F
1076	" "	11	SWSE	1840-10-10		A1
1113	BRADLEY, Stephen	11	NESW	1837-08-01		A1 F
1114	" "	11	NWSE	1837-08-01		A1
1124	BRADLEY, Thomas	3	SENE	1834-10-21		A1 R1005
960	BURNS, Henry	27	NENW	1852-12-01		A1
961	" "	28	E½SE	1852-12-01		A1
1034	BURNS, John W	28	E½NE	1850-08-10		A1
1142	BURNS, William A	23	NESW	1850-04-01		A1
1144	" "	23	W½SW	1850-04-01		A1
1141	" "	22	SESE	1852-02-02		A1
1143	" "	23	SESW	1852-02-02		A1
872	CANNON, Abraham	12	W½SE	1837-04-15		A1
1057	CASSITY, Peter	3	NWNE	1845-06-01		A1
893	CASTELLAW, Benjamin F	3	NWSW	1838-07-28		A1
892	" "	20	SWSE	1852-12-01		A1

ID	Individual in Patent	Sec.	Sec. Part	Date Issued	Other Counties	For More Info . . .
894	CASTILLAW, Benjamin F	33	NENW	1858-11-01		A1
895	" "	33	NWNE	1858-11-01		A1
1007	CAUTHAN, John	6	E½SW	1834-01-21		A1
965	CAUTHEN, Hiram L	5	E½NW	1837-08-09		A1
964	" "	3	SENW	1837-08-18		A1
963	" "	10	NESW	1838-07-28		A1
947	CAUTHRAN, George M	21	W½SE	1837-08-02		A1
946	" "	18	NWNW	1837-08-14		A1
1008	CAUTHRON, John	18	NWNE	1834-08-20		A1
1010	" "	7	SWSE	1834-08-20		A1
1009	" "	7	NWSE	1834-10-21		A1
1149	CHAMPION, William	8	NWNW	1834-09-04		A1
1150	" "	8	SWNW	1835-10-14		A1
1146	" "	7	E½NE	1835-10-16		A1
1147	" "	7	NENW	1837-04-10		A1
1148	" "	7	NWNE	1837-04-10		A1
1145	" "	5	E½SW	1849-09-01		A1
1167	CHAMPION, William J	7	NWNW	1837-05-15		A1
1006	CHASSER, John C	6	NENE	1858-11-01		A1
1086	CHESHIRE, Robert T	12	NWNE	1850-04-01		A1
1032	CHESSER, John S	5	W½NW	1837-05-20		A1
1087	CHESSER, Robert T	1	NESW	1852-02-02		A1
1090	" "	1	SWSE	1852-02-02		A1
1091	" "	12	NENW	1852-02-02		A1
1088	" "	1	SESE	1852-12-01		A1
1089	" "	1	SESW	1852-12-01		A1
1092	" "	12	NWNW	1853-08-01		A1
1098	CHESSER, Samuel T	34	SWNW	1852-02-02		A1
1121	CHESSER, Tennison	18	NENW	1835-10-16		A1
1122	" "	7	SESW	1835-10-16		A1
1165	COOK, William H	19	SESE	1901-10-08		A2
1011	COTHEN, John	6	SWSW	1837-05-15		A1
951	COURTNEY, George W	20	SESE	1898-07-12		A2
1059	COX, Pleasant	19	NWNW	1858-11-01		A1
1018	CRITINTUN, John L	11	SENW	1862-01-01		A1
987	DANIEL, James	32	E½SE	1837-08-18		A1
953	DILLARD, George W	17	W½SE	1833-11-14		A1
952	" "	17	E½SE	1835-10-16		A1
954	" "	21	SWNW	1835-10-16		A1
955	" "	15	W½NW	1837-08-18		A1 G17
996	DUKE, Joel	10	NENE	1834-08-20		A1
997	" "	10	SENW	1837-04-15		A1
1137	DUKE, Tyre	2	NESW	1845-07-01		A1
1160	DUKE, William	2	SWSE	1834-09-04		A1
1158	" "	2	SESE	1835-09-12		A1
1156	" "	11	W½NW	1837-04-15		A1
1154	" "	11	NENW	1838-07-28		A1
1155	" "	11	NWNE	1838-07-28		A1
1157	" "	2	NWSE	1838-07-28		A1
1153	" "	11	NENE	1858-11-01		A1
1159	" "	2	SESW	1858-11-01		A1
1161	DUKES, William	1	W½SW	1835-10-16		A1
994	DUNCAN, Jeremiah	10	SENE	1834-08-05		A1
993	" "	10	E½SE	1834-08-20		A1
995	DUNKIN, Jeremiah	33	E½SW	1831-11-30		A1
1042	EVANS, Josiah J	28	NWSE	1854-07-15		A1
1043	" "	28	SESE	1854-07-15		A1
1044	" "	28	SWSW	1854-07-15		A1
944	FORREST, George J	10	W½NW	1837-08-07		A1
880	FRAZER, Allen	14	NENE	1853-11-15		A1
881	" "	14	SESW	1853-11-15		A1
902	GAMBLE, Charles M	11	SESE	1854-07-15		A1
1102	GATLIN, Sarah	5	NESE	1834-09-04		A1
1103	" "	5	SESE	1835-10-08		A1
899	GOGGANS, Bluford M	32	SWSW	1860-04-02		A1
1012	GOODSON, John	24	NESE	1852-02-02		A1
1058	GOODSON, Peter	20	NWSE	1860-09-01		A1
981	GORE, Isaac	9	SE	1837-08-08		A1
982	HALL, Isaac N	25	NESE	1834-08-20		A1
983	" "	25	SENE	1834-08-20		A1
984	" "	25	SESE	1834-10-21		A1
1013	HILL, John	19	SWSW	1852-02-02		A1
1015	HOLLEY, John	31	SESE	1852-02-02		A1

ID	Individual in Patent	Sec.	Sec. Part	Date Issued	Other Counties	For More Info . . .
1014	HOLLEY, John (Cont'd)	31	NWSE	1858-11-01		A1
886	HOOD, Alston C	7	SESE	1835-10-16		A1
885	" "	7	NESE	1837-04-10		A1
1016	HOOD, John	8	SWSW	1834-08-20		A1
915	HUGHES, David	23	SENE	1837-08-02		A1
916	" "	23	W½SE	1837-08-02		A1
917	" "	24	W½SW	1837-08-09		A1
918	" "	26	NWNE	1841-05-20		A1
1082	HUGHES, Robert	35	SWNE	1852-02-02		A1
1081	" "	35	NENE	1852-12-01		A1
1069	ISOM, Richard	6	NESE	1850-08-10		A1 R931
1066	JETER, Ransom	13	SWNW	1858-11-01		A1
1095	JOHNSTON, Samuel A	10	NWSW	1854-07-15		A1
922	JORDAN, Felix	17	NESW	1834-08-05		A1
926	" "	21	NWNE	1834-08-05		A1
931	" "	6	NESE	1834-10-21		A1 R1069
921	" "	17	E½NW	1835-10-16		A1
932	" "	6	NWSE	1835-10-16		A1
933	" "	6	W½NE	1835-10-16		A1
930	" "	6	E½NW	1837-05-15		A1
934	" "	8	E½SW	1837-05-15		A1
914	" "	4	E½SW	1837-05-20		A1 G6
925	" "	21	E½SW	1837-08-07		A1
935	" "	9	E½NE	1837-08-07		A1
923	" "	20	E½NE	1837-08-09		A1
924	" "	20	W½NE	1837-08-09		A1
955	" "	15	W½NW	1837-08-18		A1 G17
927	" "	21	NWNW	1852-02-02		A1
928	" "	3	SE	1852-02-02		A1
936	" "	3	SWSW	1852-12-01		A1 G27
937	" "	33	E½NE	1852-12-01		A1 G27
929	" "	33	NWSE	1858-11-01		A1
936	JORDAN, Thomas	3	SWSW	1852-12-01		A1 G27
937	" "	33	E½NE	1852-12-01		A1 G27
1125	" "	21	SWSW	1854-07-15		A1
1045	KEENER, Lawson J	3	W½NW	1837-08-18		A1
942	KELLEY, Gallant	30	SWNE	1850-04-01		A1
943	KELLY, Gallant	31	NENE	1853-08-01		A1
901	KING, Charles L	29	NWSW	1834-08-05		A1 G29
884	KNIGHT, Allen	17	SWNE	1835-04-02		A1
882	" "	17	E½NE	1837-08-02		A1
883	" "	17	NWNE	1837-08-02		A1
901	KNIGHT, John W	29	NWSW	1834-08-05		A1 G29
1035	" "	17	SESW	1837-08-02		A1
1036	" "	20	SENW	1838-07-28		A1
1025	LANSDON, John M	13	NESE	1837-05-20		A1
1024	" "	13	NE	1837-08-10		A1
1107	LANSDON, Sion M	36	NESE	1852-02-02		A1
1108	" "	36	SENE	1852-02-02		A1
1138	LANSDON, Wiley J	14	S½NW	1835-10-16		A1
1139	" "	35	SESE	1850-08-10		A1
1140	" "	35	SWSE	1850-08-10		A1
898	LAWRENCE, Benjamin	23	NENE	1835-10-15		A1
897	" "	14	SESE	1837-08-08		A1
1116	LAWRENCE, Stephen	25	SWSW	1837-04-10		A1
1118	" "	34	NESE	1837-04-10		A1
1117	" "	27	E½SE	1837-08-09		A1
1115	" "	14	SWNE	1849-09-01		A1
1053	LEAKE, Newton B	36	SESE	1858-11-01		A1
1037	LEFLORE, John W	4	SENE	1858-11-01		A1
970	LEWIS, Ira H	29	NESW	1852-02-02		A1
971	" "	29	SWSW	1852-02-02		A1
1119	LEWIS, Stephen	30	NWNW	1852-02-02		A1
1070	MARCHANT, Richard	6	SWNW	1835-10-16		A1
900	MARSH, Canzada	8	NWSW	1837-04-10		A1
896	MARTIN, Benjamin J	35	NWSE	1841-05-20		A1
985	MARTIN, Isaiah	26	SESE	1838-07-28		A1
986	" "	35	NWNE	1838-07-28		A1
1054	MARTIN, Noah	25	NWSW	1834-08-12		A1
1055	" "	25	W½NW	1834-08-12		A1
1056	" "	26	NESE	1834-08-12		A1
1170	MARTIN, William	26	SWSE	1837-05-20		A1
1169	" "	25	SENW	1837-08-18		A1

ID	Individual in Patent	Sec.	Sec. Part	Date Issued	Other Counties	For More Info . . .
1168	MARTIN, William (Cont'd)	25	NENW	1841-05-20		A1
989	MAY, James	24	E½NE	1852-02-02		A1
988	"	13	SESE	1854-07-15		A1
1104	MAY, Simeon R	12	SWSW	1852-02-02		A1
1105	"	13	SWSE	1852-12-01		A1
889	MCDANIEL, Archibald	5	N½NE	1843-02-01		A1
876	MCDONALD, Alexander	10	NENW	1837-08-02		A1
878	"	3	E½SW	1837-08-02		A1
877	"	18	NESE	1837-08-08		A1
990	MCDONALD, James	18	SESE	1838-07-28		A1
1127	MCILWAIN, Thomas	31	NWNE	1838-07-28		A1
1126	MCILWAIN, Thomas L	30	W½SE	1838-07-28		A1
1068	MELTON, Rasha	22	W½NW	1838-07-28		A1
905	MITCHELL, Daniel	35	E½NW	1841-05-20		A1
906	"	35	NWSW	1841-05-20		A1
938	MITCHELL, Forest	23	E½NW	1837-08-02		A1
1109	MITCHELL, Sion	36	W½NE	1858-11-01		A1
1046	MOORE, Mark E	2	NESE	1854-07-15		A1
1047	"	36	NW	1854-10-02		A1
1162	MOSELEY, William E	9	NWNE	1837-08-14		A1
1163	MOSELY, William E	9	W½SW	1837-08-02		A1
888	MOTES, Andrew J	14	NESE	1849-09-01		A1
907	NEVES, Daniel	27	W½NW	1840-10-10		A1 G35
908	"	28	W½NE	1840-10-10		A1 G35
909	"	4	E½NW	1840-10-10		A1 G35
910	"	4	W½SE	1840-10-10		A1 G35
999	OWEN, John B	36	NENE	1837-08-01		A1
1064	OWEN, Randolph	27	SWSW	1852-12-01		A1
1065	"	28	SWSE	1852-12-01		A1
1078	OWEN, Robert F	27	SWNE	1852-12-01		A1
1079	"	34	SENE	1852-12-01		A1
1080	"	35	NESW	1852-12-01		A1
1026	PARHAM, John M	32	NENE	1882-12-20		A1
1060	PAYNE, Powell	11	NESE	1852-02-02		A1
1174	PAYNE, William	22	NWNE	1837-05-20		A1
1173	"	22	NESE	1838-07-28		A1
869	PENTON, Abner	7	W½SW	1834-10-21		A1
867	"	7	NESW	1835-04-15		A1
868	"	7	SENW	1835-10-16		A1
948	PETRY, George	35	NESE	1853-08-01		A1
950	"	36	SWSW	1853-08-01		A1
949	"	36	NWSW	1860-12-01		A1
998	PETRY, John A	35	SESW	1858-11-01		A1
870	PINTON, Abner	7	SWNE	1837-05-15		A1
871	"	7	SWNW	1837-05-15		A1
1048	POWELL, Martin	12	E½SE	1834-08-20		A1
1093	POWELL, Roland	24	NESW	1841-05-20		A1
1094	"	25	NENE	1841-05-20		A1
887	REYNOLDS, Anderson H	34	SESE	1840-10-10		A1
939	ROGERS, Francis A	17	NWSW	1837-08-01		A1
940	"	17	SWSW	1837-08-02		A1
941	"	18	SWSW	1838-07-28		A1
1027	ROGERS, John	17	W½NW	1834-01-21		A1
1028	"	18	NENE	1834-08-20		A1
1030	"	18	SENE	1835-10-16		A1
1031	"	18	SWNE	1837-08-08		A1
1029	"	18	NWSE	1837-08-18		A1
1166	RYLANDER, William I	27	SENW	1854-07-15		A1
1151	SANKEY, William D	32	SENE	1852-02-02		A1
1152	"	32	W½SE	1852-02-02		A1
962	SHOWS, Henry W	3	SWNE	1843-02-01		A1
1033	SKINNER, John	24	SWSE	1838-07-28		A1
1084	SMILIE, Robert L	1	SENE	1854-07-15		A1
1085	"	24	SESE	1858-09-01		A1
992	SPRADLEY, James	23	NWNE	1854-07-15		A1
1083	STAGGERS, Robert J	6	SENE	1843-02-01		A1
1164	STARK, William G	2	NWNE	1852-12-01		A1
1038	STINSON, Jordan B	6	NWNW	1837-04-10		A1
1052	STOUGH, Michael	18	S½NW	1858-11-01		A1
1106	STOUGH, Simeon	18	E½SW	1858-11-01		A1
919	SUMMERLIN, Evan	14	W½SW	1837-05-15		A1
958	SUMMERLIN, Glisson	9	SENW	1835-10-15		A1
959	"	9	SWNE	1837-04-10		A1

ID	Individual in Patent	Sec.	Sec. Part	Date Issued	Other Counties	For More Info . . .
957	SUMMERLIN, Glisson (Cont'd)	9	E½SW	1837-05-15		A1
907	TAYLOR, Job	27	W½NW	1840-10-10		A1 G35
908	" "	28	W½NE	1840-10-10		A1 G35
909	" "	4	E½NW	1840-10-10		A1 G35
910	" "	4	W½SE	1840-10-10		A1 G35
1061	TAYLOR, Randal	30	SESW	1854-07-15		A1
1062	TAYLOR, Randall	30	NWSW	1850-04-01		A1
1063	TAYLOR, Randle	30	SWSW	1852-12-01		A1
1071	TAYLOR, Richard	31	NENW	1850-04-01		A1
1072	" "	31	NESW	1858-11-01		A1
1073	" "	31	NWNW	1858-11-01		A1
1074	" "	32	SWNW	1858-11-01		A1
1067	TETER, Ranson	12	SESW	1852-12-01		A1
1128	THAWER, Thomas	15	NENE	1852-02-02		A1
1111	THROWER, Sion	15	SENW	1835-10-14		A1
1110	" "	10	SWSW	1837-05-20		A1
1135	THROWER, Thomas W	15	SWNE	1834-08-20		A1
1133	" "	15	SENE	1835-10-08		A1
1132	" "	15	NWNE	1837-04-10		A1
1136	" "	15	W½SE	1837-04-10		A1
1129	" "	14	NWNW	1837-05-20		A1
1130	" "	15	E½SE	1837-05-20		A1
1131	" "	15	NENW	1837-05-20		A1
1134	" "	15	SW	1837-08-09		A1
879	TUCKER, Alexander	12	NENE	1837-08-12		A1
903	TUCKER, Charles	13	SESW	1852-02-02		A1
904	" "	24	E½NW	1852-02-02		A1
967	TUCKER, Hiram	1	W½NE	1837-08-08		A1
966	" "	1	NENW	1852-02-02		A1
972	TUCKER, Ira J	11	S½NE	1852-02-02		A1
973	" "	12	N½SW	1852-02-02		A1
975	" "	13	NWNW	1852-02-02		A1
974	" "	12	SWNW	1852-12-01		A1
976	" "	2	SENW	1852-12-01		A1
977	" "	2	SWNE	1852-12-01		A1
979	TUCKER, Isaac D	1	NWSE	1853-08-01		A1
978	" "	1	NENE	1854-07-15		A1
980	" "	1	SENE	1854-07-15		A1
991	TUCKER, James S	1	NESE	1837-08-08		A1
1171	VENDERVEER, William P	28	W½NW	1838-07-28		A1
1172	" "	29	E½NE	1838-07-28		A1
1017	WALLER, John J	3	NENW	1834-10-21		A1
1041	WARD, Joseph	24	W½NW	1837-08-08		A1
1175	WARD, William	23	SESE	1834-08-20		A1
1176	" "	26	E½NE	1834-08-20		A1
920	WATKINS, Everit	32	E½SW	1896-11-21		A1
956	WATSON, Gilbert	32	NWSW	1852-02-02		A1
1120	WETHERFORD, Stephen	29	W½NE	1858-11-01		A1
1099	WILLHELM, Samuel	18	SWSE	1858-11-01		A1
1100	" "	19	N½NE	1858-11-01		A1
1101	" "	19	NENW	1858-11-01		A1
1019	WILLIAMSON, John L	5	W½SE	1838-07-28		A1
1020	" "	5	W½SW	1838-07-28		A1
1021	" "	8	E½NW	1838-07-28		A1
1022	" "	8	SE	1838-07-28		A1
1023	" "	8	W½NE	1838-07-28		A1

Patent Map

T11-N R18-E
St Stephens Meridian

Map Group 4

Township Statistics

Parcels Mapped	:	312
Number of Patents	:	293
Number of Individuals	:	161
Patentees Identified	:	163
Number of Surnames	:	109
Multi-Patentee Parcels	:	9
Oldest Patent Date	:	11/30/1831
Most Recent Patent	:	10/8/1901
Block/Lot Parcels	:	0
Parcels Re - Issued	:	2
Parcels that Overlap	:	0
Cities and Towns	:	3
Cemeteries	:	1

Section 6
STINSON Jordan B 1837
MARCHANT Richard 1835
JORDAN Felix 1837
JORDAN Felix 1835
CHASSER John C 1858
STAGGERS Robert J 1843
BEST Benedict 1837
JORDAN Felix 1835
JORDAN Felix 1834 / ISOM Richard 1850
COTHEN John 1837
CAUTHAN John 1834
BEST Benedict 1835
BEST Humphrey 1835

Section 5
CHESSER John S 1837
CAUTHEN Hiram L 1837
MCDANIEL Archibald 1843
ATKINSON Howell 1837
WILLIAMSON John L 1838
CHAMPION William 1849
WILLIAMSON John L 1838
GATLIN Sarah 1834
GATLIN Sarah 1835

Section 4
NEVES [35] Daniel 1840
BRADLEY David 1837
BRADLEY [6] David 1837
NEVES [35] Daniel 1840
LEFLORE John W 1858

Section 7
CHAMPION William J 1837
CHAMPION William 1837
CHAMPION William 1837
CHAMPION William 1835
PINTON Abner 1837
PENTON Abner 1835
PINTON Abner 1837
PENTON Abner 1834
PENTON Abner 1835
CAUTHRON John 1834
HOOD Alston C 1837
CHESSER Tennison 1835
CAUTHRON John 1834
HOOD Alston C 1835

Section 8
CHAMPION William 1834
WILLIAMSON John L 1838
WILLIAMSON John L 1838
CHAMPION William 1835
ATKINSON Alexander 1834
MARSH Canzada 1837
HOOD John 1834
JORDAN Felix 1837
WILLIAMSON John L 1838

Section 9
ATKINSON Alexander 1834
ATKINSON Alexander 1837
MOSELEY William E 1837
JORDAN Felix 1837
SUMMERLIN Glisson 1835
SUMMERLIN Glisson 1837
MOSELY William E 1837
SUMMERLIN Glisson 1837
GORE Isaac 1837

Section 18
CAUTHRAN George M 1837
CHESSER Tennison 1835
CAUTHRON John 1834
ROGERS John 1834
STOUGH Michael 1858
ROGERS John 1837
ROGERS John 1835
ROGERS Francis A 1838
STOUGH Simeon 1858
ROGERS John 1837
MCDONALD Alexander 1837
WILLHELM Samuel 1858
MCDONALD James 1838

Section 17
ROGERS John 1834
JORDAN Felix 1835
KNIGHT Allen 1837
KNIGHT Allen 1837
KNIGHT Allen 1835
ROGERS Francis A 1837
JORDAN Felix 1834
ROGERS Francis A 1837
KNIGHT John W 1837
DILLARD George W 1833
DILLARD George W 1835

Section 16

Section 19
COX Pleasant 1858
WILLHELM Samuel 1858
WILLHELM Samuel 1858
HILL John 1852
COOK William H 1901

Section 20
KNIGHT John W 1838
JORDAN Felix 1837
JORDAN Felix 1837
GOODSON Peter 1860
CASTELLAW Benjamin F 1852
COURTNEY George W 1898

Section 21
JORDAN Felix 1852
JORDAN Felix 1834
DILLARD George W 1835
JORDAN Felix 1837
CAUTHRAN George M 1837
JORDAN Thomas 1854

Section 30
LEWIS Stephen 1852
BODIFORD Wright 1891
BODIFORD Wright 1891
KELLEY Gallant 1850
TAYLOR Randall 1850
MCILWAIN Thomas L 1838
TAYLOR Randle 1852
TAYLOR Randal 1854

Section 29
WETHERFORD Stephen 1858
VENDERVEER William P 1838
KING [29] Charles L 1834
LEWIS Ira H 1852
LEWIS Ira H 1852

Section 28
VENDERVEER William P 1838
NEVES [35] Daniel 1840
BURNS John W 1850
EVANS Josiah J 1854
EVANS Josiah J 1854
EVANS Josiah J 1854
OWEN Randolph 1852
BURNS Henry 1852

Section 31
TAYLOR Richard 1858
TAYLOR Richard 1850
MCILWAIN Thomas 1838
KELLY Gallant 1853
TAYLOR Richard 1858
HOLLEY John 1858
HOLLEY John 1852

Section 32
TAYLOR Richard 1858
WATSON Gilbert 1852
WATKINS Everit 1896
GOGGANS Bluford M 1860
SANKEY William D 1852
PARHAM John M 1882
SANKEY William D 1852
DANIEL James 1837

Section 33
CASTILLAW Benjamin F 1858
CASTILLAW Benjamin F 1858
JORDAN [27] Felix 1852
JORDAN Felix 1858
DUNKIN Jeremiah 1831
BIRD George L 1854

Map Grid (Section Patentees)

Section 3 / 2 / 1 row (top)

	WALLER John J 1834	CASSITY Peter 1845		BLACKMON Solomon 1837	STARK William G 1852			TUCKER Hiram 1852	TUCKER Hiram 1837	TUCKER Isaac D 1854	
KEENER Lawson J 1837	CAUTHEN Hiram L 1837	SHOWS Henry W 1843	BRADLEY John 1852 / BRADLEY Thomas 1834	BRADLEY John 1852	TUCKER Ira J 1852	TUCKER Ira J 1852		SMILIE Robert L 1854	**1**	TUCKER Isaac D 1854	
CASTELLAW Benjamin F 1838	MCDONALD Alexander 1837	**3**	JORDAN Felix 1852	DUKE Tyre 1845	DUKE William 1838	MOORE Mark E 1854	DUKES William 1835	CHESSER Robert T 1852	TUCKER Isaac D 1853	TUCKER James S 1837	
JORDAN [27] Felix 1852				DUKE William 1858	DUKE William 1834	DUKE William 1835		CHESSER Robert T 1852	CHESSER Robert T 1852	CHESSER Robert T 1852	

Section 10 / 11 / 12 row

FORREST George J 1837	MCDONALD Alexander 1837	BRADLEY John 1845	DUKE Joel 1834	DUKE William 1837	DUKE William 1838	DUKE William 1838	DUKE William 1858	CHESSER Robert T 1853	CHESSER Robert T 1852	CHESHIRE Robert T 1850	TUCKER Alexander 1837
	DUKE Joel 1837		DUNCAN Jeremiah 1834	CRITINTUN John L 1862	**11**	TUCKER Ira J 1852	TUCKER Ira J 1852	**12**		BRADLEY Mary C 1852	
JOHNSTON Samuel A 1854	CAUTHEN Hiram L 1838	**10**		BRADLEY Stephen 1837	BRADLEY Stephen 1837	PAYNE Powell 1852	TUCKER Ira J 1852		CANNON Abraham 1837	POWELL Martin 1834	
THROWER Sion 1837	BOYETT David 1837	BOYETT David 1837	DUNCAN Jeremiah 1834	BRADLEY John 1837	BRADLEY Robert 1837	BRADLEY Robert 1840	GAMBLE Charles M 1854	MAY Simeon R 1852	TETER Ranson 1852		

Section 15 / 14 / 13 row

DILLARD [17] George W 1837	THROWER Thomas W 1837	THROWER Thomas W 1837	THAWER Thomas 1852	THROWER Thomas W 1837	BRADLEY Robert 1837		FRAZER Allen 1853	TUCKER Ira J 1852		LANSDON John M 1837	
	THROWER Sion 1835	THROWER Thomas W 1834	THROWER Thomas W 1835	LANSDON Wiley J 1835	LAWRENCE Stephen 1849		JETER Ransom 1858	**13**			
15	THROWER Thomas W 1837	THROWER Thomas W 1837	SUMMERLIN Evan 1837	**14**		MOTES Andrew J 1849		BALDWIN Joseph A 1858	BALDWIN Joseph A 1858	LANSDON John M 1837	
THROWER Thomas W 1837				FRAZER Allen 1853		LAWRENCE Benjamin 1837		TUCKER Charles 1852	MAY Simeon R 1852	MAY James 1854	

Section 22 / 23 / 24 row

MELTON Rasha 1838	BOONE Samuel 1837	PAYNE William 1837		MITCHELL Forest 1837	SPRADLEY James 1854	LAWRENCE Benjamin 1835	WARD Joseph 1837	TUCKER Charles 1852		MAY James 1852	
	BOONE Samuel 1845	BOON Mathew 1854			BOONE Mathew 1852	HUGHES David 1837			**24**		
BRADLEY John 1837		**22**	PAYNE William 1838	BURNS William A 1850	BURNS William A 1850	**23**		POWELL Roland 1841		GOODSON John 1852	
BRADLEY John 1837			BURNS William A 1852	BURNS William A 1852	HUGHES David 1837	WARD William 1834	HUGHES David 1837		SKINNER John 1838	SMILIE Robert L 1858	

Section 27 / 26 / 25 row

NEVES [35] Daniel 1840	BURNS Henry 1852				HUGHES David 1841	WARD William 1834		MARTIN William 1841		POWELL Roland 1841	
	RYLANDER William I 1854	OWEN Robert F 1852			BLACKBURN Thomas 1852		MARTIN Noah 1834	MARTIN William 1837		HALL Isaac N 1834	
27		LAWRENCE Stephen 1837		**26**		MARTIN Noah 1834	MARTIN Noah 1834	**25**		HALL Isaac N 1834	
OWEN Randolph 1852					MARTIN William 1837	MARTIN Isaiah 1838	LAWRENCE Stephen 1837			HALL Isaac N 1834	

Section 34 / 35 / 36 row

		MITCHELL Daniel 1841	MARTIN Isaiah 1838	HUGHES Robert 1852			OWEN John B 1837				
CHESSER Samuel T 1852	OWEN Robert F 1852	**35**	HUGHES Robert 1852	MOORE Mark E 1854	MITCHELL Sion 1858	LANSDON Sion M 1852					
	34	LAWRENCE Stephen 1837	MITCHELL Daniel 1841	OWEN Robert F 1852	MARTIN Benjamin J 1841	PETRY George 1853	PETRY George 1860	**36**		LANSDON Sion M 1852	
		REYNOLDS Anderson H 1840	PETRY John A 1858	LANSDON Wiley J 1850	LANSDON Wiley J 1850	PETRY George 1853				LEAKE Newton B 1858	

Helpful Hints

1. This Map's INDEX can be found on the preceding pages.

2. Refer to Map "C" to see where this Township lies within Crenshaw County, Alabama.

3. Numbers within square brackets [ ] denote a multi-patentee land parcel (multi-owner). Refer to Appendix "C" for a full list of members in this group.

4. Areas that look to be crowded with Patentees usually indicate multiple sales of the same parcel (Re-issues) or Overlapping parcels. See this Township's Index for an explanation of these and other circumstances that might explain "odd" groupings of Patentees on this map.

Legend

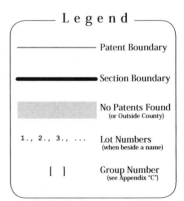

————	Patent Boundary
▬▬▬▬	Section Boundary
▨	No Patents Found (or Outside County)
1., 2., 3., ...	Lot Numbers (when beside a name)
[ ]	Group Number (see Appendix "C")

Scale: Section = 1 mile X 1 mile
(generally, with some exceptions)

Road Map

T11-N R18-E
St Stephens Meridian

Map Group 4

Cities & Towns

Bradleyton
Helicon
Magnolia Shores

Cemeteries

Hudson Cemetery

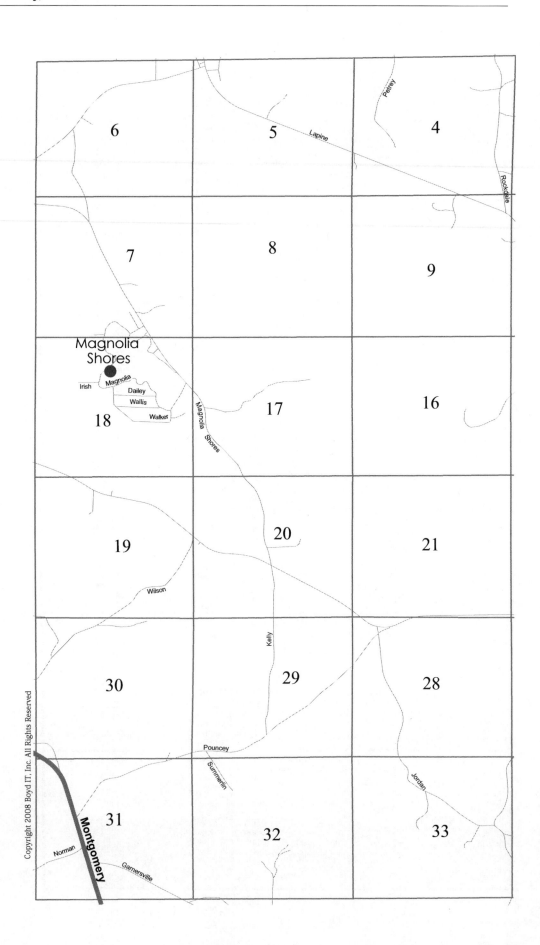

| 3 | 2 | 1 |

Athey

Tucker

| 10 | 11 | 12 |

Fairview   Church

✝ *Hudson Cem.*

May

Burnett

Matthews

| 15 | 14 | 13 |

Nekosa

| 22 | 23 | 24 |

●Helicon

Oliver   Myers   Helicon

Bradleyton ●

| 27 | 26 | 25 |

Provitt

Bradleyton

Browder

Old Petrey

Rising Star

| 34 | 35 | 36 |

Lapine

Smith
Chapel

Fork

Helpful Hints

1. This road map has a number of uses, but primarily it is to help you: a) find the present location of land owned by your ancestors (at least the general area), b) find cemeteries and city-centers, and c) estimate the route/roads used by Census-takers & tax-assessors.

2. If you plan to travel to Crenshaw County to locate cemeteries or land parcels, please pick up a modern travel map for the area before you do. Mapping old land parcels on modern maps is not as exact a science as you might think. Just the slightest variations in public land survey coordinates, estimates of parcel boundaries, or road-map deviations can greatly alter a map's representation of how a road either does or doesn't cross a particular parcel of land.

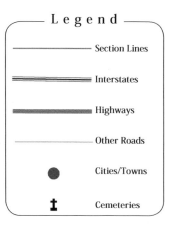

L e g e n d	
————————	Section Lines
════════	Interstates
▨▨▨▨▨▨	Highways
————————	Other Roads
●	Cities/Towns
✝	Cemeteries

Scale: Section = 1 mile X 1 mile
(generally, with some exceptions)

Historical Map

T11-N R18-E
St Stephens Meridian

Map Group 4

Cities & Towns
Bradleyton
Helicon
Magnolia Shores

Cemeteries
Hudson Cemetery

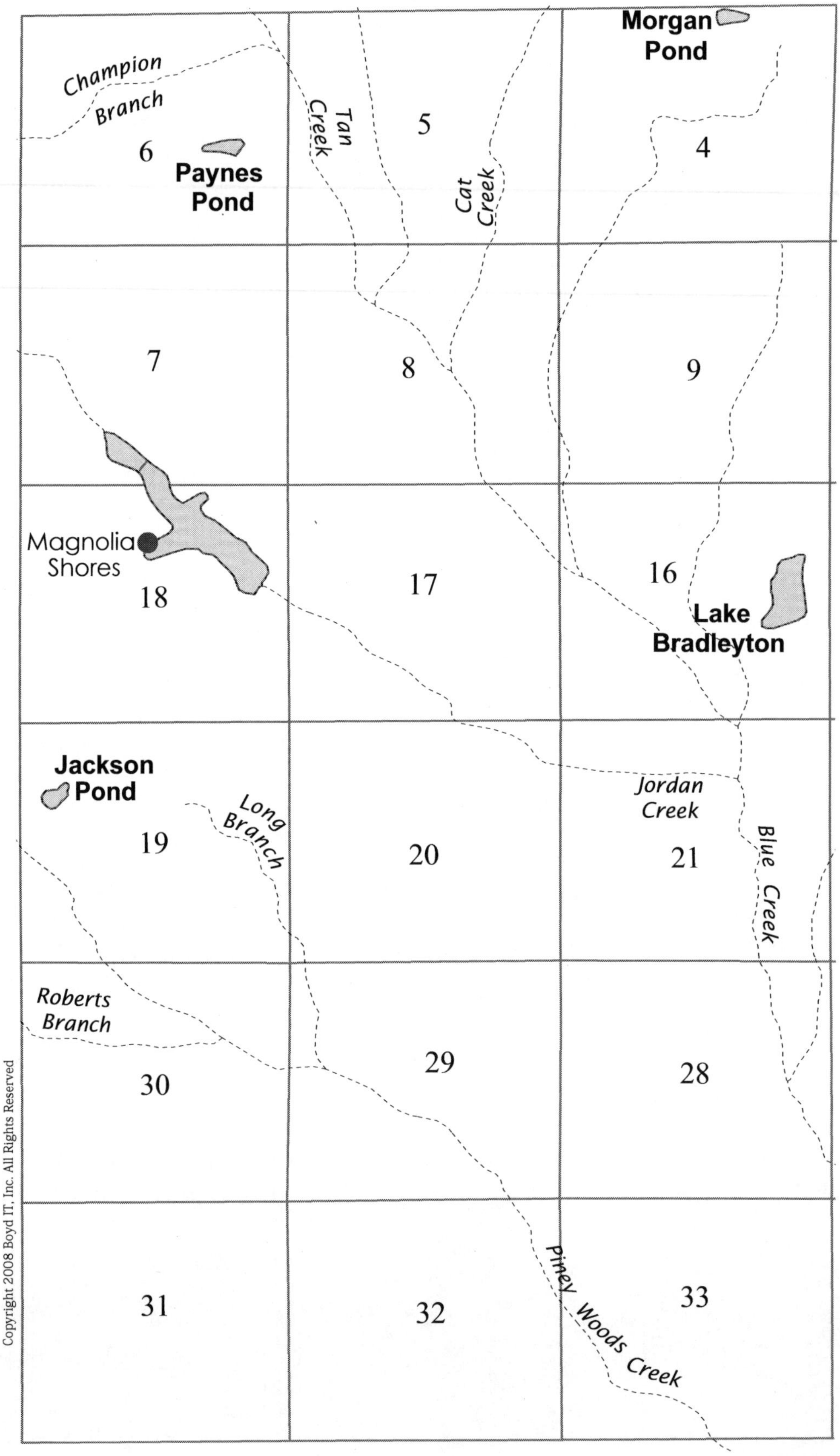

Champion Branch

Morgan Pond

Tan Creek

Cat Creek

6   Paynes Pond

5

4

7

8

9

Magnolia Shores

18

17

16   Lake Bradleyton

Jackson Pond

Long Branch

Jordan Creek

Blue Creek

19

20

21

Roberts Branch

30

29

28

Piney Woods Creek

31

32

33

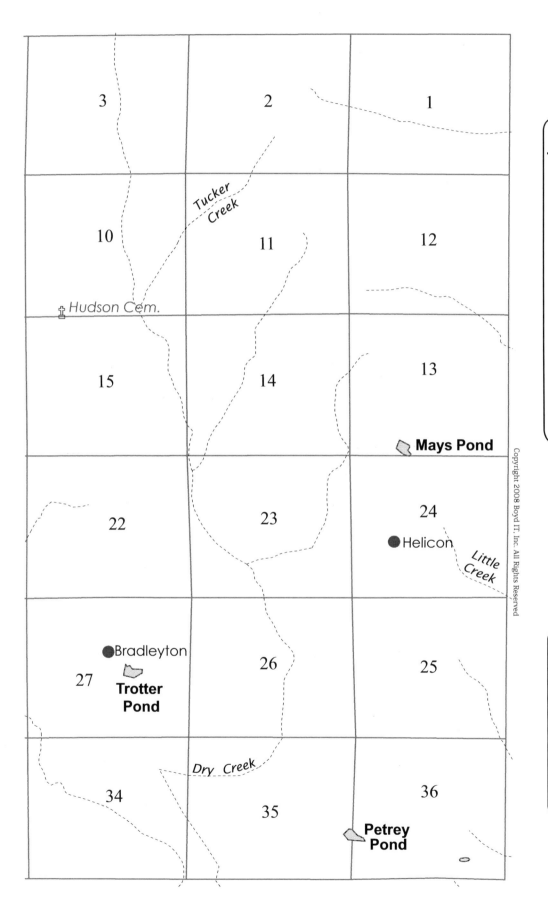

3

2

1

Tucker Creek

10

11

12

✝ *Hudson Cem.*

15

14

13

🔶 **Mays Pond**

22

23

24

● Helicon

Little Creek

●Bradleyton

26

25

27

🔶 **Trotter Pond**

Dry Creek

34

35

36

🔶 **Petrey Pond**

Helpful Hints

1. This Map takes a different look at the same Congressional Township displayed in the preceding two maps. It presents features that can help you better envision the historical development of the area: a) Water-bodies (lakes & ponds), b) Water-courses (rivers, streams, etc.), c) Railroads, d) City/town center-points (where they were oftentimes located when first settled), and e) Cemeteries.

2. Using this "Historical" map in tandem with this Township's Patent Map and Road Map, may lead you to some interesting discoveries. You will often find roads, towns, cemeteries, and waterways are named after nearby landowners: sometimes those names will be the ones you are researching. See how many of these research gems you can find here in Crenshaw County.

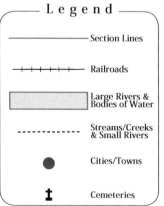

Legend

————————	Section Lines
+-+-+-+-+	Railroads
▭	Large Rivers & Bodies of Water
- - - - - -	Streams/Creeks & Small Rivers
●	Cities/Towns
✝	Cemeteries

Scale: Section = 1 mile X 1 mile
(there are some exceptions)

Map Group 5: Index to Land Patents

Township 11-North Range 19-East (St Stephens)

After you locate an individual in this Index, take note of the Section and Section Part then proceed to the Land Patent map on the pages immediately following. You should have no difficulty locating the corresponding parcel of land.

The "For More Info" Column will lead you to more information about the underlying Patents. See the *Legend* at right, and the "How to Use this Book" chapter, for more information.

```
                    LEGEND
          "For More Info . . ." column
A = Authority (Legislative Act, See Appendix "A")
B = Block or Lot (location in Section unknown)
C = Cancelled Patent
F = Fractional Section
G = Group  (Multi-Patentee Patent, see Appendix "C")
V = Overlaps another Parcel
R = Re-Issued (Parcel patented more than once)

(A & G items require you to look in the Appendixes referred
to above. All other Letter-designations followed by a number
require you to locate line-items in this index that possess
the ID number found after the letter).
```

ID	Individual in Patent	Sec.	Sec. Part	Date Issued	Other Counties	For More Info . . .
1231	BODIE, John	32	NESW	1852-02-02	Pike	A1
1232	" "	32	SWNE	1852-02-02	Pike	A1
1263	BURGESS, William	17	W½SE	1833-09-16	Pike	A1
1264	" "	19	NENE	1834-10-21		A1
1265	" "	19	W½NE	1834-10-21		A1
1266	" "	30	W½NE	1837-05-15		A1
1267	" "	8	E½SE	1837-08-01	Pike	A1 F
1268	" "	8	NENE	1850-08-10	Pike	A1
1262	" "	17	NENE	1852-02-02	Pike	A1
1269	" "	8	NESW	1852-02-02	Pike	A1
1270	" "	8	NWNE	1852-02-02	Pike	A1 R1244
1271	" "	8	SENW	1852-02-02	Pike	A1
1272	" "	8	SESW	1852-02-02	Pike	A1
1273	" "	8	SWSE	1852-02-02	Pike	A1
1181	CANNON, Abraham	6	NENE	1837-08-12	Pike	A1
1190	CANNON, David	31	SESE	1835-10-14		A1
1191	" "	31	SESW	1835-10-14		A1
1201	CANNON, Henry	17	W½SW	1845-07-01	Pike	A1
1202	" "	18	E½NE	1848-04-01		A1
1200	" "	17	SENW	1852-02-02	Pike	A1
1243	CHESSER, John W	29	SWSW	1845-07-01	Pike	A1
1275	CHESSER, William	31	NENE	1835-10-16		A1
1274	" "	30	SWSE	1837-08-18		A1
1276	" "	31	SENE	1837-08-18		A1
1277	" "	32	NWNW	1854-07-15	Pike	A1
1283	CHESSER, William N	31	NWNE	1837-05-20		A1
1278	DEAN, William	32	NENW	1852-12-01	Pike	A1 R1207
1229	DUKE, Joel	7	E½SW	1838-07-28		A1
1230	" "	7	SWSW	1838-07-28		A1
1260	FAIRCLOTH, Thomas	18	NWSE	1837-04-10		A1
1183	GAMBLE, Charles M	7	NWSE	1852-12-01		A1
1184	" "	7	SESE	1852-12-01		A1
1233	GOLDTHWAITE, John	19	E½SE	1834-10-21		A1
1234	" "	29	W½NW	1834-10-21	Pike	A1
1235	" "	30	E½NE	1834-10-21		A1
1236	" "	30	E½SE	1834-10-21		A1
1237	" "	6	W½NW	1835-10-08	Pike	A1
1245	GOODSON, Josiah	20	W½SW	1852-02-02	Pike	A1
1250	GRAHAM, Mary H	6	SWSW	1848-05-03	Pike	A1 R1205
1182	HALL, Adam N	30	W½NW	1834-10-21		A1
1219	HALL, Isaac N	30	W½SW	1833-11-14		A1
1218	" "	18	E½NW	1837-08-02		A1
1221	HENDERSON, James	8	SENE	1837-08-02	Pike	A1
1238	HURTT, John	19	SENE	1834-08-20		A1
1247	HURTT, Kindred A	20	SWNW	1835-10-16	Pike	A1
1246	" "	19	E½NW	1837-08-02		A1

ID	Individual in Patent	Sec.	Sec. Part	Date Issued	Other Counties	For More Info . . .
1281	HURTT, William	18	E½SW	1837-08-02		A1
1180	JACKSON, Abner M	31	NWNW	1834-10-21		A1
1279	JEFCOAT, William E	32	N½NE	1843-02-01	Pike	A1
1179	JONES, Aaron M	18	E½SE	1833-09-16		A1
1193	JORDAN, Felix	30	E½NW	1837-05-15		A1
1282	LANDERS, William	31	SWNW	1837-08-02		A1
1239	LANSDON, John M	18	SWNW	1834-08-12		A1
1251	LEAK, Newton B	31	SWSW	1858-11-01		A1
1261	LEAK, William B	6	SENE	1858-11-01	Pike	A1
1206	LEWIS, Ira H	31	SWNE	1841-05-20		A1
1207	" "	32	NENW	1860-10-01	Pike	A1 R1278
1220	MARTIN, Jackson	18	NWNW	1850-04-01		A1
1225	MAY, James	17	SWNW	1852-12-01	Pike	A1
1226	" "	18	SWSW	1852-12-01		A1
1224	" "	17	E½SW	1858-11-01	Pike	A1
1222	MAY, James M	17	N½NW	1896-10-28	Pike	A1
1223	" "	8	W½SW	1896-10-28	Pike	A1
1259	MAY, Simeon R	18	NWSW	1852-12-01		A1
1248	MCCURRY, Lauchlin B	8	NWSE	1850-04-01	Pike	A1
1185	MITCHELL, Daniel	30	E½SW	1852-02-02		A1
1186	" "	32	NESE	1852-02-02	Pike	A1
1188	" "	32	SWSE	1852-02-02	Pike	A1
1187	" "	32	NWSE	1858-11-01	Pike	A1
1227	MITCHELL, James	19	SWSW	1852-02-02		A1
1249	MITCHELL, Lloyd	32	SESE	1858-11-01	Pike	A1
1240	NOBLES, John	29	SESW	1852-12-01	Pike	A1
1192	OWEN, David	30	NWSE	1837-08-09		A1
1189	OWEN, David A	31	NWSW	1838-07-28		A1
1242	OWEN, John	19	NWSE	1835-10-14		A1
1241	" "	19	E½SW	1837-05-15		A1
1252	OWEN, Priscilla S	31	NESW	1835-04-02		A1
1253	OWEN, Rachel C	31	E½NW	1835-04-02		A1
1258	OWEN, Samuel T	31	NWSE	1837-08-01		A1
1257	POWELL, Rowland	18	SWSE	1834-08-12		A1
1194	PRUITT, George A	20	E½SW	1896-10-21	Pike	A1
1195	ROBINSON, George	17	NESE	1835-10-01	Pike	A1
1196	" "	17	SENE	1835-10-01	Pike	A1
1197	" "	17	W½NE	1835-10-01	Pike	A1
1284	SANDERS, William	31	SWSE	1841-05-20		A1
1256	SMILIE, Robert L	19	NWSW	1858-11-01		A1
1255	STANLEY, Robert H	32	NWSW	1860-12-01		A1
1198	TUCKER, George W	6	SESW	1852-02-02	Pike	A1
1199	" "	7	NWNW	1852-02-02		A1
1204	TUCKER, Hiram	6	SWNE	1837-08-08	Pike	A1
1205	" "	6	SWSW	1841-05-20	Pike	A1 R1250
1203	" "	6	NWNE	1858-09-01	Pike	A1
1211	TUCKER, Ira	8	W½NW	1833-06-04	Pike	A1
1210	" "	8	NENW	1834-08-05	Pike	A1
1209	" "	7	S½NW	1834-10-21		A1
1208	TUCKER, Ira J	7	NWSW	1843-02-01		A1
1214	TUCKER, Isaac D	6	SENW	1852-02-02	Pike	A1
1215	" "	6	SESE	1852-02-02	Pike	A1
1216	" "	6	SWSE	1852-02-02	Pike	A1
1217	" "	7	NENE	1852-02-02		A1
1213	" "	6	NWSE	1852-12-01	Pike	A1
1212	" "	6	NENW	1853-08-01	Pike	A1
1228	TUCKER, James S	6	NWSW	1837-08-08	Pike	A1
1254	TUCKER, Richard T	6	NESW	1858-11-01	Pike	A1
1280	TUCKER, William H	7	NESE	1848-04-01		A1
1288	WINGARD, William	20	W½SE	1833-09-16	Pike	A1
1294	" "	29	W½NE	1833-09-16	Pike	A1
1286	" "	20	E½SE	1833-11-14	Pike	A1
1285	" "	20	E½NE	1835-10-01	Pike	A1
1287	" "	20	W½NE	1835-10-01	Pike	A1
1293	" "	29	SWSE	1835-10-01	Pike	A1
1291	" "	29	NWSE	1835-10-14	Pike	A1
1290	" "	29	NENE	1835-10-16	Pike	A1
1292	" "	29	SENE	1837-08-08	Pike	A1 F
1289	" "	29	E½SE	1838-07-28	Pike	A1
1244	WOOD, John	8	NWNE	1852-02-02	Pike	A1 R1270

95

Patent Map

T11-N R19-E
St Stephens Meridian

Map Group 5

Township Statistics

Parcels Mapped	:	116
Number of Patents	:	109
Number of Individuals	:	61
Patentees Identified	:	61
Number of Surnames	:	37
Multi-Patentee Parcels	:	0
Oldest Patent Date	:	6/4/1833
Most Recent Patent	:	10/28/1896
Block/Lot Parcels	:	0
Parcels Re - Issued	:	3
Parcels that Overlap	:	0
Cities and Towns	:	0
Cemeteries	:	0

Note: the area contained in this map amounts to far less than a full Township. Therefore, its contents are completely on this single page (instead of a "normal" 2-page spread).

Legend

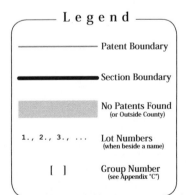

	Patent Boundary
	Section Boundary
	No Patents Found (or Outside County)
1., 2., 3., ...	Lot Numbers (when beside a name)
[ ]	Group Number (see Appendix "C")

Scale: Section = 1 mile X 1 mile (generally, with some exceptions)

GOLDTHWAITE John 1835

TUCKER Isaac D 1853

TUCKER Hiram 1858

CANNON Abraham 1837

TUCKER Isaac D 1852

TUCKER Hiram 1837

LEAK William B 1858

6

TUCKER James S 1837

TUCKER Richard T 1858

TUCKER Isaac D 1852

Pike

5

GRAHAM Mary H 1848 / TUCKER Hiram 1841

TUCKER George W 1852

TUCKER Isaac D 1852

TUCKER Isaac D 1852

TUCKER George W 1852

Crenshaw

TUCKER Isaac D 1852

TUCKER Ira 1833

TUCKER Ira 1834

BURGESS William 1852 / WOOD John 1852

BURGESS William 1850

TUCKER Ira 1834

BURGESS William 1852

8

HENDERSON James 1837

TUCKER Ira J 1843

7

GAMBLE Charles M 1852

TUCKER William H 1848

BURGESS William 1852

MCCURRY Lauchlin B 1850

DUKE Joel 1838

MAY James M 1896

BURGESS William 1837

DUKE Joel 1838

GAMBLE Charles M 1852

BURGESS William 1852

BURGESS William 1852

MARTIN Jackson 1850

HALL Isaac N 1837

CANNON Henry 1848

MAY James M 1896

BURGESS William 1852

LANSDON John M 1834

18

MAY James 1852

CANNON Henry 1852

ROBINSON George 1835

ROBINSON George 1835

MAY Simeon R 1852

HURTT William 1837

FAIRCLOTH Thomas 1837

JONES Aaron M 1833

CANNON Henry 1845

17

ROBINSON George 1835

MAY James 1852

POWELL Rowland 1834

MAY James 1858

BURGESS William 1833

BURGESS William 1834

HURTT Kindred A 1837

BURGESS William 1834

HURTT John 1834

HURTT Kindred A 1835

20

WINGARD William 1835

WINGARD William 1835

SMILIE Robert L 1858

19

OWEN John 1835

GOODSON Josiah 1852

PRUIT George A 1896

WINGARD William 1833

WINGARD William 1833

MITCHELL James 1852

OWEN John 1837

GOLDTHWAITE John 1834

HALL Adam N 1834

JORDAN Felix 1837

30

BURGESS William 1837

GOLDTHWAITE John 1834

GOLDTHWAITE John 1834

WINGARD William 1833

WINGARD William 1835

WINGARD William 1837

HALL Isaac N 1833

MITCHELL Daniel 1852

OWEN David 1837

GOLDTHWAITE John 1834

29

WINGARD William 1835

CHESSER William 1837

CHESSER John W 1845

NOBLES John 1852

WINGARD William 1835

WINGARD William 1838

JACKSON Abner M 1834

OWEN Rachel C 1835

CHESSER William N 1837

CHESSER William 1835

CHESSER William 1854

DEAN William 1852

LEWIS Ira H 1860

JEFCOAT William E 1843

LANDERS William 1837

31

LEWIS Ira H 1841

CHESSER William 1837

32

BODIE John 1852

OWEN David A 1838

OWEN Priscilla S 1835

OWEN Samuel T 1837

STANLEY Robert H 1860

BODIE John 1852

MITCHELL Daniel 1858

MITCHELL Daniel 1852

LEAK Newton B 1858

CANNON David 1835

SANDERS William 1841

CANNON David 1835

MITCHELL Daniel 1852

MITCHELL Lloyd 1858

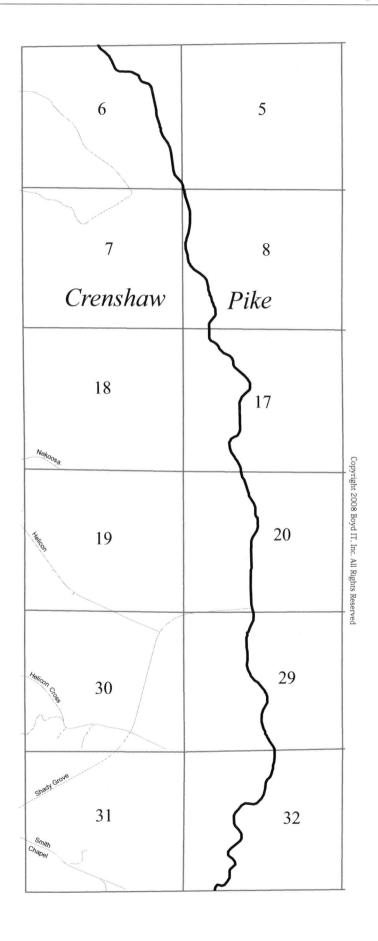

6

5

7

8

Crenshaw

Pike

18

17

Nekoosa

19

20

Helicon

Helicon Cross

30

29

Shady Grove

31

32

Smith Chapel

Road Map

T11-N R19-E
St Stephens Meridian

Map Group 5

Note: the area contained in this map amounts to far less than a full Township. Therefore, its contents are completely on this single page (instead of a "normal" 2-page spread).

Cities & Towns
None

Cemeteries
None

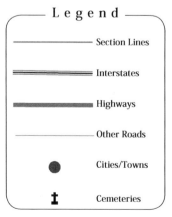

L e g e n d

———— Section Lines

══════ Interstates

━━━━━ Highways

———— Other Roads

● Cities/Towns

† Cemeteries

Scale: Section = 1 mile X 1 mile
(generally, with some exceptions)

Historical Map

T11-N R19-E
St Stephens Meridian

Map Group 5

Note: the area contained in this map amounts to far less than a full Township. Therefore, its contents are completely on this single page (instead of a "normal" 2-page spread).

Cities & Towns
None

Cemeteries
None

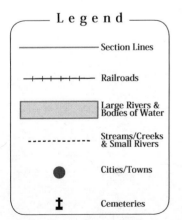

Legend

Section Lines

Railroads

Large Rivers & Bodies of Water

Streams/Creeks & Small Rivers

● Cities/Towns

✝ Cemeteries

Scale: Section = 1 mile X 1 mile
(there are some exceptions)

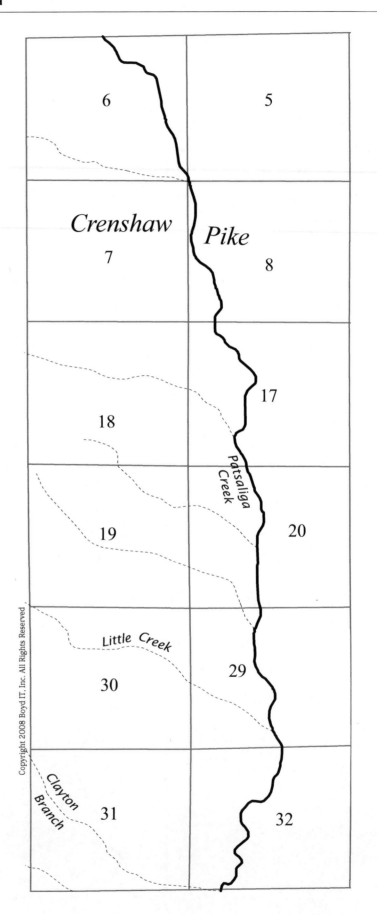

Crenshaw *Pike*

6 5

7 8

18 17

19 Patsaliga Creek 20

Little Creek

30 29

Clayton Branch 31 32

Map Group 6: Index to Land Patents

Township 10-North Range 16-East (St Stephens)

After you locate an individual in this Index, take note of the Section and Section Part then proceed to the Land Patent map on the pages immediately following. You should have no difficulty locating the corresponding parcel of land.

The "For More Info" Column will lead you to more information about the underlying Patents. See the *Legend* at right, and the "How to Use this Book" chapter, for more information.

```
┌─────────────────────────────────────────────────────────┐
│                        LEGEND                            │
│            "For More Info . . . " column                 │
│  A = Authority (Legislative Act, See Appendix "A")       │
│  B = Block or Lot (location in Section unknown)          │
│  C = Cancelled Patent                                    │
│  F = Fractional Section                                  │
│  G = Group  (Multi-Patentee Patent, see Appendix "C")    │
│  V = Overlaps another Parcel                             │
│  R = Re-Issued (Parcel patented more than once)          │
│                                                          │
│  (A & G items require you to look in the Appendixes      │
│  referred to above. All other Letter-designations        │
│  followed by a number require you to locate line-items   │
│  in this index that possess the ID number found after    │
│  the letter).                                            │
└─────────────────────────────────────────────────────────┘
```

ID	Individual in Patent	Sec.	Sec. Part	Date Issued	Other Counties	For More Info . . .
1343	ACREE, John E	15	NESE	1858-11-01	Butler	A1
1344	" "	15	SENE	1858-11-01	Butler	A1
1395	ALLEN, Washington W	3	NENW	1852-02-02		A1
1394	" "	27	SESW	1858-11-01		A1
1396	" "	34	NENW	1858-11-01		A1
1397	" "	34	SWNW	1858-11-01		A1
1351	ANTHONY, Lemuel B	1	S½	1897-02-04		A1
1352	" "	1	W½N½	1897-02-04		A1
1353	" "	2	SESE	1897-02-04		A1
1359	ANTHONY, Middleton W	11	N½	1858-11-01		A1
1329	BELL, James W	27	SESE	1858-11-01		A1 F
1330	" "	34	NENE	1858-11-01		A1 F
1331	" "	34	S½NE	1858-11-01		A1
1384	BELL, Thomas W	34	N½SE	1858-11-01		A1
1385	" "	34	N½SW	1858-11-01		A1
1386	" "	34	S½SW	1858-11-01		A1
1387	" "	34	SWSE	1858-11-01		A1
1388	" "	35	NWSW	1858-11-01		A1
1393	BELL, Washington	2	NE	1858-11-01		A1
1367	CALLENS, Robert H	11	S½	1858-11-01		A1
1313	DANIEL, Francis	3	NWSW	1837-05-20		A1
1338	DANIEL, John A	12	N½	1858-11-01		A1
1363	DANIEL, Nathaniel R	3	SWSW	1837-08-09		A1
1378	DANIEL, Thomas	26	E½NW	1858-11-01		A1
1379	" "	26	W½NE	1858-11-01		A1
1354	DAVIS, Levi	22	S½NE	1858-11-01		A1
1355	" "	22	SESE	1858-11-01		A1
1356	" "	23	NESW	1858-11-01		A1
1357	" "	23	W½NW	1858-11-01		A1
1358	" "	23	W½SW	1858-11-01		A1
1327	DAVISON, James T	35	NW	1858-09-01		A1
1326	" "	35	E½SW	1860-04-02		A1
1328	" "	35	NWNE	1860-04-02		A1
1380	DEAN, Thomas	14	S½	1858-11-01		A1
1304	EDWARDS, David	12	S½	1858-11-01		A1
1305	FAIL, Dixon N	10	SESE	1858-11-01		A1
1306	" "	10	SESW	1858-11-01		A1
1307	" "	10	W½SE	1858-11-01		A1
1308	" "	15	NENE	1858-11-01	Butler	A1
1309	" "	15	NENW	1858-11-01	Butler	A1
1310	" "	15	W½NE	1858-11-01	Butler	A1
1368	FAIL, Samuel W	2	E½NW	1858-11-01		A1
1369	" "	2	E½SW	1858-11-01		A1
1370	" "	2	SWSW	1858-11-01		A1
1371	" "	2	W½SE	1858-11-01		A1
1372	" "	3	SESE	1858-11-01		A1

ID	Individual in Patent	Sec.	Sec. Part	Date Issued	Other Counties	For More Info . . .
1303	FICKLING, Christopher	23	E½	1858-11-01		A1
1361	GATLIN, Moses	2	SWNW	1835-10-16		A1
1360	"	2	NWSW	1837-08-18		A1
1407	GHOLSON, William S	3	NWNW	1852-12-01		A1
1314	GLASS, Francis	1	NE	1860-04-02		A1 F
1319	GREGG, Henry M	3	NWSE	1854-07-15		A1
1320	" "	3	SENE	1854-07-15		A1
1381	GRIFFIN, Thomas	15	NWSE	1858-11-01	Butler	A1
1382	" "	15	SESE	1858-11-01	Butler	A1
1383	" "	22	NENE	1858-11-01		A1
1398	KIRKPATRICK, William	14	N½	1858-11-01		A1
1345	MCCARTER, John S	25	S½	1875-04-20		A1 F
1298	MCCORMACK, Barney B	27	N½	1858-11-01		A1
1321	MCCORMACK, Isabella	26	SESE	1860-04-02		A1
1322	" "	35	E½NE	1860-04-02		A1
1323	" "	35	NESE	1860-04-02		A1
1324	" "	36	S½	1860-04-02		A1
1374	MCCORMACK, Shadrach	34	NWNE	1837-08-18		A1
1375	" "	34	SENW	1837-08-18		A1
1325	MCGINNEY, James A	24	S½	1858-11-01		A1
1346	MCMULLAN, John S	13		1860-04-02		A1 F
1299	MORGAN, Charles	10	NENE	1860-09-01		A1
1347	MORGAN, John W	35	SWSW	1858-11-01		A1
1399	MORGAN, William M	10	N½SW	1858-11-01		A1
1400	" "	10	NESE	1858-11-01		A1
1401	" "	10	S½NE	1858-11-01		A1
1402	" "	10	SENW	1858-11-01		A1
1403	" "	10	W½NW	1858-11-01		A1
1315	PARKER, Gardner G	34	NWNW	1861-05-01		A1
1350	PERDUE, Joshua A	3	SWNW	1852-12-01		A1
1389	REAVES, Varnal G	22	NESE	1838-07-28		A1
1390	" "	22	NWNE	1838-07-28		A1
1300	REEVES, Cheselin M	35	SWNE	1858-09-01		A1
1301	" "	35	W½SE	1858-09-01		A1
1302	REEVES, Cheslen M	35	SESE	1858-11-01		A1
1348	REEVES, Joseph E	34	SESE	1895-01-31		A2
1349	REEVES, Joseph M	24	N½	1858-11-01		A1
1391	REEVES, Varnal G	36	N½	1875-04-20		A1
1404	REEVES, William	3	NENE	1858-11-01		A1
1405	" "	3	NESE	1858-11-01		A1
1406	" "	3	W½NE	1858-11-01		A1
1362	RIVES, Moses	27	W½SE	1837-08-18		A1
1339	ROPER, John B	10	NWNE	1858-11-01		A1
1340	" "	3	NESW	1858-11-01		A1
1341	" "	3	SENW	1858-11-01		A1
1342	" "	3	SWSE	1858-11-01		A1
1373	SEARCY, Sarah	27	SWSW	1858-11-01		A1
1295	SKIPPER, Barnabas	15	SESW	1837-08-18	Butler	A1
1297	" "	22	NW	1837-08-18		A1
1296	" "	15	SWSE	1838-07-28	Butler	A1
1364	SKIPPER, Needham	26	E½NE	1858-11-01		A1
1365	" "	26	NESE	1858-11-01		A1
1376	SKIPPER, Sion	22	SW	1858-11-01		A1
1377	" "	22	W½SE	1858-11-01		A1
1392	SPRADLEY, Warren C	2	NESE	1860-09-01		A1
1336	VEAZEY, Jesse H	15	SWNW	1852-02-02	Butler	A1
1332	" "	10	SWSW	1858-11-01		A1
1333	" "	15	N½SW	1858-11-01	Butler	A1
1334	" "	15	NWNW	1858-11-01	Butler	A1
1335	" "	15	SENW	1858-11-01	Butler	A1
1337	" "	15	SWSW	1858-11-01	Butler	A1
1311	WHIDDON, Elias	3	SESW	1853-11-15		A1
1312	WHIDON, Elias	10	NENW	1852-12-01		A1
1316	WYCHE, George D	26	SW	1858-11-01		A1
1317	" "	26	W½NW	1858-11-01		A1
1318	" "	26	W½SE	1858-11-01		A1
1366	WYCHE, Peter	25	N½	1858-11-01		A1

Patent Map

T10-N R16-E
St Stephens Meridian

Map Group 6

Township Statistics

Parcels Mapped	:	113
Number of Patents	:	64
Number of Individuals	:	55
Patentees Identified	:	55
Number of Surnames	:	36
Multi-Patentee Parcels	:	0
Oldest Patent Date	:	10/16/1835
Most Recent Patent	:	2/4/1897
Block/Lot Parcels	:	0
Parcels Re-Issued	:	0
Parcels that Overlap	:	0
Cities and Towns	:	2
Cemeteries	:	1

Note: the area contained in this map amounts to far less than a full Township. Therefore, its contents are completely on this single page (instead of a "normal" 2-page spread).

Legend

— Patent Boundary

— Section Boundary

No Patents Found
(or Outside County)

1., 2., 3., ... Lot Numbers
(when beside a name)

[ ] Group Number
(see Appendix "C")

Scale: Section = 1 mile X 1 mile
(generally, with some exceptions)

GHOLSON William S 1852

ALLEN Washington W 1852

REEVES William 1858

FAIL Samuel W 1858

ANTHONY Lemuel B 1897

GLASS Francis 1860

REEVES William 1858

PERDUE Joshua A 1852

ROPER John B 1858

3

GREGG Henry M 1854

GATLIN Moses 1835

2

BELL Washington 1858

1

DANIEL Francis 1837

ROPER John B 1858

GREGG Henry M 1854

REEVES William 1858

GATLIN Moses 1837

FAIL Samuel W 1858

FAIL Samuel W 1858

SPRADLEY Warren C 1860

ANTHONY Lemuel B 1897

DANIEL Nathaniel R 1837

WHIDDON Elias 1853

ROPER John B 1858

FAIL Samuel W 1858

FAIL Samuel W 1858

ANTHONY Lemuel B 1897

MORGAN William M 1858

WHIDON Elias 1852

ROPER John B 1858

MORGAN Charles 1860

ANTHONY Middleton W 1858

DANIEL John A 1858

12

MORGAN William M 1858

MORGAN William M 1858

MORGAN William M 1858

10

MORGAN William M 1858

11

CALLENS Robert H 1858

EDWARDS David 1858

VEAZEY Jesse H 1858

FAIL Dixon N 1858

FAIL Dixon N 1858

FAIL Dixon N 1858

VEAZEY Jesse H 1858

FAIL Dixon N 1858

FAIL Dixon N 1858

FAIL Dixon N 1858

KIRKPATRICK William 1858

VEAZEY Jesse H 1852

VEAZEY Jesse H 1858

15

ACREE John E 1858

14

13

Butler

Crenshaw

VEAZEY Jesse H 1858

GRIFFIN Thomas 1858

ACREE John E 1858

MCMULLAN John S 1860

VEAZEY Jesse H 1858

SKIPPER Barnabas 1837

SKIPPER Barnabas 1838

GRIFFIN Thomas 1858

DEAN Thomas 1858

SKIPPER Barnabas 1837

REAVES Varnal G 1838

GRIFFIN Thomas 1858

REEVES Joseph M 1858

DAVIS Levi 1858

23

22

DAVIS Levi 1858

DAVIS Levi 1858

24

SKIPPER Sion 1858

SKIPPER Sion 1858

REAVES Varnal G 1838

FICKLING Christopher 1858

DAVIS Levi 1858

MCGINNEY James A 1858

DAVIS Levi 1858

MCCORMACK Barney B 1858

WYCHE George D 1858

DANIEL Thomas 1858

SKIPPER Needham 1858

WYCHE Peter 1858

25

27

DANIEL Thomas 1858

SEARCY Sarah 1858

RIVES Moses 1837

BELL James W 1858

WYCHE George D 1858

26

WYCHE George D 1858

SKIPPER Needham 1858

MCCARTER John S 1875

ALLEN Washington W 1858

MCCORMACK Isabella 1860

PARKER Gardner G 1861

ALLEN Washington W 1858

MCCORMACK Shadrach 1837

BELL James W 1858

DAVISON James T 1860

MCCORMACK Isabella 1860

REEVES Varnal G 1875

ALLEN Washington W 1858

MCCORMACK Shadrach 1837

34

BELL James W 1858

DAVISON James T 1858

REEVES Cheselin M 1858

36

BELL Thomas W 1858

BELL Thomas W 1858

BELL Thomas W 1858

35

MCCORMACK Isabella 1860

MCCORMACK Isabella 1860

DAVISON James T 1860

BELL Thomas W 1858

BELL Thomas W 1858

REEVES Joseph E 1895

MORGAN John W 1858

REEVES Cheselin M 1858

REEVES Cheslen M 1858

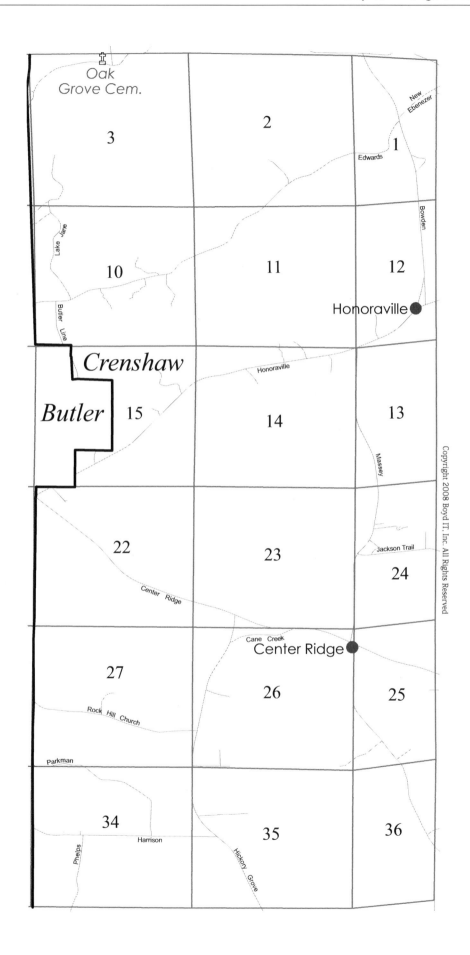

Road Map

T10-N R16-E
St Stephens Meridian

Map Group 6

Note: the area contained in this map amounts to far less than a full Township. Therefore, its contents are completely on this single page (instead of a "normal" 2-page spread).

Cities & Towns
Center Ridge
Honoraville

Cemeteries
Oak Grove Cemetery

Legend

———— Section Lines

═══════ Interstates

━━━━━━ Highways

———— Other Roads

● Cities/Towns

✝ Cemeteries

Scale: Section = 1 mile X 1 mile
(generally, with some exceptions)

Historical Map

T10-N R16-E
St Stephens Meridian

Map Group 6

Note: the area contained in this map amounts to far less than a full Township. Therefore, its contents are completely on this single page (instead of a "normal" 2-page spread).

Cities & Towns
Center Ridge
Honoraville

Cemeteries
Oak Grove Cemetery

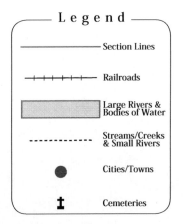

Legend

——————— Section Lines

+++++++ Railroads

� Large Rivers & Bodies of Water

- - - - - Streams/Creeks & Small Rivers

● Cities/Towns

☦ Cemeteries

Scale: Section = 1 mile X 1 mile
(there are some exceptions)

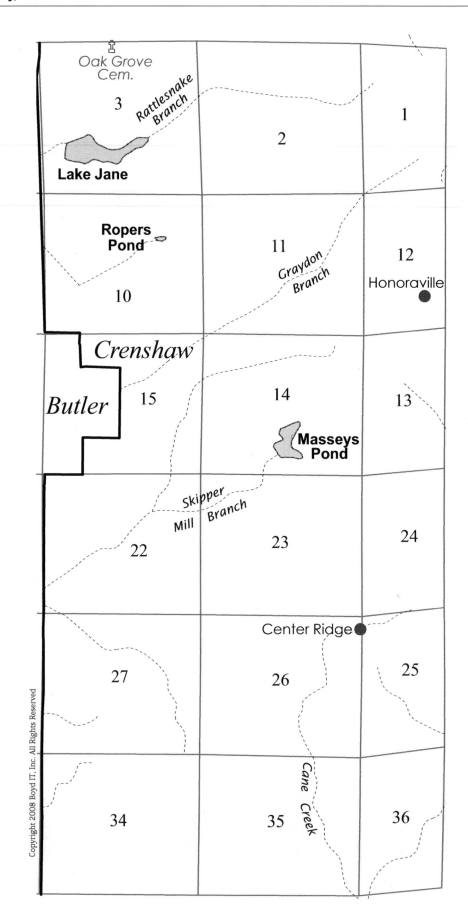

Oak Grove Cem.

3

Rattlesnake Branch

Lake Jane

Ropers Pond

10

11

Graydon Branch

2

1

12

Honoraville ●

Crenshaw

Butler

15

14

13

Masseys Pond

Skipper Mill Branch

22

23

24

Center Ridge ●

27

26

25

Cane Creek

34

35

36

Map Group 7: Index to Land Patents

Township 10-North Range 17-East (St Stephens)

After you locate an individual in this Index, take note of the Section and Section Part then proceed to the Land Patent map on the pages immediately following. You should have no difficulty locating the corresponding parcel of land.

The "For More Info" Column will lead you to more information about the underlying Patents. See the *Legend* at right, and the "How to Use this Book" chapter, for more information.

```
LEGEND
        "For More Info . . . " column
A = Authority (Legislative Act, See Appendix "A")
B = Block or Lot (location in Section unknown)
C = Cancelled Patent
F = Fractional Section
G = Group  (Multi-Patentee Patent, see Appendix "C")
V = Overlaps another Parcel
R = Re-Issued (Parcel patented more than once)

(A & G items require you to look in the Appendixes referred
to above. All other Letter-designations followed by a number
require you to locate line-items in this index that possess
the ID number found after the letter).
```

ID	Individual in Patent	Sec.	Sec. Part	Date Issued	Other Counties	For More Info . . .
1601	ANDERSON, Leonden C	14	SWSE	1860-10-01		A1
1544	BALL, John	10	NWSW	1852-02-02		A1
1546	" "	10	SWNW	1852-02-02		A1
1548	" "	9	NESE	1852-02-02		A1
1545	" "	10	SESW	1852-12-01		A1
1547	" "	9	E½NE	1858-09-01		A1
1646	BISHOP, Stephen	26	NWNW	1858-11-01		A1
1506	BODIFORD, Iva A	12	NENW	1908-09-03		A2
1444	BOLAN, Drury	35	SWSE	1858-11-01		A1
1511	BOLAN, James	35	SESE	1858-11-01		A1
1512	" "	36	SWSW	1858-11-01		A1
1585	BOON, Kinchen P	25	NWSW	1896-10-28		A1
1586	" "	25	S½SW	1896-10-28		A1
1587	" "	25	SESE	1896-10-28		A1
1588	" "	36	N½NE	1896-10-28		A1
1589	" "	36	N½NW	1896-10-28		A1
1438	BRIDGES, Daniel B	12	NWNW	1858-11-01		A1
1465	BRYAN, George	27	SWSE	1837-08-10		A1
1672	BRYAN, Thomas	20	SWSW	1858-11-01		A1
1673	" "	29	N½NE	1858-11-01		A1
1674	" "	29	N½NW	1858-11-01		A1
1647	CANDLE, Stephen	11	NESE	1837-08-08		A1
1632	CHAMPION, Robert G	2	NWNW	1852-02-02		A1
1513	CHESHIRE, James	27	NESE	1837-08-18		A1
1514	" "	27	NESW	1837-08-18		A1
1515	" "	27	W½NE	1837-08-18		A1
1413	DANIEL, Abel	4	SESW	1835-04-15		A1
1415	" "	4	SWSE	1837-05-15		A1
1410	" "	4	NESW	1837-08-08		A1
1408	" "	3	SWNW	1852-02-02		A1
1409	" "	4	E½SE	1852-02-02		A1
1414	" "	4	SWNE	1852-12-01		A1
1411	" "	4	NWNE	1858-09-01		A1
1412	" "	4	NWSE	1858-09-01		A1
1416	" "	4	SWSW	1858-09-01		A1
1418	" "	5	SESE	1858-09-01		A1
1417	" "	5	NESE	1862-01-01		A1
1450	DANIEL, Ephraim	22	NWSE	1837-08-10		A1
1449	" "	22	NESW	1837-08-18		A1
1451	" "	26	N½NE	1852-02-02		A1
1452	DANIEL, Ephraim F	6	SESE	1850-08-10		A1
1453	" "	7	NENE	1852-02-02		A1
1460	DANIEL, Francis	5	W½SW	1837-08-09		A1
1461	" "	6	E½NE	1837-08-09		A1
1462	" "	6	NWSE	1837-08-09		A1
1538	DANIEL, John A	7	N½SW	1858-11-01		A1

ID	Individual in Patent	Sec.	Sec. Part	Date Issued	Other Counties	For More Info . . .
1539	DANIEL, John A (Cont'd)	7	SWNW	1858-11-01		A1
1591	DANIEL, Leonard	17	S½NE	1849-09-01		A1
1590	" "	17	NWNW	1850-08-10		A1
1596	" "	7	NESE	1850-08-10		A1
1598	" "	8	NESW	1850-08-10		A1
1599	" "	8	SESW	1850-08-10		A1
1600	" "	8	SWSW	1850-08-10		A1
1595	" "	18	SENW	1852-02-02		A1
1594	" "	18	NWNE	1854-07-15		A1
1592	" "	18	NENW	1858-11-01		A1
1593	" "	18	NESW	1858-11-01		A1
1597	" "	7	SWSE	1858-11-01		A1
1655	DANIEL, Theophilas	9	W½NW	1849-09-01		A1
1663	DANIEL, Theophilus	9	SESW	1835-10-14		A1
1662	" "	8	SENE	1837-08-12		A1
1664	" "	9	W½SW	1837-08-12		A1
1661	" "	8	SE	1838-07-28		A1
1657	" "	17	SWNW	1852-02-02		A1
1656	" "	17	NWSW	1858-11-01		A1
1658	" "	18	NESE	1858-11-01		A1
1660	" "	18	SENE	1858-11-01		A1
1659	" "	18	S½SE	1860-10-01		A1
1665	DANIEL, Theophilus J	17	SESW	1852-02-02		A1
1676	DANIEL, Thomas F	17	NWNE	1850-08-10		A1
1675	" "	17	NESE	1852-02-02		A1
1722	DANIEL, William J	5	NWNW	1852-02-02		A1
1749	DANIEL, Zachariah	9	NESW	1852-02-02		A1
1748	" "	9	E½NW	1858-11-01		A1
1750	" "	9	W½NE	1858-11-01		A1
1751	" "	9	W½SE	1858-11-01		A1
1500	DAVIS, Isaac	11	SESW	1850-08-10		A1
1501	" "	14	NENE	1854-07-15		A1
1499	" "	11	S½SE	1858-11-01		A1
1502	" "	14	SENW	1860-12-01		A1
1565	DAVIS, John T	24	SWNE	1892-01-18		A2
1434	DENDY, Buford W	36	NWSW	1860-09-01		A1
1435	" "	36	SENE	1860-09-01		A1
1436	" "	36	SWNE	1860-09-01		A1
1604	DEPRIEST, Martin	18	NWSE	1860-10-01		A1
1605	" "	18	NWSW	1860-10-01		A1
1606	" "	18	SWNE	1860-10-01		A1
1607	" "	18	W½NW	1860-10-01		A1
1477	DILLARD, George W	15	E½SW	1837-08-18		A1 G17
1639	DOCKINS, Silas	14	NWSW	1837-08-08		A1
1640	" "	3	W½SW	1837-08-08		A1
1638	" "	14	NESW	1837-08-14		A1
1718	DOCKINS, William	11	W½SW	1838-07-28		A1
1441	ELLINGTON, David	22	NESE	1837-05-15		A1
1442	" "	22	SENE	1837-05-15		A1
1440	" "	22	NENE	1850-08-10		A1 R1424
1443	" "	22	SWNE	1852-02-02		A1
1574	ELLINGTON, Joseph	23	NWNE	1852-02-02		A1
1571	" "	13	W½SW	1896-10-28		A1
1572	" "	14	E½SE	1896-10-28		A1
1573	" "	23	E½NE	1896-10-28		A1
1714	ELLINGTON, William D	25	N½SE	1858-11-01		A1
1715	" "	25	NESW	1858-11-01		A1
1716	" "	25	SWNW	1858-11-01		A1
1717	" "	25	SWSE	1858-11-01		A1
1437	FICKLIN, Christopher	17	NWSE	1850-08-10		A1
1679	FICKLIN, Thomas	4	SWNW	1850-08-10		A1
1677	" "	4	NWSW	1858-11-01		A1
1678	" "	4	SENW	1860-10-01		A1
1463	FICKLING, Francis	20	E½SW	1837-08-18		A1
1464	" "	20	W½SE	1837-08-18		A1
1680	FICKLING, Thomas	4	N½NW	1858-11-01		A1
1681	" "	5	NENE	1858-11-01		A1
1425	FLOWERS, Benjamin	23	NWSE	1838-07-28		A1
1426	" "	23	SWNE	1838-07-28		A1
1552	FLOWERS, John	23	SESE	1837-08-14		A1
1648	FLOWERS, Stephen	24	E½SW	1837-05-20		A1
1649	" "	24	NWSW	1837-05-20		A1
1650	" "	24	SWNW	1837-05-20		A1

ID	Individual in Patent	Sec.	Sec. Part	Date Issued	Other Counties	For More Info . . .
1651	FLOWERS, Stephen (Cont'd)	25	E½NW	1838-07-28		A1
1489	FULLER, Henry C	13	SESW	1858-11-01		A1
1490	" "	24	N½NE	1858-11-01		A1
1491	" "	24	N½NW	1858-11-01		A1
1492	" "	24	N½SE	1858-11-01		A1
1493	" "	24	SENE	1858-11-01		A1
1575	FULLER, Joseph	1	NESE	1858-11-01		A1
1576	" "	1	NWSE	1858-11-01		A1
1577	" "	1	SWNE	1858-11-01		A1
1503	GREEN, Isaac	35	SWNW	1852-12-01		A1
1433	HALL, Bolling	10	W½SE	1825-04-16		A1 G20
1683	HANSHAW, Thomas	11	W½NE	1837-05-15		A1
1635	HARRISON, Samuel C	28	SWSE	1858-11-01		A1
1636	" "	33	NWNE	1858-11-01		A1
1641	HARRISON, Simeon L	32	NESW	1874-02-20		A1
1642	" "	32	NW	1874-02-20		A1
1643	" "	32	NWSE	1874-02-20		A1
1644	" "	32	W½NE	1874-02-20		A1
1496	HARTEN, Hugh	19	SENE	1852-02-02		A1
1498	HARTIN, Hugh	19	W½NE	1852-02-02		A1
1497	" "	18	S½SW	1861-05-01		A1
1516	HATHHORN, James E	12	E½SW	1837-08-08		A1
1517	HATHORN, James E	12	NWSE	1838-07-28		A1
1518	" "	12	W½SW	1838-07-28		A1
1519	" "	13	NWNW	1838-07-28		A1
1720	HIGHTOWER, William H	24	SESE	1854-07-15		A1
1721	" "	25	NENE	1854-07-15		A1
1536	HOLLAND, Jasper J	14	SESW	1862-04-10		A1
1507	JETER, Jackson	15	E½NW	1896-10-21		A1
1634	JOHNSON, Rufus G	15	NESE	1860-10-01		A1
1724	JOHNSON, William	17	NENE	1850-08-10		A1
1723	" "	10	SESE	1852-02-02		A1
1553	JONES, John	10	NWNW	1852-02-02		A1
1554	" "	10	SENW	1858-11-01		A1
1637	JONES, Seaborne	28	E½NW	1837-08-18		A1
1477	JORDAN, Felix	15	E½SW	1837-08-18		A1 G17
1458	" "	15	W½SW	1837-08-18		A1
1459	" "	22	W½NW	1837-08-18		A1
1423	KENT, Arnold	15	SWSE	1852-02-02		A1
1424	" "	22	NENE	1852-02-02		A1 R1440
1487	LILES, Hampton	11	NENE	1852-02-02		A1
1488	" "	11	SENE	1858-11-01		A1
1725	LILES, William	12	SENW	1854-10-02		A1
1578	LOFTIN, Joseph	14	NWNW	1837-08-18		A1
1579	" "	15	E½NE	1837-08-18		A1
1580	" "	15	NWSE	1837-08-18		A1
1726	LOFTIN, William	2	NWSE	1837-08-15		A1
1727	" "	2	SWNE	1837-08-15		A1
1522	LOWREY, James	21	E½NE	1831-11-30		A1
1524	" "	21	E½SE	1831-11-30		A1
1527	" "	21	NWSE	1837-08-18		A1
1528	" "	21	SWNE	1837-08-18		A1
1531	" "	5	NESW	1850-08-10		A1
1520	" "	12	NWNE	1852-02-02		A1
1530	" "	22	NWSW	1852-02-02		A1
1521	" "	14	SWSW	1854-10-02		A1
1523	" "	21	E½NW	1858-09-01		A1
1525	" "	21	E½SW	1858-09-01		A1
1526	" "	21	NWNE	1858-09-01		A1
1529	" "	21	SWSE	1860-10-01		A1
1684	LOWREY, Thomas	15	SWNW	1852-02-02		A1
1685	" "	9	SESE	1852-02-02		A1
1682	LOWREY, Thomas H	28	E½NE	1843-02-01		A1 V1694
1432	LOWRY, Bob	22	NWNE	1880-02-20		A2
1728	MAPES, William	2	N½SW	1850-08-10		A1
1729	" "	2	SESW	1852-02-02		A1
1419	MCCARTY, Alexander	29	NWSW	1858-11-01		A1
1422	" "	30	SWNE	1858-11-01		A1
1420	" "	29	SWNW	1860-04-02		A1
1421	" "	30	SENE	1860-04-02		A1
1557	MCMULLEN, John S	22	SENW	1852-02-02		A1
1540	MENEES, John B	12	SENE	1858-11-01		A1
1541	MERREES, John B	12	SWSE	1860-10-01		A1

ID	Individual in Patent	Sec.	Sec. Part	Date Issued	Other Counties	For More Info . . .
1633	MILIGAN, Robert	34	E½NE	1831-11-30		A1
1427	MILLER, Benjamin	34	NWSE	1891-06-08		A2
1454	MILLER, Ezra	26	SESW	1858-11-01		A1
1455	" "	26	SWNW	1858-11-01		A1
1456	" "	26	W½SE	1858-11-01		A1
1457	" "	26	W½SW	1858-11-01		A1
1533	MINYARD, James	5	SENE	1837-08-10		A1
1428	MITCHEL, Benjamin	24	SENW	1853-11-15		A1
1623	MITCHELL, Peter	11	SENW	1850-08-10		A1
1621	" "	11	NESW	1852-02-02		A1
1622	" "	11	NWSE	1852-02-02		A1
1624	" "	3	N½SE	1852-02-02		A1
1625	" "	3	SENE	1852-02-02		A1
1620	" "	10	NWNE	1854-07-15		A1
1730	NEWMAN, William	36	SE	1860-10-01		A1
1731	NICHOLLS, William	7	SENE	1852-02-02		A1
1735	NICHOLS, William	8	W½NW	1837-08-18		A1
1734	" "	8	NWSW	1850-08-10		A1
1732	" "	7	SENW	1858-11-01		A1
1733	" "	7	W½NE	1858-11-01		A1
1534	OWENS, James	30	NWSW	1860-10-01		A1
1535	" "	30	SWNW	1860-10-01		A1
1555	PATTERSON, John	27	SWNW	1837-08-10		A1
1509	PETTY, James A	18	NENE	1850-08-10		A1
1510	" "	28	W½SW	1874-02-20		A1
1608	PETTY, Matthew	28	E½SE	1858-11-01		A1
1609	" "	28	NESW	1858-11-01		A1
1610	" "	28	NWSE	1858-11-01		A1
1611	" "	28	SESW	1858-11-01		A1
1654	PETTY, Theophalus	7	SESE	1850-08-10		A1
1686	PHARAOH, Thomas	17	SESE	1852-02-02		A1
1687	" "	21	NWNW	1852-02-02		A1
1688	" "	25	SWNE	1852-02-02		A1 V1504
1692	PHARAOH, Thomas S	20	E½NE	1838-07-28		A1
1690	" "	17	SWSE	1850-08-10		A1
1694	" "	28	SENE	1850-08-10		A1 V1682
1691	" "	17	SWSW	1852-02-02		A1
1693	" "	20	N½NW	1852-02-02		A1
1689	PHAROAH, Thomas	28	NWNE	1853-08-01		A1
1695	PHAROAH, Thomas S	20	SWNE	1858-11-01		A1
1696	" "	28	SWNW	1858-11-01		A1
1697	PHAROH, Thomas S	20	NWNE	1858-11-01		A1
1698	" "	21	SWNW	1858-11-01		A1
1699	" "	21	W½SW	1858-11-01		A1
1700	" "	28	NWNW	1858-11-01		A1
1447	POLLARD, Elizabeth	3	NWNW	1858-11-01		A1
1448	" "	4	E½NE	1858-11-01		A1
1612	POLLARD, Nathaniel	5	SWNW	1854-07-15		A1
1616	" "	6	NWNW	1854-07-15		A1
1617	" "	6	SENW	1854-07-15		A1
1613	" "	6	NENW	1858-11-01		A1
1614	" "	6	NESE	1858-11-01		A1
1615	" "	6	NESW	1858-11-01		A1
1618	" "	6	W½NE	1858-11-01		A1
1702	POLLARD, Thomas W	3	NENW	1860-12-01		A1
1738	POLLARD, William	5	SWSE	1835-04-15		A1
1743	" "	8	W½NE	1837-05-15		A1
1741	" "	8	E½NW	1837-08-18		A1
1737	" "	5	SESW	1838-07-28		A1
1742	" "	8	NENE	1838-07-28		A1
1736	" "	5	NWSE	1852-02-02		A1
1739	" "	6	SESW	1852-02-02		A1
1740	" "	6	SWSW	1852-02-02		A1
1439	POUNCEY, Daniel N	3	NENE	1838-07-28		A1
1537	REAVES, Jesse W	27	NWSW	1852-12-01		A1
1542	REAVES, John B	33	SESE	1896-10-28		A1
1543	" "	34	SWSW	1896-10-28		A1
1631	REAVES, Richard	33	NESE	1896-10-28		A1
1630	REAVES, Richard R	34	NWSW	1852-12-01		A1
1466	REESE, George	27	SESE	1852-02-02		A1
1433	REESE, Littleton	10	W½SE	1825-04-16		A1 G20
1478	RHOADES, George W	27	NENW	1852-02-02		A1
1479	RHODES, George W	22	SWSE	1852-02-02		A1

ID	Individual in Patent	Sec.	Sec. Part	Date Issued	Other Counties	For More Info . . .
1480	RHODES, George W (Cont'd)	27	NENE	1854-07-15		A1
1481	" "	27	NWNW	1862-01-01		A1
1482	" "	27	SENW	1862-01-01		A1
1508	RIALS, Jacob	11	W½NW	1838-07-28		A1
1704	RODGERS, Wesley	29	E½SW	1858-11-01		A1
1705	" "	29	NESE	1858-11-01		A1
1706	" "	29	S½NE	1858-11-01		A1
1707	" "	29	SESE	1858-11-01		A1
1708	" "	29	SWSW	1858-11-01		A1
1709	" "	29	W½SE	1858-11-01		A1
1744	RODGERS, William	2	NENW	1852-02-02		A1
1429	ROGERS, Berry M	1	N½SW	1860-04-02		A1
1430	" "	1	S½NW	1860-04-02		A1
1431	" "	2	E½NE	1860-04-02		A1
1495	ROGERS, Henry	12	NENE	1852-02-02		A1
1494	" "	1	SESW	1854-10-02		A1
1505	ROGERS, Isaac	12	SWNW	1837-08-09		A1
1556	ROGERS, John	10	NENW	1854-07-15		A1
1619	ROGERS, Nathaniel	2	SWSE	1860-10-01		A1
1710	ROGERS, Westley	30	S½SE	1861-05-01		A1
1745	ROGERS, William	2	NWNE	1852-02-02		A1
1566	RUSSELL, John W	6	SWNW	1860-10-01		A1
1549	SCIPPER, John E	26	NESW	1858-11-01		A1
1550	" "	26	SENW	1858-11-01		A1
1504	SEWELL, Isaac Q	25	W½NW	1835-04-15		A1 V1688
1532	SEXTON, James M	33	SWNE	1896-01-30		A2
1602	SEXTON, Madison D	35	N½SE	1900-11-28		A2
1603	" "	35	S½NE	1900-11-28		A2
1666	SHELL, Thomas B	20	NWSW	1860-10-01		A1
1667	" "	20	S½NW	1860-10-01		A1
1668	" "	30	E½SW	1860-10-01		A1
1669	" "	30	N½SE	1860-10-01		A1
1670	" "	30	NWNE	1860-10-01		A1
1671	" "	30	SWSW	1860-10-01		A1
1558	SHOWES, John	2	SWSW	1852-02-02		A1
1562	SHOWS, John	27	SENE	1837-05-15		A1
1561	" "	27	NWSE	1837-08-10		A1
1559	" "	22	SESE	1838-07-28		A1
1560	" "	23	SWNW	1838-07-28		A1
1581	SHOWS, Joseph	3	NESW	1837-08-08		A1
1582	" "	3	SENW	1837-08-08		A1
1583	" "	3	SESW	1837-08-14		A1
1584	" "	3	W½NE	1841-05-20		A1
1701	SIKES, Thomas	26	S½NE	1860-10-01		A1
1567	SIMS, John W	32	SESW	1891-06-29		A2
1568	" "	32	SWSE	1891-06-29		A2
1569	" "	32	W½SW	1891-06-29		A2
1564	SKIPPER, John	23	NWSW	1837-08-09		A1
1563	" "	22	SESW	1837-08-12		A1
1645	SKIPPER, Sion	33	SENE	1837-08-15		A1
1703	SPRADLEY, Warren C	6	NWSW	1860-12-01		A1
1711	STRINGER, William A	33	NWNW	1899-07-15		A2
1468	THAGARD, George	34	NESE	1837-08-09		A1
1469	" "	34	NESW	1843-02-01		A1
1467	" "	34	E½NW	1852-02-02		A1
1470	" "	34	SESE	1852-02-02		A1
1473	" "	35	NESW	1852-02-02		A1
1475	" "	35	SWSW	1852-02-02		A1
1471	" "	34	SESW	1858-11-01		A1
1472	" "	34	SWSE	1858-11-01		A1
1474	" "	35	NWSW	1858-11-01		A1
1483	THAGARD, George W	34	NWNE	1858-11-01		A1
1484	" "	34	NWNW	1858-11-01		A1
1485	" "	34	SWNW	1860-10-01		A1
1652	TIMS, Stephen O	32	E½NE	1890-07-03		A2
1653	" "	32	E½SE	1890-07-03		A2
1476	TRANUM, George	23	NWNW	1858-09-01		A1
1445	VINSON, Elija M	1	NENW	1858-11-01		A1
1446	VINSON, Elijah M	1	NWNW	1852-02-02		A1
1486	WELCH, Green	3	SWSE	1852-02-02		A1
1747	WELCH, William	3	SESE	1852-02-02		A1
1746	" "	11	NENW	1854-10-02		A1
1712	WELCH, William B	33	E½SW	1894-05-11		A2

ID	Individual in Patent	Sec.	Sec. Part	Date Issued	Other Counties	For More Info . . .
1713	WELCH, William B (Cont'd)	33	SWSW	1894-05-11		A2
1570	WESTER, Jorden B	10	SWNE	1852-02-02		A1
1551	WRIGHT, John E	26	E½SE	1860-10-01		A1
1627	WYCHE, Peter	27	SESW	1852-12-01		A1
1626	" "	19	SESW	1858-11-01		A1
1628	" "	30	E½NW	1858-11-01		A1
1629	" "	30	NWNW	1858-11-01		A1
1719	WYCHE, William F	19	NWSE	1860-04-02		A1

Patent Map

T10-N R17-E
St Stephens Meridian

Map Group 7

Township Statistics

Parcels Mapped	:	344
Number of Patents	:	261
Number of Individuals	:	145
Patentees Identified	:	144
Number of Surnames	:	89
Multi-Patentee Parcels	:	2
Oldest Patent Date	:	4/16/1825
Most Recent Patent	:	9/3/1908
Block/Lot Parcels	:	0
Parcels Re - Issued	:	1
Parcels that Overlap	:	4
Cities and Towns	:	1
Cemeteries	:	2

Section 6
POLLARD Nathaniel 1854 · POLLARD Nathaniel 1858 · POLLARD Nathaniel 1858 · DANIEL Francis 1837
RUSSELL John W 1860 · POLLARD Nathaniel 1854
SPRADLEY Warren C 1860 · POLLARD Nathaniel 1858 · DANIEL Francis 1837 · POLLARD Nathaniel 1858 · DANIEL Francis 1837
POLLARD William 1852 · POLLARD William 1852 · DANIEL Ephraim F 1850

Section 5
DANIEL William J 1852 · FICKLING Thomas 1858
MINYARD James 1837
LOWREY James 1850 · POLLARD William 1852 · DANIEL Abel 1862
POLLARD William 1838 · POLLARD William 1835 · DANIEL Abel 1858

Section 4
FICKLING Thomas 1858 · DANIEL Abel 1858 · POLLARD Elizabeth 1858
FICKLIN Thomas 1850 · FICKLIN Thomas 1860 · DANIEL Abel 1852
FICKLIN Thomas 1858 · DANIEL Abel 1837 · DANIEL Abel 1858 · DANIEL Abel 1852
DANIEL Abel 1858 · DANIEL Abel 1835 · DANIEL Abel 1837

Section 7
NICHOLS William 1858 · DANIEL Ephraim F 1852
DANIEL John A 1858 · NICHOLS William 1858 · NICHOLLS William 1852
DANIEL John A 1858 · DANIEL Leonard 1850 · NICHOLS William 1850
DANIEL Leonard 1858 · PETTY Theophalus 1850

Section 8
NICHOLS William 1837 · POLLARD William 1837
NICHOLS William 1837 · DANIEL Leonard 1850 · DANIEL Theophilus 1838
NICHOLS William 1850 · DANIEL Leonard 1850 · DANIEL Leonard 1850
POLLARD William 1837 · POLLARD William 1837

Section 9
POLLARD William 1838 · DANIEL Theophilas 1849 · DANIEL Zachariah 1858 · DANIEL Zachariah 1858 · DANIEL Zachariah 1858 · BALL John 1858
DANIEL Theophilus 1837 · DANIEL Zachariah 1852 · DANIEL Zachariah 1858 · BALL John 1852
DANIEL Theophilus 1835 · LOWREY Thomas 1852

Section 18
DANIEL Leonard 1858 · DANIEL Leonard 1854
DEPRIEST Martin 1860 · DANIEL Leonard 1852 · DEPRIEST Martin 1860 · DANIEL Theophilus 1858
DEPRIEST Martin 1860 · DANIEL Leonard 1858 · DEPRIEST Martin 1860 · DANIEL Theophilus 1858
HARTIN Hugh 1861 · DANIEL Theophilus 1860

Section 17
PETTY James A 1850 · DANIEL Leonard 1850 · DANIEL Thomas F 1850 · JOHNSON William 1850
DANIEL Theophilus 1852 · DANIEL Leonard 1849
DANIEL Theophilus 1852 · FICKLIN Christopher 1850 · DANIEL Thomas F 1852
PHARAOH Thomas S 1852 · DANIEL Theophilus J 1852 · PHARAOH Thomas S 1850 · PHARAOH Thomas 1852

Section 16

Section 19
HARTIN Hugh 1852 · HARTEN Hugh 1852
WYCHE William F 1860
WYCHE Peter 1858

Section 20
PHARAOH Thomas S 1852
SHELL Thomas B 1860
SHELL Thomas B 1860
BRYAN Thomas 1858 · FICKLING Francis 1837

Section 21
PHARAOH Thomas 1852 · LOWREY James 1858
PHAROH Thomas S 1858 · LOWREY James 1858 · LOWREY James 1837
PHAROH Thomas S 1858 · LOWREY James 1837
LOWREY James 1858 · LOWREY James 1860

Section 28 (upper right)
PHAROH Thomas S 1858 · LOWREY James 1831
PHARAOH Thomas S 1858 · PHARAOH Thomas 1853 · LOWREY Thomas H 1843
JONES Seaborne 1837 · PHARAOH Thomas S 1850

Section 30
WYCHE Peter 1858 · WYCHE Peter 1858 · SHELL Thomas B 1860
OWENS James 1860 · MCCARTY Alexander 1858 · MCCARTY Alexander 1860
OWENS James 1860 · SHELL Thomas B 1860
SHELL Thomas B 1860 · MCCARTY Alexander 1858 · ROGERS Westley 1861

Section 29
MCCARTY Alexander 1860
BRYAN Thomas 1858 · BRYAN Thomas 1858
RODGERS Wesley 1858
RODGERS Wesley 1858 · RODGERS Wesley 1858 · RODGERS Wesley 1858

Section 28
PHAROH Thomas S 1858 · PHAROAH Thomas S 1858 · PETTY Matthew 1858 · PETTY Matthew 1858
PETTY James A 1874 · PETTY Matthew 1858 · HARRISON Samuel C 1858 · PETTY Matthew 1858

Section 31

Section 32
HARRISON Simeon L 1874
HARRISON Simeon L 1874 · TIMS Stephen O 1890
SIMS John W 1891 · HARRISON Simeon L 1874 · HARRISON Simeon L 1874 · TIMS Stephen O 1890
SIMS John W 1891 · SIMS John W 1891

Section 33
STRINGER William A 1899 · HARRISON Samuel C 1858
SEXTON James M 1896 · SKIPPER Sion 1837
WELCH William B 1894 · REAVES Richard 1896
WELCH William B 1894 · REAVES John B 1896

Map Grid

Section 3 / 2 / 1 (top row)

POLLARD Elizabeth 1858	POLLARD Thomas W 1860	SHOWS Joseph 1841	POUNCEY Daniel N 1838	CHAMPION Robert G 1852	RODGERS William 1852	ROGERS William 1852	ROGERS Berry M 1860	VINSON Elijah M 1852 — VINSON Elija M 1858

DANIEL Abel 1852 — SHOWS Joseph 1837 — **3** — MITCHELL Peter 1852 — **2** — LOFTIN William 1837 — ROGERS Berry M 1860 — FULLER Joseph 1858

DOCKINS Silas 1837 — SHOWS Joseph 1837 — MITCHELL Peter 1852 — MAPES William 1850 — LOFTIN William 1837 — ROGERS Berry M 1860 — **1** — FULLER Joseph 1858 — FULLER Joseph 1858

SHOWS Joseph 1837 — WELCH Green 1852 — WELCH William 1852 — SHOWES John 1852 — MAPES William 1852 — ROGERS Nathaniel 1860 — ROGERS Henry 1854

Section 10 / 11 / 12

JONES John 1852 — ROGERS John 1854 — MITCHELL Peter 1854 — WELCH William 1854 — HANSHAW Thomas 1837 — LILES Hampton 1852 — BRIDGES Daniel B 1858 — BODIFORD Iva A 1908 — LOWREY James 1852 — ROGERS Henry 1852

BALL John 1852 — JONES John 1858 — WESTER Jorden B 1852 — RIALS Jacob 1838 — MITCHELL Peter 1850 — **11** — LILES Hampton 1858 — ROGERS Isaac 1837 — LILES William 1854 — MENEES John B 1858

BALL John 1852 — **10** — HALL [20] Bolling 1825 — DOCKINS William 1838 — MITCHELL Peter 1852 — MITCHELL Peter 1852 — CANDLE Stephen 1837 — **12** — HATHORN James E 1838 — HATHORN James E 1837

BALL John 1852 — JOHNSON William 1852 — DAVIS Isaac 1850 — DAVIS Isaac 1858 — HATHORN James E 1838 — MERREES John B 1860

Section 15 / 14 / 13

LOWREY Thomas 1852 — JETER Jackson 1896 — LOFTIN Joseph 1837 — LOFTIN Joseph 1837 — DAVIS Isaac 1860 — DAVIS Isaac 1854 — HATHORN James E 1838

15 — LOFTIN Joseph 1837 — JOHNSON Rufus G 1860 — DOCKINS Silas 1837 — DOCKINS Silas 1837 — **14** — ELLINGTON Joseph 1896 — ELLINGTON Joseph 1896 — **13**

DILLARD [17] George W 1837

JORDAN Felix 1837 — KENT Arnold 1852 — LOWREY James 1854 — HOLLAND Jasper J 1862 — ANDERSON Leonden C 1860 — FULLER Henry C 1858

Section 22 / 23 / 24

JORDAN Felix 1837 — LOWRY Bob 1880 — ELLINGTON David KENT Arnold 1850 1852 — TRANUM George 1858 — ELLINGTON Joseph 1852 — ELLINGTON Joseph 1896 — FULLER Henry C 1858 — FULLER Henry C 1858

MCMULLEN John S 1852 — **22** — ELLINGTON David 1852 — ELLINGTON David 1837 — SHOWS John 1838 — FLOWERS Benjamin 1838 — FLOWERS Stephen 1837 — MITCHEL Benjamin 1853 — DAVIS John T 1892 — FULLER Henry C 1858

LOWREY James 1852 — DANIEL Ephraim 1837 — ELLINGTON David 1837 — SKIPPER John 1837 — **23** — FLOWERS Benjamin 1838 — FLOWERS Stephen 1837 — **24** — FULLER Henry C 1858

SKIPPER John 1837 — RHODES George W 1852 — SHOWS John 1838 — FLOWERS John 1837 — FLOWERS Stephen 1837 — HIGHTOWER William H 1854

Section 27 / 26 / 25

RHODES George W 1862 — RHOADES George W 1852 — CHESHIRE James 1837 — RHODES George W 1854 — BISHOP Stephen 1858 — DANIEL Ephraim 1852 — FLOWERS Stephen 1838 — SEWELL Isaac Q 1835 — HIGHTOWER William H 1854

PATTERSON John 1837 — RHODES George W 1862 — **27** — SHOWS John 1837 — MILLER Ezra 1858 — SCIPPER John E 1858 — SIKES Thomas 1860 — ELLINGTON William D 1858 — PHARAOH Thomas 1852 — **25**

REAVES Jesse W 1852 — CHESHIRE James 1837 — SHOWS John 1837 — CHESHIRE James 1837 — MILLER Ezra 1858 — SCIPPER John E 1858 — **26** — WRIGHT John E 1860 — BOON Kinchen P 1896 — ELLINGTON William D 1858 — ELLINGTON William D 1858

WYCHE Peter 1837 — BRYAN George 1837 — REESE George 1852 — MILLER Ezra 1858 — MILLER Ezra 1858 — BOON Kinchen P 1896 — ELLINGTON William D 1858 — BOON Kinchen P 1896

Section 34 / 35 / 36

THAGARD George W 1858 — THAGARD George 1852 — THAGARD George W 1858 — MILIGAN Robert 1831 — BOON Kinchen P 1896 — BOON Kinchen P 1896

THAGARD George W 1860 — **34** — GREEN Isaac 1852 — **35** — SEXTON Madison D 1900 — **36** — DENDY Buford W 1860 — DENDY Buford W 1860

REAVES Richard R 1852 — THAGARD George 1843 — MILLER Benjamin 1891 — THAGARD George 1837 — THAGARD George 1858 — THAGARD George 1852 — SEXTON Madison D 1900 — DENDY Buford W 1860 — NEWMAN William 1860

REAVES John B 1896 — THAGARD George 1858 — THAGARD George 1858 — THAGARD George 1852 — THAGARD George 1852 — BOLAN Drury 1858 — BOLAN James 1858 — BOLAN James 1858

Helpful Hints

1. This Map's INDEX can be found on the preceding pages.

2. Refer to Map "C" to see where this Township lies within Crenshaw County, Alabama.

3. Numbers within square brackets [ ] denote a multi-patentee land parcel (multi-owner). Refer to Appendix "C" for a full list of members in this group.

4. Areas that look to be crowded with Patentees usually indicate multiple sales of the same parcel (Re-issues) or Overlapping parcels. See this Township's Index for an explanation of these and other circumstances that might explain "odd" groupings of Patentees on this map.

Legend

— Patent Boundary

— Section Boundary

░ No Patents Found (or Outside County)

1., 2., 3., ... Lot Numbers (when beside a name)

| | Group Number (see Appendix "C")

Scale: Section = 1 mile X 1 mile (generally, with some exceptions)

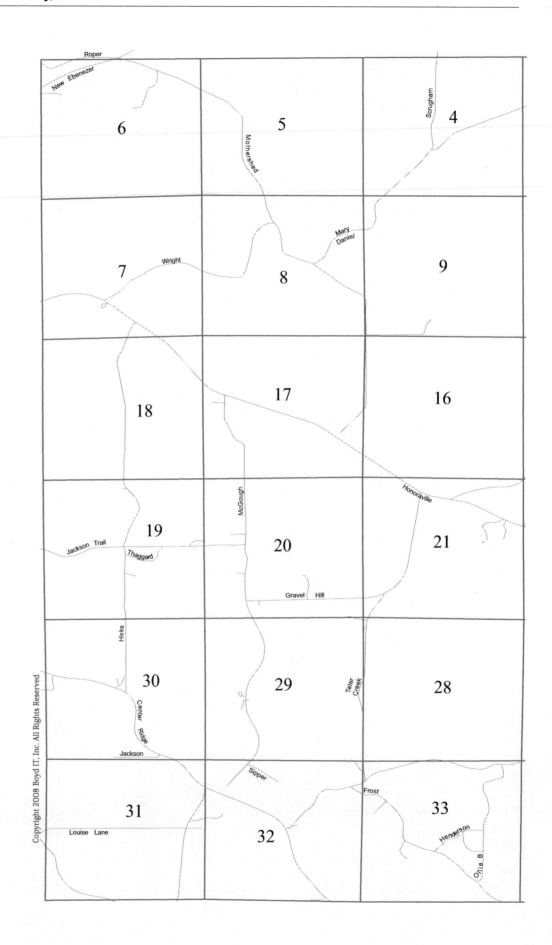

Road Map

T10-N R17-E
St Stephens Meridian

Map Group 7

Cities & Towns
Fullers Crossroads

Cemeteries
Mitchell Cemetery
Mount Pleasant Cemetery

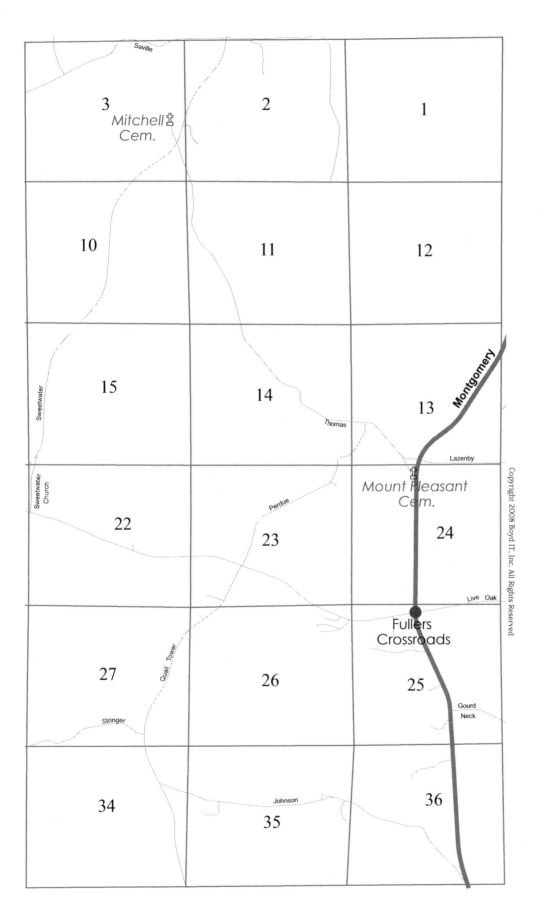

Saville

3

*Mitchell ☦
Cem.*

2

1

10

11

12

Sweetwater

15

14

13

Montgomery

Thomas

Lazenby

Sweetwater
Church

*Mount Pleasant
Cem.*

Perdue

22

23

24

Live   Oak

Quail Tower

Fullers
Crossroads

27

26

25

Gourd
Neck

Stringer

Johnson

34

35

36

Copyright 2008 Boyd IT, Inc. All Rights Reserved

Helpful Hints

1. This road map has a number of uses, but primarily it is to help you: a) find the present location of land owned by your ancestors (at least the general area), b) find cemeteries and city-centers, and c) estimate the route/roads used by Census-takers & tax-assessors.

2. If you plan to travel to Crenshaw County to locate cemeteries or land parcels, please pick up a modern travel map for the area before you do. Mapping old land parcels on modern maps is not as exact a science as you might think. Just the slightest variations in public land survey coordinates, estimates of parcel boundaries, or road-map deviations can greatly alter a map's representation of how a road either does or doesn't cross a particular parcel of land.

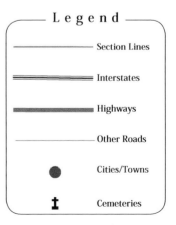

Legend

——————— Section Lines

══════════ Interstates

━━━━━━━━ Highways

———————— Other Roads

●   Cities/Towns

☦   Cemeteries

Scale: Section = 1 mile X 1 mile
(generally, with some exceptions)

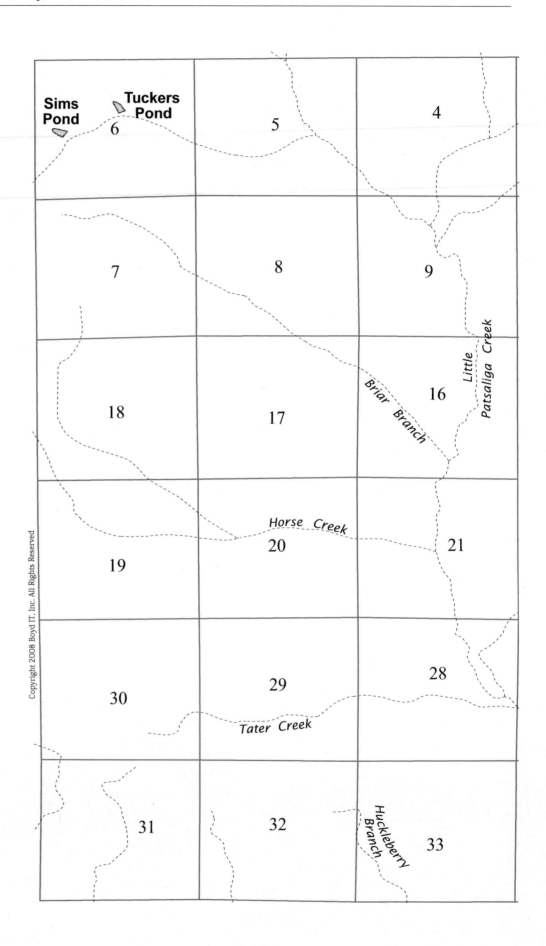

Historical Map

T10-N R17-E
St Stephens Meridian

Map Group 7

Cities & Towns
Fullers Crossroads

Cemeteries
Mitchell Cemetery
Mount Pleasant Cemetery

Sims
Pond

Tuckers
Pond

6

5

4

7

8

9

18

17

16

Briar Branch

Little Patsaliga Creek

19

20

21

Horse Creek

30

29

28

Tater Creek

31

32

33

Huckleberry Branch

Copyright 2008 Boyd IT. Inc. All Rights Reserved

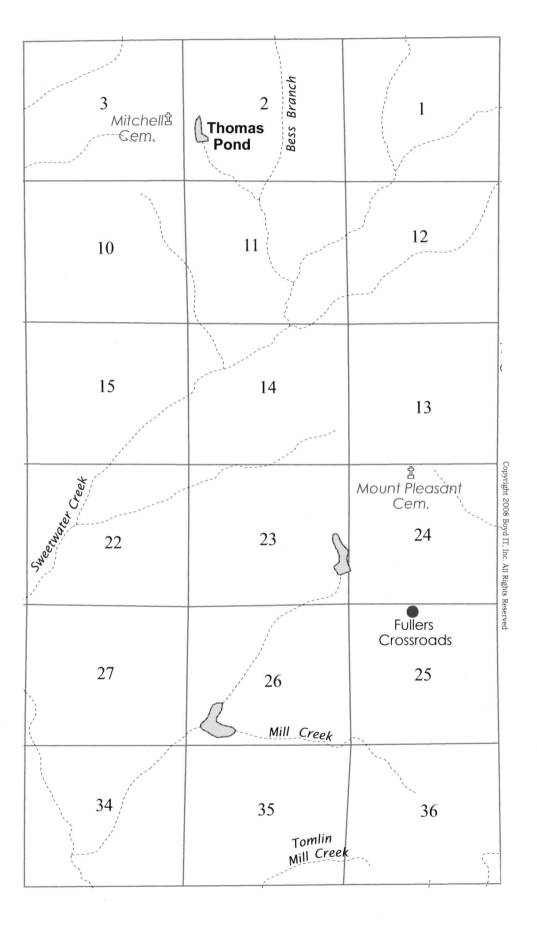

3
Mitchell‡ *Cem.*

2
Thomas Pond

Bess Branch

1

10

11

12

15

14

13

Sweetwater Creek

Mount Pleasant Cem.

22

23

24

Fullers Crossroads

27

26

25

34

35
Mill Creek

36

Tomlin Mill Creek

Helpful Hints

1. This Map takes a different look at the same Congressional Township displayed in the preceding two maps. It presents features that can help you better envision the historical development of the area: a) Water-bodies (lakes & ponds), b) Water-courses (rivers, streams, etc.), c) Railroads, d) City/town center-points (where they were oftentimes located when first settled), and e) Cemeteries.

2. Using this "Historical" map in tandem with this Township's Patent Map and Road Map, may lead you to some interesting discoveries. You will often find roads, towns, cemeteries, and waterways are named after nearby landowners: sometimes those names will be the ones you are researching. See how many of these research gems you can find here in Crenshaw County.

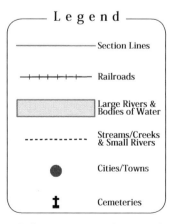

Legend

————	Section Lines
+++++	Railroads
▭	Large Rivers & Bodies of Water
- - - - -	Streams/Creeks & Small Rivers
●	Cities/Towns
‡	Cemeteries

Scale: Section = 1 mile X 1 mile
(there are some exceptions)

Map Group 8: Index to Land Patents

Township 10-North Range 18-East (St Stephens)

After you locate an individual in this Index, take note of the Section and Section Part then proceed to the Land Patent map on the pages immediately following. You should have no difficulty locating the corresponding parcel of land.

The "For More Info" Column will lead you to more information about the underlying Patents. See the *Legend* at right, and the "How to Use this Book" chapter, for more information.

```
LEGEND
           "For More Info . . . " column
A = Authority (Legislative Act, See Appendix "A")
B = Block or Lot (location in Section unknown)
C = Cancelled Patent
F = Fractional Section
G = Group  (Multi-Patentee Patent, see Appendix "C")
V = Overlaps another Parcel
R = Re-Issued (Parcel patented more than once)

(A & G items require you to look in the Appendixes referred
to above. All other Letter-designations followed by a number
require you to locate line-items in this index that possess
the ID number found after the letter).
```

ID	Individual in Patent	Sec.	Sec. Part	Date Issued	Other Counties	For More Info . . .
1761	ATKINSON, Alexander	24	SESE	1854-10-02		A1
1762	ATKISON, Alexander	25	S½SE	1898-06-27		A1
1763	" "	36	NESW	1898-06-27		A1
1764	" "	36	NWSE	1898-06-27		A1
1765	" "	36	S½NW	1898-06-27		A1
1766	" "	36	W½NE	1898-06-27		A1
1790	BARNES, Augustus	26	NENW	1860-09-01		A1
1791	" "	26	SENW	1860-09-01		A1
2010	BIRD, Wiley M	3	NWNE	1858-11-01		A1
2052	BIRD, Wylie M	3	S½NW	1858-11-01		A1
2053	" "	3	S½SE	1858-11-01		A1
2054	" "	3	SW	1858-11-01		A1
1802	BOLLING, Drewry	20	SWSW	1837-08-15		A1
1968	BONNER, Robert A	8	N½SE	1860-04-02		A1
1969	" "	8	NESW	1860-04-02		A1
1915	BOOTHE, Kitty	5	NWNW	1897-03-18		A1
1825	BUCKELEW, George D	6	E½NW	1858-11-01		A1
1826	" "	6	E½SE	1858-11-01		A1
1827	" "	6	NE	1858-11-01		A1
2039	BURKS, William P	18	E½SE	1858-11-01		A1
1984	CAMPBELL, Seaborn J	17	N½SW	1862-01-01		A1
1985	" "	17	SWSW	1862-01-01		A1
2024	CAMPBELL, William F	31	W½NW	1900-11-28		A2
2025	" "	31	W½SW	1900-11-28		A2
1840	CANNON, Henry	14	NWNE	1841-05-20		A1
1841	" "	14	SENW	1841-05-20		A1
1846	CANNON, Hilliary F	23	NESW	1901-01-23		A2
1994	CHESSER, Stephen	2	SENE	1858-11-01		A1
1853	CHURCHWELL, James	19	NESW	1858-11-01		A1
1854	"	19	NWNW	1858-11-01		A1
1855	"	19	SENW	1858-11-01		A1
1856	"	19	W½NE	1858-11-01		A1
2014	CHURCHWELL, William	29	N½SE	1854-07-15		A1
2012	" "	20	S½NW	1860-10-01		A1
2011	" "	20	S½NE	1862-01-01		A1
2013	" "	20	SE	1862-01-01		A1
1906	CLANCY, Joseph E	26	N½SW	1860-10-01		A1
1907	" "	26	NWSE	1860-10-01		A1
1908	" "	26	W½NE	1860-10-01		A1
1752	CLARK, Aaron J	7	E½NE	1862-01-01		A1
1753	" "	7	NESE	1862-01-01		A1
1754	" "	7	NWNE	1862-01-01		A1
1759	CLARK, Alden	30	E½NW	1837-08-15		A1
1760	" "	30	W½NE	1837-08-15		A1
1828	CLARK, George W	18	NENE	1860-10-01		A1
1829	" "	18	W½NE	1860-10-01		A1

ID	Individual in Patent	Sec.	Sec. Part	Date Issued	Other Counties	For More Info . . .
1758	CLAYTON, Adolphus B	1	NENE	1903-12-17		A2
2015	COOPER, William	21	NENW	1858-11-01		A1
2016	" "	21	NWNE	1858-11-01		A1
1921	DANIEL, Leonard	7	SW½NE	1854-07-15		A1
1937	DAVIS, Micajah	8	S½NE	1858-11-01		A1
1934	" "	8	E½NW	1860-04-02		A1
1935	" "	8	NWNE	1860-04-02		A1
1936	" "	8	NWNW	1860-04-02		A1
2026	FLOWERS, William	30	NWSE	1838-07-28		A1
1799	FOWLER, Daniel	19	NENW	1838-07-28		A1
1900	FOWLER, John T	18	W½SW	1890-07-03		A2
1901	FOWLER, John W	8	NWSW	1858-11-01		A1
1902	" "	8	SWNW	1858-11-01		A1
1756	FULLER, Abner S	6	SESW	1862-01-01		A1
1757	" "	6	SWSE	1862-01-01		A1
1839	FULLER, Henry C	17	SESW	1862-01-01		A1
1909	FULLER, Joseph	6	SWSW	1858-11-01		A1
1904	FULLER, Joseph C	7	NWSE	1862-01-01		A1
1905	" "	7	SWNE	1862-01-01		A1
2006	FULLER, Warren	7	SESW	1862-01-01		A1
1998	GARDNER, Thomas J	17	NESE	1852-02-02		A1
1999	" "	17	NWSE	1862-01-01		A1
2000	" "	17	SWNE	1862-01-01		A1
1903	GIBBS, John W	27	SWSW	1858-11-01		A1
1847	GORE, Isaac	13	E½NW	1845-07-01		A1
1848	" "	14	E½NE	1845-07-01		A1
1849	" "	9	SESE	1858-11-01		A1
1886	GORE, John A	15	E½SE	1860-04-02		A1
1995	GREEN, Thomas	10	SESE	1892-06-30		A2
1858	GUY, James	15	NESW	1853-08-01		A1
1860	" "	15	SENE	1858-11-01		A1
1861	" "	22	NENW	1858-11-01		A1
1859	" "	15	S½NW	1860-04-02		A1
1876	HAMRICK, Jason H	29	SWSW	1852-02-02		A1
1877	" "	30	SESE	1854-07-15		A1
1880	" "	32	NENW	1854-07-15		A1
1878	" "	31	N½NE	1858-11-01		A1
1879	" "	31	SWNE	1858-11-01		A1
2027	HAMRICK, William J	28	SWNE	1861-05-01		A1
1892	HARWELL, John	8	SESE	1860-10-01		A1
1962	HAYNES, Richard D	13	SWNW	1858-11-01		A1
1963	" "	13	W½SW	1858-11-01		A1
1964	" "	23	E½NE	1858-11-01		A1
1965	" "	23	NWNE	1858-11-01		A1
1966	" "	24	NWNW	1858-11-01		A1
1894	HEAD, John M	8	SWSW	1860-12-01		A1
1792	HOWARD, Benjamin	11	SESW	1858-11-01		A1
1793	" "	13	NWNW	1858-11-01		A1
1794	" "	14	NENW	1858-11-01		A1
1927	HUGHES, Marion	7	SWSW	1852-02-02		A1
1922	HUTTO, Levi	28	NESW	1858-09-01		A1
1923	" "	28	SENW	1858-09-01		A1
1755	JACKSON, Abner	2	NESE	1837-08-02		A1
1767	JACKSON, Alexander	1	NESW	1837-08-01		A1
1768	" "	1	NWSE	1837-08-02		A1
1810	JEFCOAT, Elijah	14	SWSE	1860-09-01		A1
1808	JEFCOAT, Elijah A	26	NWNW	1860-09-01		A1
1809	" "	26	SWNW	1860-09-01		A1
1896	JEFCOAT, John P	10	SESW	1860-09-01		A1
1897	" "	10	SWSE	1860-09-01		A1
2009	JOHNSON, Wiley	35	SE	1858-09-01		A1
1883	JONES, Jeremiah	32	SENE	1852-02-02		A1
1884	" "	33	NWNW	1852-02-02		A1
1881	" "	28	SESW	1858-11-01		A1
1882	" "	29	SESE	1858-11-01		A1
1924	JONES, Levi	21	SENE	1852-12-01		A1
2029	JONES, William K	14	SESW	1858-11-01		A1
2030	" "	14	W½SW	1858-11-01		A1
2031	" "	22	NENE	1858-11-01		A1
2032	" "	23	NWNW	1858-11-01		A1
1823	JORDAN, Felix	3	NWNW	1858-11-01		A1
1824	" "	4	SE	1858-11-01		A1 G26
1824	JORDAN, George M	4	SE	1858-11-01		A1 G26

ID	Individual in Patent	Sec.	Sec. Part	Date Issued	Other Counties	For More Info . . .
1971	JORDAN, Robert	1	NW	1854-10-02		A1
1974	" "	2	NENE	1858-11-01		A1
1972	" "	1	NWSW	1862-01-01		A1
1973	" "	1	W½NE	1862-01-01		A1
2003	JORDAN, Turner E	2	NWSE	1852-02-02		A1
2004	" "	2	NWSW	1852-02-02		A1
2005	" "	2	SWNE	1852-02-02		A1
2028	JORDAN, William	3	NENW	1853-11-15		A1
1862	KENT, James L	20	N½NE	1858-11-01		A1
1863	" "	21	NWNW	1858-11-01		A1
1957	KENT, Randolph	27	NENW	1849-09-01		A1
1955	" "	22	SESW	1852-02-02		A1
1956	" "	22	SWNE	1852-02-02		A1
1958	" "	35	SESW	1854-10-02		A1
1959	" "	36	NWSW	1858-09-01		A1
1960	" "	36	SWSW	1860-09-01		A1
1981	KING, Rufus L	10	NWSE	1852-12-01		A1
1939	KNOTTS, Nancy	21	SENW	1858-11-01		A1
1940	" "	21	SWNE	1858-11-01		A1
1941	" "	22	SWNW	1858-11-01		A1
1795	LANSDON, Benjamin J	10	N½NW	1896-04-23		A2
1986	LANSDON, Sion M	4	SENW	1890-08-29		A2
2017	LANSDON, William D	22	S½SE	1858-11-01		A1
2018	" "	27	N½NE	1858-11-01		A1
2034	LEAIRD, William	14	NESW	1837-04-10		A1
2033	" "	11	E½NW	1837-08-18		A1
2035	" "	2	E½SW	1837-08-18		A1
2036	" "	2	SWSE	1837-08-18		A1 R1970
1885	LEVERETT, Jesse N	31	E½SW	1862-01-01		A1
1805	LEWIS, Eldred S	4	N½NE	1862-01-01		A1
1806	" "	4	SWNW	1862-01-01		A1
1807	" "	5	N½NE	1862-01-01		A1
1943	LEWIS, Owen L	34	S½	1858-09-01		A1
1944	" "	34	SENE	1858-09-01		A1
1945	" "	35	NE	1858-09-01		A1
1946	" "	35	NESW	1858-09-01		A1
1947	" "	35	NW	1858-09-01		A1
1948	" "	35	W½SW	1858-09-01		A1
1949	" "	36	E½NE	1858-09-01		A1
1950	" "	36	NESE	1858-09-01		A1
1951	" "	36	S½SE	1858-09-01		A1
1952	" "	36	SESW	1858-09-01		A1
1796	MARTIN, Bird	12	SWNW	1852-02-02		A1
1837	MARTIN, Green B	10	SWNW	1858-11-01		A1
1836	" "	10	SENW	1860-04-02		A1
1864	MCNEAL, James	1	NESE	1858-11-01		A1
1865	" "	1	SENE	1858-11-01		A1
1866	" "	1	SESE	1858-11-01		A1
1867	" "	12	NENE	1858-11-01		A1
1868	" "	12	SENE	1858-11-01		A1
1869	" "	24	E½NW	1858-11-01		A1
1870	" "	24	N½SE	1858-11-01		A1
1871	" "	24	SWNE	1858-11-01		A1
1895	MCNEIL, John	24	SWSW	1861-05-01		A1
1800	MCNEILL, Daniel	14	SWNE	1860-10-01		A1
1888	MENEES, John B	7	NESW	1858-11-01		A1
1889	" "	7	NWSW	1858-11-01		A1
1852	MIDDLEBROOKS, Isaac	32	NWNW	1909-09-09		A2
1850	MILLS, Isaac L	19	E½SE	1858-11-01		A1
1851	" "	20	N½SW	1858-11-01		A1
1916	MIMS, Larkin N	12	SWNE	1837-08-01		A1
1801	MITCHELL, Daniel	2	W½NW	1841-05-20		A1
1798	MOODY, Charles W	33	E½SE	1858-11-01		A1
1928	MOORE, Mark E	20	SESW	1854-07-15		A1
1929	" "	29	SWSE	1854-07-15		A1
1930	" "	30	NESE	1854-07-15		A1
1931	" "	30	SENE	1854-07-15		A1
2019	MOSELEY, William E	13	NWSE	1852-02-02		A1
2020	" "	13	SESW	1852-02-02		A1
2021	" "	28	E½NE	1858-11-01		A1
2022	MOSELY, William E	10	W½SW	1860-09-01		A1
2037	NEWMAN, William	19	SWSW	1858-11-01		A1
2038	" "	30	NWNW	1858-11-01		A1

ID	Individual in Patent	Sec.	Sec. Part	Date Issued	Other Counties	For More Info . . .
1961	OWEN, Randolph	2	SESE	1852-12-01		A1
1970	OWEN, Robert F	2	SWSE	1845-06-01		A1 R2036
1910	PARMER, Joseph M	4	SW	1862-01-01		A1
1911	"	5	SESE	1862-01-01		A1
1811	PATENT, Elizabeth	22	SWSW	1858-11-01		A1
1954	PAYNE, Powell	12	SENW	1862-01-01		A1
2040	PERRITT, William	21	SESW	1862-01-01		A1
2041	"	21	W½SW	1862-01-01		A1
1887	PETRY, John A	2	NENW	1858-11-01		A1
1769	REYNOLDS, Anderson H	3	NENE	1840-10-10		A1
1834	RHODES, George W	29	SWNW	1842-02-02		A1
1835	"	30	NENE	1852-02-02		A1
1831	"	28	NWSW	1858-11-01		A1
1832	"	28	SWNW	1858-11-01		A1
1833	"	29	SENE	1858-11-01		A1
1830	"	28	N½NW	1860-10-01		A1
1912	RHODES, Joseph	29	E½NW	1837-08-09		A1
1913	"	32	W½SE	1837-08-09		A1
1918	RHODES, Lemuel	27	SENW	1875-04-20		A1
1919	"	27	W½NW	1875-04-20		A1
1982	RHODES, Sarah	28	SWSW	1854-07-15		A1
1983	"	32	NENE	1854-07-15		A1
1917	RICHARDSON, Lee A	34	NWNE	1903-11-24		A2
1803	RUTLEDGE, Dudley A	28	W½SE	1860-10-01		A1
1804	"	32	NWNE	1860-10-01		A1
1770	SELLERS, Anderson M	34	SWNE	1885-06-03		A1
2007	SHOWS, Warren S	17	NW	1862-01-01		A1
2008	"	8	SESW	1862-01-01		A1
1996	SIKES, Thomas H	17	N½NE	1860-04-02		A1
1997	"	8	SWSE	1860-04-02		A1
1932	SKIPPER, Martha	9	NWSW	1862-01-01		A1
1842	SOLOMAN, Henry	30	SWNW	1860-10-01		A1
1838	SOLOMON, Hartwell	19	SESW	1837-08-15		A1
1843	SOLOMON, Henry	30	NESW	1847-05-01		A1
1845	"	30	S½SW	1860-10-01		A1
1844	"	30	NWSW	1862-01-01		A1
1938	SPRADLEY, Michael D	25	SENW	1852-12-01		A1
1898	SPURLOCK, John	21	NENE	1860-04-02		A1
1899	"	22	NWNW	1860-04-02		A1
1993	STEPHENSON, Squire T	26	SWSE	1854-10-02		A1
1992	"	26	SESW	1858-11-01		A1
1933	STEVENSON, Matilda A	25	SWSW	1850-05-01		A1
1991	STEVENSON, Squire J	26	SWSW	1860-10-01		A1
1977	STOUGH, Robert W	11	N½NE	1854-07-15		A1
1978	"	11	S½NE	1858-11-01		A1
1979	"	12	NENW	1858-11-01		A1
1980	"	12	NWNW	1858-11-01		A1
1771	STURGIS, Andrew M	10	NENE	1858-11-01		A1
1772	"	10	NESE	1858-11-01		A1
1773	"	10	NESW	1858-11-01		A1
1774	"	10	S½NE	1858-11-01		A1
1775	"	11	NESW	1858-11-01		A1
1776	"	11	SWNW	1858-11-01		A1
1777	"	11	SWSW	1858-11-01		A1
1942	SUMMERLIN, Needham D	22	NWSW	1882-10-30		A1
1989	SUMMERLIN, Smith	24	SWNW	1848-05-03		A1
1988	"	23	SESE	1852-02-02		A1
1987	"	23	N½SE	1860-04-02		A1
2023	SUMMERLIN, William E	22	NWNE	1895-06-03		A2
2042	SUMMERLIN, William R	14	SESE	1852-02-02		A1
2047	"	23	NENW	1852-12-01		A1
2043	"	22	N½SE	1858-11-01		A1
2045	"	22	SENE	1858-11-01		A1
2044	"	22	NESW	1860-04-02		A1
2046	"	22	SENW	1860-04-02		A1
1990	SUMMERLINE, Smith	24	N½SW	1852-12-01		A1
1953	TALLEY, Page	21	NWSE	1837-08-12		A1
1914	TARVER, Joseph	14	NWSE	1854-10-02		A1
1975	TAYLOR, Robert	13	NESE	1852-02-02		A1
1976	"	13	SESE	1852-02-02		A1
2002	TAYLOR, Thomas	18	SENE	1860-04-02		A1
1967	THOMPSON, Richard H	18	NW	1862-01-01		A1
1872	WELCH, James	32	NESW	1837-08-09		A1

ID	Individual in Patent	Sec.	Sec. Part	Date Issued	Other Counties	For More Info . . .
1874	WELCH, James (Cont'd)	32	SENW	1837-08-09		A1
1873	" "	32	NWSW	1854-07-15		A1
1875	" "	32	SWNW	1858-11-01		A1
1893	WELCH, John L	32	S½SW	1858-11-01		A1
1820	WILLIAMSON, Erasmus	33	NWSW	1837-08-12		A1
1814	" "	32	NESE	1852-02-02		A1
1819	" "	33	NWSE	1854-10-02		A1
1815	" "	32	SESE	1858-11-01		A1
1816	" "	32	SWNE	1858-11-01		A1
1817	" "	33	E½SW	1858-11-01		A1
1821	" "	33	SWSE	1858-11-01		A1
1813	" "	28	E½SE	1860-04-02		A1
1818	" "	33	NENE	1860-04-02		A1
1822	WILLIAMSON, Esquire T	34	NW	1860-09-01		A1
1857	WILLIAMSON, James D	30	SWSE	1847-05-01		A1
2050	WILLIAMSON, William	14	NESE	1852-02-02		A1
2051	" "	25	NESE	1854-10-02		A1
1812	WINDHAM, Erasmus W	13	SWSE	1852-12-01		A1
1925	WRIGHT, Levi	24	NWNE	1852-02-02		A1
1926	" "	24	SENE	1852-02-02		A1
2048	WRIGHT, William W	9	E½SW	1900-11-28		A2
2049	" "	9	S½NW	1900-11-28		A2
1891	WYATT, John D	13	NWNE	1850-08-10		A1
1890	" "	13	NESW	1853-08-01		A1
1782	WYROSDICK, Andrew	24	SESW	1854-10-02		A1
1783	" "	24	SWSE	1854-10-02		A1
1788	" "	34	NENE	1854-10-02		A1
1781	" "	23	SWSE	1858-11-01		A1
1784	" "	25	E½SW	1858-11-01		A1
1785	" "	25	NENW	1858-11-01		A1
1786	" "	25	NWSE	1858-11-01		A1
1787	" "	25	W½NE	1858-11-01		A1
1789	" "	36	NENW	1858-11-01		A1
1778	WYROSDICK, Andrew P	25	SENE	1850-08-10		A1
1779	" "	25	SWNW	1858-11-01		A1
1780	" "	26	E½NE	1858-11-01		A1
1797	WYROSDICK, Catharine V	25	NWSW	1852-02-02		A1
1920	WYROSDICK, Lenora M	25	NENE	1852-02-02		A1
2001	WYROSDICK, Thomas R	26	NESE	1850-08-10		A1

Patent Map

T10-N R18-E
St Stephens Meridian

Map Group 8

Township Statistics

Parcels Mapped	:	303
Number of Patents	:	217
Number of Individuals	:	141
Patentees Identified	:	141
Number of Surnames	:	94
Multi-Patentee Parcels	:	1
Oldest Patent Date	:	4/10/1837
Most Recent Patent	:	9/9/1909
Block/Lot Parcels	:	0
Parcels Re - Issued	:	1
Parcels that Overlap	:	0
Cities and Towns	:	3
Cemeteries	:	2

Map Grid

Section 3
- JORDAN Felix 1858
- JORDAN William 1853
- BIRD Wiley M 1858
- REYNOLDS Anderson H 1840
- BIRD Wylie M 1858
- BIRD Wylie M 1858
- BIRD Wylie M 1858

Section 2
- MITCHELL Daniel 1841
- PETRY John A 1858
- JORDAN Turner E 1852
- CHESSER Stephen 1858
- JORDAN Turner E 1852
- LEAIRD William 1837
- JORDAN Turner E 1852
- JACKSON Abner 1837
- LEAIRD William 1837 OWEN Robert F 1845
- OWEN Randolph 1852

Section 1
- JORDAN Robert 1858
- JORDAN Robert 1854
- JORDAN Robert 1862
- JORDAN Robert 1862
- JACKSON Alexander 1837
- JACKSON Alexander 1837
- CLAYTON Adolphus B 1903
- MCNEAL James 1858
- MCNEAL James 1858
- MCNEAL James 1858

Section 10
- LANSDON Benjamin J 1896
- STURGIS Andrew M 1858
- MARTIN Green B 1858
- MARTIN Green B 1860
- STURGIS Andrew M 1858
- STURGIS Andrew M 1858
- KING Rufus L 1852
- STURGIS Andrew M 1858
- MOSELY William E 1860
- JEFCOAT John P 1860
- JEFCOAT John P 1860
- GREEN Thomas 1892

Section 11
- STURGIS Andrew M 1858
- LEAIRD William 1837
- STOUGH Robert W 1854
- STOUGH Robert W 1858
- STURGIS Andrew M 1858
- HOWARD Benjamin 1858

Section 12
- STOUGH Robert W 1858
- STOUGH Robert W 1858
- MARTIN Bird 1852
- PAYNE Powell 1862
- MIMS Larkin N 1837
- MCNEAL James 1858
- MCNEAL James 1858
- MCNEAL James 1858

Section 15
- GUY James 1860
- GUY James 1858
- GUY James 1853

Section 14
- HOWARD Benjamin 1858
- CANNON Henry 1841
- CANNON Henry 1841
- MCNEILL Daniel 1860
- GORE Isaac 1845
- LEAIRD William 1837
- TARVER Joseph 1854
- WILLIAMSON William 1852
- JONES William K 1858
- JONES William K 1858
- JEFCOAT Elijah 1860
- SUMMERLIN William 1852
- GORE John A 1860

Section 13
- HOWARD Benjamin 1858
- GORE Isaac 1845
- WYATT John D 1850
- HAYNES Richard D 1858
- HAYNES Richard D 1858
- WYATT John D 1853
- MOSELEY William E 1852
- TAYLOR Robert 1852
- MOSELEY William E 1852
- WINDHAM Erasmus W 1852
- TAYLOR Robert 1852

Section 22
- SPURLOCK John 1860
- GUY James 1858
- SUMMERLIN William E 1895
- JONES William K 1858
- KNOTTS Nancy 1858
- SUMMERLIN William R 1860
- KENT Randolph 1852
- SUMMERLIN William R 1858
- SUMMERLIN Needham D 1882
- SUMMERLIN William R 1860
- SUMMERLIN William R 1858
- PATENT Elizabeth 1858
- KENT Randolph 1852
- LANSDON William D 1858

Section 23
- JONES William K 1858
- SUMMERLIN William R 1852
- HAYNES Richard D 1858
- HAYNES Richard D 1858
- CANNON Hilliary F 1901
- SUMMERLIN Smith 1860
- WYROSDICK Andrew 1858
- SUMMERLIN Smith 1852

Section 24
- HAYNES Richard D 1858
- MCNEAL James 1858
- WRIGHT Levi 1852
- SUMMERLIN Smith 1848
- MCNEAL James 1858
- WRIGHT Levi 1852
- SUMMERLINE Smith 1852
- MCNEAL James 1858
- MCNEIL John 1861
- WYROSDICK Andrew 1854
- WYROSDICK Andrew 1854
- ATKINSON Alexander 1854

Section 27
- RHODES Lemuel 1875
- KENT Randolph 1849
- LANSDON William D 1858
- RHODES Lemuel 1875
- GIBBS John W 1858

Section 26
- JEFCOAT Elijah A 1860
- BARNES Augustus 1860
- CLANCY Joseph E 1860
- WYROSDICK Andrew P 1858
- JEFCOAT Elijah A 1860
- BARNES Augustus 1860
- CLANCY Joseph E 1860
- CLANCY Joseph E 1860
- WYROSDICK Thomas R 1850
- STEVENSON Squire J 1860
- STEPHENSON Squire T 1858
- STEPHENSON Squire T 1854

Section 25
- WYROSDICK Andrew P 1858
- WYROSDICK Andrew 1858
- WYROSDICK Andrew P 1858
- WYROSDICK Andrew P 1858
- SPRADLEY Michael D 1852
- WYROSDICK Catharine V 1852
- WYROSDICK Andrew 1858
- WYROSDICK Andrew 1858
- WILLIAMSON William 1854
- STEVENSON Matilda A 1850
- WYROSDICK Andrew 1858
- ATKISON Alexander 1898

Section 34
- WILLIAMSON Esquire T 1860
- RICHARDSON Lee A 1903
- WYROSDICK Andrew 1854
- SELLERS Anderson M 1885
- LEWIS Owen L 1858
- LEWIS Owen L 1858

Section 35
- LEWIS Owen L 1858
- LEWIS Owen L 1858
- LEWIS Owen L 1858
- LEWIS Owen L 1858
- LEWIS Owen L 1858
- KENT Randolph 1854
- JOHNSON Wiley 1858

Section 36
- WYROSDICK Andrew 1858
- LEWIS Owen L 1858
- ATKISON Alexander 1898
- ATKISON Alexander 1898
- LEWIS Owen L 1858
- KENT Randolph 1858
- ATKISON Alexander 1898
- ATKISON Alexander 1898
- LEWIS Owen L 1858
- KENT Randolph 1860
- LEWIS Owen L 1858
- LEWIS Owen L 1858

Helpful Hints

1. This Map's INDEX can be found on the preceding pages.

2. Refer to Map "C" to see where this Township lies within Crenshaw County, Alabama.

3. Numbers within square brackets [ ] denote a multi-patentee land parcel (multi-owner). Refer to Appendix "C" for a full list of members in this group.

4. Areas that look to be crowded with Patentees usually indicate multiple sales of the same parcel (Re-issues) or Overlapping parcels. See this Township's Index for an explanation of these and other circumstances that might explain "odd" groupings of Patentees on this map.

Legend

- ——— Patent Boundary
- ■■■ Section Boundary
- ░░░ No Patents Found (or Outside County)
- 1., 2., 3., ... Lot Numbers (when beside a name)
- [ ] Group Number (see Appendix "C")

Scale: Section = 1 mile X 1 mile (generally, with some exceptions)

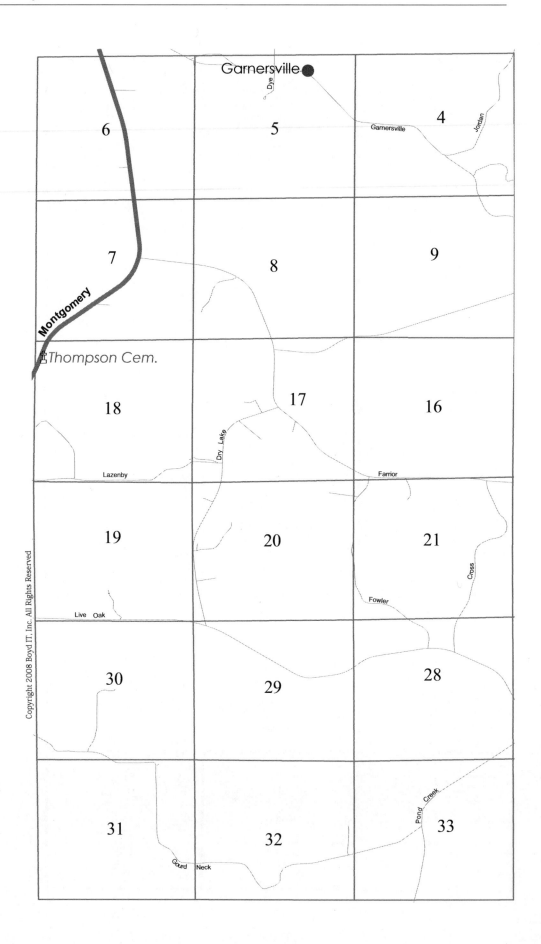

Road Map

T10-N R18-E
St Stephens Meridian

Map Group 8

Cities & Towns
Garnersville
Live Oak
Petrey

Cemeteries
Petrey Cemetery
Thompson Cemetery

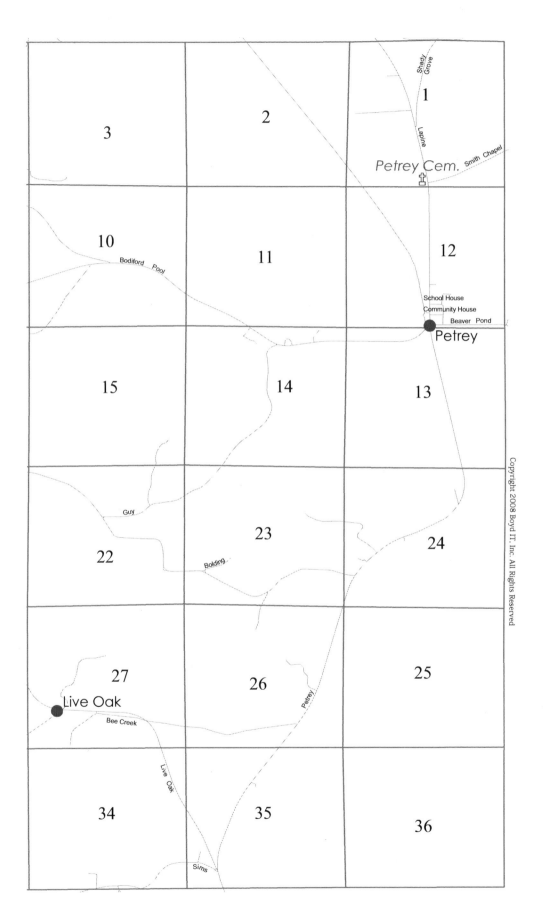

3

2

1

Shady Grove

Lapine

Petrey Cem. ♰ Smith Chapel

10

Bodiford   Pool

11

12

School House
Community House
Beaver   Pond

● Petrey

15

14

13

22

Guy

23

Bolding

24

27

Live Oak ●

Bee Creek

26

Petrey

25

34

Live Oak

35

Sims

36

Helpful Hints

1. This road map has a number of uses, but primarily it is to help you: a) find the present location of land owned by your ancestors (at least the general area), b) find cemeteries and city-centers, and c) estimate the route/roads used by Census-takers & tax-assessors.

2. If you plan to travel to Crenshaw County to locate cemeteries or land parcels, please pick up a modern travel map for the area before you do. Mapping old land parcels on modern maps is not as exact a science as you might think. Just the slightest variations in public land survey coordinates, estimates of parcel boundaries, or road-map deviations can greatly alter a map's representation of how a road either does or doesn't cross a particular parcel of land.

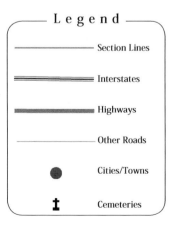

L e g e n d

——————— Section Lines

═══════ Interstates

▨▨▨▨▨▨ Highways

——————— Other Roads

● Cities/Towns

♰ Cemeteries

Scale: Section = 1 mile X 1 mile
(generally, with some exceptions)

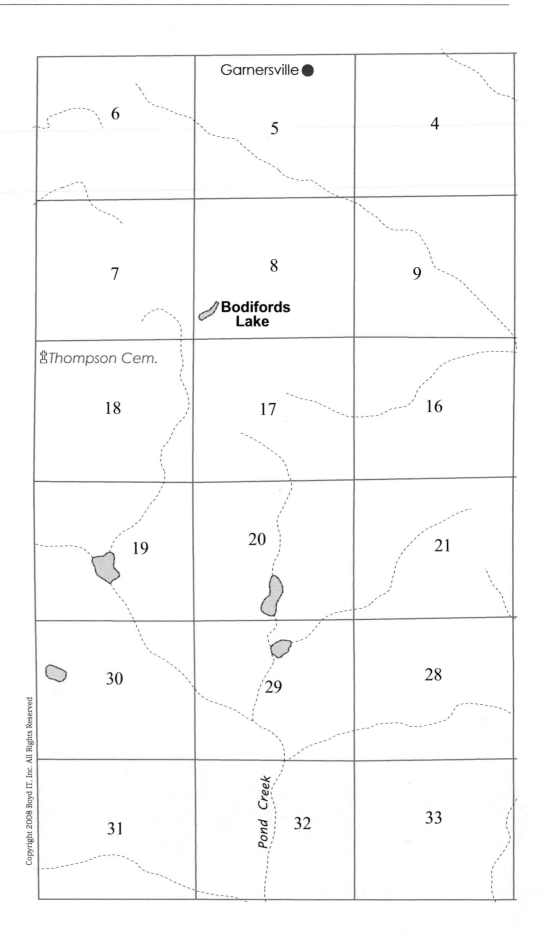

Historical Map

T10-N R18-E
St Stephens Meridian

Map Group 8

Cities & Towns
Garnersville
Live Oak
Petrey

Cemeteries
Petrey Cemetery
Thompson Cemetery

Garnersville ●

6

5

4

7

8

9

Bodifords
Lake

✝Thompson Cem.

18

17

16

19

20

21

30

29

28

31

Pond Creek

32

33

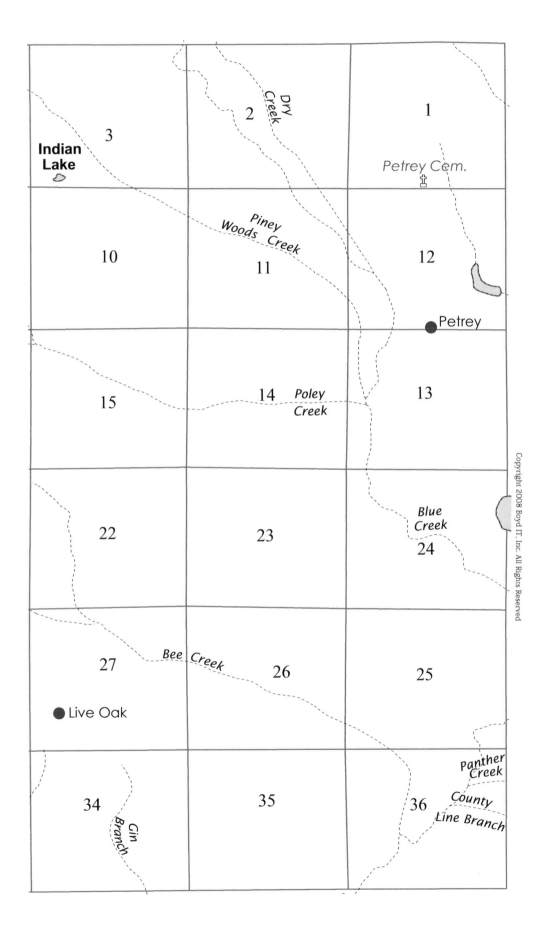

Indian
Lake

3

2

Dry Creek

1

Petrey Cem.
☨

10

*Piney
Woods   Creek*

11

12

● Petrey

15

14 *Poley
Creek*

13

22

23

*Blue
Creek*
24

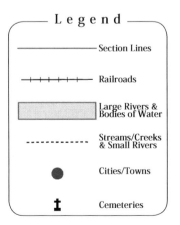

27

Bee Creek

26

25

● Live Oak

34

*Gin
Branch*

35

*Panther
Creek*

36 *County
Line Branch*

Helpful Hints

1. This Map takes a different look at the same Congressional Township displayed in the preceding two maps. It presents features that can help you better envision the historical development of the area: a) Water-bodies (lakes & ponds), b) Water-courses (rivers, streams, etc.), c) Railroads, d) City/town center-points (where they were oftentimes located when first settled), and e) Cemeteries.

2. Using this "Historical" map in tandem with this Township's Patent Map and Road Map, may lead you to some interesting discoveries. You will often find roads, towns, cemeteries, and waterways are named after nearby landowners: sometimes those names will be the ones you are researching. See how many of these research gems you can find here in Crenshaw County.

Legend

———————	Section Lines
+++++++++	Railroads
�	Large Rivers & Bodies of Water
- - - - - - -	Streams/Creeks & Small Rivers
●	Cities/Towns
☨	Cemeteries

Scale: Section = 1 mile X 1 mile
(there are some exceptions)

Map Group 9: Index to Land Patents

Township 10-North Range 19-East (St Stephens)

After you locate an individual in this Index, take note of the Section and Section Part then proceed to the Land Patent map on the pages immediately following. You should have no difficulty locating the corresponding parcel of land.

The "For More Info" Column will lead you to more information about the underlying Patents. See the *Legend* at right, and the "How to Use this Book" chapter, for more information.

```
                      LEGEND
           "For More Info . . . " column
A = Authority (Legislative Act, See Appendix "A")
B = Block or Lot (location in Section unknown)
C = Cancelled Patent
F = Fractional Section
G = Group  (Multi-Patentee Patent, see Appendix "C")
V = Overlaps another Parcel
R = Re-Issued (Parcel patented more than once)

(A & G items require you to look in the Appendixes referred
to above. All other Letter-designations followed by a number
require you to locate line-items in this index that possess
the ID number found after the letter).
```

ID	Individual in Patent	Sec.	Sec. Part	Date Issued	Other Counties	For More Info . . .
2055	ATKINSON, Alexander	30	W½NW	1854-10-02	Pike	A1
2096	BERRY, Larkin S	5	SWNW	1858-11-01	Pike	A1
2121	BOND, William B	8	NESW	1858-09-01	Pike	A1
2122	"	8	NWSE	1858-09-01	Pike	A1
2117	"	18	N½NE	1858-11-01	Pike	A1 V2065
2119	"	7	E½SE	1858-11-01	Pike	A1
2120	"	8	E½NE	1858-11-01	Pike	A1
2123	"	8	SWNW	1858-11-01	Pike	A1
2124	"	8	W½SW	1858-11-01	Pike	A1
2116	"	18	E½SE	1860-10-01	Pike	A1
2118	"	18	SENE	1860-10-01	Pike	A1 V2065
2056	DAVIS, Archibald R	18	SWSW	1850-08-10	Pike	A1
2071	DYER, George A	5	SWNE	1837-08-08	Pike	A1
2092	DYER, Josiah	17	NWNE	1835-10-01	Pike	A1
2094	"	8	SENW	1835-10-16	Pike	A1
2093	"	17	W½SE	1837-08-08	Pike	A1
2089	HUGHES, John W	6	SW	1858-11-01		A1
2095	HUNT, Kindred A	6	E½NE	1858-11-01		A1
2100	HYNES, Mary	30	SESE	1860-04-02	Pike	A1
2101	JAMES, Mary	8	SESE	1858-11-01	Pike	A1
2102	"	8	SESW	1858-11-01	Pike	A1
2103	"	8	SWSE	1858-11-01	Pike	A1
2069	JEFCOAT, Elijah	5	SENE	1852-12-01	Pike	A1
2074	JEFCOAT, Henry	30	SWSE	1858-11-01	Pike	A1
2075	"	30	SWSW	1858-11-01	Pike	A1
2072	"	30	NWSW	1860-10-01	Pike	A1
2073	"	30	SESW	1860-10-01	Pike	A1
2106	JEFCOAT, Reuben	5	NESE	1858-11-01	Pike	A1
2115	JEFCOAT, Samuel	8	SWNE	1850-08-10	Pike	A1
2110	"	5	NESW	1852-02-02	Pike	A1
2112	"	5	SWSW	1852-02-02	Pike	A1
2114	"	8	NWNE	1852-02-02	Pike	A1
2111	"	5	NWSE	1858-11-01	Pike	A1
2113	"	8	N½NW	1858-11-01	Pike	A1
2107	JEFFCOATE, Reuben	5	SENW	1852-02-02	Pike	A1
2104	LEAK, Newton B	5	NWSW	1858-11-01	Pike	A1
2105	"	6	NW	1858-11-01		A1
2065	MCKINZIE, Charles	18	E½NE	1848-05-03	Pike	A1 V2117, 2118
2066	"	18	SWNE	1848-05-03	Pike	A1 R2091
2078	MCNEAL, James	19	E½NE	1858-11-01	Pike	A1
2079	"	19	N½SW	1858-11-01	Pike	A1
2080	"	19	NWSE	1858-11-01	Pike	A1
2081	"	19	S½SW	1858-11-01	Pike	A1
2082	"	19	SENW	1858-11-01	Pike	A1
2083	"	19	SWNE	1858-11-01	Pike	A1
2084	"	19	W½NW	1858-11-01	Pike	A1

ID	Individual in Patent	Sec.	Sec. Part	Date Issued	Other Counties	For More Info . . .
2126	MEASLES, William	6	NWNE	1852-02-02		A1
2067	MITCHELL, Daniel	5	NENW	1852-02-02	Pike	A1
2068	"	5	NWNE	1852-02-02	Pike	A1
2097	MITCHELL, Lloyd	7	NESW	1852-12-01	Pike	A1
2099	MOORE, Mark E	7	NWSW	1853-11-15	Pike	A1
2098	" "	18	NWNW	1854-05-11	Pike	A1
2057	OGLESBE, Benjamin	5	NENE	1852-02-02	Pike	A1
2076	OLIVER, James C	17	NESW	1850-08-10	Pike	A1
2077	"	17	SESW	1852-02-02	Pike	A1
2125	OLIVER, William H	17	NENE	1854-10-02	Pike	A1
2088	SCOFIELD, John	19	SESE	1837-05-15	Pike	A1
2070	SIMS, Elvin	8	NESE	1852-02-02	Pike	A1
2064	STEWART, Cado P	7	S½SW	1852-12-01	Pike	A1
2090	TARVER, Joseph	18	NESW	1852-12-01	Pike	A1
2091	" "	18	SWNE	1854-10-02	Pike	A1 R2066
2108	TAYLOR, Robert	18	NWSW	1852-02-02	Pike	A1
2109	" "	18	SESW	1852-02-02	Pike	A1
2085	TUNNELL, James	18	SWSE	1849-09-01	Pike	A1
2086	"	19	NENW	1849-09-01	Pike	A1
2063	WINGARD, Benjamin	30	SWNE	1852-02-02	Pike	A1
2062	" "	30	NWNE	1854-10-02	Pike	A1
2058	" "	19	SWSE	1858-11-01	Pike	A1
2059	" "	30	E½NW	1858-11-01	Pike	A1
2060	" "	30	NESE	1858-11-01	Pike	A1
2061	" "	30	NESW	1858-11-01	Pike	A1
2135	WINGARD, William	30	E½NE	1837-08-12	Pike	A1
2127	" "	17	E½SE	1852-12-01	Pike	A1
2130	" "	17	SENW	1852-12-01	Pike	A1
2133	" "	17	W½SW	1852-12-01	Pike	A1
2136	" "	30	NWSE	1852-12-01	Pike	A1
2128	" "	17	NENW	1854-10-02	Pike	A1
2129	" "	17	SENE	1854-10-02	Pike	A1
2132	" "	17	W½NW	1854-10-02	Pike	A1
2134	" "	19	NESE	1854-10-02	Pike	A1
2131	" "	17	SWNE	1858-11-01	Pike	A1
2087	WYATT, John D	18	NWSE	1850-08-10	Pike	A1

Patent Map

T10-N R19-E
St Stephens Meridian

Map Group 9

Township Statistics

Parcels Mapped	:	82
Number of Patents	:	69
Number of Individuals	:	34
Patentees Identified	:	34
Number of Surnames	:	27
Multi-Patentee Parcels	:	0
Oldest Patent Date	:	10/1/1835
Most Recent Patent	:	10/1/1860
Block/Lot Parcels	:	0
Parcels Re-Issued	:	1
Parcels that Overlap	:	3
Cities and Towns	:	0
Cemeteries	:	0

Note: the area contained in this map amounts to far less than a full Township. Therefore, its contents are completely on this single page (instead of a "normal" 2-page spread).

Legend

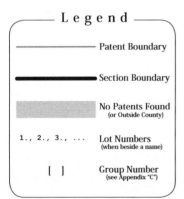

——— Patent Boundary

▬▬▬ Section Boundary

▨ No Patents Found
(or Outside County)

1., 2., 3., ... Lot Numbers
(when beside a name)

[ ] Group Number
(see Appendix "C")

Scale: Section = 1 mile X 1 mile
(generally, with some exceptions)

Map

6

LEAK Newton B 1858

MEASLES William 1852

HUNT Kindred A 1858

MITCHELL Daniel 1852

MITCHELL Daniel 1852

OGLESBE Benjamin 1852

BERRY Larkin 1858

JEFFCOATE Reuben 1852

DYER George A 1837

5

JEFCOAT Elijah 1852

HUGHES John W 1858

LEAK Newton B 1858

JEFCOAT Samuel 1852

JEFCOAT Samuel 1858

JEFCOAT Reuben 1858

JEFCOAT Samuel 1852

Crenshaw

7

JEFCOAT Samuel 1858

JEFCOAT Samuel 1852

BOND William B 1858

BOND William B 1858

DYER Josiah 1835

JEFCOAT Samuel 1850

8

MOORE Mark E 1853

MITCHELL Lloyd 1852

BOND William B 1858

BOND William B 1858

BOND William B 1858

BOND William B 1858

SIMS Elvin 1852

STEWART Cado P 1852

JAMES Mary 1858

JAMES Mary 1858

JAMES Mary 1858

MOORE Mark E 1854

BOND William B 1858

MCKINZIE Charles 1848

WINGARD William 1854

DYER Josiah 1835

OLIVER William H 1854

18

TARVER Joseph 1854
MCKINZIE Charles 1848

BOND William B 1860

WINGARD William 1854

WINGARD William 1852

WINGARD William 1858

WINGARD William 1854

TAYLOR Robert 1852

TARVER Joseph 1852

WYATT John D 1850

OLIVER James C 1850

17

DAVIS Archibald R 1850

TAYLOR Robert 1852

TUNNELL James 1849

BOND William B 1860

WINGARD William 1852

OLIVER James C 1852

DYER Josiah 1837

WINGARD William 1852

TUNNELL James 1849

MCNEAL James 1858

MCNEAL James 1858

Pike

20

MCNEAL James 1858

MCNEAL James 1858

MCNEAL James 1858

MCNEAL James 1858

19

MCNEAL James 1858

WINGARD William 1854

MCNEAL James 1858

WINGARD Benjamin 1858

SCOFIELD John 1837

WINGARD Benjamin 1858

WINGARD Benjamin 1854

ATKINSON Alexander 1854

30

WINGARD Benjamin 1852

WINGARD William 1837

29

JEFCOAT Henry 1860

WINGARD Benjamin 1858

WINGARD William 1852

WINGARD Benjamin 1858

JEFCOAT Henry 1858

JEFCOAT Henry 1860

JEFCOAT Henry 1858

HYNES Mary 1860

31

32

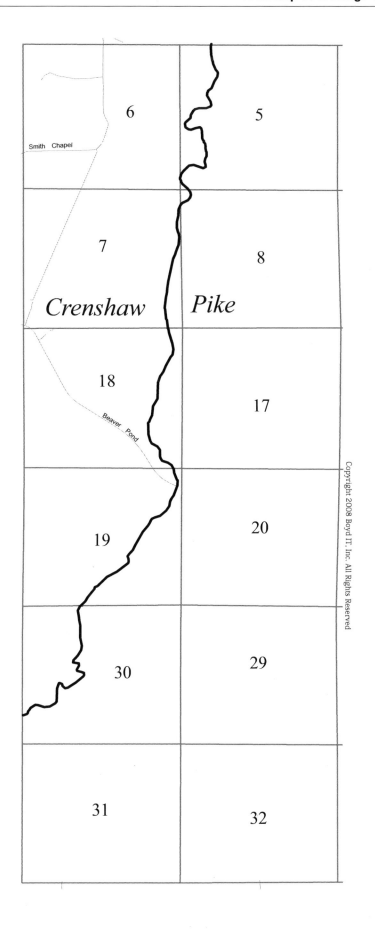

Road Map

T10-N R19-E
St Stephens Meridian

Map Group 9

Note: the area contained in this map amounts to far less than a full Township. Therefore, its contents are completely on this single page (instead of a "normal" 2-page spread).

Cities & Towns
None

Cemeteries
None

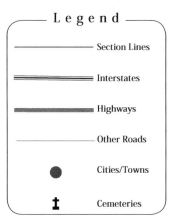

L e g e n d

———	Section Lines
═══	Interstates
▬▬▬	Highways
———	Other Roads
●	Cities/Towns
✝	Cemeteries

Scale: Section = 1 mile X 1 mile
(generally, with some exceptions)

Historical Map

T10-N R19-E
St Stephens Meridian

Map Group 9

Note: the area contained in this map amounts to far less than a full Township. Therefore, its contents are completely on this single page (instead of a "normal" 2-page spread).

Cities & Towns
None

Cemeteries
None

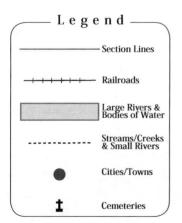

Legend

———— Section Lines

+—+—+—+— Railroads

▨ Large Rivers & Bodies of Water

------- Streams/Creeks & Small Rivers

● Cities/Towns

✝ Cemeteries

Scale: Section = 1 mile X 1 mile
(there are some exceptions)

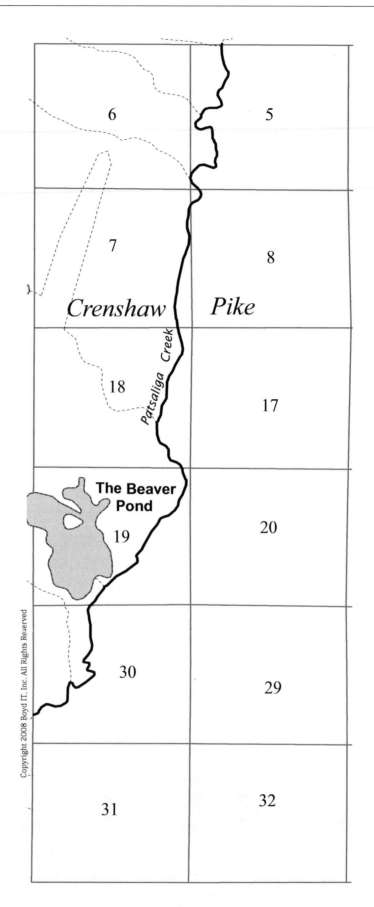

Crenshaw   *Pike*

Patsaliga Creek

The Beaver Pond

Map Group 10: Index to Land Patents

Township 9-North Range 16-East (St Stephens)

After you locate an individual in this Index, take note of the Section and Section Part then proceed to the Land Patent map on the pages immediately following. You should have no difficulty locating the corresponding parcel of land.

The "For More Info" Column will lead you to more information about the underlying Patents. See the *Legend* at right, and the "How to Use this Book" chapter, for more information.

```
                    LEGEND
          "For More Info . . . " column
A = Authority (Legislative Act, See Appendix "A")
B = Block or Lot (location in Section unknown)
C = Cancelled Patent
F = Fractional Section
G = Group  (Multi-Patentee Patent, see Appendix "C")
V = Overlaps another Parcel
R = Re-Issued (Parcel patented more than once)

(A & G items require you to look in the Appendixes referred
to above. All other Letter-designations followed by a number
require you to locate line-items in this index that possess
the ID number found after the letter).
```

ID	Individual in Patent	Sec.	Sec. Part	Date Issued	Other Counties	For More Info . . .
2267	BEASLEY, William A	34	N½	1858-11-01		A1
2197	BEDGOOD, John	22	SESW	1854-07-15		A1
2198	" "	22	SWSE	1854-07-15		A1
2199	" "	27	E½NE	1858-09-01		A1
2248	BEDGOOD, Richmond	22	NWNW	1843-02-01		A1
2175	BLACK, Francis M	10	SESE	1858-09-01	Butler	A1
2176	" "	10	SW	1858-09-01	Butler	A1
2177	" "	10	W½SE	1858-09-01	Butler	A1
2178	" "	15	NENW	1858-09-01		A1
2252	BLACK, Robert W	11	SESE	1858-09-01		A1
2253	" "	11	SWSE	1858-09-01		A1
2254	" "	14	N½SE	1858-09-01		A1
2255	" "	14	NE	1858-09-01		A1
2180	BOAN, Frederick	36	N½NW	1852-12-01		A1
2179	" "	25	W½SW	1853-10-01		A1 F
2209	BOAN, John D	24	W½SW	1848-05-03		A1
2208	" "	24	SWSE	1853-08-01		A1
2204	" "	23	SWSE	1854-07-15		A1
2205	" "	24	E½SE	1858-09-01		A1
2206	" "	24	E½SW	1858-09-01		A1
2207	" "	24	NWSE	1858-09-01		A1
2210	" "	25	NE	1858-09-01		A1
2211	" "	25	SENW	1858-09-01		A1
2202	" "	23	N½SE	1858-11-01		A1
2203	" "	23	SENW	1858-11-01		A1
2182	BOYETT, Gibson	2	NWSW	1858-11-01		A1
2183	" "	2	SWNW	1858-11-01		A1
2184	" "	3	E½SW	1858-11-01		A1
2185	" "	3	NESE	1858-11-01		A1
2186	" "	3	SWSW	1858-11-01		A1
2187	" "	3	W½SE	1858-11-01		A1
2261	BOYETT, Thomas	2	N½SE	1858-11-01		A1
2262	" "	2	NESW	1858-11-01		A1
2263	" "	2	SENE	1858-11-01		A1
2242	BURNS, Lauchlin	10	NENE	1858-11-01	Butler	A1
2243	" "	10	NW	1858-11-01	Butler	A1
2244	" "	10	W½NE	1858-11-01	Butler	A1
2245	" "	3	SESE	1858-11-01		A1
2200	BUTLER, John	14	W½SW	1823-12-01		A1
2201	" "	15	E½SE	1823-12-01		A1
2171	CALDWELL, Elizabeth G	25	NENW	1849-09-01		A1
2170	" "	23	SW	1858-11-01		A1
2172	" "	26	E½NW	1858-11-01		A1
2173	" "	26	NWNE	1858-11-01		A1 V2235
2174	" "	26	NWNW	1858-11-01		A1
2158	CHILDRES, David	23	SESE	1837-08-14		A1

ID	Individual in Patent	Sec.	Sec. Part	Date Issued	Other Counties	For More Info . . .
2160	CHILDRES, David (Cont'd)	26	NENE	1837-08-14		A1 V2235
2159	" "	26	E½SE	1837-08-18		A1
2138	COOK, Alexander H	1		1858-11-01		A1 F
2223	COOK, John P	22	E½SE	1860-10-01		A1
2259	COOK, Stephen H	26	SWSE	1837-08-18		A1
2260	" "	35	NENE	1837-08-18		A1
2191	COWART, James A	34	E½SE	1858-11-01		A1
2192	" "	35	N½SW	1858-11-01		A1
2193	" "	35	S½SW	1858-11-01		A1
2143	DAVIS, Benjamin	36	W½SW	1838-07-28		A1
2142	DAVIS, Benjamin B	35	NESE	1845-07-01		A1
2268	DAVIS, William	26	NWSE	1837-08-18		A1
2269	" "	26	SENE	1837-08-18		A1 V2235
2196	DAVISON, James T	2	NENW	1860-04-02		A1
2145	DENDY, Buford W	22	NESW	1860-09-01		A1
2190	FROST, Hillrey	22	SWSW	1850-08-10		A1
2219	GILLIS, John L	14	S½SE	1858-11-01		A1
2220	" "	23	NWNE	1858-11-01		A1
2239	GRAHAM, Joseph J	11	S½SW	1858-11-01		A1
2240	" "	14	NENW	1858-11-01		A1
2217	HAMMONDS, John	15	S½NW	1848-04-01		A1
2218	" "	15	SWNE	1849-09-01		A1
2144	HASTING, Benjamin	27	W½NW	1858-11-01		A1
2194	HESTER, James	15	SWSW	1838-07-28		A1
2249	JAMES, Robert A	26	SESW	1861-05-01		A1
2250	" "	26	SWNW	1861-05-01		A1
2251	" "	26	W½SW	1861-05-01		A1
2264	JAMES, Thomas F	22	NENW	1850-04-01		A1
2169	KELLEY, Elisha	12	SE	1858-11-01		A1
2140	KENNINGTON, Arnold	34	SW	1858-11-01		A1
2141	" "	34	W½SE	1858-11-01		A1
2265	KETTLER, Thomas S	22	SENE	1854-07-15		A1
2266	" "	23	W½NW	1854-07-15		A1
2195	LONG, James J	26	SWNE	1837-08-18		A1 V2235
2246	LONG, Mary	35	E½NW	1858-11-01		A1
2247	" "	35	W½NE	1858-11-01		A1
2221	MARLOW, John	3	NWSW	1858-11-01		A1
2222	" "	3	W½NW	1858-11-01		A1
2258	MOORE, Solomon G	27	E½SE	1911-03-01		A1
2236	MORGAN, John W	2	NWNW	1858-11-01		A1
2237	" "	3	E½NW	1858-11-01		A1
2238	" "	3	NE	1858-11-01		A1
2165	NIX, Edward	27	SENW	1858-11-01		A1
2166	" "	27	SESW	1858-11-01		A1
2167	" "	27	W½SE	1858-11-01		A1
2168	" "	27	W½SW	1858-11-01		A1
2224	PICKETT, John	35	SENE	1858-09-01		A1
2225	" "	35	SESE	1858-09-01		A1
2226	" "	36	N½SE	1858-11-01		A1
2227	" "	36	NESW	1858-11-01		A1
2137	POWELL, Abraham C	13	S½	1858-11-01		A1
2156	POWELL, Coulman	14	W½NW	1860-04-02		A1
2157	" "	15	NENE	1860-04-02		A1
2256	QUARLES, Samuel	15	W½SE	1823-12-01		A1
2155	REAVES, Chisling M	14	SESW	1849-09-01		A1
2181	REESE, George	15	SENE	1852-12-01		A1
2152	REEVES, Cheselin M	2	N½NE	1858-09-01		A1
2153	" "	2	SENW	1858-09-01		A1
2154	REEVES, Cheslen M	14	SENW	1858-11-01		A1
2241	REEVES, Joseph J	12	N½	1858-11-01		A1
2270	REEVES, William W	23	E½NE	1858-09-01		A1
2271	" "	24	N½	1858-11-01		A1
2150	RHODES, Charlotte	36	S½SE	1849-09-01		A1
2151	" "	36	SESW	1849-09-01		A1
2212	ROAN, John D	25	W½NW	1849-09-01		A1
2149	SHEPHERD, Charles H	15	NWSW	1848-04-01		A1
2257	SKIPPER, Samuel	13	N½	1858-11-01		A1
2139	SMITH, Ambrose A	15	NWNE	1858-09-01		A1
2161	SMITH, David	11	N½SE	1858-11-01		A1
2162	" "	12	SW	1858-11-01		A1
2229	SMITH, John	36	S½NE	1849-09-01		A1
2230	" "	36	S½NW	1849-09-01		A1 F
2228	" "	25	SESE	1850-04-01		A1

ID	Individual in Patent	Sec.	Sec. Part	Date Issued	Other Counties	For More Info . . .
2231	SMYTH, John	25	E½SW	1858-11-01		A1
2232	" "	25	NESE	1858-11-01		A1
2233	" "	25	W½SE	1858-11-01		A1
2234	" "	36	NENE	1858-11-01		A1
2189	STAGGERS, Henry S	22	NENE	1838-07-28		A1
2188	" "	15	E½SW	1850-04-01		A1
2213	THOMAS, John F	10	NESE	1858-09-01	Butler	A1
2214	" "	10	SENE	1858-09-01	Butler	A1
2215	" "	11	N½SW	1858-09-01		A1
2216	" "	11	NW	1858-09-01		A1
2147	VANN, Calvin	27	NWNE	1858-09-01		A1
2146	" "	27	NENW	1858-11-01		A1
2148	" "	27	SWNE	1858-11-01		A1
2235	WHITTINGTON, John T	26	NE	1891-06-19		A2 V2160, 2195, 2269
2163	WILLIAMS, Drucilla	22	NWSE	1858-11-01		A1
2164	" "	22	W½NE	1858-11-01		A1

Map (Township Grid)

Section 3 / 2 / 1 (top row)

- MARLOW John 1858
- MORGAN John W 1858
- **3**
- MORGAN John W 1858
- MORGAN John W 1858
- DAVISON James T 1860
- REEVES Cheselin M 1858
- BOYETT Gibson 1858
- REEVES Cheselin M 1858
- **2**
- BOYETT Thomas 1858
- **1**

- MARLOW John 1858
- BOYETT Gibson 1858
- BOYETT Gibson 1858
- BOYETT Gibson 1858
- BOYETT Gibson 1858
- BOYETT Thomas 1858
- BOYETT Thomas 1858
- COOK Alexander H 1858

- BOYETT Gibson 1858
- BURNS Lauchlin 1858

Crenshaw

Sections 10 / 11 / 12

- *Butler*
- BURNS Lauchlin 1858
- BURNS Lauchlin 1858
- BURNS Lauchlin 1858
- THOMAS John F 1858
- **11**
- REEVES Joseph J 1858
- **12**

- BURNS Lauchlin 1858
- **10**
- THOMAS John F 1858

- BLACK Francis M 1858
- THOMAS John F 1858
- THOMAS John F 1858
- SMITH David 1858
- SMITH David 1858
- KELLEY Elisha 1858

- BLACK Francis M 1858
- BLACK Francis M 1858
- GRAHAM Joseph J 1858
- BLACK Robert W 1858
- BLACK Robert W 1858

Sections 15 / 14 / 13

- BLACK Francis M 1858
- SMITH Ambrose A 1858
- POWELL Coulman 1860
- POWELL Coulman 1860
- GRAHAM Joseph J 1858
- BLACK Robert W 1858
- SKIPPER Samuel 1858

- HAMMONDS John 1848
- HAMMONDS John 1849
- REESE George 1852
- REEVES Cheslen M 1858
- **13**

- SHEPHERD Charles H 1848
- **15**
- BUTLER John 1823
- BUTLER John 1823
- BLACK Robert W 1858
- POWELL Abraham C 1858

- HESTER James 1838
- STAGGERS Henry S 1850
- QUARLES Samuel 1823
- REAVES Chisling M 1849
- GILLIS John L 1858
- **14**

Sections 22 / 23 / 24

- BEDGOOD Richmond 1843
- JAMES Thomas F 1850
- STAGGERS Henry S 1838
- KETTLER Thomas S 1854
- GILLIS John L 1858
- REEVES William W 1858
- REEVES William W 1858

- WILLIAMS Drucilla 1858
- KETTLER Thomas S 1854
- BOAN John D 1858
- **24**

- **22**
- DENDY Buford W 1860
- WILLIAMS Drucilla 1858
- COOK John P 1860
- CALDWELL Elizabeth G 1858
- **23**
- BOAN John D 1858
- BOAN John D 1848
- BOAN John D 1858

- BOAN John D 1858

- FROST Hillrey 1850
- BEDGOOD John 1854
- BEDGOOD John 1854
- BOAN John D 1854
- CHILDRES David 1837
- BOAN John D 1853
- BOAN John D 1858

Sections 27 / 26 / 25

- HASTING Benjamin 1858
- VANN Calvin 1858
- VANN Calvin 1858
- BEDGOOD John 1858
- CALDWELL Elizabeth G 1858
- CALDWELL Elizabeth G 1858
- CALDWELL Elizabeth G 1858
- CHILDRES David
- CALDWELL Elizabeth G 1849
- BOAN John D 1858

- WHITTINGTON John 1891
- BOAN John D 1849

- NIX Edward 1858
- VANN Calvin 1858
- JAMES Robert A 1861
- **26**
- LONG James J 1837
- DAVIS William 1837
- BOAN John D 1858
- **25**

- **27**
- NIX Edward 1858
- JAMES Robert A 1861
- DAVIS William 1837
- CHILDRES David 1837
- SMYTH John 1858
- SMYTH John 1858

- NIX Edward 1858
- NIX Edward 1858
- MOORE Solomon G 1911
- JAMES Robert A 1861
- COOK Stephen H 1837
- SMYTH John 1858
- BOAN Frederick 1853
- SMITH John 1850

Sections 34 / 35 / 36

- BEASLEY William A 1858
- **34**
- LONG Mary 1858
- LONG Mary 1858
- COOK Stephen H 1837
- BOAN Frederick 1852
- SMYTH John 1858

- **35**
- PICKETT John 1858
- SMITH John 1849
- SMITH John 1849
- **36**

- KENNINGTON Arnold 1858
- COWART James A 1858
- DAVIS Benjamin B 1845
- PICKETT John 1858

- KENNINGTON Arnold 1858
- COWART James A 1858
- COWART James A 1858
- PICKETT John 1858
- DAVIS Benjamin 1838
- RHODES Charlotte 1849
- RHODES Charlotte 1849

Patent Map

T9-N R16-E
St Stephens Meridian

Map Group 10

Township Statistics

Parcels Mapped	:	135
Number of Patents	:	84
Number of Individuals	:	62
Patentees Identified	:	62
Number of Surnames	:	46
Multi-Patentee Parcels	:	0
Oldest Patent Date	:	12/1/1823
Most Recent Patent	:	3/1/1911
Block/Lot Parcels	:	0
Parcels Re - Issued	:	0
Parcels that Overlap	:	5
Cities and Towns	:	0
Cemeteries	:	1

Note: the area contained in this map amounts to far less than a full Township. Therefore, its contents are completely on this single page (instead of a "normal" 2-page spread).

Legend

——— Patent Boundary

——— Section Boundary

No Patents Found (or Outside County)

1., 2., 3., ... Lot Numbers (when beside a name)

[ ] Group Number (see Appendix "C")

Scale: Section = 1 mile X 1 mile (generally, with some exceptions)

Road Map

T9-N R16-E
St Stephens Meridian

Map Group 10

Note: the area contained in this map amounts to far less than a full Township. Therefore, its contents are completely on this single page (instead of a "normal" 2-page spread).

Cities & Towns
None

Cemeteries
Black Rock Cemetery

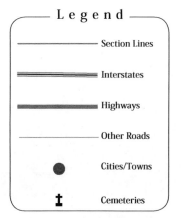

Legend

————————	Section Lines
≡≡≡≡≡≡≡≡	Interstates
━━━━━━━━	Highways
————————	Other Roads
●	Cities/Towns
✝	Cemeteries

Scale: Section = 1 mile X 1 mile
(generally, with some exceptions)

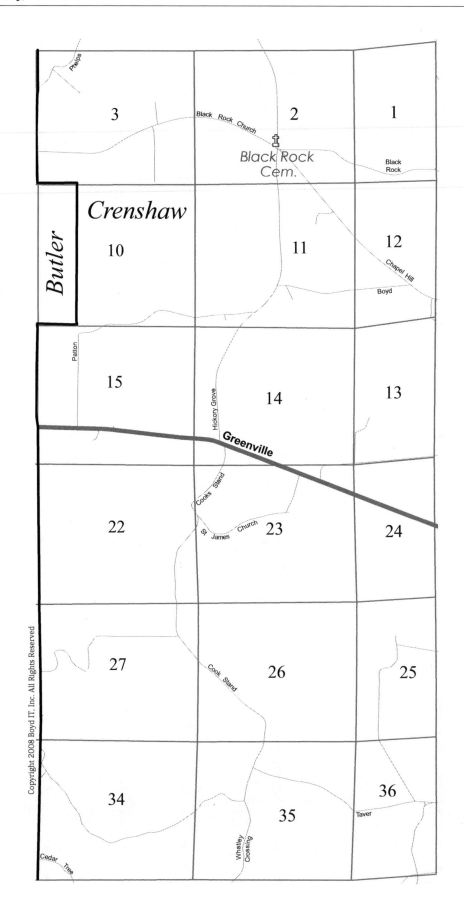

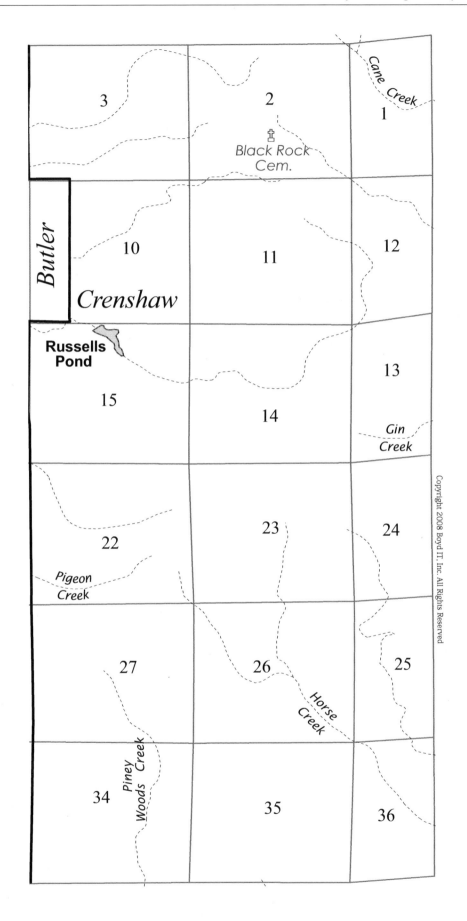

Note: the area contained in this map amounts to far less than a full Township. Therefore, its contents are completely on this single page (instead of a "normal" 2-page spread).

Cities & Towns
None

Cemeteries
Black Rock Cemetery

Legend
- Section Lines
- Railroads
- Large Rivers & Bodies of Water
- Streams/Creeks & Small Rivers
- Cities/Towns
- Cemeteries

Scale: Section = 1 mile X 1 mile
(there are some exceptions)

Map Group 11: Index to Land Patents

Township 9-North Range 17-East (St Stephens)

After you locate an individual in this Index, take note of the Section and Section Part then proceed to the Land Patent map on the pages immediately following. You should have no difficulty locating the corresponding parcel of land.

The "For More Info" Column will lead you to more information about the underlying Patents. See the *Legend* at right, and the "How to Use this Book" chapter, for more information.

```
┌─────────────────────────────────────────────────────────┐
│                        LEGEND                           │
│           "For More Info . . . " column                 │
│  ─────────────────────────────────────────────────────  │
│  A = Authority (Legislative Act, See Appendix "A")      │
│  B = Block or Lot (location in Section unknown)         │
│  C = Cancelled Patent                                   │
│  F = Fractional Section                                 │
│  G = Group (Multi-Patentee Patent, see Appendix "C")    │
│  V = Overlaps another Parcel                            │
│  R = Re-Issued (Parcel patented more than once)         │
│                                                         │
│  (A & G items require you to look in the Appendixes     │
│  referred to above. All other Letter-designations       │
│  followed by a number require you to locate line-items  │
│  in this index that possess the ID number found after   │
│  the letter).                                           │
└─────────────────────────────────────────────────────────┘
```

ID	Individual in Patent	Sec.	Sec. Part	Date Issued	Other Counties	For More Info . . .
2404	ARNOLD, John	8	NWSE	1837-08-12		A1
2403	" "	8	E½SW	1838-07-28		A1
2317	BENNETT, Frank	28	NWSE	1892-06-10		A2
2525	BENNETT, Toney	28	SWNW	1892-10-18		A2
2457	BENTLEY, Mary	21	NESW	1858-11-01		A1
2459	" "	21	SWNW	1858-11-01		A1
2460	" "	21	W½SW	1858-11-01		A1
2461	" "	28	NENW	1858-11-01		A1
2458	" "	21	NWSE	1862-01-01		A1
2462	" "	28	NWNW	1862-01-01		A1
2463	" "	28	SENW	1862-01-01		A1
2315	BLACKMON, Eze H	35	NESW	1858-11-01		A1
2316	"	35	SESW	1858-11-01		A1
2318	BOAN, Frederick	22	SWSE	1838-07-28		A1
2371	BOAN, Hicks C	30	NWNW	1891-09-15		A2
2308	BOLAN, Drury	2	NWNE	1858-11-01		A1
2440	BOYETER, Lemuel T	6	W½SE	1858-11-01		A1
2499	BOYETER, Thomas	4	SWSW	1853-08-01		A1
2500	"	8	S½NE	1858-11-01		A1
2501	"	9	SWNW	1858-11-01		A1
2311	BRIGGS, Elkanah	32	SESE	1837-08-02		A1
2466	BRIGGS, Michael	33	SWSW	1837-05-15		A1
2502	BRIGGS, Thomas H	17	NENE	1837-08-12		A1
2504	"	17	W½NE	1838-07-28		A1
2507	"	8	SESE	1838-07-28		A1
2505	"	21	SWNE	1841-05-20		A1
2503	"	17	S½NW	1858-11-01		A1
2506	"	8	NESE	1858-11-01		A1
2508	"	8	SWSE	1858-11-01		A1
2305	BROWDER, David	7	SWSE	1854-07-15		A1
2302	" "	19	E½SE	1862-01-01		A1
2303	" "	29	NWNW	1862-01-01		A1
2304	" "	30	NENE	1862-01-01		A1
2569	BROWDER, William T	20	E½SW	1860-04-02		A1
2570	" "	20	NW	1860-04-02		A1
2571	" "	20	NWSE	1860-04-02		A1
2572	" "	20	NWSW	1860-04-02		A1
2275	BROWN, Angus	26	SENE	1837-05-20		A1
2276	" "	26	W½NE	1837-05-20		A1
2274	" "	25	NWNW	1837-08-15		A1
2324	BRYAN, George	24	E½SW	1858-11-01		A1
2325	" "	24	NW	1858-11-01		A1
2326	" "	24	NWSW	1858-11-01		A1
2293	BURK, Daniel J	34	E½NW	1860-04-02		A1
2294	" "	34	E½SE	1860-04-02		A1
2295	" "	34	E½SW	1860-04-02		A1

ID	Individual in Patent	Sec.	Sec. Part	Date Issued	Other Counties	For More Info . . .
2296	BURK, Daniel J (Cont'd)	34	NWNW	1860-04-02		A1
2297	" "	34	SWSE	1860-04-02		A1
2312	BURK, Elzathan	21	E½NE	1831-11-30		A1
2430	BURK, Joseph M	31	SENW	1858-11-01		A1
2313	BURKE, Elzathan	34	SWNW	1834-09-04		A1
2319	BUSH, Frederick	32	E½NE	1862-01-01		A1
2320	" "	33	NENE	1862-01-01		A1
2321	" "	33	SENW	1862-01-01		A1
2322	" "	33	W½NE	1862-01-01		A1
2323	" "	33	W½NW	1862-01-01		A1
2306	CATHCART, David	14	W½NW	1837-04-10		A1 F
2472	CHILDERS, Paschael W	8	SWNW	1854-07-15		A1
2470	" "	8	E½NW	1858-11-01		A1
2471	" "	8	NWNW	1858-11-01		A1
2286	CLANCY, Daniel	26	W½SE	1837-08-14		A1
2288	" "	35	NWNE	1837-08-14		A1
2282	" "	22	NESE	1848-05-03		A1
2287	" "	35	NENW	1852-12-01		A1
2285	" "	26	SESW	1853-11-15		A1
2283	" "	25	S½NW	1858-11-01		A1
2284	" "	26	SESE	1858-11-01		A1
2289	" "	35	NWNW	1858-11-01		A1
2290	" "	35	SENW	1858-11-01		A1
2291	" "	35	SWNE	1858-11-01		A1
2292	" "	35	W½SE	1858-11-01		A1
2278	DAVIS, Benjamin	31	NESW	1838-07-28		A1
2373	DAVIS, Isaac	29	NE	1900-11-28		A2
2385	DAVIS, James	31	SWSE	1837-08-15		A1
2383	" "	31	SESE	1838-07-28		A1
2381	" "	31	NWSE	1858-11-01		A1
2382	" "	31	SENE	1858-11-01		A1
2384	" "	31	SESW	1858-11-01		A1
2386	" "	31	W½NE	1858-11-01		A1
2433	DAVIS, Joshiah	21	NESE	1838-07-28		A1
2434	" "	22	NWSW	1838-07-28		A1
2438	DAVIS, Josiah	22	W½NW	1837-08-02		A1
2439	" "	28	W½NE	1838-07-28		A1
2437	" "	22	E½SW	1847-05-01		A1
2497	DYKES, Stephen	14	SENW	1858-11-01		A1
2498	" "	14	W½SE	1858-11-01		A1
2417	FOWLE, John S	25	S½SE	1835-10-08		A1
2477	GABLE, Rachael A	29	S½SW	1860-04-02		A1
2478	" "	29	W½SE	1860-04-02		A1
2479	" "	31	NENE	1860-04-02		A1
2480	" "	32	N½NW	1860-04-02		A1
2481	" "	32	NWNE	1860-04-02		A1
2450	GIPSON, Lewis E	23	NENE	1858-11-01		A1
2452	" "	23	SWNE	1858-11-01		A1
2449	" "	14	SESW	1860-04-02		A1
2451	" "	23	SESW	1860-04-02		A1
2453	" "	23	W½NW	1860-04-02		A1
2454	" "	23	W½SW	1860-04-02		A1
2448	" "	14	NENW	1860-10-01		A1
2273	GOULD, Alexander	6	SENW	1892-01-18		A2
2400	GREEN, Jesse	4	NWNE	1891-05-29		A2
2486	HALE, Richard	10	NESW	1837-08-09		A1
2455	HARRELL, Louis	25	NWSE	1858-11-01		A1
2546	HARRIS, William	1	E½SE	1862-01-01		A1
2432	HERNDON, Joseph W	19	W½NW	1858-11-01		A1
2340	INGRAM, Green	6	E½NE	1860-10-01		A1
2363	JACKSON, Henry F	2	SESE	1860-10-01		A1
2359	" "	12	N½SE	1860-12-01		A1
2360	" "	12	NESW	1860-12-01		A1
2361	" "	12	SENW	1860-12-01		A1
2362	" "	12	SWNE	1860-12-01		A1
2547	JACKSON, William	10	W½NE	1860-04-02		A1
2548	" "	2	E½SW	1860-04-02		A1
2549	" "	2	SWNE	1860-04-02		A1
2550	" "	2	W½SE	1860-04-02		A1
2456	JAMES, Mahala	33	NENW	1858-11-01		A1
2429	JONES, Joseph	32	SENW	1858-09-01		A1
2551	JONES, William K	10	NENE	1858-11-01		A1
2552	" "	11	E½NE	1858-11-01		A1

ID	Individual in Patent	Sec.	Sec. Part	Date Issued	Other Counties	For More Info . . .
2307	JORDAN, David M	11	NWNW	1852-02-02		A1
2530	JORDAN, Wiley	33	SENE	1858-11-01		A1
2309	KELLEY, Elisha	7	W½SW	1858-11-01		A1
2526	KELLEY, Wade H	6	SWNE	1885-03-16		A1
2493	KELLY, Sarah A	6	E½SE	1896-02-10		A2
2412	KENT, John	8	NWSW	1854-07-15		A1
2410	" "	7	N½SE	1858-09-01		A1
2411	" "	7	NESW	1858-09-01		A1
2445	KENT, Levi	21	E½NW	1831-08-01		A1
2441	" "	17	E½SE	1837-08-02		A1
2446	" "	21	NWNE	1837-08-02		A1
2447	" "	21	NWNW	1837-08-02		A1
2442	" "	17	SW	1838-07-28		A1
2443	" "	17	W½SE	1838-07-28		A1
2444	" "	20	NE	1853-11-15		A1
2464	KENT, Mary	21	SESW	1838-07-28		A1
2465	" "	21	SWSE	1838-07-28		A1
2553	KNIGHT, William	10	SENE	1860-10-01		A1
2554	" "	2	NESE	1860-10-01		A1
2367	LEAIRD, Henry	22	SESE	1848-04-01		A1
2369	" "	27	NENE	1848-04-01		A1
2368	" "	26	SENW	1849-09-01		A1
2388	LEE, James H	4	NWSE	1891-11-23		A2
2389	" "	4	SWNE	1891-11-23		A2
2372	LINTON, Hugh	23	NWSE	1837-05-20		A1
2413	LINTON, John	23	SENE	1838-07-28		A1
2365	LONG, Henry J	10	SENW	1860-09-01		A1
2366	" "	10	SWSW	1860-09-01		A1
2364	" "	10	NENW	1860-12-01		A1
2488	LONG, Robert B	10	NWSW	1862-01-01		A1
2489	" "	10	SESW	1862-01-01		A1
2494	LONG, Sarah	15	N½NW	1862-01-01		A1
2555	LONG, William	15	SW	1837-04-15		A1
2559	" "	22	NWNE	1837-08-14		A1
2557	" "	22	E½NE	1841-05-20		A1
2558	" "	22	E½NW	1841-05-20		A1
2560	" "	22	SWNE	1841-05-20		A1
2556	" "	15	SWNW	1850-04-01		A1
2561	LONGFELLOW, William	15	W½SE	1834-10-21		A1
2510	MAHONE, Thomas	14	E½SE	1860-04-02		A1 V2511, 2512
2511	" "	14	NESE	1860-04-02		A1 V2510
2512	" "	14	SESE	1860-04-02		A1 V2510
2513	" "	15	SENE	1860-04-02		A1
2517	" "	26	NENE	1860-04-02		A1
2509	" "	12	SENE	1862-01-01		A1
2514	" "	15	SENW	1862-01-01		A1
2515	" "	15	SWNE	1862-01-01		A1
2516	" "	23	SENW	1862-01-01		A1
2532	MARSHALL, William B	19	SESW	1860-04-02		A1
2531	" "	19	NE	1862-01-01		A1
2533	" "	20	E½SE	1862-01-01		A1
2534	" "	20	SWSE	1862-01-01		A1
2535	" "	29	NENW	1862-01-01		A1
2536	" "	3	E½NW	1862-01-01		A1
2537	" "	3	SW	1862-01-01		A1
2538	" "	3	W½NE	1862-01-01		A1
2539	" "	30	SESW	1862-01-01		A1
2540	" "	30	SWSE	1862-01-01		A1
2541	" "	4	E½NE	1862-01-01		A1
2542	" "	4	E½SE	1862-01-01		A1
2543	" "	8	SWSW	1862-01-01		A1
2468	MASH, Nathan	4	E½SW	1860-10-01		A1
2469	" "	4	NWSW	1860-10-01		A1
2277	MCCARTY, Beckey	4	SWSE	1892-01-18		A2
2405	MCGEHEE, John H	1	E½SW	1862-01-01		A1
2406	" "	1	SENW	1862-01-01		A1
2407	" "	1	W½SE	1862-01-01		A1
2408	" "	12	N½NE	1862-01-01		A1
2409	" "	12	NENW	1862-01-01		A1
2435	MILES, Joshua	8	NENE	1837-08-09		A1
2436	" "	9	NWNW	1837-08-09		A1
2487	MILLER, Richard	2	SENE	1891-06-29		A2
2414	MILLS, John	18		1838-07-28		A1

ID	Individual in Patent	Sec.	Sec. Part	Date Issued	Other Counties	For More Info . . .
2496	MOORE, Solomon G	36	NWNE	1901-12-17		A2
2331	MOYE, George W	19	W½SE	1858-11-01		A1
2332	"	30	NWNE	1858-11-01		A1
2280	ODWYER, Cornelius	32	SESW	1858-11-01		A1
2281	" "	32	W½SE	1858-11-01		A1
2467	PERDUE, Milton A	31	SWNW	1849-09-01		A1
2544	PERKINS, William H	28	E½SW	1860-10-01		A1
2545	" "	28	NWSW	1862-04-10		A1
2483	PERRITT, Rebecca	14	NWSW	1837-05-20		A1
2484	" "	14	SWNW	1837-05-20		A1
2485	" "	14	W½NE	1858-11-01		A1
2482	" "	14	E½NE	1860-04-02		A1
2398	PETTY, James	4	S½NW	1891-06-10		A2
2415	PICKETT, John	31	W½SW	1848-04-01		A1
2310	PITMAN, Elizabeth B	24	SWSW	1852-02-02		A1
2376	RAINER, James D	31	NESE	1858-11-01		A1
2377	" "	32	SWNE	1858-11-01		A1
2378	" "	32	SWNW	1858-11-01		A1
2379	" "	32	SWSW	1862-01-01		A1
2416	RAMBO, John R	30	E½SE	1893-07-24		A2
2395	REAVES, James M	7	NENW	1853-11-15		A1
2402	REAVES, Jesse W	3	NWNW	1858-11-01		A1
2387	REEVES, James E	8	NWNE	1858-11-01		A1
2401	RIDGWAY, Jesse H	32	NWSW	1849-09-01		A1
2562	RIDGWAY, William	22	NWSE	1850-04-01		A1
2565	" "	27	NWNE	1850-04-01		A1
2566	" "	27	SENE	1850-04-01		A1
2563	" "	26	SWSW	1858-11-01		A1
2564	" "	27	NESE	1858-11-01		A1
2567	" "	27	SESE	1858-11-01		A1
2568	" "	34	NENE	1858-11-01		A1
2490	ROBBINS, Sampson R	34	NWNE	1860-10-01		A1
2279	ROBINSON, Burrill L	28	SWSW	1884-03-20		A1
2341	RODGERS, Harvy	25	SWNE	1858-11-01		A1
2342	" "	26	NENW	1858-11-01		A1
2344	" "	27	E½SW	1858-11-01		A1
2345	" "	27	NWSE	1858-11-01		A1
2347	" "	27	SENW	1858-11-01		A1
2348	" "	27	SWNE	1858-11-01		A1
2350	" "	9	NWSE	1858-11-01		A1
2351	" "	9	SENW	1858-11-01		A1
2352	" "	9	SWNE	1858-11-01		A1
2343	" "	26	NWNW	1862-01-01		A1
2346	" "	27	NWSW	1862-01-01		A1
2349	" "	27	SWNW	1862-01-01		A1
2473	RODGERS, Peter	28	E½NE	1888-01-21		A2
2358	ROGERS, Harvy	9	SWSE	1837-08-12		A1
2353	" "	22	SWSW	1853-11-15		A1
2354	" "	25	NENW	1853-11-15		A1
2355	" "	25	NWNE	1853-11-15		A1
2357	" "	27	NENW	1853-11-15		A1
2356	" "	26	NESW	1854-10-02		A1
2390	ROGERS, James H	4	N½NW	1896-05-21		A2
2431	SCIPPER, Joseph	2	E½NW	1884-12-05		A2
2492	SCIPPER, Samuel	3	NESE	1852-02-02		A1
2491	" "	2	NWSW	1860-10-01		A1
2524	SKAINS, Thomas	34	W½SW	1838-07-28		A1
2314	SKIPPER, Evander	9	SW	1901-01-23		A2
2418	SKIPPER, John	3	SWNW	1862-01-01		A1
2419	SMITH, John	30	W½SW	1843-02-01		A1
2422	SMYTH, John	32	NESW	1850-08-10		A1
2420	" "	30	SWNW	1858-11-01		A1
2421	" "	31	NWNW	1858-11-01		A1
2370	SOLOMON, Henry	26	NESE	1837-08-14		A1
2272	SORRELLS, Albert J	9	E½SE	1900-11-28		A2
2423	SOWELL, John	12	NWSW	1860-04-02		A1
2424	" "	12	S½SE	1860-04-02		A1
2425	" "	12	S½SW	1860-04-02		A1
2426	" "	12	W½NW	1860-04-02		A1
2427	" "	13	NENE	1860-04-02		A1
2428	" "	13	W½	1862-01-01		A1
2495	SPIVEY, Sherwood	25	NESW	1837-08-15		A1
2328	STAGGERS, George J	36	NENW	1852-12-01		A1

ID	Individual in Patent	Sec.	Sec. Part	Date Issued	Other Counties	For More Info . . .
2327	STAGGERS, George J (Cont'd)	25	SESW	1858-11-01		A1
2329	" "	36	SE	1858-11-01		A1
2330	" "	36	SESW	1858-11-01		A1
2399	STAGGERS, James	13	E½SE	1837-08-15		A1
2396	STAGGERS, James M	25	NESE	1837-08-14		A1
2397	STARLING, James M	14	NESW	1849-09-01		A1
2298	STARR, Daniel S	32	NESE	1840-10-10		A1
2299	" "	33	E½SW	1840-10-10		A1
2300	" "	33	NWSW	1840-10-10		A1
2301	" "	33	W½SE	1840-10-10		A1
2393	THAGARD, James L	25	NENE	1849-09-01		A1
2391	" "	24	E½SE	1858-11-01		A1
2392	" "	24	W½SE	1858-11-01		A1
2394	" "	25	SENE	1858-11-01		A1
2518	THAGARD, Thomas S	35	E½NE	1858-11-01		A1
2519	" "	35	E½SE	1858-11-01		A1
2520	" "	36	NESW	1858-11-01		A1
2521	" "	36	SENW	1858-11-01		A1
2522	" "	36	W½NW	1858-11-01		A1
2523	" "	36	W½SW	1858-11-01		A1
2527	THAGARD, Warren R	13	W½SE	1858-11-01		A1
2528	" "	24	NE	1858-11-01		A1
2529	THAGGARD, Warren R	34	SENE	1860-10-01		A1
2573	WATSON, Willis	28	E½SE	1860-10-01		A1
2574	" "	28	SWSE	1860-10-01		A1
2380	WILLIAMSON, James D	10	W½NW	1894-06-15		A2
2474	WILLIAMSON, Prince A	9	E½NE	1900-11-28		A2
2475	" "	9	NENW	1900-11-28		A2
2476	" "	9	NWNE	1900-11-28		A2
2334	WRIGHT, George W	10	SESE	1858-11-01		A1
2337	" "	11	SWSW	1858-11-01		A1
2338	" "	14	NWNW	1858-11-01		A1
2333	" "	10	NESE	1860-04-02		A1
2335	" "	10	W½SE	1860-04-02		A1
2336	" "	11	SESW	1862-01-01		A1
2339	" "	15	NWNE	1862-01-01		A1
2374	WYCHE, Isaac	6	NENW	1891-05-29		A2
2375	" "	6	NWNE	1891-05-29		A2

Patent Map

T9-N R17-E
St Stephens Meridian

Map Group 11

Township Statistics

Parcels Mapped	:	303
Number of Patents	:	200
Number of Individuals	:	119
Patentees Identified	:	119
Number of Surnames	:	87
Multi-Patentee Parcels	:	0
Oldest Patent Date	:	8/1/1831
Most Recent Patent	:	12/17/1901
Block/Lot Parcels	:	0
Parcels Re-Issued	:	0
Parcels that Overlap	:	3
Cities and Towns	:	6
Cemeteries	:	2

Patent map grid:

Section 6: WYCHE Isaac 1891; WYCHE Isaac 1891; GOULD Alexander 1892; KELLEY Wade H 1885; INGRAM Green 1860; BOYETER Lemuel T 1858; KELLY Sarah A 1896

Section 5

Section 4: ROGERS James H 1896; GREEN Jesse 1891; MARSHALL William B 1862; PETTY James 1891; LEE James H 1891; MASH Nathan 1860; LEE James H 1891; MASH Nathan 1860; BOYTER Thomas 1853; MCCARTY Beckey 1892; MARSHALL William B 1862

Section 7: REAVES James M 1853; KELLEY Elisha 1858; KENT John 1858; KENT John 1858; BROWDER David 1854

Section 8: CHILDERS Paschael W 1858; CHILDERS Paschael W 1854; CHILDERS Paschael W 1858; KENT John 1854; KENT John 1858; MARSHALL William B 1862; ARNOLD John 1838; REEVES James E 1858; MILES Joshua 1837; BOYTER Thomas 1858; ARNOLD John 1837; BRIGGS Thomas H 1858; BRIGGS Thomas H 1858

Section 9: MILES Joshua 1837; WILLIAMSON Prince A 1900; WILLIAMSON Prince A 1900; WILLIAMSON Prince A 1900; BOYTER Thomas 1858; RODGERS Harvy 1858; RODGERS Harvy 1858; SKIPPER Evander 1901; RODGERS Harvy 1858; SORRELLS Albert J 1900; ROGERS Harvy 1837

Section 18: MILLS John 1838

Section 17: BRIGGS Thomas H 1838; BRIGGS Thomas H 1837; BRIGGS Thomas H 1858; KENT Levi 1838; KENT Levi 1838; KENT Levi 1838; KENT Levi 1837

Section 16

Section 19: HERNDON Joseph W 1858; MARSHALL William B 1862; MOYE George W 1858; MARSHALL William B 1860; BROWDER David 1862

Section 20: BROWDER William T 1860; KENT Levi 1853; BROWDER William T 1860; BROWDER William T 1860; BROWDER William T 1860; MARSHALL William B 1862; MARSHALL William B 1862

Section 21: KENT Levi 1837; KENT Levi 1831; KENT Levi 1837; BURK Elzathan 1831; BENTLEY Mary 1858; BRIGGS Thomas H 1841; BENTLEY Mary 1858; BENTLEY Mary 1862; DAVIS Joshiah 1838; BENTLEY Mary 1858; KENT Mary 1838; KENT Mary 1838

Section 30: BOAN Hicks C 1891; SMYTH John 1858; SMITH John 1843; MOYE George W 1858; BROWDER David 1862; RAMBO John R 1893; MARSHALL William B 1862; MARSHALL William B 1862

Section 29: BROWDER David 1862; MARSHALL William B 1862; DAVIS Isaac 1900; GABLE Rachael A 1860; GABLE Rachael A 1860

Section 28: BENTLEY Mary 1862; BENTLEY Mary 1858; DAVIS Josiah 1838; RODGERS Peter 1888; BENNETT Toney 1892; BENTLEY Mary 1862; PERKINS William H 1862; PERKINS William H 1860; BENNETT Frank 1892; WATSON Willis 1860; ROBINSON Burrill L 1884; WATSON Willis 1860

Section 31: SMYTH John 1858; DAVIS James 1858; GABLE Rachael A 1860; PERDUE Milton A 1849; BURK Joseph M 1858; DAVIS James 1858; PICKETT John 1848; DAVIS Benjamin 1838; DAVIS James 1858; RAINER James D 1858; DAVIS James 1858; DAVIS James 1837; DAVIS James 1838

Section 32: GABLE Rachael A 1860; GABLE Rachael A 1860; RAINER James D 1858; JONES Joseph 1858; RAINER James D 1858; BUSH Frederick 1862; RIDGWAY Jesse H 1849; SMYTH John 1850; ODWYER Cornelius 1858; STARR Daniel S 1840; RAINER James D 1862; ODWYER Cornelius 1858; BRIGGS Elkanah 1837

Section 33: BUSH Frederick 1862; JAMES Mahala 1858; BUSH Frederick 1862; BUSH Frederick 1862; BUSH Frederick 1862; JORDAN Wiley 1858; STARR Daniel S 1840; STARR Daniel S 1840; STARR Daniel S 1840; BRIGGS Michael 1837; STARR Daniel S 1840

Section 3
REAVES Jesse W 1858
SKIPPER John 1862
MARSHALL William B 1862
MARSHALL William B 1862
MARSHALL William B 1862

Section 2
SCIPPER Joseph 1884
BOLAN Drury 1858
JACKSON William 1860
MILLER Richard 1891
SCIPPER Samuel 1852
SCIPPER Samuel 1860
JACKSON William 1860
2
KNIGHT William 1860
JACKSON William 1860
JACKSON Henry F 1860

Section 1
MCGEHEE John H 1862
1
MCGEHEE John H 1862
MCGEHEE John H 1862
MCGEHEE John H 1862
HARRIS William 1862

Section 10
WILLIAMSON James D 1894
LONG Henry J 1860
LONG Henry J 1860
JONES William K 1858
JACKSON William 1860
KNIGHT William 1860
LONG Robert B 1862
HALE Richard 1837
10
WRIGHT George W 1860
LONG Henry J 1860
LONG Robert B 1862
WRIGHT George W 1860
WRIGHT George W 1858

Section 11
JORDAN David M 1852
11
JONES William K 1858
WRIGHT George W 1862
WRIGHT George W 1858

Section 12
MCGEHEE John H 1862
SOWELL John 1860
MCGEHEE John H 1862
JACKSON Henry F 1860
JACKSON Henry F 1860
MAHONE Thomas 1862
SOWELL John 1860
JACKSON Henry F 1860
12
JACKSON Henry F 1860
SOWELL John 1860
SOWELL John 1860

Section 15
LONG Sarah 1862
WRIGHT George W 1862
LONG William 1850
MAHONE Thomas 1862
MAHONE Thomas 1862
MAHONE Thomas 1860
15
LONGFELLOW William 1834
LONG William 1837

Section 14
WRIGHT George W 1858
CATHCART David 1837
PERRITT Rebecca 1837
GIPSON Lewis E 1860
PERRITT Rebecca 1858
DYKES Stephen 1858
14
PERRITT Rebecca 1837
STARLING James M 1849
GIPSON Lewis E 1860
DYKES Stephen 1858

Section 13
PERRITT Rebecca 1860
SOWELL John 1862
SOWELL John 1860
13
MAHONE Thomas 1860
MAHONE Thomas 1860
MAHONE Thomas 1860
THAGARD Warren R 1858
STAGGERS James 1837

Section 22
DAVIS Josiah 1837
LONG William 1841
LONG William 1837
22
DAVIS Josiah 1838
DAVIS Josiah 1847
RIDGWAY William 1850
ROGERS Harvy 1853
BOAN Frederick 1838

Section 23
LONG William 1837
LONG William 1841
LONG William 1841
GIPSON Lewis E 1860
MAHONE Thomas 1862
GIPSON Lewis E 1858
CLANCY Daniel 1848
LEAIRD Henry 1848
23
GIPSON Lewis E 1860
GIPSON Lewis E 1860

Section 24
GIPSON Lewis E 1858
LINTON John 1838
LINTON Hugh 1837
BRYAN George 1858
BRYAN George 1858
BRYAN George 1858
PITMAN Elizabeth B 1852
THAGARD Warren R 1858
24
THAGARD James L 1858
THAGARD James L 1858

Section 27
ROGERS Harvy 1853
RIDGWAY William 1850
LEAIRD Henry 1848
RODGERS Harvy 1862
RODGERS Harvy 1858
27
RODGERS Harvy 1858
RIDGWAY William 1850
RODGERS Harvy 1862
RODGERS Harvy 1858
RODGERS Harvy 1858
RIDGWAY William 1858
RIDGWAY William 1858

Section 26
RODGERS Harvy 1862
RODGERS Harvy 1862
BROWN Angus 1837
LEAIRD Henry 1849
26
ROGERS Harvy 1854
RIDGWAY William 1858
CLANCY Daniel 1853

Section 25
MAHONE Thomas 1860
BROWN Angus 1837
BROWN Angus 1837
CLANCY Daniel 1837
ROGERS Harvy 1853
CLANCY Daniel 1858
25
ROGERS Harvy 1853
RODGERS Harvy 1858
SOLOMON Henry 1837
SPIVEY Sherwood 1837
HARRELL Louis 1858
CLANCY Daniel 1858
THAGARD James L 1849
THAGARD James L 1858
STAGGERS James M 1837
STAGGERS George J 1858
FOWLE John S 1835

Section 34
BURK Daniel J 1860
BURK Daniel J 1860
ROBBINS Sampson R 1860
RIDGWAY William 1858
BURKE Elzathan 1834
THAGGARD Warren R 1860
34
SKAINS Thomas 1838
BURK Daniel J 1860
BURK Daniel J 1860
BURK Daniel J 1860

Section 35
CLANCY Daniel 1852
CLANCY Daniel 1858
CLANCY Daniel 1837
CLANCY Daniel 1858
BLACKMON Eze H 1858
35
CLANCY Daniel 1858
BLACKMON Eze H 1858
THAGARD Thomas S 1858
THAGARD Thomas S 1858

Section 36
STAGGERS George J 1852
MOORE Solomon G 1901
THAGARD Thomas S 1858
THAGARD Thomas S 1858
THAGARD Thomas S 1858
36
THAGARD Thomas S 1858
STAGGERS George J 1858
STAGGERS George J 1858

Helpful Hints

1. This Map's INDEX can be found on the preceding pages.

2. Refer to Map "C" to see where this Township lies within Crenshaw County, Alabama.

3. Numbers within square brackets [ ] denote a multi-patentee land parcel (multi-owner). Refer to Appendix "C" for a full list of members in this group.

4. Areas that look to be crowded with Patentees usually indicate multiple sales of the same parcel (Re-issues) or Overlapping parcels. See this Township's Index for an explanation of these and other circumstances that might explain "odd" groupings of Patentees on this map.

Legend

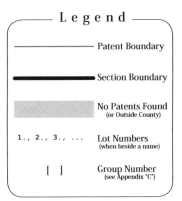

———— Patent Boundary

━━━━ Section Boundary

No Patents Found (or Outside County)

1., 2., 3., ... Lot Numbers (when beside a name)

[ ] Group Number (see Appendix "C")

Scale: Section = 1 mile X 1 mile (generally, with some exceptions)

Road Map

T9-N R17-E
St Stephens Meridian

Map Group 11

Cities & Towns

Centenary
Cherokee Village
Ivy Creek
Moodys Crossroads
Robinson Crossroads
Rutledge

Cemeteries

Lightfoot Cemetery
Siloam Cemetery

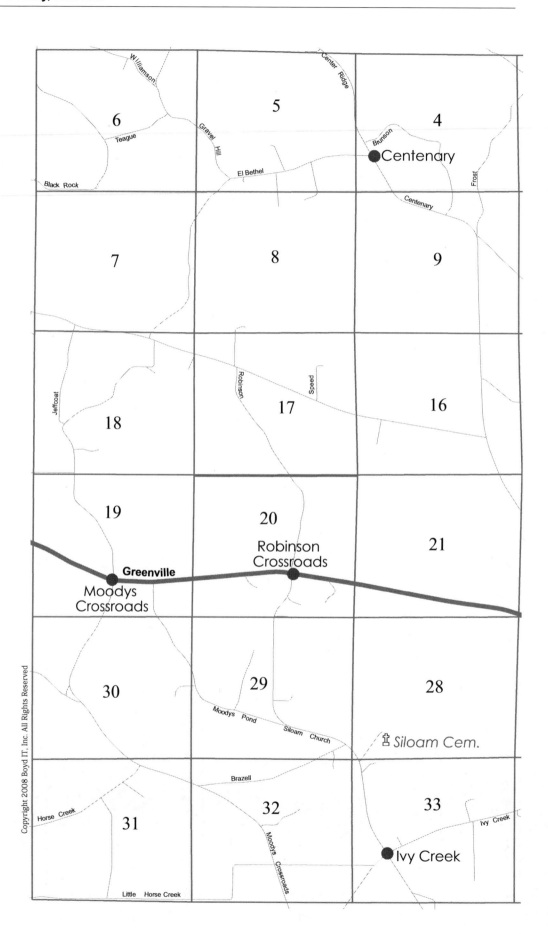

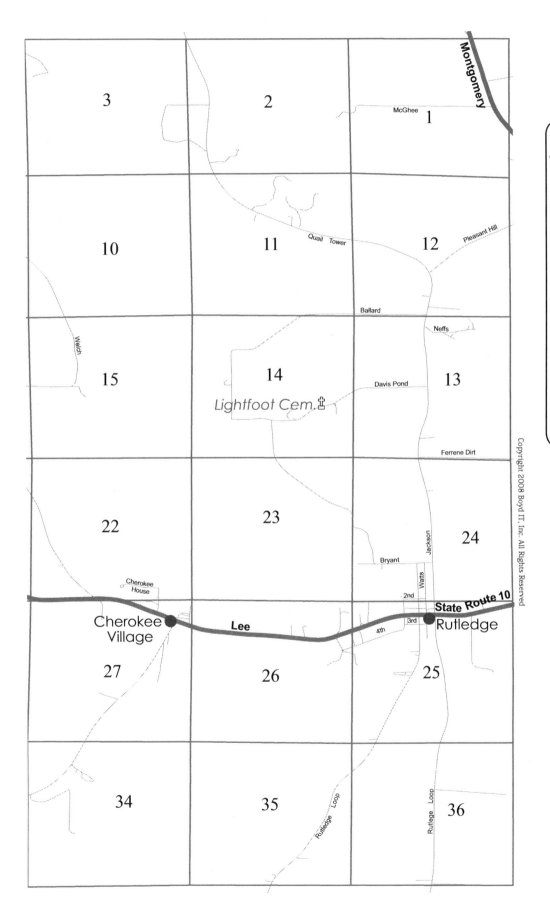

3

2

McGhee 1

Montgomery

10

11

Quail   Tower

12

Pleasant Hill

Ballard

Neffs

Welch

15

14

13

Davis Pond

Lightfoot Cem. ☩

Ferrene Dirt

22

23

24

Jackson

Bryant

Watts

2nd

Cherokee
House

Cherokee
Village

Lee

3rd

Rutledge

State Route 10

4th

27

26

25

34

35

Rutledge Loop

Rutledge Loop

36

Helpful Hints

1. This road map has a number of uses, but primarily it is to help you: a) find the present location of land owned by your ancestors (at least the general area), b) find cemeteries and city-centers, and c) estimate the route/roads used by Census-takers & tax-assessors.

2. If you plan to travel to Crenshaw County to locate cemeteries or land parcels, please pick up a modern travel map for the area before you do. Mapping old land parcels on modern maps is not as exact a science as you might think. Just the slightest variations in public land survey coordinates, estimates of parcel boundaries, or road-map deviations can greatly alter a map's representation of how a road either does or doesn't cross a particular parcel of land.

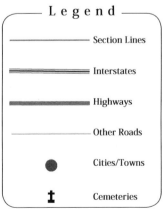

L e g e n d

—————— Section Lines

════════ Interstates

▬▬▬▬▬ Highways

—————— Other Roads

● Cities/Towns

☩ Cemeteries

Scale: Section = 1 mile X 1 mile
(generally, with some exceptions)

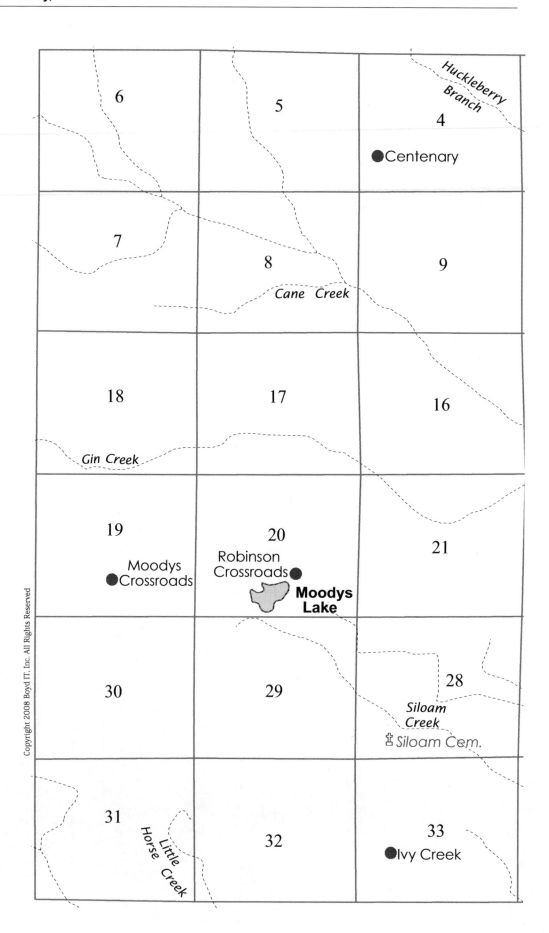

Historical Map

T9-N   R17-E
St Stephens Meridian

Map Group 11

Cities & Towns
Centenary
Cherokee Village
Ivy Creek
Moodys Crossroads
Robinson Crossroads
Rutledge

Cemeteries
Lightfoot Cemetery
Siloam Cemetery

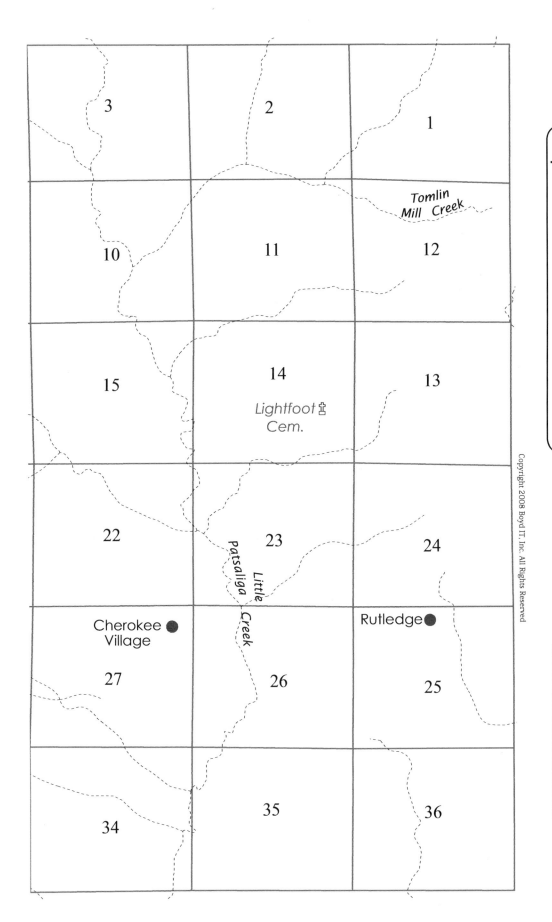

3

2

1

Tomlin Mill Creek

10

11

12

15

14

13

Lightfoot ⚰ Cem.

22

23

24

Little Patsaliga Creek

Cherokee Village ●

Rutledge ●

27

26

25

34

35

36

Helpful Hints

1. This Map takes a different look at the same Congressional Township displayed in the preceding two maps. It presents features that can help you better envision the historical development of the area: a) Water-bodies (lakes & ponds), b) Water-courses (rivers, streams, etc.), c) Railroads, d) City/town center-points (where they were oftentimes located when first settled), and e) Cemeteries.

2. Using this "Historical" map in tandem with this Township's Patent Map and Road Map, may lead you to some interesting discoveries. You will often find roads, towns, cemeteries, and waterways are named after nearby landowners: sometimes those names will be the ones you are researching. See how many of these research gems you can find here in Crenshaw County.

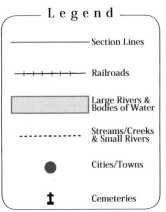

L e g e n d

──────── Section Lines

┼┼┼┼┼┼ Railroads

▭ Large Rivers & Bodies of Water

------- Streams/Creeks & Small Rivers

● Cities/Towns

⚰ Cemeteries

Scale: Section = 1 mile X 1 mile
(there are some exceptions)

Map Group 12: Index to Land Patents

Township 9-North Range 18-East (St Stephens)

After you locate an individual in this Index, take note of the Section and Section Part then proceed to the Land Patent map on the pages immediately following. You should have no difficulty locating the corresponding parcel of land.

The "For More Info" Column will lead you to more information about the underlying Patents. See the *Legend* at right, and the "How to Use this Book" chapter, for more information.

```
LEGEND
              "For More Info . . . " column
A = Authority (Legislative Act, See Appendix "A")
B = Block or Lot (location in Section unknown)
C = Cancelled Patent
F = Fractional Section
G = Group (Multi-Patentee Patent, see Appendix "C")
V = Overlaps another Parcel
R = Re-Issued (Parcel patented more than once)

(A & G items require you to look in the Appendixes referred
to above. All other Letter-designations followed by a number
require you to locate line-items in this index that possess
the ID number found after the letter).
```

ID	Individual in Patent	Sec.	Sec. Part	Date Issued	Other Counties	For More Info . . .
2807	AXSON, Thomas D	13	S½NE	1897-02-17		A1
2725	BOGGS, Joseph J	18	SWSW	1875-04-20		A1
2768	BONHAM, Nathaniel S	17	E½NW	1858-11-01		A1
2769	" "	17	N½SW	1858-11-01		A1
2770	" "	17	NWSE	1858-11-01		A1
2771	" "	17	W½NE	1858-11-01		A1
2772	" "	18	NESW	1858-11-01		A1
2586	BRADLEY, Anna	24	E½NE	1888-02-04		A2 G5
2586	BRADLEY, James C	24	E½NE	1888-02-04		A2 G5
2629	BROWN, George	30	E½NW	1831-08-01		A1
2700	BROWN, John	30	SW	1831-12-01		A1 G7
2699	" "	9	W½SW	1831-12-01		A1
2672	CANNON, James F	25	NWSW	1858-11-01		A1
2791	CAPPS, Samuel J	24	NWSW	1897-01-29		A1
2609	CLEMENTS, David	3	SW	1837-08-15		A1
2610	" "	4	SESE	1837-08-15		A1
2673	CLEMENTS, James F	9	E½NE	1837-08-15		A1
2613	CODY, Edmund	30	NE	1831-08-01		A1
2623	CODY, Francis M	33	E½NE	1858-11-01		A1
2624	" "	33	NENW	1858-11-01		A1
2625	" "	33	NWNE	1858-11-01		A1
2626	" "	33	SENW	1858-11-01		A1
2627	" "	33	SWNE	1858-11-01		A1
2703	CODY, John	31	E½SE	1831-11-30		A1
2704	" "	32	SESE	1834-08-05		A1
2757	CONE, Martha	4	SWNW	1862-01-01		A1
2620	CORNET, Francis	27	NWSE	1858-11-01		A1
2621	" "	27	SESE	1858-11-01		A1
2622	" "	34	NENW	1858-11-01		A1
2859	COURTNEY, William R	6	SENW	1858-11-01		A1
2860	" "	6	W½NE	1858-11-01		A1
2705	DAVIS, John	11	NENE	1834-08-05		A1
2706	DE BREE, JOHN	1	E½NW	1838-07-28		A1
2707	" "	1	E½SW	1838-07-28		A1
2708	" "	11	E½NW	1838-07-28		A1
2709	" "	2	SE	1838-07-28		A1
2693	DEWITT, James W	11	NWNW	1852-12-01		A1
2732	DORMAN, Lemach	14	E½NE	1858-11-01		A1
2733	" "	14	NWNE	1858-11-01		A1
2783	DUKE, Ransome	6	NENW	1858-11-01		A1
2784	" "	6	W½NW	1858-11-01		A1
2592	FRANKLIN, Barnett	35	E½SW	1852-02-02		A1
2593	" "	35	W½SE	1852-02-02		A1
2604	HALL, Clemmons	3	S½NE	1858-11-01		A1
2605	" "	4	N½SE	1858-11-01		A1 V2744, 2787
2632	HANCHEY, George L	24	W½SE	1888-11-08		A1

ID	Individual in Patent	Sec.	Sec. Part	Date Issued	Other Counties	For More Info . . .
2759	HANCHEY, Martin	24	W½NE	1883-08-13		A2
2758	" "	24	SENW	1884-03-20		A2
2616	HARDCASTLE, Eli	9	SESE	1849-09-01		A1
2614	" "	10	W½SW	1852-02-02		A1
2615	" "	15	NWNW	1852-02-02		A1
2749	HARRELL, Louis	17	S½SW	1858-11-01		A1
2750	" "	17	SWSE	1858-11-01		A1
2751	" "	20	E½NW	1858-11-01		A1
2752	" "	20	NESW	1858-11-01		A1
2753	" "	20	W½NE	1858-11-01		A1
2756	" "	29	SESE	1858-11-01		A1
2754	" "	28	SESW	1860-10-01		A1
2755	" "	28	SWNW	1860-10-01		A1
2710	HARRIS, John	21	N½NW	1858-11-01		A1
2711	" "	21	SWNW	1858-11-01		A1
2766	HARRIS, Milley A	11	W½NE	1862-01-01		A1
2845	HARRIS, William	6	W½SW	1862-01-01		A1
2670	HATHHORN, James E	19	E½NE	1852-02-02		A1
2788	HAWKINS, Robert F	34	NWSW	1890-08-29		A2
2846	HAWKINS, William	10	NESW	1860-10-01		A1
2671	HAWTHORNE, James E	20	NWNW	1852-02-02		A1
2648	HIGHNATE, Henry	15	NWSW	1854-10-02		A1
2581	HILL, Alsa G	32	W½SE	1833-09-16		A1
2580	" "	32	NESE	1837-08-18		A1
2738	HILL, Lewis	32	SW	1831-11-30		A1 G22
2734	" "	32	E½NW	1833-09-16		A1
2735	" "	32	SENE	1834-06-12		A1
2736	" "	32	SWNE	1837-08-18		A1
2737	" "	33	W½NW	1837-08-18		A1
2760	HILL, Martin	14	E½SW	1860-10-01		A1
2761	" "	14	NESE	1860-10-01		A1
2762	" "	14	SWSW	1860-10-01		A1
2763	" "	14	W½SE	1860-10-01		A1
2764	HILL, Martin M	32	NWNE	1837-05-20		A1
2597	JEFCOAT, Benjamin C	12	SESW	1897-02-17		A1
2598	" "	13	E½NW	1897-02-17		A1
2611	JEFCOAT, David H	12	NESE	1858-11-01		A1
2617	JEFCOAT, Elijah G	1	NESE	1852-12-01		A1
2644	JEFCOAT, George W	34	NESW	1858-11-01		A1
2645	" "	34	SENW	1858-11-01		A1
2664	JEFCOAT, Jacob	12	NENE	1858-11-01		A1
2712	JEFCOAT, John	1	W½SE	1837-08-10		A1
2740	JEFCOAT, Lewis	1	W½SW	1837-04-10		A1
2739	" "	1	SESE	1837-08-14		A1
2765	JEFCOAT, Mary A	12	SENE	1854-10-02		A1
2747	JONES, Littleton	9	NW	1837-08-12		A1
2743	" "	4	SESW	1840-10-10		A1
2745	" "	8	NWSE	1853-08-01		A1
2746	" "	8	SWNE	1853-08-01		A1
2741	" "	4	NE	1858-11-01		A1
2742	" "	4	NESW	1858-11-01		A1
2744	" "	4	W½SE	1858-11-01		A1 V2605
2748	" "	9	W½NE	1858-11-01		A1
2847	JONES, William	5	NENE	1858-11-01		A1
2848	" "	5	SWNE	1858-11-01		A1
2836	JONES, William H	21	NWNE	1852-02-02		A1
2777	KENT, Randolph	2	NENW	1854-10-02		A1
2779	" "	2	SENW	1854-10-02		A1
2778	" "	2	NWNE	1858-09-01		A1
2776	" "	2	NENE	1860-09-01		A1
2780	" "	2	SWNE	1860-09-01		A1
2803	KERSEY, Stephen A	36	E½SE	1907-04-05		A1
2804	" "	36	SENE	1907-04-05		A1
2823	KING, Wiley	29	NESE	1849-09-01		A1
2822	" "	28	SWSW	1858-11-01		A1
2824	" "	29	SENE	1858-11-01		A1
2840	KING, William H	35	S½NW	1852-12-01		A1
2839	" "	35	N½NW	1858-11-01		A1
2841	" "	35	W½NE	1858-11-01		A1
2837	" "	12	NWSW	1860-09-01		A1
2838	" "	12	SWSW	1860-09-01		A1
2849	LARANCE, William	12	SENW	1860-10-01		A1 V2576
2850	" "	12	SWNE	1860-10-01		A1

155

ID	Individual in Patent	Sec.	Sec. Part	Date Issued	Other Counties	For More Info . . .
2851	LAWRENCE, William	12	NWSE	1896-11-21		A1
2775	LEAIRD, Patrick B	7	N½NE	1862-01-01		A1
2731	LEVERETT, Kiziah	17	SWNW	1852-02-02		A1
2773	LEWIS, Owen L	2	NWNW	1858-09-01		A1
2774	" "	3	N½NE	1858-09-01		A1
2825	MAHONE, William F	17	E½SE	1858-11-01		A1
2826	" "	18	NWSW	1858-11-01		A1
2827	" "	18	SESW	1858-11-01		A1
2828	" "	18	W½NW	1858-11-01		A1
2829	" "	29	NENE	1858-11-01		A1
2830	" "	29	NENW	1858-11-01		A1
2831	" "	29	W½NE	1858-11-01		A1
2834	" "	7	NW	1858-11-01		A1
2835	" "	7	W½SW	1858-11-01		A1
2832	" "	31	NWSE	1862-01-01		A1
2833	" "	31	SESW	1862-01-01		A1
2854	MAPES, William	5	SESW	1847-05-01		A1
2599	MARTIN, Benjamin G	27	N½SW	1858-11-01		A1
2600	" "	27	NW	1858-11-01		A1 R2601
2602	" "	27	W½NE	1858-11-01		A1
2601	" "	27	NW	1897-02-23		A1 R2600
2659	MARTIN, Jackson	27	SWSW	1858-11-01		A1
2660	" "	28	E½NW	1858-11-01		A1
2661	" "	28	N½NE	1858-11-01		A1
2662	" "	28	NWNW	1858-11-01		A1
2663	" "	28	S½SE	1858-11-01		A1
2702	MARTIN, John C	15	SENW	1858-11-01		A1
2701	" "	15	NESW	1862-01-01		A1
2810	MARTIN, Thomas	15	S½SW	1858-11-01		A1
2635	MCADAMS, George	1	NE	1837-08-02		A1 G32
2634	" "	13	NWNW	1837-08-02		A1
2633	" "	11	SESE	1837-08-14		A1
2635	MCADAMS, Robert	1	NE	1837-08-02		A1 G32
2811	MCADAMS, Thomas	22	SWSE	1834-08-05		A1
2813	" "	27	E½NE	1834-08-05		A1
2812	" "	26	SWNE	1837-08-14		A1
2814	" "	34	NE	1837-08-14		A1
2790	MCDONALD, Rube	14	SESE	1888-02-04		A2
2575	MCGINNEY, Albert J	26	SENW	1858-11-01		A1
2696	MOODY, Jesse T	33	SESE	1852-02-02		A1
2719	MOODY, John M	33	NESE	1852-02-02		A1
2855	MOODY, William	34	SESW	1858-11-01		A1
2856	" "	34	SWSE	1858-11-01		A1
2607	MORELAND, Daniel	34	NWSE	1884-03-10		A2
2584	MORRISON, Angus G	7	E½SW	1862-01-01		A1
2585	" "	7	S½SE	1862-01-01		A1
2694	OWEN, James W	26	N½SW	1860-04-02		A1
2695	" "	26	NWSE	1860-04-02		A1
2674	PATE, James H	36	SENW	1889-11-21		A2
2726	PATE, Joshua J	36	E½SW	1883-08-13		A2
2863	PATE, William T	36	N½NE	1885-06-30		A2
2864	" "	36	SWNE	1885-06-30		A2
2700	PATTERSON, John	30	SW	1831-12-01		A1 G7
2697	PONDER, Joel B	29	SESW	1840-10-10		A1
2698	" "	29	SWSE	1840-10-10		A1
2808	POTTER, Thomas F	12	SWNW	1860-10-01		A1
2809	" "	2	SENE	1860-10-01		A1
2608	PRESCOAT, Daniel	11	SENE	1834-08-05		A1
2628	PYNES, Francis M	13	NWSW	1901-01-23		A2
2657	RABB, Hezekiah	20	E½NE	1858-11-01		A1
2861	RABB, William	20	N½SE	1852-12-01		A1
2862	" "	20	S½SE	1858-11-01		A1
2785	REDMON, Robert A	10	NENW	1860-12-01		A1
2786	REDMOND, Robert A	10	NWNW	1860-10-01		A1
2787	" "	4	NESE	1860-10-01		A1 V2605
2767	REED, Nathan B	26	N½NW	1858-11-01		A1
2641	REESE, George	29	NWSE	1849-09-01		A1
2636	" "	17	NWNW	1858-11-01		A1
2637	" "	17	SENE	1858-11-01		A1
2638	" "	18	E½NW	1858-11-01		A1
2639	" "	18	NENE	1858-11-01		A1
2640	" "	18	NESE	1858-11-01		A1
2642	" "	7	NWSE	1858-11-01		A1

ID	Individual in Patent	Sec.	Sec. Part	Date Issued	Other Counties	For More Info . . .
2643	REESE, George (Cont'd)	7	S½NE	1858-11-01		A1
2603	RHODES, Charlotte	4	W½SW	1835-04-15		A1
2646	RHODES, George W	5	SENE	1854-10-02		A1
2720	RHODES, John	5	E½SE	1831-08-01		A1
2721	" "	5	W½SE	1835-04-15		A1
2806	RHODES, Telitha	9	E½SW	1835-04-15		A1
2649	RICHARDSON, Henry	20	SWNW	1837-08-15		A1
2658	RICHBURG, Hugh	14	SWNE	1837-08-14		A1
2579	ROSTICK, Alexander Y	12	NESW	1852-12-01		A1
2612	RUTLEDGE, Dudley A	8	SWSE	1860-10-01		A1
2606	SALTER, Coleman F	24	S½SW	1890-07-03		A2
2801	SILER, Solomon	35	W½SW	1837-08-12		A1
2800	" "	34	E½SE	1837-08-15		A1
2789	SIMS, Robert	33	SESW	1834-09-04		A1
2675	SMITH, James H	10	SWSE	1854-07-15		A1
2676	" "	14	SWNW	1854-07-15		A1
2677	" "	15	S½NE	1854-07-15		A1
2679	" "	22	E½SE	1854-07-15		A1
2680	" "	22	NE	1854-07-15		A1
2681	" "	22	NWSE	1854-07-15		A1
2682	" "	22	W½	1854-07-15		A1
2678	" "	21	E½SE	1858-11-01		A1
2738	SOLOMON, Henry	32	SW	1831-11-30		A1 G22
2630	STAGGERS, George J	31	NESW	1858-11-01		A1
2631	" "	31	SWNE	1858-11-01		A1
2690	STAGGERS, James M	30	NWSE	1837-08-02		A1
2691	" "	30	SWNW	1837-08-02		A1
2689	" "	19	W½SW	1837-08-18		A1
2692	STEPHENS, James T	24	E½SE	1860-04-02		A1
2669	STEPHENSON, James C	14	NENW	1854-07-15		A1
2795	STEPHENSON, Samuel	24	NESW	1888-02-04		A2
2796	" "	24	W½NW	1888-02-04		A2
2587	STEWART, Archibald D	14	NWSW	1858-11-01		A1
2588	" "	15	NESE	1858-11-01		A1
2589	" "	15	W½SE	1858-11-01		A1
2590	" "	25	SWNW	1858-11-01		A1
2591	" "	25	SWSW	1858-11-01		A1
2852	STEWART, William M	11	SESW	1858-11-01		A1
2853	" "	11	W½SW	1858-11-01		A1
2722	STOCKARD, Joseph C	21	E½SW	1858-11-01		A1
2723	" "	21	NWSE	1858-11-01		A1
2724	" "	21	SWSW	1858-11-01		A1
2857	STREET, William N	6	E½SW	1860-10-01		A1
2858	" "	6	S½SE	1860-10-01		A1
2618	STRICKLAN, Elizabeth	26	N½NE	1858-11-01		A1
2582	SWANNER, Amariah	31	W½SW	1858-11-01		A1
2686	THAGARD, James L	30	SWSE	1858-11-01		A1
2687	" "	31	NENW	1858-11-01		A1
2688	" "	31	NWNE	1858-11-01		A1
2820	THAGARD, Warren R	19	NW	1858-11-01		A1
2842	TIPPET, William H	8	E½NW	1858-11-01		A1
2843	" "	8	SWNW	1858-11-01		A1
2844	TIPPETT, William H	8	SW	1858-11-01		A1
2781	TISDALE, Ransom S	36	NWSE	1858-11-01		A1
2782	" "	36	SWSE	1858-11-01		A1
2596	TUCKER, Bartley M	33	W½SW	1837-08-10		A1
2594	" "	33	NESW	1837-08-14		A1
2595	" "	33	W½SE	1837-08-14		A1
2792	TUCKER, Samuel M	26	S½SW	1854-10-02		A1
2793	" "	26	SESE	1854-10-02		A1
2794	" "	26	SWNW	1858-11-01		A1
2805	TYPETT, Susan	8	NWNW	1858-11-01		A1
2730	UNDERWOOD, Josiah	19	SWNE	1834-10-21		A1
2727	" "	18	W½NE	1837-08-15		A1
2728	" "	18	W½SE	1837-08-15		A1
2729	" "	19	NWNE	1837-08-15		A1
2815	UNDERWOOD, Thomas	19	E½SE	1831-08-01		A1
2816	" "	19	W½SE	1831-08-01		A1
2818	UNDERWOOD, Vincent A	20	W½SW	1837-08-15		A1
2819	" "	29	NWNW	1837-08-15		A1
2665	WEIL, Jacob	29	N½SW	1858-11-01		A1
2666	" "	29	S½NW	1858-11-01		A1
2667	" "	30	E½SE	1858-11-01		A1

ID	Individual in Patent	Sec.	Sec. Part	Date Issued	Other Counties	For More Info . . .
2668	WEIL, Jacob (Cont'd)	31	E½NE	1858-11-01		A1
2714	WELCH, John L	5	NESW	1847-05-01		A1
2716	" "	5	SENW	1847-05-01		A1
2713	" "	5	NENW	1854-07-15		A1
2715	" "	5	NWNW	1858-11-01		A1
2717	" "	6	E½NE	1858-11-01		A1
2718	" "	6	N½SE	1858-11-01		A1
2798	WELCH, Seaborn	8	NWNE	1849-09-01		A1
2799	" "	8	SENE	1849-09-01		A1
2797	" "	8	NENE	1854-07-15		A1
2821	WILLIAMS, Wiley G	24	NENW	1860-12-01		A1
2619	WILLIAMSON, Erasmus	4	NWNW	1854-10-02		A1
2647	WILLIAMSON, George	36	N½NW	1888-02-04		A2
2653	WILLIAMSON, Henry	35	E½NE	1852-12-01		A1
2654	" "	35	E½SE	1852-12-01		A1
2656	" "	36	W½SW	1852-12-01		A1
2650	" "	10	SESW	1854-10-02		A1
2651	" "	15	NENW	1854-10-02		A1
2655	" "	36	SWNW	1858-11-01		A1
2652	" "	26	SWSE	1860-10-01		A1
2867	WILLIAMSON, William	21	NWSW	1852-02-02		A1
2865	" "	13	SESW	1858-11-01		A1
2866	" "	13	SWSE	1858-11-01		A1
2583	WIROSDICK, Andrew	2	SW	1837-08-02		A1 G39
2583	WIROSDICK, Thomas	2	SW	1837-08-02		A1 G39
2683	WRIGHT, James H	28	N½SW	1852-02-02		A1
2684	" "	29	SWSW	1858-11-01		A1
2685	" "	32	NWNW	1858-11-01		A1
2802	WRIGHT, Spencer	25	NWNW	1858-11-01		A1
2868	WRIGHT, William	32	SWNW	1852-02-02		A1
2576	WYROSDICK, Alexander	12	E½NW	1858-11-01		A1 V2849
2577	" "	12	NWNE	1858-11-01		A1
2578	" "	12	SESE	1858-11-01		A1
2817	WYROSDICK, Thomas Z	2	SWNW	1858-09-01		A1

Patent Map

T9-N R18-E
St Stephens Meridian

Map Group 12

Township Statistics

Parcels Mapped	:	294
Number of Patents	:	217
Number of Individuals	:	141
Patentees Identified	:	139
Number of Surnames	:	91
Multi-Patentee Parcels	:	5
Oldest Patent Date	:	8/1/1831
Most Recent Patent	:	4/5/1907
Block/Lot Parcels	:	0
Parcels Re - Issued	:	1
Parcels that Overlap	:	5
Cities and Towns	:	3
Cemeteries	:	4

The patent map grid contains the following entries:

Section 6 / 5 / 4 area (top row):
- DUKE Ransome 1858
- DUKE Ransome 1858
- COURTNEY William R 1858
- WELCH John L 1858
- WELCH John L 1854
- JONES William 1858
- WILLIAMSON Erasmus 1854
- JONES Littleton 1858
- COURTNEY William R 1858
- WELCH John L 1858
- WELCH John L 1847
- JONES William 1858
- RHODES George W 1854
- CONE Martha 1862
- 4
- HARRIS William 1862
- STREET William N 1860
- 6
- WELCH John L 1858
- WELCH John L 1847
- 5
- RHODES John 1831
- RHODES Charlotte 1835
- JONES Littleton 1858
- HALL Clemmons 1858
- REDMOND Robert A 1860
- STREET William N 1860
- MAPES William 1847
- RHODES John 1835
- JONES Littleton 1840
- JONES Littleton 1858
- CLEMENTS David 1837

Section 7 / 8 / 9 area:
- MAHONE William F 1858
- LEAIRD Patrick B 1862
- TYPETT Susan 1858
- TIPPET William H 1858
- WELCH Seaborn 1849
- WELCH Seaborn 1854
- JONES Littleton 1837
- JONES Littleton 1858
- 7
- REESE George 1858
- TIPPET William H 1858
- 8
- JONES Littleton 1853
- WELCH Seaborn 1849
- 9
- CLEMENTS James F 1837
- MAHONE William F 1858
- MORRISON Angus G 1862
- REESE George 1858
- TIPPETT William H 1858
- JONES Littleton 1853
- BROWN John 1831
- RHODES Telitha 1835
- HARDCASTLE Eli 1849
- MORRISON Angus G 1862
- RUTLEDGE Dudley A 1860

Section 18 / 17 / 16 area:
- MAHONE William F 1858
- REESE George 1858
- UNDERWOOD Josiah 1837
- REESE George 1858
- REESE George 1858
- BONHAM Nathaniel S 1858
- 18
- BONHAM Nathaniel S 1858
- REESE George 1858
- LEVERETT Kiziah 1852
- 17
- 16
- MAHONE William F 1858
- BONHAM Nathaniel S 1858
- UNDERWOOD Josiah 1837
- REESE George 1858
- BONHAM Nathaniel S 1858
- BONHAM Nathaniel S 1858
- MAHONE William F 1858
- BOGGS Joseph J 1875
- MAHONE William F 1858
- HARRELL Louis 1858
- HARRELL Louis 1858

Section 19 / 20 / 21 area:
- THAGARD Warren R 1858
- UNDERWOOD Josiah 1837
- HATHHORN James E 1852
- HAWTHORNE James E 1852
- HARRELL Louis 1858
- RABB Hezekiah 1858
- HARRIS John 1858
- JONES William H 1852
- 19
- UNDERWOOD Josiah 1834
- HARRELL Louis 1858
- 20
- HARRIS John 1858
- 21
- STAGGERS James M 1837
- UNDERWOOD Thomas 1831
- UNDERWOOD Thomas 1831
- RICHARDSON Henry 1837
- HARRELL Louis 1858
- RABB William 1852
- WILLIAMSON William 1852
- STOCKARD Joseph C 1858
- STOCKARD Joseph C 1858
- SMITH James H 1858
- UNDERWOOD Vincent A 1837
- RABB William 1858
- STOCKARD Joseph C 1858

Section 30 / 29 / 28 area:
- BROWN George 1831
- CODY Edmund 1831
- UNDERWOOD Vincent A 1837
- MAHONE William F 1858
- MAHONE William F 1858
- MAHONE William F 1858
- MARTIN Jackson 1858
- MARTIN Jackson 1858
- MARTIN Jackson 1858
- STAGGERS James M 1837
- 30
- WEIL Jacob 1858
- KING Wiley 1858
- HARRELL Louis 1860
- BROWN [7] John 1831
- STAGGERS James M 1837
- WEIL Jacob 1858
- WEIL Jacob 1858
- 29
- REESE George 1849
- KING Wiley 1849
- WRIGHT James H 1852
- 28
- THAGARD James L 1858
- WRIGHT James H 1858
- PONDER Joel B 1840
- PONDER Joel B 1840
- HARRELL Louis 1858
- KING Wiley 1860
- HARRELL Louis 1858
- MARTIN Jackson 1858

Section 31 / 32 / 33 area:
- THAGARD James L 1858
- THAGARD James L 1858
- WEIL Jacob 1858
- WRIGHT James H 1858
- HILL Martin M 1837
- CODY Francis M 1858
- CODY Francis M 1858
- 31
- STAGGERS George J 1858
- WRIGHT William 1852
- HILL Lewis 1833
- HILL Lewis 1837
- HILL Lewis 1834
- HILL Lewis 1837
- CODY Francis M 1858
- CODY Francis M 1858
- CODY Francis M 1858
- SWANNER Amariah 1858
- STAGGERS George J 1858
- MAHONE William F 1862
- CODY John 1831
- HILL [22] Lewis 1831
- 32
- HILL Alsa G 1833
- HILL Alsa G 1837
- TUCKER Bartley M 1837
- 33
- MOODY John M 1852
- MAHONE William F 1862
- CODY John 1834
- TUCKER Bartley M 1837
- SIMS Robert 1834
- TUCKER Bartley M 1837
- MOODY Jesse T 1852

Map Grid

Section 3
LEWIS Owen L 1858
HALL Clemmons 1858
CLEMENTS David 1837

Section 2
LEWIS Owen L 1858
WYROSDICK Thomas Z 1858
KENT Randolph 1854
KENT Randolph 1858
KENT Randolph 1860
KENT Randolph 1854
KENT Randolph 1860
POTTER Thomas F 1860
WIROSDICK [39] Andrew 1837
BREE John De 1838

Section 1
BREE John De 1838
MCADAMS [32] George 1837
BREE John De 1838
JEFCOAT Elijah G 1852
JEFCOAT John 1837
JEFCOAT Jacob 1858
JEFCOAT Mary A 1854
JEFCOAT Lewis 1837

Section 10
REDMOND Robert A 1860
REDMON Robert A 1860
HARDCASTLE Eli 1852
HAWKINS William 1860
WILLIAMSON Henry 1854
SMITH James H 1854

Section 11
DEWITT James W 1852
BREE John De 1838
HARRIS Milley A 1862
DAVIS John 1834
PRESCOAT Daniel 1834
STEWART William M 1858
STEWART William M 1858
MCADAMS George 1837

Section 12
JEFCOAT Lewis 1837
WYROSDICK Alexander 1858
WYROSDICK Alexander 1858
POTTER Thomas F 1860
LARANCE William 1860
LARANCE William 1860
KING William H 1860
ROSTICK Alexander Y 1852
LAWRENCE William 1896
JEFCOAT Jacob 1858
JEFCOAT David H 1858
KING William H 1860
JEFCOAT Benjamin C 1897
WYROSDICK Alexander 1858

Section 15
HARDCASTLE Eli 1852
WILLIAMSON Henry 1854
MARTIN John C 1858
HIGHNATE Henry 1854
MARTIN John C 1862
MARTIN Thomas 1858
SMITH James H 1854
STEWART Archibald D 1858
STEWART Archibald D 1858

Section 14
STEPHENSON James C 1854
SMITH James H 1854
STEWART Archibald D 1858
HILL Martin 1860
HILL Martin 1860

Section 13
DORMAN Lemach 1858
RICHBURG Hugh 1837
DORMAN Lemach 1858
HILL Martin 1860
MCDONALD Rube 1888
MCADAMS George 1837
JEFCOAT Benjamin C 1897
PYNES Francis M 1901
WILLIAMSON William 1858
WILLIAMSON William 1858
AXSON Thomas D 1897

Section 22
SMITH James H 1854
SMITH James H 1854
SMITH James H 1854
SMITH James H 1854
MCADAMS Thomas 1834

Section 23

Section 24
WILLIAMS Wiley G 1860
HANCHEY Martin 1883
STEPHENSON Samuel 1888
HANCHEY Martin 1884
BRADLEY [5] Anna 1888
CAPPS Samuel J 1897
STEPHENSON Samuel 1888
SALTER Coleman F 1890
HANCHEY George L 1888
STEPHENS James T 1860

Section 27
MARTIN Benjamin G 1897
MARTIN Benjamin G 1858
MARTIN Benjamin G 1858
MARTIN Benjamin G 1858
MARTIN Jackson 1858
MARTIN Benjamin G 1858
MCADAMS Thomas 1834
CORNET Francis 1858
CORNET Francis 1858

Section 26
REED Nathan B 1858
TUCKER Samuel M 1858
MCGINNEY Albert J 1858
MCADAMS Thomas 1837
OWEN James W 1860
OWEN James W 1860
TUCKER Samuel M 1854
WILLIAMSON Henry 1860
TUCKER Samuel M 1854
STRICKLAN Elizabeth 1858

Section 25
WRIGHT Spencer 1858
STEWART Archibald D 1858
CANNON James F 1858
STEWART Archibald D 1858

Section 34
CORNET Francis 1858
JEFCOAT George W 1858
HAWKINS Robert F 1890
JEFCOAT George W 1858
MCADAMS Thomas 1837
MORELAND Daniel 1884
SILER Solomon 1837
MOODY William 1858
MOODY William 1858

Section 35
KING William H 1858
KING William H 1852
SILER Solomon 1837
KING William H 1858
FRANKLIN Barnett 1852
FRANKLIN Barnett 1852
WILLIAMSON Henry 1852
WILLIAMSON Henry 1852
WILLIAMSON Henry 1852

Section 36
WILLIAMSON George 1888
PATE William T 1885
WILLIAMSON Henry 1858
PATE James H 1889
PATE William T 1885
KERSEY Stephen A 1907
PATE Joshua J 1883
TISDALE Ransom S 1858
TISDALE Ransom S 1858
KERSEY Stephen A 1907

Helpful Hints

1. This Map's INDEX can be found on the preceding pages.

2. Refer to Map "C" to see where this Township lies within Crenshaw County, Alabama.

3. Numbers within square brackets [ ] denote a multi-patentee land parcel (multi-owner). Refer to Appendix "C" for a full list of members in this group.

4. Areas that look to be crowded with Patentees usually indicate multiple sales of the same parcel (Re-issues) or Overlapping parcels. See this Township's Index for an explanation of these and other circumstances that might explain "odd" groupings of Patentees on this map.

Legend

— Patent Boundary

━ Section Boundary

▨ No Patents Found (or Outside County)

1., 2., 3., ... Lot Numbers (when beside a name)

[ ] Group Number (see Appendix "C")

Scale: Section = 1 mile X 1 mile (generally, with some exceptions)

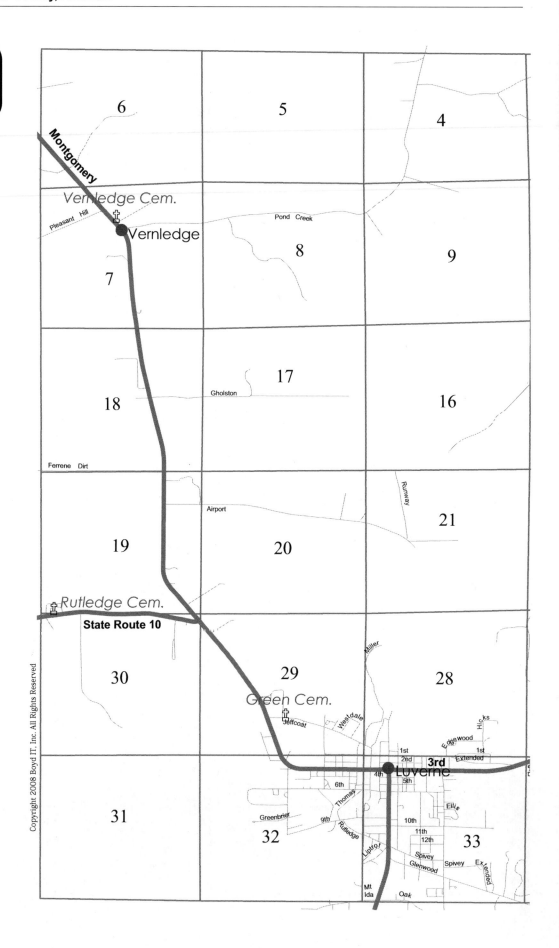

Road Map

T9-N R18-E
St Stephens Meridian

Map Group 12

Cities & Towns

Luverne
Patsburg
Vernledge

Cemeteries

Emmaus Cemetery
Green Cemetery
Rutledge Cemetery
Vernledge Cemetery

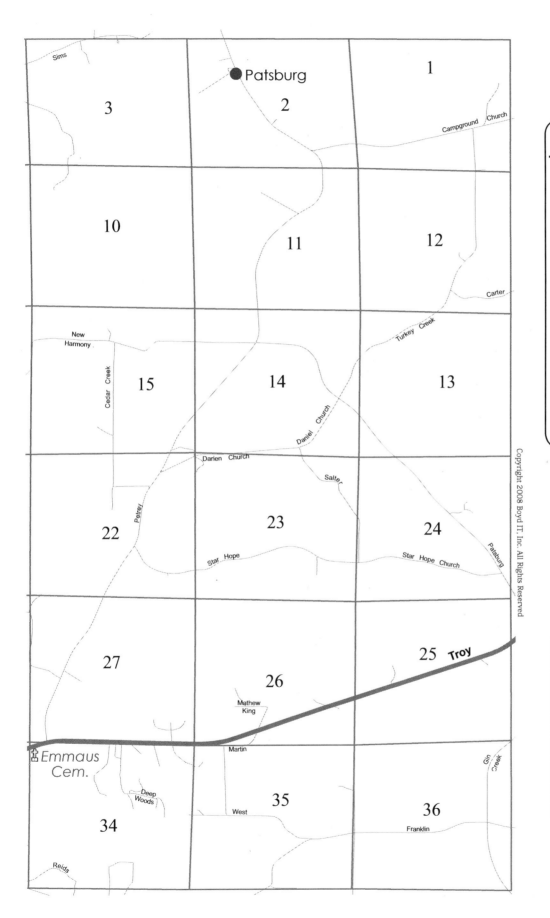

Sims

Patsburg

1

3

2

Campground Church

10

11

12

Carter

New Harmony

Turkey Creek

15

14

13

Cedar Creek

Daniel Church

Darien Church

Salte

Petrey

23

24

22

Star Hope

Star Hope Church

Patsburg

27

25 **Troy**

26

Mathew King

Emmaus Cem.

Martin

Gin Creek

Deep Woods

35

36

34

West

Franklin

Reids

Helpful Hints

1. This road map has a number of uses, but primarily it is to help you: a) find the present location of land owned by your ancestors (at least the general area), b) find cemeteries and city-centers, and c) estimate the route/roads used by Census-takers & tax-assessors.

2. If you plan to travel to Crenshaw County to locate cemeteries or land parcels, please pick up a modern travel map for the area before you do. Mapping old land parcels on modern maps is not as exact a science as you might think. Just the slightest variations in public land survey coordinates, estimates of parcel boundaries, or road-map deviations can greatly alter a map's representation of how a road either does or doesn't cross a particular parcel of land.

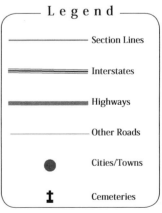

L e g e n d

————	Section Lines
════	Interstates
▬▬▬	Highways
————	Other Roads
●	Cities/Towns
⚑	Cemeteries

Scale: Section = 1 mile X 1 mile
(generally, with some exceptions)

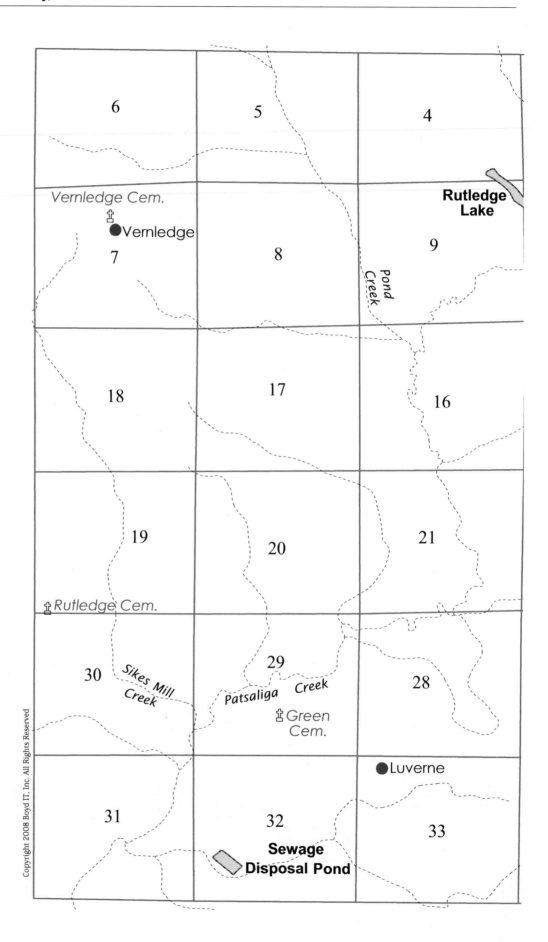

Historical Map

T9-N R18-E
St Stephens Meridian

Map Group 12

Cities & Towns

Luverne
Patsburg
Vernledge

Cemeteries

Emmaus Cemetery
Green Cemetery
Rutledge Cemetery
Vernledge Cemetery

6

5

4

Vernledge Cem.

●Vernledge

7

8

Rutledge Lake

9

Pond Creek

18

17

16

19

20

21

Rutledge Cem.

30

Sikes Mill Creek

29

Patsaliga Creek

28

Green Cem.

●Luverne

31

32

Sewage Disposal Pond

33

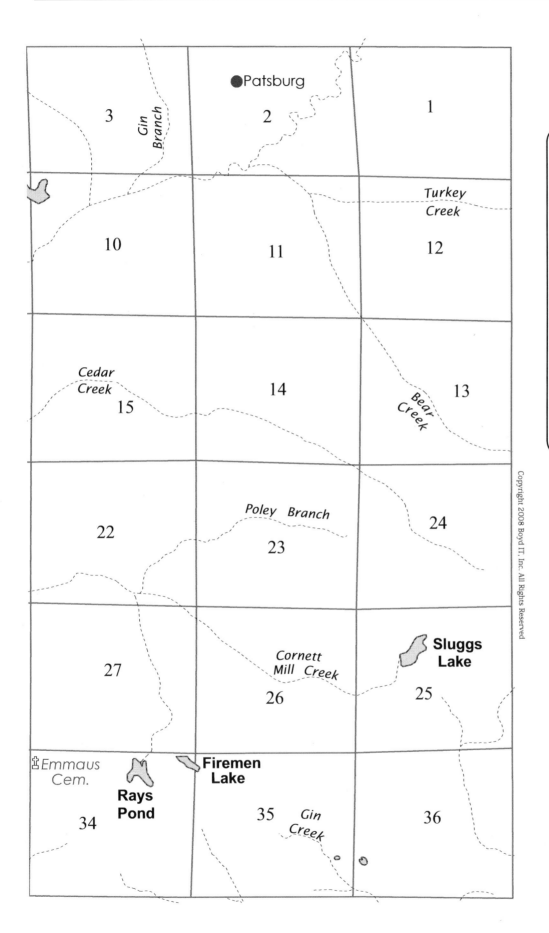

●Patsburg

3

Gin Branch

2

1

Turkey Creek

10

11

12

Cedar Creek

15

14

13

Bear Creek

22

Poley Branch

23

24

27

Cornett Mill Creek

26

Sluggs Lake

25

⚱ *Emmaus Cem.*

Rays Pond

Firemen Lake

34

35

Gin Creek

36

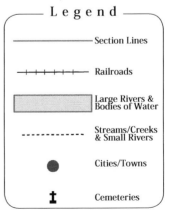

Helpful Hints

1. This Map takes a different look at the same Congressional Township displayed in the preceding two maps. It presents features that can help you better envision the historical development of the area: a) Water-bodies (lakes & ponds), b) Water-courses (rivers, streams, etc.), c) Railroads, d) City/town center-points (where they were oftentimes located when first settled), and e) Cemeteries.

2. Using this "Historical" map in tandem with this Township's Patent Map and Road Map, may lead you to some interesting discoveries. You will often find roads, towns, cemeteries, and waterways are named after nearby landowners: sometimes those names will be the ones you are researching. See how many of these research gems you can find here in Crenshaw County.

L e g e n d

—————— Section Lines

+++++++ Railroads

▭ Large Rivers & Bodies of Water

- - - - - - Streams/Creeks & Small Rivers

● Cities/Towns

⚱ Cemeteries

Scale: Section = 1 mile X 1 mile
(there are some exceptions)

Map Group 13: Index to Land Patents

Township 9-North Range 19-East (St Stephens)

After you locate an individual in this Index, take note of the Section and Section Part then proceed to the Land Patent map on the pages immediately following. You should have no difficulty locating the corresponding parcel of land.

The "For More Info" Column will lead you to more information about the underlying Patents. See the *Legend* at right, and the "How to Use this Book" chapter, for more information.

```
┌─────────────────────────────────────────────────┐
│                  LEGEND                          │
│       "For More Info . . . " column              │
│ A = Authority (Legislative Act, See Appendix "A")│
│ B = Block or Lot (location in Section unknown)   │
│ C = Cancelled Patent                             │
│ F = Fractional Section                           │
│ G = Group  (Multi-Patentee Patent, see Appendix "C")│
│ V = Overlaps another Parcel                      │
│ R = Re-Issued (Parcel patented more than once)   │
│                                                  │
│ (A & G items require you to look in the Appendixes referred│
│ to above. All other Letter-designations followed by a number│
│ require you to locate line-items in this index that possess│
│ the ID number found after the letter).           │
└─────────────────────────────────────────────────┘
```

ID	Individual in Patent	Sec.	Sec. Part	Date Issued	Other Counties	For More Info . . .
2893	AMASON, Eli	21	E½NE	1838-07-28		A1
2993	ANDERSON, Thomas	18	SWNW	1891-01-15		A2 R2968
2957	BARTON, Joshua	5	SENE	1852-02-02		A1
2954	" "	4	SENE	1858-11-01		A1
2955	" "	4	W½NW	1858-11-01		A1
2956	" "	5	NESE	1858-11-01		A1
2958	" "	5	SWNE	1858-11-01		A1
2952	BARTON, Joshua A	4	SENW	1852-12-01		A1
2953	" "	4	SWNE	1852-12-01		A1
2942	BOAN, John D	20	E½NE	1894-05-15		A2 G4
2942	BOAN, Smithey	20	E½NE	1894-05-15		A2 G4
2984	BOZEMAN, Samuel R	20	S½NW	1883-08-13		A2
3015	BOZEMAN, Zimri C	20	SWSW	1883-10-20		A1
2988	BRADLEY, Stephen E	17	NESW	1900-11-28		A2
2989	" "	17	S½NW	1900-11-28		A2
2869	BRISTOW, Abner L	4	S½SE	1880-02-20		A2
2892	BRISTOW, Edwin J	4	N½SE	1858-11-01		A1
2981	BRISTOW, Robertson	4	NESW	1860-04-02		A1
2950	BYRD, Joseph H	18	N½SE	1888-02-04		A2
2951	" "	18	S½SE	1888-02-04		A2
2990	CARTER, Stephen T	18	N½NE	1891-06-30		A2
2973	CLEMENTS, Peter	6	SWNW	1880-02-20		A2
3014	CLEMENTS, Zilpha S	6	NWNE	1895-08-08		A2
2902	COMPTON, Francis A	17	E½SE	1905-09-21		A2
2903	" "	17	SENE	1905-09-21		A2
2871	COOK, Arthur R	21	SWSE	1838-07-28		A1
2949	COOPER, Joseph E	33	SESE	1858-11-01		A1
2910	CORNETT, George W	18	S½NE	1891-06-30		A2
2887	DAVIS, Darcas	8	SWSW	1860-04-02		A1
2898	DAVIS, Enoch	5	NENW	1858-11-01		A1
2904	DAVIS, Francis	8	NWSE	1858-11-01		A1
2905	" "	8	SWSE	1858-11-01		A1
2929	DAVIS, James W	7	E½SW	1907-04-05		A1
2930	" "	7	SENW	1907-04-05		A1
2931	" "	7	W½SE	1907-04-05		A1
2948	DAVIS, John T	8	SESW	1858-11-01		A1
2986	DAVIS, Solomon	7	SWNE	1858-11-01		A1
2891	DEASON, Edmond R	29	N½NE	1858-11-01		A1
2936	DICKERSON, Jim	17	SESW	1901-01-23		A2
2922	DORMAN, James	33	NENW	1854-07-15		A1
2880	EDDINS, Daniel J	5	SENW	1858-11-01		A1
2881	" "	5	W½NW	1858-11-01		A1
2882	" "	6	NENE	1858-11-01		A1
2883	" "	6	NESE	1858-11-01		A1
2884	" "	6	S½NE	1858-11-01		A1
2899	EDDINS, Ephraim	5	NWNE	1852-02-02		A1

ID	Individual in Patent	Sec.	Sec. Part	Date Issued	Other Counties	For More Info . . .
2900	EDDINS, Ephraim (Cont'd)	5	NWSE	1852-12-01		A1
2901	" "	8	W½NE	1852-12-01		A1
2888	FINLAY, David	31	SWSE	1845-07-01		A1
2907	FOLMAR, George S	9	E½NE	1858-11-01		A1
2908	" "	9	NWSE	1858-11-01		A1
2909	" "	9	SWNE	1858-11-01		A1
2937	FOLMAR, Joel	8	E½SE	1858-11-01		A1
2938	" "	9	SESW	1858-11-01		A1
2939	" "	9	W½SW	1858-11-01		A1
2940	FOLMAR, John A	32	SENE	1885-07-27		A1
2947	FOLMAR, John N	9	E½SE	1838-07-28		A1
2889	GARDNER, Derry A	5	SWSE	1854-07-15		A1
2890	" "	9	W½NW	1858-11-01		A1
2991	GARDNER, Stephen W	4	S½SW	1885-03-25		A1
2992	" "	9	E½NW	1885-03-25		A1
2994	GILMER, Thomas M	8	SENE	1852-12-01		A1
3002	GODWIN, William	32	SESE	1852-12-01		A1
3010	GOLDEN, William J	32	SWSE	1896-04-23		A2
3003	GOODWIN, William	32	N½SE	1858-11-01		A1
3004	" "	32	SWNE	1858-11-01		A1
2870	GREEN, Allen	28	SENE	1858-11-01		A1
2906	HIGHTOWER, George H	4	NENW	1895-08-08		A2
2923	HOOKS, James M	20	N½NW	1883-08-13		A2
2941	HOOKS, John A	18	E½SW	1883-08-13		A2
3011	JACKSON, Willis	30	NESW	1891-06-30		A2
3012	" "	30	SENW	1891-06-30		A2
2886	JEFCOAT, Daniel W	7	NENW	1852-02-02		A1
2896	JEFCOAT, Elijah	6	NENW	1858-11-01		A1
2894	JEFCOAT, Elijah G	6	NWSW	1858-11-01		A1
2895	" "	6	SWSW	1858-11-01		A1
2919	JEFCOAT, Jacob	7	NWNW	1858-11-01		A1
2924	JEFCOAT, James O	6	SESE	1858-11-01		A1
2925	" "	6	SWSE	1858-11-01		A1
2926	" "	7	NWNE	1858-11-01		A1
2927	" "	8	NWNW	1858-11-01		A1
2982	JEFCOAT, Samuel O	8	NESW	1858-11-01		A1
2983	" "	8	SENW	1858-11-01		A1
2872	JOHNSON, Brazill	30	S½SW	1888-02-04		A2
2914	JOHNSON, Harriett	17	W½SW	1901-01-23		A2
2985	JONES, Samuel T	6	SESW	1885-06-20		A2
2885	JORDAN, Daniel	8	SWNW	1883-10-01		A2
2987	KERSEY, Stephen A	31	SW	1907-04-05		A1
2943	KING, John F	29	SE	1907-04-05		A1
2944	" "	32	N½NE	1907-04-05		A1
2945	" "	33	W½NW	1907-04-05		A1
2912	LONG, Gilbert	21	SWNE	1838-07-28		A1
2977	MCADAMS, Robert	6	NWNW	1837-08-10		A1
2979	" "	6	SENW	1852-02-02		A1
2976	" "	6	NESW	1852-12-01		A1
2978	" "	6	NWSE	1858-11-01		A1
2915	MCLEOD, Hugh	20	NESW	1858-11-01		A1
2916	" "	20	NWSE	1858-11-01		A1
2918	" "	20	W½NE	1858-11-01		A1
2917	" "	20	NWSW	1883-08-13		A2
2965	MCLEOD, Martha R	20	E½SE	1894-12-07		A2 G33
2966	" "	20	SESW	1894-12-07		A2 G33
2967	" "	20	SWSE	1894-12-07		A2 G33
2965	MCLEOD, Thomas W	20	E½SE	1894-12-07		A2 G33
2966	" "	20	SESW	1894-12-07		A2 G33
2967	" "	20	SWSE	1894-12-07		A2 G33
2913	MILLS, Green A	18	N½NW	1891-06-29		A2
2932	MITCHELL, James W	19	N½SW	1858-11-01		A1
2946	MITCHELL, John	17	N½NW	1858-11-01		A1
2873	NEIL, Burrell	28	S½NW	1880-02-20		A2
2963	NICHOLS, Kinchen E	7	E½SE	1907-04-05		A1
2964	" "	8	NWSW	1907-04-05		A1
2933	PELHAM, James W	21	NENW	1837-08-08		A1
2934	" "	21	NWNE	1837-08-08		A1 F
2878	RHODES, Daniel B	17	W½NE	1901-12-17		A2
2879	" "	17	W½SE	1901-12-17		A2
2897	RHODES, Elisabeth J	4	NENE	1898-03-21		A2
2969	RIEVES, Moses D	31	E½SE	1907-04-05		A1
2970	" "	31	NWSE	1907-04-05		A1

ID	Individual in Patent	Sec.	Sec. Part	Date Issued	Other Counties	For More Info . . .
2971	RIEVES, Moses D (Cont'd)	32	NW	1907-04-05		A1
2972	" "	32	NWSW	1907-04-05		A1
3005	ROUSE, William H	21	NWSE	1858-11-01		A1
3006	" "	21	SESE	1858-11-01		A1
3007	" "	28	NENE	1858-11-01		A1
3008	" "	28	W½NE	1858-11-01		A1
2920	SEALS, James D	5	NENE	1858-11-01		A1
2980	SMILIE, Robert	33	E½NE	1837-08-09		A1
2928	STEPHENS, James T	19	S½SW	1860-04-02		A1
2995	STEVENS, Thomas R	4	NWSW	1898-06-01		A2
2874	STEWART, Cader P	28	E½SE	1852-02-02		A1
2875	" "	28	SW	1858-11-01		A1
2876	" "	28	W½SE	1858-11-01		A1
2877	" "	33	W½NE	1858-11-01		A1
2921	STEWART, James D	29	NW	1858-11-01		A1
2959	STEWART, Joshua W	33	SESW	1858-11-01		A1
2960	" "	33	W½SE	1858-11-01		A1
3009	TAYLOR, William H	8	NENW	1893-03-03		A2
2996	THOMPSON, Valentine Y	30	NENW	1883-04-10		A2
2997	" "	30	SWNE	1883-04-10		A2
2998	THOMPSON, Vince	30	SENE	1891-06-29		A2
2999	THOMPSON, Voluntine Y	30	N½NE	1880-02-20		A2
2961	TISDALE, July	30	NWSW	1888-02-04		A2
2962	" "	30	SWNW	1888-02-04		A2
3000	UNDERWOOD, Wiley	32	E½SW	1858-11-01		A1
3001	" "	32	SWSW	1858-11-01		A1
2968	WILLIAMS, Miles P	18	SWNW	1883-10-01		A2 R2993
2935	WILSON, James	4	NWNE	1858-11-01		A1
2974	WOOD, Peter	30	E½SE	1883-10-01		A2
2975	" "	30	W½SE	1884-12-05		A2
3013	WOODS, Willis	28	N½NW	1882-10-20		A2
2911	WORTHINGTON, George W	18	W½SW	1883-08-13		A2

Copyright 2008 Boyd IT, Inc. All Rights Reserved

Map Grid

Section 6
MCADAMS Robert 1837	JEFCOAT Elijah 1858	CLEMENTS Zilpha S 1895	EDDINS Daniel J 1858
CLEMENTS Peter 1880	MCADAMS Robert 1852	EDDINS Daniel J	
JEFCOAT Elijah G 1858	MCADAMS Robert 1852	MCADAMS Robert 1858	EDDINS Daniel J 1858
JEFCOAT Elijah G 1858	JONES Samuel T 1885	JEFCOAT James O 1858	JEFCOAT James O 1858

Section 5
EDDINS Daniel J 1858	DAVIS Enoch 1858	EDDINS Ephraim 1852	SEALS James D 1858
	EDDINS Daniel J 1858	BARTON Joshua 1858	BARTON Joshua 1852
	EDDINS Ephraim 1852	BARTON Joshua 1858	
	GARDNER Derry A 1854		

Section 4
BARTON Joshua 1858	HIGHTOWER George H 1895	WILSON James 1858	RHODES Elisabeth J 1898
	BARTON Joshua A 1852	BARTON Joshua A 1852	BARTON Joshua 1858
STEVENS Thomas R 1898	BRISTOW Robertson 1860	BRISTOW Edwin J 1858	
GARDNER Stephen W 1885		BRISTOW Abner L 1880	

Section 7
JEFCOAT Jacob 1858	JEFCOAT Daniel W 1852	JEFCOAT James O 1858	
	DAVIS James W 1907	DAVIS Solomon 1858	
	DAVIS James W 1907	DAVIS James W 1907	NICHOLS Kinchen E 1907

Section 8
JEFCOAT James O 1858	TAYLOR William H 1893	EDDINS Ephraim 1852	
JORDAN Daniel 1883	JEFCOAT Samuel O 1858	GILMER Thomas M 1852	
NICHOLS Kinchen E 1907	JEFCOAT Samuel O 1858	DAVIS Francis 1858	FOLMAR Joel 1858
DAVIS Darcas 1860	DAVIS John T 1858	DAVIS Francis	

Section 9
GARDNER Derry A 1858	GARDNER Stephen W 1885	FOLMAR George S 1858	FOLMAR George S 1858
FOLMAR Joel 1858		FOLMAR George S 1858	FOLMAR John N 1838
	FOLMAR Joel 1858		

Section 18
MILLS Green A 1891	CARTER Stephen T 1891		
WILLIAMS Miles P 1883 / ANDERSON Thomas 1891	CORNETT George W 1891		
WORTHINGTON George W 1883	BYRD Joseph H 1888		
HOOKS John A 1883	BYRD Joseph H 1888		

Section 17
MITCHELL John 1858			
BRADLEY Stephen E 1900	RHODES Daniel B 1901	COMPTON Francis A 1905	
	BRADLEY Stephen E 1900		
JOHNSON Harriett 1901	DICKERSON Jim 1901	RHODES Daniel B 1901	COMPTON Francis A 1905

Section 16 — (No Patents Found)

Section 19 — (No Patents Found)
| MITCHELL James W 1858 | |
| STEPHENS James T 1860 | |

Section 20
HOOKS James M 1883		BOAN [4] John D 1894	
BOZEMAN Samuel R 1883	MCLEOD Hugh 1858		
MCLEOD Hugh 1883	MCLEOD Hugh 1858	MCLEOD Hugh 1858	MCLEOD [33] Martha R 1894
BOZEMAN Zimri C 1883	MCLEOD [33] Martha R 1894	MCLEOD [33] Martha R 1894	

Section 21
PELHAM James W 1837	PELHAM James W 1837	AMASON Eli 1838
	LONG Gilbert 1838	
	ROUSE William H 1858	
COOK Arthur R 1838	ROUSE William H 1858	

Section 30
THOMPSON Valentine Y 1883	THOMPSON Voluntine Y 1880		
TISDALE July 1888	JACKSON Willis 1891	THOMPSON Valentine Y 1883	THOMPSON Vince 1891
TISDALE July 1888	JACKSON Willis 1891		
	JOHNSON Brazill 1888	WOOD Peter 1884	WOOD Peter 1883

Section 29
	DEASON Edmond R 1858	
STEWART James D 1858		
		KING John F 1907

Section 28
WOODS Willis 1882	ROUSE William H 1858	ROUSE William H 1858
	NEIL Burrell 1880	GREEN Allen 1858
STEWART Cader P 1858		
STEWART Cader P 1858	STEWART Cader P 1852	

Section 31 — (No Patents Found)
| | RIEVES Moses D 1907 | RIEVES Moses D 1907 |
| | KERSEY Stephen A 1907 | FINLAY David 1845 |

Section 32
RIEVES Moses D 1907	KING John F 1907	
	GOODWIN William 1858	FOLMAR John A 1885
RIEVES Moses D 1907	UNDERWOOD Wiley 1858	GOODWIN William 1858
UNDERWOOD Wiley 1858	GOLDEN William J 1896	GODWIN William 1852

Section 33
KING John F 1907	DORMAN James 1854	STEWART Cader P 1858	SMILIE Robert 1837
STEWART Joshua W 1858	STEWART Joshua W 1858	COOPER Joseph E 1858	

Patent Map

T9-N R19-E
St Stephens Meridian

Map Group 13

Township Statistics

Parcels Mapped	:	147
Number of Patents	:	108
Number of Individuals	:	92
Patentees Identified	:	90
Number of Surnames	:	61
Multi-Patentee Parcels	:	4
Oldest Patent Date	:	8/8/1837
Most Recent Patent	:	4/5/1907
Block/Lot Parcels	:	0
Parcels Re - Issued	:	1
Parcels that Overlap	:	0
Cities and Towns	:	4
Cemeteries	:	0

Note: the area contained in this map amounts to far less than a full Township. Therefore, its contents are completely on this single page (instead of a "normal" 2-page spread).

Legend

————	Patent Boundary
━━━━	Section Boundary
▓▓▓▓	No Patents Found (or Outside County)
1., 2., 3., ...	Lot Numbers (when beside a name)
[ ]	Group Number (see Appendix "C")

Scale: Section = 1 mile X 1 mile
(generally, with some exceptions)

Road Map

T9-N R19-E
St Stephens Meridian

Map Group 13

Note: the area contained in this map amounts to far less than a full Township. Therefore, its contents are completely on this single page (instead of a "normal" 2-page spread).

Cities & Towns

Joquin
Shirleys Crossroads
Social Town
Vidette

Cemeteries

None

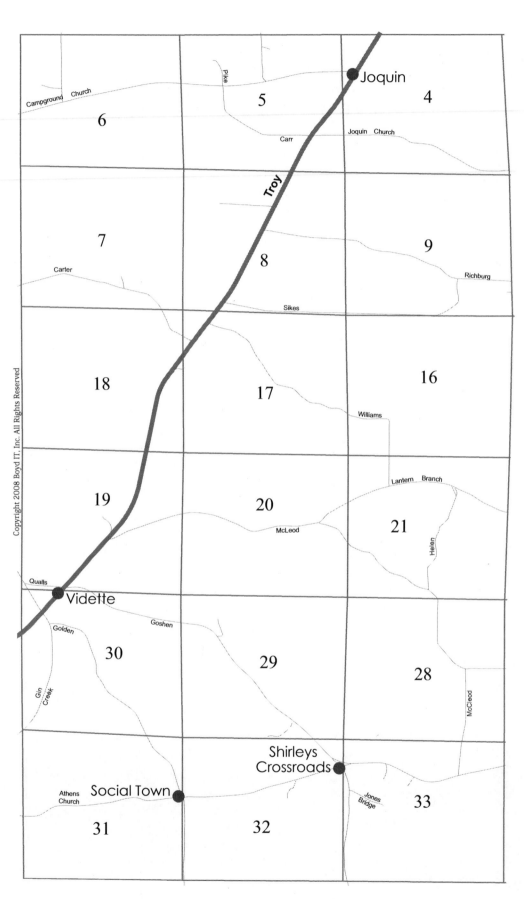

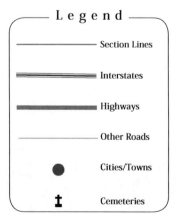

Legend

Section Lines

Interstates

Highways

Other Roads

● Cities/Towns

✝ Cemeteries

Scale: Section = 1 mile X 1 mile
(generally, with some exceptions)

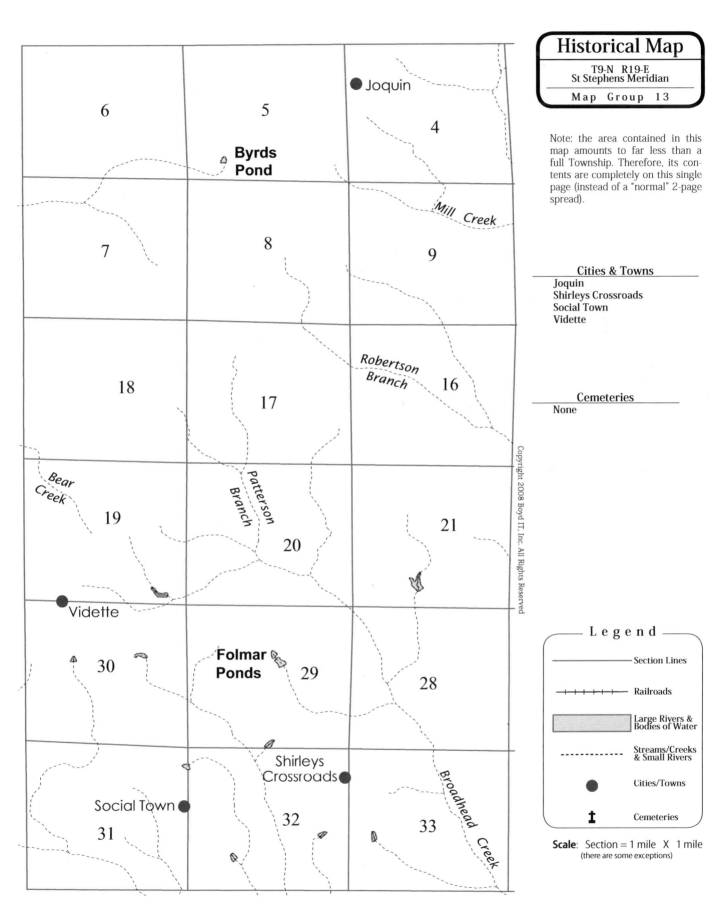

Note: the area contained in this map amounts to far less than a full Township. Therefore, its contents are completely on this single page (instead of a "normal" 2-page spread).

Cities & Towns

Joquin
Shirleys Crossroads
Social Town
Vidette

Cemeteries

None

6

5

Joquin

4

Byrds Pond

Mill Creek

7

8

9

18

17

Robertson Branch

16

Bear Creek

Patterson Branch

19

20

21

Vidette

30

Folmar Ponds

29

28

Shirleys Crossroads

Social Town

31

32

Broadhead Creek

33

Legend

———— Section Lines

+–+–+–+ Railroads

Large Rivers & Bodies of Water

- - - - Streams/Creeks & Small Rivers

● Cities/Towns

† Cemeteries

Scale: Section = 1 mile X 1 mile
(there are some exceptions)

Map Group 14: Index to Land Patents

Township 8-North Range 16-East (St Stephens)

After you locate an individual in this Index, take note of the Section and Section Part then proceed to the Land Patent map on the pages immediately following. You should have no difficulty locating the corresponding parcel of land.

The "For More Info" Column will lead you to more information about the underlying Patents. See the *Legend* at right, and the "How to Use this Book" chapter, for more information.

```
┌─────────────────────────────────────────────────────┐
│                    LEGEND                           │
│         "For More Info . . . " column               │
├─────────────────────────────────────────────────────┤
│ A = Authority (Legislative Act, See Appendix "A")   │
│ B = Block or Lot (location in Section unknown)      │
│ C = Cancelled Patent                                │
│ F = Fractional Section                              │
│ G = Group  (Multi-Patentee Patent, see Appendix "C")│
│ V = Overlaps another Parcel                         │
│ R = Re-Issued (Parcel patented more than once)      │
│                                                     │
│ (A & G items require you to look in the Appendixes  │
│ referred to above. All other Letter-designations    │
│ followed by a number require you to locate line-    │
│ items in this index that possess the ID number      │
│ found after the letter).                            │
└─────────────────────────────────────────────────────┘
```

ID	Individual in Patent	Sec.	Sec. Part	Date Issued	Other Counties	For More Info . . .
3073	ARMSTRONG, Maximillian	34	E½SW	1860-10-01		A1
3074	" "	34	NW	1860-10-01		A1
3075	" "	34	W½NE	1860-12-01		A1
3016	ARNOLD, Albert P	28	NESE	1858-11-01		A1
3019	BARRETT, Benjamin J	2	E½SW	1861-05-01		A1
3020	" "	2	SE	1861-05-01		A1
3021	" "	2	SWSW	1861-05-01		A1
3037	BASS, Elbert	25	E½NW	1903-12-17		A2
3038	" "	25	W½NE	1903-12-17		A2
3114	BENNETT, Toney	2	E½NW	1894-11-28		A2
3115	" "	2	SWNW	1894-11-28		A2
3101	BENSON, Sarah	25	E½SE	1860-04-02		A1
3102	" "	25	NESW	1860-04-02		A1
3103	" "	25	NWSE	1860-04-02		A1
3104	" "	36	E½NE	1860-04-02		A1
3105	" "	36	E½SE	1860-04-02		A1
3118	BENSON, William C	20	E½NE	1860-09-01		A1
3119	" "	20	SE	1860-09-01		A1
3120	" "	20	W½NE	1860-09-01		A1
3048	BROWN, James	33	NW	1897-02-17		A1
3049	" "	33	W½NE	1897-02-17		A1
3050	" "	33	W½SE	1897-02-17		A1
3116	BURGIN, William	34	E½NE	1861-05-01		A1
3117	" "	34	SE	1861-05-01		A1
3127	BUSH, William F	11	N½NW	1901-11-06		A2
3128	" "	11	W½NE	1901-11-06		A2
3035	CALLAWAY, Claborn	19	NW	1858-11-01		A1
3059	CAMPBELL, Jessee	20	SWSW	1860-12-01		A1
3121	CARR, William	12	NESW	1858-11-01		A1
3122	" "	12	NWSE	1858-11-01		A1
3123	" "	12	SESE	1858-11-01		A1
3124	" "	12	SESW	1858-11-01		A1
3125	" "	12	SWSE	1858-11-01		A1
3126	" "	12	SWSW	1858-11-01		A1
3060	CLAGHORN, John	15	NWSE	1858-11-01		A1
3051	CLEGHORN, James C	36	NWNW	1898-03-21		A2
3099	CLEGHORN, Samuel O	24	S½SE	1861-05-01		A1
3100	" "	24	SESW	1861-05-01		A1
3052	COOK, James C	36	E½NW	1860-09-01		A1
3053	" "	36	NWNE	1860-09-01		A1
3054	" "	36	SWNW	1860-09-01		A1
3055	" "	36	W½SW	1860-09-01		A1
3017	COOPER, Benjamin	15	SENE	1901-04-22		A2
3018	" "	15	W½NE	1901-04-22		A2
3067	COWART, John W	10	SESE	1860-04-02		A1
3068	" "	10	W½SE	1860-04-02		A1

ID	Individual in Patent	Sec.	Sec. Part	Date Issued	Other Counties	For More Info . . .
3069	COWART, John W (Cont'd)	15	NENE	1860-04-02		A1
3033	DAVIS, Cap	2	NWNW	1903-06-17		A2
3070	DAVIS, Josiah C	13	NE	1900-11-28		A2
3022	DENDY, Buford W	10	NESE	1860-09-01		A1
3023	" "	12	NESE	1860-09-01		A1
3024	" "	12	NWSW	1860-09-01		A1
3025	" "	13	W½SE	1860-09-01		A1
3026	" "	14	SENW	1860-09-01		A1
3027	" "	14	W½NW	1860-09-01		A1
3028	" "	24	SWSW	1860-09-01		A1
3029	" "	32	W½NW	1860-09-01		A1
3042	FRANKLIN, Green B	36	SESW	1858-11-01		A1
3044	" "	36	SWSE	1858-11-01		A1
3040	" "	36	NESW	1875-04-20		A1
3041	" "	36	NWSE	1875-04-20		A1
3043	" "	36	SWNE	1875-04-20		A1
3087	GOODSON, Peter	30	E½NW	1860-09-01		A1
3088	" "	30	E½SE	1860-09-01		A1
3089	" "	30	E½SW	1860-09-01		A1
3090	" "	30	W½NE	1860-09-01		A1
3071	JACKSON, Lafayette	32	E½SE	1897-02-17		A1
3072	" "	33	W½SW	1897-02-17		A1
3098	JOHNSON, Robert	15	NWSW	1858-11-01		A1
3076	KILCREASE, Minor	15	E½SW	1860-04-02		A1
3077	" "	15	SENW	1860-04-02		A1
3078	" "	15	SWSW	1860-04-02		A1
3079	" "	15	W½NW	1860-04-02		A1
3080	" "	21	NENE	1860-04-02		A1
3081	" "	22	NWNW	1860-04-02		A1
3058	MCLEAN, James	30	NENE	1860-12-01		A1
3039	MCNEAL, George T	14	SWNE	1893-08-14		A2
3045	MILLER, Henry	2	NWSW	1897-11-05		A2
3091	MITCHELL, Peter	29	SESW	1858-11-01		A1
3092	" "	29	SWSE	1858-11-01		A1
3093	" "	32	E½NW	1858-11-01		A1
3094	" "	32	NE	1858-11-01		A1
3131	PARMER, William K	28	SESE	1860-10-01		A1
3064	PICKETT, John	1	NWNW	1858-11-01		A1
3065	" "	2	NENE	1862-01-01		A1
3106	PICKETT, Stephen A	11	N½SW	1900-11-12		A2
3107	" "	11	NWSE	1900-11-12		A2
3108	" "	11	SENW	1900-11-12		A2
3109	POTTER, Thomas F	34	W½SW	1860-10-01		A1
3030	POUNCY, Calvin B	26	E½NE	1860-09-01		A1
3031	" "	26	SE	1860-09-01		A1
3032	" "	26	W½NE	1860-09-01		A1
3056	PRIER, James M	24	E½	1860-10-01		A1 C
3057	" "	24	NESW	1860-10-01		A1 C
3129	PRIER, William F	14	NENW	1860-10-01		A1
3130	" "	14	NWNE	1860-10-01		A1
3082	REAVES, Molley	13	W½SW	1860-04-02		A1
3083	" "	14	E½NE	1860-04-02		A1
3084	" "	14	E½SE	1860-04-02		A1
3085	" "	24	NWSW	1860-04-02		A1
3086	" "	24	W½NW	1860-04-02		A1
3034	RHODES, Charlotte	1	NESE	1852-02-02		A1
3066	RHODES, John	1	E½NE	1837-08-15		A1
3095	RICHARDSON, Richard	12	N½	1860-10-01		A1
3132	ROGERS, William	29	NWSW	1858-11-01		A1
3133	" "	29	SWNW	1858-11-01		A1
3134	" "	30	SENE	1858-11-01		A1
3046	SHOWS, Henry W	11	E½NE	1900-11-12		A2
3047	" "	11	E½SE	1900-11-12		A2
3061	SMITH, John H	20	N½SW	1860-09-01		A1
3062	" "	20	NW	1860-09-01		A1
3063	" "	20	SESW	1860-12-01		A1
3096	SMYTH, Robert B	2	SENE	1896-11-21		A1
3097	" "	2	W½NE	1896-11-21		A1
3112	SPRAGGINS, Thomas	27	SWNW	1858-11-01		A1
3113	" "	28	SWNE	1858-11-01		A1
3110	" "	27	NESW	1897-02-17		A1
3111	" "	27	SENW	1897-02-17		A1
3036	WOOD, David A	11	S½SW	1900-11-12		A2

Patent Map

T8-N R16-E
St Stephens Meridian

Map Group 14

Township Statistics

Parcels Mapped	:	119
Number of Patents	:	63
Number of Individuals	:	48
Patentees Identified	:	48
Number of Surnames	:	42
Multi-Patentee Parcels	:	0
Oldest Patent Date	:	8/15/1837
Most Recent Patent	:	12/17/1903
Block/Lot Parcels	:	0
Parcels Re - Issued	:	0
Parcels that Overlap	:	0
Cities and Towns	:	0
Cemeteries	:	0

6	5	4
7	8	9
18	17	16

Butler

Crenshaw

KILCREASE Minor 1860

19
CALLAWAY Claborn 1858

20
SMITH John H 1860
BENSON William C 1860
BENSON William C 1860

SMITH John H 1860
BENSON William C 1860

CAMPBELL Jessee 1860
SMITH John H 1860

21

30
GOODSON Peter 1860
GOODSON Peter 1860
MCLEAN James 1860
ROGERS William 1858
GOODSON Peter 1860
GOODSON Peter 1860

29
ROGERS William 1858
ROGERS William 1858
MITCHELL Peter 1858
MITCHELL Peter 1858

28
SPRAGGINS Thomas 1858
ARNOLD Albert P 1858
PARMER William K 1860

31

32
DENDY Buford W 1860
MITCHELL Peter 1858
MITCHELL Peter 1858
JACKSON Lafayette 1897

33
BROWN James 1897
BROWN James 1897
JACKSON Lafayette 1897
BROWN James 1897

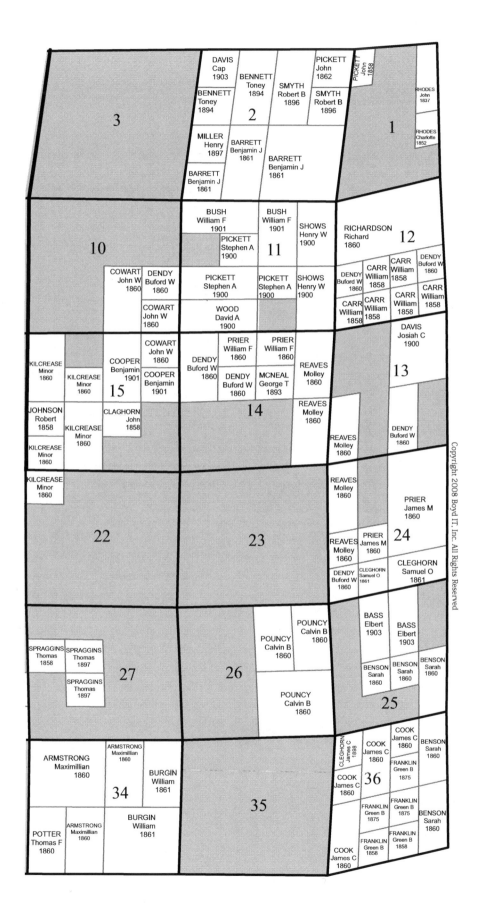

Helpful Hints

1. This Map's INDEX can be found on the preceding pages.

2. Refer to Map "C" to see where this Township lies within Crenshaw County, Alabama.

3. Numbers within square brackets [ ] denote a multi-patentee land parcel (multi-owner). Refer to Appendix "C" for a full list of members in this group.

4. Areas that look to be crowded with Patentees usually indicate multiple sales of the same parcel (Re-issues) or Overlapping parcels. See this Township's Index for an explanation of these and other circumstances that might explain "odd" groupings of Patentees on this map.

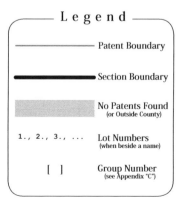

L e g e n d

——————— Patent Boundary

━━━━━━━ Section Boundary

░░░░░░░ No Patents Found (or Outside County)

1., 2., 3., ... Lot Numbers (when beside a name)

[ ] Group Number (see Appendix "C")

Scale: Section = 1 mile X 1 mile (generally, with some exceptions)

Road Map

T8-N R16-E
St Stephens Meridian

Map Group 14

Cities & Towns
None

Cemeteries
None

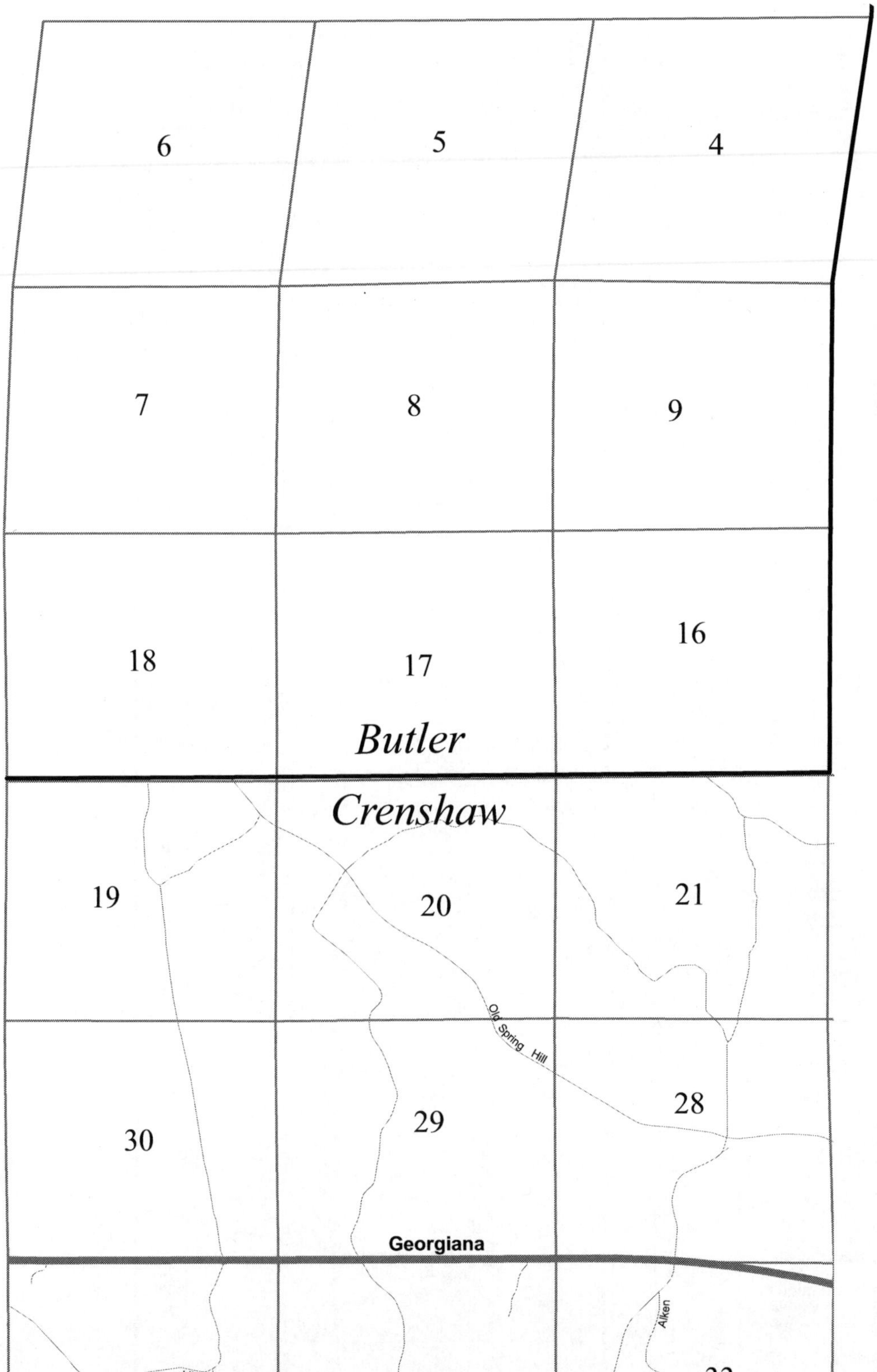

6

5

4

7

8

9

18

17

16

Butler

Crenshaw

19

20

21

Old Spring Hill

30

29

28

Georgiana

Franklin

Aiken

31

32

33

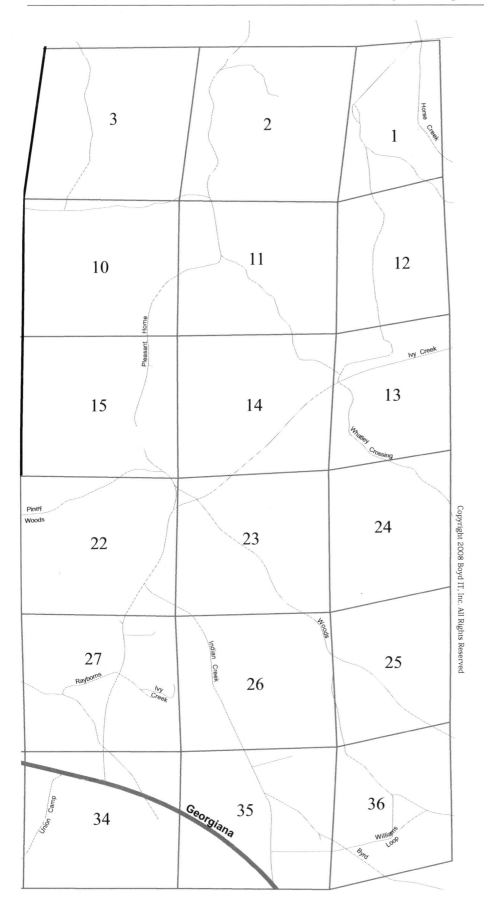

Helpful Hints

1. This road map has a number of uses, but primarily it is to help you: a) find the present location of land owned by your ancestors (at least the general area), b) find cemeteries and city-centers, and c) estimate the route/roads used by Census-takers & tax-assessors.

2. If you plan to travel to Crenshaw County to locate cemeteries or land parcels, please pick up a modern travel map for the area before you do. Mapping old land parcels on modern maps is not as exact a science as you might think. Just the slightest variations in public land survey coordinates, estimates of parcel boundaries, or road-map deviations can greatly alter a map's representation of how a road either does or doesn't cross a particular parcel of land.

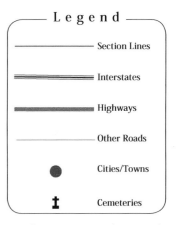

Legend

————	Section Lines
▬▬▬▬	Interstates
▬▬▬▬	Highways
————	Other Roads
●	Cities/Towns
☦	Cemeteries

Scale: Section = 1 mile X 1 mile
(generally, with some exceptions)

Historical Map

T8-N R16-E
St Stephens Meridian

Map Group 14

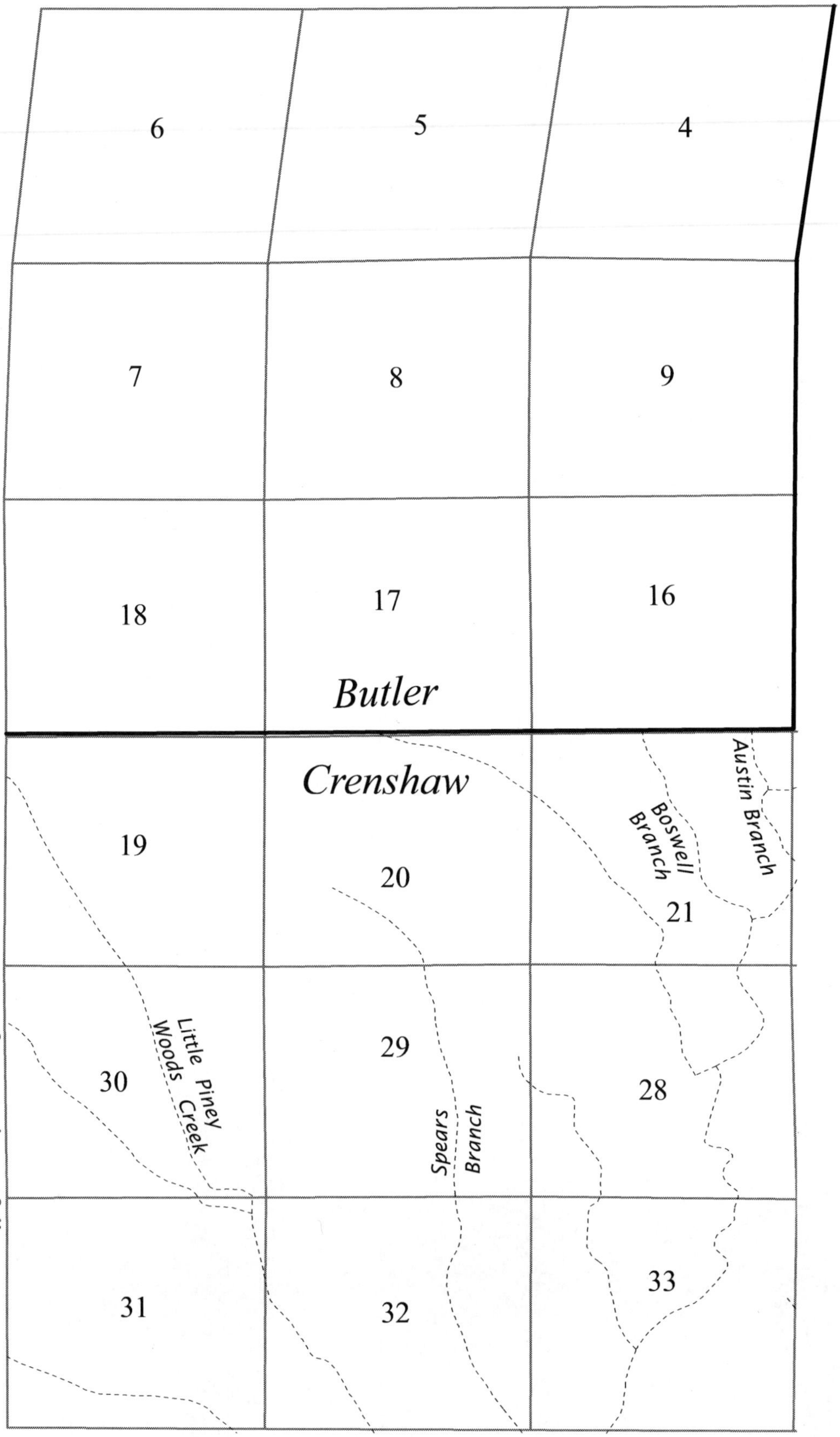

Cities & Towns
None

Cemeteries
None

6	5	4
7	8	9
18	17	16

Butler

Crenshaw

19	20	21
30	29	28
31	32	33

Austin Branch

Boswell Branch

Little Piney Woods Creek

Spears Branch

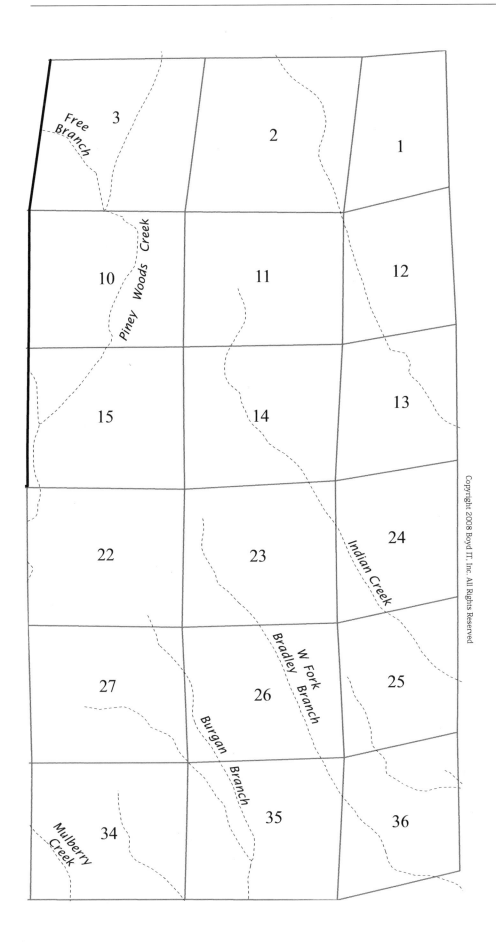

Helpful Hints

1. This Map takes a different look at the same Congressional Township displayed in the preceding two maps. It presents features that can help you better envision the historical development of the area: a) Water-bodies (lakes & ponds), b) Water-courses (rivers, streams, etc.), c) Railroads, d) City/town center-points (where they were oftentimes located when first settled), and e) Cemeteries.

2. Using this "Historical" map in tandem with this Township's Patent Map and Road Map, may lead you to some interesting discoveries. You will often find roads, towns, cemeteries, and waterways are named after nearby landowners: sometimes those names will be the ones you are researching. See how many of these research gems you can find here in Crenshaw County.

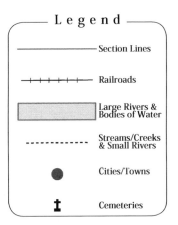

L e g e n d

——————— Section Lines

+–+–+–+–+ Railroads

▨ Large Rivers & Bodies of Water

- - - - - - - Streams/Creeks & Small Rivers

● Cities/Towns

⸸ Cemeteries

Scale: Section = 1 mile X 1 mile
(there are some exceptions)

Map Group 15: Index to Land Patents

Township 8-North Range 17-East (St Stephens)

After you locate an individual in this Index, take note of the Section and Section Part then proceed to the Land Patent map on the pages immediately following. You should have no difficulty locating the corresponding parcel of land.

The "For More Info" Column will lead you to more information about the underlying Patents. See the *Legend* at right, and the "How to Use this Book" chapter, for more information.

```
┌─────────────────────────────────────────────────────────┐
│                      LEGEND                             │
│            "For More Info . . . " column                │
├─────────────────────────────────────────────────────────┤
│ A = Authority (Legislative Act, See Appendix "A")       │
│ B = Block or Lot (location in Section unknown)          │
│ C = Cancelled Patent                                    │
│ F = Fractional Section                                  │
│ G = Group  (Multi-Patentee Patent, see Appendix "C")    │
│ V = Overlaps another Parcel                             │
│ R = Re-Issued (Parcel patented more than once)          │
├─────────────────────────────────────────────────────────┤
│ (A & G items require you to look in the Appendixes      │
│ referred to above. All other Letter-designations        │
│ followed by a number require you to locate line-items   │
│ in this index that possess the ID number found after    │
│ the letter).                                            │
└─────────────────────────────────────────────────────────┘
```

ID	Individual in Patent	Sec.	Sec. Part	Date Issued	Other Counties	For More Info . . .
3459	ALFORD, William H	29	SWSE	1858-11-01		A1
3460	" "	32	NENE	1858-11-01		A1
3461	" "	32	NWNE	1858-11-01		A1
3462	" "	32	SWNE	1858-11-01		A1
3342	AMASON, Josiah J	33	E½SW	1880-11-20		A1
3343	" "	33	NENW	1880-11-20		A1
3344	" "	33	NWSE	1880-11-20		A1
3345	" "	33	W½NE	1880-11-20		A1
3430	AMASON, Thomas W	28	W½SW	1862-01-01		A1
3431	" "	32	SENE	1862-01-01		A1
3432	" "	33	NWSW	1862-01-01		A1
3433	" "	33	W½NW	1862-01-01		A1
3365	ARMSTRONG, Melville J	18	SESE	1901-04-22		A2
3366	" "	19	E½NE	1901-04-22		A2
3241	ATHEY, Henry	12	SESW	1858-11-01		A1
3242	" "	13	NWNW	1858-11-01		A1
3439	ATHEY, William	13	NENW	1834-08-05		A1
3441	" "	13	SWNW	1834-08-05		A1
3440	" "	13	SENW	1837-05-20		A1
3137	BANKS, Abner	18	E½NW	1862-01-01		A1
3138	" "	18	N½NE	1862-01-01		A1
3410	BARROW, Thomas J	31	SESE	1902-02-03		A2
3337	BAYGENTS, Joshua H	23	NENE	1834-08-05		A1
3266	BOGGS, James	3	SWNE	1858-11-01		A1 R3267
3267	" "	3	SWNE	1858-11-01		A1 R3266
3472	BOSWELL, William J	3	SWSE	1862-01-01		A1
3409	BOYD, Theodore G	14	SESE	1834-08-05		A1
3399	BRADLEY, Samuel C	31	W½SE	1896-10-28		A1
3361	BREWER, Matthew W	26	E½SW	1862-01-01		A1
3362	" "	26	W½SE	1862-01-01		A1
3219	BRIGGS, Elkanah	5	E½NE	1837-08-15		A1
3218	" "	3	SW	1838-07-28		A1
3164	BROOKS, Baley M	36	E½SW	1860-04-02		A1
3165	" "	36	SWSE	1860-04-02		A1
3227	BROWN, George R	7	SESE	1901-01-23		A2
3398	BROWNING, Samuel	25	NENE	1858-11-01		A1
3482	BROWNING, William R	25	NW	1875-04-20		A1
3182	BRUNSON, Benjamin	13	NE	1831-12-01		A1 G8
3179	" "	22	E½SW	1837-04-10		A1
3181	" "	22	SWNE	1837-04-10		A1
3180	" "	22	SENE	1837-08-18		A1
3182	BRUNSON, David	13	NE	1831-12-01		A1 G8
3206	" "	15	W½SE	1837-08-18		A1
3207	" "	21	SWSE	1837-08-18		A1
3202	BRUNSON, David A	22	NW	1862-01-01		A1
3307	BRUNSON, John R	21	SESW	1858-11-01		A1

ID	Individual in Patent	Sec.	Sec. Part	Date Issued	Other Counties	For More Info . . .
3308	BRUNSON, John R (Cont'd)	28	NENW	1858-11-01		A1
3338	BRUNSON, Josiah	22	W½SW	1840-10-10		A1
3369	BURKE, Nancy	4	SWSE	1858-11-01		A1
3370	" "	9	NENW	1862-01-01		A1
3371	" "	9	NWNE	1862-01-01		A1
3139	CAPPS, Alexander	1	SESW	1852-02-02		A1
3140	" "	1	SWSW	1858-11-01		A1
3141	" "	12	NENW	1858-11-01		A1
3142	" "	12	NWNW	1858-11-01		A1
3143	" "	12	SENW	1858-11-01		A1
3222	CAPPS, Frank M	7	SESE	1900-11-12		A2
3223	" "	7	SWSE	1900-11-12		A2
3224	" "	7	W½SW	1900-11-12		A2
3287	CAPPS, Jane S	26	SWSW	1891-09-01		A2 G10
3363	CAPPS, Melissa A	35	SWNW	1899-11-04		A2
3364	" "	35	W½SW	1899-11-04		A2
3287	CAPPS, Robert H	26	SWSW	1891-09-01		A2 G10
3397	CAPPS, Sallie A	3	SENW	1904-03-19		A2 G11
3400	CAPPS, Samuel I	11	SENE	1858-11-01		A1
3397	CAPPS, Spencer W	3	SENW	1904-03-19		A2 G11
3463	CAPPS, William H	1	NWSE	1858-11-01		A1
3464	" "	1	SENW	1858-11-01		A1
3465	" "	1	SESE	1858-11-01		A1
3466	" "	1	SWNE	1858-11-01		A1
3467	" "	12	NWNE	1858-11-01		A1
3473	CAPPS, William J	27	NWNW	1858-11-01		A1
3474	" "	27	S½NW	1858-11-01		A1
3475	" "	27	SWNE	1858-11-01		A1
3260	CARNES, Herschel M	29	SESE	1901-01-23		A2
3298	CARTER, John	25	NESE	1858-11-01		A1
3176	CARTLIDGE, Bazdell M	17	NWSE	1860-04-02		A1
3178	" "	17	SWNE	1860-04-02		A1
3175	" "	17	NWNE	1862-01-01		A1
3177	" "	17	SENW	1862-01-01		A1
3161	CHESTER, Asa C	27	SW	1897-03-18		A1
3162	" "	28	NESE	1897-03-18		A1
3163	" "	34	NENW	1897-03-18		A1
3144	CLANCY, Alfred J	23	SWNW	1858-11-01		A1
3174	CLANCY, Bartley	23	SWNE	1835-10-15		A1
3170	" "	23	NENW	1837-04-10		A1
3172	" "	23	NWNE	1837-04-10		A1
3169	" "	23	E½SE	1837-08-18		A1
3173	" "	23	NWSE	1854-07-15		A1
3167	" "	22	NENE	1858-11-01		A1
3168	" "	22	NWNE	1858-11-01		A1
3171	" "	23	NESW	1858-11-01		A1
3199	CLANCY, Daniel	10	SESW	1852-02-02		A1
3225	COMPTON, Friendly L	24	NWNE	1860-04-02		A1
3313	COMPTON, John S	24	NESW	1896-10-28		A1
3314	" "	24	SENW	1896-10-28		A1
3367	COMPTON, Milton S	27	E½NE	1897-03-18		A1
3368	" "	27	NWNE	1897-03-18		A1
3436	COMPTON, Walter D	13	SESW	1834-08-05		A1
3437	" "	24	NENW	1834-08-05		A1
3329	COOK, Joseph M	19	S½SW	1900-11-28		A2
3315	CORDRAY, John S	25	SWSW	1858-11-01		A1
3316	" "	26	SESE	1858-11-01		A1
3317	" "	35	E½NE	1858-11-01		A1
3318	" "	36	NW	1858-11-01		A1
3495	COURTNEY, Willie M	36	NWSE	1898-04-18		A2
3184	DANIEL, Carlton L	34	S½SW	1896-05-21		A2
3135	DAVIS, Abiah	7	NENW	1837-08-15		A1
3136	" "	7	W½NW	1837-08-15		A1
3149	DAVIS, Andrew C	10	SWSW	1848-05-03		A1
3146	" "	10	NESW	1852-12-01		A1
3147	" "	10	NWSW	1852-12-01		A1
3145	" "	10	N½NW	1860-09-01		A1
3148	" "	10	S½NW	1862-01-01		A1
3150	" "	9	SESE	1862-01-01		A1
3183	DAVIS, Bose	26	N½NE	1897-07-03		A2
3239	DAVIS, Helton	5	NWNW	1860-04-02		A1
3240	" "	6	NENE	1860-04-02		A1
3268	DAVIS, James	6	SE	1837-08-12		A1

ID	Individual in Patent	Sec.	Sec. Part	Date Issued	Other Counties	For More Info . . .
3269	DAVIS, James (Cont'd)	7	W½NE	1837-08-14		A1
3302	DAVIS, John	4	E½NW	1837-08-15		A1
3303	" "	4	NWNW	1837-08-15		A1
3304	" "	4	W½NE	1837-08-15		A1
3301	" "	4	E½NE	1837-08-18		A1
3300	" "	15	W½SW	1841-05-20		A1
3299	" "	15	W½NW	1848-05-03		A1
3305	" "	12	E½NE	1858-09-01		A1 G16
3306	DAVIS, John J	1	NESE	1852-02-02		A1
3382	DAVIS, Robert B	9	SWSE	1854-10-02		A1
3381	" "	9	N½SE	1858-11-01		A1
3456	DAVIS, William	6	NWNE	1837-08-18		A1
3478	DAVIS, William M	6	SWNW	1858-11-01		A1
3220	DUKE, Euthademus M	29	NESE	1858-11-01		A1
3234	DUKE, Green S	14	E½NE	1858-11-01		A1
3235	" "	14	NENW	1858-11-01		A1
3236	" "	14	NWNE	1858-11-01		A1
3221	EDWARDS, Fannie	24	SESW	1892-01-18		A2
3326	ELLINGTON, Joseph	5	NESE	1837-08-02		A1
3327	" "	5	SWNE	1837-08-02		A1
3328	" "	8	W½SW	1838-07-28		A1
3295	FOSTER, John B	18	SWNE	1891-05-29		A2
3166	FRANKLIN, Barnett	12	SWSE	1837-04-10		A1
3245	FRANKLIN, Henry C	20	NESE	1858-11-01		A1
3247	" "	21	NWSW	1858-11-01		A1
3243	" "	17	SESE	1862-01-01		A1
3246	" "	21	NESW	1862-01-01		A1
3248	" "	21	SENW	1862-01-01		A1
3244	" "	20	E½NE	1896-10-28		A1
3249	" "	21	W½NW	1896-10-28		A1
3356	FRANKLIN, Margaret	13	SE	1831-08-01		A1 G18
3442	FRANKLIN, William B	13	NESW	1837-04-10		A1
3214	GAINEY, Elizabeth	4	NESW	1858-11-01		A1
3215	" "	4	NWSW	1858-11-01		A1
3216	" "	4	SWSW	1858-11-01		A1
3396	GANEY, Ryal E	22	E½SE	1858-11-01		A1
3258	GARRETT, Henry L	31	SW	1900-11-12		A2
3256	GIBSON, Henry J	34	N½SE	1892-04-01		A2
3257	" "	34	S½NE	1892-04-01		A2
3340	GIBSON, Josiah H	27	W½SE	1858-11-01		A1
3339	" "	27	E½SE	1860-04-02		A1
3341	" "	34	N½NE	1860-04-02		A1
3357	GIBSON, Maria J	8	SWSE	1837-08-15		A1
3393	GIBSON, Rufus	35	E½NW	1907-04-05		A1
3394	" "	35	E½SW	1907-04-05		A1
3395	" "	35	NWNW	1907-04-05		A1
3252	GILCREASE, Henry	31	NENE	1862-01-01		A1
3253	" "	31	NENW	1862-01-01		A1
3254	" "	31	W½NE	1862-01-01		A1
3255	" "	32	NWNW	1862-01-01		A1
3373	GOODSON, Peter	30	NESW	1860-09-01		A1
3374	" "	30	W½SW	1860-09-01		A1
3230	HALL, Glover	24	SWNW	1858-11-01		A1
3231	" "	24	W½SW	1858-11-01		A1
3296	HANCOCK, John B	4	N½SE	1860-08-01		A1
3297	" "	4	SESE	1860-08-01		A1
3263	HARDIN, Jacob	17	SESW	1862-01-01		A1
3264	" "	17	SWSE	1862-01-01		A1
3265	" "	17	W½SW	1862-01-01		A1
3186	HILL, Charles T	28	S½SE	1860-10-01		A1
3187	" "	28	SENE	1860-10-01		A1 V3185
3185	" "	28	S½NE	1862-01-01		A1 V3187, 3477
3387	HILL, Robert J	21	SWSW	1858-11-01		A1
3388	" "	28	SENW	1858-11-01		A1
3389	" "	28	W½NW	1858-11-01		A1
3390	" "	29	S½NE	1858-11-01		A1
3271	HOLLAND, James	20	SESW	1858-11-01		A1
3272	" "	20	SWSE	1858-11-01		A1
3274	" "	29	N½NW	1858-11-01		A1
3275	" "	30	NENE	1858-11-01		A1
3277	" "	30	SENE	1860-10-01		A1
3273	" "	20	SWSW	1862-01-01		A1
3276	" "	30	NWNE	1862-01-01		A1

ID	Individual in Patent	Sec.	Sec. Part	Date Issued	Other Counties	For More Info . . .
3458	HOLLAND, William G	19	S½SE	1900-11-12		A2
3356	HOPPER, Samuel J	13	SE	1831-08-01		A1 G18
3346	HUDSON, Lawson A	19	S½NW	1904-05-05		A2
3386	HURT, Robert	24	SWSE	1891-06-29		A2
3385	" "	24	NWSE	1896-09-04		A2
3232	INGRAM, Green	17	NENW	1860-04-02		A1
3233	" "	8	SESW	1860-04-02		A1
3159	JAMES, Arnoldus	8	SENW	1848-05-03		A1
3157	" "	8	NENW	1854-07-15		A1
3158	" "	8	NWSE	1862-01-01		A1
3160	" "	9	NWNW	1862-01-01		A1
3372	JOHNSON, Osborn S	25	SENE	1897-03-18		A1
3391	JOHNSON, Robert	12	SWNW	1837-08-14		A1
3406	JONSON, Sarah	35	W½SE	1907-04-05		A1
3438	JOURDAN, Wiley	21	SESE	1840-10-10		A1
3151	KENNEDY, Andrew J	18	E½SW	1862-01-01		A1
3152	" "	18	NESE	1862-01-01		A1
3153	" "	18	SENE	1862-01-01		A1
3154	" "	18	SWSW	1862-01-01		A1
3155	" "	18	W½SE	1862-01-01		A1
3156	" "	19	NWNE	1862-01-01		A1
3468	LANE, William H	30	SESW	1860-09-01		A1
3469	" "	30	SWNW	1860-09-01		A1
3278	LITTLE, James M	32	E½SW	1896-12-11		A1
3279	" "	32	SE	1896-12-11		A1
3280	" "	32	SENW	1896-12-11		A1
3281	" "	33	SWSW	1896-12-11		A1
3434	LOCK, Union	25	SESE	1907-04-05		A1
3457	MAHONE, William F	11	E½SE	1862-01-01		A1
3358	MAINOR, Marshel	36	S½NE	1889-08-02		A2
3470	MANNING, William H	17	NESE	1841-05-20		A1
3471	" "	17	SENE	1841-05-20		A1
3443	MARSHALL, William B	10	NE	1862-01-01		A1
3444	" "	10	SWSE	1862-01-01		A1
3445	" "	11	E½NW	1862-01-01		A1
3446	" "	11	S½SW	1862-01-01		A1
3447	" "	11	SWSE	1862-01-01		A1
3448	" "	14	N½SW	1862-01-01		A1
3449	" "	14	NWSE	1862-01-01		A1
3450	" "	14	SENW	1862-01-01		A1
3451	" "	14	SWNE	1862-01-01		A1
3452	" "	14	W½NW	1862-01-01		A1
3453	" "	15	E½SW	1862-01-01		A1
3454	" "	15	NE	1862-01-01		A1
3455	" "	15	SENW	1862-01-01		A1
3197	MILLS, Clara G	33	E½SE	1901-04-22		A2 G34
3198	" "	33	SWSE	1901-04-22		A2 G34
3392	MILLS, Robert M	24	SESE	1858-11-01		A1
3197	MILLS, Warren W	33	E½SE	1901-04-22		A2 G34
3198	" "	33	SWSE	1901-04-22		A2 G34
3213	NICHOLS, Elias S	26	NESE	1899-04-17		A2 G36
3293	NICHOLS, Joel	26	E½NW	1878-04-09		A2
3294	" "	26	S½NE	1889-11-21		A2
3292	NICHOLS, Joel L	34	NWNW	1905-11-08		A2
3213	NICHOLS, Mozelle G	26	NESE	1899-04-17		A2 G36
3479	NICHOLS, William M	34	N½SW	1888-02-04		A2
3480	" "	34	S½NW	1888-02-04		A2
3496	NICHOLS, Zellar	25	NWSW	1909-10-28		A2
3347	PARDUE, Leroy	13	SWSW	1835-04-15		A1
3348	" "	14	NESE	1835-04-15		A1
3204	PARMER, David B	30	SWNE	1860-10-01		A1
3203	" "	30	SESE	1861-09-10		A1
3205	" "	30	W½SE	1861-09-10		A1
3330	PARMER, Joseph M	20	N½SW	1862-01-01		A1
3331	" "	20	NWSE	1862-01-01		A1
3332	" "	20	SESE	1862-01-01		A1
3333	" "	20	W½NE	1862-01-01		A1
3377	PATTERSON, Peter	7	SENE	1838-07-28		A1
3414	PAUL, Thomas	36	W½SW	1890-10-11		A2
3282	PENDREY, James P	14	S½SW	1858-11-01		A1
3283	" "	15	SESE	1858-11-01		A1
3334	PERDUE, Joseph	24	NWNW	1837-08-18		A1
3335	PERDUE, Joseph R	14	SWSE	1837-08-18		A1

ID	Individual in Patent	Sec.	Sec. Part	Date Issued	Other Counties	For More Info . . .
3336	PERDUE, Joseph R (Cont'd)	22	W½SE	1837-08-18		A1
3350	PERDUE, Leroy	23	NWNW	1834-08-20		A1
3352	" "	23	SENW	1837-04-10		A1
3349	" "	13	NWSW	1837-08-18		A1
3351	" "	23	SENE	1837-08-18		A1
3359	PERRY, Mary	19	N½SE	1896-10-28		A1
3360	" "	19	SWNE	1896-10-28		A1
3261	PHILLIPS, Howard P	33	SENW	1909-10-11		A2
3237	PLATT, Harman	12	E½SE	1833-07-18		A1
3288	POPE, Jeptha	31	SENW	1900-11-12		A2
3289	" "	31	W½NW	1900-11-12		A2
3228	REESE, George	11	NWSE	1837-08-18		A1
3190	RHODES, Charlotte	6	NWNW	1848-04-01		A1
3189	" "	6	E½NW	1858-11-01		A1
3191	" "	6	SWNE	1858-11-01		A1
3192	" "	6	SWSW	1862-01-01		A1
3310	RHODES, John	6	E½SW	1837-08-15		A1
3311	" "	6	NWSW	1837-08-15		A1
3312	" "	8	SWNW	1837-08-15		A1
3208	ROACH, David	8	E½SE	1837-05-15		A1
3210	" "	9	NWSW	1837-05-15		A1
3211	" "	9	SENW	1837-08-14		A1
3212	" "	9	SESW	1837-08-14		A1
3209	" "	8	W½NE	1837-08-18		A1
3378	ROACH, Peter	21	NENW	1860-04-02		A1
3376	ROACH, Peter P	21	NWNE	1858-11-01		A1
3375	" "	21	NENE	1862-01-01		A1
3476	SANDERS, William J	28	NWSE	1896-07-09		A2
3477	" "	28	SWNE	1896-07-09		A2 V3185
3484	SKAIN, William	8	E½NE	1837-08-09		A1
3485	" "	9	NESW	1837-08-09		A1
3486	" "	9	SWNW	1837-08-09		A1
3487	" "	9	SWSW	1837-08-09		A1
3483	" "	17	NENE	1838-07-28		A1
3194	SKAINS, Charner T	24	NENE	1853-11-15		A1
3195	" "	24	NESE	1853-11-15		A1
3193	" "	12	SWNE	1858-11-01		A1
3196	" "	24	SENE	1858-11-01		A1
3401	SKAINS, Samuel S	1	E½NE	1858-11-01		A1
3402	" "	1	N½NW	1858-11-01		A1
3403	" "	1	N½SW	1858-11-01		A1
3404	" "	1	NWNE	1858-11-01		A1
3405	" "	1	SWNW	1858-11-01		A1
3418	SKAINS, Thomas	5	E½SW	1837-08-09		A1
3423	" "	5	W½SE	1837-08-09		A1
3420	" "	5	NWNE	1837-08-14		A1
3421	" "	5	SENW	1837-08-14		A1
3422	" "	5	SESE	1837-08-14		A1
3419	" "	5	NENW	1840-10-10		A1
3424	" "	5	W½SW	1841-05-20		A1
3425	" "	8	NWNW	1841-05-20		A1
3305	" "	12	E½NE	1858-09-01		A1 G16
3415	" "	11	N½NE	1858-11-01		A1
3416	" "	2	S½NE	1858-11-01		A1
3417	" "	2	SE	1858-11-01		A1
3481	SKAINS, William M	9	SWNE	1860-04-02		A1
3354	SMITH, Major L	26	NWSW	1897-11-22		A2
3355	" "	26	W½NW	1897-11-22		A2
3217	SPURLIN, Elizabeth	36	E½SE	1884-03-20		A2 G38
3217	SPURLIN, William	36	E½SE	1884-03-20		A2 G38
3259	STAGGERS, Henry S	2	N½NE	1860-12-01		A1
3383	STAGGERS, Robert E	17	SWNW	1904-05-05		A2
3200	STARR, Daniel S	21	N½SE	1841-05-20		A1
3201	" "	21	S½NE	1841-05-20		A1
3250	STOKES, Henry D	23	SESW	1903-12-31		A2
3251	" "	23	SWSE	1903-12-31		A2
3188	STYRON, Charley	3	N½NW	1903-12-31		A2
3262	SWANNER, Ira	3	SESE	1854-07-15		A1 R3325
3324	SWANNER, John	3	NESE	1850-08-10		A1
3320	" "	2	NWSW	1852-02-02		A1
3319	" "	2	NESW	1858-11-01		A1
3323	" "	2	SWSW	1858-11-01		A1
3325	" "	3	SESE	1858-11-01		A1 R3262

ID	Individual in Patent	Sec.	Sec. Part	Date Issued	Other Counties	For More Info . . .
3321	SWANNER, John (Cont'd)	2	SENW	1862-01-01		A1
3322	" "	2	SESW	1862-01-01		A1
3426	SWANNER, Thomas	31	NESE	1858-11-01		A1
3427	" "	31	SENE	1862-01-01		A1
3428	" "	32	SWNW	1862-01-01		A1
3429	" "	32	W½SW	1862-01-01		A1
3489	SWANNER, William	11	N½SW	1850-08-10		A1
3491	" "	11	W½NW	1858-11-01		A1
3488	" "	10	NESE	1862-01-01		A1
3490	" "	11	SWNE	1862-01-01		A1
3290	TATE, Jepthah V	25	E½SW	1858-11-01		A1
3291	" "	25	W½SE	1858-11-01		A1
3226	TAYLOR, Furney G	28	E½SW	1878-04-09		A2
3229	THAGARD, George W	2	SWNW	1852-02-02		A1
3270	THOMASSON, James F	19	N½NW	1858-11-01		A1
3238	TOMLINSON, Harris	35	W½NE	1858-11-01		A1
3284	TURNER, James T	24	SWNE	1885-03-30		A2
3435	UNDERWOOD, Vincent A	29	N½NE	1858-11-01		A1
3353	UPSHAW, Leroy	4	SWNW	1862-01-01		A1
3380	UPSHAW, Rebecca	10	NWSE	1862-01-01		A1
3407	UPTING, Simon	34	S½SE	1889-08-16		A2
3286	WAYNE, James W	36	NWNE	1860-12-01		A1
3285	" "	36	NENE	1907-04-05		A1
3411	WEBB, Thomas J	29	E½SW	1860-04-02		A1
3412	" "	29	NWSE	1860-04-02		A1
3413	" "	32	NENW	1860-04-02		A1
3408	WELCH, Solomon M	23	W½SW	1858-11-01		A1
3309	WILLIAMS, John R	17	NESW	1908-07-27		A2
3384	WILLIAMS, Robert E	29	S½NW	1914-01-17		A2
3379	WOOD, Pluvus C	9	NENE	1908-09-10		A1
3492	WREN, William	7	NENE	1858-11-01		A1
3493	" "	7	NESE	1858-11-01		A1
3494	" "	8	NESW	1858-11-01		A1

Patent Map

T8-N R17-E
St Stephens Meridian

Map Group 15

Township Statistics

Parcels Mapped	:	362
Number of Patents	:	246
Number of Individuals	:	165
Patentees Identified	:	161
Number of Surnames	:	102
Multi-Patentee Parcels	:	9
Oldest Patent Date	:	8/1/1831
Most Recent Patent	:	1/17/1914
Block/Lot Parcels	:	0
Parcels Re - Issued	:	2
Parcels that Overlap	:	3
Cities and Towns	:	0
Cemeteries	:	1

STYRON Charley 1903					STAGGERS Henry S 1860	SKAINS Samuel S 1858	SKAINS Samuel S 1858	SKAINS Samuel S 1858
	CAPPS [11] Sallie A 1904	BOGGS James 1858	THAGARD George W 1852	SWANNER John 1862	SKAINS Thomas 1858	SKAINS Samuel S 1858	CAPPS William H 1858	CAPPS William H 1858
3		SWANNER John 1850	SWANNER John 1852	SWANNER John 1858	**2**	SKAINS Samuel S 1858	**1** CAPPS William H 1858	DAVIS John J 1852
BRIGGS Elkanah 1838	BOSWELL William J 1862	SWANNER Ira 1854 SWANNER John 1858	SWANNER John 1858	SWANNER John 1862	SKAINS Thomas 1858	CAPPS Alexander 1858	CAPPS Alexander 1852	CAPPS William H 1858
DAVIS Andrew C 1860		MARSHALL William B 1862	SWANNER William 1858	MARSHALL William B 1862	SKAINS Thomas 1858	CAPPS Alexander 1858	CAPPS Alexander 1858	CAPPS William H 1858	DAVIS [16] John 1858
DAVIS Andrew C 1862		**10**		**11**	SWANNER William 1862	CAPPS Samuel I 1858	JOHNSON Robert 1837	CAPPS Alexander 1858	SKAINS Charner T 1858
DAVIS Andrew C 1852	DAVIS Andrew C 1852	UPSHAW Rebecca 1862	SWANNER William 1862	SWANNER William 1850	REESE George 1837	MAHONE William F 1862		**12**	
DAVIS Andrew C 1848	CLANCY Daniel 1852	MARSHALL William B 1862		MARSHALL William B 1862	MARSHALL William B 1862		ATHEY Henry 1858	FRANKLIN Barnett 1837	PLATT Harman 1833
DAVIS John 1848	MARSHALL William B 1862	MARSHALL William B 1862	MARSHALL William B 1862	DUKE Green S 1858	DUKE Green S 1858	ATHEY Henry 1858	ATHEY William 1834	BRUNSON [8] Benjamin 1831	
		15		**14** MARSHALL William B 1862	MARSHALL William B 1862	DUKE Green S 1858	ATHEY William 1834	ATHEY William 1837	**13**
DAVIS John 1841	MARSHALL William B 1862	BRUNSON David 1837	MARSHALL William B 1862	PENDREY James P 1858	MARSHALL William B 1862	PARDUE Leroy 1835	PERDUE Leroy 1837	FRANKLIN William B 1837	FRANKLIN [18] Margaret 1831
			PENDREY James P 1858		PERDUE Joseph R 1837	BOYD Theodore G 1834	PARDUE Leroy 1835	COMPTON Walter D 1834	
BRUNSON David A 1862	CLANCY Bartley 1858	CLANCY Bartley 1858	PERDUE Leroy 1834	CLANCY Bartley 1837	CLANCY Bartley 1837	BAYGENTS Joshua H 1834	PERDUE Joseph 1837	COMPTON Walter D 1834	COMPTON Friendly L 1860	SKAINS Charner T 1853
	22	BRUNSON Benjamin 1837	BRUNSON Benjamin 1837	CLANCY Alfred J 1858	PERDUE Leroy 1837	CLANCY Bartley 1835	PERDUE Leroy 1837	HALL Glover 1858	COMPTON John S 1896	**24**	TURNER James T 1885	SKAINS Charner T 1853
BRUNSON Josiah 1840	BRUNSON Benjamin 1837	PERDUE Joseph R 1837	GANEY Ryal E 1858	WELCH Solomon M 1858	CLANCY Bartley 1858	CLANCY Bartley 1854	CLANCY Bartley 1837	HALL Glover 1858	COMPTON John S 1896	HURT Robert 1896	SKAINS Charner T 1853
				STOKES Henry D 1903	STOKES Henry D 1903			EDWARDS Fannie 1892	HURT Robert 1891	MILLS Robert M 1858
CAPPS William J 1858		COMPTON Milton S 1897		NICHOLS Joel 1878	DAVIS Bose 1897					BROWNING Samuel 1858
	CAPPS William J 1858	CAPPS William J 1858	COMPTON Milton S 1897	SMITH Major L 1897		**26**	NICHOLS Joel 1889		BROWNING William R 1875	**25**	JOHNSON Osborn S 1897
27	GIBSON Josiah H 1858		SMITH Major L 1897	BREWER Matthew W 1862	BREWER Matthew W 1862	NICHOLS [36] Elias S 1899	NICHOLS Zellar 1909	TATE Jepthah V 1858	TATE Jepthah V 1858	CARTER John 1858
CHESTER Asa C 1897		GIBSON Josiah H 1860	CAPPS [10] Jane S 1891			CORDRAY John S 1858	CORDRAY John S 1858			LOCK Union 1907
NICHOLS Joel L 1905	CHESTER Asa C 1897	GIBSON Josiah H 1860	GIBSON Rufus 1907	GIBSON Rufus 1907	TOMLINSON Harris 1858	CORDRAY John S 1858	CORDRAY John S 1858		WAYNE James W 1860	WAYNE James W 1907
NICHOLS William M 1888	**34**	GIBSON Henry J 1892	CAPPS Melissa A 1899	**35**				**36**	MAINOR Marshel 1889	
NICHOLS William M 1888		GIBSON Henry J 1892	CAPPS Melissa A 1899		JONSON Sarah 1907		PAUL Thomas 1890		COURTNEY Willie M 1898	SPURLIN [38] Elizabeth 1884
DANIEL Carlton L 1896		UPTING Simon 1889		GIBSON Rufus 1907				BROOKS Baley M 1860	BROOKS Baley M 1860	

Helpful Hints

1. This Map's INDEX can be found on the preceding pages.

2. Refer to Map "C" to see where this Township lies within Crenshaw County, Alabama.

3. Numbers within square brackets [ ] denote a multi-patentee land parcel (multi-owner). Refer to Appendix "C" for a full list of members in this group.

4. Areas that look to be crowded with Patentees usually indicate multiple sales of the same parcel (Re-issues) or Overlapping parcels. See this Township's Index for an explanation of these and other circumstances that might explain "odd" groupings of Patentees on this map.

Legend

————————	Patent Boundary
━━━━━━━━	Section Boundary
░░░░░░░░	No Patents Found (or Outside County)
1., 2., 3., ...	Lot Numbers (when beside a name)
[ ]	Group Number (see Appendix "C")

Scale: Section = 1 mile X 1 mile (generally, with some exceptions)

Road Map

T8-N R17-E
St Stephens Meridian

Map Group 15

Cities & Towns
None

Cemeteries
Clarke Cemetery

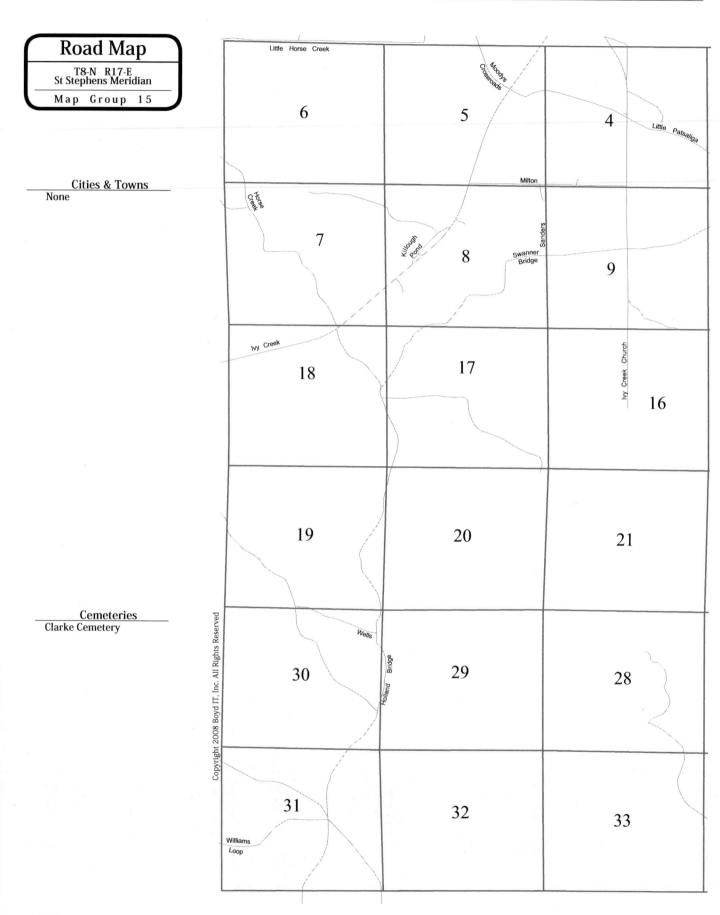

Little Horse Creek

Moodys Crossroads

Little Patsaliga

6

5

4

Horse Creek

Milton

Sanders

7

8

Killough Pond

Swanner Bridge

9

Ivy Creek

Ivy Creek Church

18

17

16

19

20

21

Wells

Holland Bridge

30

29

28

31

32

33

Williams Loop

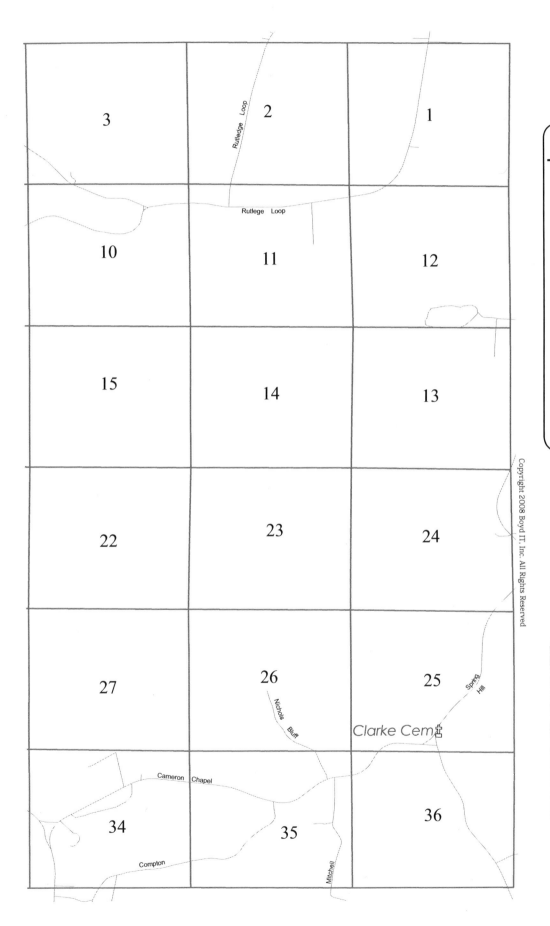

3	2	1
10	11	12
15	14	13
22	23	24
27	26	25
34	35	36

Rutledge Loop

Rutlege Loop

Nichols Bluff

Clarke Cem

Spring Hill

Cameron Chapel

Compton

Mitchell

Helpful Hints

1. This road map has a number of uses, but primarily it is to help you: a) find the present location of land owned by your ancestors (at least the general area), b) find cemeteries and city-centers, and c) estimate the route/roads used by Census-takers & tax-assessors.

2. If you plan to travel to Crenshaw County to locate cemeteries or land parcels, please pick up a modern travel map for the area before you do. Mapping old land parcels on modern maps is not as exact a science as you might think. Just the slightest variations in public land survey coordinates, estimates of parcel boundaries, or road-map deviations can greatly alter a map's representation of how a road either does or doesn't cross a particular parcel of land.

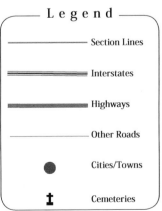

L e g e n d

———— Section Lines

═══ Interstates

▬▬▬ Highways

——— Other Roads

● Cities/Towns

✝ Cemeteries

Scale: Section = 1 mile X 1 mile
(generally, with some exceptions)

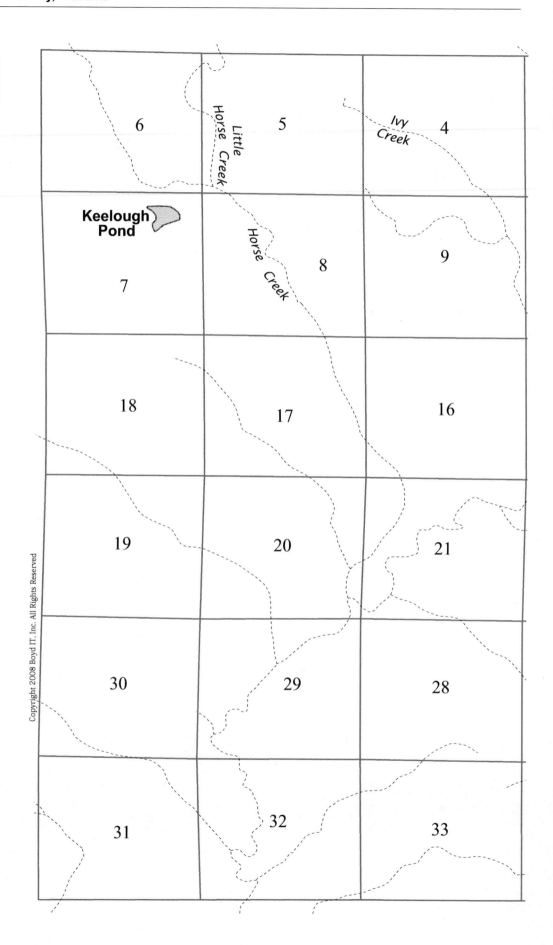

Historical Map

T8-N R17-E
St Stephens Meridian

Map Group 15

Cities & Towns
None

Cemeteries
Clarke Cemetery

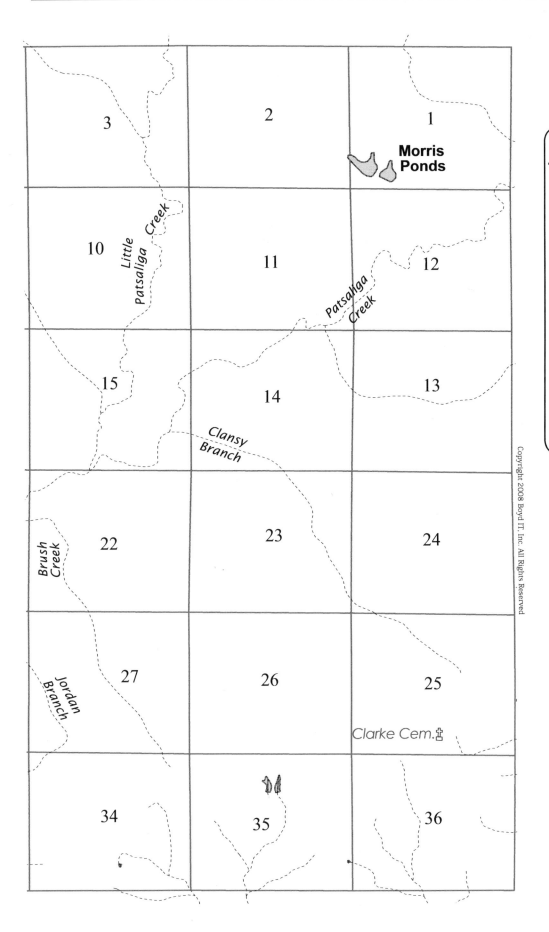

3

2

1

Morris Ponds

10

Little Patsaliga Creek

11

12

Patsaliga Creek

15

14

13

Clansy Branch

Brush Creek

22

23

24

Jordan Branch

27

26

25

Clarke Cem. ☦

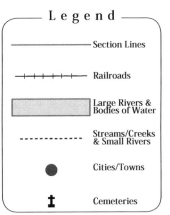

34

35

36

Helpful Hints

1. This Map takes a different look at the same Congressional Township displayed in the preceding two maps. It presents features that can help you better envision the historical development of the area: a) Water-bodies (lakes & ponds), b) Water-courses (rivers, streams, etc.), c) Railroads, d) City/town center-points (where they were oftentimes located when first settled), and e) Cemeteries.

2. Using this "Historical" map in tandem with this Township's Patent Map and Road Map, may lead you to some interesting discoveries. You will often find roads, towns, cemeteries, and waterways are named after nearby landowners: sometimes those names will be the ones you are researching. See how many of these research gems you can find here in Crenshaw County.

L e g e n d

————————— Section Lines

+++++++++ Railroads

▭ Large Rivers & Bodies of Water

- - - - - - - Streams/Creeks & Small Rivers

● Cities/Towns

☦ Cemeteries

Scale: Section = 1 mile X 1 mile
(there are some exceptions)

Map Group 16: Index to Land Patents

Township 8-North Range 18-East (St Stephens)

After you locate an individual in this Index, take note of the Section and Section Part then proceed to the Land Patent map on the pages immediately following. You should have no difficulty locating the corresponding parcel of land.

The "For More Info" Column will lead you to more information about the underlying Patents. See the *Legend* at right, and the "How to Use this Book" chapter, for more information.

```
┌─────────────────────────────────────────────────┐
│                      LEGEND                       │
│          "For More Info . . . " column            │
│ A = Authority (Legislative Act, See Appendix "A") │
│ B = Block or Lot (location in Section unknown)    │
│ C = Cancelled Patent                              │
│ F = Fractional Section                            │
│ G = Group  (Multi-Patentee Patent, see Appendix "C") │
│ V = Overlaps another Parcel                       │
│ R = Re-Issued (Parcel patented more than once)    │
│                                                   │
│ (A & G items require you to look in the Appendixes referred │
│ to above. All other Letter-designations followed by a number │
│ require you to locate line-items in this index that possess │
│ the ID number found after the letter).            │
└─────────────────────────────────────────────────┘
```

ID	Individual in Patent	Sec.	Sec. Part	Date Issued	Other Counties	For More Info . . .
3654	ALBRITTON, Joseph L	36	E½NW	1892-05-26		A1
3655	" "	36	E½SW	1892-05-26		A1
3579	ANDERSON, Henry	15	E½NW	1900-11-28		A2
3497	BAKER, Abner	34	NESW	1892-06-10		A2
3498	" "	34	NWSE	1892-06-10		A2
3499	" "	34	S½SW	1892-06-10		A2
3741	BATTLE, Stephen B	32	N½NE	1895-11-25		A2
3742	" "	32	N½NW	1895-11-25		A2
3624	BENBOW, Joel L	20	NESE	1858-11-01		A1
3625	" "	20	SENE	1858-11-01		A1
3626	" "	28	N½NW	1858-11-01		A1
3702	BENBOW, Richard	8	W½NW	1834-08-05		A1
3704	BENBOW, Richard M	30	NESE	1896-04-23		A2
3705	" "	30	S½SE	1896-04-23		A2
3523	BENNETT, Bose	20	W½SW	1897-07-27		A2
3676	BERRY, Matthew A	9	SESE	1907-04-05		A1
3677	" "	9	SWNE	1907-04-05		A1
3678	" "	9	W½SE	1907-04-05		A1
3683	BISHOP, Noble P	33	E½	1901-10-09		A1 G2
3684	" "	33	E½NW	1901-10-09		A1 G2 R3649
3685	" "	33	E½SW	1901-10-09		A1 G2 R3738
3656	BODIFORD, Joseph M	31	SESW	1900-10-12		A2
3657	" "	31	SWSE	1900-10-12		A2
3658	" "	31	W½SW	1900-10-12		A2
3641	BREAKER, John W	10	NENW	1897-03-18		A1
3642	" "	3	S½SW	1897-03-18		A1
3719	BROWNING, Samuel	19	NWNW	1858-11-01		A1
3531	BRUNSON, Daniel	18	NWNE	1834-08-05		A1
3534	BRUNSON, Daniel H	9	NESW	1858-11-01		A1
3535	" "	9	SWSW	1858-11-01		A1
3532	" "	22	S½SW	1892-01-18		A2
3533	" "	22	W½SE	1892-01-18		A2
3545	BRUNSON, David	18	NWNW	1834-08-12		A1
3586	BRUNSON, Isaac J	10	NENE	1858-11-01		A1
3619	BRUNSON, Jasper P	10	SENW	1891-06-30		A2
3620	" "	10	W½NE	1891-06-30		A2
3635	BRUNSON, John R	32	N½SW	1891-06-08		A2
3636	" "	32	S½NW	1891-06-08		A2
3634	" "	27	NW	1901-01-23		A2
3706	BRUNSON, Richard M	34	NWSW	1890-03-19		A2
3707	" "	34	W½NW	1890-03-19		A2
3761	BRUNSON, William G	27	SE	1900-11-28		A2
3597	BUCKELEW, James	6	E½SE	1833-07-18		A1
3599	" "	7	E½NE	1833-07-18		A1
3600	" "	7	SENW	1834-08-12		A1
3598	" "	6	SWSE	1834-08-20		A1

ID	Individual in Patent	Sec.	Sec. Part	Date Issued	Other Counties	For More Info . . .
3584	BURK, Isaac	34	E½NW	1890-03-19		A2
3585	" "	34	W½NE	1890-03-19		A2
3601	CAPPS, James	20	SESE	1898-03-08		A2 G9
3643	CAPPS, John W	28	E½SW	1899-02-06		A2
3644	" "	28	S½SE	1899-02-06		A2
3601	CAPPS, Mary C	20	SESE	1898-03-08		A2 G9
3716	CAPPS, Robert H	8	NESW	1837-05-20		A1
3697	COLEMAN, Peter	5	E½NW	1832-08-08		A1
3698	COLEMAN, Peter E	5	SW	1831-08-01		A1 G13
3621	COMPTON, Jefferson E	30	NENE	1896-04-23		A2
3622	" "	30	SENE	1896-04-23		A2
3623	" "	30	SWNE	1896-04-23		A2
3679	COMPTON, Milt	32	S½SW	1896-05-06		A2
3680	" "	32	W½SE	1896-05-06		A2
3580	COX, Henry	35	NE	1900-11-28		A2
3569	CURTIS, George	11	W½NE	1838-07-28		A1
3581	CURTIS, Henry D	24	W½SW	1883-10-20		A1
3602	CURTIS, James	22	N½SW	1891-06-19		A2
3603	" "	22	S½NW	1891-06-19		A2
3627	CURTIS, John B	11	E½NW	1840-10-10		A1
3628	CURTIS, John D	24	NESE	1837-08-08		A1
3712	CURTIS, Robert	26	NW	1891-06-29		A2
3720	CURTIS, Samuel	22	NE	1891-06-08		A2
3703	DEMING, Richard	22	E½SE	1891-06-08		A2
3718	DEMING, Sam	28	NE	1892-01-18		A2
3753	DEVLIN, William	11	NENE	1840-10-10		A1
3652	DOWNING, Joseph	5	W½NW	1832-08-08		A1
3653	" "	6	E½NE	1832-08-08		A1
3645	DRIVER, John W	14	NENW	1897-07-03		A2
3646	" "	14	W½NW	1897-07-03		A2 V3764, 3613
3589	FIELDER, Jack	20	NENW	1896-04-23		A2
3548	FINLAY, Duncan	12	SENE	1837-08-12		A1
3549	" "	12	W½NE	1837-08-12		A1
3547	" "	1	E½SW	1837-08-15		A1
3683	FOSKETT, William A	33	E½	1901-10-09		A1 G2
3684	" "	33	E½NW	1901-10-09		A1 G2 R3649
3685	" "	33	E½SW	1901-10-09		A1 G2 R3738
3513	FRANKLIN, Barnett	18	NENW	1834-08-05		A1
3516	" "	18	SWNE	1834-08-05		A1
3512	" "	18	E½NE	1835-09-12		A1
3515	" "	18	SENW	1837-04-10		A1
3511	" "	12	NESW	1838-07-28		A1
3514	" "	18	NWSE	1838-07-28		A1
3517	" "	2	NENW	1852-02-02		A1
3518	" "	2	NWNE	1852-02-02		A1
3604	FRANKLIN, James E	12	NWSW	1848-05-03		A1
3715	FRANKLIN, Robert	8	NE	1831-08-01		A1
3714	" "	12	S½SW	1835-10-01		A1
3524	GALLOPS, Charlotte T	32	E½SE	1895-01-31		A2
3525	" "	32	S½NE	1895-01-31		A2
3649	GALLOPS, Joseph D	33	E½NW	1906-05-23		A2 R3684
3650	" "	33	W½NE	1906-05-23		A2 V3683
3738	HALL, Stanley	33	E½SW	1906-05-23		A2 R3685
3739	" "	33	W½SE	1906-05-23		A2 V3683
3681	HAMMONS, Moses	14	SESW	1891-06-08		A2
3682	" "	14	SWSE	1891-06-08		A2
3659	HANCOCK, Joseph M	14	SWSW	1895-06-03		A2
3754	HARRELL, William F	27	NE	1900-11-12		A2 V3701
3520	HOLLADAY, Benjamin H	14	N½SE	1868-04-02		A1
3521	" "	14	SENE	1868-04-02		A1
3661	HOLLAND, Julian	30	NENW	1891-06-19		A2
3662	" "	30	NWNE	1891-06-19		A2
3638	HOLMES, John S	3	SWNW	1854-07-15		A1
3637	" "	3	N½SW	1858-11-01		A1
3537	HOOKS, Daniel	22	N½NW	1891-06-08		A2 G23
3537	HOOKS, Mary	22	N½NW	1891-06-08		A2 G23
3651	HOPPER, Joseph D	18	W½SW	1834-05-12		A1
3721	HOPPER, Samuel J	18	SESW	1834-08-05		A1
3530	HORN, Christopher C	24	NESW	1852-02-02		A1
3669	HORN, Lewis	13	SESW	1852-02-02		A1
3670	" "	36	W½NE	1858-11-01		A1
3686	HORN, Oliver W	13	SWNW	1852-02-02		A1
3688	" "	24	SWNW	1854-07-15		A1

ID	Individual in Patent	Sec.	Sec. Part	Date Issued	Other Counties	For More Info . . .
3687	HORN, Oliver W (Cont'd)	24	SESW	1854-10-02		A1
3689	" "	25	E½NE	1858-11-01		A1
3690	" "	25	NENW	1858-11-01		A1
3691	" "	25	NWNE	1858-11-01		A1
3746	HOUGH, Thaddeus	14	NENE	1888-02-04		A2
3729	HUGHES, Solomon	18	NESW	1837-08-14		A1
3730	" "	18	SWSE	1837-08-14		A1
3592	JOHNSON, James A	34	NESE	1891-05-29		A2 G24
3593	" "	34	S½SE	1891-05-29		A2 G24
3594	" "	34	SENE	1891-05-29		A2 G24
3590	" "	14	SESE	1897-03-18		A1
3591	" "	23	NENE	1897-03-18		A1
3592	JOHNSON, Laura L	34	NESE	1891-05-29		A2 G24
3593	" "	34	S½SE	1891-05-29		A2 G24
3594	" "	34	SENE	1891-05-29		A2 G24
3692	JOHNSON, Osborn S	19	SWSW	1897-03-18		A1
3693	" "	30	N½SW	1897-03-18		A1
3694	" "	30	NWSE	1897-03-18		A1
3695	" "	30	SENW	1897-03-18		A1
3696	" "	30	W½NW	1897-03-18		A1
3605	JUNE, James H	12	NWSE	1849-09-01		A1
3501	KENT, Alexander	10	W½NW	1903-07-14		A2
3740	KERSEY, Stephen A	6	NWNW	1907-04-05		A1 R3509
3699	KING, Prince H	26	NE	1890-03-19		A2
3700	KING, Ransom	10	W½SE	1895-09-04		A2
3574	KITES, Grandison	28	SENW	1892-02-08		A2 G30
3575	" "	28	SWNW	1892-02-08		A2 G30
3574	KITES, Mary	28	SENW	1892-02-08		A2 G30
3575	" "	28	SWNW	1892-02-08		A2 G30
3663	LOCKHART, Julius C	36	NESE	1858-11-01		A1
3664	" "	36	W½SE	1858-11-01		A1
3570	LOWREY, George	5	SE	1831-08-01		A1
3571	LOWRY, George	5	E½NE	1832-08-08		A1
3572	" "	5	W½NE	1832-08-08		A1
3755	MAHONE, William F	6	E½NW	1862-01-01		A1
3756	" "	6	E½SW	1862-01-01		A1
3757	" "	6	NWSE	1862-01-01		A1
3758	" "	6	W½NE	1862-01-01		A1
3759	" "	7	NENW	1862-01-01		A1
3760	" "	7	SWNW	1862-01-01		A1
3502	MCDUGALD, Alexander	12	NENW	1852-02-02		A1
3500	MCDUGALD, Alexander D	12	SWNW	1858-11-01		A1
3536	MCDUGALD, Daniel H	13	NWNW	1858-11-01		A1
3583	MCDUGALD, Hugh K	12	SENW	1850-08-10		A1
3632	MCDUGALD, John D	12	NENE	1837-08-12		A1
3630	" "	1	SESE	1850-08-10		A1
3629	" "	1	NWSE	1858-11-01		A1
3631	" "	1	SWNE	1858-11-01		A1
3667	MCKEE, Lazarus	14	NESW	1902-02-03		A2
3668	" "	14	SENW	1902-02-03		A2
3770	MOODY, William	4	SWNE	1837-08-02		A1
3769	" "	4	NENE	1837-08-10		A1
3765	" "	3	NENW	1858-11-01		A1
3766	" "	3	NWNE	1858-11-01		A1
3767	" "	3	SENW	1907-04-05		A1
3768	" "	3	SWNE	1907-04-05		A1
3587	MOORE, Isam	12	E½SE	1838-07-28		A1
3588	MOORE, Isham	13	NENE	1850-04-01		A1
3647	MOORE, John W	13	S½NE	1858-11-01		A1
3648	" "	13	SENW	1858-11-01		A1
3519	MOUNT, Beckey	26	W½SW	1893-05-26		A2
3717	MOUNT, Robert	27	SW	1900-11-12		A2
3561	NELSON, Fed	17	SW	1901-12-30		A2
3671	OLIVE, Littleton	18	SESE	1897-03-18		A1
3672	" "	19	NE	1897-03-18		A1
3673	" "	19	NWSE	1897-03-18		A1
3674	" "	20	W½NW	1897-03-18		A1
3610	PENDREY, James P	21	NWSE	1858-11-01		A1
3611	" "	21	SESW	1858-11-01		A1
3724	PENDREY, Samuel	21	N½SW	1858-11-01		A1
3725	" "	21	S½NW	1858-11-01		A1
3665	PERKINS, Kit	15	E½SW	1900-11-12		A2
3666	" "	15	W½SE	1900-11-12		A2

ID	Individual in Patent	Sec.	Sec. Part	Date Issued	Other Counties	For More Info . . .
3727	PERKINS, Simon	35	NW	1900-11-28		A2
3577	PLATT, Harman	7	W½SW	1833-07-18		A1
3576	"	7	E½SW	1837-05-20		A1
3578	PLATT, Harmon	7	W½SE	1837-08-02		A1
3564	PONDER, Francis M	17	SWNW	1858-11-01		A1
3565	" "	18	NESE	1858-11-01		A1
3606	PONDER, James H	18	SWNW	1837-05-20		A1
3607	" "	7	NESE	1837-05-20		A1
3608	" "	8	NWSW	1837-05-20		A1
3553	RICHARDSON, Elihu E	20	E½SW	1896-11-21		A1
3554	" "	20	SENW	1896-11-21		A1
3555	" "	20	SWNE	1896-11-21		A1
3556	" "	20	W½SE	1896-11-21		A1
3557	" "	29	NENW	1896-11-21		A1
3558	" "	29	NWNE	1896-11-21		A1
3713	ROGERS, Robert D	19	NWSW	1838-07-28		A1
3539	SARTON, Daniel	4	SW	1831-08-01		A1
3543	SARTOR, Daniel	9	NW	1832-08-08		A1
3542	" "	4	W½NW	1833-09-16		A1
3541	" "	4	SENW	1834-06-12		A1
3544	" "	9	NWNE	1834-06-12		A1
3540	" "	4	NENW	1837-08-10		A1
3560	SARTOR, Ephraim	10	E½SW	1891-06-19		A2
3559	SILER, Elijah	28	W½SW	1895-06-03		A2
3731	SILER, Solomon	13	SE	1837-08-09		A1
3734	" "	24	E½NW	1837-08-09		A1
3735	" "	24	NE	1837-08-09		A1
3732	" "	2	W½NW	1837-08-12		A1
3733	" "	2	W½SW	1837-08-12		A1
3736	" "	3	E½NE	1838-07-28		A1
3737	" "	3	E½SE	1838-07-28		A1
3526	SKAINS, Charner T	19	NENW	1858-11-01		A1
3527	" "	19	NESW	1858-11-01		A1
3528	" "	19	S½NW	1858-11-01		A1
3639	SMITH, John	8	E½NW	1833-08-02		A1
3609	SPENCER, James M	25	SESE	1849-09-01		A1
3617	STINSON, Jason	24	SESE	1837-08-02		A1
3618	" "	24	W½SE	1837-08-02		A1
3640	STINSON, John	36	E½NE	1837-08-02		A1
3508	SWANER, Amariah	6	SWNW	1858-11-01		A1
3509	SWANNER, Amariah	6	NWNW	1858-11-01		A1 R3740
3538	THOMAS, Daniel R	21	NENW	1907-04-05		A1
3546	THOMAS, David J	21	SWNE	1907-04-05		A1
3529	THOMPSON, Charner	10	W½SW	1898-06-01		A2
3550	TISDALE, Edward	11	NESE	1852-02-02		A1
3551	" "	11	NESW	1858-11-01		A1
3552	" "	11	NWSE	1858-11-01		A1
3566	TISDALE, Furney G	21	SWSW	1848-05-03		A1
3633	TISDALE, John E	10	SENE	1895-02-23		A2
3701	TISDALE, Rebecca	27	NENE	1840-10-10		A1 V3754
3749	TISDALE, William D	11	SENE	1854-10-02		A1
3750	" "	13	NENW	1858-11-01		A1
3751	" "	2	E½SW	1858-11-01		A1
3752	" "	2	NESE	1858-11-01		A1
3762	TISDALE, William J	10	E½SE	1860-04-02		A1
3763	" "	11	W½SW	1860-04-02		A1
3764	" "	14	NWNW	1860-04-02		A1 V3646
3567	UNDERWOOD, Furney G	2	SENW	1897-03-18		A1
3568	" "	2	SWNE	1897-03-18		A1
3613	WALKER, James R	14	SWNW	1884-03-20		A2 V3646
3612	" "	14	NWSW	1899-07-15		A1
3614	" "	15	W½NE	1904-07-15		A2
3615	WAYNE, James W	30	S½SW	1907-04-05		A1 R3563
3616	" "	31	N½NW	1907-04-05		A1
3562	WEBB, Fortunatus	7	SESE	1858-11-01		A1
3748	WEBB, Thomas J	8	SWSW	1854-07-15		A1
3747	" "	8	SESW	1860-04-02		A1
3510	WEST, Andrew	34	NENE	1904-07-15		A2
3522	WEST, Benjamin J	12	SWSE	1849-09-01		A1
3660	WEST, Joseph W	11	SESE	1850-08-10		A1
3728	WEST, Simon	36	W½NW	1895-09-04		A2
3503	WHITE, Alfred	26	E½SW	1894-05-04		A2
3504	" "	26	W½SE	1894-05-04		A2

ID	Individual in Patent	Sec.	Sec. Part	Date Issued	Other Counties	For More Info . . .
3563	WILLIAMS, Frances M	30	S½SW	1860-10-01		A1 R3615
3771	WILLIAMS, William P	35	SESW	1907-04-05		A1
3772	" "	35	SWSE	1907-04-05		A1
3573	WILLIAMSON, George W	17	W½SE	1900-11-28		A2
3582	WILLIAMSON, Henry	2	NENE	1858-11-01		A1
3595	WILLIAMSON, James A	33	E½NE	1906-05-23		A2 V3683
3596	" "	33	E½SE	1906-05-23		A2 V3683
3726	WILLIAMSON, Samuel W	36	W½SW	1897-03-18		A1
3743	WILLIAMSON, Stephen	17	E½SE	1858-11-01		A1
3744	" "	20	NWNE	1858-11-01		A1
3745	" "	21	NWNW	1858-11-01		A1
3698	WISE, Richard	5	SW	1831-08-01		A1 G13
3709	" "	7	NWNE	1834-08-05		A1
3710	" "	7	SWNE	1834-08-05		A1
3711	" "	8	W½SE	1838-07-28		A1
3708	" "	17	N½NE	1907-04-05		A1
3723	WISE, Samuel J	8	SESE	1854-10-02		A1
3722	" "	8	NESE	1862-01-01		A1
3506	WOOD, Altamont	4	E½SE	1875-04-20		A1
3507	" "	9	NENE	1875-04-20		A1
3505	YOUNG, Allen	26	E½SE	1897-09-22		A2
3675	YOUNG, Lucinda H	28	N½SE	1895-08-08		A2

Patent Map

T8-N R18-E
St Stephens Meridian

Map Group 16

Township Statistics

Parcels Mapped	:	276
Number of Patents	:	197
Number of Individuals	:	149
Patentees Identified	:	145
Number of Surnames	:	86
Multi-Patentee Parcels	:	11
Oldest Patent Date	:	8/1/1831
Most Recent Patent	:	4/5/1907
Block/Lot Parcels	:	0
Parcels Re-Issued	:	4
Parcels that Overlap	:	9
Cities and Towns	:	0
Cemeteries	:	1

Township map showing land patents. Section grid and patentee names:

Section 3
- HOLMES John S 1854
- MOODY William 1858
- MOODY William 1858
- MOODY William 1907
- MOODY William 1907
- SILER Solomon 1838
- HOLMES John S 1858
- BREAKER John W 1897
- SILER Solomon 1838

Section 2
- SILER Solomon 1837
- FRANKLIN Barnett 1852
- UNDERWOOD Furney G 1897
- FRANKLIN Barnett 1852
- UNDERWOOD Furney G 1897
- WILLIAMSON Henry 1858
- SILER Solomon 1837
- TISDALE William D 1858
- TISDALE William D 1858

Section 1
- MCDUGALD John D 1858
- MCDUGALD John D 1858
- FINLAY Duncan 1837
- MCDUGALD John D 1850

Section 10
- KENT Alexander 1903
- BREAKER John W 1897
- BRUNSON Jasper P 1891
- BRUNSON Isaac J 1858
- BRUNSON Jasper P 1891
- TISDALE John E 1895
- THOMPSON Charner 1898
- SARTOR Ephraim 1891
- TISDALE William J 1860
- KING Ransom 1895

Section 11
- CURTIS John B 1840
- CURTIS George 1838
- DEVLIN William 1840
- TISDALE William D 1854
- TISDALE William J 1860
- TISDALE Edward 1858
- TISDALE Edward 1858
- TISDALE Edward 1852
- WEST Joseph W 1850

Section 12
- MCDUGALD Alexander 1852
- FINLAY Duncan 1837
- MCDUGALD John D 1837
- MCDUGALD Alexander D 1858
- MCDUGALD Hugh K 1850
- FINLAY Duncan 1837
- FRANKLIN James E 1848
- FRANKLIN Barnett 1849
- JUNE James H 1849
- MOORE Isam 1838
- FRANKLIN Robert 1835
- WEST Benjamin J 1849

Section 15
- ANDERSON Henry 1900
- WALKER James R 1904
- PERKINS Kit 1900
- PERKINS Kit 1900

Section 14
- TISDALE William J 1860
- DRIVER John W 1897
- DRIVER John W WALKER James R 1884
- MCKEE Lazarus 1902
- WALKER James R 1899
- MCKEE Lazarus 1902
- HOLLADAY Benjamin H 1868
- HANCOCK Joseph M 1895
- HAMMONS Moses 1891
- HAMMONS Moses 1891
- HOUGH Thaddeus 1888
- HOLLADAY Benjamin H 1868
- JOHNSON James A 1897
- MCDUGALD Daniel H 1858
- HORN Oliver W 1852

Section 13
- TISDALE William D 1858
- MOORE John W 1858
- MOORE John W 1858
- MOORE Isham 1850
- MOORE John W 1858
- HORN Lewis 1852
- SILER Solomon 1837

Section 22
- HOOKS [23] Daniel 1891
- CURTIS Samuel 1891
- CURTIS James 1891
- CURTIS James 1891
- BRUNSON Daniel H 1892
- DEMING Richard 1891
- BRUNSON Daniel H 1892

Section 23
- JOHNSON James A 1897

Section 24
- SILER Solomon 1837
- SILER Solomon 1837
- HORN Oliver W 1854
- HORN Christopher C 1852
- STINSON Jason 1837
- CURTIS Henry D 1883
- HORN Oliver W 1854
- CURTIS John D 1837
- STINSON Jason 1837

Section 27
- BRUNSON John R 1901
- TISDALE Rebecca 1840
- HARRELL William F 1900
- MOUNT Robert 1900
- BRUNSON William G 1900

Section 26
- CURTIS Robert 1891
- KING Prince H 1890
- MOUNT Beckey 1893
- WHITE Alfred 1894
- WHITE Alfred 1894
- YOUNG Allen 1897

Section 25
- HORN Oliver W 1858
- HORN Oliver W 1858
- HORN Oliver W 1858
- SPENCER James M 1849

Section 34
- BRUNSON Richard M 1890
- BURK Isaac 1890
- BURK Isaac 1890
- WEST Andrew 1904
- JOHNSON [24] James A 1891
- BRUNSON Richard M 1890
- BAKER Abner 1892
- BAKER Abner 1892
- JOHNSON [24] James A 1891
- BAKER Abner 1892
- JOHNSON [24] James A 1891

Section 35
- PERKINS Simon 1900
- COX Henry 1900
- WILLIAMS William P 1907
- WILLIAMS William P 1907

Section 36
- ALBRITTON Joseph L 1892
- STINSON John 1837
- WEST Simon 1895
- HORN Lewis 1858
- WILLIAMSON Samuel W 1897
- ALBRITTON Joseph L 1892
- LOCKHART Julius C 1858
- LOCKHART Julius C 1858

Copyright 2008 Boyd IT, Inc. All Rights Reserved

Helpful Hints

1. This Map's INDEX can be found on the preceding pages.

2. Refer to Map "C" to see where this Township lies within Crenshaw County, Alabama.

3. Numbers within square brackets [ ] denote a multi-patentee land parcel (multi-owner). Refer to Appendix "C" for a full list of members in this group.

4. Areas that look to be crowded with Patentees usually indicate multiple sales of the same parcel (Re-issues) or Overlapping parcels. See this Township's Index for an explanation of these and other circumstances that might explain "odd" groupings of Patentees on this map.

Legend

— Patent Boundary

— Section Boundary

▓ No Patents Found (or Outside County)

1., 2., 3., ... Lot Numbers (when beside a name)

[ ] Group Number (see Appendix "C")

Scale: Section = 1 mile X 1 mile (generally, with some exceptions)

Road Map

T8-N R18-E
St Stephens Meridian

Map Group 16

Cities & Towns
None

Cemeteries
Bethel Cemetery

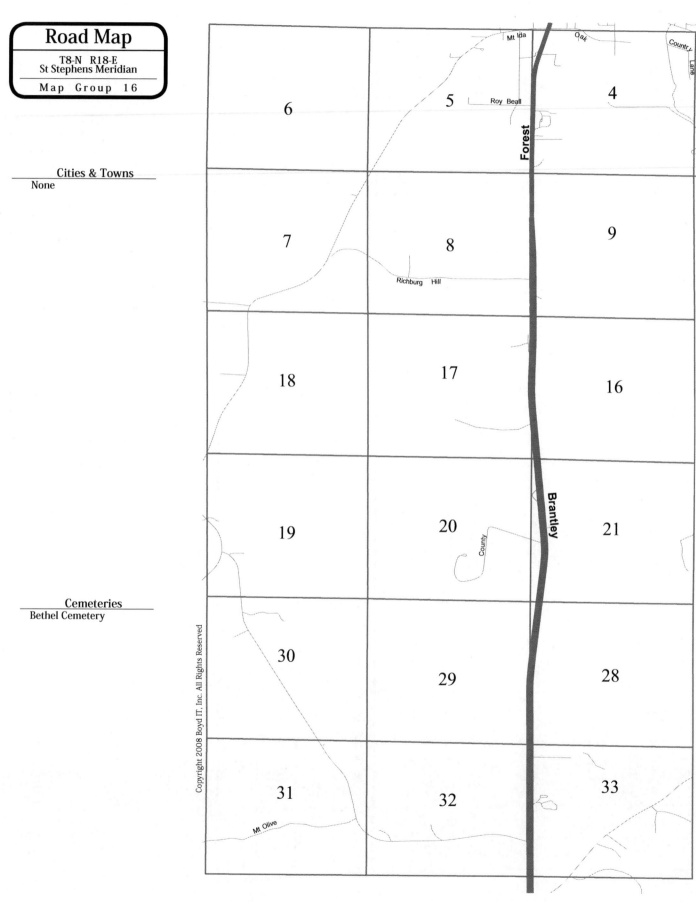

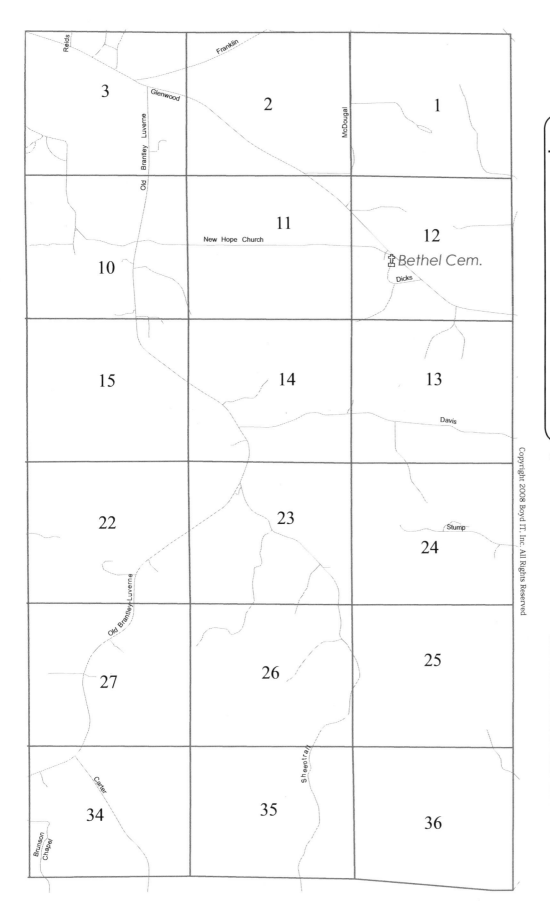

3

2

1

Reids

Franklin

Glenwood

Old Brantley Luverne

McDougal

11

New Hope Church

12

10

✝ *Bethel Cem.*

Dicks

15

14

13

Davis

22

23

24

Stump

Old Brantley Luverne

27

26

25

Carter

34

35

36

Sheeptrail

Brunson Chapel

Helpful Hints

1. This road map has a number of uses, but primarily it is to help you: a) find the present location of land owned by your ancestors (at least the general area), b) find cemeteries and city-centers, and c) estimate the route/roads used by Census-takers & tax-assessors.

2. If you plan to travel to Crenshaw County to locate cemeteries or land parcels, please pick up a modern travel map for the area before you do. Mapping old land parcels on modern maps is not as exact a science as you might think. Just the slightest variations in public land survey coordinates, estimates of parcel boundaries, or road-map deviations can greatly alter a map's representation of how a road either does or doesn't cross a particular parcel of land.

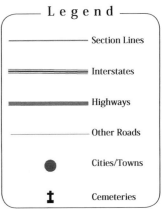

Legend

———————	Section Lines
══════════	Interstates
▓▓▓▓▓▓▓▓	Highways
—————	Other Roads
●	Cities/Towns
✝	Cemeteries

Scale: Section = 1 mile X 1 mile
(generally, with some exceptions)

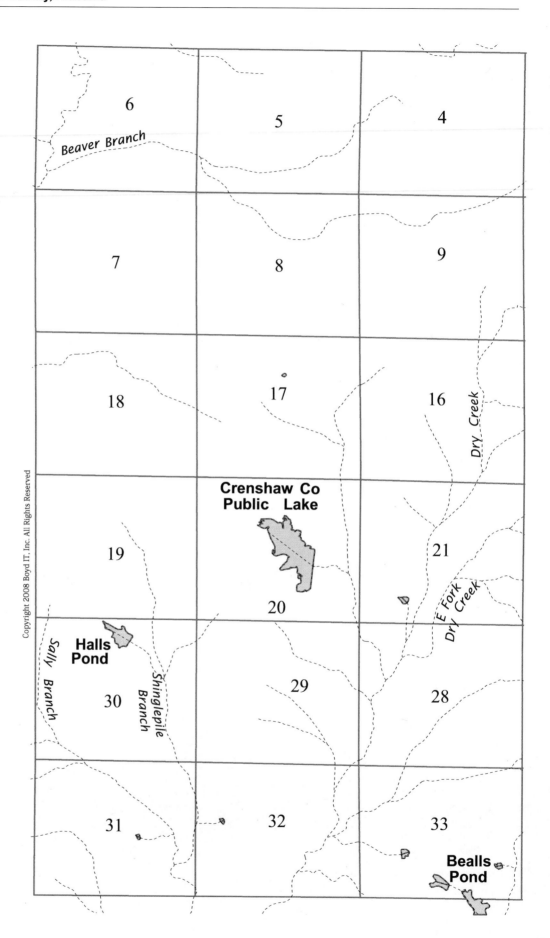

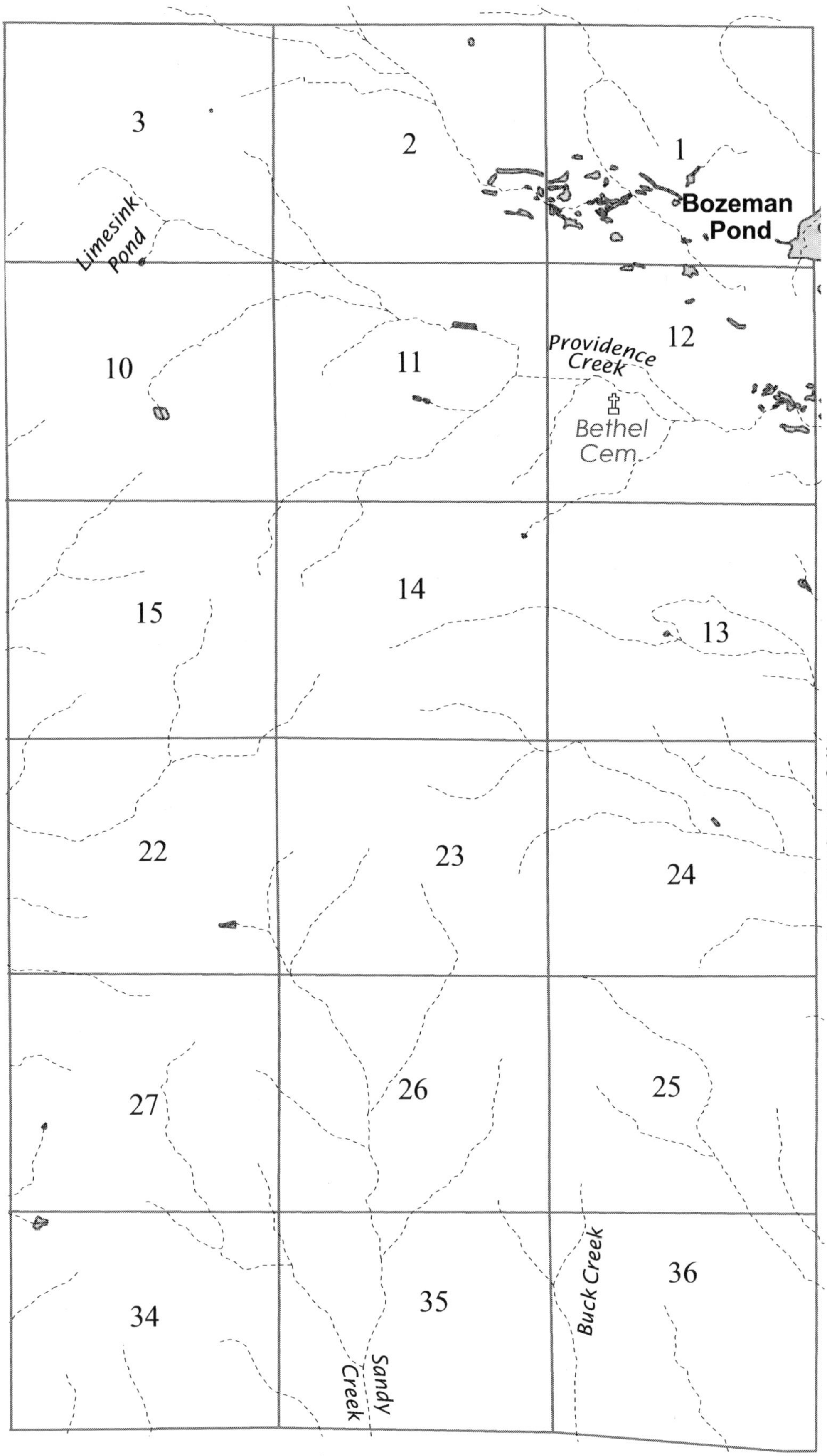
3
2
1
Bozeman Pond
Limesink Pond
10
11
12
Providence Creek
Bethel Cem
15
14
13
22
23
24
27
26
25
34
35
36
Sandy Creek
Buck Creek

Helpful Hints

1. This Map takes a different look at the same Congressional Township displayed in the preceding two maps. It presents features that can help you better envision the historical development of the area: a) Water-bodies (lakes & ponds), b) Water-courses (rivers, streams, etc.), c) Railroads, d) City/town center-points (where they were oftentimes located when first settled), and e) Cemeteries.
2. Using this "Historical" map in tandem with this Township's Patent Map and Road Map, may lead you to some interesting discoveries. You will often find roads, towns, cemeteries, and waterways are named after nearby landowners: sometimes those names will be the ones you are researching. See how many of these research gems you can find here in Crenshaw County.

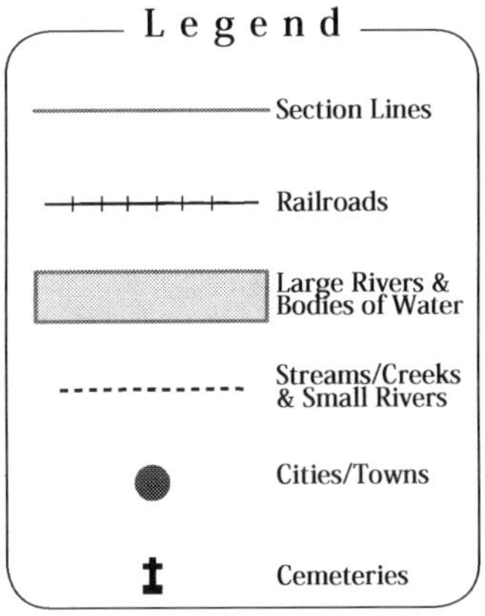
Legend
Section Lines
Railroads
Large Rivers & Bodies of Water
Streams/Creeks & Small Rivers
Cities/Towns
Cemeteries

Scale: Section = 1 mile X 1 mile
(there are some exceptions)

Map Group 17: Index to Land Patents

Township 8-North Range 19-East (St Stephens)

After you locate an individual in this Index, take note of the Section and Section Part then proceed to the Land Patent map on the pages immediately following. You should have no difficulty locating the corresponding parcel of land.

The "For More Info" Column will lead you to more information about the underlying Patents. See the *Legend* at right, and the "How to Use this Book" chapter, for more information.

```
┌─────────────────────────────────────────────────────────────┐
│                        LEGEND                                │
│            "For More Info . . . " column                     │
├─────────────────────────────────────────────────────────────┤
│ A = Authority (Legislative Act, See Appendix "A")            │
│ B = Block or Lot (location in Section unknown)               │
│ C = Cancelled Patent                                         │
│ F = Fractional Section                                       │
│ G = Group (Multi-Patentee Patent, see Appendix "C")          │
│ V = Overlaps another Parcel                                  │
│ R = Re-Issued (Parcel patented more than once)               │
│                                                              │
│ (A & G items require you to look in the Appendixes referred  │
│ to above. All other Letter-designations followed by a number │
│ require you to locate line-items in this index that possess  │
│ the ID number found after the letter).                       │
└─────────────────────────────────────────────────────────────┘
```

ID	Individual in Patent	Sec.	Sec. Part	Date Issued	Other Counties	For More Info . . .
3878	BECK, Jourdan	28	SESE	1860-04-02	Pike	A1
3879	" "	29	SENE	1860-04-02	Pike	A1
3880	" "	29	W½NE	1860-04-02	Pike	A1
3913	BIRD, Thomas	20	NWSE	1911-03-30		A2
3829	CAPPS, James W	32	SENE	1852-02-02	Pike	A1
3827	" "	32	NENE	1858-11-01	Pike	A1
3830	" "	32	SWNE	1858-11-01	Pike	A1
3828	" "	32	NWNE	1860-04-02	Pike	A1
3858	CHISSER, John W	8	NENE	1860-04-02		A1
3859	" "	9	NWNW	1860-04-02		A1
3914	COKER, Thomas	28	E½NE	1840-10-10	Pike	A1
3834	COMPTON, Jesse	9	E½NW	1837-08-18		A1
3863	COOPER, Joseph E	4	NWNE	1858-09-01		A1
3864	" "	4	SENW	1858-09-01		A1
3865	" "	4	SWNE	1858-11-01		A1
3924	CRAWFORD, William L	32	S½SE	1860-04-02	Pike	A1
3925	" "	32	SW	1860-04-02	Pike	A1
3835	CURTIS, John D	18	NWSW	1837-08-08		A1
3836	" "	20	W½NW	1840-10-10		A1
3775	DAVIS, Abel	17	NW	1837-08-08		A1 G15
3774	" "	9	NWSW	1837-08-09		A1
3773	" "	8	NESE	1838-07-28		A1
3782	DEAY, Andrew O	7	NESE	1850-08-10		A1
3887	DORMAN, Lovett	18	N½SE	1831-12-01		A1
3888	" "	18	NESW	1837-05-15		A1
3801	DYER, Edward F	17	E½SW	1860-04-02		A1
3862	DYER, Joseph	17	NWSW	1837-08-02		A1
3911	DYER, Sarah	17	SWSW	1837-08-02		A1
3873	EILAND, Josephus	28	NENW	1850-08-10	Pike	A1
3912	EILAND, Stephen	28	SWNW	1850-08-10	Pike	A1
3842	EUBANKS, John	31	E½SW	1840-10-10	Pike	A1
3844	" "	31	W½SW	1840-10-10	Pike	A1
3843	" "	31	SESE	1841-05-20	Pike	A1
3788	FINLAY, Archibald	7	W½SE	1837-04-10		A1
3787	" "	7	SWNW	1837-04-15		A1
3785	" "	7	NWNW	1837-08-12		A1
3786	" "	7	SENW	1850-08-10		A1
3798	FINLAY, David H	7	NENW	1858-11-01		A1
3799	" "	7	NWNE	1858-11-01		A1
3800	" "	8	SESW	1858-11-01		A1
3797	FINLEY, David	7	SWNE	1852-02-02		A1
3901	FRANKLIN, Robert	18	E½NE	1833-09-16		A1
3926	FUTRILL, Winburn	7	W½SW	1834-09-04		A1
3795	GIBSON, Cincinnati	32	NENW	1904-07-15	Pike	A2
3796	" "	32	S½NW	1904-07-15	Pike	A2
3861	GODIN, Jordan	19	E½NE	1833-09-16		A1

ID	Individual in Patent	Sec.	Sec. Part	Date Issued	Other Counties	For More Info . . .
3922	GODWIN, William	5	NENE	1850-08-10		A1
3886	GOLDEN, Levi H	8	NWNE	1903-11-24		A2
3840	GOODWIN, John E	4	SWNW	1860-04-02		A1 R3895
3841	"	5	SENE	1860-04-02		A1
3882	GRANT, Larkin M	5	SWSW	1860-04-02		A1
3883	"	7	NENE	1860-04-02		A1
3884	"	8	N½NW	1860-04-02		A1
3885	"	8	SENW	1860-04-02		A1
3897	HOLMES, Reuben	4	NWSE	1858-11-01		A1
3923	HOLMES, William	4	SESE	1858-11-01		A1
3898	HOLMS, Reuben	4	NWSW	1884-04-02		A1
3899	HORN, Richard W	18	S½SE	1831-12-01		A1
3900	"	18	SESW	1837-08-08		A1
3915	HORN, Thomas G	20	E½NE	1860-04-02		A1
3916	"	20	NESE	1860-04-02		A1
3831	HUTCHISON, Jesse B	5	SE	1907-04-05		A1
3832	"	5	SWNW	1907-04-05		A1
3833	"	5	W½NE	1907-04-05		A1
3876	JONES, Josiah	29	SWSW	1860-04-02	Pike	A1
3877	"	32	NWNW	1860-04-02	Pike	A1
3790	JUNE, Aurelia V	6	SWNE	1903-11-24		A2
3816	JUNE, James H	6	NENW	1860-04-02		A1
3817	"	6	NESE	1860-04-02		A1
3819	"	6	NWSW	1860-04-02		A1
3820	"	6	SESE	1860-04-02		A1
3821	"	6	SWNW	1860-04-02		A1
3818	"	6	NWSE	1897-03-18		A1
3775	KING, James	17	NW	1837-08-08		A1 G15
3822	"	7	SESE	1837-08-09		A1
3807	LEE, Isaiah	17	SENE	1838-07-28		A1
3808	"	17	SWSE	1838-07-28		A1
3791	LINTON, Briton	4	NESE	1837-08-12		A1
3823	LINTON, James	4	NESW	1858-11-01		A1
3918	LINTON, Thomas N	4	S½SE	1858-11-01		A1
3881	LOCKHART, Julius C	31	NESE	1858-11-01	Pike	A1
3917	LOWRIE, Thomas	18	NWNE	1837-05-15		A1
3824	MCDANIEL, James M	17	NESE	1858-09-01		A1
3825	"	17	SESE	1858-11-01		A1
3837	MCDUGALD, John D	6	NESW	1858-11-01		A1
3838	"	6	S½SW	1858-11-01		A1
3839	"	6	SWSE	1858-11-01		A1
3920	MCHENRY, William D	4	NENW	1852-02-02		A1
3921	"	4	NWNW	1860-04-02		A1
3789	MOORE, Asham	31	NE	1841-05-20	Pike	A1
3809	MOORE, Isam	18	W½NW	1838-07-28		A1
3810	"	30	E½SE	1840-10-10		A1
3811	"	30	W½SE	1840-10-10		A1
3812	"	31	W½NW	1840-10-10	Pike	A1
3813	MOORE, Isham	18	E½NW	1837-08-18		A1
3814	"	18	SWNE	1837-08-18		A1
3815	"	30	W½SW	1840-10-10		A1
3860	MOORE, John W	4	SWSW	1884-04-02		A1
3783	ODEAY, Andrew	7	SENE	1858-11-01		A1
3784	"	8	SWNW	1858-11-01		A1
3895	REAVES, Moses	4	SWNW	1840-10-10		A1 R3840
3896	REEVES, Moses	17	SWNE	1860-04-02		A1
3894	REIVES, Moses D	17	NWSE	1852-12-01		A1
3826	RICHBOURG, James	9	NE	1875-04-20		A1
3845	ROZEAR, John L	17	NWNE	1860-04-02		A1
3846	"	8	SWSE	1860-04-02		A1
3777	SHAW, Alexander	28	NWSW	1850-05-01	Pike	A1
3779	"	29	NESE	1850-05-01	Pike	A1
3776	"	28	E½SW	1850-08-10	Pike	A1
3778	"	28	SENW	1850-08-10	Pike	A1
3780	"	29	SESE	1850-08-10	Pike	A1
3781	"	29	W½SE	1860-04-02	Pike	A1
3847	SPEAR, John M	21	NWNE	1849-09-01	Pike	A1
3848	SPEIR, John M	21	E½NE	1840-10-10	Pike	A1
3849	"	21	E½SE	1840-10-10	Pike	A1
3851	"	21	SWNE	1853-11-15	Pike	A1
3852	"	28	W½NE	1854-07-15	Pike	A1
3850	"	21	E½SW	1858-11-01	Pike	A1
3869	STINSON, Joseph T	8	SESE	1858-11-01		A1

ID	Individual in Patent	Sec.	Sec. Part	Date Issued	Other Counties	For More Info . . .
3870	STINSON, Joseph T (Cont'd)	9	E½SW	1858-11-01		A1
3871	" "	9	SWNW	1858-11-01		A1
3866	" "	17	NENE	1860-04-02		A1
3867	" "	8	NWSE	1860-04-02		A1
3868	" "	8	S½NE	1860-04-02		A1
3889	STINSON, Micajah B	19	SW	1837-08-02		A1
3890	" "	20	SESE	1858-11-01		A1
3891	" "	21	SWSW	1858-11-01	Pike	A1
3892	" "	28	NWNW	1858-11-01	Pike	A1
3893	" "	29	NENE	1858-11-01	Pike	A1
3792	SWANNER, Canna	5	NWNW	1858-11-01		A1
3793	" "	6	E½NE	1858-11-01		A1
3794	" "	6	NWNE	1858-11-01		A1
3874	SWANNER, Joshua	9	E½SE	1837-08-18		A1
3875	" "	9	SWSE	1838-07-28		A1
3927	TUTRILL, Winburn	7	E½SW	1832-08-08		A1
3919	UNDERWOOD, Wiley	5	NENW	1858-11-01		A1
3804	WARREN, Henry D	28	NESE	1850-05-01	Pike	A1
3806	" "	28	SWSW	1850-05-01	Pike	A1
3805	" "	28	SWSE	1897-03-18	Pike	A1
3872	WEST, Joseph W	9	NWSE	1852-02-02		A1
3802	WILLIAMSON, George W	29	NESW	1860-04-02	Pike	A1
3803	" "	29	SESW	1860-04-02	Pike	A1
3853	WILLIAMSON, John T	19	W½NE	1837-08-07		A1
3854	" "	20	SENW	1852-02-02		A1
3855	" "	20	SESW	1858-11-01		A1
3856	" "	20	SWSE	1858-11-01		A1
3857	" "	20	W½SW	1858-11-01		A1
3904	WILLIAMSON, Robert	19	W½SE	1834-10-21		A1
3902	" "	19	E½SE	1837-08-02		A1
3903	" "	19	NW	1837-08-07		A1
3907	" "	30	E½NW	1840-10-10		A1
3908	" "	30	E½SW	1840-10-10		A1
3910	" "	30	W½NW	1840-10-10		A1
3909	" "	30	NE	1841-05-20		A1
3905	" "	29	NW	1845-06-01	Pike	A1
3906	" "	29	NWSW	1845-06-01	Pike	A1

Patent Map

T8-N R19-E
St Stephens Meridian

Map Group 17

Section 6
JUNE James H 1860	SWANNER Canna 1858	
JUNE James H 1860	**6** JUNE Aurelia V 1903	SWANNER Canna 1858
JUNE James H 1860	MCDUGALD John D 1858	JUNE James H 1897 / JUNE James H 1860
MCDUGALD John D 1858	MCDUGALD John D 1858	JUNE James H 1860

Section 5
SWANNER Canna 1858	UNDERWOOD Wiley 1858
HUTCHISON Jesse B 1907	
5	
HUTCHISON Jesse B 1907	

Section 4
GODWIN William 1850	MCHENRY William D 1860	MCHENRY William D 1852	COOPER Joseph E 1858
GOODWIN John E 1860	REAVES Moses 1840 / GOODWIN John E 1860	COOPER Joseph E 1858	COOPER Joseph E 1858
HOLMS Reuben 1884	LINTON James 1858	HOLMES Reuben 1858 / LINTON Briton 1837
MOORE John W 1884	HOLMES William 1858	LINTON Thomas N 1858

Section 7
FINLAY Archibald 1837	FINLAY David H 1858	FINLAY David H 1858	GRANT Larkin M 1860
FINLAY Archibald 1837	FINLAY Archibald 1850	FINLEY David 1852	ODEAY Andrew 1858
FUTRILL Winburn 1834	TUTRILL Winburn 1832	**7** FINLAY Archibald 1837	DEAY Andrew O 1850 / KING James 1837

Section 8
GRANT Larkin M 1860	GOLDEN Levi H 1903	CHISSER John W 1860	
ODEAY Andrew 1858	GRANT Larkin M 1860	**8** STINSON Joseph T 1860	
STINSON Joseph T 1860	DAVIS Abel 1838		
FINLAY David H 1858	ROZEAR John L 1860	STINSON Joseph T 1858	

Section 9
CHISSER John W 1860	COMPTON Jesse 1837	
STINSON Joseph T 1858	**9**	RICHBOURG James 1875
DAVIS Abel 1837	STINSON Joseph T 1858	WEST Joseph W 1852	SWANNER Joshua 1837
		SWANNER Joshua 1838

Section 18
MOORE Isam 1838	MOORE Isham 1837	LOWRIE Thomas 1837	FRANKLIN Robert 1833
	18	MOORE Isham 1837	
CURTIS John D 1837	DORMAN Lovett 1837	DORMAN Lovett 1831	
	HORN Richard W 1837	HORN Richard W 1831	

Section 17
DAVIS [15] Abel 1837	ROZEAR John L 1860	STINSON Joseph T 1860
17	REEVES Moses 1860	LEE Isaiah 1838
DYER Joseph 1837	REIVES Moses D 1852	MCDANIEL James M 1858
DYER Sarah 1837 / DYER Edward F 1860	LEE Isaiah 1838	MCDANIEL James M 1858

Section 16
16

Crenshaw

Section 19
WILLIAMSON Robert 1837	WILLIAMSON John T 1837	GODIN Jordan 1833
19		
STINSON Micajah B 1837	WILLIAMSON Robert 1837	WILLIAMSON Robert 1837

Section 20
CURTIS John D 1840	**20**	HORN Thomas G 1860
	WILLIAMSON John T 1852	
	BIRD Thomas 1911	HORN Thomas G 1860
WILLIAMSON John T 1858	WILLIAMSON John T 1858	WILLIAMSON John T 1858 / STINSON Micajah B 1858

Section 21
Pike

SPEAR John M 1849	SPEIR John M 1840
SPEIR John M 1853	
21	SPEIR John M 1840
SPEIR John M 1858	

Section 30
WILLIAMSON Robert 1840	WILLIAMSON Robert 1840	WILLIAMSON Robert 1841
WILLIAMSON Robert 1840	**30**	WILLIAMSON Robert 1840 / MOORE Isam 1840
MOORE Isham 1840	MOORE Isam 1840	

Section 29
WILLIAMSON Robert 1845	STINSON Micajah B 1858	
29	BECK Jourdan 1860	BECK Jourdan 1860
WILLIAMSON Robert 1845	WILLIAMSON George W 1860	SHAW Alexander 1860
JONES Josiah 1860	WILLIAMSON George W 1860	SHAW Alexander 1860

Section 28
STINSON Micajah B 1858	EILAND Josephus 1850	SPEIR John M 1854	COKER Thomas 1840
EILAND Stephen 1850	SHAW Alexander 1850		
SHAW Alexander 1850	SHAW Alexander 1850	**28**	WARREN Henry D 1850
WARREN Henry D 1850	SHAW Alexander 1850	WARREN Henry D 1897	BECK Jourdan 1860

Section 31
MOORE Isham 1840	MOORE Asham 1841	
MOORE Isam 1840	**31**	
EUBANKS John 1840	EUBANKS John 1840	

Section 32
JONES Josiah 1860	GIBSON Cincinnati 1904	CAPPS James W 1860	CAPPS James W 1858
GIBSON Cincinnati 1904	CAPPS James W 1858	CAPPS James W 1852
LOCKHART Julius C 1858	**32**	
EUBANKS John 1841	CRAWFORD William L 1860	CRAWFORD William L 1860

Section 33
33

Township Statistics

Parcels Mapped	:	155
Number of Patents	:	120
Number of Individuals	:	72
Patentees Identified	:	73
Number of Surnames	:	56
Multi-Patentee Parcels	:	1
Oldest Patent Date	:	12/1/1831
Most Recent Patent	:	3/30/1911
Block/Lot Parcels	:	0
Parcels Re - Issued	:	1
Parcels that Overlap	:	0
Cities and Towns	:	2
Cemeteries	:	1

Note: the area contained in this map amounts to far less than a full Township. Therefore, its contents are completely on this single page (instead of a "normal" 2-page spread).

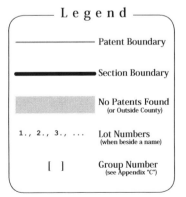

L e g e n d

——————— Patent Boundary

━━━━━━━ Section Boundary

░░░░░░░ No Patents Found (or Outside County)

1., 2., 3., ... Lot Numbers (when beside a name)

[ ] Group Number (see Appendix "C")

Scale: Section = 1 mile X 1 mile (generally, with some exceptions)

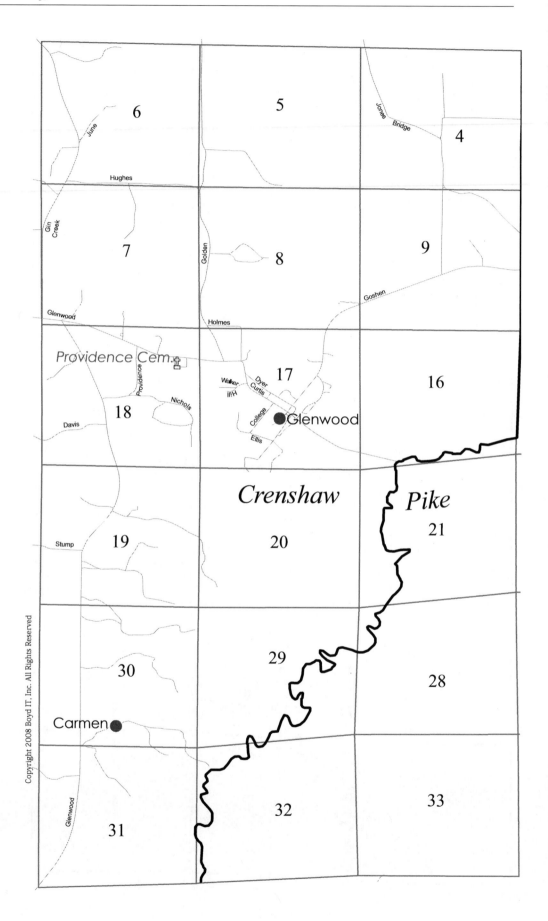

Road Map

T8-N R19-E
St Stephens Meridian

Map Group 17

Note: the area contained in this map amounts to far less than a full Township. Therefore, its contents are completely on this single page (instead of a "normal" 2-page spread).

Cities & Towns
Glenwood
Carmen

Cemeteries
Providence Cemetery

Legend

Section Lines

Interstates

Highways

Other Roads

● Cities/Towns

✝ Cemeteries

Scale: Section = 1 mile X 1 mile
(generally, with some exceptions)

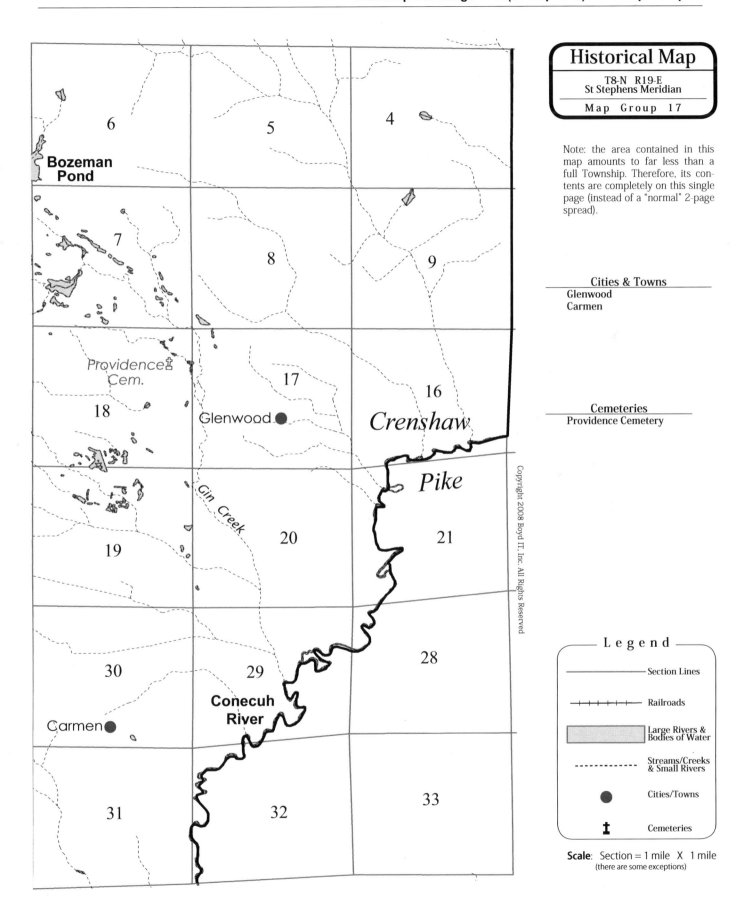

Copyright 2008 Boyd IT, Inc. All Rights Reserved

Historical Map

T8-N R19-E
St Stephens Meridian

Map Group 17

Note: the area contained in this map amounts to far less than a full Township. Therefore, its contents are completely on this single page (instead of a "normal" 2-page spread).

Cities & Towns
Glenwood
Carmen

Cemeteries
Providence Cemetery

Legend

———	Section Lines
—+—+—+—	Railroads
▨	Large Rivers & Bodies of Water
- - - - -	Streams/Creeks & Small Rivers
●	Cities/Towns
✝	Cemeteries

Scale: Section = 1 mile X 1 mile
(there are some exceptions)

Map Group 18: Index to Land Patents

Township 7-North Range 15-East (St Stephens)

After you locate an individual in this Index, take note of the Section and Section Part then proceed to the Land Patent map on the pages immediately following. You should have no difficulty locating the corresponding parcel of land.

The "For More Info" Column will lead you to more information about the underlying Patents. See the *Legend* at right, and the "How to Use this Book" chapter, for more information.

```
                    LEGEND
            "For More Info . . . " column
A = Authority (Legislative Act, See Appendix "A")
B = Block or Lot (location in Section unknown)
C = Cancelled Patent
F = Fractional Section
G = Group  (Multi-Patentee Patent, see Appendix "C")
V = Overlaps another Parcel
R = Re-Issued (Parcel patented more than once)

(A & G items require you to look in the Appendixes referred
to above. All other Letter-designations followed by a number
require you to locate line-items in this index that possess
the ID number found after the letter).
```

ID	Individual in Patent	Sec.	Sec. Part	Date Issued	Other Counties	For More Info . . .
3931	HUGHES, Benjamin	24	SWNW	1835-10-01	Butler	A1
3930	REID, Archibald M	24	W½SW	1837-08-15	Butler	A1
3928	"	24	NWNW	1840-10-10	Butler	A1
3929	"	24	SESW	1860-10-01	Butler	A1
3934	ROGERS, John	24	NESW	1843-02-01	Butler	A1
3935	"	24	SENW	1843-02-01	Butler	A1
3936	"	24	SWNE	1843-02-01	Butler	A1
3937	SHINE, William P	24	E½NE	1858-11-01	Butler	A1
3938	"	24	NESE	1858-11-01	Butler	A1
3932	STALLINGS, Daniel	24	NENW	1843-02-01	Butler	A1
3933	"	24	NWNE	1858-11-01	Butler	A1

2

1

11

12

14

13

Crenshaw

REID Archibald M 1840	STALLINGS Daniel 1843	STALLINGS Daniel 1858	
HUGHES Benjamin 1835	ROGERS John 1843	ROGERS John 1843	SHINE William P 1858
REID Archibald M 1837	ROGERS John 1843		SHINE William P 1858
	REID Archibald M 1860		

24

23

Butler

26

25

35

36

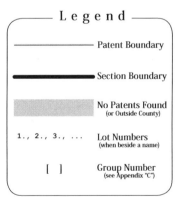

Patent Map

T7-N R15-E
St Stephens Meridian

Map Group 18

Township Statistics

Parcels Mapped	:	11
Number of Patents	:	9
Number of Individuals	:	5
Patentees Identified	:	5
Number of Surnames	:	5
Multi-Patentee Parcels	:	0
Oldest Patent Date	:	10/1/1835
Most Recent Patent	:	10/1/1860
Block/Lot Parcels	:	0
Parcels Re - Issued	:	0
Parcels that Overlap	:	0
Cities and Towns	:	0
Cemeteries	:	0

Note: the area contained in this map amounts to far less than a full Township. Therefore, its contents are completely on this single page (instead of a "normal" 2-page spread).

L e g e n d

——————— Patent Boundary

━━━━━━━ Section Boundary

No Patents Found
(or Outside County)

1., 2., 3., ...   Lot Numbers
(when beside a name)

[ ]   Group Number
(see Appendix "C")

Scale: Section = 1 mile X 1 mile
(generally, with some exceptions)

Road Map

T7-N R15-E
St Stephens Meridian

Map Group 18

Note: the area contained in this map amounts to far less than a full Township. Therefore, its contents are completely on this single page (instead of a "normal" 2-page spread).

Cities & Towns
None

Cemeteries
None

Legend

————————	Section Lines
════════════	Interstates
▬▬▬▬▬▬▬▬	Highways
————————	Other Roads
●	Cities/Towns
✝	Cemeteries

Scale: Section = 1 mile X 1 mile
(generally, with some exceptions)

2	1
11	12
14	13
23	*Butler* 24
26	25
35	36

Crenshaw

2

1

11

12

14

13

Butler
24

23

Crenshaw

26

25

35

36

Historical Map

T7-N R15-E
St Stephens Meridian

Map Group 18

Note: the area contained in this map amounts to far less than a full Township. Therefore, its contents are completely on this single page (instead of a "normal" 2-page spread).

Cities & Towns
None

Cemeteries
None

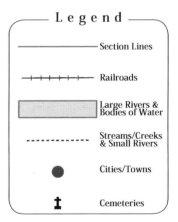

L e g e n d

———————— Section Lines

+ + + + + + Railroads

Large Rivers &
Bodies of Water

- - - - - - - Streams/Creeks
& Small Rivers

● Cities/Towns

✝ Cemeteries

Scale: Section = 1 mile X 1 mile
(there are some exceptions)

Map Group 19: Index to Land Patents

Township 7-North Range 16-East (St Stephens)

After you locate an individual in this Index, take note of the Section and Section Part then proceed to the Land Patent map on the pages immediately following. You should have no difficulty locating the corresponding parcel of land.

The "For More Info" Column will lead you to more information about the underlying Patents. See the *Legend* at right, and the "How to Use this Book" chapter, for more information.

```
┌─────────────────────────────────────────────────────────┐
│                       LEGEND                            │
│            "For More Info . . . " column                │
│  ───────────────────────────────────────────────        │
│  A = Authority (Legislative Act, See Appendix "A")      │
│  B = Block or Lot (location in Section unknown)         │
│  C = Cancelled Patent                                   │
│  F = Fractional Section                                 │
│  G = Group  (Multi-Patentee Patent, see Appendix "C")   │
│  V = Overlaps another Parcel                            │
│  R = Re-Issued (Parcel patented more than once)         │
│                                                         │
│  (A & G items require you to look in the Appendixes     │
│  referred to above. All other Letter-designations       │
│  followed by a number require you to locate line-items  │
│  in this index that possess the ID number found after   │
│  the letter).                                           │
└─────────────────────────────────────────────────────────┘
```

ID	Individual in Patent	Sec.	Sec. Part	Date Issued	Other Counties	For More Info . . .
4053	ADAMS, John	4	SE	1860-04-02		A1
4054	" "	9	W½NE	1860-04-02		A1
4055	" "	9	W½SE	1860-04-02		A1
4113	ADAMS, Samuel	18	NE	1860-09-01		A1
4114	" "	18	SE	1860-09-01		A1
4130	ADKISON, Theophilus	28	W½SE	1858-11-01		A1
4131	" "	33	NWNE	1858-11-01		A1
4045	ARMSTRONG, James W	5	E½NE	1858-11-01		A1
4092	ARMSTRONG, Maximilian	15	NWNW	1858-11-01		A1
4093	" "	15	SENW	1858-11-01		A1
4094	ARMSTRONG, Maximillian	15	NENW	1850-08-10		A1
4032	BEDGOOD, James M	25	E½SE	1860-04-02		A1
4099	BISHOP, Noble P	35	W½	1901-10-09		A1 G2 V4056, 4143
3948	BLAKENEY, Andrew J	26	NWSW	1897-03-18		A1
4016	BRIGHT, James G	24	E½NW	1858-11-01		A1
4017	" "	24	NESE	1858-11-01		A1
4018	" "	24	S½SW	1858-11-01		A1
4019	" "	24	SWNE	1858-11-01		A1
4020	" "	24	W½SE	1858-11-01		A1
4142	BRUNDIGE, Wiley	2	N½SW	1888-02-04		A2
4036	BURNETT, James R	10	W½	1860-09-01		A1
4103	CATLIN, Richard	17	E½NE	1837-08-18		A1
4104	" "	17	E½SW	1837-08-18		A1
4105	" "	17	SE	1837-08-18		A1
4106	" "	20	E½	1837-08-18		A1
4107	" "	21	NE	1837-08-18		A1
4109	" "	21	W½	1837-08-18		A1
4108	" "	21	SE	1843-02-01		A1
4110	" "	22	W½NW	1843-02-01		A1
3972	CLARK, David	26	NWNW	1858-11-01		A1
3973	" "	27	E½NE	1858-11-01		A1
4071	CONNOR, John H	1	NE	1895-08-08		A2
4057	DE BREE, JOHN	13	SW	1838-07-28		A1
4058	" "	14	W½NE	1838-07-28		A1
4059	" "	14	W½NW	1838-07-28		A1
4060	" "	14	W½SE	1838-07-28		A1
4061	" "	14	W½SW	1838-07-28		A1
4062	" "	15	S½	1838-07-28		A1
4063	" "	22	E½NE	1838-07-28		A1
4064	" "	22	SW	1838-07-28		A1
4065	" "	22	W½NE	1838-07-28		A1
4066	" "	23	E½NE	1838-07-28		A1
4067	" "	23	SWNW	1838-07-28		A1
4077	DEES, John T	29	NWSW	1850-04-01		A1
4078	" "	29	SWNW	1850-08-10		A1
3950	DENDY, Buford W	22	E½NW	1860-09-01		A1

ID	Individual in Patent	Sec.	Sec. Part	Date Issued	Other Counties	For More Info . . .
3951	DENDY, Buford W (Cont'd)	32	E½NW	1860-09-01		A1
3952	" "	32	NWSW	1860-09-01		A1
3953	" "	32	W½NW	1860-09-01		A1
3954	" "	8	E½SE	1860-09-01		A1
3955	" "	8	NESW	1860-09-01		A1
3956	" "	8	NWSW	1860-09-01		A1
3957	" "	8	W½SE	1860-09-01		A1
3939	FEAGIN, Aaron	24	N½NE	1858-11-01		A1
3940	" "	32	SESW	1858-11-01		A1
4144	FINKLEA, William	36	W½NW	1894-11-21		A2
4099	FOSKETT, William A	35	W½	1901-10-09		A1 G2 V4056, 4143
3979	FOWLER, Eli	20	SWNW	1858-11-01		A1
3978	" "	20	NWNW	1860-10-01		A1
4086	FRANKLIN, June	36	E½NW	1885-06-20		A2
4087	" "	36	W½NE	1885-06-20		A2
3971	GODWIN, Daniel W	34	NW	1902-09-15		A2
4068	GODWIN, John	23	E½SE	1860-04-02		A1
4069	" "	23	SWSE	1860-04-02		A1
4070	" "	24	N½SW	1860-04-02		A1
4056	GODWIN, John C	35	NW	1906-05-23		A2 V4099
4021	GREGORY, James G	28	NWSW	1838-07-28		A1
4022	" "	29	NE	1838-07-28		A1
3941	HALL, Aaron	9	SW	1897-03-18		A1
3990	HAMIL, George W	10	SE	1897-06-14		A1
3991	" "	11	SW	1897-06-14		A1
4157	HARRELSON, William P	34	SE	1895-09-04		A2
4095	HART, Moses	3	N½SW	1901-04-22		A2
4096	" "	3	SESW	1901-04-22		A2
4097	" "	3	SWSE	1901-04-22		A2
4100	HELTOR, Peter	36	NENE	1858-11-01		A1
4148	HIGHSMITH, William	11	NW	1897-03-18		A1
4149	" "	2	S½SW	1897-03-18		A1
4150	" "	2	W½SE	1897-03-18		A1
4023	HOLLAND, James	12	E½NE	1838-07-28		A1
4048	HOLLAND, Jasper J	1	SWSE	1843-02-01		A1
3980	HOLLY, Elias H	36	SENE	1861-05-01		A1
3963	JACKSON, Chrissey	4	NESW	1860-10-01		A1
4088	JACKSON, Lafayette	4	E½NW	1897-02-17		A1
4089	" "	4	NWNE	1897-02-17		A1
4090	" "	4	NWNW	1897-02-17		A1
4141	JOHNS, Warren R	36	NESE	1913-07-22		A2
3958	JORDAN, Charles B	20	NENW	1858-11-01		A1
3959	" "	20	NESW	1858-11-01		A1
3960	" "	20	SENW	1858-11-01		A1
3961	" "	20	SESW	1858-11-01		A1
4033	JORDAN, James M	18	SW	1858-11-01		A1
4049	JORDAN, Jesse	19	S½NW	1858-11-01		A1
4072	JORDAN, John	19	SESE	1858-11-01		A1
4043	LANE, James T	31	SESW	1837-08-18		A1
4044	" "	31	W½SW	1837-08-18		A1
3988	LLOYD, Eugene E	6	E½SW	1860-09-01		A1
3989	" "	6	W½SW	1860-09-01		A1
4029	LONG, James	32	SWNE	1852-02-02		A1
4027	" "	32	NESE	1860-10-01		A1
4028	" "	32	SESE	1862-01-01		A1
4030	" "	32	W½SE	1862-01-01		A1
4031	" "	33	SWSW	1862-01-01		A1
4120	LONG, Solomon	32	N½NE	1838-07-28		A1
4123	" "	33	SWNE	1852-02-02		A1
4121	" "	32	SENE	1858-11-01		A1
4122	" "	33	E½SW	1858-11-01		A1
4124	" "	33	W½NW	1858-11-01		A1
4125	" "	33	W½SE	1858-11-01		A1
4034	MAJOR, James	28	SESE	1860-10-01		A1
4035	" "	28	SESW	1860-10-01		A1
4111	MANSELL, Robert	23	NWSW	1852-02-02		A1
4112	" "	23	SESW	1852-02-02		A1
4073	MCTYEIRE, John	26	NENW	1860-10-01		A1
4140	MERRELL, W J	12	SESW	1885-06-30		A1
3997	MERRILL, Greenberry	25	N½NW	1858-11-01		A1
3998	" "	25	SWNW	1858-11-01		A1
4000	" "	26	SENW	1858-11-01		A1
3999	" "	26	N½NE	1860-12-01		A1

ID	Individual in Patent	Sec.	Sec. Part	Date Issued	Other Counties	For More Info . . .
4001	MERRILL, Henry M	23	NWSE	1858-11-01		A1
4005	MERRILL, Jacob	13	E½NW	1833-06-04		A1
4008	" "	13	W½NE	1837-08-09		A1
4010	" "	14	E½SE	1837-08-09		A1
4007	" "	13	SENE	1838-07-28		A1
4009	" "	13	W½SE	1838-07-28		A1
4011	" "	23	E½NW	1838-07-28		A1
4012	" "	23	NWNW	1838-07-28		A1
4013	" "	23	W½NE	1838-07-28		A1
4004	" "	12	W½SE	1841-05-20		A1
4006	" "	13	NENE	1858-11-01		A1
4152	MERRILL, William	13	W½NW	1833-06-04		A1
4153	" "	14	E½NE	1837-08-07		A1
4155	" "	24	SENE	1837-08-07		A1
4154	" "	14	E½SW	1837-08-12		A1
4156	" "	24	W½NW	1837-08-12		A1
4151	" "	13	E½SE	1841-05-20		A1
4079	MOORE, Joseph J	25	E½SW	1900-11-12		A2
4080	" "	25	SENW	1900-11-12		A2
4081	" "	25	SWNE	1900-11-12		A2
4050	MORGAN, John A	30	E½SE	1858-11-01		A1
4051	" "	30	NWSE	1858-11-01		A1
4052	" "	30	S½NE	1858-11-01		A1
4084	MORRIS, Julia A	36	S½SE	1860-04-02		A1
4085	" "	36	SESW	1860-04-02		A1
4163	OWEN, Zachariah	27	NESW	1852-02-02		A1
4164	" "	27	SWNE	1852-02-02		A1
3946	OWENS, Ada	1	SENW	1897-08-30		A2
3947	" "	1	W½NW	1897-08-30		A2
4126	OWENS, Thaddeus C	1	SWSW	1897-03-18		A1
4127	" "	11	NWNE	1897-03-18		A1
4128	" "	11	S½NE	1897-03-18		A1
4129	" "	12	NW	1897-03-18		A1
4165	OWENS, Zachariah	20	NWSW	1852-02-02		A1
4132	POTTER, Thomas F	12	W½SW	1860-10-01		A1
4133	" "	14	E½NW	1860-10-01		A1
4082	RHOADES, Josiah	11	NENE	1858-11-01		A1
4083	" "	2	NESE	1858-11-01		A1
4002	RIDGEWAY, Jack	3	E½SE	1900-11-28		A2
4003	" "	3	NWSE	1900-11-28		A2
4143	RODGERS, William D	35	SW	1906-05-23		A2 V4099
4024	ROGERS, James L	36	N½SW	1890-07-03		A2
4025	" "	36	NWSE	1890-07-03		A2
4026	" "	36	SWSW	1890-07-03		A2
4091	SCIPPER, Mary A	34	NE	1891-06-30		A2
4160	SHEHEAN, William	25	NWNE	1907-04-05		A1
3965	SHINE, Daniel B	30	NWSW	1850-08-10		A1
3964	" "	30	NESW	1858-11-01		A1
3966	" "	30	SWSW	1858-11-01		A1
4046	SHINE, James W	30	SENW	1858-11-01		A1
4047	" "	30	W½NW	1858-11-01		A1
4158	SHINE, William P	19	W½SW	1858-11-01		A1
4159	" "	30	NENW	1862-04-10		A1
3949	SKIPPER, Barnet B	30	NWNE	1858-11-01		A1
4119	SKIPPER, Silas	29	SENW	1852-12-01		A1
4118	" "	29	NWNW	1858-11-01		A1
3984	SMITH, Elizabeth	31	NESW	1858-11-01		A1
3985	" "	31	SENW	1858-11-01		A1
3986	" "	31	SWSE	1858-11-01		A1
3987	" "	31	W½NW	1858-11-01		A1
4014	SMITH, James D	29	NENW	1852-12-01		A1
4074	SMITH, John	30	NENE	1849-09-01		A1
4075	SMYTH, John	28	SWNW	1849-09-01		A1
4076	" "	29	NESE	1849-09-01		A1
3976	SOLOMON, David W	27	E½NW	1860-04-02		A1
3977	" "	27	NWNW	1860-04-02		A1
3968	STALLINGS, Daniel	18	NWNW	1858-11-01		A1
3969	" "	18	SWNW	1858-11-01		A1
3970	" "	7	SWSW	1858-11-01		A1
3967	" "	18	E½NW	1860-09-01		A1
4038	STALLINGS, James	30	SWSE	1854-07-15		A1
4041	" "	31	NENW	1854-07-15		A1
4037	" "	30	SESW	1858-11-01		A1

ID	Individual in Patent	Sec.	Sec. Part	Date Issued	Other Counties	For More Info . . .
4039	STALLINGS, James (Cont'd)	31	E½NE	1858-11-01		A1
4040	" "	31	N½SE	1858-11-01		A1
4042	" "	31	SWNE	1858-11-01		A1
4145	STANLEY, William H	8	E½NW	1860-09-01		A1
4146	" "	8	W½NE	1860-09-01		A1
4147	" "	8	W½NW	1860-09-01		A1
4015	TAYLOR, James E	32	SWSW	1852-02-02		A1
3974	UNDERWOOD, David H	26	S½SE	1897-07-03		A2
3975	"	26	S½SW	1897-07-03		A2
3942	VAN PELT, ABRAHAM C	6	E½NW	1860-09-01		A1
3943	" "	6	W½NW	1860-09-01		A1
4115	VAN PELT, SARAH A	17	NW	1898-06-27		A1
4116	" "	17	W½NE	1898-06-27		A1
4117	" "	8	S½SW	1898-06-27		A1
3944	WALL, Absalom	22	SWSE	1837-08-12		A1
3945	" "	27	NWNE	1837-08-12		A1
4098	WALL, Nancy	28	NENE	1850-08-10		A1
4134	WALL, Thomas G	28	E½NW	1860-04-02		A1
4135	" "	28	NESE	1860-04-02		A1
4136	" "	28	NESW	1860-04-02		A1
4137	" "	28	NWNW	1860-04-02		A1
4138	" "	28	SENE	1860-04-02		A1
4139	" "	28	W½NE	1860-04-02		A1
4161	WALL, Wright	28	SWSW	1837-08-12		A1
4162	"	33	NENE	1837-08-12		A1
3962	WILLIAMS, Charles	26	S½NE	1875-06-01		A2
3981	WILLIAMS, Elisha	24	SESE	1858-11-01		A1
3982	" "	25	NENE	1858-11-01		A1
3992	WILLIAMS, George	4	SESW	1860-04-02		A1
3993	" "	4	SWNW	1860-04-02		A1
3994	" "	4	W½SW	1860-04-02		A1
3995	" "	8	E½NE	1860-04-02		A1
3996	" "	9	W½NW	1860-04-02		A1
3983	WILLS, Eliza	34	SW	1885-06-20		A2
4101	WRIGHT, Rebecca J	26	N½SE	1900-08-09		A2
4102	" "	26	NESW	1900-08-09		A2

Patent Map

T7-N R16-E
St Stephens Meridian

Map Group 19

Township Statistics

Parcels Mapped	:	227
Number of Patents	:	153
Number of Individuals	:	95
Patentees Identified	:	94
Number of Surnames	:	67
Multi-Patentee Parcels	:	1
Oldest Patent Date	:	6/4/1833
Most Recent Patent	:	7/22/1913
Block/Lot Parcels	:	0
Parcels Re - Issued	:	0
Parcels that Overlap	:	3
Cities and Towns	:	2
Cemeteries	:	2

Copyright 2008 Boyd IT, Inc. All Rights Reserved

Helpful Hints

1. This Map's INDEX can be found on the preceding pages.

2. Refer to Map "C" to see where this Township lies within Crenshaw County, Alabama.

3. Numbers within square brackets [ ] denote a multi-patentee land parcel (multi-owner). Refer to Appendix "C" for a full list of members in this group.

4. Areas that look to be crowded with Patentees usually indicate multiple sales of the same parcel (Re-issues) or Overlapping parcels. See this Township's Index for an explanation of these and other circumstances that might explain "odd" groupings of Patentees on this map.

Legend

- Patent Boundary
- Section Boundary
- No Patents Found (or Outside County)
- 1., 2., 3., ... Lot Numbers (when beside a name)
- [ ] Group Number (see Appendix "C")

Scale: Section = 1 mile X 1 mile (generally, with some exceptions)

Road Map

T7-N R16-E
St Stephens Meridian

Map Group 19

Cities & Towns
Merrill Mill
Mulberry

Cemeteries
Friendship Cemetery
Saint Lukes Cemetery

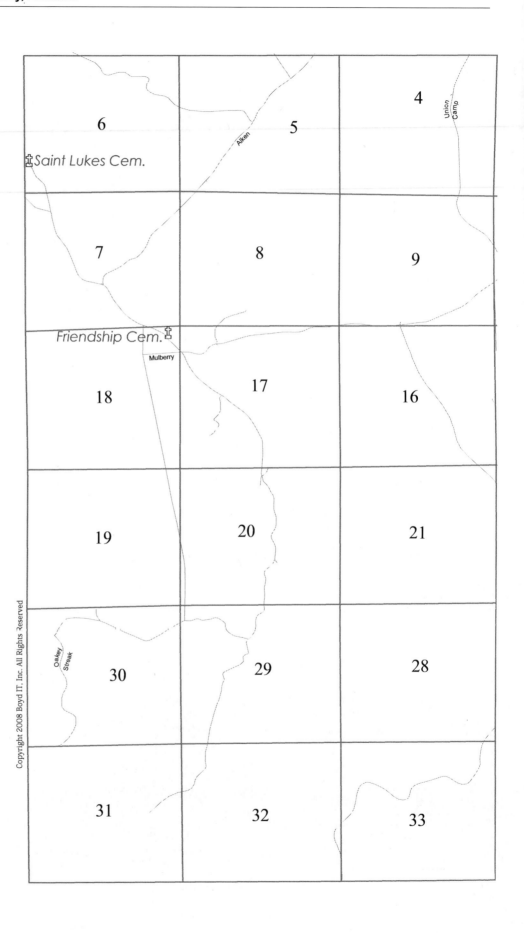

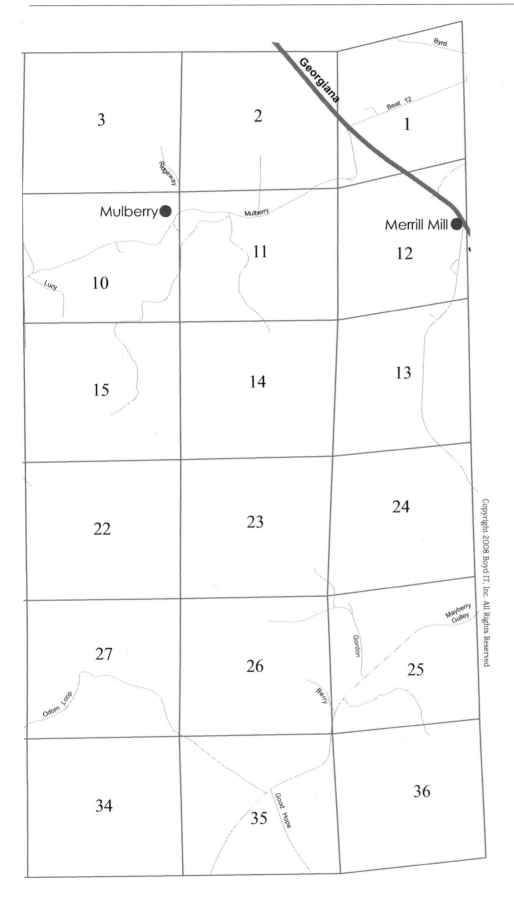

3

2

Byrd

Georgiana

Beat 12

1

Ridgeway

Mulberry●

Mulberry

Merrill Mill●

10

Lucy

11

12

15

14

13

22

23

24

Mayberry Gulley

27

26

Gordon

25

Berry

Odom Loop

34

35

Good Hope

36

Helpful Hints

1. This road map has a number of uses, but primarily it is to help you: a) find the present location of land owned by your ancestors (at least the general area), b) find cemeteries and city-centers, and c) estimate the route/roads used by Census-takers & tax-assessors.

2. If you plan to travel to Crenshaw County to locate cemeteries or land parcels, please pick up a modern travel map for the area before you do. Mapping old land parcels on modern maps is not as exact a science as you might think. Just the slightest variations in public land survey coordinates, estimates of parcel boundaries, or road-map deviations can greatly alter a map's representation of how a road either does or doesn't cross a particular parcel of land.

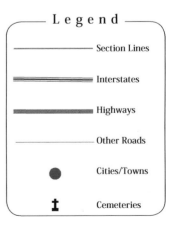

L e g e n d

————————	Section Lines
════════════	Interstates
▨▨▨▨▨▨▨▨	Highways
————————	Other Roads
●	Cities/Towns
✝	Cemeteries

Scale: Section = 1 mile X 1 mile
(generally, with some exceptions)

Historical Map

T7-N R16-E
St Stephens Meridian

Map Group 19

Cities & Towns
Merrill Mill
Mulberry

Cemeteries
Friendship Cemetery
Saint Lukes Cemetery

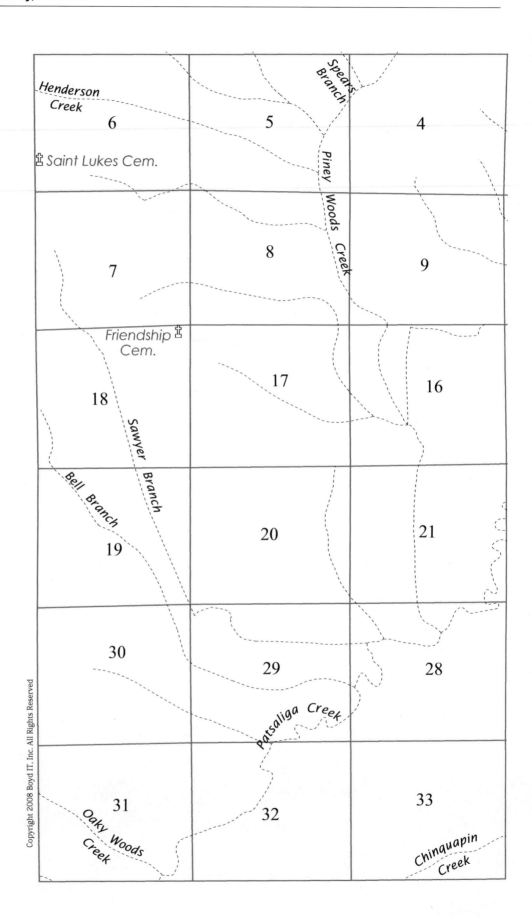

Henderson Creek

6

5

4

Spears Branch

✝ Saint Lukes Cem.

Piney Woods Creek

7

8

9

Friendship ✝ Cem.

18

17

16

Sawyer Branch

Bell Branch

19

20

21

30

29

28

Patsaliga Creek

31

32

33

Oaky Woods Creek

Chinquapin Creek

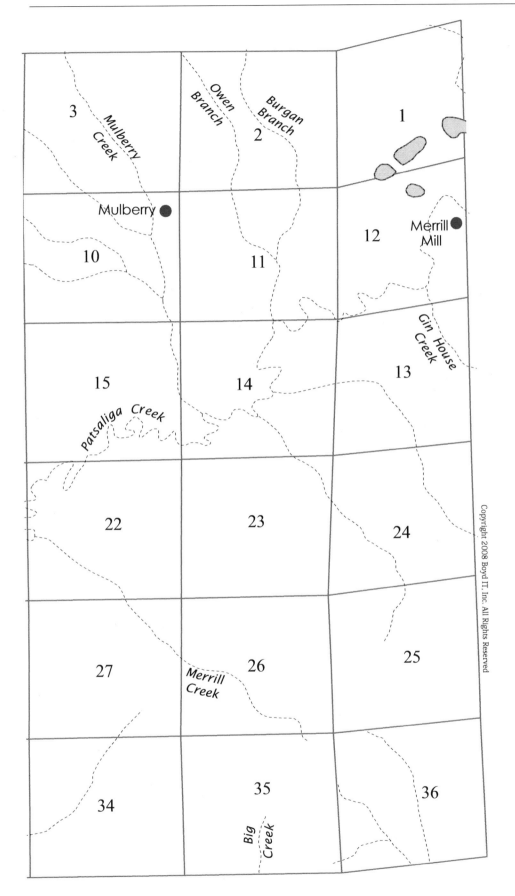

3

Mulberry Creek

Owen Branch

Burgan Branch

2

1

Mulberry ●

12

Merrill Mill ●

10

11

15

14

Gin House Creek

13

Patsaliga Creek

22

23

24

25

27

Merrill Creek

26

34

35

36

Big Creek

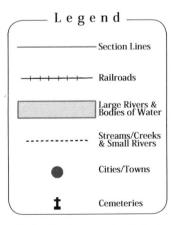

Helpful Hints

1. This Map takes a different look at the same Congressional Township displayed in the preceding two maps. It presents features that can help you better envision the historical development of the area: a) Water-bodies (lakes & ponds), b) Water-courses (rivers, streams, etc.), c) Railroads, d) City/town center-points (where they were oftentimes located when first settled), and e) Cemeteries.

2. Using this "Historical" map in tandem with this Township's Patent Map and Road Map, may lead you to some interesting discoveries. You will often find roads, towns, cemeteries, and waterways are named after nearby landowners: sometimes those names will be the ones you are researching. See how many of these research gems you can find here in Crenshaw County.

Legend

———— Section Lines

+++++++ Railroads

▬▬▬ Large Rivers & Bodies of Water

- - - - - Streams/Creeks & Small Rivers

● Cities/Towns

♰ Cemeteries

Scale: Section = 1 mile X 1 mile
(there are some exceptions)

Map Group 20: Index to Land Patents

Township 7-North Range 17-East (St Stephens)

After you locate an individual in this Index, take note of the Section and Section Part then proceed to the Land Patent map on the pages immediately following. You should have no difficulty locating the corresponding parcel of land.

The "For More Info" Column will lead you to more information about the underlying Patents. See the *Legend* at right, and the "How to Use this Book" chapter, for more information.

```
┌─────────────────────────────────────────────────────┐
│                        LEGEND                        │
│         "For More Info . . . " column                │
├─────────────────────────────────────────────────────┤
│ A = Authority (Legislative Act, See Appendix "A")    │
│ B = Block or Lot (location in Section unknown)       │
│ C = Cancelled Patent                                 │
│ F = Fractional Section                               │
│ G = Group  (Multi-Patentee Patent, see Appendix "C") │
│ V = Overlaps another Parcel                          │
│ R = Re-Issued (Parcel patented more than once)       │
│                                                       │
│ (A & G items require you to look in the Appendixes    │
│ referred to above. All other Letter-designations      │
│ followed by a number require you to locate            │
│ line-items in this index that possess the ID number   │
│ found after the letter).                              │
└─────────────────────────────────────────────────────┘
```

ID	Individual in Patent	Sec.	Sec. Part	Date Issued	Other Counties	For More Info . . .
4362	ALBRITTON, Moses	4	NWSW	1894-12-07		A2
4408	ANDERSON, Super	24	SWSE	1860-04-02		A1
4409	" "	25	NENE	1860-04-02		A1
4410	" "	25	NWNE	1860-04-02		A1
4388	BAYGENTS, Rufus F	26	S½NW	1860-04-02		A1
4183	BELL, Barney E	27	NWSW	1900-11-28		A2
4184	" "	27	SENW	1900-11-28		A2
4185	" "	27	W½NW	1900-11-28		A2
4392	BRADLEY, Samuel C	7	NENE	1860-04-02		A1
4394	" "	7	NWNE	1860-04-02		A1
4389	" "	6	N½NE	1896-11-21		A1
4390	" "	6	NWSE	1896-11-21		A1
4391	" "	6	S½NW	1896-11-21		A1
4393	" "	7	NENW	1896-11-21		A1
4177	BRANNAN, Alexander	19	SESE	1860-04-02		A1
4178	" "	20	SWSW	1860-04-02		A1
4182	BROOKS, Baley M	1	NENW	1860-04-02		A1
4271	BROWNING, James A	15	NWSE	1858-11-01		A1
4270	" "	15	NENW	1860-04-02		A1
4272	" "	15	W½NE	1860-04-02		A1
4173	BRUNSON, Albert	10	E½NE	1891-06-08		A2
4174	" "	10	NESE	1891-06-08		A2
4175	" "	10	SWNE	1891-06-08		A2
4239	BRUNSON, Henry D	11	N½SW	1900-11-12		A2
4240	" "	11	NWSE	1900-11-12		A2
4241	" "	11	SENW	1900-11-12		A2
4370	BRUNSON, Otis S	11	N½NW	1900-11-28		A2
4371	" "	11	W½NE	1900-11-28		A2
4331	BRYAN, Joseph F	28	NWSW	1892-06-10		A2
4332	" "	28	SWNW	1892-06-10		A2
4342	BURNETTE, Judy	30	NESW	1899-08-16		A2
4196	BUSH, Charles W	24	NW	1890-03-19		A2
4181	CAMERON, Archibald H	18	NENW	1878-04-09		A2
4197	CANNON, Charlie B	17	NENE	1907-05-01		A2
4403	CARTER, Shadrach	29	SESE	1838-07-28		A1
4404	CARTER, Shadrick	15	SESE	1860-04-02		A1
4302	CHAPMAN, John D	25	SENW	1860-04-02		A1
4303	" "	25	SWNE	1860-04-02		A1
4300	" "	24	E½SW	1897-02-17		A1
4301	" "	24	NWSE	1897-02-17		A1
4422	COMPTON, William	10	SESE	1893-07-24		A2
4180	CUMBIE, Andrew J	1	SWSW	1900-11-28		A2
4186	DANIEL, Benjamin F	4	N½SE	1891-06-19		A2
4187	" "	4	SENE	1891-06-19		A2
4188	" "	4	SESE	1891-06-19		A2
4217	DANIEL, Edward	20	E½NE	1894-06-09		A2

ID	Individual in Patent	Sec.	Sec. Part	Date Issued	Other Counties	For More Info . . .
4318	DAVIDSON, John L	4	E½SW	1883-09-15		A2
4411	DOZIER, Thomas H	26	E½SE	1897-07-27		A2
4412	" "	26	NESW	1897-07-27		A2
4413	" "	26	NWSE	1897-07-27		A2
4218	ENGRAM, Edward E	20	W½NE	1878-04-09		A2
4227	FAISON, Eugene L	17	E½SE	1899-11-04		A2
4167	FANNIN, Abram W	8	E½SE	1860-04-02		A1
4168	" "	8	N½SW	1860-04-02		A1
4169	" "	8	NWSE	1860-04-02		A1
4170	" "	8	SWSE	1860-04-02		A1 R4256
4171	" "	9	NWSW	1860-04-02		A1
4172	" "	9	SWSW	1860-04-02		A1
4166	FEAGIN, Aaron	30	E½NW	1843-02-01		A1
4245	FROST, Hilrey	31	SWSE	1858-11-01		A1
4244	" "	31	NESE	1860-04-02		A1
4252	GALLOPS, Isom	17	E½SW	1860-04-02		A1
4253	" "	17	NWSW	1860-04-02		A1
4254	" "	17	SENW	1860-04-02		A1
4255	" "	17	W½NW	1860-04-02		A1
4256	" "	8	SWSE	1860-04-02		A1 R4170
4306	GALLUPS, John	33	NWSW	1860-04-02		A1
4307	" "	33	SWNW	1860-04-02		A1
4385	GALLUPS, Robert	28	SWSE	1860-04-02		A1
4386	" "	33	NWNE	1860-04-02		A1
4377	HALLFORD, Reddin	18	E½SW	1858-11-01		A1
4378	" "	18	NWSW	1858-11-01		A1
4379	" "	18	S½NW	1858-11-01		A1
4380	" "	18	SWSE	1858-11-01		A1
4381	" "	18	SWSW	1858-11-01		A1
4333	HANDLEY, Joseph J	22	SENW	1898-06-17		A2
4449	HARRISON, Williamson	19	N½SW	1858-11-01		A1
4450	" "	19	NESE	1858-11-01		A1
4451	" "	19	NW	1858-11-01		A1
4452	" "	19	NWNE	1858-11-01		A1
4216	HATHEWAY, Ebenezer B	36	SWSE	1841-05-20		A1
4308	HAYGOOD, John H	14	N½NE	1895-06-03		A2
4375	HELTON, Peter	31	SWNW	1854-07-15		A1
4374	" "	30	W½SW	1858-11-01		A1
4373	" "	30	SWNW	1860-04-02		A1
4202	HENDERSON, Daniel	35	NESE	1860-04-02		A1
4330	HENDERSON, Johnson	25	SWSW	1907-04-05		A1
4293	HICKS, Jesse T	28	SENW	1884-12-05		A2
4294	" "	28	SWNE	1884-12-05		A2
4292	" "	28	E½NE	1885-03-30		A2
4397	HIGHSMITH, Sarah A	12	N½NE	1888-01-21		A2
4208	HOLLAND, David	31	NENW	1850-08-10		A1
4209	" "	31	NWNW	1854-07-15		A1
4207	" "	31	NENE	1858-11-01		A1
4211	" "	31	SENW	1858-11-01		A1
4212	" "	31	SWNE	1858-11-01		A1
4210	" "	31	NWSE	1860-04-02		A1
4319	HOLLAND, John N	6	NESE	1858-11-01		A1
4320	" "	6	SENE	1858-11-01		A1
4321	" "	6	SESE	1860-04-02		A1
4322	" "	6	SWNE	1860-04-02		A1
4358	HOLLAND, Mary	5	NWNW	1860-04-02		A1
4359	" "	5	W½SW	1860-04-02		A1
4352	HOLLEY, Louisa	22	NESE	1896-06-15		A2
4297	HOLLIS, John A	22	NE	1888-02-04		A2
4426	HOLLIS, William	22	E½SW	1888-02-04		A2
4427	" "	22	W½SE	1888-02-04		A2
4453	HOLLIS, Williard H	20	E½SE	1890-10-11		A2
4249	HUGHES, Isaiah W	23	NESW	1900-11-28		A2
4250	" "	23	S½NE	1900-11-28		A2
4251	" "	23	SENW	1900-11-28		A2
4311	JOHNSON, John J	2	E½NW	1858-11-01		A1
4312	" "	2	NESW	1858-11-01		A1
4313	" "	2	NWNW	1858-11-01		A1
4314	" "	2	SWNE	1860-04-02		A1
4315	JONES, John	4	SWSW	1858-11-01		A1
4316	" "	5	SWSE	1858-11-01		A1
4317	" "	8	SWNE	1860-04-02		A1
4360	JONES, Matthew P	19	E½NE	1858-11-01		A1

ID	Individual in Patent	Sec.	Sec. Part	Date Issued	Other Counties	For More Info . . .
4361	JONES, Matthew P (Cont'd)	19	SWNE	1858-11-01		A1
4407	KIMBRO, Simon P	34	W½NW	1880-02-20		A2
4405	" "	34	NENW	1889-11-21		A2
4406	" "	34	NWNE	1889-11-21		A2
4324	KIRKLAND, John P	17	NWNE	1907-05-01		A2
4325	" "	17	NWSE	1907-05-01		A2
4326	" "	17	S½NE	1907-05-01		A2
4424	KIRKLAND, William G	9	W½NE	1900-11-28		A2
4425	" "	9	W½SE	1900-11-28		A2
4226	LEE, Emma	26	NENW	1896-10-07		A2
4213	MCDONALD, Delodius N	14	N½SW	1891-06-29		A2
4214	" "	14	SWSW	1891-06-29		A2
4298	MCMICHEL, John C	15	NESW	1860-04-02		A1
4299	" "	15	SENW	1860-04-02		A1
4260	MERRILL, Jacob	7	N½SW	1858-11-01		A1
4259	" "	18	W½NE	1860-04-02		A1
4261	" "	7	S½SW	1860-04-02		A1
4262	" "	7	SWSE	1860-04-02		A1
4415	MERRILL, Thomas L	8	SESW	1883-10-20		A1
4414	" "	18	NENE	1884-03-10		A2
4433	MERRILL, William	19	SESW	1837-08-07		A1
4434	" "	19	W½SE	1837-08-12		A1
4430	MERRILL, William J	32	NWSE	1854-07-15		A1
4432	" "	32	SWNW	1854-07-15		A1
4428	" "	29	SWSW	1860-04-02		A1
4429	" "	32	NESW	1860-04-02		A1
4431	" "	32	SWNE	1860-04-02		A1
4203	MILLS, Daniel R	3	NW	1900-11-28		A2
4417	MILLS, William A	3	SW	1900-11-12		A2
4454	MILLS, Wilson	10	NW	1895-06-19		A2
4237	MONTGOMERY, Green	24	E½NE	1860-04-02		A1
4238	MONTGOMERY, Hampton	24	E½SE	1860-04-02		A1
4354	MOON, Martha J	29	NWNW	1858-11-01		A1
4355	" "	30	NENE	1858-11-01		A1
4347	NEESE, Lewallen	34	SENW	1889-08-02		A2
4348	" "	34	SWNE	1889-08-02		A2
4179	NEWSOM, Alfred	34	SESE	1884-04-02		A1
4296	NICKOLS, Job F	3	NE	1900-10-12		A2
4290	OGDEN, Jesse	29	SWNW	1837-08-12		A1
4291	" "	30	SESW	1837-08-12		A1
4221	PARKER, Eli	36	SESW	1852-12-01		A1
4220	" "	36	NESW	1860-04-02		A1
4222	" "	36	W½SW	1860-04-02		A1
4219	" "	35	SESE	1884-04-02		A1
4384	PEEK, Robert C	14	S½SE	1897-08-30		A2
4437	PERRY, William	18	E½SE	1860-04-02		A1
4438	" "	18	NWSE	1860-04-02		A1
4439	" "	18	SENE	1860-04-02		A1
4421	PHILLIPS, William C	4	NENE	1906-09-26		A2
4192	PRICE, Bridges	29	NESE	1858-11-01		A1
4193	" "	29	SESW	1858-11-01		A1
4194	" "	29	SWSE	1858-11-01		A1
4191	" "	28	SWSW	1860-04-02		A1
4195	" "	33	NWNW	1860-04-02		A1
4337	RHODES, Josiah	20	E½SW	1860-04-02		A1
4338	" "	20	NWSW	1860-04-02		A1
4339	" "	29	NENW	1860-04-02		A1
4340	" "	29	NWNE	1860-04-02		A1
4341	" "	30	NWNE	1860-04-02		A1
4334	RICHBURG, Joseph L	1	NWSE	1900-11-28		A2
4335	" "	1	SENW	1900-11-28		A2
4336	" "	1	W½NE	1900-11-28		A2
4279	ROACH, James	31	SWSW	1854-07-15		A1
4280	" "	32	SESW	1858-11-01		A1
4281	" "	32	SWSE	1860-04-02		A1
4282	" "	32	W½SW	1860-04-02		A1
4327	ROBBINS, John	35	SWSE	1860-04-02		A1
4349	RODGERS, Littleberry	31	SESE	1852-02-02		A1
4350	" "	32	SENW	1852-02-02		A1
4351	ROGERS, Littleberry	31	SESW	1837-08-10		A1
4372	ROGERS, Patterson	32	SENE	1854-07-15		A1
4204	ROYAL, Datus D	13	NW	1860-04-02		A1
4205	" "	13	NWNE	1860-04-02		A1

ID	Individual in Patent	Sec.	Sec. Part	Date Issued	Other Counties	For More Info . . .
4206	ROYAL, Datus D (Cont'd)	13	NWSW	1860-04-02		A1
4228	SANDERS, Franklin J	27	N½NE	1900-11-28		A2
4229	" "	27	NESE	1900-11-28		A2
4230	" "	27	SENE	1900-11-28		A2
4273	SASSEN, James J	25	NWSW	1884-04-02		A1
4215	SASSER, Dennis G	24	W½SW	1895-06-03		A2
4274	SASSER, James J	25	SWNW	1860-04-02		A1
4286	SASSER, Jesse B	36	S½NE	1854-10-02		A1
4283	" "	25	SESE	1858-11-01		A1
4284	" "	36	NENE	1858-11-01		A1
4285	" "	36	NESE	1860-04-02		A1
4287	SASSER, Jesse J	26	SESW	1889-08-02		A2
4288	" "	26	SWSE	1889-08-02		A2
4289	" "	26	W½SW	1889-08-02		A2
4295	SASSER, Jessee B	36	SESE	1860-04-02		A1
4356	SASSER, Martha	25	NESW	1860-04-02		A1
4357	" "	25	SESW	1907-04-05		A1
4246	SAUNDERS, Howell J	1	E½SW	1901-01-23		A2
4247	" "	1	NWSW	1901-01-23		A2
4248	" "	1	SWNW	1901-01-23		A2
4328	SAUNDERS, John	2	N½NE	1891-06-29		A2
4382	SAUNDERS, Richard	12	E½SW	1860-04-02		A1
4383	" "	12	SE	1860-04-02		A1
4440	SCARBOROUGH, William	6	N½NW	1860-04-02		A1
4275	SMITH, James J	30	SWSE	1893-03-03		A2
4329	SMITH, John	12	SENW	1860-04-02		A1
4276	SORRELL, James M	28	N½SE	1886-03-10		A2
4277	" "	28	SESE	1886-03-10		A2
4418	SPENCER, William B	12	NENW	1860-04-02		A1
4419	" "	12	NWNW	1860-04-02		A1
4420	" "	12	SWNW	1860-04-02		A1
4236	SPURLIN, Georgeann L	1	NENE	1900-11-12		A2
4198	STANLEY, Daniel E	34	E½NE	1860-04-02		A1
4199	" "	35	E½NW	1860-04-02		A1
4200	" "	35	W½NE	1860-04-02		A1
4201	" "	35	W½NW	1860-04-02		A1
4400	STANLEY, Sarah	35	SENE	1860-04-02		A1
4398	" "	25	W½SE	1862-01-01		A1
4399	" "	35	NENE	1862-01-01		A1
4401	" "	36	NW	1862-01-01		A1
4402	" "	36	NWNE	1862-01-01		A1
4376	STOKES, Ransom D	30	SESE	1923-11-16		A2
4304	STRIPLING, John D	14	N½SE	1891-06-08		A2
4305	" "	14	S½NE	1891-06-08		A2
4363	TAUNTON, Newton	33	E½SW	1860-04-02		A1
4364	" "	33	NENW	1860-04-02		A1
4365	" "	33	SE	1860-04-02		A1
4366	" "	33	SENE	1860-04-02		A1
4367	" "	33	SENW	1860-04-02		A1
4368	" "	33	SWNE	1860-04-02		A1
4369	" "	33	SWSW	1860-04-02		A1
4231	TAYLOR, Furney G	2	NWSW	1860-04-02		A1
4232	" "	2	SWNW	1860-04-02		A1
4263	TAYLOR, Jacob	5	E½NW	1841-05-20		A1
4266	" "	5	NWNE	1841-05-20		A1
4269	" "	8	E½NE	1854-10-02		A1
4264	" "	5	E½SE	1858-11-01		A1
4265	" "	5	NESW	1860-04-02		A1
4267	" "	5	NWSE	1860-04-02		A1
4268	" "	5	SWNE	1860-04-02		A1
4278	TAYLOR, James R	8	NENW	1854-10-02		A1
4309	TAYLOR, John H	12	S½NE	1897-10-28		A2
4441	TAYLOR, William W	19	SWSW	1858-11-01		A1
4442	" "	29	NESW	1858-11-01		A1
4444	" "	29	SENW	1858-11-01		A1
4446	" "	30	NWNW	1858-11-01		A1
4443	" "	29	NWSE	1860-04-02		A1
4445	" "	29	SWNE	1860-04-02		A1
4423	THURSTON, William F	4	SWSE	1897-09-22		A2
4257	TISON, Jack	13	E½SW	1900-11-28		A2
4258	" "	13	W½SE	1900-11-28		A2
4176	TURNER, Albert R	23	SE	1900-11-28		A2
4235	TURNER, George G	2	S½SW	1896-07-09		A2

ID	Individual in Patent	Sec.	Sec. Part	Date Issued	Other Counties	For More Info . . .
4343	TYSON, Justin	4	E½NW	1860-04-02		A1
4344	" "	4	W½NE	1860-04-02		A1
4345	" "	4	W½NW	1860-04-02		A1
4346	" "	5	E½NE	1860-04-02		A1
4189	UNDERWOOD, Benjamin F	28	E½SW	1891-06-08		A2
4310	WADDILL, John H	26	NE	1891-09-01		A2
4447	WALLACE, William	22	NWSW	1895-02-23		A2
4448	" "	22	SWNW	1895-02-23		A2
4223	WALLIS, Elisha A	21	SESE	1900-11-28		A2
4224	" "	21	SWNE	1900-11-28		A2
4225	" "	21	W½SE	1900-11-28		A2
4233	WALLIS, Gabriel M	28	N½NW	1894-03-17		A2
4234	" "	28	NWNE	1894-03-17		A2
4242	WALLIS, Henry E	9	E½NE	1900-11-12		A2
4243	" "	9	E½SE	1900-11-12		A2
4435	WALLIS, William N	21	N½NE	1901-04-22		A2
4436	" "	21	N½NW	1901-04-22		A2
4455	WARRICK, Wily	11	S½SE	1901-01-23		A2
4456	" "	11	S½SW	1901-01-23		A2
4416	WILLIAMS, Thomas	22	N½NW	1891-06-10		A2
4190	WILLIAMSON, Benjamin M	2	NESE	1898-06-01		A2
4323	WILLIAMSON, John O	10	NWNE	1904-05-05		A2
4353	WILLIAMSON, Lucy J	12	W½SW	1901-12-04		A2
4387	WILLIAMSON, Robert H	3	SE	1900-11-12		A2
4395	WILSON, Samuel H	22	SESE	1860-04-02		A1
4396	" "	26	NWNW	1860-04-02		A1

Patent Map

T7-N R17-E
St Stephens Meridian

Map Group 20

Township Statistics

Parcels Mapped	:	291
Number of Patents	:	190
Number of Individuals	:	133
Patentees Identified	:	133
Number of Surnames	:	94
Multi-Patentee Parcels	:	0
Oldest Patent Date	:	8/7/1837
Most Recent Patent	:	11/16/1923
Block/Lot Parcels	:	0
Parcels Re-Issued	:	1
Parcels that Overlap	:	0
Cities and Towns	:	3
Cemeteries	:	1

Copyright 2008 Boyd IT, Inc. All Rights Reserved

Section 3
MILLS
Daniel R
1900

NICKOLS
Job F
1900

JOHNSON
John J
1858

JOHNSON
John J
1858

TAYLOR
Furney G
1860

SAUNDERS
John
1891

JOHNSON
John J
1860

Section 2

BROOKS
Baley M
1860

RICHBURG
Joseph L
1900

SPURLIN
Georgeann L
1900

SAUNDERS
Howell J
1901

RICHBURG
Joseph L
1900

MILLS
William A
1900

WILLIAMSON
Robert H
1900

TAYLOR
Furney G
1860

JOHNSON
John J
1858

WILLIAMSON
Benjamin M
1898

SAUNDERS
Howell J
1901

Section 1

RICHBURG
Joseph L
1900

TURNER
George G
1896

SAUNDERS
Howell J
1901

CUMBIE
Andrew J
1900

Section 10
MILLS
Wilson
1895

WILLIAMSON
John O
1904

BRUNSON
Albert
1891

BRUNSON
Albert
1891

BRUNSON
Otis S
1900

BRUNSON
Henry D
1900

Section 11

BRUNSON
Otis S
1900

SPENCER
William B
1860

SPENCER
William B
1860

HIGHSMITH
Sarah A
1888

SPENCER
William B
1860

SMITH
John
1860

Section 12

TAYLOR
John H
1897

BRUNSON
Albert
1891

COMPTON
William
1893

WARRICK
Wily
1901

BRUNSON
Henry D
1900

BRUNSON
Henry D
1900

WARRICK
Wily
1901

WILLIAMSON
Lucy J
1901

SAUNDERS
Richard
1860

SAUNDERS
Richard
1860

Section 15
BROWNING
James A
1860

BROWNING
James A
1860

MCMICHEL
John C
1860

MCMICHEL
John C
1860

BROWNING
James A
1858

CARTER
Shadrick
1860

Section 14

MCDONALD
Delodius N
1891

MCDONALD
Delodius N
1891

HAYGOOD
John H
1895

STRIPLING
John D
1891

STRIPLING
John D
1891

PEEK
Robert C
1897

Section 13

ROYAL
Datus D
1860

ROYAL
Datus D
1860

ROYAL
Datus D
1860

TISON
Jack
1900

TISON
Jack
1900

Section 22
WILLIAMS
Thomas
1891

WALLACE
William
1895

HANDLEY
Joseph J
1898

HOLLIS
John A
1888

HOLLEY
Louisa
1896

WALLACE
William
1895

HOLLIS
William
1888

HOLLIS
William
1888

WILSON
Samuel H
1860

Section 23

HUGHES
Isaiah W
1900

HUGHES
Isaiah W
1900

HUGHES
Isaiah W
1900

TURNER
Albert R
1900

Section 24

BUSH
Charles W
1890

MONTGOMERY
Green
1860

SASSER
Dennis G
1895

CHAPMAN
John D
1897

CHAPMAN
John D
1897

ANDERSON
Super
1860

MONTGOMERY
Hampton
1860

Section 27
BELL
Barney E
1900

BELL
Barney E
1900

BELL
Barney E
1900

SANDERS
Franklin J
1900

SANDERS
Franklin J
1900

SANDERS
Franklin J
1900

Section 26

WILSON
Samuel H
1860

LEE
Emma
1896

BAYGENTS
Rufus F
1860

WADDILL
John H
1891

SASSER
Jesse J
1889

DOZIER
Thomas H
1897

DOZIER
Thomas H
1897

DOZIER
Thomas H
1897

SASSER
Jesse J
1889

SASSER
Jesse J
1889

Section 25

SASSER
James J
1860

CHAPMAN
John D
1860

CHAPMAN
John D
1860

SASSEN
James J
1884

SASSER
Martha
1860

ANDERSON
Super
1860

ANDERSON
Super
1860

STANLEY
Sarah
1862

HENDERSON
Johnson
1907

SASSER
Martha
1907

SASSER
Jesse B
1858

Section 34
KIMBRO
Simon P
1880

KIMBRO
Simon P
1889

NEESE
Lewallen
1889

KIMBRO
Simon P
1889

NEESE
Lewallen
1889

STANLEY
Daniel E
1860

NEWSOM
Alfred
1884

Section 35

STANLEY
Daniel E
1860

STANLEY
Daniel E
1860

STANLEY
Daniel E
1860

STANLEY
Sarah
1862

STANLEY
Sarah
1860

HENDERSON
Daniel
1860

ROBBINS
John
1860

PARKER
Eli
1884

Section 36

STANLEY
Sarah
1862

STANLEY
Sarah
1862

SASSER
Jesse B
1854

PARKER
Eli
1860

PARKER
Eli
1860

PARKER
Eli
1852

STANLEY
Sarah
1862

SASSER
Jesse B
1858

SASSER
Jesse B
1860

HATHEWAY
Ebenezer B
1841

SASSER
Jessee B
1860

Helpful Hints

1. This Map's INDEX can be found on the preceding pages.

2. Refer to Map "C" to see where this Township lies within Crenshaw County, Alabama.

3. Numbers within square brackets [ ] denote a multi-patentee land parcel (multi-owner). Refer to Appendix "C" for a full list of members in this group.

4. Areas that look to be crowded with Patentees usually indicate multiple sales of the same parcel (Re-issues) or Overlapping parcels. See this Township's Index for an explanation of these and other circumstances that might explain "odd" groupings of Patentees on this map.

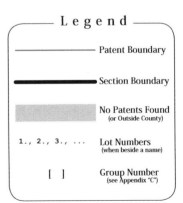

Legend

— Patent Boundary

— Section Boundary

No Patents Found
(or Outside County)

1., 2., 3., ... Lot Numbers
(when beside a name)

[ ] Group Number
(see Appendix "C")

Scale: Section – 1 mile X 1 mile
(generally, with some exceptions)

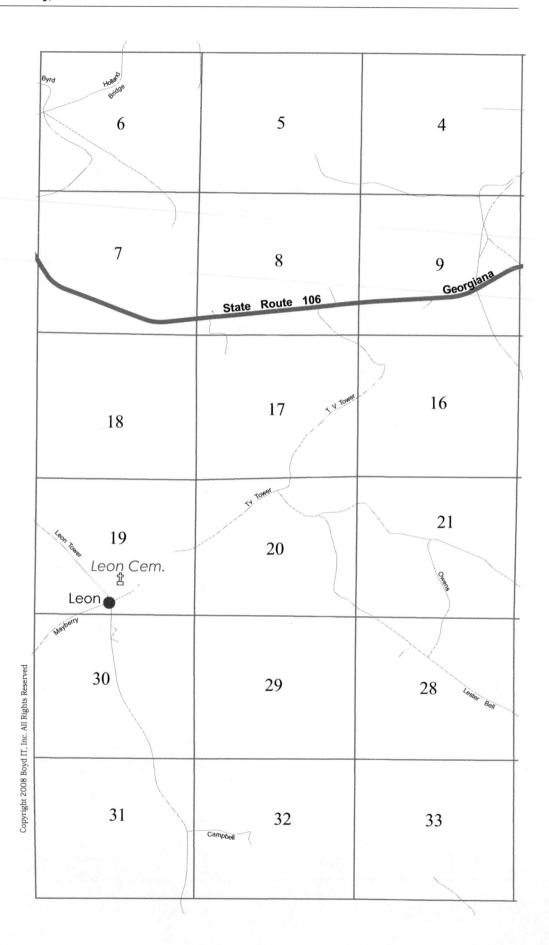

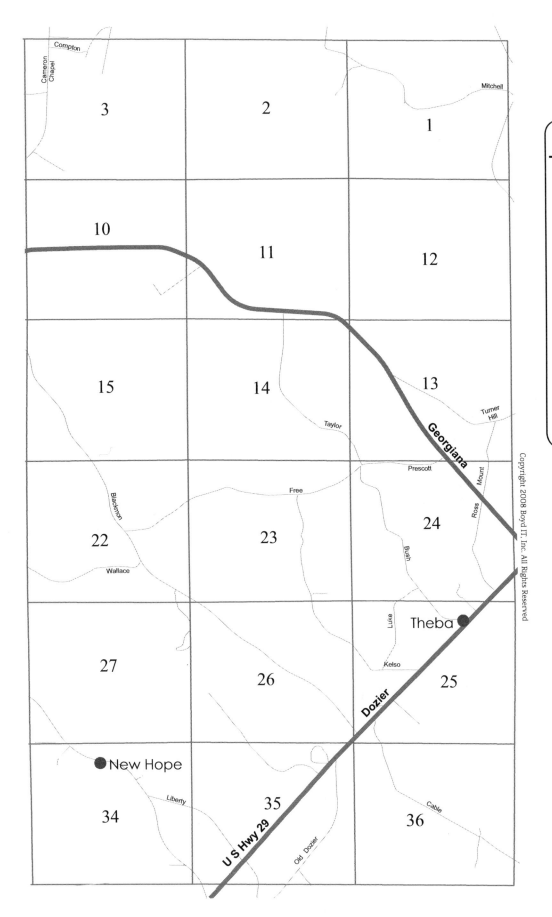

3

2

1

Compton

Cameron Chapel

Mitchell

10

11

12

15

14

13

Taylor

Turner Hill

Georgiana

Prescott

Mount

Ross

22

23

24

Blackmon

Free

Wallace

Bush

27

26

25

Luke

Theba

Kelso

Dozier

New Hope

34

35

36

Liberty

Old Dozier

Cable

U S Hwy 29

Copyright 2008 Boyd IT, Inc. All Rights Reserved

Helpful Hints

1. This road map has a number of uses, but primarily it is to help you: a) find the present location of land owned by your ancestors (at least the general area), b) find cemeteries and city-centers, and c) estimate the route/roads used by Census-takers & tax-assessors.

2. If you plan to travel to Crenshaw County to locate cemeteries or land parcels, please pick up a modern travel map for the area before you do. Mapping old land parcels on modern maps is not as exact a science as you might think. Just the slightest variations in public land survey coordinates, estimates of parcel boundaries, or road-map deviations can greatly alter a map's representation of how a road either does or doesn't cross a particular parcel of land.

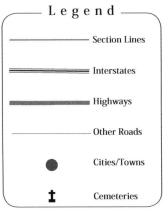

L e g e n d

———————	Section Lines
═══════════	Interstates
▓▓▓▓▓▓▓▓▓	Highways
———————	Other Roads
●	Cities/Towns
✝	Cemeteries

Scale: Section = 1 mile X 1 mile
(generally, with some exceptions)

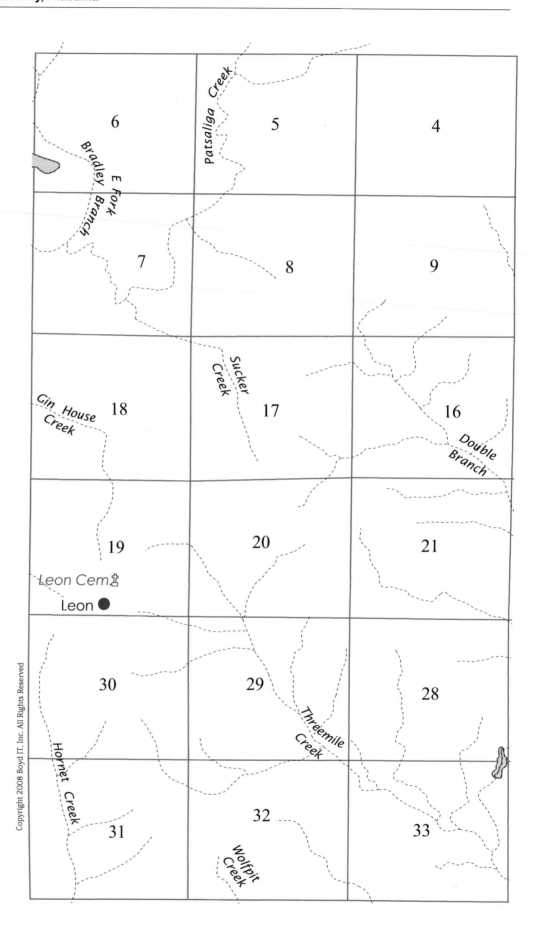

Historical Map

T7-N R17-E
St Stephens Meridian

Map Group 20

Cities & Towns

Leon
New Hope
Theba

Cemeteries

Leon Cemetery

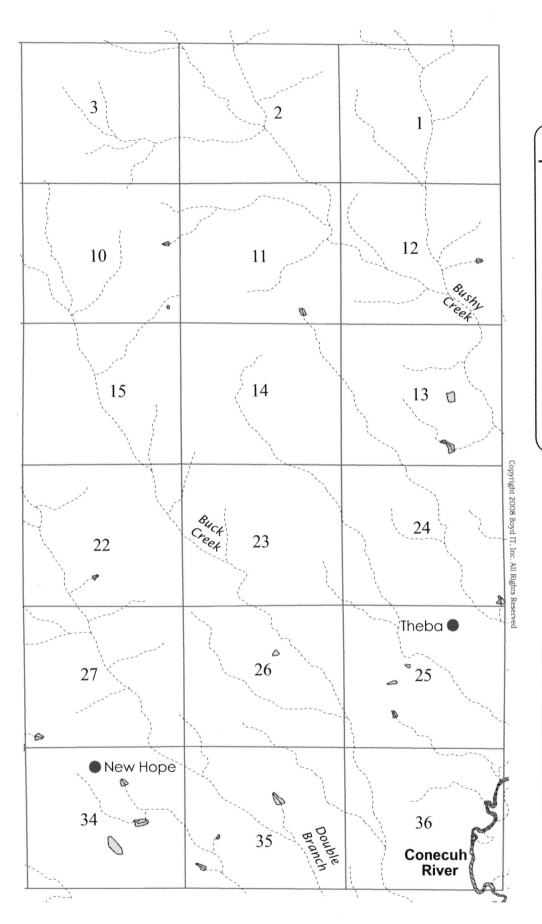

3
2
1
10
11
12
Bushy Creek
15
14
13
22
Buck Creek
23
24
27
26
Theba
25
New Hope
34
35
Double Branch
36
Conecuh River

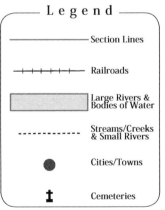

Helpful Hints

1. This Map takes a different look at the same Congressional Township displayed in the preceding two maps. It presents features that can help you better envision the historical development of the area: a) Water-bodies (lakes & ponds), b) Water-courses (rivers, streams, etc.), c) Railroads, d) City/town center-points (where they were oftentimes located when first settled), and e) Cemeteries.
2. Using this "Historical" map in tandem with this Township's Patent Map and Road Map, may lead you to some interesting discoveries. You will often find roads, towns, cemeteries, and waterways are named after nearby landowners: sometimes those names will be the ones you are researching. See how many of these research gems you can find here in Crenshaw County.

Legend

- Section Lines
- Railroads
- Large Rivers & Bodies of Water
- Streams/Creeks & Small Rivers
- Cities/Towns
- Cemeteries

Scale: Section = 1 mile X 1 mile
(there are some exceptions)

Map Group 21: Index to Land Patents

Township 7-North Range 18-East (St Stephens)

After you locate an individual in this Index, take note of the Section and Section Part then proceed to the Land Patent map on the pages immediately following. You should have no difficulty locating the corresponding parcel of land.

The "For More Info" Column will lead you to more information about the underlying Patents. See the *Legend* at right, and the "How to Use this Book" chapter, for more information.

```
                    LEGEND
              "For More Info . . . " column
A = Authority (Legislative Act, See Appendix "A")
B = Block or Lot (location in Section unknown)
C = Cancelled Patent
F = Fractional Section
G = Group  (Multi-Patentee Patent, see Appendix "C")
V = Overlaps another Parcel
R = Re-Issued (Parcel patented more than once)

(A & G items require you to look in the Appendixes referred
to above. All other Letter-designations followed by a number
require you to locate line-items in this index that possess
the ID number found after the letter).
```

ID	Individual in Patent	Sec.	Sec. Part	Date Issued	Other Counties	For More Info . . .
4467	ALSABROOKS, Andrew J	35	S½SW	1901-01-23		A2 G1
4467	ALSABROOKS, Mariah A	35	S½SW	1901-01-23		A2 G1
4741	ANDERSON, Super	30	N½NW	1896-10-21		A1
4742	" "	30	NWSE	1896-10-21		A1
4743	" "	30	SENW	1896-10-21		A1
4744	" "	30	SWNE	1896-10-21		A1
4687	BENBOW, Martha G	3	NENW	1900-11-28		A2
4688	" "	3	NWSW	1900-11-28		A2
4689	" "	3	W½NW	1900-11-28		A2
4787	BOOTH, Wilson	25	E½SW	1854-07-15		A1
4788	" "	25	SENW	1854-07-15		A1
4789	BOOTHE, Wilson	25	NWSE	1860-04-02		A1
4790	" "	25	SENE	1860-04-02		A1
4791	BOOTHE, Wilson L	25	SWNE	1854-10-02		A1
4776	BOSWELL, William J	30	SESW	1860-04-02		A1
4485	BOYETT, Bennet	19	E½SE	1860-04-02		A1
4486	" "	19	SENE	1860-04-02		A1
4488	BOYETT, Bennett	19	NENE	1838-07-28		A1
4490	" "	20	SWNE	1838-07-28		A1
4487	" "	18	SE	1858-11-01		A1
4489	" "	20	NWNW	1858-11-01		A1
4778	BRANDON, William N	26	NWNE	1860-04-02		A1
4779	" "	26	W½NW	1860-04-02		A1
4780	" "	27	NENE	1860-04-02		A1
4781	" "	27	NESE	1860-04-02		A1
4782	" "	27	SWNE	1860-04-02		A1
4527	BRUNSON, Francis A	6	E½NE	1903-05-19		A2
4528	" "	6	NESE	1903-05-19		A2
4583	BRYANT, James F	34	NWSE	1889-08-16		A2
4644	BRYANT, John L	24	W½NE	1895-01-31		A2
4643	" "	13	SWSE	1900-11-28		A2
4655	CAMPBELL, Johua C	27	NWSE	1902-07-03		A2
4512	CAPPS, Daniel D	4	NENE	1895-06-03		A2
4587	CARLILE, James J	3	SWSW	1860-04-02		A1
4588	"	4	SESE	1860-04-02		A1
4476	CARPENTER, Benjamin	14	W½NE	1837-08-14		A1
4767	CARPENTER, William	31	SWSW	1835-09-12		A1
4695	CARTER, Mary M	10	NENW	1895-08-08		A2 G12
4696	" "	10	W½NE	1895-08-08		A2 G12
4695	CARTER, William H	10	NENW	1895-08-08		A2 G12
4696	" "	10	W½NE	1895-08-08		A2 G12
4514	CAULEY, David S	31	SENW	1843-02-01		A1
4616	CHAPMAN, John D	30	NESW	1897-02-17		A1
4617	" "	30	S½SE	1897-02-17		A1
4768	COMPTON, William	19	SESW	1903-05-19		A2
4769	" "	30	NWSW	1916-04-26		A2

ID	Individual in Patent	Sec.	Sec. Part	Date Issued	Other Counties	For More Info . . .
4770	COMPTON, William (Cont'd)	30	SWNW	1916-04-26		A2
4465	COOK, Alonzo	17	E½NW	1901-01-23		A2
4466	" "	17	SWNW	1901-01-23		A2
4566	DAVIS, Isaac	26	SENE	1852-02-02		A1
4567	" "	27	NESW	1860-04-02		A1
4568	" "	27	SESW	1860-04-02		A1
4652	DAVIS, John W	7	E½NW	1899-11-04		A2
4653	" "	7	W½NE	1899-11-04		A2
4584	DELOACH, James F	6	NWSW	1890-08-29		A2
4585	" "	6	S½SW	1890-08-29		A2
4586	" "	6	SWSE	1890-08-29		A2
4674	EILAND, Levi	13	SESW	1852-02-02		A1
4594	ELLIS, James W	13	NWSW	1860-04-02		A1
4595	" "	13	S½NW	1860-04-02		A1
4596	" "	13	SWNE	1860-04-02		A1
4597	" "	23	E½SE	1860-04-02		A1
4598	" "	24	SESW	1860-04-02		A1
4599	" "	24	SWSW	1860-04-02		A1
4600	" "	25	NENW	1860-04-02		A1
4656	ETHERIDGE, Jonathan	33	SWNE	1852-02-02		A1
4618	EUBANKES, John	1	E½NE	1837-08-18		A1
4619	" "	1	E½SE	1837-08-18		A1
4654	EVERAGE, John W	10	NENE	1883-10-20		A1
4582	EVERIDGE, James	8	NESE	1860-04-02		A1
4657	EVERIDGE, Jonathan	17	SENE	1860-04-02		A1
4658	" "	17	SWSE	1860-04-02		A1
4659	EVRIDGE, Jonathan	17	E½SE	1862-12-20		A1
4660	" "	17	NWSE	1862-12-20		A1
4661	" "	20	NWNE	1862-12-20		A1
4746	FAGIN, Thomas	29	NESE	1858-11-01		A1
4500	FLOYD, Charles	25	SWSW	1854-07-15		A1
4499	" "	25	NWSW	1854-10-02		A1
4501	" "	36	NWSE	1860-04-02		A1
4720	FLOYD, Samuel J	35	SESE	1900-11-28		A2
4721	" "	35	SWNE	1900-11-28		A2
4722	" "	35	W½SE	1900-11-28		A2
4571	FRANKLIN, Jacob B	3	S½NE	1900-11-12		A2
4572	" "	3	W½SE	1900-11-12		A2
4609	GAINER, Jesse	25	S½SE	1852-02-02		A1
4612	" "	36	NWNE	1852-02-02		A1
4611	" "	36	NENE	1853-08-01		A1
4615	" "	36	SWNE	1854-07-15		A1
4608	" "	24	NESW	1854-10-02		A1
4610	" "	25	W½NW	1854-10-02		A1
4614	" "	36	SENW	1854-10-02		A1
4607	" "	24	NESE	1858-11-01		A1
4613	" "	36	NWNW	1858-11-01		A1
4700	GAINER, Nathan	36	E½SE	1905-03-30		A2
4539	GAINES, Green L	10	NESW	1885-05-25		A2
4540	" "	10	SENW	1885-05-25		A2
4675	GAINES, Levingston	10	SWSW	1860-04-02		A1
4676	" "	15	NWSE	1860-04-02		A1
4677	GAINES, Levington	15	NENW	1907-04-05		A1
4678	" "	15	NWSW	1907-04-05		A1
4679	" "	15	W½NW	1907-04-05		A1
4715	GIBSON, Robert M	5	W½NW	1904-09-16		A2
4686	GILCHRIST, Malcom	24	NENW	1896-10-28		A1
4664	HALL, Joseph M	35	E½NW	1913-07-22		A2
4665	" "	35	N½SW	1913-07-22		A2
4620	HAMILTON, John F	11	NENW	1858-11-01		A1
4621	" "	2	SESW	1858-11-01		A1
4622	" "	2	SWSE	1858-11-01		A1
4704	HAMILTON, Richard S	9	N½SE	1860-04-02		A1
4705	" "	9	S½SE	1860-04-02		A1
4706	" "	9	SENE	1860-04-02		A1
4707	" "	9	SWNE	1860-04-02		A1
4524	HATHORN, Eli S	2	NWSW	1895-08-08		A2
4525	" "	2	W½NW	1895-08-08		A2
4684	HIGHSMITH, Louis B	6	N½NW	1891-06-29		A2
4685	" "	6	W½NE	1891-06-29		A2
4458	HOLLEY, Alfred	31	NENW	1907-04-05		A1
4459	" "	32	E½SW	1907-04-05		A1
4515	HURLEY, Edmond	13	NESW	1858-11-01		A1

ID	Individual in Patent	Sec.	Sec. Part	Date Issued	Other Counties	For More Info . . .
4516	HURLEY, Edmond (Cont'd)	13	NWSE	1858-11-01		A1
4683	JACKSON, Littleberry	20	SESE	1860-04-02		A1
4650	JAY, John S	1	SESW	1854-07-15		A1
4651	" "	1	SWSE	1854-07-15		A1
4724	JAYROE, Sarah A	4	E½NW	1892-06-10		A2
4725	" "	4	W½NE	1892-06-10		A2
4517	JOHNSON, Edmond	34	NESE	1860-04-02		A1
4518	" "	34	SENE	1860-04-02		A1
4562	JOHNSON, Hiram	24	NWNW	1837-08-09		A1
4561	" "	13	SWSW	1852-02-02		A1
4563	" "	24	SWNW	1852-02-02		A1
4564	" "	26	NENE	1852-02-02		A1
4646	JOHNSON, John M	10	NWNW	1889-11-21		A2
4647	" "	10	NWSW	1889-11-21		A2
4648	" "	10	SWNW	1889-11-21		A2
4751	JOHNSON, Washington P	4	SW	1891-11-23		A2
4785	JOHNSON, William S	10	NESE	1890-03-19		A2
4786	" "	10	SENE	1890-03-19		A2
4526	JONES, Fed	36	SWNW	1911-08-24		A2
4550	JONES, Harvey	32	NENE	1858-11-01		A1
4551	JONES, Harvy	32	SENE	1860-04-02		A1
4552	" "	33	NWNW	1860-04-02		A1
4635	JONES, John	29	E½SW	1833-06-04		A1
4636	" "	29	W½SE	1837-08-15		A1
4639	" "	32	E½NW	1837-08-15		A1
4642	" "	33	W½SE	1837-08-15		A1
4638	" "	30	NESE	1838-07-28		A1
4637	" "	29	W½SW	1860-04-02		A1
4641	" "	32	W½NE	1860-04-02		A1
4640	" "	32	SWSE	1861-05-01		A1
4624	JONES, John J	34	E½SW	1894-10-22		A2
4625	" "	34	SWSE	1894-10-22		A2
4626	" "	34	SWSW	1894-10-22		A2
4666	JONES, Joseph W	33	NWNE	1904-07-02		A2
4668	JONES, Josiah	31	NWSE	1838-07-28		A1
4669	" "	33	NESW	1838-07-28		A1
4667	" "	31	NESW	1843-02-01		A1
4733	JONES, Seaborn	27	SESE	1860-04-02		A1
4734	" "	34	NENE	1860-04-02		A1
4603	JOSEY, Jeremiah J	14	SW	1858-11-01		A1
4604	" "	14	W½SE	1858-11-01		A1
4605	" "	15	E½SE	1858-11-01		A1
4502	KENNEDY, Charles K	14	NENW	1902-03-07		A2
4503	" "	14	SWNW	1902-03-07		A2
4713	KILCREASE, Robert J	26	NWSW	1895-06-19		A2
4544	LANIER, H Manuel	22	SWNE	1923-08-20		A2
4750	LAWSON, Walter T	24	E½NE	1876-12-01		A2
4460	LAYTON, Alfred	1	E½NW	1900-11-12		A2
4461	" "	1	NESW	1900-11-12		A2
4477	LOCKHART, Benjamin F	11	NWNW	1858-11-01		A1
4478	" "	2	SWSW	1858-11-01		A1
4479	" "	33	NESE	1860-04-02		A1
4480	" "	33	SESE	1860-04-02		A1
4670	LOCKHART, Julius C	14	SENE	1860-04-02		A1
4662	LOLLIS, Jones	26	SWSE	1854-10-02		A1
4663	" "	35	NENE	1854-10-02		A1
4470	MALLOY, Anguish	26	NESW	1854-10-02		A1
4471	" "	26	SWNE	1860-04-02		A1
4472	" "	26	SWSW	1860-04-02		A1
4513	MALLOY, Daniel	35	NWNW	1854-10-02		A1
4473	MALOY, Anguish	26	SENW	1860-04-02		A1
4474	" "	26	SESW	1860-04-02		A1
4649	MALOY, John	34	SESE	1861-05-01		A1
4481	MARTIN, Benjamin G	4	NESE	1893-03-03		A2
4482	" "	4	SENE	1893-03-03		A2
4483	" "	4	W½SE	1893-03-03		A2
4570	MATTHEWS, Jacob A	22	NESW	1897-09-22		A2
4716	MAYHAR, Robert	7	E½NE	1858-11-01		A1
4717	" "	8	NWSW	1858-11-01		A1
4718	" "	8	W½NW	1858-11-01		A1
4671	MCDUGALD, Levi D	5	E½SE	1901-01-23		A2
4672	" "	5	SENE	1901-01-23		A2
4673	" "	5	SWSE	1901-01-23		A2

ID	Individual in Patent	Sec.	Sec. Part	Date Issued	Other Counties	For More Info . . .
4690	MERRITT, Mary A	28	NWNW	1860-04-02		A1
4691	" "	28	S½NW	1860-04-02		A1
4692	" "	28	SWNE	1860-04-02		A1
4693	" "	28	W½SE	1860-04-02		A1
4475	MITCHELL, Ben	17	NESW	1919-11-07		A2
4542	MONTGOMERY, Green	19	NW	1858-11-01		A1
4543	" "	19	NWNE	1858-11-01		A1
4541	" "	18	SESW	1896-10-28		A1
4545	MONTGOMERY, Hampton	19	N½SE	1858-11-01		A1
4546	" "	19	SWNE	1858-11-01		A1
4547	" "	19	W½SE	1858-11-01		A1
4548	" "	30	NWNE	1860-04-02		A1
4740	MOUNT, Stephen E	3	E½SE	1900-11-28		A2
4735	NICHOLS, Shadrick	20	NESE	1860-04-02		A1
4736	" "	20	SWSE	1860-04-02		A1
4737	" "	21	SWSW	1860-04-02		A1
4745	OGLESBY, Tabitha	32	SESE	1860-04-02		A1
4555	PAYNE, Henry W	36	SESW	1891-06-29		A2
4556	" "	36	SWSE	1891-06-29		A2
4752	PEACOCK, Washington	1	NWNE	1858-11-01		A1
4753	" "	12	NENW	1860-04-02		A1
4754	" "	12	NWNW	1860-04-02		A1
4756	PEAVY, Washington	23	NESW	1858-11-01		A1
4757	" "	23	NWSE	1858-11-01		A1
4758	" "	23	SENW	1858-11-01		A1
4755	" "	23	NENW	1860-04-02		A1
4627	PERKINS, John J	28	SW	1858-11-01		A1
4765	PETERSON, William B	5	NESW	1860-04-02		A1
4766	" "	5	NWSE	1860-04-02		A1
4714	PHILLIPS, Robert J	5	NWSW	1905-12-01		A2
4747	PORTER, Virginia C	6	NESW	1891-06-08		A2 G37
4748	" "	6	NWSE	1891-06-08		A2 G37
4749	" "	6	S½NW	1891-06-08		A2 G37
4759	POTTER, Wesley	36	W½SW	1891-06-10		A2
4592	PRIESTER, James U	24	S½SE	1860-04-02		A1
4593	" "	25	N½NE	1860-04-02		A1
4777	RILEY, William J	31	NE	1858-11-01		A1
4519	ROGERS, Edward J	11	SESE	1858-11-01		A1
4520	" "	12	S½SW	1858-11-01		A1
4521	" "	13	NENW	1860-04-02		A1
4522	" "	13	NESE	1860-04-02		A1
4493	SASSER, Byrd	31	SESW	1835-09-12		A1
4494	" "	31	SWSE	1835-09-12		A1
4491	" "	31	E½SE	1837-08-15		A1
4495	" "	32	W½SW	1841-05-20		A1
4492	" "	31	NWSW	1843-02-01		A1
4565	SASSER, Howell	20	NWSE	1838-07-28		A1
4606	SASSER, Jesse B	30	SWSW	1858-11-01		A1
4554	SCOTT, Henry	18	NENW	1898-03-08		A2
4697	SHANKS, Mathew	18	W½NE	1860-04-02		A1
4698	" "	7	E½SW	1860-04-02		A1
4699	" "	7	SE	1860-04-02		A1
4457	SHAW, Alexander	36	SENE	1854-10-02		A1
4569	SMITH, Isaac	8	SWSW	1904-01-27		A2
4726	SMITH, Seaborn J	1	NWSW	1858-11-01		A1
4727	" "	1	W½NW	1858-11-01		A1
4729	" "	2	NESE	1858-11-01		A1
4728	" "	2	NENE	1860-04-02		A1
4730	" "	2	NESW	1896-11-21		A1
4731	" "	2	NWSE	1896-11-21		A1
4732	" "	2	SENE	1896-11-21		A1
4800	SMITH, Zachariah	15	SWSE	1858-11-01		A1
4801	" "	22	N½NE	1858-11-01		A1
4575	SORRELLS, James A	4	W½NW	1894-06-09		A2
4576	" "	5	NENE	1901-04-22		A2
4577	STANALAND, James D	20	SWSW	1884-04-02		A1
4578	" "	29	NWNW	1884-04-02		A1
4579	" "	29	S½NE	1884-04-02		A1
4580	" "	29	S½NW	1884-04-02		A1
4581	" "	30	E½NE	1884-04-02		A1
4529	STRICKLIN, Francis M	23	NWSW	1860-04-02		A1
4530	" "	23	SWSW	1860-04-02		A1
4682	STRICKLIN, Lewis	26	SESE	1838-07-28		A1

ID	Individual in Patent	Sec.	Sec. Part	Date Issued	Other Counties	For More Info . . .
4680	STRICKLIN, Lewis (Cont'd)	23	SWSE	1860-04-02		A1
4681	" "	26	NENW	1860-04-02		A1
4589	TAYLOR, James R	20	E½SW	1860-04-02		A1
4590	" "	20	NWSW	1860-04-02		A1
4591	" "	20	SWNW	1860-04-02		A1
4710	TAYLOR, Robert B	11	SENE	1852-12-01		A1
4711	" "	12	NWNW	1852-12-01		A1
4709	" "	11	NENE	1854-07-15		A1
4708	" "	1	SWSW	1854-10-02		A1
4712	" "	2	SESE	1858-11-01		A1
4747	TAYLOR, Virginia C	6	NESW	1891-06-08		A2 G37
4748	" "	6	NWSE	1891-06-08		A2 G37
4749	" "	6	S½NW	1891-06-08		A2 G37
4719	THOMPKINS, Samuel B	13	E½NE	1900-11-28		A2
4723	THOMPKINS, Samuel S	12	E½SE	1911-11-27		A2
4462	TILLERY, Alfred	17	NWSW	1860-04-02		A1
4463	" "	17	S½SW	1860-04-02		A1
4464	" "	20	E½NW	1860-04-02		A1
4484	TISDALE, Benjamin W	10	NWSE	1888-08-05		A1
4523	TISDALE, Edward	11	NWSE	1843-02-01		A1
4534	TISDALE, Furney G	21	E½NW	1837-08-09		A1
4535	" "	21	NWSE	1837-08-09		A1
4531	" "	10	S½SE	1860-04-02		A1
4532	" "	14	NWNW	1860-04-02		A1
4533	" "	15	SENW	1860-04-02		A1
4536	TISDALE, Furny G	11	SW	1858-11-01		A1
4628	TISDALE, John J	21	E½SW	1860-04-02		A1
4629	" "	21	NWNE	1860-04-02		A1
4630	" "	21	NWNW	1860-04-02		A1
4631	" "	21	SENE	1860-04-02		A1
4632	" "	27	NWSW	1860-04-02		A1
4633	" "	28	NESE	1860-04-02		A1
4634	" "	28	SENE	1860-04-02		A1
4703	TISDALE, Rebecca	21	SESE	1840-10-10		A1
4772	TISDALE, William D	15	W½NE	1838-07-28		A1
4771	" "	11	SWSE	1852-02-02		A1
4553	TURNER, Henry J	10	SESW	1894-11-21		A2
4601	TURNER, Jasper N	18	NESW	1890-10-11		A2
4602	" "	18	SENW	1890-10-11		A2
4760	UNDERWOOD, Wiley	20	NENE	1837-08-09		A1
4496	VINES, Caswell	20	SENE	1858-11-01		A1
4497	" "	21	NWSW	1858-11-01		A1
4498	" "	21	SWNW	1858-11-01		A1
4775	VINES, William H	2	E½NW	1860-04-02		A1
4504	WADE, Columbus W	27	SWSE	1860-04-02		A1
4505	" "	27	SWSW	1860-04-02		A1
4506	" "	33	NENE	1860-04-02		A1
4507	" "	33	SENE	1860-04-02		A1
4508	" "	34	E½NW	1860-04-02		A1
4509	" "	34	NWNW	1860-04-02		A1
4510	" "	34	NWSW	1860-04-02		A1
4511	" "	34	W½NE	1860-04-02		A1
4537	WILKERSON, Gabriel C	35	NESE	1901-12-04		A2
4538	" "	35	SENE	1901-12-04		A2
4702	WILKINSON, Oscar C	35	NWNE	1911-08-10		A1
4549	WILLIAMS, Hannah	22	NWSE	1854-10-02		A1
4560	WILLIAMS, Henry	29	SESE	1852-02-02		A1
4557	" "	22	E½SE	1858-11-01		A1
4558	" "	22	SESW	1858-11-01		A1
4559	" "	22	SWSE	1858-11-01		A1
4694	WILLIAMS, Mary A	28	SESE	1852-02-02		A1
4701	WILLIAMS, Oliver P	28	NENW	1850-08-10		A1
4738	WILLIAMS, Simon	33	SENW	1852-02-02		A1
4739	" "	33	SWNW	1852-02-02		A1
4761	WILLIAMS, Wiley	21	NESE	1841-05-20		A1
4764	" "	28	NWNE	1841-05-20		A1
4762	" "	22	NENW	1860-04-02		A1
4763	" "	22	SENW	1860-04-02		A1
4774	WILLIAMS, William G	21	SWNE	1840-10-10		A1
4773	" "	21	NENE	1841-05-20		A1
4784	WILLIAMS, William P	2	SWNE	1860-04-02		A1
4783	" "	2	NWNE	1907-04-05		A1
4792	WILLIAMS, Wilson	27	NENW	1854-10-02		A1

ID	Individual in Patent	Sec.	Sec. Part	Date Issued	Other Counties	For More Info . . .
4793	WILLIAMS, Wilson (Cont'd)	27	NWNE	1858-11-01		A1
4794	" "	27	NWNW	1860-04-02		A1
4795	" "	27	SENW	1860-04-02		A1
4796	" "	27	SWNW	1860-04-02		A1
4797	WILLIAMS, Wily	21	SWSE	1838-07-28		A1
4798	" "	22	W½NW	1838-07-28		A1
4799	" "	22	W½SW	1838-07-28		A1
4468	WILLIAMSON, Andrew S	17	N½NE	1860-04-02		A1
4469	" "	17	SWNE	1860-04-02		A1
4645	WILLIAMSON, John L	14	NENE	1860-04-02		A1
4573	WISE, Jacob	3	E½SW	1900-11-28		A2
4574	" "	3	SENW	1900-11-28		A2
4623	WRIGHT, John H	26	N½SE	1895-06-19		A2

Patent Map

T7-N R18-E
St Stephens Meridian

Map Group 21

Township Statistics

Parcels Mapped	:	345
Number of Patents	:	230
Number of Individuals	:	153
Patentees Identified	:	150
Number of Surnames	:	99
Multi-Patentee Parcels	:	6
Oldest Patent Date	:	6/4/1833
Most Recent Patent	:	8/20/1923
Block/Lot Parcels	:	0
Parcels Re - Issued	:	0
Parcels that Overlap	:	0
Cities and Towns	:	2
Cemeteries	:	2

Copyright 2008 Boyd IT, Inc. All Rights Reserved

Map

Section 3
- BENBOW Martha G 1900
- BENBOW Martha G 1900
- WISE Jacob 1900
- FRANKLIN Jacob B 1900
- BENBOW Martha G 1900
- FRANKLIN Jacob B 1900
- MOUNT Stephen E 1900
- WISE Jacob 1900
- CARLILE James J 1860

Section 2
- HATHORN Eli S 1895
- VINES William H 1860
- WILLIAMS William P 1907
- SMITH Seaborn J 1860
- WILLIAMS William P 1860
- SMITH Seaborn J 1896
- HATHORN Eli S 1895
- SMITH Seaborn J 1896
- SMITH Seaborn J 1896
- SMITH Seaborn J 1858
- LOCKHART Benjamin F 1858
- HAMILTON John F 1858
- HAMILTON John F 1858
- TAYLOR Robert B 1858

Section 1
- SMITH Seaborn J 1858
- LAYTON Alfred 1900
- PEACOCK Washington 1858
- EUBANKES John 1837
- SMITH Seaborn J 1858
- LAYTON Alfred 1900
- EUBANKES John 1837
- TAYLOR Robert B 1854
- JAY John S 1854
- JAY John S 1854

Section 10
- JOHNSON John M 1889
- CARTER [12] Mary M 1895
- CARTER [12] Mary M 1895
- EVERAGE John W 1883
- JOHNSON John M 1889
- GAINES Green L 1885
- JOHNSON William S 1890
- JOHNSON John M 1889
- GAINES Green L 1885
- TISDALE Benjamin W 1888
- JOHNSON William S 1890
- GAINES Levingston 1860
- TURNER Henry J 1894
- TISDALE Furney G 1860

Section 11
- LOCKHART Benjamin F 1858
- HAMILTON John F 1858
- TISDALE Furny G 1858
- TISDALE Edward 1843
- TISDALE William D 1852
- ROGERS Edward J 1858

Section 12
- TAYLOR Robert B 1854
- TAYLOR Robert B 1852
- PEACOCK Washington 1860
- PEACOCK Washington 1860
- TAYLOR Robert B 1852
- ROGERS Edward J 1858
- THOMPKINS Samuel S 1911

Section 15
- GAINES Levington 1907
- GAINES Levington 1907
- TISDALE William D 1838
- TISDALE Furney G 1860
- GAINES Levington 1907
- GAINES Levingston 1860
- SMITH Zachariah 1858

Section 14
- TISDALE Furney G 1860
- KENNEDY Charles K 1902
- CARPENTER Benjamin 1837
- WILLIAMSON John L 1860
- KENNEDY Charles K 1902
- LOCKHART Julius C 1860
- JOSEY Jeremiah J 1858
- JOSEY Jeremiah J 1858

Section 13
- ROGERS Edward J 1860
- ELLIS James W 1860
- ELLIS James W 1860
- THOMPKINS Samuel B 1900
- ELLIS James W 1860
- HURLEY Edmond 1858
- HURLEY Edmond 1858
- ROGERS Edward J 1860
- JOHNSON Hiram 1852
- EILAND Levi 1852
- BRYANT John L 1900

Section 22
- WILLIAMS Wily 1838
- WILLIAMS Wiley 1860
- SMITH Zachariah 1858
- WILLIAMS Wiley 1860
- LANIER H Manuel 1923
- MATTHEWS Jacob A 1897
- WILLIAMS Hannah 1854
- WILLIAMS Wily 1838
- WILLIAMS Henry 1858
- WILLIAMS Henry 1858
- WILLIAMS Henry 1858

Section 23
- PEAVY Washington 1860
- PEAVY Washington 1858
- STRICKLIN Francis M 1860
- PEAVY Washington 1858
- PEAVY Washington 1858
- STRICKLIN Francis M 1860
- STRICKLIN Lewis 1860
- ELLIS James W 1860

Section 24
- JOHNSON Hiram 1837
- GILCHRIST Malcom 1896
- JOHNSON Hiram 1852
- BRYANT John L 1895
- LAWSON Walter T 1876
- GAINER Jesse 1854
- GAINER Jesse 1858
- ELLIS James W 1860
- ELLIS James W 1860
- PRIESTER James U 1860

Section 27
- WILLIAMS Wilson 1860
- WILLIAMS Wilson 1854
- WILLIAMS Wilson 1858
- BRANDON William N 1860
- WILLIAMS Wilson 1860
- WILLIAMS Wilson 1860
- BRANDON William N 1860
- TISDALE John J 1860
- DAVIS Isaac 1860
- CAMPBELL Johua C 1902
- BRANDON William N 1860

Section 26
- BRANDON William N 1860
- STRICKLIN Lewis 1860
- BRANDON William N 1860
- JOHNSON Hiram 1852
- MALLOY Anguish 1860
- MALLOY Anguish 1860
- DAVIS Isaac 1852
- KILCREASE Robert J 1895
- MALLOY Anguish 1854
- WRIGHT John H 1895
- MALLOY Anguish 1860
- MALOY Anguish 1860
- LOLLIS Jones 1854
- STRICKLIN Lewis 1838

Section 25
- GAINER Jesse 1854
- ELLIS James W 1860
- PRIESTER James U 1860
- BOOTH Wilson 1854
- BOOTHE Wilson L 1854
- BOOTHE Wilson 1860
- FLOYD Charles 1854
- BOOTHE Wilson 1860
- FLOYD Charles 1854
- BOOTH Wilson 1854
- GAINER Jesse 1852

Section 34
- WADE Columbus W 1860
- DAVIS Isaac 1860
- WADE Columbus W 1860
- JONES Seaborn 1860
- WADE Columbus W 1860
- WADE Columbus W 1860
- JONES Seaborn 1860
- JOHNSON Edmond 1860
- WADE Columbus W 1860
- JONES John J 1894
- BRYANT James F 1889
- JOHNSON Edmond 1860
- JONES John J 1894
- MALOY John 1861

Section 35
- MALLOY Anguish 1860
- MALOY Anguish 1860
- LOLLIS Jones 1854
- STRICKLIN Lewis 1838
- MALLOY Daniel 1854
- HALL Joseph M 1913
- WILKINSON Oscar C 1911
- LOLLIS Jones 1854
- FLOYD Samuel J 1900
- WILKERSON Gabriel C 1901
- HALL Joseph M 1913
- FLOYD Samuel J 1900
- WILKERSON Gabriel C 1901
- ALSABROOKS [1] Andrew J 1901
- FLOYD Samuel J 1900

Section 36
- GAINER Jesse 1858
- JONES Fed 1911
- GAINER Jesse 1852
- GAINER Jesse 1853
- GAINER Jesse 1854
- GAINER Jesse 1854
- SHAW Alexander 1854
- POTTER Wesley 1891
- FLOYD Charles 1860
- GAINER Nathan 1905
- PAYNE Henry W 1891
- PAYNE Henry W 1891

Helpful Hints

1. This Map's INDEX can be found on the preceding pages.

2. Refer to Map "C" to see where this Township lies within Crenshaw County, Alabama.

3. Numbers within square brackets [ ] denote a multi-patentee land parcel (multi-owner). Refer to Appendix "C" for a full list of members in this group.

4. Areas that look to be crowded with Patentees usually indicate multiple sales of the same parcel (Re-issues) or Overlapping parcels. See this Township's Index for an explanation of these and other circumstances that might explain "odd" groupings of Patentees on this map.

Legend

- —— Patent Boundary
- —— Section Boundary
- No Patents Found (or Outside County)
- 1., 2., 3., ... Lot Numbers (when beside a name)
- [ ] Group Number (see Appendix "C")

Scale: Section = 1 mile X 1 mile (generally, with some exceptions)

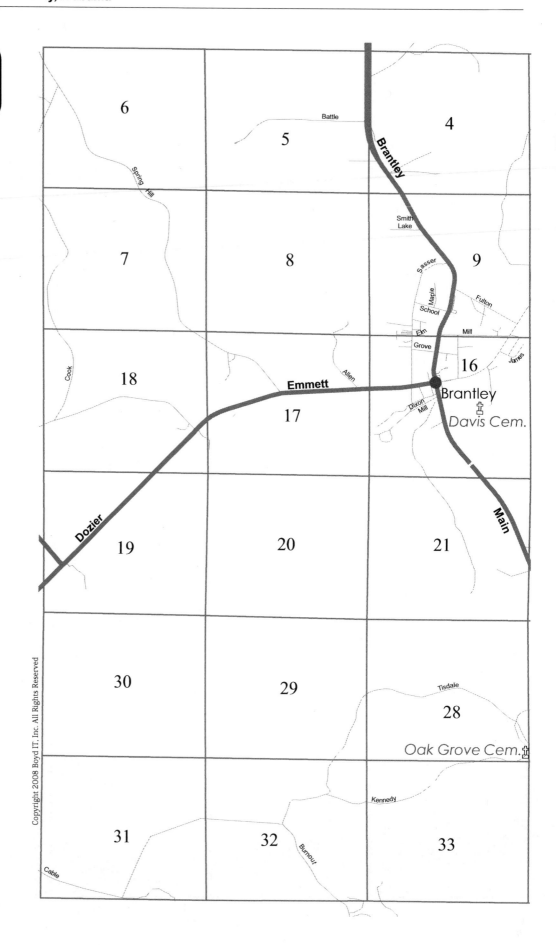

Road Map

T7-N R18-E
St Stephens Meridian

Map Group 21

Cities & Towns
Brantley
Peacock (historical)

Cemeteries
Davis Cemetery
Oak Grove Cemetery

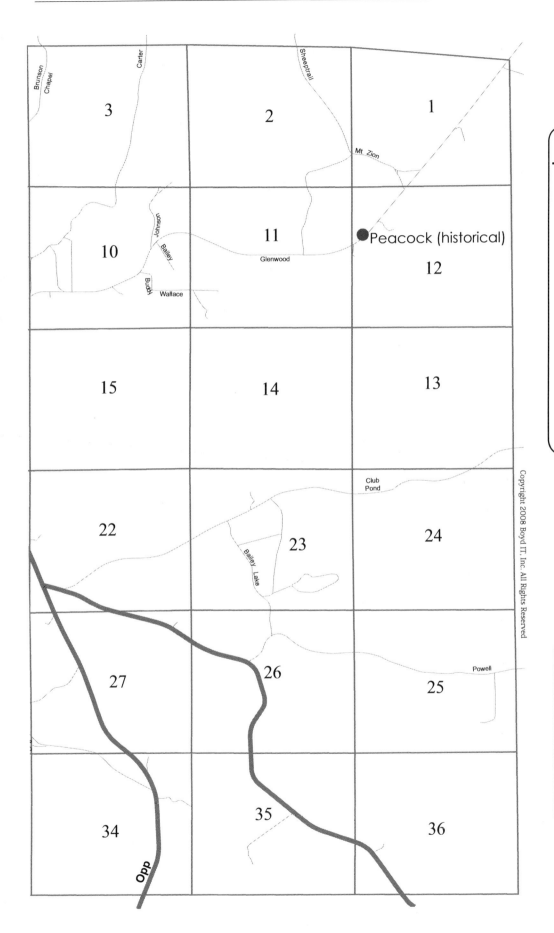

●Peacock (historical)

Helpful Hints

1. This road map has a number of uses, but primarily it is to help you: a) find the present location of land owned by your ancestors (at least the general area), b) find cemeteries and city-centers, and c) estimate the route/roads used by Census-takers & tax-assessors.

2. If you plan to travel to Crenshaw County to locate cemeteries or land parcels, please pick up a modern travel map for the area before you do. Mapping old land parcels on modern maps is not as exact a science as you might think. Just the slightest variations in public land survey coordinates, estimates of parcel boundaries, or road-map deviations can greatly alter a map's representation of how a road either does or doesn't cross a particular parcel of land.

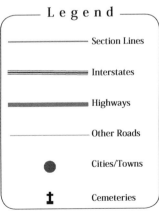

L e g e n d

————	Section Lines
═══════	Interstates
▬▬▬▬	Highways
————	Other Roads
●	Cities/Towns
✝	Cemeteries

Scale: Section = 1 mile X 1 mile
(generally, with some exceptions)

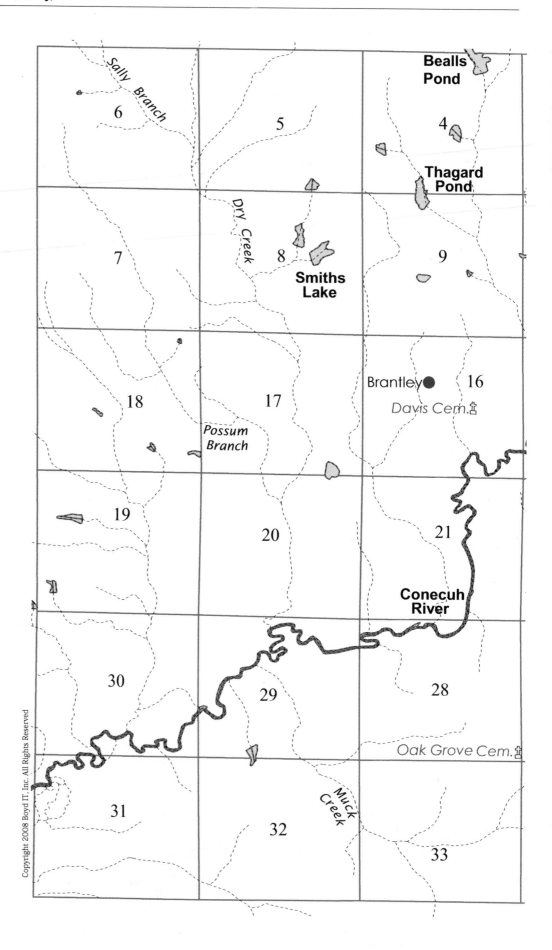

Historical Map

T7-N   R18-E
St Stephens Meridian

Map Group 21

Cities & Towns
Brantley
Peacock (historical)

Cemeteries
Davis Cemetery
Oak Grove Cemetery

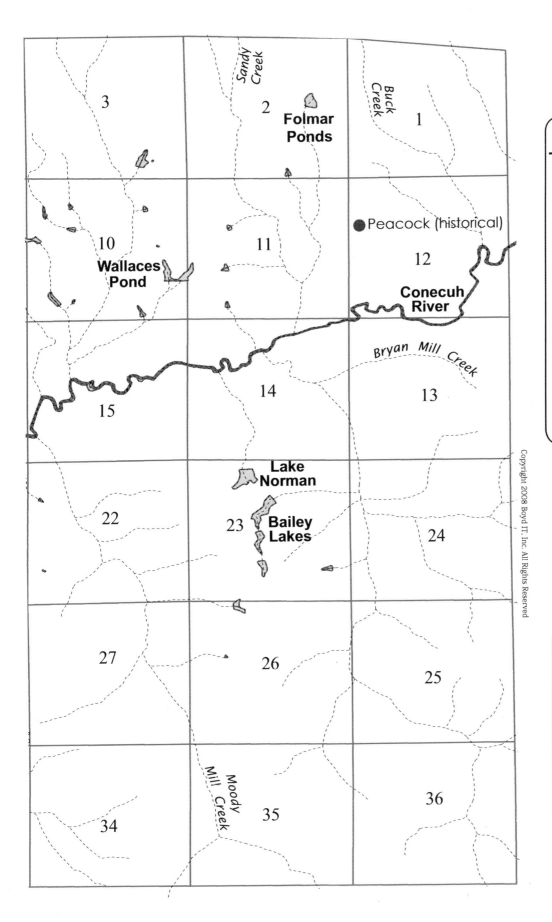

3

2

**Folmar
Ponds**

*Sandy
Creek*

*Buck
Creek*

1

10

11

● Peacock (historical)

12

**Wallaces
Pond**

**Conecuh
River**

Bryan Mill Creek

15

14

13

**Lake
Norman**

22

23

**Bailey
Lakes**

24

27

26

25

*Moody
Mill Creek*

34

35

36

Copyright 2008 Boyd IT, Inc. All Rights Reserved

Helpful Hints

1. This Map takes a different look at the same Congressional Township displayed in the preceding two maps. It presents features that can help you better envision the historical development of the area: a) Water-bodies (lakes & ponds), b) Water-courses (rivers, streams, etc.), c) Railroads, d) City/town center-points (where they were oftentimes located when first settled), and e) Cemeteries.

2. Using this "Historical" map in tandem with this Township's Patent Map and Road Map, may lead you to some interesting discoveries. You will often find roads, towns, cemeteries, and waterways are named after nearby landowners: sometimes those names will be the ones you are researching. See how many of these research gems you can find here in Crenshaw County.

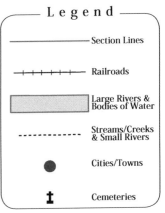

L e g e n d

——————— Section Lines

+–+–+–+–+–+ Railroads

Large Rivers &
Bodies of Water

– – – – – – Streams/Creeks
& Small Rivers

● Cities/Towns

✝ Cemeteries

Scale: Section = 1 mile X 1 mile
(there are some exceptions)

Map Group 22: Index to Land Patents

Township 7-North Range 19-East (St Stephens)

After you locate an individual in this Index, take note of the Section and Section Part then proceed to the Land Patent map on the pages immediately following. You should have no difficulty locating the corresponding parcel of land.

The "For More Info" Column will lead you to more information about the underlying Patents. See the *Legend* at right, and the "How to Use this Book" chapter, for more information.

```
┌─────────────────────────────────────────────────────────┐
│                        LEGEND                            │
│              "For More Info . . . " column               │
│  A = Authority (Legislative Act, See Appendix "A")       │
│  B = Block or Lot (location in Section unknown)          │
│  C = Cancelled Patent                                    │
│  F = Fractional Section                                  │
│  G = Group  (Multi-Patentee Patent, see Appendix "C")    │
│  V = Overlaps another Parcel                             │
│  R = Re-Issued (Parcel patented more than once)          │
│                                                          │
│  (A & G items require you to look in the Appendixes      │
│  referred to above. All other Letter-designations        │
│  followed by a number require you to locate line-items    │
│  in this index that possess the ID number found after    │
│  the letter).                                            │
└─────────────────────────────────────────────────────────┘
```

ID	Individual in Patent	Sec.	Sec. Part	Date Issued	Other Counties	For More Info . . .
4805	ADAMS, Benjamin	33	NENE	1860-04-02	Coffee	A1
4851	ADAMS, Jesse	19	NWNE	1860-04-02		A1
4863	ADAMS, John Q	4	S½SE	1854-07-15		A1
4862	" "	4	NENE	1858-11-01		A1
4892	ADAMS, Noah	8	SESW	1860-04-02		A1
4934	ADAMS, William M	9	E½SE	1900-11-28		A2
4935	" "	9	NWSE	1900-11-28		A2
4936	" "	9	SENE	1900-11-28		A2
4804	ASKEW, Andrew J	20	W½NW	1891-06-30		A2
4893	BISHOP, Noble P	19	E½NE	1902-06-12		A1 G2 V4888, 4889
4894	" "	19	SE	1902-06-12		A1 G2 R4810
4895	" "	19	SESW	1902-06-12		A1 G2
4896	" "	19	SWNE	1902-06-12		A1 G2 V4889
4925	BLAIR, William	5	E½SW	1837-08-12		A1
4926	" "	8	NWNW	1837-08-12		A1
4879	BOOTHE, Legrand	30	NWSE	1862-01-01		A1
4880	" "	30	SWNE	1862-01-01		A1
4848	BRANAN, James H	33	S½NW	1860-04-02	Coffee	A1
4811	BRANTLEY, Charles G	4	SWSW	1860-04-02		A1
4844	BRIDGES, Jacob	17	SESE	1860-04-02		A1
4845	" "	17	SWSE	1860-04-02		A1
4846	" "	20	NENW	1860-04-02		A1
4847	" "	20	NWNE	1860-04-02		A1
4927	BRYAN, William C	5	E½NW	1860-04-02		A1
4902	BUCKELEW, Richard C	5	N½NE	1854-07-15		A1
4903	" "	8	NWSE	1860-04-02		A1
4904	" "	8	SESE	1860-04-02		A1
4905	" "	9	NWSW	1860-04-02		A1
4906	BUCKELEW, Robert	4	W½NE	1841-05-20		A1
4891	BURT, Matthew	31	NESE	1837-08-12		A1
4866	CARLILE, John W	19	NESW	1860-04-02		A1
4806	CARPENTER, Benjamin	30	SENW	1837-08-14		A1
4807	" "	6	SESE	1837-08-14		A1
4808	" "	7	W½NE	1837-08-14		A1
4929	CARPENTER, William	5	W½SW	1837-08-12		A1
4907	CARTER, Stephen	31	NWSE	1838-07-28		A1
4840	CODY, Green	4	NENW	1860-04-02		A1
4841	" "	4	SENE	1860-04-02		A1
4938	COOK, William N	20	NENE	1891-11-23		A2
4850	COSBY, James M	19	NW	1901-11-16		A2
4897	COX, Octavia	6	N½SE	1910-10-13		A1 G14
4898	" "	6	SWSE	1910-10-13		A1 G14
4899	DRISKELL, Presley	32	SESW	1858-11-01		A1
4900	" "	32	SWSE	1858-11-01		A1
4901	DRISKILL, Presley	32	SESE	1860-04-02		A1
4802	EILAND, Alexander J	9	NESW	1860-04-02		A1

ID	Individual in Patent	Sec.	Sec. Part	Date Issued	Other Counties	For More Info . . .
4874	EILAND, Josephus	4	NWNW	1852-02-02		A1
4872	" "	18	NENE	1858-11-01		A1
4875	" "	7	SENE	1858-11-01		A1
4876	" "	7	SESE	1858-11-01		A1
4869	" "	17	NWSE	1860-04-02		A1
4870	" "	17	S½NW	1860-04-02		A1
4871	" "	17	SWNE	1860-04-02		A1
4873	" "	18	SENE	1860-04-02		A1
4882	EILAND, Levi	8	NESE	1858-11-01		A1
4908	EILAND, Stephen	8	S½NW	1860-04-02		A1
4909	" "	8	W½NE	1860-04-02		A1
4910	EILAND, Thomas C	30	SWSW	1920-06-14		A2
4930	EILAND, William E	17	SW	1900-11-28		A2
4809	ELLIS, Benjamin F	18	W½NW	1897-05-03		A2
4859	EUBANKS, John	6	N½	1837-08-07		A1
4860	"	6	SW	1837-08-07		A1
4881	EYLAND, Levi D	4	SWNW	1849-09-01		A1
4893	FOSKETT, William A	19	E½NE	1902-06-12		A1 G2 V4888, 4889
4894	" "	19	SE	1902-06-12		A1 G2 R4810
4895	" "	19	SESW	1902-06-12		A1 G2
4896	" "	19	SWNE	1902-06-12		A1 G2 V4889
4854	GAINER, Jesse	30	NENE	1854-10-02		A1
4852	" "	19	W½SW	1858-11-01		A1
4853	" "	29	NWNW	1858-11-01		A1
4810	GILCHRIST, Benjamin L	19	SE	1906-05-23		A2 R4894
4826	GILCHRIST, Eliza	20	E½SW	1885-03-16		A2 G19
4827	"	20	NWSE	1885-03-16		A2 G19
4826	GILCHRIST, Malcolm	20	E½SW	1885-03-16		A2 G19
4827	" "	20	NWSE	1885-03-16		A2 G19
4886	GILCHRIST, Malcom	30	SESW	1854-07-15		A1
4887	" "	31	NENE	1854-07-15		A1
4885	" "	20	NWSW	1875-06-01		A2
4888	GILCHRIST, Mansfield R	19	NENE	1909-05-11		A2 V4893
4889	" "	19	S½NE	1909-05-11		A2 V4893, 4896
4931	GREEN, William	4	N½SW	1849-09-01		A1
4932	" "	5	NESE	1849-09-01		A1
4933	" "	5	SWNE	1849-09-01		A1
4864	HAMILTON, John S	20	SENW	1860-04-02		A1
4814	HARRIS, Dennis	28	S½NW	1891-01-15		A2 G21
4814	HARRIS, Jacob	28	S½NW	1891-01-15		A2 G21
4834	HEMPHILL, Franklin P	28	NESE	1891-06-30		A2
4835	" "	28	SESE	1891-06-30		A2
4842	HENDERSON, Henry C	28	NE	1892-01-20		A2
4828	HUETT, Elizabeth	7	NWSE	1837-08-14		A1
4877	HURLEY, Joshua	21	NESW	1860-04-02		A1
4878	" "	21	NWSW	1860-04-02		A1
4921	JACKSON, William A	8	SWSE	1850-08-10		A1
4944	JONES, Wright P	18	S½SE	1884-03-20		A2
4843	KENT, Isaac R	20	SWSW	1860-04-02		A1
4939	KETCHAND, William P	30	SWSE	1860-04-02		A1
4940	" "	31	W½NE	1860-04-02		A1
4837	KING, George	29	W½SW	1837-08-15		A1
4838	" "	30	E½SE	1837-08-15		A1
4849	KING, James	28	SWSE	1860-04-02		A1
4920	KOLB, Triphena	8	W½SW	1883-09-15		A2
4922	KOLB, William A	18	NWNE	1899-04-17		A2
4803	LANGLEY, Amos J	8	E½NE	1896-05-21		A2
4857	LEGGETT, John C	9	E½NW	1900-11-12		A2
4858	" "	9	W½NE	1900-11-12		A2
4861	LIGHTFOOT, John	29	SWNW	1837-08-14		A1
4867	LOLLIS, Jones	30	SENE	1854-10-02		A1
4829	MACK, Ezra R	33	SESW	1860-04-02	Coffee	A1
4830	" "	33	W½SW	1860-04-02	Coffee	A1
4833	MCALPIN, Franklin A	7	E½SW	1858-11-01		A1
4831	" "	18	E½NW	1896-10-21		A1
4832	" "	18	E½SW	1896-10-21		A1
4937	MILLER, William	21	NWSE	1860-04-02		A1
4923	MULLINS, William B	30	NENW	1858-11-01		A1
4924	" "	30	SWNW	1858-11-01		A1
4941	SHAW, William	8	NENW	1852-02-02		A1
4890	SMITH, Martha	28	W½SW	1892-03-23		A2
4883	SPIVEY, Madison G	20	E½SE	1899-02-06		A2
4884	" "	20	SWSE	1899-02-06		A2

ID	Individual in Patent	Sec.	Sec. Part	Date Issued	Other Counties	For More Info . . .
4928	SPIVEY, William C	20	S½NE	1898-10-04		A2
4836	STANDLEY, Garrett	5	SENE	1852-02-02		A1
4812	STANLEY, Cullen	4	NWSE	1852-02-02		A1
4813	"	4	SENW	1852-02-02		A1
4839	STRINGER, Gib	28	N½NW	1890-03-19		A2
4897	STRINGER, Octavia	6	N½SE	1910-10-13		A1 G14
4898	" "	6	SWSE	1910-10-13		A1 G14
4942	THURMAN, William	29	NE	1900-11-12		A2
4943	TRUM, William	32	NESW	1860-04-02		A1
4816	TURMAN, Edwin	31	SESE	1852-02-02		A1
4818	" "	31	SWSE	1854-10-02		A1
4815	" "	31	NWSW	1858-11-01		A1
4817	" "	31	SESW	1858-11-01		A1
4819	" "	31	SWSW	1858-11-01		A1
4915	TURMAN, Tilmon	29	SESW	1858-11-01		A1
4916	" "	32	NENW	1858-11-01		A1
4917	TURMON, Tilmon	18	NESE	1891-11-03		A2
4918	" "	18	NWSE	1891-11-03		A2
4919	" "	18	SWNE	1891-11-03		A2
4822	WARREN, Elison	31	SWNW	1854-10-02		A1
4820	" "	31	E½NW	1858-11-01		A1
4821	" "	31	NESW	1858-11-01		A1
4824	" "	32	SWNW	1858-11-01		A1
4823	" "	32	SENW	1860-04-02		A1
4825	" "	32	W½SW	1860-04-02		A1
4912	WASDIN, Thomas	33	NESW	1858-11-01	Coffee	A1
4913	" "	33	NWSE	1858-11-01	Coffee	A1
4914	" "	33	S½SE	1858-11-01	Coffee	A1
4911	" "	33	NESE	1860-04-02	Coffee	A1
4865	WELLBORN, John S	4	SESW	1897-11-05		A2
4868	WHALEY, Joseph H	9	NENE	1860-04-02		A1
4855	WICKER, John A	32	N½SE	1858-11-01		A1
4856	" "	32	NE	1858-11-01		A1

Patent Map

T7-N R19-E
St Stephens Meridian

Map Group 22

Map Parcels

Section 6
EUBANKS John 1837
COX [14] Octavia 1910
EUBANKS John 1837
COX [14] Octavia 1910
CARPENTER Benjamin 1837

Section 5
CARPENTER William 1837
BLAIR William 1837

Section 4
BRYAN William C 1860
BUCKELEW Richard C 1854
GREEN William 1849
STANDLEY Garrett 1852
EILAND Josephus 1852
CODY Green 1860
BUCKELEW Robert 1841
ADAMS John Q 1858
EYLAND Levi D 1849
STANLEY Cullen 1852
CODY Green 1860
GREEN William 1849
GREEN William 1849
STANLEY Cullen 1852
BRANTLEY Charles G 1860
WELLBORN John S 1897
ADAMS John Q 1854

Section 7
CARPENTER Benjamin 1837
EILAND Josephus 1858
MCALPIN Franklin A 1858
HUETT Elizabeth 1837
EILAND Josephus 1858

Section 8
BLAIR William 1837
SHAW William 1852
EILAND Stephen 1860
LANGLEY Amos J 1896
EILAND Stephen 1860
KOLB Triphena 1883
ADAMS Noah 1860
BUCKELEW Richard C 1860
EILAND Levi 1858
JACKSON William A 1850
BUCKELEW Richard C 1860

Section 9
LEGGETT John C 1900
LEGGETT John C 1900
WHALEY Joseph H 1860
ADAMS William M 1900
BUCKELEW Richard C 1860
EILAND Alexander J 1860
ADAMS William M 1900
ADAMS William M 1900

Section 18
ELLIS Benjamin F 1897
MCALPIN Franklin A 1896
KOLB William A 1899
EILAND Josephus 1858
TURMON Tilmon 1891
EILAND Josephus 1860
TURMON Tilmon 1891
TURMON Tilmon 1891
MCALPIN Franklin A 1896
JONES Wright P 1884

Section 17
EILAND Josephus 1860
EILAND Josephus 1860
EILAND Josephus 1860
EILAND William E 1900
BRIDGES Jacob 1860
BRIDGES Jacob 1860

Section 16
Crenshaw

Section 19
COSBY James M 1901
ADAMS Jesse 1860
GILCHRIST Mansfield R 1909
GILCHRIST Mansfield R 1909
BISHOP [2] Noble P 1902
GAINER Jesse 1858
CARLILE John W 1860
GILCHRIST Benjamin L 1906
BISHOP [2] Noble P 1902
BISHOP [2] Noble P 1902

Section 20
ASKEW Andrew J 1891
GILCHRIST Malcom 1875
GILCHRIST [19] Eliza 1885
GILCHRIST [19] Eliza 1885
KENT Isaac R 1860
BRIDGES Jacob 1860
HAMILTON John S 1860
BRIDGES Jacob 1860
COOK William N 1891
SPIVEY William C 1898
SPIVEY Madison G 1899
SPIVEY Madison G 1899

Section 21
HURLEY Joshua 1860
HURLEY Joshua 1860
MILLER William 1860

Section 30
MULLINS William B 1858
CARPENTER Benjamin 1837
BOOTHE Legrand 1862
GAINER Jesse 1854
LOLLIS Jones 1854
MULLINS William B 1858
BOOTHE Legrand 1862
KING George 1837
EILAND Thomas C 1920
GILCHRIST Malcom 1854
KETCHAND William P 1860

Section 29
GAINER Jesse 1858
LIGHTFOOT John 1837
KING George 1837
THURMAN William 1900
TURMAN Tilmon 1858

Section 28
STRINGER Gib 1890
HENDERSON Henry C 1892
HARRIS [21] Dennis 1891
SMITH Martha 1892
KING James 1860
HEMPHILL Franklin P 1891
HEMPHILL Franklin P 1891

Section 31
WARREN Elison 1858
KETCHAND William P 1860
GILCHRIST Malcom 1854
WARREN Elison 1854
TURMAN Edwin 1858
WARREN Elison 1858
CARTER Stephen 1838
BURT Matthew 1837
TURMAN Edwin 1858
TURMAN Edwin 1858
TURMAN Edwin 1854
TURMAN Edwin 1852

Section 32
TURMAN Tilmon 1858
WICKER John A 1858
WARREN Elison 1858
WARREN Elison 1860
WARREN Elison 1860
TRUM William 1860
WICKER John A 1858
DRISKELL Presley 1858
DRISKELL Presley 1858
DRISKILL Presley 1860

Section 33
ADAMS Benjamin 1860
BRANAN James H 1860
MACK Ezra R 1860
WASDIN Thomas 1858
WASDIN Thomas 1858
WASDIN Thomas 1860
MACK Ezra R 1860
Coffee
WASDIN Thomas 1858

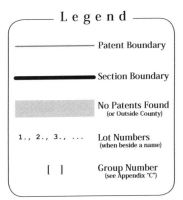

Township Statistics

Parcels Mapped	:	143
Number of Patents	:	107
Number of Individuals	:	84
Patentees Identified	:	80
Number of Surnames	:	63
Multi-Patentee Parcels	:	9
Oldest Patent Date	:	8/7/1837
Most Recent Patent	:	6/14/1920
Block/Lot Parcels	:	0
Parcels Re - Issued	:	1
Parcels that Overlap	:	4
Cities and Towns	:	1
Cemeteries	:	0

Note: the area contained in this map amounts to far less than a full Township. Therefore, its contents are completely on this single page (instead of a "normal" 2-page spread).

Legend

— Patent Boundary

— Section Boundary

▓ No Patents Found (or Outside County)

1., 2., 3., ... Lot Numbers (when beside a name)

[ ] Group Number (see Appendix "C")

Scale: Section = 1 mile X 1 mile (generally, with some exceptions)

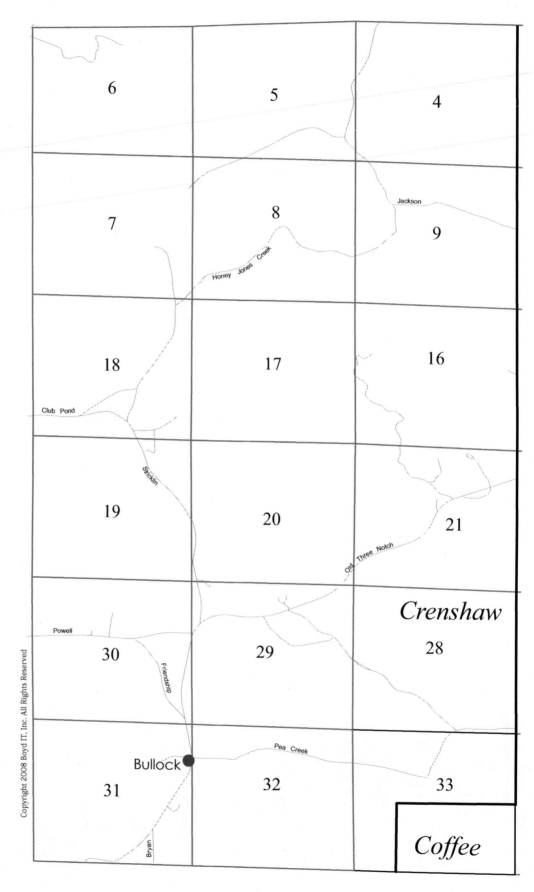

Road Map

T7-N R19-E
St Stephens Meridian

Map Group 22

Note: the area contained in this map amounts to far less than a full Township. Therefore, its contents are completely on this single page (instead of a "normal" 2-page spread).

Cities & Towns
Bullock

Cemeteries
None

Legend

———— Section Lines

━━━━ Interstates

━━━━ Highways

——— Other Roads

● Cities/Towns

✝ Cemeteries

Scale: Section = 1 mile X 1 mile
(generally, with some exceptions)

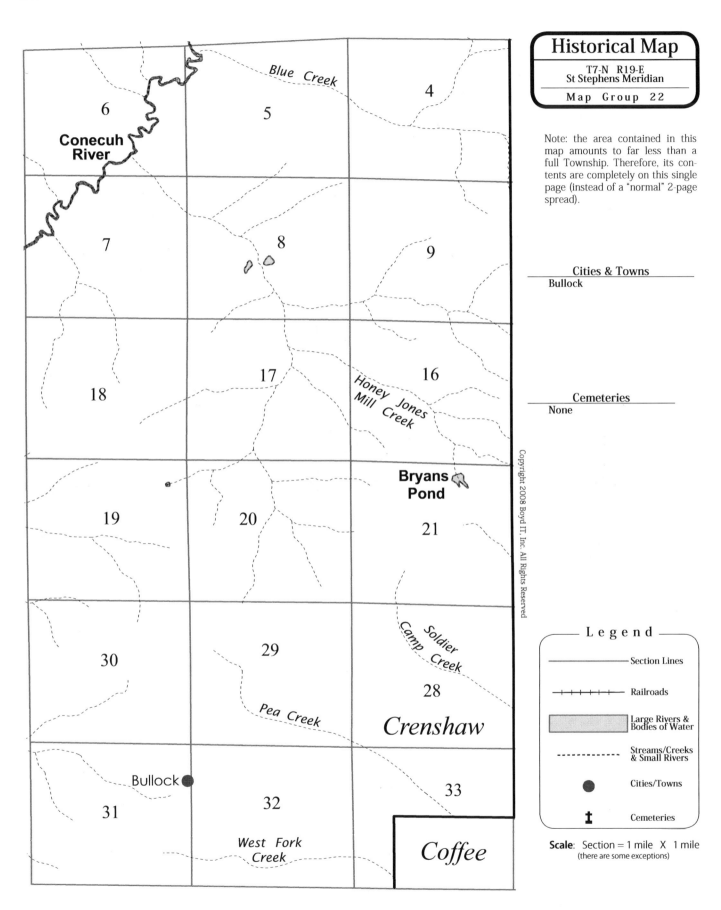

Note: the area contained in this map amounts to far less than a full Township. Therefore, its contents are completely on this single page (instead of a "normal" 2-page spread).

Cities & Towns
Bullock

Cemeteries
None

Copyright 2008 Boyd IT, Inc. All Rights Reserved

Legend

Section Lines

Railroads

Large Rivers & Bodies of Water

Streams/Creeks & Small Rivers

Cities/Towns

Cemeteries

Scale: Section = 1 mile X 1 mile
(there are some exceptions)

Map Group 23: Index to Land Patents

Township 6-North Range 17-East (St Stephens)

After you locate an individual in this Index, take note of the Section and Section Part then proceed to the Land Patent map on the pages immediately following. You should have no difficulty locating the corresponding parcel of land.

The "For More Info" Column will lead you to more information about the underlying Patents. See the *Legend* at right, and the "How to Use this Book" chapter, for more information.

```
┌─────────────────────────────────────────────────────────┐
│                      LEGEND                              │
│             "For More Info . . . " column                │
│  A = Authority (Legislative Act, See Appendix "A")       │
│  B = Block or Lot (location in Section unknown)          │
│  C = Cancelled Patent                                    │
│  F = Fractional Section                                  │
│  G = Group  (Multi-Patentee Patent, see Appendix "C")    │
│  V = Overlaps another Parcel                             │
│  R = Re-Issued (Parcel patented more than once)          │
│                                                          │
│  (A & G items require you to look in the Appendixes      │
│  referred to above. All other Letter-designations        │
│  followed by a number require you to locate line-items   │
│  in this index that possess the ID number found after    │
│  the letter).                                            │
└─────────────────────────────────────────────────────────┘
```

ID	Individual in Patent	Sec.	Sec. Part	Date Issued	Other Counties	For More Info . . .
5110	BELL, Samuel	10	E½NE	1860-04-02		A1
5111	" "	11	NWNW	1860-04-02	Covington	A1
4961	BOYKIN, Burrell	3	SENE	1858-11-01		A1
5016	BRANEN, Harris	15	NESW	1848-05-03	Covington	A1
5017	" "	15	W½NE	1848-05-03	Covington	A1
5041	BRYAN, Jesse	11	SWSE	1837-08-02	Covington	A1
5026	CARPENTER, Holley	3	SWNW	1860-04-02		A1
5027	" "	4	SENE	1860-04-02		A1
5060	CARTER, John	17	SWSE	1838-07-28		A1
5115	CARTER, Seaborn	10	NESE	1860-04-02		A1
5116	" "	11	NENW	1860-04-02	Covington	A1
5117	" "	11	NESW	1860-04-02	Covington	A1
5118	" "	11	NWSE	1860-04-02	Covington	A1
5119	" "	11	SWNW	1860-04-02	Covington	A1
5120	" "	11	W½SW	1860-04-02	Covington	A1
5121	" "	15	NENE	1860-04-02	Covington	A1
5139	CHILDRE, William	19	NENE	1854-07-15		A1
5140	" "	20	NENW	1854-07-15	Covington	A1
5137	" "	17	NWSW	1858-11-01		A1
5138	" "	18	E½SE	1858-11-01		A1
5141	" "	20	NWNE	1858-11-01	Covington	A1
5003	CLARK, George	17	SESW	1853-11-15		A1
5004	" "	17	SWSW	1858-11-01		A1
5061	CLARK, John	6	NWSE	1858-11-01		A1
5062	" "	6	W½NW	1858-11-01		A1
5063	" "	7	NWNW	1858-11-01		A1
5005	CLARKE, George	17	NESW	1858-11-01		A1
5006	" "	17	SESE	1858-11-01		A1
5007	" "	17	SWNW	1858-11-01		A1
4948	CURETON, Albert	4	W½SW	1860-04-02		A1
4949	" "	8	S½NE	1860-04-02		A1
4950	" "	8	SENW	1860-04-02		A1
4951	" "	9	SENW	1860-04-02		A1
4952	" "	9	W½NW	1860-04-02		A1
4962	DANIEL, Bushrod W	6	NESW	1852-02-02		A1
5145	DANNELLY, William H	1	NESE	1854-07-15	Covington	A1
5067	DAUPHIN, John J	30	NESW	1858-11-01	Covington	A1
5068	" "	30	S½SW	1858-11-01	Covington	A1
5128	DAUPHIN, Thomas D	31	SENW	1854-07-15	Covington	A1
5127	" "	31	NENW	1858-11-01	Covington	A1
5129	" "	31	SWNE	1858-11-01	Covington	A1
4959	DOZIER, Benjamin	15	SESW	1852-02-02	Covington	A1
4960	" "	15	SWSE	1858-11-01	Covington	A1
4976	DOZIER, Daniel	17	SWNE	1838-07-28		A1
4979	" "	8	NWSW	1838-07-28		A1
4980	" "	8	SWNW	1838-07-28		A1

ID	Individual in Patent	Sec.	Sec. Part	Date Issued	Other Counties	For More Info . . .
4973	DOZIER, Daniel (Cont'd)	17	E½NW	1843-02-01		A1
4977	" "	8	N½SE	1858-11-01		A1
4978	" "	8	NESW	1858-11-01		A1
4981	" "	8	SWSE	1858-11-01		A1
4974	" "	17	NWNE	1860-04-02		A1
4975	" "	17	NWSE	1860-04-02		A1
4982	" "	9	SWSW	1860-04-02		A1
4985	DOZIER, Daniel T	18	NWSE	1858-11-01		A1
4993	DOZIER, Elias	17	E½NE	1860-04-02		A1
5078	ETHERIDGE, John M	18	SENE	1895-06-19		A2
5142	FAIL, William	1	SESE	1860-04-02	Covington	A1
4945	FEAGIN, Aaron	21	W½SW	1837-08-15	Covington	A1
4946	" "	29	SENE	1837-08-15	Covington	A1
4947	" "	29	SENW	1837-08-15	Covington	A1
4956	FEAGIN, Andrew	31	NWNE	1838-07-28	Covington	A1
4957	FEAGIN, Andrew J	20	S½SE	1858-11-01	Covington	A1
5009	FEAGIN, George	29	W½NE	1834-08-12	Covington	A1
5008	" "	29	NENE	1838-07-28	Covington	A1
5010	" "	29	W½SE	1838-07-28	Covington	A1
5106	FEAGIN, Richardson	21	E½NW	1841-05-20	Covington	A1
5107	" "	21	SWNE	1845-07-01	Covington	A1
5024	FROST, Hilrey	6	NWNE	1858-11-01		A1
5025	" "	6	SWNE	1860-04-02		A1
5056	FROST, John B	20	NESW	1921-08-26	Covington	A1
5057	" "	20	NWSE	1921-08-26	Covington	A1
5058	" "	20	SENW	1921-08-26	Covington	A1
5059	" "	20	SWNE	1921-08-26	Covington	A1
5131	GANEY, Thomas J	10	N½NW	1860-04-02		A1
5132	" "	10	S½NW	1860-04-02		A1
5133	" "	10	SESE	1860-04-02		A1
5134	" "	10	SWNE	1860-04-02		A1
5135	" "	10	W½SE	1860-04-02		A1
5109	GARDNER, Ruth	21	NENE	1852-12-01	Covington	A1
5018	HANDLEY, Hesekiah B	17	NWNW	1860-04-02		A1
5019	" "	18	N½NE	1860-04-02		A1
5021	" "	7	NWSE	1860-04-02		A1
5020	" "	7	E½NE	1896-10-26		A1
5022	HANDLEY, Hezekiah B	7	SESE	1858-11-01		A1
5023	" "	8	SESW	1858-11-01		A1
5028	HANDLEY, Irwin	19	E½SW	1860-04-02		A1
5029	" "	19	W½SW	1860-04-02		A1
5030	" "	30	NENW	1860-04-02	Covington	A1
5042	HANDLEY, Jesse	19	SWNW	1860-04-02		A1
5047	HANDLEY, John A	7	NWSW	1858-11-01		A1
5048	" "	7	SWNW	1858-11-01		A1
5130	HENLEY, Thomas	2	S½SE	1858-11-01		A1
5150	HILL, William J	31	SESE	1860-04-02	Covington	A1
4953	HOLLEY, Alfred	21	NWNE	1834-08-12	Covington	A1
4963	HOLLEY, Calvin	15	SWSW	1837-08-10	Covington	A1
4994	HOLLEY, Elias H	10	SWSW	1860-04-02		A1
4995	" "	9	NENE	1860-04-02		A1
4996	" "	9	SESE	1860-04-02		A1
4997	HOLLY, Elias H	9	NESE	1858-11-01		A1
4998	" "	9	SENE	1858-11-01		A1
5043	HURT, Joel	5	E½SW	1860-04-02		A1
5044	" "	5	NWSW	1860-04-02		A1
5045	" "	5	SE	1860-04-02		A1
5046	" "	5	SWNW	1860-04-02		A1
5031	JACKSON, James M	21	E½SW	1858-11-01	Covington	A1
5032	" "	21	SWSE	1858-11-01	Covington	A2
5112	JEFFERS, Sarah A	31	N½SE	1860-04-02	Covington	A1
5113	" "	31	S½SW	1860-04-02	Covington	A1
5114	" "	31	SWSE	1860-04-02	Covington	A1
4964	JONES, Charles	31	NENE	1852-02-02	Covington	A1
5126	MANSILL, Simeon	19	SWSE	1837-08-10		A1
5065	MARTIN, John F	18	SWNE	1860-04-02		A1
5151	MERRILL, William	20	W½NW	1841-05-20	Covington	A1
4986	MILES, David D	10	NESW	1907-04-05		A1
4987	" "	10	NWSW	1907-04-05		A1
4988	" "	15	NW	1907-04-05	Covington	A1
4958	MILTON, Bassel M	1	W½SW	1860-04-02	Covington	A1
5146	MURPHEY, William H	9	SESW	1907-04-05		A1
5147	MURPHY, William H	9	NESW	1860-04-02		A1

ID	Individual in Patent	Sec.	Sec. Part	Date Issued	Other Counties	For More Info . . .
5148	MURPHY, William H (Cont'd)	9	SWNE	1860-04-02		A1
5149	" "	9	W½SE	1860-04-02		A1
4954	NEWSOM, Alfred	3	E½NW	1860-04-02		A1
4955	" "	3	SWNE	1860-04-02		A1
4989	NOBLES, Edmond	3	NWSW	1860-04-02		A1
4990	NOBLES, Edmund	3	NESW	1860-04-02		A1
4991	NOBLES, Elder	10	NWNE	1860-04-02		A1
5105	NORTON, Richard	21	SESE	1852-02-02	Covington	A1
5049	OWEN, John A	11	E½SE	1837-08-09	Covington	A1
5066	OWEN, John G	11	SENE	1841-05-20	Covington	A1
5037	PARKER, James	15	NESE	1854-07-15	Covington	A1
5015	PARRISH, Hamilton	19	NWNW	1858-11-01		A1
5033	PENDREY, James P	3	SESW	1860-04-02		A1
5034	" "	3	SWSE	1860-04-02		A1
5035	" "	4	NESE	1860-04-02		A1
5036	" "	4	NWNW	1860-12-01		A1
5038	ROACH, James	5	NENW	1858-11-01		A1
5040	" "	5	W½NE	1858-11-01		A1
5039	" "	5	NWNW	1860-04-02		A1
5079	ROBBINS, John	2	NWNE	1854-10-02		A1
5081	" "	2	SENW	1854-10-02		A1
5080	" "	2	SENE	1860-04-02		A1
5082	" "	2	SWNE	1860-04-02		A1
5136	ROBBINS, Thomas	31	SWNW	1854-10-02	Covington	A1
5086	RODGERS, Littleberry	5	SENW	1852-02-02		A1
5087	" "	6	SWSE	1852-02-02		A1
5088	" "	6	SWSW	1852-02-02		A1
4983	ROGERS, Daniel	6	E½NE	1860-04-02		A1
4984	" "	6	NESE	1860-04-02		A1
5093	ROGERS, Littleberry	6	SESW	1837-04-10		A1
5091	" "	6	E½NW	1837-08-10		A1
5092	" "	6	NWSW	1854-07-15		A1
5089	" "	4	SWNW	1858-11-01		A1
5090	" "	5	E½NE	1858-11-01		A1
5095	" "	7	NWNE	1858-11-01		A1
5094	" "	7	NENW	1862-01-01		A1
5014	ROWELL, Green B	21	SWNW	1858-11-01	Covington	A1
4992	SIMS, Eldredge	30	S½NW	1860-04-02	Covington	A1
5083	SPORT, Jonathan	3	NESE	1862-01-01		A1
5084	" "	3	SESE	1884-04-02		A1
5152	SPORT, William	2	NWSW	1896-10-28		A1
5070	STEWART, John L	29	NWNW	1860-04-02	Covington	A1
5071	" "	29	SWNW	1860-04-02	Covington	A1
5072	" "	30	E½NE	1860-04-02	Covington	A1
5073	" "	30	NWNW	1860-04-02	Covington	A1
5074	" "	30	NWSW	1860-04-02	Covington	A1
5075	" "	30	SE	1860-04-02	Covington	A1
5076	" "	30	SWNE	1860-04-02	Covington	A1
5077	" "	31	SENE	1860-04-02	Covington	A1
5085	STRAUGHN, Leroy M	17	NESE	1841-05-20		A1
5108	STRICKLIN, Robert M	20	NESE	1903-11-24	Covington	A2
4966	TAYLOR, Council D	19	NESE	1837-08-10		A1
4968	" "	19	SENE	1837-08-10		A1
4965	" "	18	SWSE	1858-11-01		A1
4967	" "	19	NWSE	1858-11-01		A1
4969	" "	19	SESE	1858-11-01		A1
4970	" "	19	W½NE	1858-11-01		A1
4972	" "	20	SWSW	1860-04-02	Covington	A1
4971	" "	20	NWSW	1884-04-02	Covington	A1
5054	TAYLOR, John A	7	NESE	1837-04-10		A1
5055	" "	8	SWSW	1837-04-10		A1
5052	" "	29	S½SW	1852-02-02	Covington	A1
5053	" "	29	SESE	1852-12-01	Covington	A1
5050	" "	29	NENW	1860-04-02	Covington	A1
5051	" "	29	NESE	1860-04-02	Covington	A1
5153	TAYLOR, William W	18	NENW	1858-11-01		A1
5154	TAYLOR, Windul	18	NWSW	1837-08-07		A1
5155	" "	18	W½NW	1837-08-07		A1
5156	" "	7	SWNE	1837-08-07		A1
5069	TURBEVILLE, John J	11	SESW	1852-12-01	Covington	A1
5064	WEATHERFORD, John D	20	E½NE	1921-08-26	Covington	A1
5122	WEATHERFORD, Seaborn J	4	NESW	1884-04-02		A1
5123	" "	4	NWSE	1884-04-02		A1

ID	Individual in Patent	Sec.	Sec. Part	Date Issued	Other Counties	For More Info . . .
5124	WEATHERFORD, Seaborn J (Cont'd)	4	SENW	1884-04-02		A1
5125	" "	4	SWNE	1884-04-02		A1
5100	WELLS, Michael P	19	SENW	1852-02-02		A1
5099	" "	19	NENW	1854-07-15		A1
5097	" "	18	S½SW	1858-11-01		A1
5096	" "	18	NESW	1860-04-02		A1
5098	" "	18	SENW	1860-04-02		A1
5101	" "	30	NWNE	1860-04-02	Covington	A1
5102	" "	7	NESW	1860-04-02		A1
5103	" "	7	SENW	1860-04-02		A1
5104	" "	7	SWSE	1860-04-02		A1
5000	WILLIAMS, Elisha	3	NWNW	1858-11-01		A1
5001	" "	4	N½NE	1858-11-01		A1
5002	" "	4	NENW	1858-11-01		A1
5011	WILLIAMS, George M	8	SESE	1860-04-02		A1
5012	" "	9	NWNE	1860-04-02		A1
5013	" "	9	NWSW	1860-04-02		A1
5143	WILLIAMS, William G	21	NESE	1858-11-01	Covington	A1
5144	" "	21	NWSE	1858-11-01	Covington	A1
4999	WYATT, Elijah W	2	SWNW	1854-10-02		A1

Patent Map

T6-N R17-E
St Stephens Meridian

Map Group 23

Township Statistics

Parcels Mapped	:	212
Number of Patents	:	141
Number of Individuals	:	88
Patentees Identified	:	88
Number of Surnames	:	59
Multi-Patentee Parcels	:	0
Oldest Patent Date	:	8/12/1834
Most Recent Patent	:	8/26/1921
Block/Lot Parcels	:	0
Parcels Re - Issued	:	0
Parcels that Overlap	:	0
Cities and Towns	:	2
Cemeteries	:	2

Section 6
- CLARK John 1858
- ROGERS Littleberry 1837
- FROST Hilrey 1858
- FROST Hilrey 1860
- ROGERS Daniel 1860
- ROGERS Littleberry 1854
- DANIEL Bushrod W 1852
- CLARK John 1858
- ROGERS Daniel 1860
- RODGERS Littleberry 1852
- ROGERS Littleberry 1837
- RODGERS Littleberry 1852

Section 5
- ROACH James 1860
- ROACH James 1858
- ROACH James 1858
- ROGERS Littleberry 1858
- HURT Joel 1860
- RODGERS Littleberry 1852
- HURT Joel 1860
- HURT Joel 1860
- HURT Joel 1860

Section 4
- PENDREY James P 1860
- WILLIAMS Elisha 1858
- WILLIAMS Elisha 1858
- ROGERS Littleberry 1858
- WEATHERFORD Seabom J 1884
- WEATHERFORD Seabom J 1884
- CARPENTER Holley 1860
- CURETON Albert 1860
- WEATHERFORD Seabom J 1884
- WEATHERFORD Seabom J 1884
- PENDREY James P 1860

Section 7
- CLARK John 1858
- ROGERS Littleberry 1862
- ROGERS Littleberry 1858
- HANDLEY Hesekiah B 1896
- HANDLEY John A 1858
- WELLS Michael P 1860
- TAYLOR Windul 1837
- HANDLEY John A 1858
- WELLS Michael P 1860
- HANDLEY Hesekiah B 1860
- TAYLOR John A 1837
- WELLS Michael P 1860
- HANDLEY Hezekiah B 1858

Section 8
- DOZIER Daniel 1838
- CURETON Albert 1860
- CURETON Albert 1860
- DOZIER Daniel 1838
- DOZIER Daniel 1858
- DOZIER Daniel 1858
- TAYLOR John A 1837
- HANDLEY Hezekiah B 1858
- DOZIER Daniel 1858
- WILLIAMS George M 1860

Section 9
- CURETON Albert 1860
- WILLIAMS George M 1860
- HOLLEY Elias H 1860
- CURETON Albert 1860
- MURPHY William H 1860
- HOLLY Elias H 1858
- WILLIAMS George M 1860
- MURPHY William H 1860
- HOLLY Elias H 1858
- DOZIER Daniel 1860
- MURPHEY William H 1907
- MURPHY William H 1860
- HOLLEY Elias H 1860

Section 18
- TAYLOR William W 1858
- HANDLEY Hesekiah B
- TAYLOR Windul 1837
- WELLS Michael P 1860
- MARTIN John F 1860
- ETHERIDGE John M 1895
- TAYLOR Windul 1837
- WELLS Michael P 1860
- DOZIER Daniel T 1858
- WELLS Michael P 1858
- TAYLOR Council D 1858
- CHILDRE William 1858

Section 17
- HANDLEY Hesekiah B 1860
- DOZIER Daniel 1843
- DOZIER Daniel 1860
- CLARKE George 1858
- DOZIER Daniel 1838
- CHILDRE William 1858
- CLARKE George 1858
- DOZIER Daniel 1860
- DOZIER Elias 1860
- STRAUGHN Leroy M 1841
- CLARK George 1858
- CLARK George 1853
- CARTER John 1838
- CLARKE George 1858

Crenshaw 16

Section 19
- PARRISH Hamilton 1858
- WELLS Michael P 1854
- CHILDRE William 1854
- HANDLEY Jesse 1860
- WELLS Michael P 1852
- TAYLOR Council D 1858
- TAYLOR Council D 1837
- TAYLOR Council D 1858
- TAYLOR Council D 1837
- HANDLEY Irwin 1860
- HANDLEY Irwin 1860
- MANSILL Simeon 1837
- TAYLOR Council D 1858

Section 20
- MERRILL William 1841
- CHILDRE William 1854
- CHILDRE William 1858
- FROST John B 1921
- FROST John B 1921
- TAYLOR Council D 1884
- FROST John B 1921
- FROST John B 1921
- STRICKLIN Robert M 1903
- TAYLOR Council D 1860
- FEAGIN Andrew J 1858
- WEATHERFORD John D 1921

Section 21
- ROWELL Green B 1858
- FEAGIN Richardson 1841
- HOLLEY Alfred 1834
- GARDNER Ruth 1852
- FEAGIN Richardson 1845
- FEAGIN Aaron 1837
- JACKSON James M 1858
- WILLIAMS William G 1858
- WILLIAMS William G 1858
- JACKSON James M 1858
- NORTON Richard 1852

Section 30
- STEWART John L 1860
- HANDLEY Irwin 1860
- WELLS Michael P 1860
- STEWART John L 1860
- STEWART John L 1860
- SIMS Eldredge 1860
- STEWART John L 1860
- STEWART John L 1860
- DAUPHIN John J 1858
- DAUPHIN John J 1858
- STEWART John L 1860

Section 29
- STEWART John L 1860
- TAYLOR John A 1860
- FEAGIN George 1834
- FEAGIN George 1838
- STEWART John L 1860
- FEAGIN Aaron 1837
- FEAGIN George 1838
- FEAGIN George 1834
- FEAGIN Aaron 1837
- TAYLOR John A 1860
- TAYLOR John A 1852
- TAYLOR John A 1852

Section 28

Section 31
- DAUPHIN Thomas D 1858
- FEAGIN Andrew 1838
- JONES Charles 1852
- ROBBINS Thomas 1854
- DAUPHIN Thomas D 1854
- DAUPHIN Thomas D 1858
- STEWART John L 1860
- JEFFERS Sarah A 1860
- JEFFERS Sarah A 1860
- JEFFERS Sarah A 1860
- HILL William J 1860

Section 32

Section 33

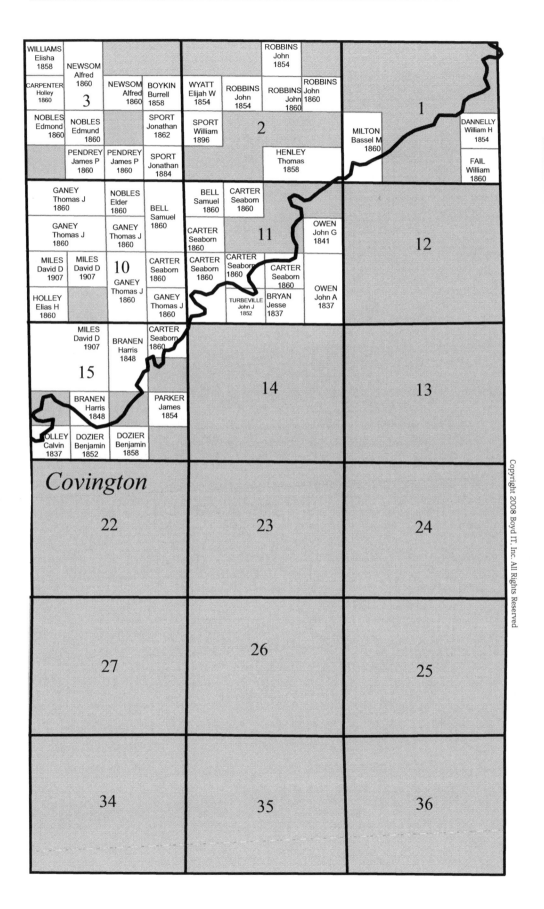

Helpful Hints

1. This Map's INDEX can be found on the preceding pages.

2. Refer to Map "C" to see where this Township lies within Crenshaw County, Alabama.

3. Numbers within square brackets [ ] denote a multi-patentee land parcel (multi-owner). Refer to Appendix "C" for a full list of members in this group.

4. Areas that look to be crowded with Patentees usually indicate multiple sales of the same parcel (Re-issues) or Overlapping parcels. See this Township's Index for an explanation of these and other circumstances that might explain "odd" groupings of Patentees on this map.

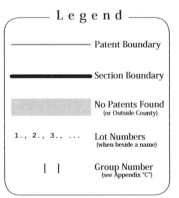

Legend

——————	Patent Boundary
▬▬▬▬▬	Section Boundary
▒▒▒▒▒	No Patents Found (or Outside County)
1., 2., 3., ...	Lot Numbers (when beside a name)
[ ]	Group Number (see Appendix "C")

Scale: Section = 1 mile X 1 mile
(generally, with some exceptions)

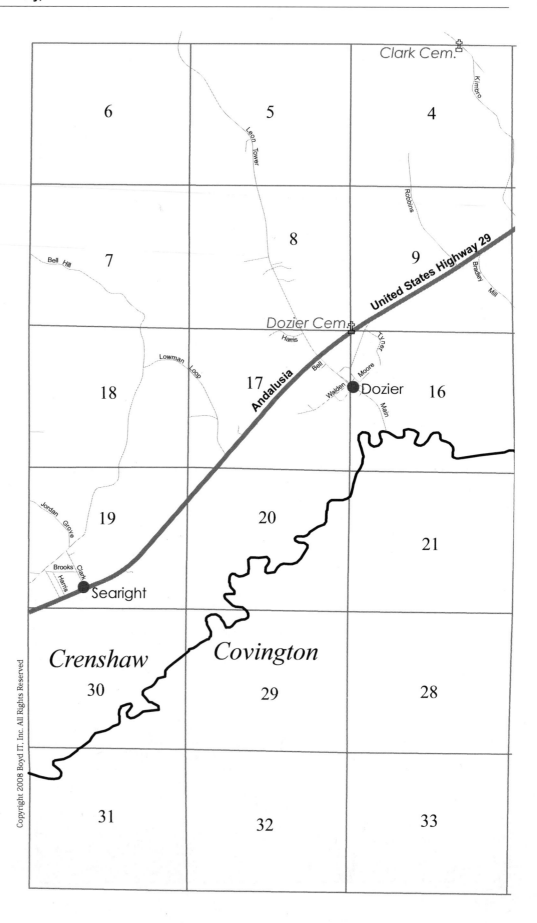

Road Map

T6-N R17-E
St Stephens Meridian

Map Group 23

Cities & Towns

Dozier
Searight

Cemeteries

Clark Cemetery
Dozier Cemetery

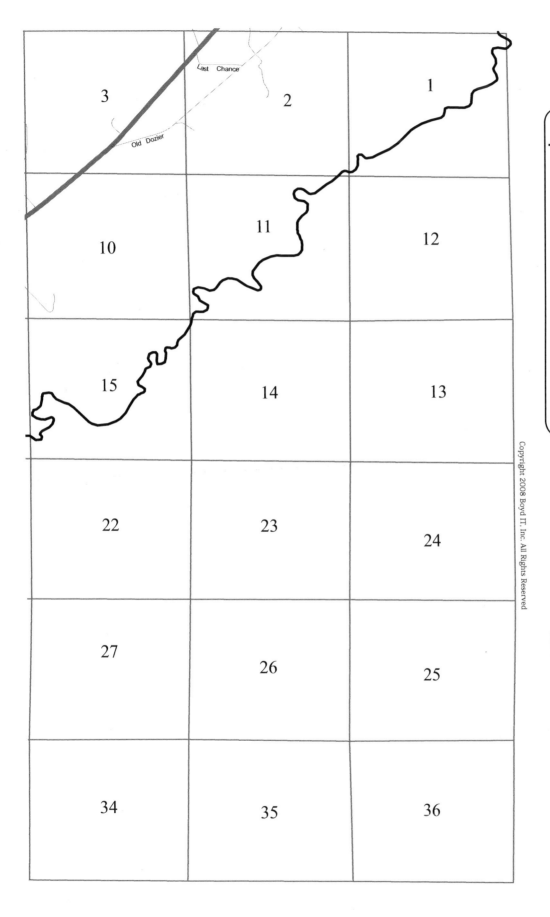

3

2

1

Last Chance

Old Dozier

10

11

12

15

14

13

22

23

24

27

26

25

34

35

36

Helpful Hints

1. This road map has a number of uses, but primarily it is to help you: a) find the present location of land owned by your ancestors (at least the general area), b) find cemeteries and city-centers, and c) estimate the route/roads used by Census-takers & tax-assessors.

2. If you plan to travel to Crenshaw County to locate cemeteries or land parcels, please pick up a modern travel map for the area before you do. Mapping old land parcels on modern maps is not as exact a science as you might think. Just the slightest variations in public land survey coordinates, estimates of parcel boundaries, or road-map deviations can greatly alter a map's representation of how a road either does or doesn't cross a particular parcel of land.

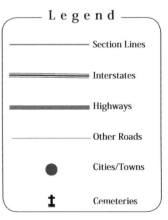

Legend

——————— Section Lines

═══════ Interstates

▨▨▨▨▨▨ Highways

——————— Other Roads

● Cities/Towns

✝ Cemeteries

Scale: Section = 1 mile X 1 mile
(generally, with some exceptions)

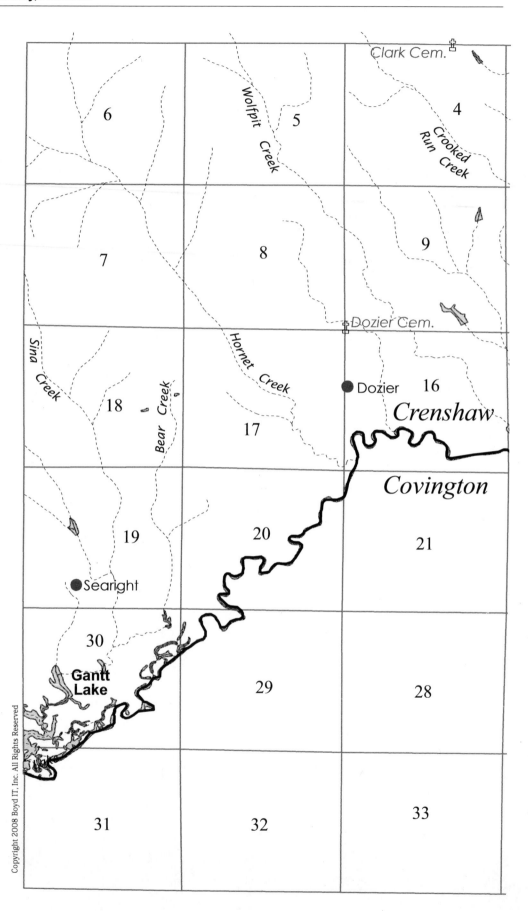

Historical Map

T6-N R17-E
St Stephens Meridian

Map Group 23

Cities & Towns
Dozier
Searight

Cemeteries
Clark Cemetery
Dozier Cemetery

Clark Cem.

6

Wolfpit Creek

5

4

Crooked Run Creek

7

8

9

Sina Creek

Dozier Cem.

18

Bear Creek

Hornet Creek

17

Dozier

16

Crenshaw

Covington

19

20

21

Searight

30

29

28

Gantt Lake

31

32

33

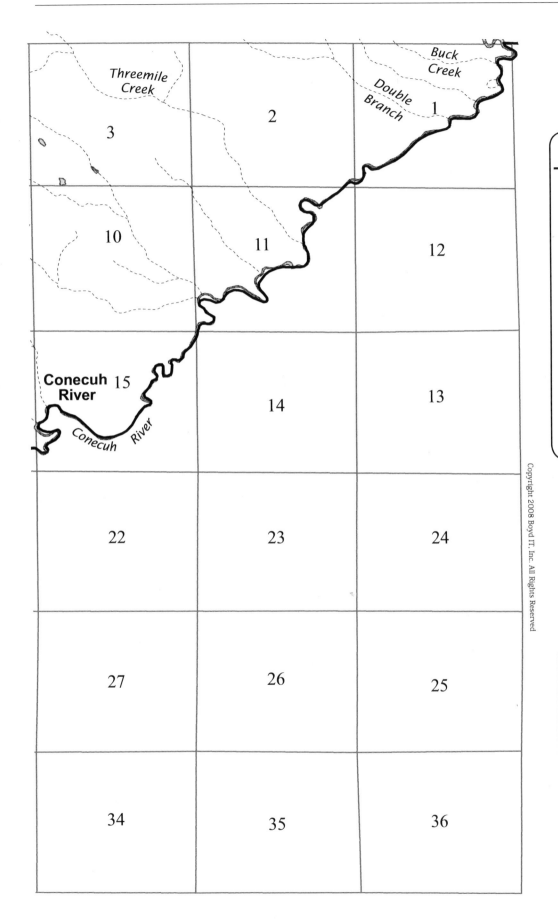

Threemile
Creek

Buck
Creek

Double
Branch

3

2

1

10

11

12

Conecuh
River 15

Conecuh River

14

13

22

23

24

27

26

25

34

35

36

Helpful Hints

1. This Map takes a different look at the same Congressional Township displayed in the preceding two maps. It presents features that can help you better envision the historical development of the area: a) Water-bodies (lakes & ponds), b) Water-courses (rivers, streams, etc.), c) Railroads, d) City/town center-points (where they were oftentimes located when first settled), and e) Cemeteries.

2. Using this "Historical" map in tandem with this Township's Patent Map and Road Map, may lead you to some interesting discoveries. You will often find roads, towns, cemeteries, and waterways are named after nearby landowners: sometimes those names will be the ones you are researching. See how many of these research gems you can find here in Crenshaw County.

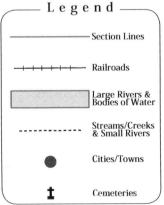

Legend

———————— Section Lines

—+—+—+—+— Railroads

� Large Rivers &
Bodies of Water

------------- Streams/Creeks
& Small Rivers

● Cities/Towns

✝ Cemeteries

Scale: Section = 1 mile X 1 mile
(there are some exceptions)

Map Group 24: Index to Land Patents

Township 6-North Range 18-East (St Stephens)

After you locate an individual in this Index, take note of the Section and Section Part then proceed to the Land Patent map on the pages immediately following. You should have no difficulty locating the corresponding parcel of land.

The "For More Info" Column will lead you to more information about the underlying Patents. See the *Legend* at right, and the "How to Use this Book" chapter, for more information.

```
                      LEGEND
            "For More Info . . . " column
A = Authority (Legislative Act, See Appendix "A")
B = Block or Lot (location in Section unknown)
C = Cancelled Patent
F = Fractional Section
G = Group  (Multi-Patentee Patent, see Appendix "C")
V = Overlaps another Parcel
R = Re-Issued (Parcel patented more than once)

(A & G items require you to look in the Appendixes referred
to above. All other Letter-designations followed by a number
require you to locate line-items in this index that possess
the ID number found after the letter).
```

ID	Individual in Patent	Sec.	Sec. Part	Date Issued	Other Counties	For More Info . . .
5245	BAILEY, Jasper M	21	E½SW	1900-11-12		A2
5246	" "	21	NWSW	1900-11-12		A2
5247	" "	21	SWNW	1900-11-12		A2
5289	BAILEY, Mathew C	20	E½NE	1892-06-10		A2
5290	" "	20	SWNE	1892-06-10		A2
5293	BAILY, Matthew C	9	NWNW	1860-04-02		A1
5221	BAIN, James M	24	E½NE	1890-07-03		A2
5222	" "	24	SENW	1890-07-03		A2
5223	" "	24	SWNE	1890-07-03		A2
5254	BLOCKER, John C	33	SE	1900-11-28		A2
5168	BOOTH, Charity	11	NW	1899-11-04		A2
5214	BOYETT, James E	22	SE	1899-11-04		A2
5326	BOYETT, William	9	E½SW	1900-11-28		A2
5327	" "	9	S½SE	1900-11-28		A2
5259	BURGIN, John M	8	NENW	1845-07-01		A1
5163	BUTLER, Bunyan	17	E½NE	1900-11-28		A2
5164	" "	17	NESE	1900-11-28		A2
5165	" "	17	NWNE	1900-11-28		A2
5281	BUTLER, Lloyd	8	NWNW	1899-07-26		A2
5282	" "	8	SENW	1899-07-26		A2
5283	CHANDLER, Lloyd	21	NENE	1900-11-12		A2
5284	" "	21	SENW	1900-11-12		A2
5285	" "	21	W½NE	1900-11-12		A2
5328	CHANDLER, William H	28	NWSW	1901-04-22		A2
5329	" "	28	SWNW	1901-04-22		A2
5178	COLQUITT, David F	14	E½NE	1901-10-08		A2
5179	" "	14	NESE	1901-10-08		A2
5219	COON, James J	26	N½NW	1897-08-05		A2
5220	" "	26	SWNW	1897-08-05		A2
5274	COSTON, Joseph	8	S½SE	1890-08-29		A2
5275	" "	8	S½SW	1890-08-29		A2
5215	COTTLE, James E	2	NE	1889-08-16		A2
5183	CULPEPPER, Edmund B	11	W½SW	1899-11-04		A2
5251	DANNELLEY, Jesse H	17	NWSE	1858-11-01		A1
5252	" "	17	SWNE	1860-04-02		A1
5286	DAVIS, Margaret	3	E½SE	1900-11-12		A2
5287	DAVIS, Mary E	10	E½SW	1891-05-29		A2
5288	" "	10	S½SE	1891-05-29		A2
5157	DUNCAN, Alexander	28	E½NE	1894-12-07		A2
5277	EILAND, Levi	34	NENE	1860-04-02		A1
5278	" "	34	SENE	1860-04-02		A1
5279	" "	35	NWNW	1860-04-02		A1
5294	FAIL, Michael F	8	NWSW	1860-04-02		A1
5295	" "	8	SWNW	1860-04-02		A1
5196	GIBBS, George W	22	NW	1916-05-19		A2
5231	GRAHAM, James P	36	SE	1898-03-21		A2

ID	Individual in Patent	Sec.	Sec. Part	Date Issued	Other Counties	For More Info . . .
5175	HATTAWAY, Daniel C	4	W½NW	1911-06-22		A2
5322	HENLY, Thomas J	29	NE	1900-11-28		A2
5332	HOLDER, William J	28	N½SE	1899-07-15		A2
5333	" "	28	SESE	1899-07-15		A2
5334	" "	28	SWNE	1899-07-15		A2
5335	HUDSON, William J	34	W½NW	1898-02-03		A2
5336	" "	34	W½SW	1898-02-03		A2
5192	JONES, George	25	NE	1900-11-28		A2
5342	JONES, Wright P	14	SESW	1860-04-02		A1
5343	" "	23	NENW	1860-04-02		A1
5232	KERBY, James P	13	E½SW	1900-11-12		A2
5233	" "	13	W½SE	1900-11-12		A2
5272	KIDD, John W	13	E½NW	1900-11-12		A2
5273	" "	13	W½NE	1900-11-12		A2
5169	KILCREASE, Charles E	3	NESW	1900-11-12		A2
5170	" "	3	SENW	1900-11-12		A2
5171	" "	3	W½SE	1900-11-12		A2
5257	KILCREASE, John J	10	W½NW	1891-11-23		A2
5258	" "	10	W½SW	1891-11-23		A2
5311	KILCREASE, Robert	10	E½NW	1894-04-19		A2
5312	" "	10	N½NE	1894-04-19		A2
5204	KNOWLEN, Henry	12	NESW	1888-08-05		A1
5184	KNOWLING, Elbert	11	SESE	1899-11-04		A2
5185	" "	11	SWNE	1899-11-04		A2
5186	" "	11	W½SE	1899-11-04		A2
5188	LASSITER, Ephraim P	36	NW	1892-08-01		A2
5276	LASSITER, Joseph M	36	SW	1892-06-10		A2
5159	LOCKHART, Benjamin F	3	NWSW	1860-04-02		A1
5160	" "	3	W½NW	1860-04-02		A1
5161	" "	4	NESE	1860-04-02		A1
5345	LOUNSBURY, Zaze	5	SWSW	1860-04-02		A1
5313	MADDOX, Seleta L	26	NESW	1898-06-17		A2 G31
5314	" "	26	S½SW	1898-06-17		A2 G31
5315	" "	26	SENW	1898-06-17		A2 G31
5337	MADDOX, William J	26	SE	1892-06-30		A2
5176	MALLOY, Daniel	2	NESW	1858-11-01		A1
5177	" "	2	SENW	1858-11-01		A1
5263	MALLOY, John	3	NWNE	1860-04-02		A1
5338	MALONE, William R	1	N½SE	1860-04-02		A1
5339	" "	1	NE	1860-04-02		A1
5200	MALOY, Hardy T	2	NWSW	1889-08-16		A2
5201	" "	2	S½SW	1889-08-16		A2
5202	" "	2	SWNW	1889-08-16		A2
5255	MALOY, John G	2	SE	1889-11-21		A2
5205	MCCURLEY, Isaac E	36	NE	1894-03-17		A2
5187	MCDANIEL, Elizabeth	20	SE	1892-01-18		A2
5181	MCMILLAN, David	2	NWNW	1885-08-05		A2
5180	" "	2	NENW	1891-11-23		A2
5162	MITCHELL, Benjamin	24	SW	1894-11-21		A2
5167	MITCHELL, Calvin T	5	SESE	1860-04-02		A1
5206	MITCHELL, Isaiah	33	NE	1901-01-23		A2
5209	MITCHELL, James A	14	SESE	1899-03-24		A2
5264	MITCHELL, John	11	E½SW	1858-11-01		A1
5265	" "	14	NENW	1858-11-01		A1
5266	" "	14	NWNE	1858-11-01		A1
5207	MOODY, Jacob	5	E½NW	1860-04-02		A1
5208	" "	5	W½NE	1860-04-02		A1
5280	MOODY, Levi	9	SWNE	1907-04-05		A1
5296	MOODY, Michael	4	NESW	1838-07-28		A1
5323	MOORE, Wesley W	15	SESE	1901-11-06		A2
5199	MORGAN, Green B	14	W½NW	1890-03-19		A2
5217	MORGAN, James H	14	NESW	1890-03-19		A2
5218	" "	14	SENW	1890-03-19		A2
5228	MORGAN, James O	24	NENW	1892-06-30		A2
5229	" "	24	NWNE	1892-06-30		A2
5230	" "	24	W½NW	1892-06-30		A2
5316	MORGAN, Snow B	12	S½NW	1893-07-31		A2
5317	" "	12	W½SW	1893-07-31		A2
5216	MORRIS, James F	4	S½SE	1893-07-24		A2
5234	MORROW, James R	12	S½SE	1893-07-31		A2
5235	" "	12	SESW	1893-07-31		A2
5158	NEIL, Amos P	27	SWNE	1860-04-02		A1
5197	NELSON, George W	22	SW	1902-02-12		A2

ID	Individual in Patent	Sec.	Sec. Part	Date Issued	Other Counties	For More Info . . .
5239	NELSON, James T	12	E½NE	1891-06-30		A2
5240	" "	12	NESE	1891-06-30		A2
5241	" "	12	NWSE	1891-06-30		A2
5321	OGLESBY, Tabitha	5	NENE	1860-04-02		A1
5256	OWENS, John H	27	NWNE	1888-07-12		A1
5330	PAYNE, William H	8	N½NE	1893-07-24		A2
5331	" "	8	SWNE	1893-07-24		A2 R5195
5189	PEACOCK, Faight	35	SE	1900-11-28		A2
5193	POPE, George M	8	N½SE	1894-06-15		A2
5194	" "	8	NESW	1894-06-15		A2
5195	" "	8	SWNE	1894-06-15		A2 R5331
5324	PRESCOTT, Wiley	11	NESE	1901-12-04		A2
5325	" "	11	SENE	1901-12-04		A2
5236	RABURN, James	15	NESE	1900-11-28		A2
5237	" "	15	SENE	1900-11-28		A2
5238	" "	15	W½NE	1900-11-28		A2
5213	RAMICK, James D	24	SE	1893-05-26		A2
5166	ROBBINS, Cade	20	NWNW	1860-04-02		A1
5291	ROBINS, Matilda	21	NENW	1900-11-28		A2
5292	" "	21	NWNW	1900-11-28		A2
5182	ROBINSON, Dixon H	29	SE	1900-11-28		A2
5313	ROGERS, Seleta L	26	NESW	1898-06-17		A2 G31
5314	" "	26	S½SW	1898-06-17		A2 G31
5315	" "	26	SENW	1898-06-17		A2 G31
5203	SASSER, Henry H	4	S½SW	1898-08-15		A2
5242	SASSER, James T	25	SE	1900-11-28		A2
5243	" "	9	S½NW	1900-11-28		A2
5244	" "	9	W½SW	1900-11-28		A2
5253	SASSER, John B	15	NW	1900-11-28		A2
5260	SASSER, John M	9	E½NE	1900-11-28		A2
5261	" "	9	NENW	1900-11-28		A2
5262	" "	9	NWNE	1900-11-28		A2
5303	SASSER, Oren W	20	E½SW	1899-03-24		A2
5308	SASSER, Robert J	28	E½NW	1893-07-24		A2
5309	" "	28	NWNE	1893-07-24		A2
5310	" "	28	NWNW	1893-07-24		A2
5224	SIMMONS, James M	1	S½SE	1900-11-28		A2
5225	" "	1	SESW	1900-11-28		A2
5190	SMITH, Frances T	34	E½NW	1898-02-03		A2
5191	" "	34	E½SW	1898-02-03		A2
5198	SMITH, George W	22	NE	1894-06-15		A2
5210	SMITH, James A	4	E½NE	1858-11-01		A1
5211	SMITH, James B	15	S½SW	1900-11-28		A2
5212	" "	15	W½SE	1900-11-28		A2
5267	SMITH, John	28	E½SW	1894-06-20		A2
5268	" "	28	SWSE	1894-06-20		A2
5269	" "	28	SWSW	1894-06-20		A2
5297	SMITH, Milton	23	NWNW	1901-01-23		A2
5298	" "	23	S½NW	1901-01-23		A2
5301	SMITH, Noah H	4	NWSW	1860-04-02		A1
5302	" "	5	NESE	1860-04-02		A1
5299	" "	34	W½NE	1885-06-20		A2
5300	" "	34	W½SE	1897-12-18		A2
5304	SMITH, Richard	4	E½NW	1837-05-20		A1
5306	" "	4	SWNE	1838-07-28		A1
5305	" "	4	NWSE	1860-04-02		A1
5307	" "	9	NESE	1907-04-05		A1
5318	SMITH, Stephen J	26	NE	1899-08-16		A2
5172	STEWART, Charles M	33	NW	1900-11-28		A2
5173	THOMASSON, Cornelius T	20	NENW	1899-11-04		A2
5174	" "	20	NWNE	1899-11-04		A2
5248	THOMASSON, Jefferson S	17	E½SW	1900-11-28		A2
5249	" "	17	SWSE	1900-11-28		A2
5250	" "	17	SWSW	1900-11-28		A2
5344	TIDWELL, Wyley	11	N½NE	1899-11-04		A2
5340	TILLIS, Wilson	12	W½NE	1896-11-09		A2
5341	TULLIS, Wilson	12	N½NW	1891-01-15		A2
5319	WAGERS, Susan A	5	N½SW	1860-04-02		A1
5320	" "	5	W½NW	1860-04-02		A1
5270	WARRICK, John T	20	S½NW	1891-06-08		A2
5271	" "	20	W½SW	1891-06-08		A2
5226	WEED, James N	10	N½SE	1891-06-30		A2
5227	" "	10	S½NE	1891-06-30		A2

Patent Map

T6-N R18-E
St Stephens Meridian

Map Group 24

Township Statistics

Parcels Mapped	:	189
Number of Patents	:	117
Number of Individuals	:	108
Patentees Identified	:	107
Number of Surnames	:	72
Multi-Patentee Parcels	:	3
Oldest Patent Date	:	5/20/1837
Most Recent Patent	:	5/19/1916
Block/Lot Parcels	:	0
Parcels Re-Issued	:	1
Parcels that Overlap	:	0
Cities and Towns	:	1
Cemeteries	:	1

Section 3

LOCKHART Benjamin F 1860

MALLOY John 1860

KILCREASE Charles E 1900 **3**

LOCKHART Benjamin F 1860

KILCREASE Charles E 1900

KILCREASE Charles E 1900

DAVIS Margaret 1900

Section 2

MCMILLAN David 1885

MCMILLAN David 1891

COTTLE James E 1889

MALOY Hardy T 1889

MALLOY Daniel 1858 **2**

MALOY Hardy T 1889

MALLOY Daniel 1858

MALOY Hardy T 1889

MALOY John G 1889

Section 1

MALONE William R 1860

MALONE William R 1860

SIMMONS James M 1900

SIMMONS James M 1900

Section 10

KILCREASE Robert 1894

KILCREASE John J 1891

KILCREASE Robert 1894

WEED James N 1891

KILCREASE John J 1891 **10**

DAVIS Mary E 1891

WEED James N 1891

DAVIS Mary E 1891

Section 11

BOOTH Charity 1899 **11**

KNOWLING Elbert 1899

PRESCOTT Wiley 1901

CULPEPPER Edmund B 1899

MITCHELL John 1858

KNOWLING Elbert 1899

PRESCOTT Wiley 1901

KNOWLING Elbert 1899

Section 12

TULLIS Wilson 1891

MORGAN Snow B 1893 **12**

TILLIS Wilson 1896

NELSON James T 1891

MORGAN Snow B 1893

KNOWLEN Henry 1888

NELSON James T 1891

NELSON James T 1891

MORROW James R 1893

MORROW James R 1893

Section 15

SASSER John B 1900

RABURN James 1900

RABURN James 1900 **15**

RABURN James 1900

SMITH James B 1900

MOORE Wesley W 1901

SMITH James B 1900

Section 14

MORGAN Green B 1890

MITCHELL John 1858

MITCHELL John 1858

COLQUITT David F 1901

MORGAN James H 1890 **14**

MORGAN James H 1890

COLQUITT David F 1901

JONES Wright P 1860

MITCHELL James A 1899

Section 13

KIDD John W 1900

KIDD John W 1900

KERBY James P 1900 **13**

KERBY James P 1900

Section 22

GIBBS George W 1916

SMITH George W 1894 **22**

NELSON George W 1902

BOYETT James E 1899

Section 23

SMITH Milton 1901

JONES Wright P 1860

SMITH Milton 1901 **23**

Section 24

MORGAN James O 1892

MORGAN James O 1892

MORGAN James O 1892

BAIN James M 1890

BAIN James M 1890

BAIN James M 1890

MITCHELL Benjamin 1894 **24**

RAMICK James D 1893

Section 27

OWENS John H 1888

NEIL Amos P 1860 **27**

Section 26

COON James J 1897

COON James J 1897

MADDOX [31] Seleta L 1898

SMITH Stephen J 1899 **26**

MADDOX [31] Seleta L 1898

MADDOX William J 1892

MADDOX [31] Seleta L 1898

Section 25

JONES George 1900 **25**

SASSER James T 1900

Section 34

HUDSON William J 1898

SMITH Frances T 1898

SMITH Noah H 1885

EILAND Levi 1860 **34**

EILAND Levi 1860

HUDSON William J 1898

SMITH Frances T 1898

SMITH Noah H 1897

Section 35

EILAND Levi 1860 **35**

PEACOCK Faight 1900

Section 36

LASSITER Ephraim P 1892

MCCURLEY Isaac E 1894 **36**

LASSITER Joseph M 1892

GRAHAM James P 1898

Helpful Hints

1. This Map's INDEX can be found on the preceding pages.

2. Refer to Map "C" to see where this Township lies within Crenshaw County, Alabama.

3. Numbers within square brackets [ ] denote a multi-patentee land parcel (multi-owner). Refer to Appendix "C" for a full list of members in this group.

4. Areas that look to be crowded with Patentees usually indicate multiple sales of the same parcel (Re-issues) or Overlapping parcels. See this Township's Index for an explanation of these and other circumstances that might explain "odd" groupings of Patentees on this map.

Legend

——— Patent Boundary

━━━ Section Boundary

No Patents Found (or Outside County)

1., 2., 3., . . . Lot Numbers (when beside a name)

[ ] Group Number (see Appendix "C")

Scale: Section = 1 mile X 1 mile (generally, with some exceptions)

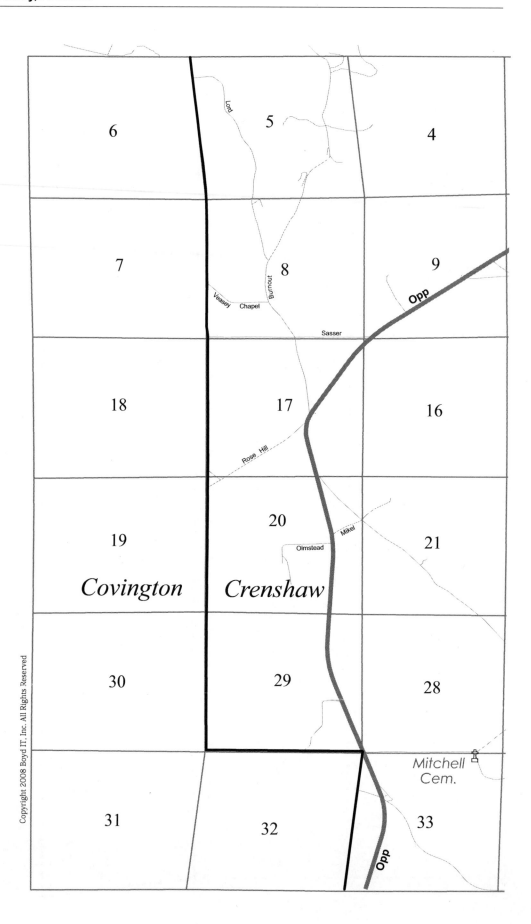

Road Map

T6-N R18-E
St Stephens Meridian

Map Group 24

Cities & Towns
Weed Crossroad

Cemeteries
Mitchell Cemetery

Copyright 2008 Boyd IT, Inc. All Rights Reserved

6

5

4

7

8

9

Veasey

Burnout

Chapel

Opp

Sasser

18

17

16

Rose Hill

19

20

21

Mikel

Olmstead

Covington

Crenshaw

30

29

28

Mitchell
Cem.

31

32

33

Opp

Lord

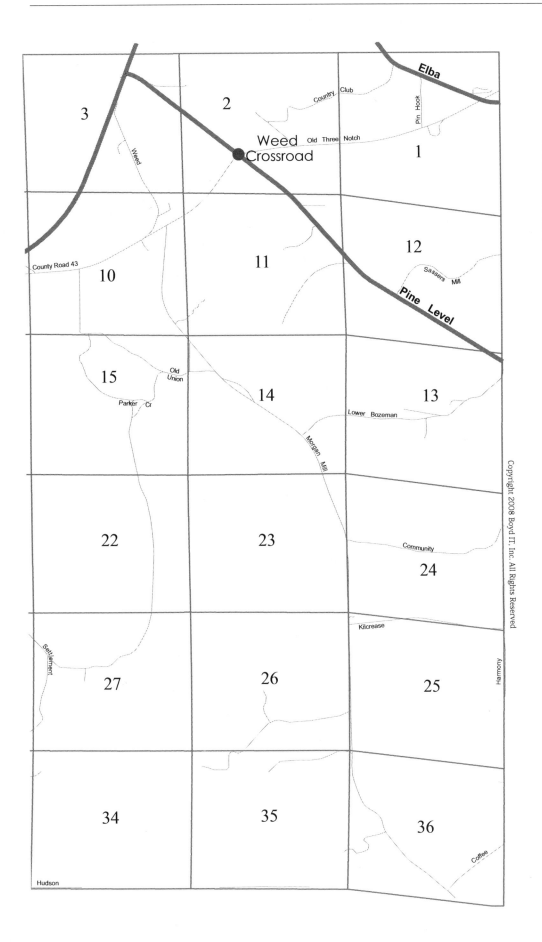

3

2

Country Club

Elba

Pin Hook

Weed
Crossroad

Old Three Notch

1

Weed

12

Sassers Mill

County Road 43

10

11

Pine Level

15

Old
Union

14

13

Parker Cr

Lower Bozeman

Morgan Mill

22

23

24

Community

Settlement

Kilcrease

27

26

25

Harmony

34

35

36

Coffee

Hudson

Helpful Hints

1. This road map has a number of uses, but primarily it is to help you: a) find the present location of land owned by your ancestors (at least the general area), b) find cemeteries and city-centers, and c) estimate the route/roads used by Census-takers & tax-assessors.

2. If you plan to travel to Crenshaw County to locate cemeteries or land parcels, please pick up a modern travel map for the area before you do. Mapping old land parcels on modern maps is not as exact a science as you might think. Just the slightest variations in public land survey coordinates, estimates of parcel boundaries, or road-map deviations can greatly alter a map's representation of how a road either does or doesn't cross a particular parcel of land.

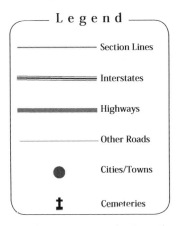

L e g e n d

———— Section Lines

▬▬▬▬ Interstates

▬▬▬▬ Highways

———— Other Roads

● Cities/Towns

✝ Cemeteries

Scale: Section = 1 mile X 1 mile
(generally, with some exceptions)

Historical Map

T6-N R18-E
St Stephens Meridian

Map Group 24

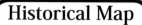

6

5

4

Cities & Towns
Weed Crossroad

7

8

9

18

17

16

Covington *Crenshaw*

19

20

21

Poley Creek

Cemeteries
Mitchell Cemetery

30

29

Pigpen Creek

28

Mitchell Cem.

31

32

33

Jolly Creek

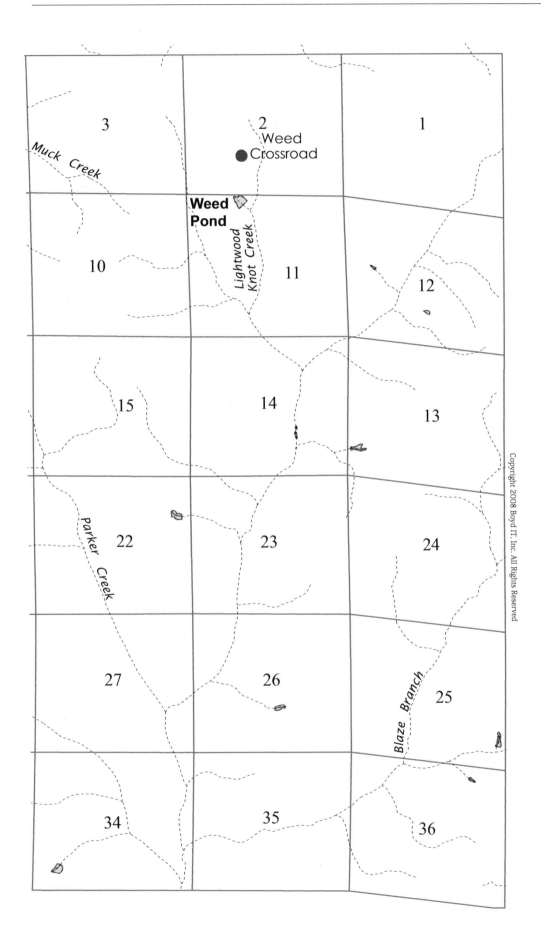

3

2
Weed
●Crossroad

1

Muck Creek

**Weed
Pond**

Lightwood
Knot Creek

10

11

12

15

14

13

Parker Creek

22

23

24

27

26

Blaze Branch

25

34

35

36

Copyright 2008 Boyd IT, Inc. All Rights Reserved

Helpful Hints

1. This Map takes a different look at the same Congressional Township displayed in the preceding two maps. It presents features that can help you better envision the historical development of the area: a) Water-bodies (lakes & ponds), b) Water-courses (rivers, streams, etc.), c) Railroads, d) City/town center-points (where they were oftentimes located when first settled), and e) Cemeteries.

2. Using this "Historical" map in tandem with this Township's Patent Map and Road Map, may lead you to some interesting discoveries. You will often find roads, towns, cemeteries, and waterways are named after nearby landowners: sometimes those names will be the ones you are researching. See how many of these research gems you can find here in Crenshaw County.

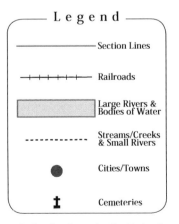

L e g e n d

——————— Section Lines

+-+-+-+-+-+ Railroads

Large Rivers &
Bodies of Water

- - - - - - Streams/Creeks
& Small Rivers

● Cities/Towns

☨ Cemeteries

Scale: Section = 1 mile X 1 mile
(there are some exceptions)

Appendices

Appendix A - Acts of Congress Authorizing the Patents Contained in this Book

The following Acts of Congress are referred to throughout the Indexes in this book. The text of the Federal Statutes referred to below can usually be found on the web. For more information on such laws, check out the publishers's web-site at *www.arphax.com*, go to the "Research" page, and click on the "Land-Law" link.

Ref. No.	Date and Act of Congress	Number of Parcels of Land
1	April 24, 1820: Sale-Cash Entry (3 Stat. 566)	4631
2	May 20, 1862: Homestead EntryOriginal (12 Stat. 392)	714

Appendix B - Section Parts (Aliquot Parts)

The following represent the various abbreviations we have found thus far in describing the parts of a Public Land Section. Some of these are very obscure and rarely used, but we wanted to list them for just that reason. A full section is 1 square mile or 640 acres.

Section Part	Description	Acres
<none>	Full Acre (if no Section Part is listed, presumed a full Section)	640
<1-??>	A number represents a Lot Number and can be of various sizes	?
E½	East Half-Section	320
E½E½	East Half of East Half-Section	160
E½E½SE	East Half of East Half of Southeast Quarter-Section	40
E½N½	East Half of North Half-Section	160
E½NE	East Half of Northeast Quarter-Section	80
E½NENE	East Half of Northeast Quarter of Northeast Quarter-Section	20
E½NENW	East Half of Northeast Quarter of Northwest Quarter-Section	20
E½NESE	East Half of Northeast Quarter of Southeast Quarter-Section	20
E½NESW	East Half of Northeast Quarter of Southwest Quarter-Section	20
E½NW	East Half of Northwest Quarter-Section	80
E½NWNE	East Half of Northwest Quarter of Northeast Quarter-Section	20
E½NWNW	East Half of Northwest Quarter of Northwest Quarter-Section	20
E½NWSE	East Half of Northwest Quarter of Southeast Quarter-Section	20
E½NWSW	East Half of Northwest Quarter of Southwest Quarter-Section	20
E½S½	East Half of South Half-Section	160
E½SE	East Half of Southeast Quarter-Section	80
E½SENE	East Half of Southeast Quarter of Northeast Quarter-Section	20
E½SENW	East Half of Southeast Quarter of Northwest Quarter-Section	20
E½SESE	East Half of Southeast Quarter of Southeast Quarter-Section	20
E½SESW	East Half of Southeast Quarter of Southwest Quarter-Section	20
E½SW	East Half of Southwest Quarter-Section	80
E½SWNE	East Half of Southwest Quarter of Northeast Quarter-Section	20
E½SWNW	East Half of Southwest Quarter of Northwest Quarter-Section	20
E½SWSE	East Half of Southwest Quarter of Southeast Quarter-Section	20
E½SWSW	East Half of Southwest Quarter of Southwest Quarter-Section	20
E½W½	East Half of West Half-Section	160
N½	North Half-Section	320
N½E½NE	North Half of East Half of Northeast Quarter-Section	40
N½E½NW	North Half of East Half of Northwest Quarter-Section	40
N½E½SE	North Half of East Half of Southeast Quarter-Section	40
N½E½SW	North Half of East Half of Southwest Quarter-Section	40
N½N½	North Half of North Half-Section	160
N½NE	North Half of Northeast Quarter-Section	80
N½NENE	North Half of Northeast Quarter of Northeast Quarter-Section	20
N½NENW	North Half of Northeast Quarter of Northwest Quarter-Section	20
N½NESE	North Half of Northeast Quarter of Southeast Quarter-Section	20
N½NESW	North Half of Northeast Quarter of Southwest Quarter-Section	20
N½NW	North Half of Northwest Quarter-Section	80
N½NWNE	North Half of Northwest Quarter of Northeast Quarter-Section	20
N½NWNW	North Half of Northwest Quarter of Northwest Quarter-Section	20
N½NWSE	North Half of Northwest Quarter of Southeast Quarter-Section	20
N½NWSW	North Half of Northwest Quarter of Southwest Quarter-Section	20
N½S½	North Half of South Half-Section	160
N½SE	North Half of Southeast Quarter-Section	80
N½SENE	North Half of Southeast Quarter of Northeast Quarter-Section	20
N½SENW	North Half of Southeast Quarter of Northwest Quarter-Section	20
N½SESE	North Half of Southeast Quarter of Southeast Quarter-Section	20

Section Part	Description	Acres
N½SESW	North Half of Southeast Quarter of Southwest Quarter-Section	20
N½SESW	North Half of Southeast Quarter of Southwest Quarter-Section	20
N½SW	North Half of Southwest Quarter-Section	80
N½SWNE	North Half of Southwest Quarter of Northeast Quarter-Section	20
N½SWNW	North Half of Southwest Quarter of Northwest Quarter-Section	20
N½SWSE	North Half of Southwest Quarter of Southeast Quarter-Section	20
N½SWSE	North Half of Southwest Quarter of Southeast Quarter-Section	20
N½SWSW	North Half of Southwest Quarter of Southwest Quarter-Section	20
N½W½NW	North Half of West Half of Northwest Quarter-Section	40
N½W½SE	North Half of West Half of Southeast Quarter-Section	40
N½W½SW	North Half of West Half of Southwest Quarter-Section	40
NE	Northeast Quarter-Section	160
NEN½	Northeast Quarter of North Half-Section	80
NENE	Northeast Quarter of Northeast Quarter-Section	40
NENENE	Northeast Quarter of Northeast Quarter of Northeast Quarter	10
NENENW	Northeast Quarter of Northeast Quarter of Northwest Quarter	10
NENESE	Northeast Quarter of Northeast Quarter of Southeast Quarter	10
NENESW	Northeast Quarter of Northeast Quarter of Southwest Quarter	10
NENW	Northeast Quarter of Northwest Quarter-Section	40
NENWNE	Northeast Quarter of Northwest Quarter of Northeast Quarter	10
NENWNW	Northeast Quarter of Northwest Quarter of Northwest Quarter	10
NENWSE	Northeast Quarter of Northwest Quarter of Southeast Quarter	10
NENWSW	Northeast Quarter of Northwest Quarter of Southwest Quarter	10
NESE	Northeast Quarter of Southeast Quarter-Section	40
NESENE	Northeast Quarter of Southeast Quarter of Northeast Quarter	10
NESENW	Northeast Quarter of Southeast Quarter of Northwest Quarter	10
NESESE	Northeast Quarter of Southeast Quarter of Southeast Quarter	10
NESESW	Northeast Quarter of Southeast Quarter of Southwest Quarter	10
NESW	Northeast Quarter of Southwest Quarter-Section	40
NESWNE	Northeast Quarter of Southwest Quarter of Northeast Quarter	10
NESWNW	Northeast Quarter of Southwest Quarter of Northwest Quarter	10
NESWSE	Northeast Quarter of Southwest Quarter of Southeast Quarter	10
NESWSW	Northeast Quarter of Southwest Quarter of Southwest Quarter	10
NW	Northwest Quarter-Section	160
NWE½	Northwest Quarter of Eastern Half-Section	80
NWN½	Northwest Quarter of North Half-Section	80
NWNE	Northwest Quarter of Northeast Quarter-Section	40
NWNENE	Northwest Quarter of Northeast Quarter of Northeast Quarter	10
NWNENW	Northwest Quarter of Northeast Quarter of Northwest Quarter	10
NWNESE	Northwest Quarter of Northeast Quarter of Southeast Quarter	10
NWNESW	Northwest Quarter of Northeast Quarter of Southwest Quarter	10
NWNW	Northwest Quarter of Northwest Quarter-Section	40
NWNWNE	Northwest Quarter of Northwest Quarter of Northeast Quarter	10
NWNWNW	Northwest Quarter of Northwest Quarter of Northwest Quarter	10
NWNWSE	Northwest Quarter of Northwest Quarter of Southeast Quarter	10
NWNWSW	Northwest Quarter of Northwest Quarter of Southwest Quarter	10
NWSE	Northwest Quarter of Southeast Quarter-Section	40
NWSENE	Northwest Quarter of Southeast Quarter of Northeast Quarter	10
NWSENW	Northwest Quarter of Southeast Quarter of Northwest Quarter	10
NWSESE	Northwest Quarter of Southeast Quarter of Southeast Quarter	10
NWSESW	Northwest Quarter of Southeast Quarter of Southwest Quarter	10
NWSW	Northwest Quarter of Southwest Quarter-Section	40
NWSWNE	Northwest Quarter of Southwest Quarter of Northeast Quarter	10
NWSWNW	Northwest Quarter of Southwest Quarter of Northwest Quarter	10
NWSWSE	Northwest Quarter of Southwest Quarter of Southeast Quarter	10
NWSWSW	Northwest Quarter of Southwest Quarter of Southwest Quarter	10
S½	South Half-Section	320
S½E½NE	South Half of East Half of Northeast Quarter-Section	40
S½E½NW	South Half of East Half of Northwest Quarter-Section	40
S½E½SE	South Half of East Half of Southeast Quarter-Section	40

Section Part	Description	Acres
S½E½SW	South Half of East Half of Southwest Quarter-Section	40
S½N½	South Half of North Half-Section	160
S½NE	South Half of Northeast Quarter-Section	80
S½NENE	South Half of Northeast Quarter of Northeast Quarter-Section	20
S½NENW	South Half of Northeast Quarter of Northwest Quarter-Section	20
S½NESE	South Half of Northeast Quarter of Southeast Quarter-Section	20
S½NESW	South Half of Northeast Quarter of Southwest Quarter-Section	20
S½NW	South Half of Northwest Quarter-Section	80
S½NWNE	South Half of Northwest Quarter of Northeast Quarter-Section	20
S½NWNW	South Half of Northwest Quarter of Northwest Quarter-Section	20
S½NWSE	South Half of Northwest Quarter of Southeast Quarter-Section	20
S½NWSW	South Half of Northwest Quarter of Southwest Quarter-Section	20
S½S½	South Half of South Half-Section	160
S½SE	South Half of Southeast Quarter-Section	80
S½SENE	South Half of Southeast Quarter of Northeast Quarter-Section	20
S½SENW	South Half of Southeast Quarter of Northwest Quarter-Section	20
S½SESE	South Half of Southeast Quarter of Southeast Quarter-Section	20
S½SESW	South Half of Southeast Quarter of Southwest Quarter-Section	20
S½SESW	South Half of Southeast Quarter of Southwest Quarter-Section	20
S½SW	South Half of Southwest Quarter-Section	80
S½SWNE	South Half of Southwest Quarter of Northeast Quarter-Section	20
S½SWNW	South Half of Southwest Quarter of Northwest Quarter-Section	20
S½SWSE	South Half of Southwest Quarter of Southeast Quarter-Section	20
S½SWSE	South Half of Southwest Quarter of Southeast Quarter-Section	20
S½SWSW	South Half of Southwest Quarter of Southwest Quarter-Section	20
S½W½NE	South Half of West Half of Northeast Quarter-Section	40
S½W½NW	South Half of West Half of Northwest Quarter-Section	40
S½W½SE	South Half of West Half of Southeast Quarter-Section	40
S½W½SW	South Half of West Half of Southwest Quarter-Section	40
SE	Southeast Quarter Section	160
SEN½	Southeast Quarter of North Half-Section	80
SENE	Southeast Quarter of Northeast Quarter-Section	40
SENENE	Southeast Quarter of Northeast Quarter of Northeast Quarter	10
SENENW	Southeast Quarter of Northeast Quarter of Northwest Quarter	10
SENESE	Southeast Quarter of Northeast Quarter of Southeast Quarter	10
SENESW	Southeast Quarter of Northeast Quarter of Southwest Quarter	10
SENW	Southeast Quarter of Northwest Quarter-Section	40
SENWNE	Southeast Quarter of Northwest Quarter of Northeast Quarter	10
SENWNW	Southeast Quarter of Northwest Quarter of Northwest Quarter	10
SENWSE	Souteast Quarter of Northwest Quarter of Southeast Quarter	10
SENWSW	Southeast Quarter of Northwest Quarter of Southwest Quarter	10
SESE	Southeast Quarter of Southeast Quarter-Section	40
SESENE	SoutheastQuarter of Southeast Quarter of Northeast Quarter	10
SESENW	Southeast Quarter of Southeast Quarter of Northwest Quarter	10
SESESE	Southeast Quarter of Southeast Quarter of Southeast Quarter	10
SESESW	Southeast Quarter of Southeast Quarter of Southwest Quarter	10
SESW	Southeast Quarter of Southwest Quarter-Section	40
SESWNE	Southeast Quarter of Southwest Quarter of Northeast Quarter	10
SESWNW	Southeast Quarter of Southwest Quarter of Northwest Quarter	10
SESWSE	Southeast Quarter of Southwest Quarter of Southeast Quarter	10
SESWSW	Southeast Quarter of Southwest Quarter of Southwest Quarter	10
SW	Southwest Quarter-Section	160
SWNE	Southwest Quarter of Northeast Quarter-Section	40
SWNENE	Southwest Quarter of Northeast Quarter of Northeast Quarter	10
SWNENW	Southwest Quarter of Northeast Quarter of Northwest Quarter	10
SWNESE	Southwest Quarter of Northeast Quarter of Southeast Quarter	10
SWNESW	Southwest Quarter of Northeast Quarter of Southwest Quarter	10
SWNW	Southwest Quarter of Northwest Quarter-Section	40
SWNWNE	Southwest Quarter of Northwest Quarter of Northeast Quarter	10
SWNWNW	Southwest Quarter of Northwest Quarter of Northwest Quarter	10

Section Part	Description	Acres
SWNWSE	Southwest Quarter of Northwest Quarter of Southeast Quarter	10
SWNWSW	Southwest Quarter of Northwest Quarter of Southwest Quarter	10
SWSE	Southwest Quarter of Southeast Quarter-Section	40
SWSENE	Southwest Quarter of Southeast Quarter of Northeast Quarter	10
SWSENW	Southwest Quarter of Southeast Quarter of Northwest Quarter	10
SWSESE	Southwest Quarter of Southeast Quarter of Southeast Quarter	10
SWSESW	Southwest Quarter of Southeast Quarter of Southwest Quarter	10
SWSW	Southwest Quarter of Southwest Quarter-Section	40
SWSWNE	Southwest Quarter of Southwest Quarter of Northeast Quarter	10
SWSWNW	Southwest Quarter of Southwest Quarter of Northwest Quarter	10
SWSWSE	Southwest Quarter of Southwest Quarter of Southeast Quarter	10
SWSWSW	Southwest Quarter of Southwest Quarter of Southwest Quarter	10
W½	West Half-Section	320
W½E½	West Half of East Half-Section	160
W½N½	West Half of North Half-Section (same as NW)	160
W½NE	West Half of Northeast Quarter	80
W½NENE	West Half of Northeast Quarter of Northeast Quarter-Section	20
W½NENW	West Half of Northeast Quarter of Northwest Quarter-Section	20
W½NESE	West Half of Northeast Quarter of Southeast Quarter-Section	20
W½NESW	West Half of Northeast Quarter of Southwest Quarter-Section	20
W½NW	West Half of Northwest Quarter-Section	80
W½NWNE	West Half of Northwest Quarter of Northeast Quarter-Section	20
W½NWNW	West Half of Northwest Quarter of Northwest Quarter-Section	20
W½NWSE	West Half of Northwest Quarter of Southeast Quarter-Section	20
W½NWSW	West Half of Northwest Quarter of Southwest Quarter-Section	20
W½S½	West Half of South Half-Section	160
W½SE	West Half of Southeast Quarter-Section	80
W½SENE	West Half of Southeast Quarter of Northeast Quarter-Section	20
W½SENW	West Half of Southeast Quarter of Northwest Quarter-Section	20
W½SESE	West Half of Southeast Quarter of Southeast Quarter-Section	20
W½SESW	West Half of Southeast Quarter of Southwest Quarter-Section	20
W½SW	West Half of Southwest Quarter-Section	80
W½SWNE	West Half of Southwest Quarter of Northeast Quarter-Section	20
W½SWNW	West Half of Southwest Quarter of Northwest Quarter-Section	20
W½SWSE	West Half of Southwest Quarter of Southeast Quarter-Section	20
W½SWSW	West Half of Southwest Quarter of Southwest Quarter-Section	20
W½W½	West Half of West Half-Section	160

Appendix C - Multi-Patentee Groups

The following index presents groups of people who jointly received patents in Crenshaw County, Alabama. The Group Numbers are used in the Patent Maps and their Indexes so that you may then turn to this Appendix in order to identify all the members of the each buying group.

Group Number 1
ALSABROOKS, Andrew J; ALSABROOKS, Mariah A

Group Number 2
BISHOP, Noble P; FOSKETT, William A

Group Number 3
BLACKMAN, William D; STINSON, Micajah

Group Number 4
BOAN, John D; BOAN, Smithey

Group Number 5
BRADLEY, Anna; BRADLEY, James C

Group Number 6
BRADLEY, David; JORDAN, Felix

Group Number 7
BROWN, John; PATTERSON, John

Group Number 8
BRUNSON, Benjamin; BRUNSON, David

Group Number 9
CAPPS, James; CAPPS, Mary C

Group Number 10
CAPPS, Jane S; CAPPS, Robert H

Group Number 11
CAPPS, Sallie A; CAPPS, Spencer W

Group Number 12
CARTER, Mary M; CARTER, William H

Group Number 13
COLEMAN, Peter E; WISE, Richard

Group Number 14
COX, Octavia; STRINGER, Octavia

Group Number 15
DAVIS, Abel; KING, James

Group Number 16
DAVIS, John; SKAINS, Thomas

Group Number 17
DILLARD, George W; JORDAN, Felix

Group Number 18
FRANKLIN, Margaret; HOPPER, Samuel J

Group Number 19
GILCHRIST, Eliza; GILCHRIST, Malcolm

Group Number 20
HALL, Bolling; REESE, Littleton

Group Number 21
HARRIS, Dennis; HARRIS, Jacob

Group Number 22
HILL, Lewis; SOLOMON, Henry

Group Number 23
HOOKS, Daniel; HOOKS, Mary

Group Number 24
JOHNSON, James A; JOHNSON, Laura L

Group Number 25
JOHNSON, William; MILLIGAN, Martha

Group Number 26
JORDAN, Felix; JORDAN, George M

Group Number 27
JORDAN, Felix; JORDAN, Thomas

Group Number 28
KELLEY, Tyre; VICKERY, James H

Group Number 29
KING, Charles L; KNIGHT, John W

Group Number 30
KITES, Grandison; KITES, Mary

Group Number 31
MADDOX, Seleta L; ROGERS, Seleta L

Group Number 32
MCADAMS, George; MCADAMS, Robert

Group Number 33
MCLEOD, Martha R; MCLEOD, Thomas W

Group Number 34
MILLS, Clara G; MILLS, Warren W

Group Number 35
NEVES, Daniel; TAYLOR, Job

Group Number 36
NICHOLS, Elias S; NICHOLS, Mozelle G

Group Number 37
PORTER, Virginia C; TAYLOR, Virginia C

Group Number 38
SPURLIN, Elizabeth; SPURLIN, William

Group Number 39
WIROSDICK, Andrew; WIROSDICK, Thomas

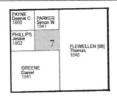

Extra! Extra! (about our Indexes)

We purposefully do not have an all-name index in the back of this volume so that our readers do not miss one of the best uses of this book: finding misspelled names among more specialized indexes.

Without repeating the text of our "How-to" chapter, we have nonetheless tried to assist our more anxious researchers by delivering a short-cut to the two county-wide Surname Indexes, the second of which will lead you to all-name indexes for each Congressional Township mapped in this volume :

For your convenience, the "How To Use this Book" Chart on page 2 is repeated on the reverse of this page.

We should be releasing new titles every week for the foreseeable future. We urge you to write, fax, call, or email us any time for a current list of titles. Of course, our web-page will always have the most current information about current and upcoming books.

Arphax Publishing Co.
2210 Research Park Blvd.
Norman, Oklahoma 73069
(800) 681-5298 toll-free
(405) 366-6181 local
(405) 366-8184 fax
info@arphax.com

www.arphax.com

How to Use This Book - A Graphical Summary

Part I
"The Big Picture"

Map A ▸ *Counties in the State*

Map B ▸ *Surrounding Counties*

Map C ▸ *Congressional Townships (Map Groups) in the County*

Map D ▸ *Cities & Towns in the County*

Map E ▸ *Cemeteries in the County*

Surnames in the County ▸ *Number of Land-Parcels for Each Surname*

Surname/Township Index ▸ *Directs you to Township Map Groups in Part II*

The Surname/Township Index can direct you to any number of **Township Map Groups**

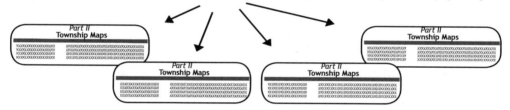

Part II
Township Map Groups
(1 for each Township in the County)

Each Township Map Group contains all four of of the following tools . . .

Land Patent Index ▸ *Every-name Index of Patents Mapped in this Township*

Land Patent Map ▸ *Map of Patents as listed in above Index*

Road Map ▸ *Map of Roads, City-centers, and Cemeteries in the Township*

Historical Map ▸ *Map of Railroads, Lakes, Rivers, Creeks, City-Centers, and Cemeteries*

Appendices

Appendix A ▸ *Congressional Authority enabling Patents within our Maps*

Appendix B ▸ *Section-Parts / Aliquot Parts (a comprehensive list)*

Appendix C ▸ *Multi-patentee Groups (Individuals within Buying Groups)*

49015173R00161